738
D0598073

# *Warman's* American Pottery & Porcelain

## 2ᴺᴰ EDITION

## SUSAN & AL BAGDADE

W. K. Woodard Memorial Library

© 2000 by
Susan and Al Bagdade


All rights reserved.
No part of this publication may be reproduced or transmitted in any form or by any means,
electronic or mechanical, including photocopy, recording or any information storage and retrieval system,
without permission in writing from the author, except by a reviewer who may quote brief passages in a
critical article or review to be printed in a magazine or newspaper or electronically transmitted on radio or
television. The author and publisher assume no liability or responsibility for any loss incurred by users of
this book because of errors, typographical, clerical, or otherwise.

## COVER PHOTO CREDITS

**Front cover:** Front row, from left: Cookie Jar, Howdy Doody, Purinton, $1,000, from the
collection of Mercedes DiRenzo, Chicago, IL; teapot, 11" l, Golden Glo, Hall China, $85.00, from
the collection of Nancy Rosenbaum and Johnny Stein, Highland Park, IL. Back row, from left: Tray,
Majolica, 13" l, ftd, unmkd, $795.00, from the collection of Randi Schwartz, Raven and Dove, Wilmette, IL;
Acoma Storage Jar, 11" h x 9" d, c1920, $3,500.00, from the collection of Susan and Jerry Steinberger,
Highland Park, IL; vase, 10 1/2" h, Pinecone pattern, Roseville, $600.00, from the collection of Doris S.
Prizant and M. Mike Goldman, Chicago, IL.

**Back cover:** Top: Dutch Jug, 6" h, "Fruit" pattern, Purinton, $40.00. Credit: The Antique Market
of Michigan City, IN. Middle: Oyster Plate, 8 1/2" w, Union Porcelain Company, $395.00. Credit:
Randi Schwartz, Raven and Dove, Wilmette, IL. Bottom: Vase, 5" h, Clifton, $350.00. Credit:
Tony McCormack, Sarasota, FL.

Published by

**krause
publications**

700 E. State Street • Iola, WI 54990-0001
Telephone: 715/445-2214


Please, call or write us for our free catalog of antiques and collectibles publications. To place an
order or receive our free catalog, call 800-258-0929. For editorial comment and further information,
use our regular business telephone at (715) 445-2214


Library of Congress Catalog Number: 94-3191
ISBN: 0-87341-822-0

Printed in the United States of America

# TABLE OF CONTENTS

# PREFACE

Since our *Warman's English and Continental Pottery and Porcelain* price guides were so well received by everyone associated with the antiques field, we decided to turn our attention to the arena of American pottery and porcelain. Once again, we found that there really was not one comprehensive volume dealing with all aspects of American ceramics.

We feel that providing helpful introductory materials such as reference books, museums, collectors' clubs, periodicals, and marks along with a concise history of the manufactory separates our books from any other American price guides, and definitely fills a void for antiques dealers and collectors.

As with our earlier tomes, this volume was a true division of labor. Al was once again in charge of the nearly eleven thousand data entries and their prices, along with taking the three hundred photographs. Susan wrote the histories for the nearly one hundred fifty manufactories which were divided into four headings: Art Pottery, Dinnerware Manufacturers, General Manufacturers, and Utilitarian Ware.

Everywhere we sought information, whether auction house, antiques show, antiques shop or mall, flea market, museum, pottery factory, and such, we found encouragement and enthusiasm for this much-needed project.

As with our other books, we invite readers to send their comments to us in care of our publisher, the Wallace-Homestead Book Company. We hope our readers are pleased with this new effort.

**Susan and Al Bagdade**
**Northbrook, Illinois**

# PREFACE TO THE SECOND EDITION

Organization is the key to the improvements in this second edition of *Warman's American Pottery and Porcelain.* Our first edition was divided into four major headings: Art Pottery, Dinnerware Manufacturers, General Manufacturers, and Utilitarian Ware. Then the manufacturers were divided under these four headings. Through trial and error, we found that this arrangement sometimes proved to be difficult for both the novice and even advanced collectors, since users were uncertain as to where to locate the manufactory that interested them within this organizational scheme.

As a result, we have written the second edition in straight alphabetical order to eliminate location difficulties. We hope that users of this price guide will find this arrangement more satisfactory and user friendly.

An important addition to this price guide is the section of color photographs featuring many important manufactories. We have used three hundred new black and white photographs, added more marks, and included some new manufactories to keep current with users' interests. All Reference Books, Museums, and Collectors' Clubs have been updated with the newest information. As always, all of our price listings are new for this second addition. We have also added Reproduction Alerts where information is available.

We would love to hear comments and suggestions from our readers. You can reach us through our publisher, Krause Publications, or e-mail us directly at ADBSDB@aol.com.

**Susan and Al Bagdade**
**Chicago, Illinois**
**September 2000**

# ACKNOWLEDGMENTS

Special thanks must go to David Rago, who allowed us to utilize color photographs from his extensive collection of American art pottery available for auction. John Toomey and Don Treadway were kind enough to allow us to photograph auction properties before they crossed the block.

A special debt of thanks must go to Rich Kleinhardt for drawing all the American pottery and porcelain marks required for the first edition, and to Donna Bagdade for drawing all the additional marks for the new categories included in the second edition.

We must thank the auction houses that provided complimentary subscriptions to their extensive catalogues. The authors express additional grateful appreciation to Tom Porter of Garth's Auctions, Inc. and Skinners from both Boston and Bolton for help above and beyond.

Our gratitude must go to all the antique shop owners, antique show dealers, and antique mall exhibitors, who allowed us to take numerous photographs and collect data for this second edition in their establishments. Everyone we encountered along the way was exceptionally helpful and generous with their time and information, in addition to encouraging us in our endeavor.

Additional thanks to Randi Schwartz, John Stein and Nancy Rosenbaum, Jerry and Susan Steinberger, Mercedes and Hillary DiRenzo, Doris S. Prizant and M. Mike Goldman for lending us pieces from their collections to photograph for the cover of this book. An extra special thanks to Charles Bagdade for taking the cover photograph, and to Gail Bagdade for assisting in the layout.

We would also like to thank Kris Manty, our editor at Krause Publications, who worked to make this American ceramics price guide a reality.

# Part One: How to Use This Book

# ORGANIZATION OF THE PRICE GUIDE

**Listings:** More than one hundred and fifty categories dealing with American pottery and porcelain are listed in this price guide.

**History:** Every category has a capsule history that details the founding of the company, its location, dates of existence, nature of the wares, and general information available on the specific company. Notes about marks are included in the history. Some company dates may not be exact since the reference materials available do not always agree about opening and closing dates of manufactories.

**References:** Reference books are listed whenever possible to encourage the collector to learn more about the category. Books are listed only if there is a substantial section on the specific category being considered, or if it is a complete book on that category. Included in the listing are author, title, publisher, (if published by a small firm or individual, we have indicated "privately printed"), date of publication, or most recent edition.

Some of the books listed may be out of print and no longer available from the publisher; these will usually be available in public libraries or through inter-library loan. Readers also may find antiques book dealers at antiques shows, flea markets, and advertising in trade papers and journals. Many book dealers provide attractive mail order services.

Additional general references books on American pottery and porcelain are listed in the Bibliographies section found in the Appendix.

**Periodicals:** In addition to publications of collectors' clubs, there are numerous general interest newspapers and magazines that devote attention to American ceramics. A sampling includes the following:

**Antique Monthly,** 2100 Powers Ferry Rd. Atlanta, GA 30339

**Antique Review,** P.O. Box 538, Worthington, OH 43085

**Antique Trader Weekly,** P.O. Box 1050, Dubuque, IA 52001

**Antique Week,** P.O. Box 90, Knightstown, IN 46148

**Antiques and Auction News,** P.O. Box 500, Mount Joy, PA 17552

**Antiques and Collecting Magazine,** 1006 S. Michigan Ave. Chicago, IL 60650

**Antiques and The Arts Weekly,** 5 Church Hill Rd., Newtown, CT 06470

**Antiques (The Magazine Antiques),** 575 Broadway, New York, NY 10012

**Collector Magazine and Price Guide,** P.O. Box 4333, Charlottesville, VA 22905

**Collector News,** Box 156, Grundy Center, IA 50638

**Maine Antique Digest,** 911 Main Street, Waldboro, ME 04572

**Mid Atlantic Antiques Monthly,** P.O. Box 908, Henderson, NC 27536

**New York-Pennsylvania Collector,** 73 Buffalo Street, Canandaiga, NY 14429

**The Daze,** P.O. Box 57, Otisville, MI 48463

**Warman's Today's Collector,** 700 East State Street, Iola, WI 54990-0001

**West Coast Peddler.** P.O. Box 5134, Whittier, CA 90607

**Yesteryear,** P.O. Box 2, Princeton, WI 54968

**Museums:** Museums are listed if significant collections in the category are on display. Many museums have large collections of American ceramics but did not provide a detailed listing for inclusion in this book. If the name of the museum and the city where it is located are the same, only the state is listed for the location of the museum. A listing of museums with significant American ceramics is located in the Appendix.

**Collectors' Clubs:** All collectors' clubs have been verified to be active. The most recent address is listed for membership information.

**Additional Listings:** When more than one category is covered by a specific listing, other listings are added to help the reader find additional information. Be sure to check the index to locate all the data.

**Marks:** When wares are marked, we have included representative marks for that manufactory. Readers should realize that there is some variation in the marks within the same manufactory. However, to see the full range of marks used by a firm, one must consult one of the marks books listed in the Bibliographies in the Appendix.

**Reproduction Alert:** If there are known reproductions or fakes for a particular category they are listed in this section. The primary source for this information came from the "Antiques and Collectors Reproduction News" that is published monthly for $32 per year. This is an excellent source of invaluable information for collectors. P.O. Box 71174, Des Moines, IA 50325.

# DERIVATION OF PRICES USED

Prices for listed items were derived from a variety of sources. Field work involving antiques shows, flea markets, antiques shops, and antiques malls were a major source for pricing. The prices listed are the actual retail prices of an item, i.e. what the collector would have to pay to purchase the piece.

General ceramics and specialized auctions were another important source for pricing. These items are identified in the guide with an (A) prior to the listed price. The price reflects the hammer price plus whatever buyer's premium was charged.

Another important source of pricing came from antiques trade papers, journals, antiques magazines, and price lists solicited from antiques dealers. These were important for determining what pieces were actually available, what their condition was, as well as what price was required to obtain the piece.

Prices for dinnerware examples are listed as individual pieces. However, the collector can often find the best value when purchasing a complete dinner service. Many more partial sets are available on the marketplace than complete sets. With this in mind, the collector can fill out a partial set with some diligent searching using the pricing found in this guide as a reference point. This also holds true for those who wish to replace or add additional pieces to a complete service.

The Internet has be come a major source of pricing that was in its infancy when the first edition of this book went to press. Web sites and Internet "auctions" or marketplaces have been a rich source for pricing and availability. This will only become more important with time.

# THE ROLE OF CONDITION
# IN PRICING AMERICAN CERAMICS

Condition is one of the major factors that dictates price. In a very few instances, where an item is extremely rare, or is a true one-of-a-kind piece, condition may not be the deciding factor in determining if a piece is worth purchasing.

The term "mint" should mean just that: factory fresh without any sign of wear or damage. "Flea bites, dings, and nicks" are just terms for damage. The same holds true for such overused words as "age cracks and hairlines" which actually indicate damaged goods.

The collector should strive to purchase the best possible examples. Due to the large quantity of material produced by the major companies, this can be accomplished with diligent shopping.

The frequent use of over the glaze transfers and decals on American ceramics makes them vulnerable to damage. Fading, splitting, and loss of body are fairly common; examples with these defects should be avoided. Since early American ceramic glazes tended to be heavy, cracking and staining of the surface and underbody are fairly common which detracts from the appearance of the piece as well as its value.

Knife scratching of the surface, if minimal is acceptable, but if the scratches pierce the glaze or design, they attract and retain dirt which is difficult to remove. By holding a plate on the horizontal and gently tilting it towards the light, the depth of scratching can usually be ascertained.

Broken, glued, or repaired pieces should be avoided unless the piece is of such merit that it belongs in a collection. However, the price should reflect the degree of damage and repair. Slight variations in color, surface texture, and glaze often indicate a repair. Be especially watchful for knobs, handles, and spouts that are easily damaged. The use of a black light can often detect repairs and should be used when a question exists.

The key element is to purchase the best example that fits comfortably within the collector's pocketbook.

# STATE OF THE MARKET

Several factors have given the American ceramics market a shot in the arm. The robust economy resulting in additional spendable income certainly has played a role in this active market. Collectors and designers, rather than investors, control this market, much to the glee of the overall antiques field. The television media certainly has had a significant impact on the field, drawing novices, serious collectors and just the curious to appraisal fairs both on public and cable television networks. The success of these shows is a fact, and not only does it expose a hitherto unknown arena to the uninitiated, it also has brought some very interesting and highly significant pieces out of the attic into the marketplace.

Internet buying and selling is the third and maybe the most important factor in determining the health of the American ceramics market. It is not the wave of the future, but in actuality, it is the wave of the present. Buying via the computer screen and communicating through e-mail introduces instant gratification. On-line auctions have become the "darling" of the antiques world, though most are more like giant marketplaces, rather than auctions. New material is added daily to create an almost limitless inventory, and such items as dinnerware sets can be assembled with a little patience and an active cursor.

In recent years, the mega antiques mall has made shopping for antiques and collectibles quite simple. A collector could move through four hundred to five hundred or more shops under one roof and enjoy lunch without leaving the building. Mega malls continue to sprout up around the country. Many dealers maintain active web sites, as well as spots in the mall, and can display their merchandise through several outlets. However, nothing beats actual physical contact with an item and though the electronic media continues to grow, the malls will still maintain a place of prominence.

All of these factors have generated life into the American ceramics market. Top-drawer antiques continue to attract interest, though most of these are sold on site. A few examples include a world's record for a Van Briggle. A Lady of the Lily vase sold for $41,250, and an impressive Teco leaf form vase went down for a spectacular $66,000, including the buyer's premium. The pottery of the "Mad Potter of Biloxi" George Ohr has done quite well, with unusual glazes and bisque examples selling well. The heavyweights in American art pottery continue to find buyers, and this certainly is the case since the last state of the market report. A Grueby table lamp with a Tiffany shade sold for a surprising $286,000. Was it the base, shade, or the combination?

Well-painted Rookwood is very strong, though commercially made pieces are not quite as attractive. Weller, Roseville, and Hull are still commanding good prices, but some of the popular modern-era categories such as Scheier and Pillin that were heading the class are often being passed over, especially at auction where they are failing to meet the opening bids.

West Coast ceramics continue to be a driving force in the American market, and Catalina Island, Kay Finch, Hedi Schoop and Howard Pierce show strong performances. New reference books have thrown a brighter light on these ceramics. The same can be said for Western style dinnerware. Products by Wallace and Syracuse with cowboy themes are drawing good prices.

One of the "piping hot" areas is the general collection called "Restaurant China." Young people are finding this heavy-duty material perfect for casual and patio dining, as well as the nostalgia factor associated with such restaurant chains as Bob's Big Boy and Chicken In The Rough, to name a couple. Bright colors and heavy ceramic bodies are factors in its desirability. In fact, several stores around the country deal in nothing but hotel and restaurant china. It is also selling very well on the Internet. A two-volume set of books dealing with this aspect of American ceramics certainly has helped in pattern and manufacturer identification.

There are many bargains in American dinnerware. Certainly such companies as Lenox and Castleton can hold their own quality-wise with most of the European manufacturers. The sets assemble easily, and since so much material is available on the Internet, beginning collectors, as well as homemakers, can put sets together over a period of time and add auxiliary pieces as needed. Replacement services also are beneficial since they keep "wants" on file. These factors help make American dinnerware very attractive.

Brightly decorated dinnerware such as Vernon Kilns, Franciscan, and Red Wing continue to be bright spots. Red Wing Bob White with its numerous accessory pieces remains a favorite and supports strong prices especially for unusual forms.

Vintage Fiesta continues to have a strong following headed by a "super" rare medium green-covered onion soup that crossed the auction block for $10,000. Rare colors on unusual shapes continue to show strong interest and very good prices. Harlequin also has its followers and remains active. Other Homer Laughlin seems to be stacking up on the shelves with no clear patterns emerging as favorites.

Well-decorated stoneware has been selling well at auction. Even minor chipping hasn't affected the pricing when strong designs such as pecking chickens and people decorate the surface. Face or grotesque jugs are making their presence known and will be added as prices stabilize in the future.

# SEEING AMERICA'S CERAMICS INDUSTRY

The collector of American ceramics is in a fortunate position. Many fine museums specializing in ceramic products of the United States are within easy reach. Several top-quality museums maintain extensive collections of work native to the region and provide a wealth of educational materials such as early company catalogs and sales material. The museums' libraries can offer a wealth of information.

One such museum that your authors visited while traveling around the country seeking material for this book is the East Liverpool Museum of Ceramics located in East Liverpool, Ohio. Situated in one of the major United States pottery and porcelain centers from the late 1800s and well into the 20th century, the museum offers a glimpse into the technology and economics of this period. It is a must stop for any serious collector of American ceramics. Museums such as this one can be found in many parts of the United States.

In addition, several working porcelain and pottery factories offer tours of their facilities. The great Homer Laughlin factory in Newell, West Virginia (across the river from East Liverpool), Hall China, and the Robinson-Ransbottom concern offer walking tours complete with demonstrations of the art of the commercial potter.

A trip to Doylestown, Pennsylvania is a must for those whose interest lies in American art tiles. The Moravian Tile Works offers a most interesting tour with demonstrations in the fine art of tile production. An interesting museum illustrates some of the factory's finest work. Finally, many studio potters across the country welcome visitors, but these can be hit or miss and communications with the studio prior to the visit may be prudent.

**Museum of Ceramics, East Liverpool, Ohio.**

# ABBREVIATIONS USED IN THE LISTINGS

| | | | |
|---|---|---|---|
| (A) | auction price | int | interior |
| AD | after dinner | irid | iridescent |
| adv | advertising | irreg | irregular |
| bkd | background | l | length |
| C | Century | lt | light |
| c | circa | lg | large |
| circ | circular | med | medium |
| cov | cover, covered | mkd | marked |
| d | diameter or depth | mk, mks | mark, marks |
| dbl | double | mtd | mounted |
| diag | diagonal | mts | mounts |
| dk | dark | # | numbered |
| dtd | dated | oct | octagonal |
| emb | embossed | opal | opalescent |
| ext | exterior | orig | original |
| ftd | footed | pr, prs | pair, pairs |
| ft | foot | rect | rectangular |
| ground | background | sgd | signed |
| h | height | sm | small |
| hex | hexagonal | sq | square |
| H-H | handle to handle | unmkd | unmarked |
| horiz | horizontal | vert | vertical |
| hp | hand painted | w | width |
| imp | impressed | yr | year |

## ABINGDON USA

Bookends, 7" h, black glaze, "ABINGDON USA" mk, pr, $110.

# Abingdon Pottery

### Abingdon, Illinois
### 1934-1950

**History:** The Abingdon Sanitary Manufacturing Company began in 1908 and made china plumbing fixtures. By 1934 Abingdon Pottery started to produce art pottery using the same equipment and material used for plumbing fixtures, a true white vitreous porcelain. Domestic and English clays were used for the high-fired china bodies.

Many skilled modelers worked on the numerous decorative and utilitarian designs made at the manufactory. Ralph Nelson, Joe Pica, and Harley Stegall created more than one thousand designs for Abingdon during its short history. Regular gloss, crazed, and mottled glazes were used. Additionally, new colors and glazes were introduced every spring and fall during the seventeen year history. They were also known for using crystalline, iridescent, and matte glazes plus unusual textures.

Art pottery production was expanded in 1945, and the name was changed to Abingdon Potteries, Inc. Controlling stock was sold to Briggs Manufacturing Company of Detroit in 1947, and three years later art pottery production was discontinued. The company reverted to producing sanitary wares, their art wares were sold to Haeger Pottery and molds were sold to Pigeon Pottery and were later used by Western Stoneware of Monmouth, Illinois.

A tremendous variety of pieces was modeled including cookie jars, teapots, lamps, figurines, bookends, pitchers, vases, candleholders, flower pots, cookie jars, small animals and much more in a wide range of colors. Shades of blue, red, yellow, pink, green, brown, and gray were used on the hand decorated examples. A total of 149 colors was produced. Blanks were also sold to other companies for decoration.

Almost all pieces of Abingdon pottery were marked, usually in blue underglaze. Some paper labels were also used.

**References:** Joe Paradis, *Abingdon Pottery Artware 1934-1950: Stepchild of the Great Depression,* Schiffer Publishing Ltd.1997; Norma Rehl, *Abingdon Pottery*, Milford, New Jersey, Published privately, 1981.

**Collectors' Club:** Abingdon Pottery Collectors, Elaine Westover, 210 Knox Highway 5, Abingdon, IL 61410, $5.00 per year, quarterly newsletter.

**Museums:** Abingdon City Library, IL; Illinois State Museum, Bloomington, IL.

Bookend
6" h, seagull, ivory, #305, pr ............................. 168.00
6 1/2" h, seated Russian figure, blond glaze, pr ................................................................. 450.00

Bowl
10" l x 7" w, flared rect shape, yellow, "ABINGDON U.S.A." mark ................................. 20.00

Jam Jar, 3 3/4" h, purple grapes, green leaves, white cov, aqua base, $25.

15" l, shell shape, blue ........................................ 35.00
Console Bowl, 11" l, wavy rim, matte pink glaze ............................................................................ 20.00
Console Set, bowl, 14 1/2 l, #532, scroll ends, 2 candleholders, 5" h, #575, blue ........................... 35.00
Cornucopia, 9" d, triple, white, #583 ........................... 50.00
Figure
4 3/4" h, squatting goose, head raised, white glaze ................................................................. 58.00
5 1/4" h, heron, tan, #574 ................................... 68.00
7" h, peacock, turquoise, #416 .......................... 95.00
10" h, Fruit Girl, Cameo Pink glaze .................. 425.00
Floor Vase, 15" h, Grecian style, lt blue, #603 ................................................................. 180.00
Flower Pot, 3 1/4" h, w/saucer, vert fluting, med blue glaze ............................................................................ 7.00
Planter
3" h x 10" l, rect w/flared top, cut corners, matte white glaze, #437 ................................... 30.00
4" h, figural puppy, blue, #670 .......................... 50.00
10" H-H, wavy rim, curled handles white flowerheads, med green glaze, #470 ................. 20.00
Shelf, 8" w, figural angel face and wings, pink glaze, #587 ................................................................. 100.00
Tea Tile, 5" sq, Geisha figure, brown glaze, #400 ........ 80.00
Urn, 9" h, "Wreath," pink, #538 ................................. 30.00
Vase
4 1/2" h, ribbon shape, pink .............................. 25.00
6 1/2" h, raised tulip design, black ext, turquoise int, #654 ........................................... 75.00

Vase, 7 1/4" h, med blue glaze, $48.

**Vase, 10 3/4" h, white glaze, $80.**

6 3/4" h, ribbed rim, 2 handles, peach-pink ext, ivory int, "ABINGDON USA 516" mark ..................... 20.00

7" h, "Sleeping Mexican and Cactus," green and maroon .......................................................... 135.00

7 1/4" h, figural star, relief of stars and clouds, med blue glaze, #463 ............................................ 30.00

7 1/2" h
  Flat shell shape, pink, "ABINGDON U.S.A." mark .................................................................... 30.00
  Sailing ship design, rope ends, matte pink glaze ..................................................................... 25.00

8" h, green seahorse, cream body, yellow int, #596D .................................................................. 75.00

8 1/2" l, fan shape, matte pink ............................. 10.00

8 3/4" h, "Berne," classic shape, multiple compound handles, matte pink ext, matte white int, #535 .................................................................... 20.00

9" h
  Corset shape, thin handles from base to middle, incised horiz lines, white glaze, #152 ......... 30.00
  Handle, black glaze, #630, pr ......................... 70.00
  Overlapped swirl design, cream with gold trim .................................................................... 45.00
  Trumpet shape, ruffled rim, painted white flowers on side, green body glaze .......................... 30.00

11" h, corset shape, 2 curled handles, relief molded vert acanthus leaves, dk green glaze ............. 20.00

11" l, dbl cornucopia shape, white .................... 30.00

Wall Pocket, 8 1/2" h, figural morning glory, matte blue glaze, #377 ......................................................... 25.00

# Advertising and Calendar Plates

### c1906-1950s

**History:** American china and pottery companies sold factory seconds and over-runs to art houses, which then produced the advertising and calendar plates. The majority of these plates were mass-produced, cheaply made, everyday kitchen porcelain or pottery overstock items. Plates were usually available in three or four sizes for decorating. Rim styles were plain, scalloped, slightly wavy, or almost crimped.

The peak years of production and distribution of advertising and calendar advertising plates which were Christmas giveaways were 1906-1915. These were the favorite advertising media for small-town businesses during the 1930s. During the years of World War II, these plates were not made. In the 1950s, many of the manufacturers attempted to recapture the popularity of these plates.

After a merchant selected the plate size and rim style, he would then select a decal for the calendar design that was usually applied to the rim, and a decal for the center of the plate. The advertiser then specified exactly how the name of his business or service would appear, his address, and perhaps a personal message that should be added to the plate. A wide range of businesses utilized advertising plates.

Decals changed every year. Sometimes they were the work of local artists, but sometimes more famous artists became involved. From 1909-15, Howard Christy created a series of his works for use on calendar plates. The Gibson girls were utilized from 1910-1921.

In addition to being used for advertising, calendar plates were ordered by individuals or families to give as gifts at holiday time. Politicians also made use of calendar plates to keep their faces in front of the public.

**References:** Lisa Didier, "Rolling Back the Tears: The Joys of Collecting Calendar Plates," *The Antique Trader Weekly*, July 8, 1998.

**Newsletter:** Alan Gumtow, 710 North Lake Shore Drive, Tower Lakes, IL 60010, *The Calendar*.

Plate
  6 1/2" d, multicolored decal of 3 babies sitting on branch fence eating w/bibs, gold "Souvenir of 3 Rivers, Mich." below, yellow luster rim w/gilt overlay, gilt line rim, Sterling ....................................... 35.00

  7" d, red cherries w/green leaves, irid lt green inner border shaded to yellow and white with pink and white flowers, scalloped and ribbed border and rim, "Compliments of Reynolds & Co. Groceries Elwood City, Pa." ......................................................... 20.00

  7 3/4" d, oct, basket of multicolored flowers at top, raised beaded shaded pink border, "Puritan Cake Co., Inc. Makers of Puritan Cakes Cambridge, Mass." ................................................................. 55.00

  8" d, purple and red berries, green leaves in center, gold "People Who Trade With Us Prosper, Hays & Collins They Like Our Prices" below, 1910 blue calendar leaves on border, gilt rim, East Liverpool, Ohio mk ........................................................... 59.00

  8 1/8" d, center multicolored decal of globe, peace and "The Great World War," blue bordered yellow 1919 calendar leaves on border w/coats of arms, gold

Plate, 7 1/2" d, multi-colored, gold trim, 1910, $55.

Plate, 9" d, "Old Glory," brown boat, blue 1917 calendar leaves and flags, tan ground, gold rim, "D.E. McNichol East Liverpool O." mk, $75.

Plate, 8 5/8" d, dk pink, yellow and white roses, brown 1908 calendar leaves, $28.

Plate, 9 1/2" d, multicolored center, green 1909 calendar leaves and border, gold "COMPLIMENTS OF THE HOME MILLING CO. USE OLD HOMESTEAD FLOUR", $50.

"LOU HAUCK OCTOBER 16, 1919, VALLEY FALLS, KS" on front, McNicol mk ................... 15.00

8 1/4" d

Brown deer in green forest in center, silver "Compliments of Haynes Co-operative Mercantile Co. Haynes, No. Dak." below, 1917 calendar leaves and flags on border .................................... 22.00

Center w/2 cherubs ringing in 1910 New Year bell, green calendar leaves around border w/florals, green scalloped rim, gold "Compliments of P.L. Kimberly General Store" ............................. 30.00

Green and magenta bird in center w/magenta ribbon, gold "COMPLIMENTS OF CENTRE TEA CO." below, magenta outlined 1909 calendar leaves and magenta ribbon on border, scalloped rim ............................................................. 39.00

Multicolored decal of Panama Canal in center, yellow and black calendar leaves for 1915 and American flags, gold "CHAS. SEEPE & SONS DRY GOODS PERU ILLINOIS" on front, flow blue border w/raised designs and gold overlay, "Limoges China" mk ................................ PRICE

Purple pansies in center, blue-green 1911 calendar leaves on inner border, brown clock faces on outer border, gold "A.W. Struve 1763 W. Chicago Ave Fine Foot Wear," worn gold rim ........... 32.00

Two magenta roses and green leaves in center, gold "1909" and "Souvenir of Betterton, MD." month leaves on border, Pope Gosser ....... 28.00

8 3/8" d, decal of 2 cherubs ringing New Year's Bell in center, border of 1910 calendar leaves w/ribbons and sm blue flowers between .......................... 75.00

8 1/2" d

Multicolored mountain lake scene, gold "THE KEDZIE BAKERY, 1510 NORTH KEDZIE AVE-

NUE, CHICAGO," rose-red 1909 calendar leaves below scene, luster border, gold rim, "American China Company, Toronto, Ohio" mk ................................................................. 90.00

Two walking brown and white elk in center, lustered yellow border w/gold hanging swags, "GREETINGS A.G. KOCH, KEWASKUM, WI." on reverse, McNicol ...................................... 10.00

8 5/8" d, multicolored decal of deer in woods in center, "gold COMPLIMENTS OF MERCANTILE DEPT. JOHANNESBURG MNFG. CO. JOHANNESBURG, MICH." below, purple 1911 calendar leaves w/wild life scenes on border .................................... 40.00

9" dOct, center brown basket of red and pink roses, blue border w/raised beading, gold "JOSEPH ZAVSKY FANCY GROCERIES CLEVELAND, OHIO" ......................................................... 19.00

Two turkeys in center, 1911 red calendar leaves on border w/turkeys between, gold "COMPLIMENTS OF SUMMIT LIQUOR CO., SEATTLE, WASH." on front, Goodwin mk .................. 55.00

9 1/8" d, multicolored rural scene in center, gold "COMPLIMENTS OF W.A. BURGIN DEALER IN STAPLES & FANCY GROCERIES SCHOOL SUPPLIES PHONE 9 DARLINGTON, IND" below, green outlined rust 1908 calendar leaves on border, gilt overlay on inner border, gilt edge, Sterling ..... 45.00

9 1/4" d

Bust of woman with brown hair and blue bonnet in center, green 1909 leaves on border, gold "Compliment of E.H. Lutt Niobrara, Neb." .......... 50.00

Center blue and green shaded decal of children swimming in hole w/rhyme and 1910 calendar leaves, green scalloped rim and border w/raised white enameled dots, "gold Compliments of W.L. Flotow, General Merchandise 600 West 10th St. Michigan City, Ind. Bell phone 619"............40.00

Children swimming in center w/rust brown 1910 calendar leaves and "For the merry days of youth...James Whitcomb Riley," gold floral inner border, green scalloped border w/raised dots, gold "Bellefontaine Ohio Second Anniversary Souvenir Syndicate Dept. Store."...............45.00

Decal of Mt. Vernon in center in colors, green 1910 leaves on border, gold "SCHREMPF BROTHERS CO. The Big Cash Store, Watertown, Wis." ........................................................................40.00

Multicolored decal of mill scene with boat in center, gold "HENRY DAUB & SON, GROCER, GRAFTON, PA." brown 1909 calendar on border, scalloped rim, "N.CCO./E.L.Q." mk....25.00

Multicolored floral center w/scattered florals, 1909 calendar leaves on border, "COMPLIMENTS of LOUIS LEHNER LEROY, WIS." scalloped gold rim, D.E. McNicol.......................18.00

9 3/8" d, multicolored decal of cottage scene and mill, 1909 calendar leaves and berries on border, scalloped rim, "BARLEY & TEEGARDEN DEALERS in GRAIN, COAL & GENERAL MERCHANDISE, MT. HERON, OHIO" below center scene ..............30.00

9 1/2" d

Floral center, gold lacy border, gold "Compliments of Star Furn Company Columbus, Ohio," Homer Laughlin blank ............................................12.00

Multicolored barn and lake scene in horseshoe, 1909 calendar leaves around border, gold "F.G. TERWILLIGER HONEDALE, PA." on reverse, KTK & Co. ..................................................38.00

9 3/4" d, brown and white horseheads in center w/horseshoes and 1911 calendar leaves, crazing ........................................................................25.00

10" d, multicolored pilot in classic airplane in center, "J.P. ALLEYS HAMBONE CIGARS" on border, Buffalo Pottery, c1911 ......................................50.00

# American Bisque Company

## Williamstown, West Virginia
## 1919-1982

**History:** The American Bisque Company began in 1919 in Williamstown, West Virginia making kewpie dolls. It soon expanded to vases, planters, and lamp bases. In 1922, B.E. Allen, a part owner of Sterling China Company, purchased American Bisque.

DESIGN
PATENT
REG 120
A.B. CO.

In 1937, the plant was destroyed by flooding. The company started over and added banks, cookie jars, and flower pots to its product line. The plant was then destroyed by fire in 1945 and rebuilt again.

Concurrently, American Pottery Company opened across the river in Marietta, Ohio and also built a plant in Byesville, Ohio. Joseph Lenhart owned American Pottery but was also sales manager of American Bisque. A portion of American Pottery was sold to the son of B.E. Allen, owner of American

Bisque. American Pottery made mixing bowls, covered casseroles, teapots, refrigerator storage containers, and wall pockets.

Molds from the Ludiwici Company of New Lexington, Ohio were sold to American Bisque and American Pottery to add to the intertwining of these companies.

The primary designer for American Bisque from the 1960s to the early 1970s was Al Dye. From 1955-1975, American Bisque pottery was sold by S.S. Kresge. American Pottery was sold in 1961 and went out of business in 1965. Several other companies also decorated American Bisque and American Pottery pieces.

In 1968, American Bisque added new products to its line. Ashtrays, hanging pots, candy dishes, salad sets, and tiered serving trays were made in vibrant colors and marketed under the name Berkeley ware with a clover logo that was sold in chain stores and Sequoia with a tree logo that was sold in gift shops.

American Bisque was sold in 1982 to Bipin Mizra. Its name was changed to American China Company and went out of business several years later.

Cookie jars were another major product for American Bisque. (See Cookie Jars). Some of the jars were novelty examples including jars with blackboards or magnets, jars with flat tops to act as serving trays, and jars with action pieces. American Bisque also made cookie jars for Cardinal China Company of Carteret, New Jersey and these were marked Cardinal.

Another company that American Bisque made pottery for was Leeds which was a Chicago based distributor who was licensed by Walt Disney Productions to use their characters in pottery pieces. Leed also had pottery produced by several other manufactures.

**References:** Mary Jane Giacomini, *American Bisque: A Collector's Guide with Prices,* Schiffer Publishing Ltd. 1994.

Bank

4" h, "Fatsy Pig," pink and blue...............................47.00

4 3/4" h, figural dancing pig, red, yellow, and green dots, red ruffled rim ......................................................35.00

6" h, standing elephant, gray and black, yellow base ........................................................................75.00

6 1/4" h, Snow White, yellow and blue, Leeds.........85.00

6 3/4" h, Mickey Mouse, black outlines, yellow shoes, pink flowers.....................................68.00

7" h, Popeye head .................................................450.00

7 1/2" h

Bambi, brown, green, and black..........................95.00

Donald Duck fishing ............................................95.00

Doorstop, 8" h, figural Siamese cat, brown shades .....35.00

Grease Jar, 6 1/2" h, churn shape, red flower petals, black leaves, brown ground ...............................................38.00

Lamp, 7 1/2" h, Davy Crocket, brown, gray, and tan ........................................................................150.00

Pitcher, 6 1/4" h, figural chick, yellow w/gold accents ........................................................................50.00

Planter

4" h, figural white stork and tan woven base ...........10.00

5 1/4" h

6 1/2" l, green gazelle, brown and green tree stump planter......................................................19.00

Bear w/clown and blocks, gray, black, and red ........................................................................35.00

5 1/2" h

Circus Elephant, yellow and pink .........................15.00

**Planter, 6" h, brown dog, rose cheeks, lime green shoe, umkd, $20.**

# American Haviland Company

### New York, New York
### 1940-1960s

**History:** In 1940, Theodore Haviland opened a factory for the manufacture of Haviland China in the United States in New York. Due to high duties on Haviland China coming to America, increasing costs in Europe, and the start of World War II, it was impossible to continue manufacturing Haviland China in France for the American markets.

Approximately fifty patterns were made in the United States. First wares were marked "THEODORE HAVILAND New York." Later wares had "Made in America" with "New York." Prior to 1950 the firm was called "Theodore Haviland & Co., Inc." After 1950 it was called "Haviland and Co., Inc."

**Collectors' Club:** Haviland Collectors Internationale Foundation, P.O. Box 11632, Milwaukee, WI, 53211.

**APPLE BLOSSOM PATTERN**
| | |
|---|---|
| Bread and Butter Plate | 16.00 |
| Cup and Saucer | 30.00 |
| Dinner Plate | 18.00 |
| Salad Plate | 16.00 |

**ARLINGTON PATTERN**
| | |
|---|---|
| Cup and Saucer | 6.00 |
| Gravy Boat, 6 1/2" l | 10.00 |
| Meat Platter, 13 3/4" l, w/well | 20.00 |

Plate
| | |
|---|---|
| 6 1/2" d | 6.00 |
| 7 1/2" d" | 8.00 |
| 10 1/2" d | 10.00 |
| Soup Plate, 7 3/4" d | 8.00 |
| Vegetable Bowl, 9 1/2" l | 15.00 |

**ASHLEY PATTERN**
| | |
|---|---|
| Cup and Saucer | 8.00 |
| Vegetable Bowl, 9 1/2" l | 20.00 |

**CAMBRIDGE PATTERN**
| | |
|---|---|
| Creamer, 2 3/4" h | 5.00 |
| Cup and Saucer | 5.00 |
| Gravy Boat w/undertray | 10.00 |

Plate
| | |
|---|---|
| 6 1/2" d | 5.00 |
| 7 1/2" d | 6.00 |
| 10 3/4" d | 10.00 |
| Meat Platter, 13 1/2" l, w/well | 20.00 |

Vegetable Bowl
| | |
|---|---|
| 6 3/4" l | 8.00 |
| 9 1/2" l | 10.00 |

**CAMELLIA PATTERN**
| | |
|---|---|
| Dinner Plate | 10.00 |
| Salad Plate | 10.00 |

**CLINTON PATTERN**
| | |
|---|---|
| Plate, 6" d | 2.00 |

**GOTHAM PATTERN**
| | |
|---|---|
| Cup and Saucer | 8.00 |

**PASADENA PATTERN**
| | |
|---|---|
| Cup and Saucer | 18.00 |
| Gravy Boat, 7" l, w/attached undertray | 40.00 |

Little pig, cream and red ..... 28.00
6 1/4" h, Dutch boy w/wooden shoe ..... 15.00
6 1/2" h, Snow White, yellow, turquoise, and black ..... 115.00
6 3/4" h
    Figural standing seal w/barrel, dk green and yellow spray ..... 20.00
    Figural swan, pink, yellow, red, and green ..... 15.00
7" h x 8" l, donkey and cart, tan and brown, gold accents ..... 18.00
7" l, figural squatting rabbit, pink and white ..... 9.00
7 1/2" h
    8 1/2" l, figural gypsy and cart, multicolored ..... 10.00
    Figural bust of praying Madonna, blue, yellow, and gold ..... 10.00
9 1/2" l, figural tugboat, tan and blue ..... 35.00
10" l, figural stalking tiger, tan w/black stripes ..... 10.00
14" l, figural swimming fish, turquoise w/glaze accents ..... 10.00
Shakers, 4 1/4" h, Dumbo elephant, sgd "Walt Disney," pr ..... 85.00
Vase
4 1/2" h
    Cornucopia, blue and white ..... 12.00
    Figural boot, drip gold glaze, mkd ..... 22.00
5" h, pitcher shape, gold stylized blossoms, green ground ..... 10.00
6" h
    Bulbous, 2 handles, raised pink morning glory and green leaves, molded swirl ground, pink-mauve ground ..... 10.00
    Molded heart, ribbon, and flowers, cream and yellow, gold trim ..... 20.00
    6 1/2" h, molded rose and green leaves, gold accents ..... 30.00
7 1/4" h, horiz ribbing, curled handles, brown-green speckling, pr ..... 35.00
8 1/2" h, squat base, tapered neck, yellow ground w/gold speckles ..... 10.00

Plate

    6" d.................................................................8.00

    7 1/2" d........................................................10.00

    10" d............................................................18.00

## ROSALINDE PATTERN

Casserole, Cov.................................................75.00

Creamer ..........................................................40.00

Cup and Saucer ..............................................50.00

Gravy Boat, attached undertray ....................65.00

Plate

    6 1/2" d......................................................15.00

    7 1/2" d......................................................20.00

    10 1/2" d....................................................40.00

Platter, 11 3/4" l..............................................75.00

Sugar Bowl, Cov..............................................60.00

## UNNAMED PATTERNS-THEODORE HAVILAND BLANKS

Maroon border w/gold overlay

    Berry Bowl, 5" d .......................................4.00

    Cup and Saucer........................................5.00

    Plate

        6 1/2" d ............................................5.00

        7 1/2" d ............................................6.00

        8 1/2" d ............................................6.00

        10 3/4" d ........................................10.00

    Soup Bowl, 7 3/4" d .................................7.00

ACOMA    Marie & Sartano

# American Indian Pottery

### Arizona, Colorado, New Mexico, South Carolina
### 1600-present

**History:** Areas in New Mexico and the southwestern United States have an uninterrupted history of pottery production, especially from the Historic Period of about 1600 until the present time.

Pottery was very important to the Pueblo Indians who made utilitarian pottery for cooking, storage, and gathering, and made other pieces for ceremonial and trading purposes. Bowls were made in a wide assortment of sizes, with the dough bowl being the largest. Jars also came in many sizes: the large storage jars were used for grain. Water jars, canteens, pitchers and other pieces all served everyday needs, while ceremonial vessels and effigy figures were for special events.

No two pieces of pottery were alike, and the Pueblos did not use a potter's wheel. The clay was rolled into ropes that were coiled to build up walls. Shaping and thinning was accomplished with a piece of gourd for a scraper. The body surface was rough and usually covered with a fine red or white clay slip. Many decorations were black or dark colors that were made by adding powdered manganese or iron to the boiled juice of plants. Shaped and decorated pieces were set out on a sheet metal or rock framework and cov-

ered with slabs of dried cow dung or slow burning fuel, which was then lit. The fire was smothered if the final pottery was supposed to be black. If not, the fire produced shades of cream, tan, red, orange or yellow. Several hours were needed for firing.

For the most part, pottery was made by women, but some men worked on pots, too. A variety of decorations was used, including feathers, star patterns, floral motifs, volutes, clouds, circles, suns, and animals, to name some. Each Pueblo area used the ceramic materials that were available in its own group of villages. Each type of pottery had a two-part name signifying the form and decoration characterized by the geographical area of distribution and the time of manufacture. There were great varieties in types, sizes, color and designs from the various pottery areas.

By about 1900, pottery production was on the decline, except for ceremonial pieces and limited utilitarian items, because it was not necessary to make cooking and eating pieces that were available in the Anglo world. During the 20th century, there was a revival of pottery making and new types and styles were developed. The Pueblos did not repeat pottery styles from earlier periods. The specific area in which a piece was made can be determined by identifying the tempering material used. Each of the six pueblos used a particular temper (the neutral ingredient added to the clay).

Many Pueblos incorporated the "ceremonial" line break in their pottery decorations, although there is not a definite reason for this break. Encircling black lines framed decorative motifs and a small interruption in the framing lines was called a break. Many forms of feather shapes were symbolic, such as round capped feathers, series of feathers and split feathers. At different times and in different areas, black or red rims were used.

In the northern Tewa Pueblos of Picuris and Taos, pottery was mostly utilitarian in nature. The other northern pueblos of San Juan and Santa Clara made unpainted red and black wares. In about 1850, Santa Clara used a sculpted bear paw trademark on jars in sets of three or more. They also made the wedding vase, which was a double-spouted jar with connecting handles.

The southern Tewa villages specialized in painted pottery. The most famous of these areas is the San Ildefonso Pueblo. From 1760-1880, the standard style on large simple storage jars was Powhodge Polychrome—black-painted geometric motifs on cream slip. Water jugs were more common than bowls. For a time, pottery making declined, but the coming of the railroad revitalized the tourist trade about 1880. San Ildefonso Polychrome and other attractive red-and-black decorated pottery was made in response to the renewed interest.

Maria Martinez and Julian, her husband, became famous in 1918 for their black wares. They were very prolific and their popular pieces had a deep glossy black background with matte-black decorations, often a stylized feather design. They also made polychrome pieces as a result of Julian's experimentation with colors.

Other southern villages included Tesuque Pueblo, where pottery was made until c1910, and Nambe Pueblo, where painted pottery was produced. In the northeast Keres Pueblos, the Cochiti used ceremonial symbols on its pottery, and the Santo Domingo used naturalistic decorations. There were six pueblos in the central area: Zia, Santa Ana, Jemez, San Felipe, Isleta, and Sandia—all making an assortment of pottery.

The Acoma, Laguna, and Zuni Pueblos were the only potters who tempered clay with finely crushed shards of pottery. Nearly every broken pottery piece was saved by these New Mexican pueblos for re-use in this way. Red banding was not used on Acoma or Laguna pottery. In 1850, McCarthys Polychrome had bird and floral motifs, while Acoma Polychrome, from the turn of the century, had geometric decorations. Laguna Polychrome decorations mostly followed Acoma traditions, but were less intricate and bolder. Zuni Polychrome, made from about 1850, had sunflowers, deer with a red arrow from the mouth to the heart, birds, and butterflies.

The Hopi villages in Arizona made pottery that was different from that of the Pueblos. Hopi pieces were yellow with mottled orange tones, had motifs that were painted on a polished paste rather than slip, and had flat or convex bases. A new school of pottery started by Nampeyo and her family about 1900 (and still in existence) revived the ancient Sikyatki polychrome style. The Hopi still make pottery for their own use, as well as to sell.

North American Indians did not use a potter's wheel to make their wares. They used a paddle and anvil to thin and compress coil or used the tools to form pieces without coils. Some northern Plains Indians also used this method. In addition, pieces were modeled or molded in a basket.

The Catawba Indians from Rock Hill, South Carolina, were the most active pottery makers of the eastern tribes. They made tablewares, vases, pitchers and flowerpots with non-characteristic designs and forms and sold the wares to support themselves in the 1900s. They used the coil method and open pit firing and their blackwares were similar to those made by the San Ildefonso Pueblo.

Several tribes comprise the Colorado River Division of the Yuman group. Early Yuman pottery had less decoration than the Pueblo wares. Mojave made painted wares with the paddle and anvil coil method.

**References:** John W. Barry, *American Indian Pottery*, Books Americana, Revised Edition, 1984; Kenneth M. Chapman, *The Pottery of Santo Domingo Pueblo*, University of New Mexico Press, 1977; ———, *The Pottery of San Ildefonso Pueblo*, University of New Mexico Press, 1970; Rick Dillingham, *Acoma and Laguna Pottery*, School of American Research Press, 1993; Larry Frank and Francis H. Harlow, *Historic Pottery of the Pueblo Indians 1600-1880*, Schiffer Publishing Ltd. 1990; Betty LeFree, *Santa Clara Pottery Today*, University of New Mexico Press, 1975; Susan Peterson, *Maria Martinez, Five Generations of Potters*, Smithsonian Institution Press, 1978.

**Museums:** Arizona State Museum, Tucson, AZ; Denver Art Museum, CO; El Pueblo Museum, Pueblo, CO; Heard Museum of Primitive Art and Anthropology, Phoenix, AZ; Koshare Indian Museum, La Junta, CO; Milwaukee Public Museum, WI; Museum of the American Indian, Heye Foundation, New York, NY; Museum of New Mexico, Santa Fe, NM; National Museum of the American Indian, Smithsonian Institution, Washington, DC; San Diego Museum of Man, CA; Southwest Museum, Los Angeles, CA; University of Arizona Museum of Art, Tucson, AZ.

**Bowl, 3 1/2" h x 4" d, black matte and polished design, sgd "Maria Martinez & Popoive," c1960, $6,500.**

**Bowl, 7 3/4" d, black designs, orange ground, c1910, $750.**

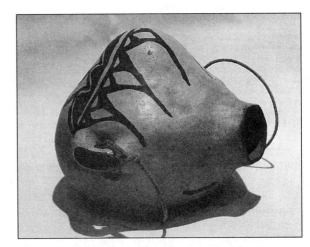

**Canteen, 7 1/2" h, black, tan ground, Cochiti Pueblo, c1875, $1,150.**

## PLAINS AND SOUTHEASTERN

Bottle
7" h, swirl painted and engraved, Mississippian
.................................................................... 1,500.00
7 1/2" h, flared rim, gray-tan, repaired neck, Mississippian
.................................................................... 465.00
Jar, 4" h x 6 3/4" d, rolled rim, gray-tan, Mississippian
.................................................................... 400.00

Effigy
5" l x 3" h, walking bear, gray, Mississippian
.................................................................... 3,500.00
9 1/2" l x 5 1/4" h, incised lips, head dress, eyelashes, smoked terra cotta earthenware, sgd "Sara Ayers Catawba," (A)........................ 385.00

## SOUTHWESTERN

Bowl
5" h, overhead handle, figural bird heads on rim, red-orange and umber geometric design on white slip ground, Acoma Pueblo, (A)............... 100.00
6" d, polished blackware, carved water serpent on recessed matte ground, sgd "Donna Tafoya, Santa Clara Pueblo," (A) .............................. 330.00
6 3/4" d
Black painted lizard on white ground int, 6 thin bands on int rim, Mimbres, c1050, (A) ................. 1,610.00
Relief carved water serpent against matte black ground, polished black body, sgd "Christina Naranjo, Santa Clara" on base, (A) .......... 1,230.00

8 1/2" d, int w/black zigzag geometric designs on white clay body, Mimbres, restored, (A) ...................... 935.00

9" w, polychrome stylized leaves, Acoma ............. 850.00

9 3/4" d, painted matte black stylized curved wing motifs and rect designs on polished black slip ext, sgd "Marie," San Ildefonso, (A) ............................ 4,025.00

10" d, brown and red painted central abstract wing and rim bands w/circ motifs on orange slip int, Hopi, (A) ................................................................ 245.00

10 1/2" d, black flowing swirls, Hopi, c1840 .......... 975.00

11" d, brown zigzags and steps on int, orange-brown ground, Hopi, c1920 ......................................... 375.00

11 1/4" d, black and red painted int w/curved wing motif on orange slip ground, Hopi, (A) ...................... 805.00

12 1/2" d, orange and black checkerboard design in center, black stylized leaves on int, orange ext and rim, San Ildefonso, c1920 .................................... 1,250.00

Chili Bowl, 7 1/8" d, panels of black leaves, orange int, cream ground, Santa Domingo .............................. 350.00

Dough Bowl

14 1/2" d, black and white triangles and geometric shapes, orange int, black rim, Santa Domingo ................................................................. 1,250.00

19 1/2" d, painted black band of triangles forming segmented star motifs between bands, cream slip ground, Santa Domingo, (A) ...................................... 2,875.00

Effigy Pot, 6 1/2" h x 7" d, handled, gray interlocking zigzag designs ................................................................ 1,750.00

Jar

4 1/4" h, blackware, rounded sides, flared rim w/incised grooves, Santa Clara, (A) .................................. 415.00

4 3/4" d, flat base, brown and red painted sq motif on rim w/4 radiating dbl feather designs, overall hatching, orange slip ground, Hopi, (A) ........................ 1,495.00

5" h, orange and gray-black zigzags, dk orange ground, Santa Clara Pueblo ......................................... 440.00

6 1/4" d, squat bowl shape, closed top, band of matte black geometrics on polished black slip ground, sgd "Marie & Santana," San Ildefonso, (A) ........... 2,185.00

6 1/2" h x 8 1/2" d, ruffled rim, umber and red ochre geometrics, diagonals, and curled designs on polished orange slip ground, sgd "Verna Nahee," Hopi, (A) ................................................................ 412.00

6 3/4" d, black painted bird figures w/oval wings and foliate elements, cream slip ground, red painted base and int, sgd "Santana Melchor," Santa Domingo, (A) ................................................................ 230.00

7" h, effigy, figural seated man w/bulbous torso, red-brown accented slit eyes and mouth and geometric pattern, Mesa Verde, (A) ............................... 4,600.00

7 1/2" d, indented base, red and black painted band of geometrics, stepped designs, and stepped arrowheads, semicircles and scrolling foliates on shoulder, cream slip ground, Zuni, (A) ............................ 2,070.00

7 3/4" d, indented base, flared sides, tapered neck, red and black painted band of foliates and triangles under scalloped band, floral motifs on neck, beige slip ground, San Ildefonso, (A) ............................. 2,760.00

8" h, bulbous shape, scalloped rim, polished and carved band of key and terraced motifs, "Lee Ann Tafoya, Santa Clara," (A) ....................................... 1,495.00

8 1/2" d, globular shape, indented base, narrow neck w/scalloped rim, orange shades and black painted bird figures alternating w/arched banding and scattered florals, white ground, Acoma, (A) ...................... 4,830.00

10" h, smoked orange slip w/curvilinear umber and red orange designs, sgd "Sahyah," Hopi, (A) ......... 358.00

12 1/4" d, squat shape, red-brown and black painted deer w/heartlines and hatched "V" designs, creamy white slip ground, Zuni, (A) .................................... 7,820.00

13 3/4" h, black and beige painted bands of foliate motifs, circ designs, joined triangles and bars on dk red-brown slip ground, Santa Domingo, (A) ......... 5,750.00

Pitcher

4" h, black stylized flowerheads, cream ground, orange int, Santa Domingo, c1930 ............................. 325.00

6" h, painted black and red overall floral designs, band of scalloping on ext border, circ designs on int border, cream slip ground, San Ildefonso, (A) .............. 518.00

Plate

5 1/2" d, blackware, matte floral motif on polished black slip body, sgd "Blue Corn," San Ildefonso, (A) ................................................................ 695.00

6 1/4" d, painted matte black band of stylized wing motifs, polished black slip ground, sgd "Maria/Popovie 1964," San Ildefonso, (A) ......................................... 3,450.00

9" d, red and brown painted stylized bird motifs in center on cream slip, banded rim, Hopi, (A) ................. 240.00

Pot

9 1/2" h, polychrome zigzags and geometrics, basketweave shoulder, Acoma ..................... 3,500.00

**Vase, 8" h, orange and black designs, tan ground, Santa Domingo, c1940, $675.**

**Jar, 11" h x 11" d, black designs, cream ground, Tesuque Pueblo, $25,000.**

13" h, orange and black deer, geometrics and arches, and lighting bolts in layers, red clay, Zuni, c1900, hairlines, (A) ....................................................... 6,160.00

Storage Jar, 18 1/4" h, black flying mythical bird, orange and black striped banding, cream ground, Zia........ 10,500.00

Teapot, 7" h, black stylized flowerheads, orange stems, orange trim, cream ground, Cochin, c1920........... 400.00

Wedding Jar

6 1/2" h, black basketweave base, orange bird, cream ground, rope twist handle, Acoma........................ 75.00

7 3/4" h, red, cream, and brown painted stylized wing motif on beige slip ground, sgd "Deloris Toya Jemez Pueblo, N.M." on base, (A)............................... 115.00

Vase

5 3/4" h, black seed pods, cream ground, lt orange int, black rim, Santa Domingo ............................... 250.00

7 1/4" h, swollen cylinder shape, redware, red, brown, cream, and gray feather motifs, polished red slip body, sgd "Yolanda Velarde, Santa Clara, Pueblo," (A) ............................................................ 420.00

8" h, ball shape with flared rim, flat circ foot, Santa Clara, black, polished vert band of wavy leaves, bands of rectangles, matte black ground, sgd "Israel Sandova" ............................................................ 425.00

# Anchor Pottery

### Trenton, New Jersey
### 1884-1927

after 1904

**History:** Israel Lacey purchased the property from the Joseph Moore Pottery estate and renamed it Anchor Pottery. James Norris operated the plant, and he produced cream colored, white granite, and semi-porcelain wares. Both dinnerwares and toilet sets were made.

After a succession of managers, the plant closed in 1927 and was taken over by Fulper Pottery Company of Flemington, New Jersey.

**Platter, 13 3/4" l, lavender and white flowers, green leaves, on lt blue ground, relief molded handles and border trim, gold curlicues outlined rim, $15.**

Bone Dish, 6 1/2" l, blue, pink, green, gray, and white floral bouquet in center, gold rim .............................. 5.00

Chamber Pot, 11" d, 5 1/2" h, painted pink roses, green leaves, raised scrolling on body and handle, worn gold trim............................................................................ 30.00

Dish, 8 3/4" l, oval, beige glaze, mkd ............................ 5.00

Pitcher, 5" h, center band of pink roses and green foliage, mkd ...................................................................... 10.00

Platter, 14" l x 10" w, oval, emb handles, wavy rim, white glaze, mkd ................................................................ 10.00

Vase, 4 1/2" h, bulbous middle, spread ft, wavy flared rim, brown floral decal, yellow to tan ground ................. 45.00

Wash Set, pitcher, 11 1/2" h, bowl, 15 3/4" d, toothbrush holder, 5 1/2" h, cov dish, 6 1/2" d, purple pansies, green and yellow foliage, gold splashed molded rims, "green anchor and wreath, Anchor, Port of Trenton" mk, c1893 ............................................................................ 425.00

1911

# Arequipa Pottery

### Fairfax, California
### 1911-1918

**History:** Arequipa Pottery was started in 1911 in a tuberculosis sanitarium in Arequipa as a project for the female patients. Frederick Rhead, art director at Roseville, and Agnes, his wife, served as instructors. Native California clays were utilized for the works.

After an attempt to incorporate the potteries, the Rheads left, and Albert Solon became pottery director in 1913. He had trained in England as a ceramic engineer and worked in a tile factory before coming to the United States. A variety of works was made by hand at the pottery. Patients were responsible for much of the decorating and hand finishing. Solon experimented with a variety of glazes. Works were exhibited at the Panama-Pacific Exposition in 1915, where they won several awards.

F.H. Wilde replaced Solon in 1915 and continued the work with glazes. With the constant turnover of patients and the frequent changes in directors, no specific style developed at Arequipa during the years of its existence. Handmade Spanish type tiles were introduced by Wilde before the pottery was forced to close due to the war in Europe in 1918.

Most pieces were marked with the jug under a tree mark along with the company name either painted, incised, or impressed. Some have the date added to the mark. Paper labels also were used.

**Museums:** National Museum of History and Technology, Smithsonian Institution, Washington, DC; New Orleans Museum of Art, LA.

**Vase, 6" h, lt yellow and white squee-zebag design on blue neck, matte purple body, imp mk, (A), $5,225.**

Bowl
  5" d, closed form
    Carved relief of primrose under matte dk green glaze, (A) ................................................1,320.00
    Matte dk green to black glaze, painted mk, (A)
    ...................................................................176.00
  6 1/2" d, Closed Shouldered Form
    Emb eucalyptus branches under matte green and dk blue glaze, (A)...............................880.00
    Matte purple glaze, dtd 1912, (A) ....................286.00
  7" d, low, faceted form, emb grass design, semi-matte blue and green glaze, "stamped AREQUIPA CALIFORNIA" mk, (A) ...........................................385.00
  9 1/2" d, low form, matte blue glaze, dtd 1912, (A)
    ...................................................................209.00
  Scarab, 3" l, incised beetle, matte maroon glaze, mkd, (A)
    ...................................................................770.00

Vase
  3 3/4" h, bulbous shape, short collar, mottled matte green glaze, "ink Arequipa, California" mk, (A)
    ...................................................................412.00
  4" h, molded floral design under matte blue and green glaze, (A) .............................................715.00
  4 1/4" h, squat shape, closed shoulder, enameled plant w/white berries, semi-matte blue-gray glaze, (A)
    ...................................................................660.00
  5 1/2" h
    Flared form w/swollen shoulder, matte rose pink glaze, chip on ft, (A) .....................................385.00
    Tapered shape, short collar, emb stylized leaves, mottled matte purple glaze, "Arequipa, California" mk, hairlines, (A)..............................................357.00
  7" h, bulbous shape, tapered cylinder neck, red, squee-zebag wreath of heart leaves on frothy green glaze, (A)...............................................................4,675.00
  7 1/2" h, gourd form, matte suspended green glaze, dtd 1913, (A)............................................1,540.00
  8" h, waisted shape, suspended matte blue glaze, mkd, (A) ...............................................................1,760.00

# Autumn Leaf

## 1930s-1970s
## East Liverpool, Ohio

**History:** The Hall China Company made the Autumn Leaf decal pattern and offered it exclusively through the Jewel Tea Company of Barrington, Illinois. This door-to-door sales firm offered Autumn Leaf pieces as premiums for the purchase of other items, such as teas, coffee, grocery items, and laundry products.

During the Depression, Autumn Leaf pieces had a lot of popular appeal. Sales people brought the groceries, along with the Autumn Leaf premiums, directly to the home. It was only possible to acquire Autumn Leaf pieces through Jewel Tea.

Many of Hall's Autumn Leaf pieces were made for several decades. In the Autumn Leaf pattern, Hall made dinnerware, kitchenware, accessories, condiments, warmers, tidbits, coffeepots, teapots, shakers, and canisters. Cookie jars were introduced in 1957, followed by butter dishes several years later. Clocks were made from an Autumn Leaf cake plate from 1956-1959.

Other companies that used the Autumn Leaf decal included the Crooksville China Company of Crooksville, Ohio, which used its pieces as a premium for *Needlecraft* magazine. Additional makers of Autumn Leaf included American Limoges, Crown, Harker, Vernon of California, Paden City, and Columbia Chinaware. Many of these pieces were made prior to 1930, and few of them have an identifying mark. The Hall pieces were marked "Superior Hall Quality Dinnerware."

Hall's first piece with the Autumn Leaf decal was a 9" mixing bowl. Two smaller bowls were added and remained in the line until Autumn Leaf was discontinued in 1976. New items were added regularly since it was developed as a premium line, and other pieces were discontinued. The incentive was to buy more products to get different premiums. Items not popular with housewives were quickly discontinued. Other companies' Autumn Leaf examples were usually not the quality of the Hall pieces.

In 1990, China Specialties of Strongville, Ohio commissioned Hall China Company to produce selected pieces of china in the Autumn Leaf pattern. They were introduced as special limited editions. Included in this list were a 6-cup Airflow teapot, the conic mug, the covered Norris water jug, and the Irish coffee mug that were marked in several different ways.

Several pieces were also commissioned by the Autumn Leaf Collectors' Club, including the NY teapot, and the Edgewater vase that are marked as such.

**References:** Jo Cunningham, *The Autumn Leaf Story*, Hafa-Production, 1976; C.L. Miller, *Jewel Tea Company, Its History and Products*, Schiffer Publishing Ltd.1994; Margaret & Ken Whitmyer, *The Collector's Encyclopedia of Hall China*, Collector Books, 1989, Values Updates, 1992, 2nd Edition, 1994, Values updated, 1997.

**Collectors' Club:** National Autumn Leaf Collectors Club, Rt #16, Box 275, Tulsa, OK 74131-9600.

Bean Pot, 6 3/8" h, 2 handles, "Hall Mary Dunbar" mk
.............................................................................180.00
Berry Bowl, 5 1/2" d.............................................8.00
Bowl
  7" d, "HALLS SUPERIOR" mk ..........................11.00

**Coffee Server, 9 1/2" h, Hall, $89.**

| | |
|---|---|
| 9" d, "HALLS SUPERIOR" mk | 30.00 |
| 10 1/2" l, Hall | 32.00 |
| Bud Vase, 5 1/2" h, Hall gold mk | 180.00 |
| Cake Plate, 9 1/2" d | 30.00 |
| Cereal Bowl, 6" d | 10.00 |
| Coffee Server, 9 1/2" h, "HALLS SUPERIOR" mk | 90.00 |
| Creamer, 4 1/4" h, old style | 45.00 |
| Cream Soup, 6 1/2" H-H | 25.00 |
| Cup and Saucer, Hall | 15.00 |
| Custard Cup, 3 3/4" d | 10.00 |
| French Baker, 7 3/4" d, "HALLS SUPERIOR" mk | 25.00 |
| Fruit Bowl, 6 1/2" d | 5.00 |
| Grease Jar, Cov, 2 3/4" h, Hall Jewel Tea | 30.00 |
| Mixing Bowl | |
| 6 1/4" d | 18.00 |
| 7 1/2" d | 32.00 |
| Pie Baker, 9" d, Columbia | 50.00 |
| Pie Plate, 9 1/2" d, Hall | 39.00 |
| Pitcher | |
| 6" h, Hall Jewel Tea | 40.00 |
| 8 3/4" h, bulbous, "HALLS SUPERIOR" mk | 58.00 |
| Plate, 10" d | 6.00 |
| Platter | |
| 11 1/2" l, Hall | 25.00 |
| 13 1/2" l, Hall | 42.00 |
| Range Shaker, 4 1/4" h, Hall Jewel Tea, pr | 38.00 |
| Sauce Dish, 5 1/2" d | 6.00 |
| Shakers, re-issue, Hall, pr | 35.00 |
| Soup Bowl, 8 1/2" d | 22.00 |
| Teapot, Aladdin shape, with infusor, Hall | 60.00 |

# Batchelder Pottery Company

**Pasadena and Los Angeles, California**
**1910-1932**
**1936-1951**

**History:** Ernest Batchelder started making tiles in his studio in Pasadena, California in 1910. He was influenced by the

Moravian tiles made by Henry Chapman Mercer from Doylestown, Pennsylvania. Batchelder became partners with Frederick Brown, while sculptors Charles and Emma Ingels made master molds for him.

The early tiles were designed in low relief and hand pressed from plaster molds. Some had medieval heraldic subjects or views of California landscapes. The relief tiles made from California clays were sprayed with slip in a variety of colors. Each tile was signed.

Their factory moved to Los Angeles in 1916 and became a full service tile factory making glazed faience tile in numerous designs. They also made architectural panels, moldings, corbels, fireplace facings, and fountains. Lucian Wilson was his new partner. Architectural terra cotta, garden pots and bookends also were made. Batchelder was able to supply a great deal of tiles for the building boom of the 1920s in a variety of colored glazes.

In 1930, the full effect of the Depression hit the company, and it went bankrupt in 1932. The stock was sold to Bauer Pottery. By 1936, Batchelder started over as Batchelder Ceramics in Pasadena. Now he made slip-cast bowls, vases, and such in modern adaptations of the classical Chinese forms in earthenware. The quality of the glazes was excellent. This was a small operation where Batchelder hand incised his name on most pieces. Batchelder ceramics were sold through department stores and gift shops. In 1951, Batchelder retired.

**Reference:** Jack Chipman, *Collector's Encyclopedia of California Pottery, 2nd Edition*, Collector Books, 1998.

| | |
|---|---|
| Bookend, 6" h, incised vert geometric designs, gray glaze, pr, (A) | 220.00 |
| Bowl | |
| 8 1/2" d, green glaze | 85.00 |
| 11" d, flared shape, ext w/lime green body and maroon overspray, int w/yellow ground and maroon overspray, "F.A. BATCHELDER PASADENA 129" mk | 85.00 |

**Tile, 2 3/4" sq, beige ground, blue accents, mkd, (A), $28.**

W. K. Woodard Memorial Library

**Tile, 2 3/4" sq, beige ground, blue accents, (A), $30.**

12 1/2" l, yellow-chartreuse glazed int, mauve ext, "E.A. Batchelder Pasadena, Made in USA 149" mk
.................................................................... 55.00

13" d, 10 sides, chartreuse ground w/maroon overglaze
.................................................................... 75.00

Planter, 12 1/4" l x 3 3/4" w x 4" h, green ext w/brown flecks, cream int .................................................................... 40.00

Tile

2 3/4" sq, matte multicolored stylized poppy pod, mkd, (A)............................................................. 22.00

3 3/4" sq, incised deer design, aqua and bisque, mkd
.................................................................... 95.00

4 1/2" sq, brown trees, blue bkd, imp mk, (A) ........ 440.00

5 1/2" w x 8" h, brown flowers in vase, blue bkd, imp mk, (A) .................................................................. 231.00

6" sq

Blue stylized floral design, brick red bkd, imp mk, (A)
.................................................................... 231.00

Incised brown poppy, black bkd, (A).................. 252.00

8" sq, rust knight on horseback, lt blue accented bkd, (A)
.................................................................... 330.00

Vase

3 1/2" h, ball shape, short collar, matte green and multi-shaded blue glaze, (A) ...................................... 412.00

5" h, cylinder shape, tapered shoulder, gloss cobalt and teal glazes, (A) ...................................... 550.00

6 1/2" h

Hex shape, dry glaze.............................. 340.00

Sq shape, olive green glaze, cream int, mkd .... 100.00

# J.A. Bauer Pottery

## Los Angeles, California
## 1909-1962

**History:** John Andrew Bauer founded the pottery company in 1909 in Los Angeles, California with workers from his Paducah Pottery in Kentucky. He started production with a line of quality flower pots made from California adobe clay.

Stonewares were started as soon as suitable clays were found. Bauer made whiskey jugs, water coolers, covered jars, butter churns, and such. Flower pots continued to be a mainstay of the pottery's business during the first two decades.

Its art pottery line of vases and flower bowls with matte green glazes won a Bronze Medal at the 1915 Panama-California Exhibition in San Diego. Bauer sold the pottery in 1922 to the Bernheim family and his son-in-law Watson Bockmon. Bockmon bought out the Bernheims and incorporated as the J.A. Bauer Pottery Company, Inc. during the Depression.

Victor Houser developed new opaque colors of green, light blue, and yellow for the California colored pottery in both plain and ring designs that were appropriate for both indoor and outdoor use in the early 1930s. Additional colors were added with its success over the years.

The Bauer company purchased the Batchelder tile factory in 1932 and used it as a second plant. Additional lines such as Monterey in the Art Moderne style were introduced in 1934.

Slip-cast vases, planters, jardinieres, candlesticks, flower bowls and figurines were called Cal-Art. They were usually marked in the mold and were made in satin-matte and regular finishes in the mid-1930s.

During the World War II period, La Linda was developed with pastel colors and leadless glazes and became a big seller. After the war and the end of restrictions, Ring Ware was redesigned with streamlined contours and new contemporary colors.

Monterey Moderne was new in 1948 in a contemporary style to compete with Russel Wright designs. Herb Brushe's lines Contempo and Al Fresco were produced by Bauer in the 1950s. Bauer's dinnerwares were practical, unembellished, and pleased the general buying public.

Bauer also introduced special pottery for florists and gardeners including vases, bowls, planters, sand jars, urns, bird baths, and jardinieres. With the loss of key employees in the 1950s along with inexpensive competing Japanese ceramic imports, the Bauer pottery finally closed in the early 1960s.

A great many different marks were used on Bauer pottery. Most were impressed on the bottom of pieces.

**References:** Jack Chipman, *Collector's Encyclopedia of Bauer Pottery*, Collector Books, 1998; _____, *Collector's Encyclopedia of California Pottery, 2nd Edition*, Collector Books, 1998; _____ and Judy Stangler, *The Complete Collectors Guide to Bauer Pottery*, Jo-D Books, 1982; Jeffrey B. Snyder, *Beautiful Bauer: A Pictorial Study with Prices*, Schiffer Publishing Ltd. 2000; *Mitch Tuchman, Bauer: Classic American Pottery*, Chronicle Books, 1995.

## ART POTTERY

Candlestick, 4 1/2" h, figural circle in circle, pink, Cal-Art, Ray Murray, pr ...................................... 225.00

Planter, 4" h x 9" l, figural swan, matte white, Cal-Art
.................................................................... 85.00

**Pitcher, 5" h, red-brown striping and strawberries, green leaves, "Cooking is an Art" under spout, $125.**

Vase

5" h, ribbed body, 2 sml handles at each side, white, Cal-Art ....................................................................... 75.00

6" h

Ribbed fan shape, cobalt, Matt Carlton
.............................................................................. 395.00

"Ruffle," ribbed body, wavy lip, cobalt, Matt Carlton
.............................................................................. 395.00

7" h x 10" d, "Indian," shouldered form, matte black glaze, (A) ............................................................ 230.00

8" h

"Ruffle," ribbed body, wavy lip, orange-red, Matt Carlton ........................................................... 450.00

Twist handles on waist, cobalt, Matt Carlton ..... 995.00

9 3/4" h, cylinder shape, flared rim, chartreuse, "Bauer 10" mk ............................................................ 150.00

12 1/2" h, flower form, leaf base, oyster white speckle glaze, "Bauer 677" mk ................................ 100.00

24" h, "Rebekah," Chinese yellow ........................ 3200.00

## ATLANTA WARE

Bowl

#12, cobalt rings.................................................... 165.00

#18, yellow rings ................................................... 125.00

Vase

8" h

Bulbous base, slender neck, ftd, lt green, "Bauer Pottery Atlanta" mk................................................. 83.00

"Lotus," brown, "Bauer Pottery Atlanta" mk ....... 120.00

10" h, flared ft, swelled body, spread rim, ringed base, yellow .............................................................. 105.00

## BRUSCHE AL FRESCO

Bowl

5" d

Burgundy............................................................ 15.00

Chartreuse.......................................................... 12.00

Gray.................................................................... 10.00

7 1/2" l, oval, coffee brown.................................... 10.00

Bowl, Divided, 9" w, gray speckled finish ..................... 35.00

Plate, 10" d

Burgundy................................................................ 12.00

Gray ...................................................................... 10.00

Platter, 10 1/4" d, gray .............................................. 18.00

**Vase, 5 1/2" h, turquoise, "Atlanta" mk, $65.**

## BRUSCHE CONTEMPO

Platter, 12 5/8" l, rect, speckled pink ............................ 20.00

## FLORIST POTTERY

Bulb Bowl, 6 1/4" d, sky blue glaze, #507 ................... 45.00

Flower Pot

3" h, Cal-Art Swirl, chartreuse ............................. 20.00

4" h

Cal-Art Swirl, yellow ........................................... 25.00

Three step Hi-Fire, white...................................... 40.00

5" h, Cal-Art Swirl, teal blue Bauer California .......... 40.00

9" h, speckled green, "Bauer 10" mk ...................... 50.00

Hanging Pot, 8" h, lt blue, undrilled ........................... 350.00

Jardiniere, 8 1/8" h, stepped shape, rolled rim, white .. 55.00

Oil Jar, 12" h, yellow, "Bauer 100" mk ...................... 1295.00

Vase

Stock

6" h, white, "imp Bauer Los Angeles" mk .......... 225.00

14 1/2" h, speckled white glaze, "imp Bauer Los Angeles" mk ....................................................... 150.00

10" h, swirl, pink glaze "BAUER USA" mk .............. 65.00

## GLOSS PASTEL KITCHEN WARE

Pitcher 6 1/4" h, 2 qt, ice lip, yellow........................... 165.00

Teapot, 13" l, Aladdin style, brown ........................... 295.00

## MISCELLANEOUS

Bowl, 10" d, Indian, matte black glaze ...................... 240.00

Figure, 8" h, standing Madonna, white, Cal-Art......... 450.00

## MISSION MODERNE

Sugar Bowl, Cov, burgundy........................................ 30.00

## MONTEREY

Creamer, Sugar Bowl, and Tray, Miniature, blue creamer and sugar bowl, yellow tray ..................................... 75.00

Cup and Saucer, burgundy ........................................ 30.00

Plate

6 1/2" d, green ....................................................... 8.00

9 1/2" d

Burgundy.............................................................. 25.00

California orange-red ........................................... 18.00

Green ................................................................... 15.00

Turquoise ............................................................. 18.00

Refrigerator Beverage Dispenser, Cov, cobalt, "imp Bauer Pottery Los Angeles" mk ..................................... 495.00

## MONTEREY MODERNE

Chop Plate, 13 1/4" d, brown and chartreuse ............. 45.00

Creamer, burgundy .................................................. 25.00

Mug, 10 oz, olive green............................................. 30.00

Pitcher, 5 1/8" h, pink ............................................... 50.00

## PLAINWARE

Ashtray

3" sq, orange-red, blue, yellow, or green, metal stand, set of 4 ................................................................ 495.00

6" d, sombrero, orange ........................................ 325.00

Bowl, 6" d, aqua ...................................................... 4.00

Plate, 10 1/4" d, aqua............................................... 3.00

## RINGWARE

Ashtray, 4" d, jade green .......................................... 185.00

Basket, 8 1/4" h, yellow............................................. 65.00

Berry Bowl, 4" d, maroon................................................65.00
Bowl, 8" d, orange .......................................................50.00
Bud Vase, 5" h, cobalt ...............................................450.00
Casserole
    6 1/2" d, cobalt ....................................................325.00
    7 1/2" d, orange ...................................................250.00
Chop Plate
    12 1/2" d, orange-red ..........................................125.00
    14" d, green .........................................................225.00
    17" d, yellow.........................................................425.00
Creamer and Cov Sugar Bowl, orange .......................85.00
Mixing Bowl
    #9, dbl ring
        Gray, "Bauer, Los Angeles" mk .........................210.00
        Yellow, "Bauer, Los Angeles" mk ......................200.00
    #12, yellow................................................................95.00
    #24, dbl ring, jade green, "Bauer, Los Angeles" mk, wear
    ..........................................................................50.00
    #30, lt green, "Bauer U.S.A." mk..............................38.00
    #36, orange ..............................................................38.00
Nappy, #8, orange .......................................................85.00
Pie Plate, 9 1/2" d, copper holder, yellow...................125.00
Pitcher
    1 1/2 pint, cobalt...................................................195.00
    2 qt, yellow ...........................................................225.00
    3 qt, jade green .....................................................350.00
Plate
    7 1/2" d
        Cobalt, 3rd period....................................................60.00
        Gray, 2nd period, "Bauer, Los Angeles" mk ........40.00
    9" d, gray, 3rd period................................................45.00
Platter, 12 1/2" l, orange..............................................78.00
Punch Bowl
    11" d, ftd, green....................................................445.00
    14" d, 3 feet, white ...............................................995.00
Relish Tray, 10 1/2" d, divided, maroon.....................395.00
Salad Bowl, 12" d, chartreuse ...................................175.00
Shakers, yellow, pr .....................................................35.00
Sherbet, orange...........................................................85.00
Tea Set, pot, 6 1/2" h, creamer, cov sugar bowl, green
................................................................................425.00
Vase, 8" h, cylinder shape, yellow .............................140.00
Vegetable Bowl, 9" d, yellow......................................75.00

1890     1886

# Edwin Bennett Pottery

### Baltimore, Maryland
### 1844-1936

**History:** Edwin Bennett founded his pottery in 1844 in Balti-more, Maryland to manufacture high quality commercial pot-

tery wares. Teapots were the most important items in the Bennett line. They were made in porcelain, whiteware, majolica, and Rockingham examples. Bennett also made yellowware, caneware, Rockingham ware, flint enamel, and queensware. By 1848, his works were in demand, and he sent for his brother William to assist him.

Charles Coxon joined the Bennett brothers in 1850. Most of his designs were made in Rockingham ware. Examples included shaving mugs, ale pitchers, water coolers, cham-ber pots, teapots and the most famous Rebekah, a ten sided pot with the words "Rebekah at the Well" below the figure of the woman.

During the post Civil War expansion period, Bennett intro-duced a line of white earthenware for both dinner and toilet sets. Some were produced with embossed designs with flower or wheat motifs, while others were transfer printed with a variety of designs. He also used these whiteware bodies for spatterware and spongeware pieces. After the country's Centennial in 1876, much of the whiteware was marked with a variety of marks and some initials. Bennett also experimented with parian wares and American Belleek tea sets.

After the Chicago Exposition of 1893 where the company received a medal of commendation, artwares were intro-duced. Henry Brunt was responsible for the firms art pottery lines.

Brubensul ware, an earthenware line, was introduced in 1894. Mostly pedestals and jardinieres were made with majolica-like glazes in browns, greens, blues, and oranges which flowed together when fired. Pieces were usually marked with paper labels.

Albion ware was introduced in 1895 as a slip painted underglaze ware predominately in greens with a transparent glaze. Designs were mostly Oriental in style. Albion was marked with the Bennett and Albion names in addition to the date and artist's cipher.

The pottery company continued to expand in the early part of the 20th century. "Bennett Bakeware" was the pri-mary line along with "Bennett S-V," a double glazed whitew-are. These pieces were produced by overglazed stenciling or hand-painted designs that were simple in nature. George Bauer became general manager during the 1920s. At this time Bennett Pottery was producing dinnerware with applied decals as were the other producers of American dinnerware. To tempt buyers during the Depression, Bauer knew that dif-ferent items had to be made.

Since dinnerwares were white or cream-colored up to that time, he introduced color. At first he used pastel tones, and then more intense colors. When decals were used they tended to dominate the plates.

Bauer contributed three patents for pottery making that allowed for significant changes in methods of decoration. In the first patent dated September 1931, Bauer introduced a pliable metal stencil for adding color to pottery examples. On some pieces, the stencil was used to block color applica-tions, and on some it provided the outline for decoration. Patterns that were stenciled included flowers, vines, figures, polka dots, and checks. Pieces made included cake ser-vices, canister sets, salt boxes, pie plates, and dinnerwares.

Bauer's other patents were utilized at Harker Pottery which he joined in 1939, though some incised and encrusted "cameo" examples were made before Bennett closed even though the patent is dated 1941.

The Edwin Bennett Pottery Company filed for bankruptcy in 1936 due to the economic climate at the time.

**Museums:** Maryland Historical Society Museum, Baltimore, MD; Museum of History and Technology, Smithsonian Insti-tution, Washington DC.

**Platter, 11 3/4" l, floral border, black ground w/yellow cartouches of blue and red flowers on border, $10.**

Butter Dish, Cov, border bands of blue overlapping and intertwined swirls, cartouches of red and blue flowers, gold rims and curled knob, "BENNETT BALTIMORE S-V" mk .............................................................. 35.00

Dish, 14" l x 11" w, shell form, 3 pink, purple, and white flowers in center, green shaded rim ............................... 10.00

Inkwell, 4 1/2" d, Rockingham glaze, "imp E & W. Bennett, Canton Ave. Baltimore, Md" label, (A) ................... 688.00

Plate, 9 3/8" d, bluebird design, "Bennett S-V Baltimore" mk .................................................................... 5.00

Syrup Pitcher, 7" h, molded border band of arches and geometrics, aqua-green, pewter lid ............................... 75.00

Vase, 15 1/2" h, bulbous base, slender tapered neck, white, blue, and purple violets, variegated leaf bkd, hole in base, mkd, (A) ..................................................... 1540.00

Vegetable Bowl, 9" d, bluebird design, "Bennett S-V Baltimore" mk ........................................................... 10.00

# Bennington Potteries

**Bennington, Vermont**
**Norton Pottery 1793-1894**
**Fenton Pottery c1835-1858**

**History:** Captain John Norton established Norton Pottery in Bennington, Vermont where he first made earthenwares for kitchens. Numerous family members continued to join the firm throughout its history.

In 1815, gray stoneware production was added, and in 1823 salt glazed stonewares were made with brushwork replacing the incised and impressed decorations. Stonewares from this period were marked with the Norton name and the town of Bennington. The mark was impressed and usually had cobalt rubbed into the letters to color them. Through the years, there were various changes in the mark, but the Norton name was always included.

During the 1850s through the 1880s, additional Norton family members were in control of the pottery. Slip trailed decorations were used on the Norton salt-glazed stonewares depicting birds, florals, pine trees, and deer. The mark used from 1861-1881 "E. and L.P. Norton, Bennington, V" was the most common mark and used for the longest period of time including the period of increased production immediately following the Civil War. Norton only marked his stonewares.

Rockingham production probably started about 1841. Solid brown examples were made for several years, and then by 1849, mottled brown pieces were made. Hound handled pitchers were the most desirable pieces made in Rockingham glaze and they came in four different sizes.

**History:** Christopher Webber Fenton leased an area of the Norton Pottery about 1835. After he married Julius Norton's sister, he was partners with Norton from 1843-1847. During this period, Norton and Fenton made crocks, jugs, six sided brown pitchers in at least four sizes and different designs with a variety of handles, and stonewares. These pieces were impressed "Norton and Fenton, Bennington, VT."

Working in Rockingham glaze, Fenton made goblets, pitchers, tea and coffeepots, sugar bowls, relish dishes, covered butter dishes, and an assortment of bowls and bakers.

After this short lived partnership, Fenton worked on his own to refine the coloring process for Rockingham ware. By sprinkling the transparent glaze he used on the bisque ware with metallic oxides, he obtained tones of blue, yellow, and orange that blended with the brown color on the Rockingham pieces. He called this variation Flint enamel and patented it in 1849.

About 1/5 of Fenton's production was marked. Fenton adopted an oval impressed mark: "Lyman, Fenton & Co./Fenton's Enamel/Bennington, VT/Patented 1849." Four variations of the "1849"mark were used on the Rockingham and Flint enamel pieces. Rockingham pieces were made from 1847-1867, while Flint enamel was made from 1849-1859.

Fenton was considered one of the greatest potters of his time. Despite the short time he was operating his pottery, he managed to work in numerous medias such as yellowware, whiteware, graniteware, brown Rockingham, Flint enamel, slip covered redwares, and scroddled ware which was made with variegated clays and resembled the veins in marble. Additionally, he was the first potter working in America to make Parian ware. His Parian ware examples were sent for exhibit to the Crystal Palace Fair in New York City.

In 1853, Fenton was incorporated as the United States Pottery Company. At other times during its existence, the pottery was called Fenton's Works, or Lyman, Fenton and Company.

Fenton made Toby bottles in Rockingham, Flint enamel and graniteware that frequently had the 1849 mark. Five different Toby pitchers were made in Rockingham and Flint enamel as well as Toby snuff jars in several varieties.

Standing poodles with baskets of fruit in their mouths were made in brown Rockingham, Flint enamel, graniteware and Parian. Additionally, there were cow creamers, door knobs, soap dishes, teapots, and seated dogs in the form of inkwells and paperweights. Parian examples included a large variety of vases and pitchers as well as statues that were all individuals. These pieces are difficult to identify as Bennington.

Despite this tremendous variety and size of his production and the peak years from 1847-1858, the Fenton factory closed in 1858 due to a combination of increased costs, poor marketing techniques, and financial instability caused by the approaching Civil War.

**References:** Richard Carter Barret, *Bennington Pottery and Porcelain*, Bonanza Books, 1958;_____*How to Identify Bennington Pottery*, Stephen Greene Press, 1964; Laura Woodside Watkins, *Early New England Potters and Their Wares*, Harvard University Press, 1950.

**Museums:** Bennington Museum, VT; Brooklyn Museum, NY; Museum of Ceramics, East Liverpool, OH; National Museum of American History, Smithsonian Institution, Washington, DC; Shelburne Museum, VT; Wadsworth Atheneum, Hartford, CT.

## POTTERY AND PORCELAIN

Candlestick, 7 3/4" h, flint enamel, hairlines, (A) ........385.00

Flask, 6 3/8" h, book-shaped, Rockingham glaze, chips, (A) .................................................................................300.00

Mug, 3 3/8" h, paneled, Rockingham glaze, dtd "1849," (A) .................................................................................800.00

Pitcher

    6 5/8" h, "Sweetheart" design, Rockingham glaze, (A) .......................................................................325.00

    9 1/2" h, green, brown, and tan flint enamel glaze, oct panels w/hearts and ribs," imp Lyman Fenton & Co., Fenton's Enamel Patented 1849, Bennington, VT" on base, (A) ..........................................715.00

    11 1/2" h, molded game animals on sides, brown flint enamel, c1840 .................................................900.00

Tobacco Jar, 7" h, ribbed design, brown flint enamel Rockingham glaze, "imp Lyman Fenton & Co., Fenton's Enamel Patented 1849, Bennington, VT" on base, c1850, (A) ..........................................................468.00

**Jar, 10 1/4" h, "imp cobalt E. NORTON & CO. BENNINGTON VT," 1 1/2" on front w/floral, tan ground, chips, $355.**

**Vase, 7 3/4" h, parian, turquoise dress, tan vase and stand, brown ground in panel, white body, $1,200.**

Toby Jar, Cov, 4 1/2" h, lt green sponging, brown amber int, imp "1849," chips, (A) .............................................660.00

Wash Basin, 13" d, brown flint enamel, molded diamond pattern, hairline, (A) ..................................................412.00

## STONEWARE

Cake Crock, 8" h, blue leaf design, "imp blue E. NORTON & CO., BENNINGTON, VT and 2," c1886, replaced handles, repairs, (A) ......................................................44.00

Crock

    9" h, blue crossed birds design, "imp blue E. & L.P. NORTON, BENNINGTON, VT," c1880, (A) ....1,320.00

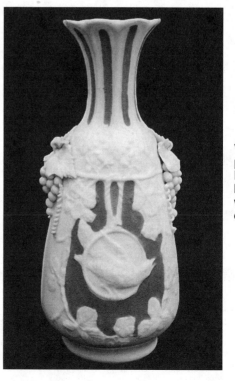

**Vase, 8 1/2" h, parian, "Song Bird" pattern, blue accents, white ground, c1850-58, $125.**

12 3/4" h, lg cobalt chicken pecking corn w/ground, "imp J.NORTON & CO., BENNINGTON, VT 5," repaired hairlines, (A) .................................................... 1,320.00

13" h

Lg blue basket of flowers, "imp blue J. NORTON & CO., BENNINGTON, VT and 6," c1880, (A) .............................................................. 3,190.00

Ovoid, cobalt dbl thistle design, "imp cobalt J. & E. NORTON BENNINGTON, VT and 3," (A) ..... 358.00

Jar

10 3/4" h, ovoid, cobalt brushed fruit, imp "L. Norton & Son, Bennington 2," applied shoulder handles, chips, (A) .................................................................. 220.00

11 1/2" h, ovoid, cobalt triple leaf design, "imp J. & E. NORTON, BENNINGTON, VT 2," repaired hairlines, (A) .................................................................. 1,320.00

Jug

3" h, Albany slip, "incised *Little Brown Jug 1876*" on front, (A) ...................................................................... 198.00

11" h, ovoid, blue bird on log, "imp J. & E. NORTON, BENNINGTON, VT," (A) .................................... 550.00

12 1/2" h, ovoid, thick blue triple flower, "NORTON & FENTON, BENNINGTON, VT," c1845, (A) ........ 578.00

# Sascha Brastoff

## West Los Angeles, California
## 1948-1973

**History:** Sascha Brastoff first worked at the Sculpture Center in Manhattan. Two of his sculptures won an award in 1939. During World War II, he was in the entertainment services. After moving to Los Angeles in 1945, he was a costume designer for Fox. Winthrop Rockefeller saw his terra cotta sculptures and wanted to finance Brastoff to produce a line of American made china.

A small plant was opened in 1948 in West Los Angeles, California. Since Brastoff was not that skilled in ceramic production, they hired technicians and decorators. At first they made earthenwares in the form of vases, bowls, and ashtrays. About 1950, they made a series of figurines.

Nearly everything made was hand painted. Sascha trained artisans to duplicate his personal, flamboyant style of decoration. Overglaze gold trim was lavish and became a hallmark of his business. Platinum also was used for decoration.

Demand continued for grow for Sascha's ceramics. In the early fifties, he joined with Tom Hamilton of American Ceramic Products and moved to a larger plant in Hawthorne. In 1952, Sascha Brastoff of California, Inc. was launched with an increasing number of employees. A fire destroyed the factory eight months later.

With Rockefeller backing, a new factory was built in Los Angeles in 1953. Sascha supervised the artist decorators and was responsible for all shapes, decorative patterns, as well as glazes. The factory produced about two hundred items twice a year.

Products made included flower bowls, vases, figurines, boxes, lamps, wall plaques, and masks along with free and formed shaped dishes. Smoking accessories were especially abundant with a great variety of ashtrays being the most popular of Sasha's work. He also made enamel on copperware articles.

In 1954, the first of ten fine china dinnerware patterns was made. The earthenware was the most successful. "Surf Ballet" was a marbleized pattern of gold or platinum with various background colors. Other patterns included "Jewel Bird," "Roof Tops," "Persian," "Pagoda," and "Star Steed." The "Alaska" ceramic series was created for the tourist trade. Porcelain dinnerware patterns included "Allegro," "Zephyr," "Winrock," and "Lame."

A variety of Sascha marks was used. The rooster trademark with his name was used after the move in 1953 and was applied overglaze in gold or platinum. Other designers signed "Sascha B." Sascha himself signed his full name on pieces. Some enamel ware was marked with paper labels.

**References:** Jack Chipman, *Collector's Encyclopedia of California Pottery, 2nd Edition*, Collector Books, 1992; _____*Collector's Encyclopedia of California Pottery*, Collector Books, 1992; Steve Conti, A. DeWayne Bethany & Bill Seay, *Collector's Encyclopedia of Sascha Brastoff*, Collector Books, 1995; Tina A. Richey, "Sascha May Again Become a Household Name," *Antique Week*, October 23, l995.

**Museums:** Cranbrook Academy, Bloomfield Hills, MI; Everson Museum of Art, Syracuse, NY; Guggenheim Museum of Art, New York, NY; Houston Art Museum, TX; Los Angeles County Museum of Art, CA; Metropolitan Museum of Art, New York, NY; Whitney Museum of American Art, New York, NY.

Ash Receiver, 6 3/4" h, triangular, blue/green igloo, brown and white ground ...................................................... 45.00

Ashtray

5 1/2" d, multicolored cabin on stilts ........................ 40.00

9 3/4" l, freeform, "Alaska," brown walrus ............... 58.00

Bowl

5 1/2" d, 3 sm feet, "Surf Ballet" pattern, pink and gold .......................................................................... 34.00

9 1/2" d, "Roofs" pattern, multicolored .................... 50.00

Box, Cov

6 1/4" sq, brown shades and gold fruit on cov, chip .......................................................................... 45.00

7" l x 5 3/4" w, freeform, turquoise or tan banding w/brown geometric ovals, cream ground ........... 90.00

7 1/2" l

Gold, tan, and turquoise geometrics and raised lines on cov, cream ground, "Compliments of Hiram

**Ashtray, 6 1/2" w, cream, black, and turquoise horse, dk turquoise ground, $55.**

Walker 1858-1958 Luncheon Romanoff's May 21, 1958" on int cov ........................................ 40.00

Tan, blue, and rose "Roofs" pattern ................... 145.00

Bud Vase

8" h, black and brown log cabin, aqua rim .............. 45.00

8 1/4" h, "Alaska," blue-green and black outlined bear ........................................................................ 75.00

Bowl, 5 1/2" d, "Surf Ballet" pattern, pink ..................... 20.00

Coffee Set, pot, 11" h, creamer, 4" h, cov sugar bowl, 6" h, scattered green leaves, white ground .................... 150.00

Charger

12" d, green and turquoise provincial rooster, gold accents, gold outlined magenta florals w/turquoise and green leaves, yellow sun, cream ground, 1947-53 ............................................................ 45.00

17" d, 3 walking camels, cream, green, and gold, matte finish, "gold SASCHA" on front .......................... 275.00

Coffee Set, pot, 10" h, creamer, 3 3/4" h, cov sugar bowl, 5" h, "Surf Ballet" pattern, yellow w/gold and pink swirls ........................................................................ 85.00

Cup and Saucer

"Alaska" pattern, blue walrus design ........................ 35.00

"Cotton Puff," black and gray tones ........................ 28.00

"Surf Ballet" pattern, pink and gold .......................... 4.00

Dish

8" l, ftd, "Alaska" pattern, gray seal, blue sky .......... 55.00

9 5/8" l, freeform

Ftd, brown log cabin on stilts, shaded green and white ........................................................................ 85.00

**Dish, 13 5/8" l, green, gold, and tan, speckled white ground, sgd, $245.**

**Plate, 8" d, brown and gold, $23.**

Gray, blue, and gold peacock ............................ 45.00

13" l, teardrop shape, multicolored "Roofs" pattern . 45.00

Flower Bowl, 11 1/2" h, vert handles from rim, multicolored "Roofs" pattern, (A) ............................................ 25.00

Flowerpot, 4 1/4" h, gold outlined green and brown oak leaves, dk green ground, wavy rim ........................ 32.00

Mug, 5 1/2" h, "Alaska" pattern, polar bear on blue-green ground ................................................................ 69.00

Pitcher, 10 1/2" h, round shape w/elongated spout, arc handle, Eskimo design on front, med blue top w/black, white, and brown accents ................................................ 195.00

Plate

6 3/4" d, "Surf Ballet" pattern, pink and gold .............. 6.00

8 1/4" d, "Surf Ballet" pattern, pink and gold .............. 6.00

9 1/2" l x 8 1/2" w, freeform shape, tan, blue, and rose rooftops ............................................................ 125.00

10" d, Eskimo with spear, wolf at side, steel blue .... 50.00

10 1/2" d, "Surf Ballet" pattern

Black and gold ................................................ 12.00

Pink and gold .................................................. 10.00

11" d

"Jade Tree" pattern .......................................... 10.00

"Vanity Fair" pattern ......................................... 10.00

16 3/4" d, relief of cowboy, bronco bull, saddle, cactus, fish, and lumber, gray ........................................ 350.00

Platter, 18 3/4" l x 14 1/2" w, "Roofs" pattern ............. 315.00

Sugar Bowl, Cov, "Surf Ballet" pattern, black and gold ........................................................................ 18.00

Teapot

6 1/4" h, "Iceburg" pattern, woven overhead handle ........................................................................ 125.00

7 1/2" h, "Surf Ballet" glaze, marbled white, pink, and lavender swirls ...................................................... 95.00

10" h, Igloo pattern ........................................... 90.00

Tray, 12 1/2" l, 3 figures in black, white, and gold, red ground, hairline, (A) ............................................ 121.00

Vase

3" h, gourd shape, serpent head handle, mint green glaze, (A) ........................................................ 15.00

5 1/2" h

Bust of brown bear on front, blue to cream ground ........................................................................ 75.00

Cylinder shape, grapes on matte white ground, sgd "Sascha B." mk ............................................... 75.00

7" h, black and dk yellow moose on front, white and yellow ground ...................................................... 115.00

7 1/2" h, sq bottle shape, brown shades of stylized horse and rider or fantasy bird, bubbled ground ......... 450.00

8" h

"Alaska," walrus design ................................... 75.00

Hourglass shape, polar bear on front ................. 30.00

Tapered cylinder shape w/wide base, wavy rim, polychrome flowing ribbons design .................... 120.00

8 1/2" h, painted horse design ............................ 250.00

10" h, tapered cylinder shape, polychrome bands of stylized leaves and geometrics ............................ 295.00

12" h, cylinder shape, olive and brown banded geometrics ................................................................ 495.00

13 1/2" h, tapered cylinder shape, wavy rim, horiz bands of green, red, tan, and cream ............................ 220.00

# Brayton Laguna Pottery

## South Laguna Beach, California
## 1927-1968

**History:** Durlin E. Brayton started his pottery working at home making hand-crafted earthenware dinnerwares in mixed colors in the late 1920s. Pieces were press molded by hand and dipped in a series of opaque glazes in colors like rose, strawberry pink, eggplant, jade green, lettuce green, chartreuse, old gold, burnt orange, lemon yellow, silky black, and white.

In addition to regular place settings, serving pieces such as teapots, pitchers, and large serving bowls were made by Brayton. He also made flower pots, vases, tea tiles, wall plates, and figurines in limited quantities.

With his second wife Webb, they expanded the business from the home into a commercial facility. They were licensed by Walt Disney from 1938-40 to produce ceramic figures of the Disney characters.

The first outside designer to work for Brayton Laguna was H.S. Anderson, a Swedish woodcarver who was responsible for humorous figurines and groups such as the English hunter with fox and hounds, the hillbilly shotgun wedding set, and the popular purple cow, bull, and calf family. Birds, animals, and human figures were made in a variety of finishes, along with planters, vases, ashtrays, candleholders, cookie jars, salt and pepper shakers, and other household items.

Eventually more than twenty-five designers worked at the pottery to make hand-decorated figurines. By the end of World War II, they supplied retail outlets all over the United States and many foreign countries. They were a major ceramics center since overseas ceramics could not be imported for giftware during the war. After the war, cheaper Japanese and Italian imports began flooding the market again, and the pottery declined. With the death of Webb in 1948 and Durlin Brayton's death in 1951, the company continued to slide and was closed in 1968.

Various marks were used on Brayton Laguna pieces, though some pieces were not marked due to size.

**References:** Jack Chipman, *Collector's Encyclopedia of California Pottery*, Collector Books, 1992 _____; *2nd Edition*, 1998; Mike Schneider, *California Potteries, The Complete Book*, Schiffer Publishing Ltd. 1995.

Ashtray, 7 1/4" sq, white duck, green curlicue leaves, maroon ground.........................................................10.00
Bowl, 7" d, indented wavy border, mint green .............42.00
Box, Cov, 5" l x 3 1/4" w, incised and yellow enameled flowerheads, pink hearts, and green leaves, matte brown ground...................................................................10.00
Dish, 6 1/4" sq, raised brown and turquoise geometric design on matte black ground, gloss gray border ....28.00
Figure
   3 1/4" h, Pluto, pink.............................................130.00
   3 1/2" h
      "Anne," little girl, pink jumper, white blouse .........75.00
      Black boy throwing dice, pr ...............................195.00
   4 1/2" h, boy and girl kissing, multicolored, pr .........95.00
   6" h
      4" h, purple cow and calf, set of 2 .....................255.00

**Figures, 4 1/2" h, 6 1/4" h, 6 1/2" h, bull, cow, and calf, purple body, white horns, black accents, set of 3, $495.**

Man w/protruding stomach, hands in pockets, long red coat, flowered vest, cream trousers, red shoes, (A) ................................................................................... 55.00
6 1/2" h, bull with head up or down, matte black, white trim, pr .............................................................. 150.00
6 1/2" l, bird w/beak pointed down, brushed brown finish, "Brayton Laguna Calif K25A" mk...................... 10.00
7" h, jazz figures, cream suits, tan instruments, brown and black accents, set of 4, (A) ......................... 560.00
7 1/2" h
   Hippopotamus, gray ........................................... 100.00
   Pelican, brown, white crackle face and bill.......... 10.00
7 3/4" h, stylized bird frosted orange w/brown comb, bill, wing tips, (A) ...................................................... 44.00
8" h, 7" h, 5" h, Ringmaster, 2 circus horses, cream and tan, set of 3, chips ............................................... 45.00
8 1/2" h
   Girl in lavender gown, basket on arm, mkd ................................................................................... 80.00
   Peasant woman w/2 tan baskets, turquoise skirt, white blouse, yellow floral vest................................. 65.00
   Sea horse, white ribbing, turquoise trim............ 115.00
8 3/4" h, "Bedtime," man in striped night shirt, black hair, woman in pink nighty, yellow braided hair ................................................................................... 150.00
9" h, standing rooster, dk brown w/white feather accents, yellow beak and feet ........................................... 25.00
9 1/2" h
   Stylized bird w/long tail, black w/gold trim ................................................................................... 155.00
   Walking drake and hen ducks, blue and white, pr ................................................................................... 145.00
10" h, woman in salmon gown, 2 Afghans at side ................................................................................... 95.00
14 3/4" h, Jamaican woman, yellow, white, and green enameled flowers and birds on dress ................ 50.00
18" l, stalking panther or seated, black, gold trim, set of 3 ................................................................................... 395.00
Flower Holder, 8" h, "Frances," figural girl wearing white dress w/red and yellow trim, holding yellow bowl .... 50.00
Pitcher, 6" h, red, green, black and gold stylized peasant couple and harvest ................................................. 30.00

Pitcher Set, pitcher, 7 1/2" h, 4 mugs, 5" h, center band of raised dk brown pretzels, dk brown bands, dk brown figural pretzel handles, tan ground ...........................225.00

Planter

   3" h, sq shape, relief molded curlicues in frame on sides, sq ft, green glaze.................................................10.00

   7" h, "Sally," green dress, white apron, brown hair
   ..................................................................................35.00

   8 1/2" l, raised dk blue flowerheads and foliage, yellow ground ..............................................................10.00

   11" h, woman w/2 wolfhounds, yellow gown
   ..................................................................................60.00

Shakers

   3 3/4", 4 1/4" h, Gingham Dog, Calico Cat, pr .........54.00

   5 1/2" h, black chef and cook, red, green, brown, and white, pr...............................................................50.00

Vase

   4 1/2" h, figural corset, pink w/red trim........................5.00

   6" h, ball shaped top, cone shaped base, dk red glaze w/gray speckles.....................................................35.00

   8" h, rect, panels of relief molded circles in squares, green glaze.........................................................10.00

Wall Hanger, 13" h, figural peasant woman, magenta hat, white dress w/green and blue peasant designs, magenta stockings and belt, yellow sq base........................235.00

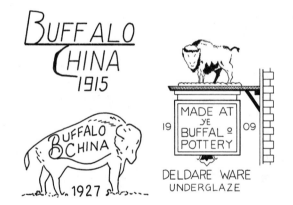

# Buffalo Pottery

### Buffalo, New York
### 1903-1983

**History:** The Buffalo Pottery was established in 1903 by the Larkin Soap Company to satisfy the premium needs of the company. Louis H. Brown, who came from Crescent Pottery in Trenton, New Jersey, was the first manager. He brought artists and craftsmen with him to Buffalo. William Rea was the first superintendent. Though most wares were made for the Larkin Company, products were also sold to outlets throughout the country.

The first wares were dinner sets in semi-vitreous china that were given away with the soap products. Buffalo also developed the first American underglaze Blue Willow pattern. Commemorative, historical, and advertising examples also were made.

From 1905-1909, Buffalo Pottery made a series of pitchers in 29 patterns of semi-vitreous china. The decorations were transfer printed and often hand decorated. Many were edged in gold.

William Rea brought Buffalo Pottery into the art pottery arena with his Deldare Ware in 1908. Pieces had a solid olive green ground with a high-gloss glaze. English literature's "Vicar of Wakefield" by Goldsmith provided the design ideas for the transfer printed scenes. Artists decorated the pieces by hand according to a rigid pattern. Each piece was signed by the artist.

"The Fallowfield Hunt" featured scenes from English fox hunting with borders of hunters on horseback. Titles were written on the face of the piece. A second pattern, "Ye Olden Days," had a continuous border of old two-story houses and local scenes of English life both indoors and out. This pattern was made in 1908-9 and then reissued in 1924-25. They were very expensive to produce and that is why they were discontinued both times. Dinner sets, tea sets, dresser sets with trays, vases, drinking sets, pitchers, chocolate sets, and other pieces were made in Deldare.

"Emerald Deldare" was made with the olive clay in 1911 with "Dr. Syntax" scenes as well as Art Nouveau motifs, geometric designs, stylized flowers and butterflies, and scenes of lakes and mountains. Due to limited production, these pieces were most sought after for their superior design and decoration.

In 1912, "Abino Ware" had hand-decorated sailing scenes, rural Dutch windmills, and other pastoral designs. It was made on the same shapes as Deldare.

The change from semi-vitreous ware to vitrified china took place in 1915. Examples were then stamped "Bufffalo China" instead of "Buffalo Pottery." Additional lines included "Luna Ware," "Cafe-au-Lait," and "Ivory Ware" in soft colors. During World War I, Buffalo Pottery made extensive china examples for the government.

After the war, production resumed on commercial dinnerwares for hotels, institutions, steamship lines, etc., as well as premiums for Larkin and direct sales to the public; 1923 was the last time that Buffalo Pottery was offered as a Larkin premium. Larkin then used imported china examples for its premiums, since it was cheaper than producing its own. Institutional ware was marked "Buffalo China" after 1930, along with the body color.

In 1940, Buffalo Pottery was reorganized, and the name changed to Buffalo Pottery Incorporated. During World War II, production was again dominated by china for the Armed Forces. In 1950, the first Christmas plates were made, and continued until 1962. Buffalo continued to mass produce hotel and industrial wares. The Chesapeake and Ohio Railroad was a major client.

In 1983, the Buffalo China, Inc. was acquired by Oneida Ltd. of Oneida, New York.

**References:** Violet and Seymour Altman, *The Book of Buffalo Pottery*, Schiffer Publishing Ltd. 1987.

**Museums:** Historical Society Museum, Buffalo, NY.

### ABINO WARE
Charger, 12" d, country scene of buildings, trees, pond, and man and sheep, brown and green shades, pierced for hanging, dtd 1913 ...................................................550.00
Plate, 7 1/4" d, sailing boat in foreground, sailboats in bkd, "Abino ware, 1912, #232" mark, (A)......................303.00

### COLORIDO WARE
Custard Cup, 3 1/4" h, loop handle, pedestal base, "Breaking Cover," multicolored on cream-yellow ground, (A)
..................................................................................358.00

Plate

   8" d, multicolored Indian transfer w/HP details on yellow banded border, "Colorido ware/Lamelle" mk, (A)
   ..................................................................................55.00

   11" d, "The Fallowfield Hunt-Breakfast at The Three Pigeons," maroon drawing, ivory-cream ground, "Colorido" mk, (A) ...................................................165.00

**Pitcher, 8" h, Deldare, "Ye Olden Days-Go Spare an old Broken Soldier," multicolored, tan ground, $500.**

## DELDARE
### The Fallowfield Hunt

Bowl, 9" d, "The Fallowfield Hunt-The Death," dtd 1909, sgd "L.Streissel," (A) .................................. 495.00

Card Tray, 8" H-H, "The Fallowfield Hunt" on front, (A) .................................. 303.00

Chop Plate, 14" d, "The Fallowfield Hunt-The Start," dtd 1908, (A) .................................. 523.00

Mug

2 1/2" h, "The Fallowfield Hunt," on base, dtd 1909, (A) .................................. 825.00

3 3/4" h, "Breaking Cover," dtd 1909, set of 4, (A) .................................. 1,100.00

4 1/2" h, "The Fallowfield Hunt," on base, dtd 1909, set of 4, (A) .................................. 990.00

Pitcher, 9" h, paneled, "Breaking Cover," (A) .............. 715.00

Plate

6 1/2" d, dtd 1908 .................................. 130.00

7 1/4" d, "Breaking Cover," dtd 1909, set of 4, (A) .................................. 715.00

9 1/4" d, "The Start," sgd "L.Newman," dtd 1908, (A) .................................. 220.00

Tea Tile, 6" d, "Breaking Cover," dtd 1909, chip on reverse, (A) .................................. 220.00

### Ye Olden Days

Bowl

8" d, "Ye Village Street" .................................. 375.00

9" d, "Ye Village Street" .................................. 395.00

Candlestick, 9" h, paneled, "Village Scene," sgd "D.Shuster," pr, (A) .................................. 1,045.00

Chamberstick, 5" d, "Village Scene" on border, circ handle, dtd 1925, (A) .................................. 385.00

Chop Plate, 13 1/2" d, "An Evening at Ye Lion Inn," 1908 .................................. 475.00

Cup and Saucer .................................. 165.00

Fern Bowl, 8 1/2" d, everted rim, "Ye Village Street," (A) .................................. 495.00

Hair Receiver, 4 1/2" d, "Ye Village Street" .................. 325.00

Humidor, 7 1/4" h, "Ye Lion Inn," (A) .................................. 825.00

Mug, 4 1/2" h, "Ye Lion Inn," artist sgd .................. 300.00

Mustard Jar, Cov, 3 3/4" h, scroll handle, "Scenes of Village Life In Ye Olden Days," sgd "N.Sheehan," dtd 1909, (A) .................................. 1,870.00

Nut Bowl, 8" d, "Ye Lion Inn," dtd 1909, (A) .............. 880.00

Plate

8 1/4" d, "Ye Town Crier," sgd "M.Broel," dtd 1908, (A) .................................. 193.00

10 1/8" d, "Ye Village Gossips" .................................. 155.00

11 3/4" d, "An Evening at Ye Lion Inn" .................. 585.00

Powder Jar, Cov, 2 3/4" h x 4 1/2" d, "Ye Village Street," dtd 1909, (A) .................................. 550.00

Relish Tray, 12" l, "Ye Olden Days," dtd 1908, (A) .................................. 825.00

Soup Bowl, 9" d, "Ye Village Street," .................. 495.00

Teapot, 4 3/4" h, "Scenes of Village Life In Ye Olden Days," dtd 1925, (A) .................................. 385.00

Tea Tile, 6 1/4" d, "Traveling in Ye Olden Days," dtd 1908 .................................. 290.00

Tray, 13 3/4" l, rect, "Heirloom," curved edges .......... 795.00

Vase, 8 1/2" h, bag shape, flared rim, "Ye Village Parson-Ye Village Schoolmaster," sgd "J.Nekola," dtd 1909, (A) .................................. 770.00

## EMERALD DELDARE

Candlestick, 9" h, berry and vine design on shaft, butterfly and florals on base, sgd "M.Broel," dtd 1911, repaired bobiche, (A) .................................. 303.00

Chamberstick, 7" h, shield back, white and celadon flowers, olive ground, chip, (A) .................................. 990.00

Fruit Bowl, 9 1/2" d, "Dr. Syntax Reading His Tour," sgd "W. Ramlus," dtd 1911, (A) .................................. 825.00

Mug

3 1/2" h, "Dr. Syntax and Companion" .................. 525.00

4 1/2" h, "Syntax Again Filled Up His Glass," sgd "M.Broel," dtd 1911, (A) .................................. 467.00

Pin Tray, 6 1/2" l, rect, "Dr. Syntax Received By The Maid Instead of The Mistress," dtd 1911, (A) .................. 550.00

Pitcher, 8" h, "Dr. Syntax Bound to a Tree by Highwayman" .................................. 1,950.00

Plaque

12" d

"Dr. Syntax Sketching The Lake," dtd 1911, (A) .................................. 1,650.00

"The Landing," lg pelican landing on grass, mallards in bkd, dtd 1911, (A) .................................. 3,300.00

13 3/4" d, "Dr. Syntax Sell's Grizzle," dtd 1911, (A) .................................. 1,320.00

Plate

8 1/4" d, "Dr. Syntax-Misfortune at Tulip Hall," .................................. 485.00

9 1/4" d, "Introduction To Courtship," dtd 1911, (A) .................................. 880.00

10" d

"Dr. Syntax Making A Discovery," sgd "J. Gerhardt," dtd 1911, (A) .................................. 880.00

"The Garden Trio," sgd "M. Gerhardt," dtd 1911, (A) .................................. 770.00

Shaker, 3" h, white flowers, geometrics, and butterfly bands, sgd "JG/HB," pr, (A) .................................. 1,100.00

Sugar Bowl, Cov, 4 1/4" h, "Dr. Syntax In The Wrong Lodging House But With His Day's Fatigue," "Death of Punch" on reverse, rim chip, (A) .................................. 330.00

Tankard, 12 1/4" h, "To Becky's Hand He Gave A Squeeze," sgd "L.Streissel," dtd 1908, crazing, (A) .......... 1,650.00

Teapot, 4 3/4" h, "Dr. Syntax Disputing His Bill With The Landlady," dtd 1911, (A) .................................. 523.00

Tea Tile, 6" d, "Dr. Syntax Taking Possession Of His Living, At Length, Dear Wife," dtd 1911, (A) ...................... 770.00

Toothpick Holder, 2 1/4" h, cylinder shape, stylized fuchsia flower design, band of butterflies at mouth, sgd "E. Missel," dtd 1911, (A) ................................................. 1,310.00

Vase, 7 3/4" h, kingfisher, iris, and dragonflies
.................................................................... 2,800.00

## LAMARE PATTERN

Platter

12" l ................................................................. 95.00

14 3/4" l ........................................................... 125.00

## MISCELLANEOUS

Bowl, 5" d, Blue Willow pattern .................................. 12.00

Butter Pat, Blue Willow pattern ................................. 15.00

Candlestick, 6 1/2" h, shield back style, Rougeware, pale pink ground, black "Buffalo Rougeware 1930" mk, (A)
.................................................................... 88.00

Game Set, platter, 15" l, 6 plates, 9" d, multicolored transfers of deer, moose, or elk in forest, green borders w/gold banding .................................................................... 495.00

Jug

5 1/2" h, Triumph, stylized poppy flowers, buds, and stems, blue shades, (A) ................................... 715.00

6 1/4" h

Cinderella, brown transfer w/yellow, mauve, blue, brown, and lt green accents, scene of Cinderella's coach or trying on slipper, dtd 1906, (A) ....... 495.00

Rip Van Winkle, brown transfer w/lt blue, mauve, green and brown accents, dtd 1907, (A) ....... 770.00

6 1/2" h, Dutch, castle on side, Dutch mother and daughter on reverse, coat of arms on base, brown transfers w/HP accents, "1907 Dutch Jug" mk, (A) .......... 770.00

7" h, "Whirl of the Town" and "Fox Hunt," HP polychromes, dtd 1908 .......................................... 450.00

7 1/4" h, George Washington, Mount Vernon, cobalt blue transfer, "Buffalo Semi-Vitreous" mk, (A) ........... 605.00

7 1/2" h, Chrysanthemum, blue transfer w/HP blue accented chrysanthemums, gold outlined scalloped rim and ft, raised beading, (A) ........................... 550.00

9 1/4" h, "Marine," blue ......................................... 985.00

Pitcher

4 1/2" h, Blue Willow pattern ................................. 115.00

5 1/2" h, gaudy willow, gold trim, dtd 1906 ............. 200.00

6 1/4" h, geranium pattern, green transfer, "Buffalo Semi-Vitreous 1906" mk, (A) ................................. 330.00

8" h

Robin Hood, brown transfer w/HP accents, gold trim, hairline, (A) ................................................. 250.00

Roosevelt Bears, multicolored ...................... 2,500.00

8 3/4" h, melon shape, white glaze, gold trimmed borders and handles, "Buffalo Pottery 1909" mark, (A)
.................................................................... 660.00

9" h, Pilgrim, John Alden and Priscilla on one side, Miles Standish and Mayflower on reverse, multicolored, dtd 1908, (A) ...................................................... 770.00

9 1/4" h, Gloriana, blue shaded Gloriana woman in meadow, animals on border, dtd 1908, (A) ....... 523.00

Plate

6" d, Blue Willow pattern ....................................... 12.00

7 1/4" d, Blue Willow pattern .................................. 10.00

7 1/2" d

Mt. Vernon, green transfer .................................. 39.00

Niagara Falls, green transfer ............................... 42.00

8" d, Blue Willow pattern ........................................ 15.00

9" d

Painted band of mauve and lavender daisies on dk green border ground, sgd "Ivory Buffalo 1927" mk, (A) ................................................................ 55.00

"The Gunner," green transfer ......................... 1100.00

10 1/4" d

American Woodcock, green transfer ................... 55.00

Capital Building, green transfer ......................... 45.00

Ivory, HP multicolored parrot on branch, lt and dk green banded border, "Ye Olde Ivory Buffalo" mk, (A) ................................................................ 275.00

Niagara Falls, blue transfer ................................. 40.00

Washington Home at Mount Vernon, green ........ 45.00

Platter

14" l, rect, "The Buffalo Hunt," green transfer
.................................................................... 370.00

14 1/2" l, "Dr. Syntax Advertising For A Wife," blue transfer, floral border, dtd 1909, (A) ......................... 880.00

Toddy Set, bowl, 9 3/4" d, 6 cups, 5" h, black transfer of devil and fire w/hp red-maroon accents, ivory-beige ground w/red-maroon striping, (A) .................................... 330.00

Vase, 8 1/8" h, Portland, lt blue bisque appliqué of flying cherubs over Roman-type figures, hairlines, (A)
.................................................................... 1,210.00

Wash Set, pitcher, 12 1/2" h, bowl, 16" d, mug, 4" h, hot water pitcher, 7 3/4" h, cov soap dish, 6" d, chamber pot, 10" d, green "Chrysanthemum" pattern ................. 450.00

# Bybee Pottery

## Bybee, Kentucky
## 1809-Present

**History:** Webster Cornelison started the pottery using his own name in 1809 in Bybee, Kentucky. James Eli, his son, started keeping records of the pottery

Plate, 9 1/8" d, "American Herring Eagle," green transfer, c1902-1911, $100.

GENUINE BYBEE

in 1845. Six generations of this family have been involved with the pottery that is still owned by Walter II. The name was changed to Bybee Pottery in 1954.

In the early years, they made salt glazed stoneware. During the 1920s and '30s, they produced fine artwares in heavy matte finish glazes with the rich clay that came from the area. Pieces were shaped on the potter's wheel. Mostly vases, candlesticks, and bowls were made.

Utilitarian wares are now made in approximately a dozen glazes. Some marks are the stamped or impressed map of Kentucky with "Genuine Bybee." Cornelison Pottery is stamped on examples from the 1930s and 40s. Some gold paper stickers were used for marks.

Baker, 12 1/2" H-H, dk blue and white splotches, "BB" mk ............................................................................ 12.00
Bank, 6" h, standing figural pig, maroon, "BB" mk.......... 8.00
Batter Bowl, 12 1/4" w, yellow, "Bybee, Ky" mk ............ 25.00
Bowl
   2 1/4" d, tan-gold sponging, Cornelison ..................... 5.00
   4 1/4" d, tab handles, pastel blue, mkd ..................... 8.00
   5" d, gloss cobalt glaze ............................................. 5.00
   8" d, scalloped rim, gray w/blue and gray splashes, "Bybee, KY" mk ...................................................... 15.00
   13 1/4" H-H, oval shape, cream glaze, mkd ........... 10.00
Butter Dish, Cov, 7" h, bell shape, blue glaze .............. 25.00
Chamberstick
   2 1/2" h, oatmeal glaze ............................................ 10.00
   4" h, mottled matte green glaze, "Cornelison Pottery, Bybee, Ky" mk ...................................................... 36.00
   6 1/2" h, shield back, yellow glaze .......................... 35.00
Chip and Dip Set, 10 1/4" d, center bowl, 3 3/4" d, med blue glaze, "imp BYBEE KY" mk.................................... 10.00
Figure
   5" l, swimming duck, dk blue mottled glaze ............ 10.00
   6 1/2" h, cat, blue glaze .......................................... 40.00
Flowerpot, 3" h, w/attached saucer, flared, piecrust rim, med brown glaze, "Cornelison Since 1845 Bybee KY" mk ................................................................................. 20.00
Garlic Jar, 4" h, pierced sides, dk red-purple glaze ...... 18.00

Jug, 4 1/2" h, maroon and lt blue sponging.................. 10.00
Juice Pitcher, 7" h, relief molded grapes on side, cranberry red glaze ................................................................. 10.00
Milk Pitcher, 7 3/4" h, applied handle, green, "CORNELISON POTTERY BYBEE KY" mk ........................... 38.00
Mixing Bowl, 11" d, blue sponging, "BB" mk................ 45.00
Paperweight, 3" d, blue and white spatter, "BB" mk ..... 10.00
Pitcher
   4 1/2" h, pinched spout, sea green, Cornelison Bybee ................................................................................ 25.00
   5 1/2" h, figural bird, blue and white sponging, mkd ................................................................................ 20.00
   5 3/4" h, pea green, "BB" mk ..................................... 5.00
   6 1/4" h, HP blue fisherman and foliage ................. 10.00
Pitcher, Cov
   5" h, med blue glaze. Cornelison ........................... 32.00
   10" h, rust brown glaze, (A) ................................... 10.00
Planter
   3 1/2" h, 3 handles, 3 open sections on lower body, delphinium blue glaze, Cornelison ........................ 30.00
   5 1/2" d, bowl shape w/closed rim, med blue glaze ................................................................................ 28.00
   6 1/4" d, bowl shape, everted rim, 2 sm handles, green and maroon glaze, "SELDON BYBEE" mk ......... 76.00
Plate
   8" d, reeded rim, med blue glaze, mkd ..................... 6.00
   10 5/8" d, purple glaze, red clay ............................... 6.00
Strawberry Jar, 5 1/2" h, brown glaze, Cornelison ....... 15.00
Teapot, 8" h, med blue glaze, "BB" mk......................... 20.00
Vase
   4 1/2" h, bulbous shape, white pitted glaze, "Cornelison Pottery Bybee, KY" mk...................................... 10.00
   4 3/4" h
      Pear shape, flared rim, pink glaze..................... 20.00
      Squat shape, sq handles, castware, red-burgundy glaze on purple ground, Seldon Bybee, (A) ................................................................................ 110.00
   5" h, crooked handles, gloss robin's egg blue glaze "gold Genuine Bybee" label........................................ 80.00
   5 1/2" h, bowl shape w/horiz handles on rim, emb flowerheads, swirling stems, metallic green and brown glazes, "1927 Seldon Bybee 509 Kentucky map" mk, (A) .......................................................................... 82.00
   6" h, ftd, cylinder shape, flat architectural handles, matte med blue glaze....................................................... 38.00
   7 1/8" h, swollen cylinder shape, spread ft, emb flowers and stems, red clay body w/green crystalline overglaze, "Seldon Bybee" mk, pr, (A) ..................... 357.00

# California Faience

## Berkeley, California
## 1916-1950s

**History:** California Faience was started in 1916 by William Bragdon and Chauncey Thomas where they made art pottery and tiles. They adopted the California Faience name in 1924.

**Vase, 6 7/9" h, matte green glaze, mkd, $275.**

The art pottery pieces were mostly cast and had monochrome matte glaze finishes. Some examples were done in high gloss. Tiles and inserts were made by pressing them into plaster molds and they were polychrome decorated. Numerous pieces were made for florist ware. In the mid-1920s, they made art porcelain molds for West Coast Porcelain Manufacturers for a short time.

No artwares were made during the Depression years. Some tiles were made for the 1932 World's Fair. Bragdon bought out Thomas in the late 1930s. He continued to operate, but no commercial art ware was made. He sold the factory in the early 1950s and worked for the new owners until he died in 1959.

Artwares have the incised California Faience mark. Tiles were marked with a hand stamp.

**Museums:** National Museum of History and Technology, Smithsonian Institution, Washington, DC; The Newark Museum, NJ; The Oakland Museum, CA.

Bookend, 5" h, emb circ geometric design, matte green glaze, pr, (A)......192.00

Bowl
4 1/2" d, closed rim, turquoise glaze, red clay, "California Faience" mk......75.00
9" d
Flared rim, turquoise glaze......128.00
Lotus shape, matte black ext, gloss yellow and turquoise int, "incised California Faience" mk, (A)......110.00
12" d, oct, sky blue int, matte black ext, cuenca yellow rim, "California Faience" mk......360.00

Cabinet Vase, 3 1/2" h, gloss raspberry red glaze, "imp California Faience" mk, (A)......220.00

Candlestick, 4 1/2" h, gloss turquoise glaze, "imp California Faience" mk, pr, (A)......250.00

Console Set, bowl, 12" d, 2 candlesticks, 4 1/2" h, faceted bowl, matte mustard yellow ext, semi-matte cobalt and turquoise int, matte black ext on candlesticks, turquoise int, "stamped California Faience" mks, (A)......220.00

Jar, 5 1/4" h, seafoam green ext, dk brown clay, "incised California Faience" mk......425.00

Lamp Base, 8 3/4" h, bulbous shape, speckled matte ochre and green glaze, "imp California Faience" mk, (A) 495.00

**Trivet, 5 1/2" d, yellow, green, and dk blue Southwest scene, turquoise ground, red clay, (A), $413.**

Trivet, 5 1/4" d
Cuenca matte and glossy blue peacock on yellow ground, turquoise border, "stamped California Faience" mk, (A)......330.00
Cuenca polychrome basket of flowers, cobalt ground, "stamped California Faience" mk, (A)......220.00

Vase
4" h x 6 1/2" w, bowl shape, short collar, matte thick burgundy glaze, (A)......913.00
4 1/2" w, bowl shape, closed top, matte royal blue glaze, (A)......187.00
5" h
Squat shape, short collar, gloss turquoise glaze, red clay body, (A)......187.00
Swollen cylinder shape, closed top, gloss med blue glaze, dk red clay body, (A)......176.00
5 1/2" h
Flared shoulder shape, matte blue glaze, (A)...660.00
Squat shape, flared rim, semi-matte white glaze, "imp California Faience" mk, (A)......200.00
6" h
Corset shape, gloss turquoise glaze......140.00
Cylinder shape, matte blue glaze, incised mk, (A)......275.00
7 1/4" h, corset shape, gloss green glaze, "imp California Faience" mk, (A)......200.00
8" h
Narrow base, bulbous body, short rim, sky blue glaze......560.00
Paneled, purple flambe glaze, "imp California Faience" mk, (A)......215.00
8 1/2" h, swollen shape, short collar, gloss turquoise glaze......220.00
12" h, bulbous base, tapered neck, multi-toned gloss blue glaze, red clay body, (A)......660.00

# Camark Pottery

### Camden, Arkansas
### 1926-1966

**History:** Camden Art and Tile Company, known as Camark for the town and state where it was located was established by Samuel J. "Jack" Carnes in 1926 in Camden, Arkansas. During the first year, it made individually created pieces by artists such as John Lessell of Ohio in luster and iridescent treatments. Lessell died after a year and his wife and daughter were hired since they knew the luster and iridescent techniques.

Lessell had worked at Owen China, J.B. Owens, and Weller before he worked for Camark. His work was very similar to art pottery being made at Weller. Camark first made vases and lamp bases by Lessell that were decorated with floral and scenic motifs in flat enamel, high gloss and luster enamel finishes and several combinations on bronze called Lessell ware.

The LeCamark line in 1927 featured art pottery and a lot of other pottery in a variety of finishes. Additional lines were done under the direction of Steven and Charles Sebaugh who came from Weller, and Alfred Tetzschner who created a new line called Futuristic/Modernistic after the Lessells left. This line was influenced by the Art Moderne movement, but these designs were discontinued by late 1928 or 1929.

Boris Trifonoff also came to Camark in the 1920s and made more than eight hundred molds for Camark until he left for Homer Laughlin in the mid 1940s. Camark mostly made molded pieces after the early 1930s. Trifonoff introduced the two most popular glazes at this time period: green over pink and green over orange.

When the Sebaughs left, changes were made to the pottery which had a matte or bright finish in simple pastel colors. Examples made included flower pots, ornamental vases, bowls, dishes, plates, cups and saucers, pitchers, condiment containers, mostly cat figurines, and novelty items.

Camark continued for another thirty years. By the 1950s, it was concentrating on mass-produced pottery for florist and giftware markets.

A variety of ink stamp marks, stickers, and mold marks was used. The company was sold shortly after Carnes died in 1966 and was operated by Mary Daniel.

**References:** David Edwin Gifford, *Collector's Guide to Camark Pottery*, Collector Books, 1997; _____, *Collector's Guide to Camark Pottery, Book II*, Collector Books, 1999.

Ashtray
   3" h, figural wood stove, aqua glaze ................ 10.00
   3 3/4" d, figural flowerhead, dk red ........................ 6.00
Bud Vase, 5 3/4" h, 3 entwined twigs, gloss black glaze
   .................................................................................... 35.00
Candleholder
   3 1/8" h, cornucopia shape, matte yellow glaze, pr
   .................................................................................... 10.00
   5" h, dbl, deep rose ............................................... 35.00
Console Bowl, 11" d, flared scalloped shape, satin ivory glaze, mkd ...................................................................... 20.00
Cup and Saucer, petal shape, celadon green glaze ..... 10.00
Dish, 6 1/4" l, shell shape w/well, green glaze ............ 13.00
Ewer, 9 1/2" h, blue w/black drip, #207 .................. 225.00
Flower Frog
   3" h, ball shape, turquoise glaze ............................. 15.00
   6 1/2" h, bowl shape with cover and handle, mint green
   .................................................................................... 33.00
   9" h, leaning nude lady with drapery, green ............. 89.00
Humidor, 5 1/2" h, oct w/flared base, blue and white stippled glaze .............................................................. 50.00
Mug, 5" h, fancy handle, apple green glaze ................ 20.00
Pin Tray, 3 1/2" d, petal shape, blue-gray ................... 10.00
Pitcher
   3" h, swirl design, matte blue glaze ........................ 15.00

**Flower Frog, 3 1/4" h x 4 1/2" d, matte turquoise glaze, $15.**

5 1/2" h, yellow, #829 .............................................. 7.00
5 3/4" h, HP blue and magenta flowerheads, green leaves, brown stems, yellow lip, handle, and base
   .................................................................................... 75.00
6" h, lt blue glaze, #474 ............................................. 6.00
7" h, figural parrot handle, red stripe on body ......... 75.00
7 1/2" h, paneled, lt aqua glaze .............................. 20.00
8" h
   Ball shape w/stopper, orange and green drip .... 145.00
   Slanted bamboo shape, med blue glaze, mkd .... 20.00
8 7/8" h, ewer shape, gloss brown glaze ................. 25.00
Pitcher, Cov, 6" h, yellow glaze ................................... 6.00
Planter
   4" h, lobed body, rolled handles, green drip over blue ground ................................................................... 58.00
   7" l x 7" h, dbl figural swans, green glaze .............. 15.00
   8 1/2" l x 4 1/2" w, rect, wavy body, med blue glaze, "imp CAMARK USA" mk ............................................. 10.00
   9 1/2" l, flared, rect shape, relief molded florals on sides, gloss white glaze .............................................. 10.00
   11" H-H, crimped and finger pressed border, curved tab handles, yellow glaze .......................................... 15.00
Teapot, 5 1/2" h, swirl body, med blue ....................... 20.00
Urn, 5 1/2" h, lobed middle, flared ft and rim, lt blue .... 10.00
Vase
   4" h, flower form, matte orange glaze .................... 15.00
   4 1/4" h x 4 1/8" w, figural quarter moon shape w/4 feet, semi-matte med blue glaze ................................... 15.00
   5" h
      Flat, pitcher shape w/handle, oval ft, pink glaze
      .............................................................................. 20.00
      Overlapped leaves, blue, #051 ......................... 10.00
      Star shaped rim, green drip over pink ground, shape #632 ................................................................. 155.00
   5 1/8" h x 7 1/8" l, molded nautilus shell, ftd, lt green
   .................................................................................... 20.00
   6" h
      Flared shape with full vert handles, green drip over pink, shape #608 ....................................... 160.00
      Lobed flower form, spread ft, lg loop handles, yellow glaze ............................................................. 20.00
      Ribbed with scrolls on rim, green drip over pink ground, shape #426 ..................................... 190.00
      Two handles, green drip, orange ground ........... 90.00
   6 1/4" h, urn shape, 2 small curved handles on shoulder, green drip over pink ground, shape #605
   .................................................................................. 160.00
   7" h, cornucopia shape, blue-green glaze .............. 20.00
   8" h, Deco style, blue and white stipple ................ 185.00
   8 1/2" h, fan shape, relief of blue iris w/yellow accents, green stems, shaded blue body, #831 ................ 70.00
   9 1/2" h, figural overlapped leaves, dbl loop handles, flared ft, aqua green ........................................... 70.00
   10" h
      Flower form, loop handles, gloss black glaze ..... 38.00
      Fluted cornucopia, leaf form base, pink glaze, pink glaze ................................................................. 40.00
   11" h
      Art Deco style figural calla lily, lt turquoise glaze 50.00
      "Old World," pitcher shape, matte white glaze, #268
      .............................................................................. 33.00

Wall Pocket, 6" h, relief molded stylized tulip head, green glaze, #105 ..................................30.00

Water Jug, 6 3/4" h, white glaze ...............................60.00

# Canonsburg Pottery

### Canonsburg, Pennsylvania
### 1901-1978

**History:** The Canonsburg China Company was started in Canonsburg, Pennsylvania in 1901 with the help of W.S. George. Semi-porcelain dinner sets, toilet sets, odd dishes, and hotel wares were made. In 1909, it was purchased by Canonsburg Pottery Company. John George was president and was followed by his son in 1920. Succession continued in the George family.

In the early years of dinnerware production, all operations were done by hand. Periodic improvements were made. Mostly it concentrated on dinnerwares in the later years. When Steubenville Pottery Company closed in 1959, Canonsburg bought its molds and equipment. "Rose Point by Steubenville" was made by Canonsburg after 1959.

In 1960, it employed a new underglaze technique for applying decals. Wares were sold through department stores, chain stores, and mail order houses. Some form of the little canon mark was used for long periods of time.

In 1976, the factory was sold to Angelo Falconi. There was a bankruptcy sale in 1978, but the plant had been idle since a fire in 1975.

### AUTUMN MIST PATTERN
Creamer ....................................................16.00
Cup and Saucer .........................................12.00
Nappy, 9" d ...............................................18.00
Platter
   11 1/2" l ................................................20.00
   15 1/2" l ................................................28.00
Sugar Bowl, Cov.........................................20.00
Teapot........................................................48.00

### GEORGELYN IVORY PATTERN
Bowl, 8 1/2" l...............................................8.00
Creamer .......................................................8.00
Platter, 13 1/2" l .........................................10.00
Vegetable Bowl, 9 1/2" d ...........................10.00

### KEYSTONE PATTERN
Creamer .......................................................5.00
Cup and Saucer ...........................................4.00
Gravy Boat .................................................10.00
Plate
   9" d...........................................................6.00
   10" d.........................................................8.00
Sugar Bowl, Cov.........................................10.00

### LADY LOCKET PATTERN
Plate, 10" d..................................................5.00

### LEAF SWIRL PATTERN
Creamer .......................................................8.00
Cup and Saucer ...........................................7.00
Dinner Plate .................................................8.00
Platter, 13 1/2" l .........................................18.00
Sugar Bowl.................................................12.00

### MADIERA PATTERN-PRISCILLA SHAPE
Berry Bowl, 5 1/2" d, olive green .................5.00
Cup and Saucer ...........................................5.00
Plate, 7" d, olive green ................................6.00
Platter, 11" l, olive green............................10.00

### MISCELLANEOUS
Vegetable Bowl, 8 1/2" l ............................75.00

### PRECIOUS PEAR PATTERN
Platter
   11 1/2" l ................................................15.00
   13" l .......................................................20.00

### REGENCY PATTERN
Butter Dish ................................................28.00
Creamer .....................................................14.00
Cup and Saucer .........................................12.00
Gravy Boat, w/undertray ..............................5.00
Pitcher, 6 1/2" h ...........................................4.00
Platter
   12" l ......................................................22.00
   14" l ......................................................28.00
Shakers, pr ................................................22.00
Sugar Bowl, Cov ........................................20.00

### ROSE CLUSTER PATTERN
Creamer .......................................................4.00
Plate, 10" d..................................................6.00
Platter, 14" l ..............................................10.00
Sugar Bowl, Cov ..........................................5.00

### TEMPORAMA PATTERN
Cereal Bowl, 6 1/8" d...................................3.00
Cup and Saucer ...........................................8.00
Fruit Bowl, 5 1/2" d.......................................3.00
Pitcher, 10 1/4" h .......................................20.00
Plate
   7 1/4" d ....................................................4.00

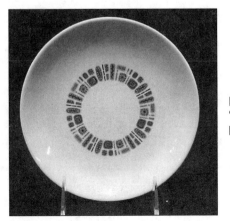

Plate, 7 1/4" d, "Temporama" pattern, $14.

**Platter, 11 3/4" l, "Wild Clover" pattern, magenta flowers, black branches, $5.**

10" d.............................................................10.00
Soup Bowl, 8 1/4" d.....................................8.00

### WESTCHESTER PATTERN
Cereal Bowl, 5" d..........................................3.00
Coffee Cup and Saucer.................................5.00
Plate
   6" d........................................................3.00
   9" d........................................................5.00
Serving Bowl, 10 1/2" d.................................5.00

### WILD CLOVER PATTERN
Chop Plate, 14" H-H....................................10.00
Creamer ......................................................12.00
Platter, 14" l................................................20.00
Soup Bowl, 8" d.............................................7.00
Vegetable Bowl, 8 3/4" d.............................12.00

### WILSHIRE PATTERN
Platter
   11 1/2" l................................................5.00
   13 7/8" l................................................5.00

1920s

c.1910-1920

# Carrollton Pottery

## Carrollton, Ohio
## 1903-late 1930s

**History:** The Carrollton Pottery Company was built by E.L. Henderson and his brother-in-law in 1903 in Carrollton, Ohio and made semi-vitreous porcelain china. After a fire in 1914, they rebuilt their factory. In 1929, they merged with seven other companies to form America China Corporation. Semi-porcelain dinner sets, teawares, and toilet sets were made

with an assortment of marks. The company operated until about 1937 and then closed. Its building was used to refine beryllium until a fire in 1955.

Blue and brown sq design border bands w/bouquets
  Plate
    8 1/4" d.............................................3.00
    9" d...................................................4.00
  Platter
    11" l.................................................15.00
    15 1/4" l...........................................18.00
  Serving Bowl, 9" l......................................7.00
  Vegetable Bowl, Cov, 10" H-H...............35.00
Bowl
  10" d, multicolored garden flowers in center, gold ribbon and circ border...........................5.00
  10 1/2" l, white w/gold trim.......................5.00
Butter Dish, Cov
  7" sq, lg red and purple poppies and green leaves on border, "CARROLLTON H CHINA" mk.................15.00
  W/drain, rect, bluebird design.................70.00
Gravy Boat, 8" l x 3 1/8" h, bluebird design, M.D. ........30.00
Plate
  Bluebird Design
    9" d.................................................30.00
    10" d...............................................30.00
  9" d, red, green, and yellow stylized floral bunches on border.........................................5.00
  10" d
    Border bunches of pink roses, blue flowers, blue band of dots and dashes, outer band of brown chevrons, M.D. ...........................12.00
    Red, green, and yellow stylized formal floral bunches on border.................5.00
Vegetable Bowl, Cov
  8" H-H, sq shape, blue border bands w/floral in oval car touches..................................10.00
  11 1/2" H-H, borders of dk blue semi-circles and leaves ......................................10.00

**Platter, 13" l, lavender, blue, and iron red birds, yellow, lavender and blue flowers on inner and outer borders, blue striping, $10.**

**Dish, 12 1/4" l x 9 3/4" w, gloss turquoise int, matte salmon ext, $45.**

# Catalina Island Pottery

### Avalon, California
### 1927-1941

**History:** William Wrigley, Jr. owned Catalina Island and started a tile plant there in 1927 with its extensive clay deposits. After several years, Harold Johnson joined the business and was responsible for many designs and glazes used on colored ornamental pottery.

The company received an award for the extensive tile work on the Catalina Casino when it was completed in 1929. Then it shifted its attention to slip casting souvenir items and numerous vases, flower bowls, lamps, candleholders and other decorative accessories using the native brown burning type clay.

Virgil Haldeman became ceramic engineer in 1930, and he made the outstanding and unusual glazes. Colors such as Mandarin yellow, Catalina blue, Descanso green, Toyon red, turquoise, pearly white, seafoam, and Monterey brown were utilized. Spanish-style wrought-iron frames and stands were made for scenic tile panels and decorative wall plates in Moorish patterns, Spanish galleons, and undersea garden designs.

A wide variety of glazes was used on the tablewares that were introduced about 1930. The three basic dinnerware designs, plus numerous serving pieces, were sold all over the country. In 1936, a new dinner service with a raised rope border in satin finish pastel colors was introduced.

There was a problem with the local brown clay which was very brittle and broke easily. A new white burning clay was brought in from Lincoln, California in 1932, but this proved to be quite costly.

In 1937, the Catalina molds and designs were sold to Gladding-McBean in Los Angeles, and they continued to make the Catalina line from 1937 until 1941.

A number of versions of "Catalina" or "Catalina Island" were used to mark the island pieces, which are more desirable especially if they were made with the brown clay. Some paper labels also were used. "Catalina Pottery" was used by Gladding-McBean to mark its Catalina pottery line.

**References:** Jack Chipman, *Collector's Encyclopedia of California Pottery, 2nd Edition*, Collector Books, 1998; Steven and Aisha Hoefs, *Catalina Island Pottery Collectors Guide*, Published Privately, 1993; Tile Heritage Foundation, *Catalina Tile of the Magic Isle*, 1993.

Ashtray
   8 1/4" l x 5" h, seated Mexican figure w/hat and blanket, mustard gold glaze ............................................ 575.00
   6 1/4" l, figural fish, blue-green body, red mouth
   .................................................................. 175.00
Bowl
   5" d, red clay
      Matte blue ..................................................... 62.00
      Yellow ........................................................... 60.00

   7 3/4" d, ftd, blue glaze ........................................ 150.00
   10" d, overlapped bamboo design, peach ext, turquoise int ...................................................... 75.00
   14" l, figural clam shell, green glaze ..................... 175.00
Box, 4 3/4" l x 3 1/2" w, rect, aqua base, white cov w/gold trim and gold figural horsehead knob ..................... 95.00
Candlestick
   3 1/4" h, blue-green glaze ...................................... 50.00
   5 1/2" h, turquoise, pr .......................................... 295.00
Carafe, 9" h, wood handle, matte green ..................... 150.00
Charger, 11 1/4" d, tan, cream, red, and gray mission scene
.......................................................................... 695.00
Chop Plate, 11" d, coupe shape, Toyon Red ............... 52.00
Console Bowl, 9 3/4" d, Mandarin Yellow ................... 100.00
Cruet, 6" h, gourd shape, semi-matte green glaze ..... 195.00
Dinnerware
   Rope pattern border-matte yellow glaze
      Bowl, 6 1/2" d ................................................. 20.00
      Chop Plate, 13" d, roped rim, mauve-blue glaze
      .................................................................. 165.00
      Cream Jug ....................................................... 18.00
      Cup and Saucer ............................................... 15.00
      Plate, 8 1/2" d ................................................. 25.00
      Platter, 13 1/2" l x 11" w .................................. 35.00
      Sugar Bowl, Cov ............................................. 25.00

**Tile, 7" l x 6" w, turquoise, red-brown and dk blue, (A), $475.**

**Vase, 11 7/8" h, seafoam green ext, salmon int, $175.**

Vegetable Bowl, 9 1/2" l, lt blue ............................ 75.00
Jar, Cov, 4" h, seafoam green body, Monterey brown cov
............................................................................ 150.00
Juice Tumbler, 2 5/8" h, matte green glaze ................. 16.00
Mug, 4" h, Toyon red ..................................................... 50.00
Pitcher, 6" h, burnt orange glaze ................................. 85.00
Planter, 10" l x 7" w, rect, ivory ................................... 60.00
Plaque, 13 3/4" d, yellow and dk blue swimming fish and jel-
lyfish, dk red and green plants, red snails, blue ground,
pierced for hanging ................................................ 1,300.00
Plate, 11 1/4" d, yellow and black painted Southwestern
scene, matte green ground, "imp Catalina Island" mk, (A)
............................................................................ 440.00
Platter, 18 1/2" l, green ............................................. 475.00
Wall Pocket, 8 3/8" h, figural sea shell, matte green
............................................................................ 300.00
Vase
4 3/4" h, squat base, flared neck, med blue glaze
........................................................................ 40.00
5" h
Stepped shape, blue ......................................... 125.00
Triangular shape, sage green ext, yellow int
.................................................................. 60.00
6" h
Oxblood glaze, Catalina Pottery ....................... 160.00
Squat base
Flared neck and rim, Toyon red ..................... 80.00
Matte green w/brown shading ...................... 135.00
7" h, pot shape, 5 vert ribs, center horiz rib, matte green
glaze ............................................................... 360.00
7 1/2" h
Cylinder shape, narrow base, short rim, Toyon red
.................................................................. 625.00
Trophy shape, orange ....................................... 325.00
7 3/4" h, bulbous w/fluted neck, lt blue glaze, "CATALINA
ISLAND 627" mk .............................................. 85.00
8" h, flared shape, white ext, turquoise int .............. 65.00
9" h, trophy shape, bulbous base, straight vert handles,
pearl white over red clay ................................... 495.00
12" h, bulbous base, flared rim, textured blue ext, lt blue
int ..................................................................... 400.00

# Ceramic Arts Studio

## Madison, Wisconsin
## Very late 1930s-early '40s-1955

**History:** Ceramic Arts Studio was started by Lawrence Rabbitt, an art student in Madison, Wisconsin, who set up a pottery using Wisconsin clays. He was soon joined by Rueben Sand, a law and business student. When they found that making hand-thrown pieces was erratic and time consuming, they experimented with slipcast pieces.

After Betty Harrington brought in a figure to be glazed, they asked her to become a designer and modeler for Ceramic Arts Studio. She was their chief designer for the remainder of the years the company was in business. More than eight hundred figures were made during the short history of the company, and Harrington made more than half of them.

The outbreak of World War II was beneficial to this company, since giftware buyers were left without their oriental and European supplies, and American potteries filled in the gap. But after the war, Japan once again focused on ceramics during the recovery period, and its examples were less expensive than its American counterparts. Ceramic Arts Studio competed until 1955 and then closed the company.

Distinctive features of Ceramic Arts Studio figures included the pink glazed cheeks on people figures and some animals, the eyes, the colors used, the detailed hand painting, and the white bisque body. Some figures were identified by the marks on the base, but many were not marked. Others had the name of the figure on the bottom. The glazes and modeling characteristics had a unique feel to them.

People figures were the company's strong feature, specifically children and adults. These had great appeal for gift buyers. The distinctive pose, size, facial expressions, colors, and decoration, along with the high quality workmanship and reasonable prices, made these very desirable. Other forms made included animals, birds, aquatic creatures, story book figures, head vases, and wall plaques.

**References:** Sabra Olson Laumbach, *Harrington Figurines*, Ferguson Communications, 1985; Mike Schneider, *Animal Figures*, Schiffer Publishing Ltd. 1990; _____, *Ceramic Arts Studio: Identification and Price Guide*, Schiffer Publishing Ltd.1994; _____, *Complete Salt & Pepper Shaker Book*, Schiffer Publishing Ltd. 1993; BA Wellman, *1992-93 Ceramic Arts Studio Price Guide*, self-published, 1993.

**Collectors' Club:** CAS Collectors Association. Jim Petzold, P.O. Box 46, Madison WI 53701-0046, bimonthly newsletter *CAS Collector*, $18.50.

**Reproduction Alert:** Many Ceramic Arts Studio pieces have been copied by overseas potteries, but these are fairly easy to spot. The quality of the decoration, the thinness of the glaze, the colors not being true, the inferior details, as well as the lighter weight, all contribute to detecting a copy.

Bank, 4 7/8" h, figural barber head, tan and gray......... 85.00
Dish, 11 3/4" l, boat shape w/raised vert ends, red-brown
glaze, divided int ...................................................... 8.00
Figure
1 7/8" h, kitten scratching, white w/orange accents
........................................................................ 45.00
2 3/8" h, 3 1/2" l, ox and wagon, brown, tan, and white
........................................................................ 195.00

**Bud Vase, 6 1/4" h, yellow-tan, mkd, $28.**

2 1/2" h, "Tembino the Elephant," black and gray
.................................................................... 125.00
2 3/4" h
    2 7/8" h, "Calico Cat" and "Gingham Dog", pr ..... 85.00
    "Fufu Poodle," white and pink ............................ 60.00
    Panda w/hat, blue, black, and white ................. 225.00
2 7/8" h, "Frisky Baby Lamb" ................................. 20.00
3" h, Scottie dog, black ......................................... 129.00
3 1/8" h, "Wee Swedish Girl," burgundy ................ 36.00
3 1/4" h, "Gentleman Turtle," brown, green, red, and blue
.................................................................... 35.00
3 3/8" h, Summer Sally, cream, orange trim ........... 85.00
3 1/2" h
    "Wee French Boy," blue trim .............................. 26.00
    "Wee Scotch Boy," green trim ............................ 36.00
3 5/8"h, 6" h, Mary and lamb, white w/orange, blue, and
    black trim, pr ..................................................... 85.00
3 7/8" h, stylized doe, brown ................................. 80.00
4" h
    5 1/2" h, "Tin-A-Ling," "Sung-To," green, pr ......... 60.00
    Elf on toadstool, white, blue, orange, and black
    .................................................................... 40.00
4" l, 6" l, fighting leopards, pr ................................ 200.00
4 1/2" h
    Billie goat, cream, black trim ............................. 68.00
    "Little Boy Blue," striped shirt ........................... 40.00
    4 1/2" l, crocodile, green .................................... 24.00
    4 5/8" h, "The Harmonica Boy," blue jacket ........... 40.00
4 3/4" h
    "Elsie the Elephant," cream, polychrome trim ... 122.00
    Sultan seated on pillow, green, white, and gold
    .................................................................... 70.00
    "Tom" cat standing, cream ................................. 125.00
4 7/8" h
    "Daisy Donkey," cream, polychrome flowers ..... 150.00
    "Young Love," olive green, black, and orange, pr
    .................................................................... 120.00

5 1/8" h
    5 5/8" h, "Pioneer Sam" and "Susie," black and cream,
    pr ................................................................... 95.00
    6 5/8" h, Gypsies, blue, dk blue, red, tan, and gold, pr
    .................................................................... 125.00
    "Spring Sue," green, yellow, and blue ................ 65.00
5 1/4" h
    "Bo-Peep," blue .................................................. 40.00
    "Summer Belle," orange, blue, black, and white
    .................................................................... 45.00
5 3/8" h, Russian couple, black, blue, white, and red, pr
.................................................................... 100.00
5 3/8" h, "Winter Belle," green coat .......................... 80.00
5 1/2" h, "Peter Pan" and "Wendy," green, white and
    orange, pr ......................................................... 195.00
6" h
    6 1/2" h, "Blythe" and "Pensive," black and chartreuse,
    pr ................................................................... 170.00
    "Budgie," turquoise ............................................ 95.00
    "Mary," green ..................................................... 30.00
6 1/4" h, "Archibald the Dragon," green ................. 200.00
6 1/2" h
    6 3/8" h, "Harry" and "Lillibeth," black, tan, green, and
    white, pr ........................................................... 60.00
    Chinese boy, yellow coat and hat ...................... 45.00
    Spanish woman dancer, green scarf .................. 60.00
6 3/4" h, Colonial woman, blue ............................... 50.00
6 7/8" h, "Miss Lucidy," green ................................. 50.00
7 1/8" h, "Rhumba" woman, dk blue, white, red, and pea
    green ................................................................ 65.00
7 1/4" h, "Colonel Jackson," black, brown, and white
.................................................................... 45.00
9 3/8" h, 9 5/8" h, Balinese dancers, flesh, yellow, green,
    and white, pr ..................................................... 200.00
10" h, "Tragedy," green .......................................... 125.00
11 1/2" h, "Fire Lady," red glaze ............................. 160.00
Pitcher
    3" h, "Adam and Eve," brown, blue, and cream ....... 45.00
    3 1/4" h, Colonial man Toby jug, blue, black, and
    yellow .............................................................. 65.00
    5" h, lt yellow body, dk green drip from rim ........... 200.00
Shakers
    1 1/2"h, 2" h, mouse and cheese, gray tones and
    yellow, pr .......................................................... 35.00
    2 1/4" h, "Oakie" and leaf, green and cream .......... 165.00
    2 3/8 h, 4 3/4" h, kangaroo and baby, yellow ........ 125.00
    2 1/2" h, 4 1/4" h, "Gorilla snuggles," black and gray
    .................................................................... 95.00
    3 1/8 h, 3 3/8" h, "Eskimo kids," pr ...................... 95.00
    3 1/4" h
        3 7/8" h, fighting cocks, multicolored ................ 50.00
        5 1/4" l, "Sambo and Tiger," brown, black, and blue
        .................................................................... 750.00
    3 1/2" h
        Elephants, turquoise, pink, and black ................ 75.00
        "Minnehaha and Hiawatha" ................................ 135.00
        "Seahorse and Coral," brown and tan ................ 70.00
    4 1/2" h, 2 1/2" h, Mom and baby polar bear .......... 48.00
Shelf-Sitter
    4" h, Chinese boy, green ...................................... 20.00

4 1/4" h, "Banjo Girl," white, orange, blue, and brown
.................................................................................... 60.00

4 3/4" h
Blackamoor, white w/black and orange, pr ........ 145.00
"Jill," green and white .......................................... 35.00

5" h, "Tomcat," white ............................................... 80.00

5 1/8" h, seated collie, brown and cream ................ 75.00

5 1/4" h, "Ballet En Pose" and "Ballet En Repose," lime
green, pr .............................................................. 170.00

5 1/2" h, 6" h, "Sun Li" and "Su Lin," black, white, and red,
pr ............................................................................. 45.00

5 3/4" h, Siamese cat ............................................... 55.00

7 1/8" h, 8 1/4" h, "Maurice" and "Michelle," green, pr
.................................................................................... 80.00

7 7/8" h, 8 1/8" h, "Pete" and "Polly" parrots, red,
yellow trim, pr .................................................... 200.00

Wall Plaque
4 7/8" h, Boy and girl, blue, white, and orange, pr ... 75.00
7 3/4" h, figural cockatoo, white w/black accents ..... 40.00

9" h
"Zor" and "Zorina," green, pr .............................. 95.00

9 1/2" h, "Attitude" and "Arabesque," white, red trim, pr
.................................................................................. 100.00

Wall Pocket, 8 1/8" h, "African Man" and "African Woman"
masks, brown, "Ceramic Arts Studio Madison, Wisc" mk,
pr, (A) ................................................................... 275.00

1900-1904
or later

MOTHER GOOSE
HAYNES
Ware
Decoration
No. 510

# Chesapeake Pottery/D.F. Haynes and Son Company

## Baltimore, Maryland
## 1880-1914

**History:** Chesapeake Pottery was started in 1880 by Henry
and Isaac Broughman and John Tunstall. In 1882, D.F.
Haynes and Company purchased Chesapeake Pottery. The
pottery was expanded until 1887, when it was bought by
Edwin Bennett. After a few years, he sold the works to his
son and David Haynes, and it was called Haynes, Bennett
and Company.

When Bennett retired in 1895, Frank Haynes joined the
firm and it became D.F. Haynes and Son in 1896. In 1914,
American Sugar Refining Company bought the pottery site
and discontinued the business.

The company made semi-porcelain toilet sets, dishes,
jardinieres, and novelties. Majolica was made between
1881-1890. Haynes first majolica dinner pattern was Clifton.
Avalon Faience was a more elegant design based on
French faience. Both of these patterns had off-white backgrounds, which was new for American majolica. A third
faience design was Real Ivory.

Parian was made after 1895, and then they made white
granite ware. Jugs, lamps, vases, and clocks also were
made. An assortment of marks was used.

**References:** Marilyn G. Karmason with Joan B. Stacke,
*Majolica*, Harry Abrams, 1989.

**Museums:** Peale Museum, one of Baltimore City Life Museums, MD.

Centerbowl, 12" d x 7 3/8" h, "Holland Sunset" pattern on int,
green ext ................................................................. 150.00
Creamer, 4" h, "Cumberland" pattern, Haynes Ware ... 10.00
Dish, Cov, 5" h x 4 3/4" d, "Holland Sunset"
pattern ....................................................................... 30.00

Pitcher
4 7/8" h, raised leaves and blackberries, gold trim, cream
ground, black "AVALON FAIENCE BALT. triangle" mk
.................................................................................... 35.00

5" h, squat shape, "Gainsborough," yellow, green, and
brown trees and cows ........................................... 60.00

6 1/4" h, "Holland Sunset" pattern, yellow, green, brown,
and red ................................................................... 30.00

7" h
Blue and copper red scattered bouquets, wide pink
scalloped border band, molded face spout,
Avalon .............................................................. 40.00

Red carnation design w/foliage on sides, gold band
accents, figural face spout, black "AVALON" mk,
hairline .............................................................. 20.00

9" h, bark-type cream ground, branch handle, relief of
blackberries and leaves ..................................... 450.00

Plate, 8" d, violet-red relief molded blackberries and leaves
on border, textured white ground, Avalon mk .......... 45.00

**Biscuit Jar, 9" H-H, "Dutch Sunrise" design pat-
tern, yellow, green, and purple, Haynes mk, $75.**

**Pitcher, 10" h, raised
tan pear, yellow
peach, and red
strawberries, black-
berries on reverse,
brown and green
leaves, textured
ground, $100.**

W. A. Woodard Memorial Library

Platter

    12" H-H, red-pink flower bouquets on border, molded rope rim, black "triangle AVALON FAIENCE BALT" mk ................................................................................. 20.00

    13" H-H, blackberry design, branch handles, green, red, and brown, cream ground, Avalon mk, (A) .......... 50.00

Vase

    5 1/2" h, squat shape, flared rim, "Cloverdale" pattern, green and yellow forest and meadow scene, "Cloverdale Decoration Haynes Ware" mk ...................... 85.00

    6 1/2" h

        Bag shape, shoulder band of white heart shapes w/blue and green leaf designs, dk matte pink ground, mkd ...................................................... 35.00

        Bulbous middle, spread ft, 2 vert handles, ruffled rim, panels of red, blue, and green flowers, red borders, gold trim, "HAYNES BALT." mk ........................ 18.00

    7" h

        Blackberry design, red, green, and brown, cream ground, Clifton mk ............................................. 175.00

        Cylinder shape, wide base, raised brown outlined bird design, green outlined leaves w/gold veining, white crackle ground ............................................. 235.00

    10" h, tapered body, bulbous shoulder, flared neck and rim, 2 fancy handles, "Cloverdale" pattern, cow in pasture, Haynes .................................................. 30.00

    12" h, corset shape, white teardrop white panels w/green and blue leaves and red center, black Greek key design on rim, dk rose ground, "Haynes Ware Myriad" mk ........................................................................ 35.00

**Vase, 9" h, imp floral design, multi-toned matte green glaze, repaired rim chips, (A), $440.**

Vase

    5" h, swollen shape, lobed body, short collar, matte feathered turquoise and olive green glazes, imp mk, (A) ........................................................................ 440.00

    6 3/4" h, dbl gourd shape w/architectural handles, relief molded Art Nouveau swirls, textured green glaze ..................................................................... 1,250.00

    7" h, tapered cylinder shape, wide shoulder w/sm rim, emb leaves, semi-matte pea green glaze, mkd, (A) ........................................................................ 550.00

    8" h, squat twisted base, stem neck, matte brown and green suspended glaze, (A) ......................................... 38.00

# Chicago Crucible Company

## Chicago, Illinois
## c1920-c1932

**History:** The Northwestern Terra Cotta Company acquired the Chicago Crucible Company in 1920 in Chicago, Illinois and discontinued its Norweta line. It expanded its facilities for Chicago Crucible and made decorative pottery vases, lamp bases, and ashtrays with mottled glazes in shades of blue and green. Additional production included wall plaques with relief portraits and whimsical open-mouthed frogs. These lines were discontinued after a few years. A raised in-mold mark was used. Some architectural terra cotta also was made.

**Reference:** Sharon S. Darling, *Chicago Ceramics and Glass: An Illustrated History from 1871-1933*, Chicago Historical Society, 1979.

Ash Receiver, 5" h, figural seated frog w/open mouth, matte green glaze .......................................................... 300.00

Ashtray, 5" sq, mottled blue glaze, "CHICAGO CRUCIBLE CHICAGO, ILL" mk ............................................... 75.00

Bud Vase, 8" h, 4 sided neck, lobed base, thick apple green and turquoise glaze, mkd, (A) .............................. 330.00

Paperweight, gold glaze figure on multicolored Persian rug ................................................................................ 450.00

# Children's Ware

**History:** Numerous American manufacturers made miniature versions of their regular-size dishes for children. These smaller-size dishes were used by children to entertain their friends at tea parties. Dinner sets in the smaller size also were made. Dishes were also made to feed babies with nursery rhymes and fairy tales for decoration.

    Production of children's ware reached a peak during World War II, since the less-costly Japanese imports were not available. After the war, production declined, and many of the firms were no longer in business.

    Manufacturers used animal themes, nursery rhymes, children's activities, and the artwork of famous illustrators such as Kate Greenaway. Knowles, Taylor, and Knowles, East Liverpool China, Buffalo Pottery, Florence Cook Pottery, Harker, Homer Laughlin, Canonsburg, Salem China, Southern Potteries, Warwick, Smith Phillips, and Roseville were some of the makers. There were also many unmarked sets.

**References:** Doris Lechler, *Children's Glass Dishes, China, and Furniture*, Collector Books, 1983 values, Volume II 1986, updated 1991; Lorraine May Punchard, *Child's Play*, published by author, 1982; Margaret and Kenn Whitmyer, *Collector's Encyclopedia of Children's Dishes: An Illustrated Value Guide*, Collector Books, 1993.

**Collectors' Clubs:** Children's Things Collectors Society, Linda Martin, P.O. Box 983, Durant, IA 52747, CTCS Newsletter; *The Tiny Times*, newsletter, Abbie Kelly, P.O. Box 351, Camillus, NY 13031.

**Museums:** Margaret Woodbury Strong Museum, Rochester, NY.

Cereal Bowl

    5" d, blue stenciled airbrushed dancing duck on int, Jackson.................................................................. 30.00

    5 1/4" d, 3 decals of dogs and children on int, aqua and pink ext lines, Crown Pottery............................. 15.00

    6 1/4" d, pumpkin decal, Salem ............................... 14.00

    6 1/2" d, Little boy blue rhyme and scene of boy sitting next to haystack, gold overlay border, Edwin Knowles .................................................................. 38.00

Creamer

    2 3/4" h, standing rabbits, Roseville...................... 150.00

    3 1/4" h, band of ivory chicks on yellow band, "black Marrianne.Her.Jug" around center, Paul Revere, (A) .................................................................. 357.00

Cup, 3" h, dbl handled, Sunbonnet girl, Roseville ...... 175.00

Dish

    4 3/4" d, multicolored decal of "This is the House Jack Built," alphabet border, "DRESDEN CHINA" mk .................................................................. 15.00

    5" d, cartoon figures of walking elephant and hippo in dress clothes, Warwick...................................... 15.00

    8" d

        Multicolored decal of "Baby Bunting and Bunch While Crossing A Log Are Boldly Stared At By An Ugly Green Frog," McNichol ................................. 35.00

        Three section, brown bunnies, nest of eggs in sections, cream-yellow ground, border band of sponged red stylized flowerheads, Limoges China .................................................................. 20.00

Feeding Bowl, 9" d, tab handles, decal of girl feeding bear sitting in highchair, gold trim, Homer Laughlin ........ 75.00

Feeding Dish

    7" d

        "Higglety, Pigglety My Black Hen, She Lays Eggs For Gentlemen," green trim, Roseville ............... 545.00

        Running ducks, rolled edge, Weller Zona ......... 140.00

    7 1/4" d, multicolored decal of 2 puppies on seesaw, alphabet border, Crown ...................................... 22.00

    7 1/2" d

        "Baby Bunting" in center, alphabet border, McNichol .................................................................. 15.00

        "Hickory-Dickory-Dock," Roseville..................... 130.00

**Feeding Dish, 8" d, yellow chicks, cream ground, "stamped RV" mk, $250.**

**Plate, 7 1/8" d, white duck, pink cameo ground, Harker, $25.**

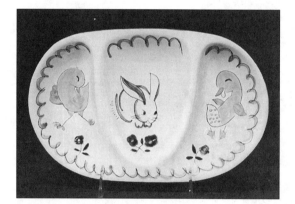

**Feeding Dish, 10 1/4" l, yellow, brown, and green, Stangl Kiddieware, $165.**

    7 3/4" d, Campbell's Kids, Buffalo Pottery ............. 100.00

    8" d

        Campbell's Kids, multicolored scene of little boy giving flower to little girl, (A)......................... 137.00

        Dogs, Roseville ................................................ 150.00

        Four sitting rabbits, Roseville ........................... 165.00

        Three section, decals of boy, girl, and doll on teeter-totter, aproned rabbit and rabbits, Salem ....... 35.00

        Three standing little girls with yellow bonnets, Roseville .................................................................. 195.00

Kiddie Set, 3 piece, cup, cereal bowl, 5 5/8" d, plate, 9 1/4" d, "Ranger Boy" design, Stangl ................... 150.00

Mug

    2 3/4" h, Little Boy Blue w/black cow, Salem .......... 10.00

    3" h

        Blue lobster design, blue lined rim, loop handle, crackle glaze, "blue stamped Dedham Pottery" mk, (A)............................................................... 770.00

        Dressed rabbit, Roseville ................................. 200.00

    3 1/2" h, white cameo of elephant on stand, blue ground, Harker .................................................................. 15.00

Pitcher, 4" h, molded brown rabbit, blue bird on branch, Weller Zona, (A)...................................................... 44.00

Plate

    5 1/2" d, "Mary and Her Lamb, Tom, Tom, Mistress Mary, Little Boy Blue" on border, Syracuse.................. 10.00

6 3/8" d, multicolored decal of "Sing a song of sixpence..." and boy w/pie, blue line on inner and outer border, scalloped rim, Salem ...........................................28.00

6 1/2" d, yellow chicks, Roseville ...........................128.00

7 1/8" d, "Little Tommy Tucker Sings For His Supper" design, Shenango .................................................40.00

7 1/4" d

Boy's face and "For A Good Little Boy," E. Knowles ...........................................................................10.00

"Old King Cole" poem and design in center, blue lined rim, East Liverpool Potteries ..........................12.00

7 1/2" d, dk blue elephant and baby border band and circ center, crackle glaze, blue stamped "Dedham Pottery" mk, (A) .......................................................... 1,650.00

8" d, pink airbrushed pig chef, Jackson ...................30.00

9 1/4" d, Kiddieware, "Little Bo Peep," Stangl ..........95.00

10" l, Kiddieware, "Pony Ride," Stangl.....................50.00

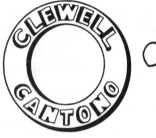

CLEWELL
Canton O.

# Clewell Art Ware

## Canton, Ohio
## 1906-1966

**History:** Charles Walter Clewell founded the studio in 1906 and continued until he died in 1966. He was a metal worker, not a potter who covered ceramic bodies with a tight covering of copper, silver, or burnished copper and made ornamental and utilitarian pieces. He purchased pottery blanks for his covered works from Weller, Cambridge, Owens, and Knowles, Taylor, and Knowles.

Clewell worked by himself and won a medal in the Paris International Exposition in 1937 for his covered artware. He made vases, lamps, complete stein sets, and pitchers in various shapes and sizes with this metal over pottery technique. He conducted experiments to study the oxidation of copper and man-made methods of producing the corrosion to eventually produce the matte green or blue-green colors he used.

Wares were usually marked with Clewell incised or impressed in the base of pieces along with numbers.

**Museums:** The Canton Art Institute, OH.

Bookend, 6 1/2" h, w/candleholder, bronze, brown, and green patina, pr, (A) ...........................................2,310.00

Bowl

3 1/2" d, ftd, faux rivet design, set of 4, (A) ............230.00

9 1/2" d, rolled, closed rim, green, brown, and blue patina, (A).....................................................523.00

Bud Vase, 10" h, hourglass shape, vertigris patina, "incised Clewell" mk, (A).....................................................715.00

Candlestick, 7" h, 4 sided, tapered, dk bronzed patina, unmkd, pr, (A) ..........................................1,430.00

Ewer, 6" h, sm flared spout, brown patina, (A) ...........440.00

Mug, 4 1/2" h, applied deer head, (A)...........................82.00

**Vase, 9" h, copper clad, original patina, (A), $350.**

**Vase, 10 1/2" h, blue-green to orange patina, incised mk, (A), $550.**

Pitcher, 9 1/2" h, faceted, faux rivet panels, int hairline, brown patina, (A) ................................................... 110.00

Vase

5" h, spherical, short neck, vertigris to bronze patina, "incised Clewell" mk, (A) ..................................825.00

5 1/4" h, ovoid, 3 sm feet, verdigris and bronze patina, "incised Clewell 411-2-6" mk, (A) ......................605.00

6" h, squat shape

Sm everted rim, overall copper finish................550.00

Two loop handles from shoulder to rim, vertigris and bronze patina, "incised Clewell 408-2-6" mk, (A) .......................................................................1,540.00

6 1/2" h, ovoid, blue-green and bronze patina, "incised Clewell 32142" mk, (A)....................................715.00

7" h

Bottle shape, incised stylized poppies, brown patina, (A) ....................................................................770.00

Swollen shape, green and orange patina, incised mk, (A) ....................................................................715.00

7 1/2" h

    Hourglass shape with bulbous base, verdigris and bronze patina, "incised Clewell 250-29" mk, (A) ...................................................................... 605.00

    Ovoid shape, verdigris to bronze patina, "incised Clewell/351-25" mk, (A) ............................. 1,100.00

7 5/8" h, ball base, straight neck, flared rim, ftd, vertigris base, copper colored neck and rim, "incised Clewell 295" mk, (A) ........................................................ 357.00

9" h, flared form, spread ft, 2 sm handles, bronze w/green and brown patina, (A) ..................................... 1,540.00

10" h, faceted sides, circ rim, verdigris and bronze patina, "incised Clewell 439-2-6" mk, (A) ................... 2,640.00

10 1/4" h, squat base, straight neck, rolled rim, verdigris patina, "incised Clewell 5-2-6" mk, (A) ........... 1,870.00

11" h

    Applied nude on vase, vert leaves, copper clad, unmkd, (A) ......................................................... 715.00

    Flat shoulder, striated gold, green, and copper patina, "incised Clewell" mk, (A) ............................. 1,065.00

11 1/4" h, tapered sides, cupped rim, verdigris and bronze patina, "incised Clewell/485-215" mk, (A) ....................................................................... 1,650.00

12 1/2" h, ovoid shape, sm flared rim, brown, blue, and green patina, (A) .............................................. 1,870.00

13" h, swollen tapered shape, short, flared rim, green, blue, and brown patina, mkd, (A) ................... 1,540.00

14 1/2" h, classic shape, bronze to verdigris patina, "incised Clewell" mk, (A) ................................ 2,575.00

Vessel

4 1/2" h, bowl shaped body, spread ft and rim, bronze and verdigris patina, "incised Clewell 417-2-g" mk, (A) ...................................................................... 495.00

5 1/2" h, lg flowing buttress handles from body to rim, bronze to verdigris patina, "incised Clewell/408-2-6" mk, (A) .................................................................. 785.00

1905

# Clifton Art Pottery

### Newark, New Jersey
### 1905-1914

**History:** Fred Tschirner and William A. Long established the factory in 1905 and made art pottery until 1911. Crystal Patina had a porcelain-like dense body that was decorated with a pale green crystalline glaze. Later semi-matte colors included green, yellow, and tan.

In 1906, they introduced Clifton Indian Ware, which was adapted from American Indian pottery utilizing unglazed New Jersey red clay for the pieces. The interiors were covered with a high-gloss black glaze so water could not penetrate the pottery. A wide variety of examples included candlesticks, vases, mugs, jardinieres, pedestals, and umbrella stands. Owens and Weller made imitations of these wares. Souvenir and cooking utensils also were made.

Other Clifton lines included Robin's Egg Blue, which used the same dense body as Crystal Patina with a matte blue glaze. Tirrube had a matte finish background with flowers covered in a light slip.

After 1911, the focus of the firm shifted to wall and floor tile using leadless glazes developed by Charles Stegmeyer. In 1914, the name of the company was changed to the Clifton Porcelain Tile Company.

Marks are incised on Crystal Patina and impressed on the Indian ware; 100 series marks are on Crystal Patina and 200 series are on the Indian ware shapes. Some early pieces are dated.

**Museums:** National Museum of History and Technology, Smithsonian Institution, Washington, DC; The Newark Museum, NJ.

Cabinet Vase, 2 1/4" h x 4" d, squat shape, "Crystal Patina," (A) ........................................................... 235.00

Coffeepot, 2 3/4" h, native American design, terra cotta matte glaze ......................................................... 225.00

Jardiniere, 8 1/2" h x 11" d, incised and painted buff and black native American "Four Mile Ruin, Arizona" design, brown ground, rim hairline, mkd, (A) ..................... 440.00

Lamp, 8 1/2" h, squat, stepped shape, gloss tan w/dk brown drip ..................................................................... 95.00

Pitcher, 4 1/2" h, native American designs, black circles and stepped blocks, red clay ground ............................. 60.00

Teapot, 7" h, funnel base tapering to bulbous body, short spout, loop handle, matte caramel "Crystal Patina" .......................................................................... 99.00

Vase

4 1/8" h, bowl shape, rust, tan, and black stepped native American designs, "imp Clifton 220 Chevlon Arizona" mk, (A) ............................................................... 137.00

4 3/8" h, squat base, straight neck, black, tan, and rust swirled native American designs, (A) ................ 137.00

4 1/2" h, 2 flared handles, "Crystal Patina," silver overlay, "incised Clifton Pottery, 1906" mk, (A) ........... 1,100.00

5" h, native American designs, artist sgd ............... 250.00

6 1/2" h, bulbous base, flared neck and rim, white "Crystal Patina" glaze, (A) ........................................ 175.00

6 3/4" h, squat shape, straight collar, native American designs, "Four-Mile Ruin, Arizona," black geometrics, reddish ground, (A) ......................................... 100.00

7" h, swollen, tapered shape, closed rim, "Crystal Patina," emb poppies under turquoise glaze, "incised Clifton Pottery 1905" mk, hairline, (A) ........................ 440.00

8 1/2" h, tapered body, trumpet neck, flared rim, green glaze w/yellow and gray accents, mkd .............. 300.00

9 1/2" h, bottle shape, "Crystal Patina" glaze, "incised Clifton" mk, (A) .................................................. 385.00

**Teapot, 8" l, mottled pea green glaze, $295.**

10" h, wide, angular handles, "Crystal Patina" glaze, "incised Clifton" mk, (A) ................................... 495.00

11" h, matte green "Crystal Patina" glaze .............385.00

Vessel, 8" h x 11" d, jar shape, Indian "Homolobi," umber bands of geometrics on terra cotta ground, "incised Clifton/233" mk, (A) ..................................... 495.00

Water Jug, 5" h, native American designs, "Four-Mile Ruin, Arizona," black crabs, red body, (A) ......... 125.00

# Cookie Jars

## 1920s-Present

**History:** Ceramic cookie jars were made by a tremendous number of potteries from the 1920s until the present time, though the majority were made during the 1940s to the 1970s. Cookie jars were usually made of white earthenware.

There are five primary methods of decoration used on cookie jars. These include: glaze, paint, glaze and paint combination, glaze and transfer combination, and a combination of all three elements. The glaze finish, whether matte or glossy, is the most durable finish. Cold paint decoration refers to paint decoration that is not fired. This causes many problems since it is either applied directly to the bisque body or on top of the glaze. The paint could deteriorate easily. Transfers are fired on decals applied over the glaze that also could be damaged by frequent use.

Nelson McCoy from Roseville, Ohio and American Bisque Company from Williamstown, West Virginia were the two biggest producers of cookie jars. More than three hundred varieties were made by McCoy from the time it started making them in the late 1930s. Plain bean pot types were its first jars. In 1939, it made its first figural Mammy with cauliflowers. McCoy jars were characterized by very detailed mold features, hand painting of details on top of the glaze, use of decals, frequent use of fruits and vegetables, and canister types for its jars. Most of its cookie jars were marked.

American Bisque was second to McCoy in numbers of jars made from 1937-1973. Important jars included the Flintstone group, Olive Oyl, and Popeye examples. These jars also showed a lot of detail in relief and in the way they were decorated. Most were glazed by air brushing. Very few solid color jars were made. They usually were marked "U.S.A."

sometimes with a number. Paper labels were also used. Frequently their jars had a wedge on the bottom to aid in firing.

The Abingdon Pottery Company from Abingdon, Illinois made 22 designs from 1939-1950. Its first one was "Little Old Lady" in solid colors and decorations. They were marked with an ink stamp "Abingdon USA," plus an impressed serial number.

Brush Pottery Company of Roseville, Ohio had many cookie jars made by Don and Russ Winton from the mid-1940s until 1971. Most were airbrushed and marked with the "W" mark. They made simple stoneware cookie jars earlier. First decorations were leaves and flowers. Figural jars with people, animals, fruits, vegetables, and other subjects started about 1940.

California Originals from Torrence mostly made animal cookie jars plus license ware for Walt Disney, Walter Lanz, DC Comics, Muppets, and such.

Hall China Company from East Liverpool, Ohio made cookie jars designed by Eva Ziesel marked "Hall's Superior Quality Kitchen Ware Made in USA." Mostly canister shapes were made as accessories to its dinnerware and kitchen utility lines. Many different back stamps were used.

The Hull Pottery Company of Crooksville, Ohio was best known for Little Red Riding Hood, patented in 1943. Though Hull owned the patent rights, much of the Red Riding Hood collection was made by Regal China of Antioch, Illinois. In addition to cookie jars, there were spice jars, sugars, creamers, match safes, salt and pepper shakers, planters, mugs, canisters, butter dishes, teapots, cracker jars, and milk pitchers. There were different varieties of Little Red Riding Hood with the basket open or closed. Most have impressed, ink stamp, or gold stamp mark.

Metlox Potteries from Manhattan Beach, California started cookie jars in 1947 and made a wide assortment of them until 1989. Many were made under the name "Poppy Trail of California."

Shawnee Pottery Company of Zanesville, Ohio had designer Rudy Gantz from 1939-1944 who made Smiley Pig, Winnie Pig, Sailor Boy, Jack and Jill and such. Shawnee molds were bought for Terrace Ceramics in 1961 and then McNicol China Company of Clarksburg, West Virginia produced them.

Robinson-Ransbottom Pottery Company of Roseville, Ohio is still in business. From 1935-1975, it made cookie jars similar to what was being made by American Bisque.

Twin Winton of Pasadena, California made cookie jars with a wood tone matte glaze finish in 1951. After moving to San Juan Capistrano in 1964, it made a "Collectors' Series" of 18 jars including an owl, Raggedy Ann, Andy, donkey, etc. In 1977, it sold its business and molds to Treasure Craft. Now located in Compton, California, Treasure Craft is one of the American potteries still making a lot of cookie jars. That company was sold to Pfaltzgraff Pottery Company in 1988.

Numerous other companies made cookie jars such as Bauer, California Cleminsons, DeForest, Fredericksburg Art Pottery Company, Frankoma, Gladding McBean and Company, Haeger Potteries, Inc., Pearl China Company, Pennsbury Pottery, Pfaltzgraff Pottery, Purinton Pottery Company, Red Wing, and Cronin China Company to name a few.

Black Americana cookie jars are highly collectible today. Brayton Laguna Pottery Company, Pearl China, Mosaic Tile Company, and Fielder and Fielder all made mammys.

Advertising cookie jars were used to advertise products, as premium offers, and as licenses using certain logos on jars.

Many decorating companies bought bisque cookie jars from potteries and then applied glaze, paint, transfer decorations, or some combinations of all three types of decors.

They sold them through their individual marketing departments or to a distributor. Studio artists such as Carol Gifford designed a series of black cookie jars such as "Watermelon Mammy." Rick Wisecarver made 32 molds from 1983-1991 in Roseville, Ohio using black and country themes. They were all signed on the back.

**References:** Harold Nichols, *McCoy Cookie Jars: From The First To The Latest*, Nichols Publishing, 1987; Fred and Joyce Roerig, *The Collector's Encyclopedia of Cookie Jars*, *Book I*, 1997 Values, *Book II*, 1998 Values, *Book III*, 1999 Values, Collector Books, 1997, 1998, 1999; Mike Schneider, *The Complete Cookie Jar Book, 2nd Edition*, Schiffer Publishing Ltd. 1999; Mark & Ellen Supnick, *Wonderful World of Cookie Jars*, L-W Publishing, 1996; Ermagene Westfall, *An Illustrated Value Guide to Cookie Jars, Books I & II*, Collector Books, 1997.

**Newsletters:** "Cookie Jarrin," Joyce Roerig, Editor, 1501 Maple Ridge Road, Walterboro, SC 9495, bimonthly; "Crazed Over Cookie Jars," Maureen Saxby, P.O. Box 254, Savanna, IL 61074.

**Museums:** The Cookie Jar Museum, Lemont, IL

**Reproduction Alert:** The original Hillbilly Frog cookie jar was made by Brush Pottery Company. The mold was sold in 1992 to a potter who made 75-80 reissues. There is also a low-quality reproduction on the market since 1992. Reproduction Hull Little Red Riding Hood cookie jars are marked the same as old originals. Height is the most reliable way to separate old from new. There are also Red Riding Hood cookie jars marked with a McCoy trademark, but these are reproductions, too, since the jars were designed and patented by Hull, not McCoy.

### ABINGDON
Bo Peep ....................................................... 300.00
Hobby Horse ................................................ 450.00
Humpty Dumpty ........................................... 385.00
Jack-In-Box ................................................. 450.00
Money Bag .................................................. 125.00
Mother Goose, (A) ....................................... 475.00

### ADVERTISING
Archway Cookie Bus ...................................... 35.00
Elsie in the Barrel ........................................ 350.00
Harley Hog .................................................. 385.00
Keebler Tree House ........................................ 70.00
Kraft T Bear ................................................ 175.00
Mrs. Field .................................................. 125.00
Nabisco Oreo Cookie Truck .............................. 85.00
Paradise Bakery ........................................... 150.00
Quaker Oats ................................................. 95.00

### AMERICAN BISQUE
Baby Girl Elephant ....................................... 150.00
Bluebird ...................................................... 40.00
Casper ..................................................... 1,450.00
Chalkboard Girl ........................................... 250.00
Clock, red, black, and white ............................. 85.00
Cookies Of The World .................................... 210.00
Cookie Truck ............................................... 110.00
Churn Boy ................................................... 220.00
Dino with Golf Clubs .................................. 1,350.00
Donald Duck, standing ................................... 375.00
Donkey and Milk Wagon .................................. 140.00
Farmer Pig .................................................. 165.00
Figaro on Ball of Yarn ................................... 395.00

Fred and Dino .......................................... 1,175.00
French Poodle, burgundy ................................ 120.00
Goofy Rabbit ................................................ 85.00
Ice Cream Freezer ........................................ 450.00
Kitten on Quilted Box .................................... 145.00
Lady Pig ..................................................... 175.00
Mohawk Indian ......................................... 2,200.00
Paddle Boat ................................................ 295.00
Puppy on Quilted Base ................................... 150.00
Sack of Cookies ............................................. 45.00
Seal on Igloo ............................................... 375.00
Spaceship ................................................... 400.00
Spool of Thread ........................................... 275.00
Standing Mickey Mouse ............................... 4,500.00
Teddy Bear ................................................. 135.00
Umbrella Kids .............................................. 375.00
Wilma on Telephone ...................................... 795.00
Yogi Bear, felt tongue .................................... 575.00

### BAUER
Swimming Fish, pink, Cemar turned ................... 180.00

### BRAYTON LAGUNA
Maid ...................................................... 4,900.00
Mammy, red dress ..................................... 1,250.00
Swedish Maiden ........................................... 450.00

### BRUSH
Davy Crocket .............................................. 225.00
Elephant with Ice Cream Cone .......................... 575.00
Formal Pig, black coat, blue vest ...................... 330.00
Happy Bunny ............................................... 225.00
Hippo and Monkey, (A) ................................... 585.00
Laughing Hippo ............................................ 850.00
Little Boy Blue ............................................. 695.00
Old Woman's Shoe .......................................... 85.00
Puppy Police ............................................... 725.00
Raggedy Ann with Patches ............................... 445.00
Smiling Bear ............................................... 300.00
Teddy Bear, dk brown ..................................... 199.00
White Bunny ................................................ 199.00

### CALIFORNIA ORIGINALS
Circus Wagon ................................................ 75.00
Clown Riding Elephant .................................... 185.00
Ernie ........................................................ 125.00
Happy Clown ................................................. 75.00
Indian With Lollipop ....................................... 90.00
Koala Bear .................................................. 200.00
Liberty Bell .................................................. 65.00
Little Girl ................................................... 195.00
Mickey Mouse with Drum ................................. 395.00
Pinocchio, arms crossed .............................. 1,400.00
Raggedy Ann ............................................... 175.00
Red Bull ...................................................... 69.00
Rooster ....................................................... 45.00
Santa on His Sack ......................................... 595.00
Space Cadet .................................................. 75.00
Superman .................................................... 595.00
Taxi with Flat Tire ........................................ 125.00
The Count ................................................... 595.00

The Grouch ................................................. 75.00
Victrola ..................................................... 450.00
Woody Woodpecker ................................... 800.00

**CHARACTER**
Benny ....................................................... 275.00
Hopalong Cassidy, Peter Pan Products ..... 550.00
Paddington Bear ........................................ 975.00
Snoopy Chef, red collar ............................. 295.00

**DEFOREST**
Cookie King ............................................... 500.00
Nun - "The Lord Helps Those Who Help Themselves"
................................................................... 425.00

**DORANNE**
Clover Bunny .............................................. 50.00
Cow Jumped Over the Moon ....................... 250.00
Donkey ...................................................... 90.00
Mother Goose ........................................... 135.00
Pinocchio Head ......................................... 225.00
Pirate and Chest ........................................ 95.00
Walrus ...................................................... 25.00

**FITZ AND FLOYD**
Cookie Thief .............................................. 129.00
Hedda Gobbler .......................................... 99.00
Mammy ..................................................... 665.00
Runaway ................................................... 325.00
Santa on Motorcycle .................................. 695.00
Southwest Santa ....................................... 695.00

**GLADDING McBEAN-FRANCISCAN**
Cafe Royale pattern ................................... 250.00

**GONDER**
Swirled aqua body, brown speckle and brush design
................................................................... 100.00

**HALL**
Autumn Leaf, 10" h, "Rayed" ...................... 195.00

**HULL**
Barefoot Boy .............................................. 299.00
Little Red Riding Hood
    Closed basket ...................................... 375.00
    Gold stars on apron .............................. 650.00
    Open Basket ........................................ 375.00
    Poinsettia ............................................ 800.00

**MCCOY**
Asparagus ................................................. 95.00
Bobby Baker .............................................. 45.00
Burlap Bag ................................................ 40.00
Chef's Head, ............................................. 195.00
Clyde Dog .................................................. 200.00
Colby Cat, black ........................................ 450.00
Colonial Fireplace ...................................... 120.00
Dalmatians ................................................ 250.00
Football Boy ............................................... 295.00
Globe ........................................................ 745.00
Harley Hog ................................................ 550.00
Kookie Kettle ............................................. 40.00
Mammy
    Red polka dot dress ............................. 375.00

Yellow ....................................................... 550.00
Pineapple .................................................. 75.00
Snoopy in Doghouse .................................. 325.00
Tepee
    Regular Top .......................................... 250.00
    Slant Top .............................................. 300.00
Touring Car ............................................... 65.00
Yosemite Sam ........................................... 175.00
W.C.Fields ................................................. 175.00
Windmill .................................................... 100.00

**METLOX**
Apple
    Dk red ................................................. 175.00
    Lt red .................................................. 75.00
Ballerina Bear ........................................... 145.00
Beaver ...................................................... 69.00
Beulah ...................................................... 425.00
Broccoli .................................................... 150.00
Brownie Girl, (A) ........................................ 750.00
Calico Cat ................................................. 275.00
Daisy Topiary ............................................ 95.00
Flamingo ................................................... 895.00
Homestead Provincial ................................ 115.00
Katy Cat .................................................... 130.00
Lighthouse ................................................ 800.00
Mousemobile ............................................ 295.00
Noah's Ark ................................................ 325.00
Panda ....................................................... 55.00
Penguin .................................................... 155.00
Pierre ....................................................... 150.00
Puddles the Duck ...................................... 95.00
Purple Cow ............................................... 575.00
Rose ......................................................... 395.00
Scottie, white ............................................ 365.00
Sir Francis Drake ...................................... 45.00
Sombrero Bear .......................................... 95.00
Squash ..................................................... 190.00
Stage Coach ............................................. 950.00
Uncle Sam Bear ........................................ 2,250.00

**MOSAIC TILE**
Mammy, blue dress .................................... 500.00

**PEARL CHINA**
Chef .......................................................... 400.00
Mammy ..................................................... 750.00

**PENNSBURY**
Red Barn ................................................... 100.00

**RED WING**
Baker, blue ................................................ 90.00
Drummer Boy ............................................ 595.00
Friar Tuck, yellow ...................................... 95.00
Katrina-The Dutch Girl ............................... 140.00
King of Tarts ............................................. 1,250.00
Round-Up pattern ...................................... 450.00

**REGAL**
Barn .......................................................... 295.00
Davy Crockett ............................................ 595.00

**Red Wing, Dutch Girl, yellow, brown trim, $95.**

**Shawnee, Winnie-bank form, brown base, gold trim, $650.**

**Regal China, Goldilocks, red sash, "#405" mk, $595**

| | |
|---|---:|
| Diaper Pin Pig | 795.00 |
| Fifi | 895.00 |
| Goldilocks | 175.00 |
| Majorette | 395.00 |
| Quaker Oats | 180.00 |
| Salad Chef | 525.00 |

**ROBINSON RANSBOTTOM**

| | |
|---|---:|
| Barrel shape, brown "*Cookie*" and sponging | 80.00 |
| Ole King Cole, red coat | 800.00 |
| Peter Peter Pumpkin Eater | 170.00 |

**ROSEVILLE**

| | |
|---|---:|
| Clematis pattern, (A) | 330.00 |

**SHAWNEE**

Cooky

| | |
|---|---:|
| Blue hat, gold trim | 350.00 |
| Green hat, gold trim | 395.00 |
| Drum Major | 310.00 |

Jojo

| | |
|---|---:|
| Gold trim | 850.00 |
| Plain | 395.00 |
| Lucky Elephant, pink collar | 275.00 |

Muggsy

| | |
|---|---:|
| Gold trim | 995.00 |
| Plain | 450.00 |

Puss and Boots

| | |
|---|---:|
| Gold, (A) | 500.00 |

| | |
|---|---:|
| Plain | 175.00 |
| Sailor Boy | 125.00 |

Smiley Pig

| | |
|---|---:|
| With shamrocks | 425.00 |
| Yellow bib | 395.00 |
| Winking Owl | 175.00 |

Winnie Pig

| | |
|---|---:|
| Blue collar | 285.00 |
| Green collar | 275.00 |
| Red collar, gold trim | 975.00 |
| With shamrocks | 400.00 |

**TREASURE CRAFT**

| | |
|---|---:|
| Football and Coach | 375.00 |
| Graniteware Coffeepot, blue and white | 20.00 |
| Pink Panther | 225.00 |
| Pluto | 225.00 |

**TWIN WINTON**

| | |
|---|---:|
| Castle | 400.00 |
| Cookie Shack | 65.00 |
| Elf on Stump | 185.00 |
| Grandma's Cookies | 65.00 |
| Gunfighter Rabbit | 195.00 |
| Jack-In-Box | 495.00 |
| Old King Cole | 595.00 |
| Pirate Fox | 85.00 |
| Raggedy Ann | 125.00 |
| Ranger Bear | 35.00 |
| Rose Petal Coach | 565.00 |
| Santa | 795.00 |
| Tommy Turtle | 125.00 |

**VANDOR**

| | |
|---|---:|
| Crocodile w/sunglasses | 95.00 |
| Fred Flintstone in Chair w/Pebbles | 500.00 |

**WELLER**

| | |
|---|---:|
| Mammy | 1,999.00 |

1912 – 1931

# Cowan Pottery

### Cleveland, Ohio
### Rocky River, Ohio
### 1912-1931

**History:** R. Guy Cowan came from a family of potters from East Liverpool, Ohio. He studied ceramics under Charles Binns at Alfred University and started his pottery studio in 1912, which was incorporated as the Cleveland Pottery and Tile Company with the encouragement from the Cleveland Chamber of Commerce. For several years he made both tiles and art wares with heavy glazes and lusters to cover the red clay body.

In 1917, Cowan won first prize at the International Show at The Art Institute of Chicago for his art pottery. He closed his studio and joined the army in that same year.

Upon returning in 1919, the studio did not meet his needs, and he moved to Rocky River in 1920 with Wendell G. Wilcox as his manager. A high-fired porcelain body made from English clays replaced the redware body he used previously. Ceramic sculpture became his focus, and he won numerous awards. The porcelain pieces were molded and figures were the most popular. These were often made in limited editions of fifty to one hundred, and then the molds were destroyed. Waylande Gregory was the leading figure artist, but many additional artists worked for Cowan.

Richard Hummel formulated an oriental red glaze which was used on art pottery vases. Inexpensive items made included lamp bases, jars, and decorative figures. There was always a struggle to keep a balance between the art pottery lines and the more commercial pieces.

Console sets with flower bowls and figural flower frogs, candlesticks, vases, compotes, nut and candy dishes were made in various sizes and shapes for the general public. The ivory glaze with a soft finish and pastel shades on the interior became a Cowan trademark. Tiles also were made.

Various pastel shades were used for tablewares in the Colonial and Federal patterns. Lusterware and crackleware glazes were popular during the 1920s. Cowan pottery examples were sold all over the country.

In 1927, an inexpensive line of flower containers called "Lakeware" was developed in four colors: oriental red, peacock green-blue, Flemish gray-blue and olive green which were used mostly by florists. Cowan Potters, Inc. was formed in 1929 with plans for new lines and expansion. The Wahl Pen Company had Cowan make paperweights, ceramic bookends, desk sets, and other accessories. Due to financial problems caused by the Depression, the firm went into receivership in 1930 and remained in business for only one additional year to use materials already on hand. When they closed in 1931, Cowan became art director of Onondaga Pottery Company in Syracuse, New York.

Cowan examples were marked in a variety of ways. From 1912-1917, the redware was incised with "Cowan Pottery" and sometimes initialed, too. On the porcelain body, "Cowan" was impressed and imprinted. Later examples had the semi-circular Cowan mark with the initials R.G.

**References:** Mark Bassett & Victoria Naumann, *Cowan Pottery and the Cleveland School*, Schiffer Publishing Ltd. 1997; Tim and Jamie Saloff, *The Collector's Encyclopedia of Cowan Pottery*, Collector Books, 1994.

**Museums:** Cleveland Museum of Art, OH: Cowan Pottery Museum at Rocky River Public Library, OH; Everson Museum of Art, Syracuse, NY; New Orleans Museum of Art, LA; The Western Reserve Historical Society, Cleveland, OH.

Bookend

4 1/2" H, "Push and Pull" elephants, ivory, #840, #841, pr ............................................................ 1,400.00

6 1/4" h, "Boy and Girl," Special Ivory glaze, "stamped Cowan" mk, pr, (A) ............................ 385.00

6 1/2" h, monk reading, matte green glaze, imp mk, pr, (A) ........................................................ 550.00

7 3/8" h, figural ram, Oriental Red glaze, Waylande Gregory, pr, (A) ...................................... 1,320.00

7 1/2" h

Standing elephant, Oriental Red glaze, "imp Cowan" mk, (A) ...................................... 1,210.00

Sunbonnet girl, green w/gold crystalline streaks, pr ............................................................ 450.00

8 1/2" h, "Flying Fish," Antique Green glaze, "stamped Cowan" mk, restored chip, pr, (A) .................... 550.00

Bowl

4" h x 6" d, flared shape, mottled matte pink ext, mottled matte green int .................................. 330.00

5 1/2" d, "Larkspur," blue luster, shape #646B ............................................................................. 75.00

11 1/2" d, flower form, spread ft, ivory and tan ext, green int, (A) .................................................... 77.00

Candelabra, 7" h x 10" w, "Pavlova," Ivory glaze, "stamped Cowan" mark, chip, (A) ............................................ 247.00

Candlestick

4 1/2" h, figural seahorse on base, column shaft, ivory glaze, pr, (A) .......................................... 44.00

6" h, figural leaping antelope, gloss caramel, glaze, hairline, pr, (A) .......................................... 220.00

10 1/2" h, blue luster glaze, (A) ............................. 110.00

Charger, 11" d, incised polo players, gloss brown and cafe-au-lait glaze, "imp V.S. Cowan" mk, (A) ................ 770.00

Cigarette Holder, 3 1/2" h, Seahorse, Apple Blossom Pink ............................................................................. 65.00

**Flower Frog, 10" h, "Laurel," white glaze, c1926, $795.**

Compote, 3 1/2" h, figural seahorse base, white ext, mottled pink int................................................................70.00

Console Bowl

9 1/2" d x 5 3/4" h, "Etruscan," Chinese Red glaze, #B-6.................................................................165.00

14 1/2" l, "Pterodactyl," Special Ivory glazed ext, April Green glazed int, #729, (A) ..............................138.00

16 1/4" d, "Seahorse," ivory ....................................128.00

17" l, ftd, lobed body, lavender int, ivory ext, (A)......30.00

Cup and Saucer, dk yellow glaze ................................35.00

Decanter, 12" h, figural King or Queen of Clubs, Oriental Red glaze, "imp Cowan" mk, pr, (A)....................1,210.00

Figure

8" h, "Pierrette," Old Ivory glaze, "stamped Cowan" mk, (A)................................................................275.00

9 1/2" h, seated Russian playing tambourine, Parchment glaze, "imp A. Blazys Cowan" mk, c1927, (A) ...935.00

9" h, Spanish Dancers, blue, tan, red, blue-green, and yellow, oval bases, Elizabeth Anderson, 1928, "imp Cowan" mk, pr, (A) .........................................1,320.00

14" h, "Antinea," Art Deco style bust of man's head, semi-matte black glaze , Drexel Jacobson, c1928, (A)
................................................................4,960.00

14 1/2" h, figural heron, Ivory Matte glaze, Waylande Gregory, c1930, imp "Cowan" mk, repairs, (A)........880.00

18" h, "Nautch Dancer," Art Deco style dancing lady, ivory and charcoal glazes, "incised Waylande Gregory, stamped Cowan" mks, (A) ..............................9,900.00

Flower Frog

6 1/4" h, "Pavlov," dancing woman with drape, Original Ivory glaze, "stamped Cowan" mk, (A) ................88.00

6 1/2" h, "Grace," Old Ivory glaze, (A) ....................575.00

7 3/4" h, Original Ivory glaze

"Duet," chip on base, (A) ..................................495.00

"Heavenward," "stamped Cowan" mk, (A) .........193.00

9 1/2" h, "Awakening," standing draped female, Original Ivory glaze, "stamped Cowen" mk, (A) ...........1,650.00

10 1/2" h, "Swirl Dancer," Original Ivory glaze, "stamped Cowan" mk, (A) ..............................................1,045.00

15" h, "Triumphant," standing draped female, raised arm, Original Ivory glaze, "Cowan" mk, (A) ...........2,310.00

Jar, Cov, 12 3/4" h, Egyptian Blue glaze, black lid w/loop knob, "imp Cowan" mk, hairline, (A)......................440.00

Lamp Base, 13 1/2" h, 4-sided, panels of lt brown classical figures in relief, parchment blue panel ground, (A)
................................................................225.00

Potpourri Jar, 7" h, textured Oriental Red glaze, imp mk, (A)
................................................................275.00

Urn

9 1/2" h, 2 loop handles, Peacock glaze, (A) ..........88.00

11 1/2" h, fluted body, 2 sm handles from shoulder to rim, Marigold glaze, "stamped Cowan" mk, (A) ..........55.00

Vase

5 3/4" h, jar shape, azure blue glaze, form #V28...340.00

6 1/4" h

Ovoid, closed rim, Arabian Night blue glaze, "imp Cowan" mk, (A)................................................412.00

Spherical, 2 sm scroll handles on neck, gloss Terra Cotta glaze, imp mk, (A) ...............................385.00

7" h, pillow, flared and fluted body, seahorse base, mint green, (A) ........................................................25.00

7 1/4" h, bulbous shape, Chinese Red glaze........165.00

Vase, 5 1/2" h, shaded magenta w/lt green ground, $125.

8" h, bulbous shape, emb stylized leaves, Persian blue crackle glaze, "imp Cowan" mk, (A) ..................880.00

8 3/4" h, bulbous shape, flared rim, lustered Delphinium Blue glaze, (A)......................................................137.00

9" h, ribbed, flared rim, Russet Brown glaze, "stamped Cowan" mk, (A) ......................................................138.00

10" d, spherical ribbed shape, lt vermillion glaze, "stamped Cowan" mk, hairlines, (A).................137.00

11 1/2" h, "Chinese Bird" design, Jade Green glaze, "stamped Cowan" mk, (A) ...............................495.00

11 3/4" h, ribbed ovoid shape, mottled gloss blue glaze, unmkd, (A)............................................................660.00

12 3/4" h, tapered cylinder shape, short collar, gunmetal drip over marigold flambe glaze, hairline, (A)....440.00

13" h, swollen tapered shape, lustered gray drip over yellow ground, mkd, (A) .........................................825.00

14" h, "Egyptian," ribbed body, flared rim, crystalline blue-green glaze, mkd, (A)........................................385.00

# Crescent Pottery

**1920-1926**

# Leigh Potters, Inc.

**1926-1931**
**Alliance, Ohio**

**History:** F.A. Sebring built a pottery in Alliance, Ohio in 1920 that was operated as the Crescent China Company until 1926. From 1926-1931, it was operated as the Leigh Potters, Inc. and run by Charles Sebring, son of F.A. Sebring.

Products made were similar to wares being made at the other Sebring potteries. Dinnerware, kitchenware, and some decorative pottery called Leigh Art Ware in semi-porcelain with decals were made.

The Depression affected the pottery business, and the plant closed in 1931.

**ADELPHIA PATTERN**
Cream Soup, 6 3/4" H-H..............................6.00

**EMPEROR PATTERN**
Cup and Saucer ........................................5.00

**FUCHSIA PATTERN**
Berry Bowl, 4 1/2" sq ...............................3.00
Casserole, Cov, 7" sq ...............................12.00
Gravy Boat, 9" w, undertray.......................12.00
Vegetable Bowl, 8 1/2" sq..........................10.00

**HOLLYWOOD PATTERN**
Plate, 7 1/4" d, multicolored desert flower in center, wide
    yellow border...........................................5.00

**MAYFAIR PATTERN**
Berry Dish, 5 1/2" d ...................................3.00
Cup and Saucer ........................................10.00
Plate, 8 3/4" sq ........................................3.00

**MEISSEN ROSE PATTERN**
Tidbit Tray, 11 1/2" l, center handle .............10.00

**MISCELLANEOUS**
Bowl, 10 3/4" d, red rose pattern on border, shaped rim
    w/gold overlay .......................................20.00
Platter
    11" l, central red, pink, and green floral design, scalloped
        shell border w/burgundy shading .........10.00
    16" l x 12 1/4" w, border band of roses, blue and yellow
        flowerheads, cream ground................10.00
Sugar Bowl, Cov, 5" h, "Suntan Ware," tan body, dk green
    handles and knob....................................10.00
Tea Set, pot, 9" h, creamer, 3" h, cov sugar bowl, 3 1/2" h,
    pink, yellow, and green exotic bird on flowering branch,
    ivory ground, mkd ..................................35.00

**NAVAJO PATTERN**
Platter, 12" l ...............................................20.00

**OLD MIRROR PATTERN**
Platter, 11" H-H ..........................................10.00

**PETIT POINT BIRD AND FLOWERS PATTERN**
Platter, 13 1/2" H-H ....................................10.00

**WILDFLOWER PATTERN**
Fruit Bowl, 5 1/4" d .....................................5.00
Plate, 9" d..................................................5.00
Platter, 11 3/4" l .........................................10.00
    Soup Bowl, 8" d .......................................4.00

COIORAMA

# Cronin China Company

**Minerva, Ohio**
**1934-1956**

**History:** The Cronin China Company was founded in 1934
in Minerva, Ohio and made semi-porcelain dinnerwares until
1956, when U.S. Ceramic Tile Company acquired all the
stock of Cronin China. Then they made wall and floor tile.

During the '30s and '40s, Cronin made hand-painted
pitchers, platters, and bowls marked Pottery Guild for the
Block China Company. Colorama was a Fiesta type ware
made by Cronin, and Bake Oven was decaled baking
dishes.

**EVERBRITE**
Berry Bowl, 5" d............................................3.00
Plate, 9 1/4" d...............................................5.00
Platter, 11 1/4" l ............................................10.00

**MISCELLANEOUS**
Range Set, cov grease jar, 5 1/2" h, 2 shakers, 4" h, "Sevilla"
    pattern, gray ...........................................10.00
Water Pitcher, 6 1/2" h, Zephyr Disc, dk green glaze
    .............................................................50.00

**PETIT POINT PATTERN**
Egg Cup, 3" h..............................................30.00

**ROSEMARIE PATTERN**
Plate, 10" d..................................................2.00

**ROYAL GOLD CREST PATTERN**
Pitcher, 7" h.................................................10.00

Plate, 9" d, "The Aris-
tocrat," red tulips,
green leaves, brown
baskets and shelf, red
lined rim, $10.

Bowl, 7 3/4" d, multicolored decal in center, gold
border, $5.

**Casserole, cov, 9 1/4" H-H, blue shades, $12.**

### ROYAL RAJAH MAROON PATTERN
Bowl, Cov, 9 1/2" d .......................................................... 25.00
Cake Plate, 10 3/4" H-H ...................................................... 6.00
Plate, 6" d ........................................................................ 3.00

### TULIP PATTERN-BLUE
Bean Pot, 3 1/4" d ............................................................ 15.00
Casserole, Cov, 8 1/4" d .................................................... 15.00
Creamer, 3 1/4" h .............................................................. 10.00
Pitcher, 6 3/4" h, ice lip .................................................... 20.00
Relish, 13" l, 3 section ...................................................... 15.00
Sugar Bowl, Cov, 2 7/8" h .................................................. 15.00
Teapot, 5 1/2" h ................................................................ 15.00
Tray, 10" l, skillet shape w/handle .................................... 10.00

### ZEPHYR SHAPE
Cereal Bowl, 6" d, cobalt .................................................... 7.00
Cup and Saucer, cobalt ...................................................... 6.00
    Plate, 6 1/4" d, maroon ................................................ 7.00

# Crooksville China Company

### Crooksville, Ohio
### 1902-1959

**History:** The Crooksville China Company was established in Crooksville, Ohio in 1902 and made semi-porcelain din-nerwares and toilet sets with old country type decorations.

"Pantry-Bak-in" was made with many different decals on the waffle sets, bowls, teapots, covered jugs, fruit juice set, coffeepots, baking dishes, cookies jars, spice jars, and such. Stinthal China was a thin semi-porcelain dinnerware. There were usually no pattern names on the dinnerwares. Competition from Japanese imports and the introduction of plastic dinnerwares forced the company to close in 1959.

**Pancake Batter Set, cov pitcher, 6" h, pitcher, 3 1/2" h, tray, 11 5/8" l, dk red, black, and gold trim, cream ground, $60.**

### APPLE BLOSSOM PATTERN
Batter Jug, Cov, 7" h ........................................................ 25.00
Berry Bowl, 5 1/2" d .......................................................... 2.00
Bowl
    8" d ............................................................................ 7.00
    11 3/4" d, pink ground ................................................ 35.00
Creamer, 5" h .................................................................. 10.00
Plate
    6" d ............................................................................ 3.00
    8" sq .......................................................................... 10.00
Teapot, 8" h .................................................................... 40.00

### BORDER ROSE PATTERN
Fruit Bowl, 5" d ................................................................ 4.00
Plate, 9 5/8" d .................................................................. 5.00
Soup Bowl, 7 1/4" d .......................................................... 3.00

### COUNTRY HOME PATTERN
Bowl, 6" d ........................................................................ 15.00
Cake Plate, 12" d .............................................................. 32.00
Cup and Saucer ................................................................ 22.00
Pitcher
    3 3/4" h ...................................................................... 18.00
Pitcher, Cov, 5 1/8" h ........................................................ 38.00

### DELMAR ROSE PATTERN
Creamer ............................................................................ 3.00
Fruit Bowl, 5 1/4" d ............................................................ 3.00
Plate
    6" d ............................................................................ 3.00
    9" d ............................................................................ 10.00
Platter, 11 3/4" H-H ............................................................ 4.00
Serving Bowl, 8" d ............................................................ 5.00
Sugar Bowl, Cov ................................................................ 3.00

### DINNER ROSE PATTERN
Berry Bowl, 5 1/4" d .......................................................... 4.00
Cup and Saucer ................................................................ 5.00
Plate
    6 1/4" d ...................................................................... 5.00
    9 1/2" d ...................................................................... 8.00

## ELEGANT PATTERN
Berry Bowl, 5 1/4" d......................................................3.00
Casserole, Cov, 10 1/2" H-H .......................................45.00
Cereal Bowl, 6 3/4" H-H ...............................................5.00
Creamer ......................................................................8.00
Cup and Saucer .........................................................5.00
Gravy Boat, 8" l, w/undertray.....................................15.00
Plate
    6" d.........................................................................4.00
    8" d.........................................................................5.00
Platter
    11 1/2" l .................................................................8.00
    14" l ......................................................................10.00

## HIBISCUS PATTERN
Berry Bowl, 5 1/2" d.....................................................3.00
Cup and Saucer ..........................................................4.00
Plate
    6" d.........................................................................2.00
    10" d.......................................................................5.00
Platter
    11 1/2" l .................................................................7.00
    13 1/2" l .................................................................9.00
Vegetable Bowl
    8" d.........................................................................7.00
    9 1/2" l ...................................................................8.00

## IVA-LURE
Chop Plate, 12" d ......................................................20.00
Plate
    7" sq.....................................................................12.00
    9 7/8" sq ...............................................................18.00
Platter, 13 1/2" l ........................................................32.00

## PANTRY BAKE-IN
Casserole, Cov, 9" d, Apple Blossom pattern..............35.00
Pie Baker, 10" d, multicolored petit point fruit in center, red
    striped rim, "Pantry Bak-in ware by Crooksville 1038" mk
    .................................................................................20.00

## PETIT POINT HOUSE PATTERN
Casserole, Cov, 7 1/4" d............................................65.00
Mixing Bowl, 6" d.......................................................10.00
Pie Plate, 10" d..........................................................20.00

Pitcher
    5 1/2" h ...............................................................30.00
    6 1/2" h ...............................................................38.00
Plate
    6" d.........................................................................5.00
    10" d.......................................................................10.00
Platter
    11" l, red lined rim ...............................................50.00
    11 1/2" l ...............................................................15.00
Salad Bowl, 11" d ......................................................35.00
Soup Bowl, 8" d..........................................................8.00
Tray, 11 3/4" H-H .......................................................22.00

## PRIMROSE PATTERN
Bowl, 8" d .................................................................10.00
Creamer ...................................................................10.00
Plate, 11" d ...............................................................12.00

## SILHOUETTE PATTERN
Coffeepot, 6" h, w/metal drip top ............................100.00
Creamer ...................................................................40.00
Mixing Bowl, 9 3/4" d.................................................30.00
Pie Plate, 10" d.........................................................30.00
Plate
    9" d.......................................................................20.00
    9 1/2" sq...............................................................15.00
Salad Bowl, 10" d ......................................................50.00
Sugar Bowl, Cov ........................................................50.00
Teapot, 6" h ..............................................................15.00

## SOUTHERN BELLE PATTERN
Berry Bowl, 5 1/4" d.....................................................3.00
Creamer ...................................................................24.00
Cup and Saucer ..........................................................4.00
Plate
    6 1/8" d...................................................................4.00
    10" d.......................................................................5.00
Sugar Bowl, Cov ........................................................24.00

**Mixing Bowl, 9 1/2" d, "Petit Point House" pattern, multicolored, $25.**

**Plate, 10" d, "Southern Belle" pattern, Iva Lure shape, $12.**

Teapot, 8 1/2" h ............................................. 49.00
Vegetable Bowl, 12" H-H ................................ 34.00

**SPRAY PATTERN**
Dessert Bowl, 4 1/2" d .................................... 2.00
Plate, 6 1/2" d ................................................ 2.00
Soup Bowl, 8" d ............................................. 3.00

**SPRING BLOSSOM PATTERN**
Berry Dish, 5" d ............................................. 3.00
Creamer, 4" h ................................................ 4.00
Cup and Saucer ............................................. 4.00
Plate
   6" d ........................................................ 4.00
   9 1/4" d ................................................. 6.00
   10" d ...................................................... 6.00
Platter, 15" l ................................................... 8.00
Serving Bowl, Cov, 10" d ............................. 10.00
Soup Bowl, 8 1/2" d ....................................... 6.00
Sugar Bowl, Cov, 4" h .................................... 6.00

**TRELLIS PATTERN**
Creamer ...................................................... 15.00
Mixing Bowl
   6 1/8" d .................................................. 8.00
   7 1/4" d ................................................ 10.00
Plate
   6" d ........................................................ 2.00
   7" d ........................................................ 3.00
   9" d ........................................................ 4.00
Serving Dish, 9" l ........................................ 10.00
Sugar Bowl, Cov ......................................... 15.00
Tray, 11 1/2" l .............................................. 10.00

**TROTTER PATTERN**
Creamer ........................................................ 4.00
Cup and Saucer ............................................. 5.00
Gravy Boat ..................................................... 5,00
Plate, 10 1/4" d .............................................. 5.00
   Sugar Bowl, Cov ....................................... 5.00

# Crown Pottery

### Evansville, Indiana
### 1891-c1955

**History:** The Flentke family organized the Crown Pottery in 1891 in Evansville, Indiana. They took over the Peoria Pottery Company in 1902 and became Crown Potteries Company.

   They made both plain and decorated ironstone china, "Crown Porcelain" dinnerware, toilet ware, and semi-porcelain using various means of china decoration. They went out of business in 1955 due to competition from the Japanese imports.

**C.P.Co.**
**WARRANTED**
**SEMI-PORCELAIN**
c.1910

**BLUE BIRD PATTERN**
Vegetable Bowl, 8 1/2" l ............................... 10.00
Vegetable Bowl, Cov, 11" H-H, "C.P.Co." mk ... 55.00

**HAWTHORNE PATTERN**
Plate, 9 1/4" d ............................................... 8.00

**MISCELLANEOUS**
Bowl
   8 3/4" d, red tulips and blue flowers on border ......... 8.00
   9 1/4" d, sm bouquet of multicolored flowers in center, molded floral border w/lustered chartreuse ........ 10.00
   9 1/2" d, multicolored decal of bust of Arab, raised border designs w/maroon ground and gold floral overlay, "C.P.Co. and crown" mk ..................................... 15.00
   10" d, yellow, red, and white roses and green leaves in center, ribbed border, pea green lustered rim, "C.P.Co. and crown" mk ..................................... 8.00

**Bowl, 10" d, red, yellow, and white roses, pea green lustered border, "crowned C.P.CO." mk, $25.**

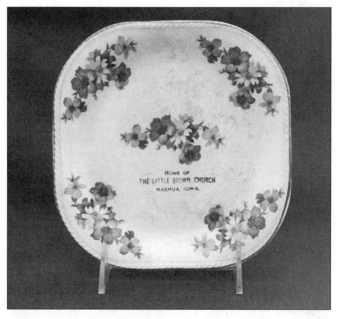

**Plate, 6 5/8" sq, blue, orange, and red flowers, yellow ground, gold "HOME OF THE LITTLE BROWN CHURCH, NASHUA, IOWA" on front, gold "crown C.P.CO." mk, $10.**

Creamer, 4 3/4" h, multicolored band of florals and fencing ................................................................... 10.00

Plate

9 3/4" d, Monarch shape, sm red, blue, and yellow stylized flowers in black dish on shelf, red lined border .................................................... 5.00

10 3/8" d, 3 apples in center, raised border design w/orange luster, "crown C.P.Co." mk ................... 24.00

Platter

11 1/2" H-H, lg red rose, yellow flowers, green leaves on side, gold outlined handles .................................. 5.00

15 1/4" H-H, pink dogwood blossoms on border, gold outlined molded handles and rim ............................ 10.00

Relish Tray, 7 5/8" l, multicolored decal of basket of fruit at each end, "crown C.P.Co." mk ................................. 6.00

**NAVAJO PATTERN**
Plate, 6 1/4" d ............................................................. 12.00

**WINDMILL PATTERN**
Plate
6 1/4" d .................................................................. 3.00
9" d ....................................................................... 15.00

1875 - 1889

# Dedham Pottery

**Dedham, Massachusetts
1896-1943**

# Chelsea Keramic Art Works

**Chelsea, Massachusetts
1866-1889**

# Chelsea Pottery US

**Chelsea, Massachusetts
1891-1895**

**History:** The Chelsea Keramic Art Works was established by Alexander W. Robertson in 1866 and Hugh, his brother, joined him two years later. They made bean pots, flower pots and simple vases. James, their father, joined the group in 1872, and they started to produce more decorative pottery. Their redwares were quite ornate.

After being influenced by the oriental art works at the 1876 Philadelphia Centennial Exposition, Hugh perfected the oxblood (sang de bouef) and craquelle glazes used in the Orient. Other colored glazes also were developed, and he won several awards at three World's Fairs.

After James died in 1880 and Alexander went to California in 1884, Hugh continued to perfect his glazes, but was forced to close the operation in 1889 since the costs of pro-

duction were too high, and there were no profits. Several years later, Hugh was hired to reopen the pottery known as Chelsea Pottery US and manage it. It stayed in business until 1895 and used the cloverleaf mark with CPUS in petals impressed. After several more years, the pottery was moved to Dedham, Massachusetts and renamed Dedham Pottery.

Works produced before 1875 were not marked. Chelsea faience was introduced in 1877, making use of the many glazes developed by the family.

**Dedham History:** In 1896, the pottery was moved from Chelsea, Massachusetts to Dedham, Massachusetts for more favorable conditions, and the name was changed from Chelsea Keramic Art Works. Hugh Robertson perfected the craquelle glaze he developed at Chelsea, and this is what Dedham became famous for, since it was made in about fifty patterns.

The blue in glaze border decoration and gray background tableware pieces had rabbits, ducks, elephants, swans, lobsters, turkeys, lions, owls, birds, turtles, irises, clover, magnolias, grapes, poppies, waterlilies, azaleas, and other animals and flowers as themes. The rabbit, designed by Joseph L. Smith was the most popular pattern and was adapted as the company trademark. The elephant, designed by Charles Davenport, head of decorating, is today a highly popular pattern.

All of the work was done freehand, without the use of stencils or decals. Each piece had the company name on it. Some of the patterns were done for special orders. The craquelle glaze was a very unique feature, and this spider web veining was produced from too rapid cooling and rubbing the piece with Cabot's lamp black powder.

William Robertson took over the pottery in 1908 after Hugh died. There were problems with the supplies during World War I, but by 1925 the operation was back to normal. When William died in 1929, J. Milton Robertson took over until 1943 when the pottery was forced to close due to increased costs and a shortage of skilled personnel.

The only other product made at Dedham was hand thrown vases with high fired glazes on a high fired base. The effect of one glaze running down over the other was called "Volcanic Ware," and it was not too popular.

**References:** Lloyd E. Hawes, *The Dedham Pottery and the Earlier Robertson's Chelsea Potteries*, Dedham Historical Society, 1968.

**Collectors' Club:** Dedham Pottery Collectors Newsletter, Jim Kaufman, 248 Highland Street, Dedham, MA 02026, quarterly journal, $18.

**Museums:** Brooklyn Museum, NY; Chrysler Museum, Norfolk, VA; Dedham Historical Society, MA; Museum of Fine Arts, Boston, MA; National Museum of History and Technology, Smithsonian Institution, Washington, DC; New Orleans Museum of Art, LA; Wadsworth Atheneum, Hartford, CT; Worcester Art Museum, MA.

Ashtray, 6 3/4" d, 3 cigar rests, dk blue flat border w/2 eared rabbit, " blue stamped Dedham Pottery" mk, (A) ... 220.00

Bottle, 8 1/2" h, sq gin shape, blue scroll "G" on front, white crackle ground, "blue stamped Dedham Pottery" mk, (A) ................................................................. 605.00

Bowl

4 1/2" d, ftd, dk blue butterfly and floral border band on ext, crackle glaze, "blue stamped Dedham Pottery" mk, (A) ................................................................ 413.00

7 1/4" d, inner border band of horse chestnuts on blue ground, crackle glaze, "blue stamped Dedham Pottery" mk, (A) ............................................................ 193.00

9" d, band of 2 eared rabbits on blue inner border, scalloped rim, "blue stamped Dedham Pottery" mk, (A) ................................................................. 1,045.00

10 3/8" d, inner border of 2 eared rabbit, med blue and white crackle......................495.00

Butter Pat, 3 1/2" d, blue outlined overlapped pansy style floral petals, crackle glaze, "blue stamped Dedham Pottery" mk, (A) ..................413.00

Charger, 12" d, 2 eared rabbit border on blue ground, crackle glaze, "blue stamped Dedham Pottery" mk, hairline, (A)...................330.00

Cream Bowl, 7 1/2" d x 2 1/2" h, band of 2 eared rabbits on blue ground on flat border, crackle glaze, "blue stamped Dedham Pottery" mk, (A) ....................468.00

Creamer, 3 1/2" h, squat shape, dk blue center band w/turkey pattern crackle glaze, #1, "blue stamped Dedham Pottery" mk, (A)...................523.00

Cup and Saucer, border bands of irises on dk blue ground, crackle glaze, "blue stamped Dedham Pottery" mk, (A) ....................220.00

Dish, 4 1/2" l, figural oyster shell, white crackleware, blue pearl, pr, (A) ...................660.00

Flower Holder

3 1/2" d, figural crawling turtle, blue accented shell, face, and feet, pierced shell, crackle glaze, "blue stamped Dedham Pottery" mk, (A)...................495.00

6 3/4" h, white figural rabbit seated on haunches, dome base, blue facial accents, crackle glaze, (A) ..1,320.00

Knife Rest, 3 1/4" d, figural crouching rabbit, blue accented face, eyes, and ears, crackle glaze, "blue stamped Dedham Pottery" mk, (A) ....................413.00

Marmalade Jar, 4" h, border band of swimming swans and cattails on blue ground at base, blue lined rims, crackle glaze, "blue Dedham Pottery" mk, (A)...................880.00

Nappy

6" d, azalea pattern outlined on dk blue border band on flared rim, crackle glaze, "blue stamped Dedham Pottery" mk, (A)....................187.00

9 1/4" d, 2 eared rabbit on blue border band, crackle glaze, "blue stamped Dedham Pottery" mk, (A) ....................330.00

Nappy, Cov, 11" d, 2 eared rabbits on blue border band, blue floral band on cov border, crackle glaze, "blue stamped Dedham Pottery" mk, (A) ....................715.00

Olive Dish, 7 3/4" l, oval, border band of 2 eared rabbits on blue ground, crackle body, "blue stamped Dedham Pottery" mk, (A) ....................550.00

Pilgrim Flask, 8" h, 4 sm feet, carved relief design of ivory hunting dog in field, blue ground, Chelsea Keramic, (A) ....................4,125.00

Pitcher

4 1/2" h, sq, dk blue 2 eared rabbit band around base, blue lined border, crackle glaze, "blue stamped Dedham Pottery" mk, (A)...................1,210.00

5" h

Bulbous and lobed body, dk blue outlined stylized leaf designs, crackle glaze, #17, "blue stamped Dedham Pottery" mk, (A) ....................715.00

Dk blue hanging grapes, crackle glaze, #2, "blue stamped Dedham Pottery" mk, (A) ...............523.00

"Night and Morning," blue and white ................525.00

Tapered shape, #6

Azalea blossoms on dk blue band on base, blue stripe on border, crackle glaze, "blue stamped Dedham Pottery" mk ...............550.00

Dbl turtles design on base, blue lined rim, crackle glaze, "blue stamped Dedham Pottery" mk, (A) ....................1,980.00

Pitcher, Cov, 5 1/2" h, bulbous shape w/loop handle, center band of 2 eared rabbit on blue ground, blue striped borders, crackle glaze, (A)...................495.00

Plate

6" d

Day Lily design on blue ground, blue lily pods on border, "blue stamped Dedham Pottery" mk, (A) ....................1,430.00

Peacock design on blue border, crackle glaze, "imp rabbit" mk, (A)....................4,675.00

Swan pattern w/cattails border on blue ground, crackle glaze, "blue stamped Dedham Pottery" mk, (A) ....................303.00

**Plate, 8 1/2" d, blue and white, $800.**

**Plate, 8 1/2" d, dk blue, blue "DEDHAM POTTERY" mk, $225.**

Wild Rose design w/leaves on dk blue border band, crackle glaze, "blue Dedham Pottery" mk, (A) ....................................................3,300.00

7 1/2" d, dk blue crab motif across center, blue wave border, crackle glaze, "blue Dedham Pottery" mk, (A) ...............................................358.00

8 1/4" d, lg flowing dk blue poppy in center, poppy buds on border, gray crackle glaze, "blue Dedham Pottery" mk, (A) ............467.00

8 1/2" d

Blue outlined azaleas on blue border band, crackle ground, "blue stamped Dedham Pottery, imp rabbit" mks, (A) .......................................330.00

Blue outlined turtles on blue border band, crackle ground, "blue stamped Dedham Pottery, imp rabbit" mks, (A) ...................................1,540.00

Blue Scottie dogs in center, blue lined rims, crackle ground, hairline, "blue stamped Dedham Pottery" mk, (A) ......................................1,650.00

Border band of flying doves on blue ground, crackle ground, rim chips and hairline, "blue Dedham Pottery" mk, (A) .............................1,540.00

Dk blue border w/turkey pattern on border, crackle ground, "blue stamped Dedham Pottery, imp rabbit" mks, (A) ...............................358.00

Med blue border of walking lions, blue rabbit mk ......................................................1,100.00

White upside down dolphin and baby on dk blue ground border, crackle glaze, "imp CPUS" mk, (A) ..........................................770.00

8 3/4" d, stylized flowing blue nasturtium motif, crackle ground, "blue stamped Dedham Pottery, imp rabbit" mk, (A) ................................5,225.00

9 3/4" d, med blue border of ducks .........................425.00

10" d

Dk blue "Bird In The Potted Orange Tree" pattern, crackle glaze, "imp rabbit" mk, (A) ...............440.00

Dk blue outlined white polar bears and jagged ice caps on border, crackle glaze, rebus "O" signature, "blue stamped Dedham Pottery, imp rabbit" mks, (A) ...........................................................660.00

Mushroom pattern on cobalt blue border band, crackle glaze, "blue Dedham Pottery, imp rabbit" mk, (A) ................................................495.00

Snowtree pattern on dk blue border band, crackle glaze, "blue Dedham Pottery" mk .................220.00

10 1/4" d, border w/greenish glazed molded cloverleaf design, blue accented band w/circ green dots on int band, crackle ground, "CUPS" mk, (A) ..............920.00

Soup Plate, 8 1/4" d, blue border band w/single eared rabbits, Maude Davenport, crackle glaze, "blue stamped Dedham Pottery, imp rabbit" mks, (A)....................525.00

Spoon, 4 1/2" l, blue elephant and baby in bowl, "blue stamped Dedham Pottery" mk, (A) .....................1,210.00

Tea Tile, 6 1/8" d, dk blue horsechestnut and stylized flower border band, crackle glaze, "blue stamped Dedham Pottery" mk, (A) ....................................385.00

Toothpick Holder, 2 1/2" h, blue accented figural tulip, white crackle ground, (A)........................................815.00

Vase

5 3/4" h, urn shape, 2 appled leaf form handles, terra cotta, "imp CKAW" mk, (A) ...............................633.00

7" h, sq, tapered shape, emb bee and floral design, applied birds on branches, carved and tooled florals

and leaves on opposite panels, olive glaze, restored rim chips, "imp Chelsea Keramic Art Works/Robertson & Sons" mk, (A)....................................660.00

8 1/4" h, baluster shape, burgundy red Dragon's Blood glaze w/green and blue drip, (A) ....................1,210.00

8 3/4" h, swollen body, straight neck, frothy oxblood glaze, "stamped CKAW" mk, (A) ....................1,760.00

9 1/2" h, bulbous shape, short collar, thick, curdled sang-de-boeuf volcanic glaze, Hugh Robertson, "incised Dedham Pottery" mk, (A) .............................3,575.00

10 3/4" h, swollen body, straight neck, mirrored drip brown and green glaze, Hugh Robertson, hairlines, (A) ......................................................990.00

c.1892 and later          c.1890

# Dresden Pottery Company

## East Liverpool, Ohio
## 1875-1927

**History:** In 1875, Brunt, Bloor, Martin and Company operated at the Dresden Pottery Works in East Liverpool, Ohio. They made white ironstone, gold decorated wares, tablewares, tea sets, toilet wares, spittoons, toys, and hotel ware. They sold the company in 1882 to avoid the labor struggle.

The Potter's Co-Operative Company was formed by a group of potters as a result of the labor dispute in East Liverpool. Headed by H.A. McNicol, they purchased the Dresden Pottery Works from Brunt, Bloor, Martin and Company. The co-operative made dinnerware, tea sets, sanitary wares, and hotel china.

The co-operative operated until 1925, when a new corporation, Dresden Pottery Company, purchased Dresden Pottery Works and incorporated. They also made semi-vitreous dinnerware, hotel china, and plain and decorated specialty wares. A variety of marks was used. This new company disbanded after two years of operation in 1927.

**References:** William C. Gates, Jr. and Dana E. Ormerod, *The East Liverpool, Ohio Pottery District: Identification of Manufacturers and Marks*, The Society for Historical Archaeology, l982.

Bone Dish, 6 1/2" l, scrolling rim, white glaze, set of 4. 24.00

Bowl, 9 1/4" d, pink and white dogwood blossoms, green foliage, gold rim, "DRESDEN CHINA" mk ................5.00

Chamber Pot, 5 5/8" h x 8 1/2" d, molded curlicues w/red roses decal on sides...............................................68.00

Fish Set

Platter, 13 1/2" l, 6 plates, 8" d, swimming trout or game fish, yellow-green shaded borders .....................70.00

Platter, 14 5/8" l, 4 plates, 9" d, multicolored freshwater game fish, dbl gold line rims ............................... 365.00

Ice Cream Set, master bowl, 9" d, 4 bowls, 5" d, small purple flowerheads, green leaves, gold dusted borders ..... 60.00

Lemonade Set, pitcher, 5 3/4" h, 5 tumblers, 4 1/2" h, rect handles, purple grapes on sides, white ground, purple borders ................................................................. 245.00

Milk Pitcher, multicolored scene of Dutchmen smoking cigars, children, and women, blue lined rim and handle ...................................................................... 100.00

Pitcher, 7 1/2" h, corset shape, wavy rim, fancy handle, white glaze, crazing, "DRESDEN CHINA" mk ......... 10.00

Plate

6 1/2" d, multicolored decal of couple seated in sailboat cockpit and "Sailing Close" below, gold "Detroit Where Life Is Worth Living" under decal, "Dresden" mk . 24.00

7 1/2" d, multicolored decal of Gibson girl in bathing suit seated on dock, gold rim .................................... 65.00

10" d

Blue transfer of wild turkeys in center, blue floral and curlicue border, shaped indented rim.............. 25.00

Grapes and peaches in center, gold curlicue border w/raised design, gold shaped rim ................... 30.00

10 1/2" d

Brown decal of bust of "William Jennings Bryant," "Dresden" mk .................................................. 45.00

Bunches of white lily of the valley and green leaves, "DRESDEN CHINA" mk .................................. 5.00

Platter

10 3/4" H-H, inner border band of pink roses and green foliage, outer border band of gold hanging stylized flowers, gold rim, mkd ........................................... 5.00

13 1/4" l, blue windmill transfer on border, blue inner and outer lines, "DRESDEN CHINA" mk .................... 10.00

Tankard, 13 1/4" h, tan transfer of nude seated on rock, shaded green ground............................................. 100.00

Vegetable Bowl, Cov, 8 1/2" l, black medallions w/pink roses and blue flowers, "DRESDEN S.V." mk

.................................................................................. 5.00

**Plate, 6 5/8" d, orange, red, and white roses, gold border, "DRESDEN" mk, $8.**

# East Liverpool Pottery Company

### 1894-1901
### East Liverpool Potteries Company

### East Liverpool, Ohio
### 1901-1907

**History:** John and Robert Hall, along with Monroe Patterson, established the East Liverpool Pottery Company in Ohio in 1894. For the first two years, they made plain and decorated ironstone china. Then they introduced semi-vitreous porcelain.

It was one of the six potteries that formed the East Liverpool Potteries Company in 1901. The other potteries were: Globe Pottery Company, Wallace and Chetwynd, East End Pottery Company, and George C. Murphy Pottery Company, all from East Liverpool. They joined with United States Pottery Company from Wellsville, Ohio to compete with the larger pottery producers. They tried to use the same mark, but there were variations.

In 1903, the Halls broke away and started Hall China Company. The others also left the merger except for Globe and United States Pottery and returned to their individual operations. By 1907, the East Liverpool Potteries was no longer since Globe and United States also pulled out.

United States Pottery continued in Wellsville under the East Liverpool Potteries name and made semi-vitreous tableware, hotel ware, and toilet ware. They named a line of dinnerware "Elpco." In 1936, the firm became Purinton Pottery Company.

**References:** William C. Gates, Jr. and Dana E. Ormerod, *The East Liverpool, Ohio, Pottery District: Identification of Manufacturers and Marks,* The Society for Historical Archaeology, 1982.

**Museums:** Museum of Ceramics at East Liverpool, OH.

Bone Dish, 6" l, kidney shape, brown transfer of flowers, buds, and foliage in center, scalloped top rim, mkd .................................................................................. 5.00

Bowl, 8 1/2" d, yellowware, center band of blue seaweed on white ground, (A) ..................................................... 385.00

Bread Tray, 12 1/2" l, multicolored scattered floral bouquets, gold outlined molded handles, scalloped rim, "East Liverpool Potteries" mk........................................................ 10.00

Chamber Pot, 6" d, yellowware, white band w/brown stripes and red seaweed, hairlines, (A) ............................ 220.00

Creamer, 3 1/2" h, bluebird design, gilt scalloped rim ................................................................................ 35.00

Figure, 6 3/8" h, redware, recumbent lion, rect base, brown Rockingham-type glaze ......................................... 250.00

Fish Platter, 13" l, decal of green swimming fish w/red dots in weeds, green border w/gold striping, "E.L.P.Co" mk .................................................................................. 75.00

Gravy Boat, 7 1/2" l, bluebird design, "ELPCO" mk ................................................................................ 45.00

Jar, Cov, 6" h, yellowware, center band of blue seaweed on white ground, (A) ................................................. 605.00

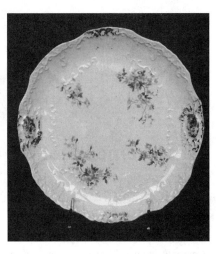

Cookie Plate, 9" d, scattered purple and yellow flowers, gray and green foliage, molded curlicues, gold accented handles and rim, $10.

Mixing Bowl, 9 1/4" d, w/spout, yellowware, white band w/blue stripes and blue seaweed design, hairlines and chips, (A) ................................................................. 468.00
Mug, 2 7/8" h, yellowware, center band of green seaweed on white ground, hairlines, (A) ............................... 385.00
Plate
    Bluebird pattern
        9" d, "ELPCO China" mk .................................... 20.00
        10" d, mkd ......................................................... 15.00
    8 1/4" d, multicolored multiple roosters and chicks, green shaded border w/relief molding, shaped rim, red mk ........................................................................ 30.00
Platter
    14" l, bunches of dogwood blossoms, leaves, and branches on border, brown transfer, molded shell design on rim, mkd ............................................... 12.00
    17" l, bunches of sm violets and green leaves on border, gold outlined shaped rim, crazing........................ 15.00
Shaker, 4 3/8" h, yellowware, center band of blue seaweed on white ground, (A).............................................. 1,320.00

# Kay Finch Ceramics

### Corona del Mar, California
### 1939-1963

**History:** After outgrowing a small home space, Kay Finch and Braden, her husband, opened a studio in Corona del Mar, California since there was a big demand for her pig, angel, and animal figurines. They soon outgrew that space and a larger studio was constructed and opened on December 7, 1941.

Kay did all the sculpting at the studio, but her staff did the decoration and production. Animals were her favorite subject. Pastel colors, especially pink, were the norm. Horses, lambs, cats, dogs, rabbits, pigs, camels, elephants, penguins, chickens, and owls all found form in Kay Finch figurines. Kay also designed people from around the world, angels, religious items, and wedding cake toppers of the bride and groom.

Pigs were the most successful figures. Grumpy, Smiley, and Sassy were done along with baby and bitsy pigs. There was also Grandpa or Gerry pig. Kay's sculptures were designed to be anatomically correct with perfect proportions along with a sense of whimsey.

World War II was a boom time for Kay Finch Ceramics. The studio continued to receive non-essential materials required for ceramic production. Stores could no longer get imports due to war restrictions and they needed merchandise. Kay Finch's works were distributed through shops and their own catalogs. They were also sold in the finest department stores. By the mid 1940s they were available in more than fifteen hundred outlets in the United States. After the war, Kay's ceramics were sold in foreign markets, and they increased their number of employees to meet the additional demand.

In the mid-1940s, Kay started making some larger pieces in limited production. One of the first, Cathay or Chinese Princess, was more than 3' tall. Only ten were made, finished, and decorated by hand. A smaller 23" version was also made. Others included Tang Horse or Stallion, Petey the Donkey, Madonna Holding Babe, and Violet the Elephant. She also made several sets of dinnerware for a short period of time.

Kay's ceramics had tremendous variety and were made in sizes ranging from 1" to 36" tall. They utilized the best materials, and were expensive for the time. Kay was the sole designer of the studio, and she never copied designs of other artists. Her brother-in-law, Alfred Schultz, produced the special clay, glazes, and colors used by the studio.

After Kay began Crown Crest Kennels in the early 1940s for dog breeding, she translated her love of dogs in the 1950s to a lot of dog sculptures including twelve American Kennel Club champions produced in natural colors. Soon other canine ceramics included trophies, banks, ashtrays, wall plaques, steins, and jewelry.

By 1950, trade agreements with foreign countries allowed inexpensive imports to flood the US market again. Many of these companies were making copies of Finch ceramics. Finch's response was to introduce new lines to stay competitive such as the Baby's First and holiday ceramics for Thanksgiving, Easter, and Christmas. They even made a line of Chrismas plates from 1950-1962. Additional experimenting was done with painting, glazing methods, as well as air brushing.

Kay's son George started making bowls, vases, and one of a kind sculptures produced in solid colors with a high glaze or matte finish. His work was architectural in design for his flower arranging bowls, petal bowls, and Ming bowls. By the late 1950s the Talisman California line all done by George Finch was marketed separately from the Finch line.

Kay and George also made bathroom wall plaques, cotton containers, kitchen canisters and large ceramic fountains.

After Kay's husband George died in 1962, the business was closed in 1963. By that time, Kay had done more than seven hundred designs from 1937-1961. Freeman McFarlin's El Monte factory purchased some of Kay's designs. After being away from the business for several years, Kay produced some original sculpture for Freeman McFarlin Potters in its San Marcos plant from the mid 1960s until about 1980.

Kay Finch ceramic marks included black and red ink stamped marks, embossed and hand written marks, as well as paper labels. Very small pieces usually were not marked.

**References:** Jack Chipman, *Collector's Encyclopedia of California Pottery, 2nd Edition*, Collector Books, 1998; Devin Frick, Jean Frick, Richard Martinez, *Collectible Kay Finch*, Collector Books, 1997; Mike Nickel & Cindy Horvath, *Kay Finch Ceramics: Her Enchanted World*, Schiffer Publishing Ltd.1996.

Bank, 3 1/2" h, "Sassy Pig" ......................................... 95.00

Box, Cov, 6" H-H, "Briar Rose," dk pink flower w/green leaves, pink ground, green handles, figural pink and green flower on cov.............................................75.00
Candlestick, 3 1/2" h, gold-yellow glaze, pr...............40.00
Compote, 3 1/2" h x 8 1/2" d, flared ft, brick red glaze . 10.00
Figures
 2 1/2" h, "Cottontail Baby Rabbit," pink and white ...85.00
 3" h
  4" h, "Jeep" and "Peep" ducks, green top knots, brown beaks and feet, pr...........................................75.00
  4 1/4" h, Mr. and Mrs. Bird, blue and white, pr .........................................................................225.00
 3 1/4" h
  Sleeping kitten, gray-blue shades, #182 .............90.00
  Squirrel, brown and gray .....................................125.00
  Standing penguin, Pee Wee, black and white ...135.00
 3 1/2" h, "Jocko" monkey, blue, brown, and white .........................................................................375.00
 3 3/4" h
  Owl, brown, and gray ............................................48.00
  "Winky," tan, brown, and rose ..............................85.00
 4" h
  Angel praying, #114A ...........................................60.00
  Standing draft horse, green..................................145.00
 4 1/4" h
  Angel, white gown, blond hair, "Kay Finch, California" mk ...............................................75.00
  "Peep," duck, green and cream...........................45.00
 5" h x 8" l, dove, turquoise, pr ...............................450.00
 5 1/2" h
  "Biddy" hen, white, green, and rose .................145.00
  Mouse seated on haunches, gold .......................50.00
 6" h, "Jezebel" cat, gray shades ...........................250.00
 6 3/8" h, "Grumpy Pig," strawberries and white flowers .........................................................................395.00
 6 1/2" h, praying lady, pink and blue, white vest ......95.00
 7 1/2" d, Christmas wreath, green leaves, red berries, brown and green bow.........................................45.00
 7 1/2" h, "Godey Lady," wearing cape, green hat, blue flowered dress, hands in muff ...........................88.00
 8 1/2" h, "Butch", brown, gold trim .........................135.00
 10" h, "Anna," seated Siamese cat, cream w/dk brown accents, blue eyes.........................................525.00
 10 3/4" h
  "Ambrosia" the Persian cat, pink and white, #155 .........................................................................695.00
  "Chanticleer," multicolored.................................650.00
 11" h
  Chinese court lady, green and pink, #400 ........225.00
  Chinese court prince, blue and pink, #451 ........200.00
  "Vickie," black and white cocker spaniel, green collar .............................................................950.00
Planter
 3" h, flared, sq shape, green ivy on sides, pink ground, green figural border drape .........................20.00
 5" h, baby and block, pink and blue .......................195.00
 6" h, Teddy Bear, blue, "Kay Finch" mk..................55.00
Plaque, 8" l, figural Siamese Fighting fish, turquoise, gold trim.........................................................................95.00

Platter, 10 3/4" l, rect, "Briar Rose" pattern .................32.00
Tumbler, 5" h, figural mule head, black ......................50.00
Vase
 3" h, tapered rect shape, green foliage, purple and dk pink flowers on sides, pink ground, mint green trim, pr .........................................................................50.00
 7 3/4" h, figural Afghan dog handle on tumbler shape, tan .........................................................................255.00
 11" h, figural turkey, brown w/gold trim, dk red head .........................................................................625.00
 19" h, "Moon," turquoise glaze.............................250.00

# Florence Ceramics

### Pasadena, California
### 1939-1964

**History:** Florence Ward started working with clay in 1939 in Pasadena, California, as therapy after her son's death. While her husband and other son were busy with the war, she started a ceramics business in her garage workshop.

Florence Ceramics was created during World War II, and Florence did all the modeling of the figurines. All of the pieces were molded and cast, and hand decorated with hand made flowers. Semi-porcelain figures were introduced twice yearly. There were ladies, gentlemen, and figural groups. After the war, her family joined her in the company, and they built a modern factory.

"The Florence Collection" included reproductions of historical couples in period costumes, fictional characters, European royalty, and subjects from paintings. Less expensive examples included figurine vases and children in period attire. Some figures were incorporated into lamps. Lace decoration was used on figurines.

Other ceramic items made were busts, wall plaques, wall pockets, vases, smoking sets, picture frames, clock frames, candleholders, and a large assortment of birds.

In 1956, sculptor Betty Davenport Ford modeled a line of bisque finished animal figures including highly stylized rabbits, dogs, cats, doves, and squirrels. These were made for only two years.

Names were usually incised in the base of figures when possible, or paper labels were used. The company name also was ink stamped.

After Florence's husband died in 1964, production was stopped, and the company was sold to Scripto Corporation. It retained the Florence name, but made advertising specialty ware such as mugs, cups, and ashtrays. In 1977, all production was stopped.

**References:** Jack Chipman, *Collector's Encyclopedia of California Pottery, 2nd Edition*, Collector Books, 1998; Doug Foland, *The Florence Collectibles: An Era of Elegance*, Schiffer Publishing Ltd.1995.

**Collectors' Club:** Florence Collector's Club, Beth Dunigan, P.O. Box 122, Richland, WA 99352, bimonthly newletter *Florence of Pasadena,* $20 per year.

Ashtray, figural shell, pink glaze, S3..........................100.00

W. K. Woodard Memorial Library

**Figure, 3 3/4" h, "Tootsie," white body, med blue eyes and tail, $48.**

**Figure, 7 1/4" h, "Rebecca," brown dress, green muff, dk brown hair, $495.**

Box, Cov

    3 1/4" d, bust of blond girl w/green bow and "Bobby Pins" on cov ................................................................ 25.00

    6 1/4" l, bust of lady's head on cov, teal ................ 175.00

Dish, 11 1/2" l x 5 1/2" w, 2 pink roses, green leaves on side, cream ground ........................................................... 10.00

Figure

    4 1/2" h, 7" h, shelf sitter mermaid, blond hair, kneeling mermaid, brown hair, irid purple gowns, pr ....... 175.00

    5 1/2" h

        Becky, blue and white ........................................ 175.00

        Joyce, cream and pink ......................................... 75.00

        Peter, blue and white ......................................... 170.00

    6" h

        Ann, beige, green hat ......................................... 85.00

        Choir Boys, black and white, dk brown, med brown, or blond hair, set of 3 ....................................... 350.00

        Elaine, white w/gold trim .................................... 50.00

        Irene

            Aqua and gold ............................................... 70.00

            Gray ............................................................. 72.00

        Joy, teal blue ................................................... 100.00

    6 1/4" h, Jim, white .............................................. 65.00

    6 3/4" h x 7 3/4" w, Catherine, blue ........................ 95.00

    7" h

        Ballerina, brown hair, pink and gold body .......... 145.00

        Rebecca, teal, gold, and ivory ........................... 230.00

        Sally, peach gown ............................................ 180.00

    7 1/4" h

        Delia, blonde hair, gray with burgundy trim ....... 165.00

        Edith, brown hair, purple dress ......................... 225.00

        Lillian, rose dress ............................................ 120.00

    7 1/2" h

        Betsy, ivory, gold lace trim ............................... 110.00

        David, white and gold ...................................... 100.00

        Grace, lt green ................................................ 220.00

        Green parakeet on stump w/dogwood blossoms .................................................... 195.00

        Jeanette, olive green ........................................ 140.00

        Laura, blue ....................................................... 85.00

        Melanie, beige w/green .................................... 110.00

        Sarah, blue gown ............................................ 125.00

    7 3/4" h

        Chinese boy or girl

            Black and white, pr ...................................... 100.00

            Green, pr .................................................... 85.00

        Clarissa, pale pink rose dress with green trim ................................................................ 155.00

    8" h

        Abigail, tan w/rust trim .................................... 185.00

        Annabel, pink .................................................. 400.00

        Douglas, tan ................................................... 195.00

        Marsie, brown hair, moss green and white ........ 195.00

        Richard, turquoise jacket ................................. 475.00

        Sue Ellen, gray and maroon ............................ 160.00

    8 1/4" h, Lantern Boy, white and gold ..................... 75.00

    8 1/2" h

        Elizabeth on Sofa, violet and gray ..................... 500.00

        Camille, articulated hand, blue ......................... 235.00

        Claudia, gray and pink ..................................... 250.00

        Joyce, white w/gold trim .................................. 225.00

        Matilda, blonde hair, gray dress with violet trim ................................................................ 175.00

        Roberta, blue dress, red gloves ....................... 225.00

    8 3/4" h, Musette, blue ....................................... 200.00

    9" h, Eugenia, maroon ........................................ 339.00

    9 1/4" h

        Deborah, magenta dress .................................. 345.00

        Victor, black lined cape, brown hair .................. 115.00

    9 1/2" h, bust of Pamela, white bisque ................. 165.00

    9 3/4" h, bust of David, sand .............................. 200.00

    10" h

        Deborah, green gown ..................................... 1039.00

        Georgette, burgundy dress .............................. 295.00

        Louis XVI, white and gold ................................. 175.00

        Prima Donna, pink .......................................... 475.00

        Vivian, rose .................................................... 375.00

10 1/4" h, Leading Man, pink suit..........................275.00
10 1/2" h
    Ava, tan and rust ...........................................200.00
    Princess, burgundy gown, (A) ..........................500.00
Flower Holder
  6" h
    Mimi, white and pink..........................................50.00
    Polly, dk red trim, blue underskirt ......................60.00
  6 1/4" h, Bee, white and flowered gown..................65.00
  7" h, Kay, white dress........................................60.00
Lamp, 9" h, Dear Ruth, green, blond hair.................1000.00
Planter
  5 1/2" h, May, standing girl, pink flowered dress......40.00
  6 1/2" h.............................................................85.00
  7" h
    June.................................................................50.00
    Kay .................................................................50.00
  8" h, Emily .......................................................50.00
Platter, 15" H-H, 3 section, wavy separators, matte white
  glaze ..............................................................15.00
Serving Dish, 9 1/2" l, 3 curved feet, Floraline, gold and
  champagne .......................................................85.00
Vase, 9" h, cornucopia shape, curlicue base, cream w/gold
  trim, Floraline, R-5 ............................................45.00
Wall Plaque
  7 1/4" h, oval, cameo, bust of woman w/feathered hat,
    brown ruffled rim............................................135.00
  8" h x 6 1/2" w, Floraline .........................................75.00
  9 1/2" h x 6 1/2" w, rect, woman in dk green bonnet,
    maroon dress, holding purse, taupe bkd...........100.00

FRANKOMA POTTERY

FRANKOMA

# Frankoma Pottery

### Sapulpa, Oklahoma
### 1933-Present

**History:** In 1933, John Frank established a small studio in his home in Norman, Oklahoma to make pottery. He left his teaching position at the University of Oklahoma in 1936 and moved to Sapulpa, Oklahoma and set up a small factory. He utilized the local-red brown clay that showed through the glaze finish.

Frank developed the once-fired process for pottery where the clay body and colored glazes were fused. Many designs reflected the local heritage of the Southwest Indians and local flora and fauna.

Working with J.W. Daugherty, John developed the "Rutile art glazes" that were characteristic of Frankoma ware. Colors on the earthenware clay body were Prairie Green, Desert Gold, Woodland Moss, Peach Glow, Terra Cotta Rose, Clay Blue, White Sand, and others. The red body showed through the glaze and produced a mottled effect. Green, gold, and black were introduced first in 1933 and uti-

lized until the present time. The other colors were added over a period of years.

The pottery started with the production of sculptures done by a series of fine artists. Subjects included Fan Dancer, Seated Figure, Seated Indian Bowl Maker, Indian Chief, Red Irish Setter, Indian Head, Phoebe, Afro Girl and Man, and such. Ray Murray was one of the most prolific artists and was responsible for Indian Chief, Fan Dancer, Mountain Girl and numerous others.

Due to a series of setbacks, they switched to dinnerwares and numerous series of collectibles. A separate sculpture catalog was reintroduced in 1972, but discontinued after 1974.

Dinnerware patterns included Mayan-Aztec that was inspired from the American Indian tribes of the Southwest that was introduced in 1936-38 with pitchers, mugs, and coffee mugs. In 1948 it was made in full sets in Desert Gold and Bronze Green. Wagon Wheel was made in 1948, and Plainsman from the same year was the largest dinnerware line in Frankoma production. Lazybones came in 1953, and Westward in 1962 was the last new pattern made.

Grace Lee Frank, John's wife, designed the Madonna plaques in rubbed bisque which was a chocolate brown matte rub with a stain instead of glaze. "Grace Madonna" was done in 1977 and "Madonna of Love" came out in 1978.

John Frank created a line of Christmas plates beginning in 1965 that were marked "First Issue." He made them until his death in 1973, and then the designs were done by his daughter Joniece who took over. The designs were different biblical scenes done in low relief with a white semi-translucent glaze known as "Della Robbia" white where red glaze would show through.

Miniature ceramic Christmas cards were started in 1944 by John and Grace Lee and were sent out every year in the shape of ash trays, pitchers, trays, and such. Grace Lee continued them after she remarried.

Numerous collectible lines were made at Frankoma. In 1972, there were Teenagers of the Bible, political mugs were made for the National Republican Woman's Club starting in 1968 until 1979, Bicentennial Plates started in 1972 with the history of the American Revolution, Contestoga Wagon was done in a pale soft blue, 1972 saw plates for the Oklahoma Wildlife Federation, a bottle vase series started in 1969, and in 1976 Toby Mugs were started.

Additional pieces made at Frankoma included bookends, vases, windbells, bowls, trivets, canisters, salt and pepper sets, and Will Rogers plaques.

A series of marks was used over the years, and most pieces were marked. Stock numbers were also used on most pieces.

In 1983, the pottery was destroyed by fire and rebuilt.

**References:** Phyllis and Tom Bess, *Frankoma Pottery*, Schiffer Publishing Ltd.1997; Susan N. Cox, *The Collector's Guide to Frankoma Pottery, Book One, Two, & Three*, Page One Publications, 1982; Donna Frank, *Clay in the Master's Hands*, Vantage Press, 1977; Gary V. Schaum, *Collector's Guide Frankoma Pottery 1933-1990*, L-W Book Sales, 1998.

**Newsletter:** Robert Hase, "The Frankoma Collector's Newsletter," 244 Fox Lane, Belvidere, IL 61008. quarterly, free.

### LAZY BONES PATTERN
Butter Dish, Woodland Moss, Sapulpa clay, #4K

.......................................................................15.00
Plate
  7" d, Desert Gold .......................................5.00
  10" d, Desert Gold .....................................6.00

Sugar Bowl, Cov, Prairie Green, Sapulpa clay ............. 10.00

## MAYAN-AZTEC PATTERN

Bean Pot, Cov, 3 1/4" h, Prairie Green, Ada clay, (A)
.................................................................................38.00
Berry Bowl, 5 1/4" d, Desert Gold ................................. 3.00
Canister, 7" h, Woodland Moss ................................... 40.00
Casserole, Cov, 8" d, Prairie Green, (A) ..................... 30.00
Mug, 5" h, turquoise ..................................................... 15.00
Pitcher, 8" h, Prairie Green ......................................... 15.00
Plate, Desert Gold
    5 1/4" d ........................................................................ 4.00
    7" d .............................................................................. 4.00
    9 1/2" d ........................................................................ 7.00
    10 1/4" d ...................................................................... 8.00
Shakers, Pr, White Sand ............................................. 20.00
Tray, 14" l, White Sand ................................................ 50.00

## MISCELLANEOUS

Ashtray
    6" l, figural Dutch wooden shoe, Desert Gold .......... 30.00
    7 1/2" d, 3 rests, dk brown ground, brown speckled edge,
    #458 ...................................................................... 15.00
Baking Dish, 10" d, Prairie Green glaze, "FRANKOMA 91"
    mk ............................................................................ 9.00
Bowl
    7" l, leaf shape, Woodland Moss, #225 .................... 12.00
    10" l, cactus design, Prairie Green, Ada clay, #206
    .............................................................................. 45.00
Bud Vase
    8" h, spread ft, jade green glaze, #43 ..................... 45.00

**Candle holder, 11 1/2" h, yellow glaze, $150.**

**Trivet, 6 1/4" d, ftd, magenta glaze, $16.**

9 1/2" h, chalk white glaze, red Sapulpa clay .......... 18.00
Candlestick, 8" l, cactus pattern, Prairie Green, Ada clay,
    #306, pr ................................................................ 150.00
Canteen, 6 1/2" h, Thunderbird, Desert Gold, Ada clay, #59
.................................................................................65.00
Cornucopia, 6" l, Prairie Green glaze, "FRANKOMA 57S"
    mk ............................................................................ 15.00
Figure
    7" h, seated puma, green, #114 .............................. 65.00
    8" h, dancing Indian chief, onyx black, Ada clay.... 100.00
    11 1/2" h, mare and colt, rubbed bisque glaze, Salpulpa
    clay ........................................................................ 15.00
    13" l, Fan Dancer, flame orange glaze, (A)........... 110.00
Honey Pot, 4 3/4" h, Spring Green, #803 ................... 15.00
Jug, 7 1/4" h, squat shape, green shaded to brown
.................................................................................22.00
Pitcher
    6 1/4" h, horiz ribbing, brown, orange, and white mottling,
    red clay.................................................................. 22.00
    8" h, ovoid, green shading over brown ground, #835
    .............................................................................. 22.00
Planter
    5" h, figural owl, tan glaze, Ada clay ........................ 5.00
    6 1/4" h, figural swan, gloss green glaze, (A) ......... 22.00
    7" h, figural boot and horseshoes, brown glaze, pr
    .............................................................................. 45.00
    12" l
        Crescent shape, gloss blue glaze, #211 ............. 50.00
        Figural mallard duck, green/brown...................... 25.00
Plaque, 9 1/4" d, "Sequoyah's Cherokee Alphabet," Prairie
    Green, Salpulpa clay ............................................. 15.00
Toby Jug, 4" h, Uncle Sam figural, Flame Red, Sapulpa clay
.................................................................................10.00
Trivet, 6 1/2" d, "End of the Trail" design, terra cotta Sapulpa
    clay w/black glaze accents ..................................... 15.00
Urn, 16" h, rect handles, Desert Gold glaze, (A) ......... 88.00
Vase
    6" h
        Clam shell shape, blue glaze, (A) ...................... 30.00
        Ram's head, Prairie Green, Ada clay, #38 ......... 50.00
        Snail, Red Bud glaze, Ada Clay .......................... 65.00
    6 1/2" h
        Reed, Desert Gold glaze, Ada clay, #28 ............. 65.00
        Thunderbird Canteen, Desert Gold glaze, Ada clay,
        #59.......................................................................... 65.00
    6 3/4" h, goblet style, mottled brown....................... 17.00
    7" h, cactus design, Prairie Green, #4, Ada clay
    .............................................................................. 45.00
    8 3/4" h, cylinder shape, Brown Satin glaze,
    "FRANKOMA 73" mk ............................................... 10.00
    10" h, classic shape, leaf handles, Prairie Green,
    Sapulpa clay, #71 ................................................. 75.00
    10 3/4" h, lobed, tapered body, graduated discs on base,
    Prairie Green glaze, Ada Clay............................... 90.00
    12" h, black and terra cotta, #V-4 ........................... 50.00
    15" h, Prairie Green, #V-1 ....................................... 50.00
Wall Pocket, 5" h, figural boot, Satin Brown................. 60.00

## PLAINSMAN PATTERN
Bowl
    6" d, Desert Gold ..................................................... 6.00

9" sq, Dk Brown Satin ............................................ 15.00
Casserole, Cov, 11" H-H, Prairie Green glaze, 5V
................................................................................. 39.00
Creamer, Prairie Green glaze, "FRANKOMA 5DA" mk
................................................................................... 6.00
Gravy Boat, Brown Satin glaze, "FRANKOMA 5S" mk
................................................................................. 20.00
Mug, 5 3/8" h, Prairie Green glaze, Sapulpa clay
................................................................................. 10.00
Plate
   6 1/4" d, Desert Gold ................................................. 3.00
   7" d, Desert Gold ...................................................... 6.00
   10" d, Desert Gold glaze ........................................... 8.00
Platter
   9 5/8" l, Prairie Green, red clay ............................. 15.00
   15" H-H, Brown Satin glaze .................................... 15.00
Sugar Bowl, 3" h, Desert Gold ....................................... 8.00
Tray, 9 5/8" l, rect, Prairie Green ............................... 10.00
Vegetable Bowl, 9" sq, Brown Satin glaze ................... 15.00

**POLITICAL MUGS**
Democrat
   1975, Autumn gold glaze ...................................... 20.00
   1978, Woodland Moss glaze .................................. 15.00
   1979, matte brown glaze ....................................... 25.00
   1980, lt blue glaze ................................................. 18.00
Republican
   1968, white .............................................................. 35.00
   1969, NIXON-AGNEW, red ................................... 125.00
   1970, blue ............................................................... 85.00
   1971, matte black ................................................... 75.00
   1975, gloss yellow ................................................. 25.00
   1973, NIXON-AGNEW, cream and brown .............. 65.00

**WAGON WHEEL PATTERN**
Creamer, 4" h, Prairie Green ....................................... 15.00
Pitcher, 7" h, Prairie Green ......................................... 25.00
Plate
   6 3/4" d, Prairie Green .......................................... 10.00
   9" d, Prairie Green, Ada clay ................................ 10.00
   10" d, Prairie Green ............................................... 20.00
Platter
   14" l x 8 1/2" w, Prairie Green .............................. 20.00
   15 1/4" l, Desert Gold, Sapulpa clay ..................... 15.00
Teapot, 7 1/2" h, Prairie Green .................................... 70.00

**WESTWIND PATTERN**
Plate, 7" d, White Sand .................................................. 8.00
Platter, 12" l
   Flame ....................................................................... 12.00
   White Sand .............................................................. 12.00

# Ohio Pottery

**1900-1923**

# Fraunfelter China Company

**1923-1939**
**Zanesville, Ohio**

**History:** Ohio Pottery operated in Zanesville, Ohio from 1900-1923. They made hotel ware and intro-

duced hard paste dinnerware from 1918-1920. Kitchenwares also were introduced c1915.

Fraunfelter China Company took over in 1923. They also purchased American China Products Company of Chesterton, Indiana and made dinnerware in both plants. When Fraunfelter died in 1925, the Chesterton plant was closed.

Both Ohio and Fraunfelter sold large quantities of blanks for decoration since they were one of the few firms making European quality porcelains at prices that were competitive. Fraunfelter closed during the Depression, then reorganized, reopened and closed in 1939.

A wide variety of marks was used.

Baking Dish, Cov, 10" d, w/metal holder, oval, mottled tan
   glaze ....................................................................... 15.00
Bowl, 6 3/4" l, gloss brown ............................................. 5.00
Casserole, Cov
   7" d x 5" h, dk green glaze, "Ohio Pottery" mk ........ 38.00
   8 1/2" d, pearl luster body w/blue luster band on base and
     cov, metal stand, mkd .......................................... 10.00
Cereal Bowl, 5 1/2" d, 4 bouquets in baskets on inner border
   separated by band ................................................... 5.00
Coffeepot
   7 1/4" h, cream and orange bands, silver stripes, spout,
     and handle, "oval Fraunfelter-Ohio" mk .............. 35.00
   7 3/4 h, Art Deco style, green and chrome horiz banding
   ................................................................................. 22.00
Creamer, yellow body, silver trim, "oval Fraunfelter-Ohio" mk
................................................................................... 5.00
Sugar Bowl, Cov, 4" h, white vert panels w/multicolored florals separated by vert orange panels ..................... 15.00
Syrup Jug, 5 1/2" h, band of multicolored garden flowers below shoulder, lustered body, gold trim, metal cov
................................................................................. 20.00
Teapot
   3" h x 6" l, squat shape, brown-gold glaze .............. 15.00
   6" h, Art Deco style, stacked shape, brown ............. 20.00
   8 1/4" h, brown glaze, gold trim ............................. 50.00
Vase
   4 3/8" h, squat shape, ftd, flared rim, lemon yellow drip over orange body, "Fraunfelter USA 98" mk ....... 75.00
   5 3/4" h
     Bulbous middle, wide shoulder, flared rim, mottled med green glaze, "stamped Fraunfelter USA 98" mk, (A) ............................................................. 55.00
     Tapered shape, wide shoulder, flared rim, green-gold luster glaze, (A) ................................. 82.00
   7" h, blue, orange, and white luster finish ............. 150.00
   8 3/4" h, tapered cylinder shape, short, flared rim, mirror black glaze, mkd .............................................. 100.00

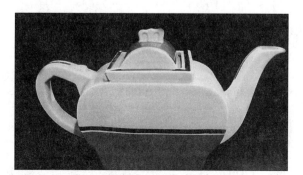

**Teapot, 7" h, orange, silver, and ivory, $75.**

UNION MADE
U.S.A.
WARRANTED
22 KT. GOLD
DUSTY ROSE

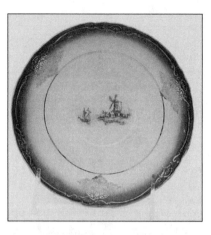

Saucer Dish, 5 1/4" d, black transfer, flowing blue border w/gold overlay, "LaFrancaise" mk, $6.

# French China Company

**East Liverpool and Sebring, Ohio**
**1898-1929**

# Saxon China Company

**Sebring, Ohio**
**1911-1929**

# French-Saxon China Company

**Sebring, Ohio**
**1935-1964**

**History:** The Sebring brothers organized the French China Company in 1898 in East Liverpool, Ohio and made semi-porcelain dinner, tea, toilet wares, and novelties. They moved the French China Company to a new plant in Sebring, Ohio in 1901 and continued to make semi-porcelains.

Saxon China Company was founded in 1911 and made plain and decorated semi-vitreous dinnerwares.

In 1916 Sebring created a holding company called Sebring Manufacturing Corporation for French China Company, Strong Manufacturing Company and Saxon China Company. Each continued to operate separately until 1929 when the holding company joined American Chinaware Corporation which failed two years later.

The Saxon China Company reopened as the French-Saxon China Company in 1935. They produced semi-porcelain dinnerware, tea sets, and various accessory pieces. In 1964 the French-Saxon China Company was purchased by Royal China Company of Sebring, Ohio.

**References:** William C. Gates, Jr. and Dana E. Ormerod, *The East Liverpool, Ohio, Pottery District: Identification of Manufacturers and Marks,* The Society for Historical Archaeology, 1982.

### ALOHA PATTERN
Plate, 12 3/4" H-H, green .............................................. 6.00

### BREEZE PATTERN
Berry Bowl, 5 1/4" d....................................................... 3.00
Cereal Bowl, 6" d........................................................... 4.00
Creamer ........................................................................ 5.00
Cup and Saucer ............................................................ 4.00
Plate
   6" d.......................................................................... 4.00
   7 1/4" d.................................................................... 5.00
   9 1/8" d.................................................................... 8.00
Platter, 10" H-H............................................................. 10.00
Soup Bowl, 7 5/8" d........................................................ 5.00

Soup Bowl, 7 3/4" d, "Breeze" pattern, $8.

Sugar Bowl, Cov ........................................................... 8.00
Vegetable Bowl, 8 5/8" d............................................... 10.00

### BURGUNDY LACE PATTERN
Creamer, 3" h ............................................................... 5.00
Cup and Saucer ............................................................ 6.00
Plate
   6 1/2" d .................................................................. 4.00
   9 1/2" d .................................................................. 5.00
Sugar Bowl, Cov, 5" h ................................................... 6.00

### MARTHA WASHINGTON PATTERN
Creamer, 3" h x 5 1/2" l ................................................ 10.00
Sugar Bowl, Cov, 4" h ................................................... 14.00

### MISCELLANEOUS
Berry Bowl, 5 1/2" d, gold medallion in center, flowing blue border w/gold hanging swag overlay ........................ 18.00
Bowl, 9 1/2" d, black sailing ship and long boat transfer in center, flowing blue border with vert ribbing and gold rim, "La Francaise" mk................................................... 165.00
Game Set, platter, 14 1/4" l, 6 plates, 8 3/8" d, pr of walking pheasants on platter, pr of quail in meadow on plates, tan borders w/gold floral overlays, sgd "R.K. Beck"..... 175.00
Pie Plate, 9 1/2" d, red and blue stylized Dutch couple and windmill................................................................... 15.00
Plate
   9" d, yellow flower in center, pink border w/gold accents, "La Francaise" mk ................................................. 8.00
   9 1/4" d, bluebird design, "La Francaise" mk .......... 15.00

Platter

10 1/2" H-H, red and white roses in center, gold swag border, "F.C.Co." mk ........................... 10.00

12 1/2" l

Flowing blue border, "La FRANCAISE SEMI VITROUS" mk ........................... 25.00

Two swimming ducks in center, cobalt border w/gold trim, lobed rim, "La Francaise" mk

........................... 35.00

13 1/2" l

Multicolored shore birds in center, "La Francaise" mk

........................... 25.00

Multicolored windmill scene in center, raised design on flowing blue border, gold fan design overlay, "La Francaise" mk ........................... 125.00

Shaving Bowl, 11 1/4" l, raised yellow bamboo w/blue and red bachelor buttons, raised shell border w/gilt trim, "La Francaise" mk ........................... 42.00

Sugar Bowl, Cov, paneled, bluebird pattern ................ 30.00

Tray, 10 5/8" l, flowing blue border w/raised curlicues and gold hanging swags, "SAXON CHINA" mk .............. 50.00

### PINECONE PATTERN

Creamer, 6 3/4" l ........................... 8.00

Cup and Saucer ........................... 6.00

Plate

7 1/4" d ........................... 6.00

9" d ........................... 8.00

Platter, 11" H-H ........................... 8.00

Serving Bowl, 8 3/4" d ........................... 30.00

### PINK DAWN PATTERN

Soup Plate, 7 3/4" d ........................... 5.00

### POND LILY PATTERN

Cereal Bowl, 7 1/2" d ........................... 3.00

### SILVER SYMPHONY PATTERN

Creamer ........................... 6.00

Sugar Bowl, Cov ........................... 8.00

Tray, 12" H-H ........................... 12.00

### THISTLE PATTERN

Plate

6" d ........................... 2.00

9" d ........................... 5.00

# Fulper

## Flemington, New Jersey
## 1805-1929

**History:** The Fulper factory was founded by Samuel Hill in 1805 as a manufacturer of drain tile and farm items using the red clays around Flemington, New Jersey. When the factory was purchased by Abraham Fulper in 1860, who worked with his three sons, they expanded their business to include water, vinegar, and pickling jars, butter churns, ginger beer bottles, and mugs.

A big seller was the Fulper Germ Proof Filter, which provided clear, cool water in public places in stoneware jars that were decorated with cobalt blue lettering and designs.

Though the name changed several times, the factory was incorporated as the Fulper Pottery Company in 1899. Its Vasekraft art pottery line was introduced in 1909 using the heavy stoneware body. Pieces included jardinieres, vases, bowls, bookends, candleholders, cooking ware, mugs, and such in a tremendous variety of glazes.

The best contribution Fulper made was its pottery lamp bases. Fulper also made ceramic shades to accompany many of the bases. Lamps came in many shapes, sizes, and glazes and were products of the Vasekraft period. The most desirable forms were the toadstools and mushrooms. The finest glazes were utilized on the lamps, and the shades were inset with leaded glass.

Martin Stangl came from Germany to New Jersey in 1910 as a chemist and plant superintendent for William Fulper. After a short stay developing an industrial art ware line for Haeger Potteries of Dundee, Illinois, Stangl returned to Fulper as general manager.

Stangl helped invent a group of famille rose glazes including Ashes of Roses, Deep Rose, Peach Bloom, Old Rose, and True Rose. Stangl was also responsible for some of the clay bodies. The Vasekraft line used classical and oriental shapes. Glazes included the expensive famille rose, "Mission Matte," "Mirror Glaze," Cat's Eye, Rouge, Mustard Matte, Bronze, Cucumber Green, Cafe au Lait, Mulberry, and such. Crystalline glazes also were used. Lamps, ashtrays, lamp shades, vases, bowls, cigarette boxes, etc. were made. Some forms were quite unusual.

John Kunsman was Fulper's master potter. Other potters also worked there. Some pieces were artist signed. Marks were raised, incised, or stamped in ink. Some Vasekraft pieces had paper labels.

During World War I since imports were limited, Fulper produced bisque dolls and dolls' heads from 1918-21 that usually were marked with the Fulper name. Stangl created a porcelain body from which a doll's head was made and is now famous as the Fulper dollhead.

Solid color green dinnerware was the first of the colored dinnerware lines made in the United States and was introduced by Stangl to bolster the Fulper Pottery. Other colors were added to the line.

Fulper made high quality porcelains with the outlined vertical mark with oriental type lettering from 1920-1928. Martin Stangl designed many porcelain forms such as perfume dolls in the form of ballerinas, powder boxes, candy boxes, bookends, candleholders, and baskets. Stangl developed the porcelain body. All the articles were hand decorated.

**References:** Harvey Duke, *Stangl Pottery*, Wallace-Homestead, 1993; John Hibel, Carole Hibel, Robert DeFalco, *The Fulper Book*, text by David Rago, The Arts and Crafts Quarterly Press, 1992.

**Museums:** Chrysler Museum, Norfolk, VA; New Jersey State Museum, Trenton, NJ; Newark Museum, NJ; New Orleans Museum of Art, LA; Philadelphia Museum of Art, PA.

**Reproduction Alert:** Fulper Glazes, Inc. of Yardley, Pennsylvania has been producing lamps similar to Fulper Pottery originals marked with a square-cornered Fulper Tile logo. There are twelve difference standard glazes available in crystalline, mirror and matte finishes. Many use the original glaze names.

Basket, 7 1/4" h, emb rose and rope handle, matte blue glaze, racetrack mk, (A) ........................... 145.00

Beverage Set, pitcher, 10 1/2" h, 6 mugs, 4 1/2" h, gunmetal gray glaze ........................... 2,200.00

Bookend

6" h, figural "Roman Mausoleum," mottled ivory and white matte glaze, restored chip, pr, (A) ........................... 605.00

**Planter, 9 3/4" H-H, luster khaki ext, blue-green luster int, printed "FULPER" mk, $340.**

8 1/2" h, seated Ramses I, verdi matte green, shape #450, pr .......................................................... 1,470.00

Bowl

7 1/2" w, metallic black and blue crystalline glazes
.................................................................... 165.00

8" d, cobalt flambe on Famille Rose, shape #437
.................................................................... 185.00

8 1/2" d, semi-spherical, 4 feet, Mahogany and Ivory flambe glaze, matte mustard yellow base, (A)
.................................................................... 468.00

10" d, Effigy, Cafe-au-lait and yellow crystalline glaze on int and gargoyles, matte mustard yellow ext, rect mk, (A) ............................................................ 550.00

11" d, "Ibis," 3 figural birds, brown flambe over mustard ext, Flemington Green flambe int, (A) .............. 935.00

Bud Vase

5 3/4" h, bullet shape, Cat's Eye flambe glaze, unmkd, (A) .................................................................. 110.00

7" h, stick shape, "Ashes of Rose" drip on "Elephant's Breath," shape #9 ............................................. 290.00

8 1/2" h, Leopard Skin Crystalline glaze, (A) ...... 1,430.00

8 3/4" h, geometric shape, matte brown glaze.... 1,400.00

Candle Sconce, 10 1/2" h, hooded, 3 glass inserts, Cucumber Crystalline glaze, racetrack mk, (A)
.................................................................. 2,200.00

Candlestick, 8" h, twisted shape, Cat's Eye flambe glaze, racetrack mk, (A) ............................................. 75.00

Centerpiece Bowl

11 1/4" d, 3 ftd, mottled rose glaze, (A) ................. 413.00

14 3/4" d, Chinese Blue crystalline flambe glaze, racetrack mk, (A) ............................................... 330.00

Charger, 12 3/4" h, ftd, blue and ivory flambe glaze on top, matte ochre and green glaze on bottom and 4 feet, chips, (A) .................................................................. 660.00

Coaster, 4" d, emb green crystalline coat of arms in center, Cafe-au-lait ground, set of 3, (A) ......................... 165.00

Doorstop, 6" h x 9" l, figural recumbent cat, Cat's Eye flambe glaze, (A) ................................................ 1,045.00

Figure, 8" h, seated stylized dog, butterscotch and blue flambe glazes, (A) .................................................. 340.00

Flower Frog

3 1/4" l, figural scarab beetle, cream, red, blue, green, and brown flambe, shape #448 ......................... 175.00

4 d, lily pad, tan, green, blue, and brown flambe, shape #424 .................................................................. 135.00

5" l, figural frog, tan, green, blue, and brown, shape #400
.................................................................... 195.00

7" h, standing penguin, white, blue, and brown matte glazes, (A) ........................................................... 303.00

Incense Burner, 6" l, Aladdin lamp shape, gloss green over matte mustard yellow body, repaired chip, (A) ....... 220.00

Inkwell

4" h x 5 1/4" l, triangular, Germanic, matte green glaze, "inked FULPER in rect" mk, (A) ......................... 330.00

5" h, Vasecraft, pen tray on front, matte ochre glaze, racetrack mk, (A) .............................................. 550.00

Jug, 11" h, dk blue crystalline flambe glaze, (A) ......... 110.00

Lamp

16" h, bell shape shade, inset w/triangular chartreuse and umber leaded glass, frothy "Elephant Breath" and "Mouse Gray" flambe glaze, (A) ..................... 8,800.00

16 3/4" h, trumpet base, mushroom shade, Flemington Green flambe glaze, green leaded slag glass inserts, hairlines on shade, (A) ................................... 7,150.00

Lantern, 12 3/4" h, Chinese style, faceted body, faux rivets and straps, dk blue flambe glaze, leaded green slag glass windows, wired, (A) ..................................... 4,400.00

Perfume Lamp, 6 1/4" h, pink ballerina figure holding spread skirt, (A) ..................................................... 120.00

Pilgrim Flask, 10" h, curdled green, Mirror Black, blue, and ivory flambe glaze, (A) .................................... 1,045.00

Powder Jar, Cov

2" h x 4" d, Famille Rose glaze, (A) ..................... 275.00

6 1/2" h, figural lady, purple jacket, red green florals on ivory skirt base, (A) .......................................... 143.00

Urn

8 1/2" h, 2 handles, Colonial Ware, brown flambe glaze, racetrack mk, (A) .............................................. 110.00

9" h, bulbous shape, ftd, ochre, mahogany, and lt blue flambe glaze, textured ground, (A) .................... 935.00

9 1/4" h, squat body, 2 flat handles from shoulder to rim, Chinese Blue Crystalline to Famille Rose glaze, (A)
.................................................................... 413.00

11" h, amphora shape, scrolled handles, rolled rim, mirror black glaze, textured body, (A) .......................... 495.00

12 1/2" h, spherical shape, ftd, short neck w/rim, horiz handles, hammered matte Cucumber green glaze, racetrack mk, (A) .............................................. 880.00

13" h, classical shape, sm loop handles on shoulder, Mirror Black glaze, incised racetrack mk, (A) ........ 467.00

Vase

4" h, blue and green flambe on mirror black, shape #011
.................................................................... 245.00

5" h, squat shape, 2 angular handles, Copperdust Crystalline glaze, (A) ................................................. 550.00

5 1/4" h, bulbous shape, rolled rim, mahogany drip over Copperdust Crystalline glaze, (A) ..................... 440.00

5 1/2" h

Gourd shape, Flemington Green flambe glaze, (A)
.................................................................... 468.00

Ovoid, dk mirrored green and blue flambe glaze, (A)
.................................................................... 330.00

6" h

Bulbous shape, 2 sm handles, Famille Rose to Matte Green drip glaze, (A) ..................................... 495.00

Spherical shape, Leopard Skin Crystalline glaze, "ink vert FULPER" mark, (A) .............................. 715.00

Straight sides, rolled shoulder and rim, green and tan mottled glaze, 1909 ...................................... 950.00

6 1/2" h

Amphora shape, 3 sm handles, green crystalline glaze
.................................................................... 325.00

Spherical, 3 sm handles on shoulder, Chinese Blue flambe glaze, (A)............................468.00

Swollen middle, flared rim, applied rose and leaves, semi-matte white glaze, racetrack mk, (A)......33.00

7" h

Bulbous shape, flared rim, flambe blue and tan glaze, "ink vert FULPER" mk....................525.00

Spherical, 2 sm handles on shoulder, Moss to Wisteria flambe glaze, (A)..........................495.00

7 1/2" h

Bulbous shape, frothy Wisteria matte glaze, (A) ............................................358.00

Gourd shape, 2 loop handles from shoulder to rim, Leopard Skin Crystalline glaze, (A) .............825.00

8" h

Bulbous base, cylinder neck, molded serpent on shoulder, green crystalline glaze, vert stamp mk, (A) ...............................................770.00

Oct, collar rim, textured ivory to blue and green flambe glaze, (A) .........................................770.00

Ovoid, Cat's Eye flambe glaze, (A) ..................413.00

9" h

Bottle shape, mottled mahogany glaze, (A) ......605.00

Four buttress handles, green crystalline glaze ....................................................495.00

9 1/2" h, tapered shape, 2 buttressed handles, frothy Copperdust to green flambe glaze, (A) .............495.00

9 3/4" h

Corset shape, Flemington Green flambe glaze, racetrack mk, (A) ................................440.00

Cylinder shape w/molded mushrooms on base, ivory and "Elephant's Breath" flambe glazes, hairline, (A) ................................................467.00

10" h

Bulbous, flared ft and rim, Moss Green drip over Rose glaze, (A) ........................................990.00

Faceted, green, blue, mahogany, and ivory flambe glaze, "vert FULPER" mk, (A) ........................825.00

Urn shape, corseted shoulder, flared rim, ivory, Cat's Eye flambe, and Chinese Blue glazes, (A) ...550.00

11" h

Amphora shape, curlicue handles from shoulder to rim, blue, brown, and yellow flambe glaze, vert mk, (A) ................................................523.00

Arts and Craft form, 2 open vert handles, brown and blue drip over matte med blue ground, (A) ...770.00

12" h

Amphora shape, flat ft and rim, frothy cobalt and purple semi-matte glaze, (A)............................550.00

Bulbous body, 2 horiz handles, hammered green glaze, c1910 ...........................................2400.00

12 1/2" h, tapered cylinder shape, frothy blue and green flambe glaze, restored rim, (A) ........................385.00

13" h, tapered shape, gunmetal, mahogany, and Copperdust Crystalline glaze, hairlines, (A) ..................660.00

13 1/4" h, bulbous body, flared ft and rim, Chinese Blue to Flemington Green flambe glaze, (A) ................770.00

16 1/4" h, tapered cylinder shape, rolled rim, frothy Moss green drip over Rose glaze, (A) ....................1,540.00

17 3/4" h, tapered cylinder shape, short, straight neck, Cucumber Green glaze, base nick, (A) ..........1,650.00

Water Pitcher, 9" h, stoneware, Pennsylvania Dutch style cobalt grapes from rim, "Room 11" in floral cartouche on side, "JK" and horseshoe on front, salt glaze finish, c1908, (A)....................................2,015.00

# Galena Pottery

## Galena, Illinois Area
## 1843-1899

**History:** The pottery from the Galena area of Illinois and southern Wisconsin was a redware pottery similar to the New England redwares with a lead glaze. Some pieces of this utilitarian pottery had a rough texture, some was smooth and glossy. Other examples had splotches or spots in reds, greens, browns, and yellows.

Galena pots were wheel thrown, partially dried, glazed and then fired once to be ready for market. Each piece was individual; no two were exactly alike in coloring. Some examples had grooved lines, some had sawtooth or cogwheel decorations. The best work on the Galena pots was done on the top edges. Galena used larger and heavier edge moldings than other potteries. The only decorative color effects were the occasional spots or the pieces that were dipped halfway into the cream colored slip. Most pieces were not marked. There were just numbers to indicate the size capacity of a specific piece.

Utilitarian pieces made included jars and pots for preserves, butter, soap, dye, lard, meats, oils, milk, dough, honey, apple butter, and such. There were pitchers, serving bowls, bottles, colanders, flower pots, and dogs. Tiles for drainage, chimney collars and roof tiles also were made to meet local needs. All the Galena area potteries used the same red clay and glazes during their fifty or so years of production. Preserve jars were the most numerous items made, and these were glazed both inside and out.

In 1843, D.A. Sachett and Company established a pottery in Galena. The following year Alfred Suckett established a pottery and soon added other sites. There were several different owners in the next thirty years, but eventually Andrew Jennings controlled the potteries until their demise.

Other areas included several locations in Elizabeth, Illinois where their pottery was characterized by the thinness of its walls, some unglazed examples, and some applied mold work. In Mineral Point, Wisconsin they made utilitarian Galena glazed redwares and several types of complex roof tiles.

**References:** Wayne B. Horney, *Pottery of the Galena Area*, published by author, 1965.

**Collectors' Club:** Collectors of Illinois Pottery and Stoneware, David McGuire, 1527 East Converse Street, Springfield, IL 62703, $15 per year, newsletter.

Churn, 4 1/2" h, miniature, green-amber glaze w/orange spots, applied handles, tooled lines on shoulder, wood lid and dasher, (A) ....................................1430.00

Herb Jar, Dk Brown Luster

**Storage Jar, 5 1/2" h, yellow glaze, $795.**

4 1/2" h, incised lines on shoulder, 19th C, chip on rim
.....................................................................235.00
5 1/4" h.........................................................275.00
5 3/4" h, incised lines on shoulder ........................325.00
Jar, 10" h, wide collar, mottled green and orange glaze, (A) . 413.00
Wall Pocket, 7 3/4" h, tooled and mottled greenish amber glaze w/brown flecks, redware, pr, (A)
.....................................................................220.00

Plate, 10" d, "Mexi-Bolero" pattern and shape, $10.

# W.S. George Pottery Company

## East Palestine, Ohio
## 1909-1955

**History:** W.S. George bought a controlling interest in the East Palestine Pottery Company in 1904 and added a new plant to it called the Continental China Company. In 1909, he changed the name to W.S. George Pottery Company.

He made semi-porcelain dinnerware, plain and decorated table and toilet ware, hotel ware and an assortment of white and decorated articles. Dinnerware was made in a great variety of shapes and designs. Some shapes included Argosy from the late 1920s, Bolero, Lido, and Rainbow from the 1930s, and Del Rio Ochre from 1934.

Though W.S. George died in 1925, his family members carried on. They used a wide variety of marks on their wares. Due to competition from cheap foreign imports, the company went bankrupt in 1955. In 1960, it was reorganized and operated by the Royal China Company of Sebring, Ohio.

### ARGOSY PATTERN

Creamer .......................................................... 4.00
Dish, Cov, 7 1/4" d............................................. 8.00
Gravy Boat, 7 1/2" l ........................................... 5.00
Plate
   6" d............................................................ 2.00
   7" d............................................................ 2.00
   9" d............................................................ 3.00
Platter
   8 3/4" l...................................................... 5.00
   11" l.......................................................... 8.00
   14 3/4" l.................................................... 10.00
Sugar Bowl, Cov................................................. 5.00
Vegetable Bowl, 9" l.......................................... 12.00

### BASKETWEAVE PATTERN

Grill Plate, 10" d, green ..................................... 9.00
Plate, Yellow
   5 1/4" d...................................................... 2.00
   6 1/4" d...................................................... 2.00
   9 1/4" d...................................................... 5.00

### BLOSSOMS PATTERN-LIDO SHAPE

Berry Bowl, 5 5/8" d........................................... 3.00
Plate
   6 1/2" d...................................................... 4.00
   7 1/2" d...................................................... 4.00
   9 1/8" d...................................................... 5.00

### BLUEBIRD PATTERN-DERWOOD SHAPE

Berry Dish, 5 1/2" d........................................... 5.00
Cream Jug, 4 3/4" h, mkd................................... 50.00
Cup and Saucer ................................................. 15.00
Plate
   7 1/4" d...................................................... 15.00
   8 1/4" d...................................................... 12.00
   9 1/4" d...................................................... 15.00
Platter, 10 3/4" l............................................... 30.00
Soup Plate, 7 3/4" d........................................... 15.00
Vegetable Bowl, 8 1/2" l.................................... 20.00

### BLUSHING ROSE PATTERN-LIDO SHAPE

Platter, 11 5/8" l............................................... 10.00
Serving Bowl, 9" d............................................. 8.00

### BOLERO SHAPE

Platter, 10 1/4" d, purple, yellow, and pink florals in center, ribbed border, gilt rim................................ 5.00

### BREAKFAST NOOK PATTERN-LIDO SHAPE

Berry Bowl, 5 1/2" d........................................... 3.00
Casserole, Cov, 9 3/4" H-H ............................... 32.00
Creamer .......................................................... 5.00
Cup and Saucer ................................................. 10.00
Gravy Boat ...................................................... 15.00
Plate
   6 3/4" d...................................................... 5.00
   7 3/4" d...................................................... 10.00
   8 1/2" d...................................................... 12.00
   9 1/4" d...................................................... 10.00
Platter
   9" l.......................................................... 10.00

12 1/2" l..................................................10.00
15 1/2" l..................................................12.00
Soup Plate, 8" sq........................................3.00
Sugar Bowl, Cov........................................10.00
Vegetable Bowl, 9 1/4" l.............................20.00

## CALICO PATTERN
Creamer ....................................................3.00
Cup and Saucer ..........................................2.00
Plate
　6 1/2" d.................................................3.00
　7 1/4" d.................................................3.00
　10 1/4" d...............................................4.00
Platter, 11 3/4" l.......................................15.00
Serving Bowl, 9 1/2" l..................................5.00
Sugar Bowl, Cov.........................................5.00

## CHEROKEE PATTERN
Platter, 15 1/2" l.......................................18.00

## CHERRY BLOSSOM PATTERN
BOLERO SHAPE
　Cup and Saucer ....................................3.00
　Plate
　　6" d..................................................3.00
　　7" d..................................................4.00
　　9" d..................................................6.00
　Serving Bowl, 9" d .................................5.00
　Soup Bowl, 7" d .....................................4.00
LIDO SHAPE
　Berry Bowl, 5 1/2" d................................2.00
　Cup and Saucer ....................................3.00
　Plate
　　6 1/2" d..............................................3.00
　　9 1/4" d..............................................4.00
　Soup Bowl, 6 5/8" d.................................5.00

## DALRYMPLE PATTERN-LIDO SHAPE
Cup and Saucer ..........................................7.00
Plate, 6 3/4" d............................................8.00
Platter, 12" l.............................................15.00
Shakers, Pr................................................8.00

## DOGWOOD PATTERN
Fruit Bowl, 5" d ...........................................4.00
Platter, 9" l..............................................12.00
Soup Bowl, 7 1/2" d......................................6.00

## FIESTA PATTERN
Platter, 14 1/2" l.........................................5.00

## FLOWER RIM PATTERN
Vegetable Bowl, 9 1/4" l.............................10.00

## GEORGETTE PATTERN
Gravy Boat, 8" l x 3" h...............................10.00
Serving Bowl, 10" d....................................15.00

## GOLDEN AUTUMN PATTERN
Cup and Saucer ..........................................6.00

## GRACIA PATTERN-BOLERO SHAPE
Berry Bowl, 5" d........................................10.00
Plate
　6 1/2" d ...............................................12.00
　7 1/4" d ...............................................16.00
　10 1/4" d ..............................................20.00

## HOPALONG CASSIDY DESIGN
Plate, 9 3/8" d, black transfer, "To My Friend, Hoppy,"
..............................................................55.00

## IROQUOIS RED PATTERN
Cup and Saucer ..........................................6.00
Plate
　6 1/4" d ................................................3.00
　7 1/4" d ................................................4.00
　10 1/8" d ...............................................5.00
Platter
　13" l.....................................................8.00
　15 1/2" l...............................................10.00
Soup Bowl, 8" d...........................................5.00
Sugar Bowl, Cov, 3 1/2" h..............................8.00

## MEXI-BOLERO PATTERN
Plate, 6 1/2" d.............................................8.00

## MEXI-LIDO PATTERN
Casserole, Cov, 8 1/2" d...............................40.00
Plate, 10" d, 14.00
Platter, 11 1/2" l........................................10.00

## PEACH BLOSSOM PATTERN-LIDO SHAPE
Plate, 10 1/4" d..........................................10.00
Platter, 11 5/8" l..........................................8.00

## PETALWARE
Bowl, 5" d, coral ..........................................3.00
Cup and Saucer, Demitasse, blue...............24.00
Dish, 5 1/2" d, forest green...........................5.00
Gravy Boat, 8 1/4" l, mint green ..................20.00

**Bowl, 9 1/2" d, orange, purple, and yellow flowers, green leaves, orange molded border, $10.**

Plate
  6 1/2" d
    Pink ...........................................................4.00
    Sapphire Blue.......................................5.00
  7 1/2" d, lt yellow.................................6.00
Platter, 13" l
  Lt green ................................................12.00
  Pink ......................................................10.00
Serving Bowl, 8 1/2" d, pink ...................3.00
Soup Bowl, 7 3/4" d, pink ........................6.00
Sugar Bowl, Cov, 3 1/2" h, yellow...........10.00

## PETIT POINT ROSE PATTERN-DERWOOD SHAPE
Platter, 13" l ............................................8.00
Sugar Bowl, Cov, 4" h.............................7.00

## RADISSON SHAPE
Platter, 14" l, border band of multicolored garden flowers,
  "RADISSON, W.S.GEORGE" mk...........35.00

## SHORTCAKE PATTERN
Berry Bowl, 5 1/2" d..................................5.00
Coffee Service, pot, creamer, cov sugar bowl, 12 cups and
  saucers .............................................125.00
Cup and Saucer ......................................5.00
Gravy Boat, 2 handles............................25.00
Plate
  6 1/4" d...................................................5.00
  9" d.........................................................6.00
  10" d.....................................................10.00
Platter
  11 1/2" l ...............................................10.00
  13 1/8" l................................................10.00
Shakers, Pr, 3 3/4" h...............................12.00
Soup Plate, 8" d.......................................9.00

# Gladding, McBean and Company/Franciscan Ceramics

## Glendale and Los Angeles, California
## 1875-1984

**History:** Charles Gladding, Peter McBean, and George Chambers founded the Gladding, McBean Company in 1875. Using clay from Placer County, California, they made ornamental terra cotta and other building materials. Through rapid expansion, they became one of the largest clay products firms in the western United States by 1926.

Tropico Pottery had been making terra cotta garden pottery and tiles since 1904; it was acquired by Gladding, McBean in 1923, it became the Glendale plant, and the business was expanded. They were known for their tiles all over the country.

With the patenting of a one-fire talc body known as Malinite in 1928, they had the body for their earthenware production in 1934. El Patio was made in twenty colors and more than 103 shapes from 1934-1954. Cups and bowl handles have a distinctive, pretzel-like shape.

"Franciscan" was the trade name used, which was symbolic of California. Coronado was made from 1936-1956 in fifteen colors and more than sixty shapes. These were initially marketed with four place settings in an individual carton and designated starter sets which were exceptionally popular with brides.

The initial hand-painted Franciscan pattern on the El Patio shape was called Padua in 1937 and had six color combinations and 32 shapes. Other decorated dinnerware lines included Del Mar and Mango in 1937, and Hawthorne in 1938. Apple in 1940, Desert Rose in 1942, and Ivy in 1948 had the border design embossed in the mold and then they were hand tinted by decorators. Desert Rose was the most popular underglaze dinnerware pattern.

Gladding, McBean purchased the Catalina line and molds in 1937 and produced that line until 1941. Catalina Rancho was made from those molds. They also produced an extensive line of artware vases and bowls that were marketed as "Catalina Art Pottery" with various glaze combinations.

The Ox Blood glaze by ceramic engineer Max Compton used on Chinese style shapes for Angelino ware from 1938-1942 was produced in periwinkle blue, light bronze, and satin ivory.

A new vitrified body for hotel china was developed in 1939 and used the following year for Franciscan Fine China. The Masterpiece China line made from 1941-1979 featured more than 165 decorative patterns on nine basic shapes. Informal china called Discovery from 1958-1975 was done in a medium weight by a series of designers.

Competition from fine quality Japanese china which was inexpensive appeared in the 1950s, and the company eventually stopped china production in 1979, though the earthenware lines were continued. Due to declining sales, Gladding, McBean sold its Franciscan plant in 1962 to Lock Joint Pipe Company which became Interpace Corporation in 1968.

New patterns continued to be developed in the '60s and '70s including Tulip Time, Pebble Beach, and Hacienda to name a few. Kaleidoscope was produced in solid color glazes. Wall, floor, and decorative tiles continued to be made until 1982.

Franciscan ceramics was sold to Josiah Wedgwood and Sons Ltd. of England in 1979. Production was stopped in Los Angeles in 1984 since the wares were now made in England.

A tremendous variety of marks was used during the years of production.

**References:** Jack Chipman, *Collector's Encyclopedia of California Pottery, 2nd Edition*, Collector Books, 1998; Delleen Enge, *Franciscan Ware*, Collector Books, 1981; Jeffrey B. Snyder, *Franciscan Dining Services*, Schiffer Publishing Ltd.1996.

**Collectors' Club:** Franciscan Collectors Club, 8412 5th Avenue NE, Seattle, WA 98115.

## APPLE PATTERN
Bowl, 8 1/2" d ..........................................42.00
Butter Dish, Cov, 7 3/4" l, (A) ................40.00
Casserole, Cov, 8 1/4" d, (A)...................20.00
Chop Plate, 12" d ....................................85.00
Cup and Saucer, Demitasse ...................65.00
Grill Plate, 11" d, (A)...............................55.00
Milk Pitcher, 6" h.....................................75.00

**Plate, 9 3/4" d, "Apple" pattern, $18.**

Mug, 4 1/4" h, (A) ...................................... 15.00
Pitcher
    6 1/4" h..................................................... 15.00
    9" h........................................................... 135.00
Plate, 10 1/2" d......................................... 25.00
Platter, oval
    12" l........................................................... 40.00
    14" l........................................................... 65.00
    19" l......................................................... 290.00
Relish Dish, 10" l...................................... 48.00
Shakers, pr................................................ 85.00
Tea Set, pot, 5 3/4" h, creamer, cov sugar bowl, (A)
............................................................. 50.00
Trivet, 6" d............................................... 225.00

## ARDEN PATTERN
Cup and Saucer ........................................ 15.00
Gravy Boat ................................................ 65.00
Plate
    6 3/8" d....................................................... 6.00
    8 3/8" d....................................................... 8.00
    10 5/8" d................................................... 15.00
Shakers, Pr................................................ 18.00
Teapot...................................................... 125.00

## AUTUMN PATTERN
Creamer ..................................................... 12.00
Cup and Saucer .......................................... 4.00
Mug, 2 3/4" h ............................................. 17.00
Plate
    6 1/2" d....................................................... 5.00
    10 1/2" d................................................... 14.00
Side Salad Crescent, 8 1/2" l..................... 21.00

## BOUNTIFUL PATTERN
Cup and Saucer ........................................ 10.00

## CAFE ROYAL PATTERN
Cup and Saucer ........................................ 12.00

## CORONADO PATTERN
Creamer, white .......................................... 10.00
Sugar Bowl, Cov, white.............................. 15.00
Vase, 10 1/2" h, satin turquoise................ 115.00

## DEL MAR PATTERN
Butter Dish, Cov ........................................ 18.00

Platter, 13" l x 8 1/4" w, rect ....................... 20.00
Vegetable Bowl, 8 1/4" l x 5 1/2" w, rect. .......... 18.00

## DESERT ROSE PATTERN
Ashtray, 4 3/4" sq .................................... 220.00
Candy Dish, 7" l....................................... 225.00
Cereal Bowl, 6" d ....................................... 15.00
Chop Plate, 12" d ...................................... 55.00
Compote, 4" h ........................................... 75.00
Creamer ..................................................... 28.00
Cup and Saucer ........................................... 9.00
Cup and Saucer, Demitasse ....................... 80.00
Egg Cup, 3 1/2" h ...................................... 35.00
Fruit Bowl, 5 1/4" d .................................... 12.00
Grill Plate, 11" d ...................................... 135.00
Milk Pitcher, 6 1/2" h.................................. 70.00
Pickle Dish, 11" l........................................ 85.00
Plate
    6 1/2" d....................................................... 9.00
    8" d........................................................... 13.00
    9 1/2" d..................................................... 23.00
    10 1/2" d................................................... 20.00
Platter
    14" l........................................................... 35.00
    19" l......................................................... 225.00
Porringer Bowl, 6" d ................................. 130.00
Relish Dish, 12" l, 3 sections.................... 165.00
Salad Bowl, 7 3/4" d................................... 29.00
Serving Bowl
    8" d........................................................... 33.00
    9" d........................................................... 40.00
Soup Bowl, 8 1/2" d.................................... 18.00
Sugar Bowl, Cov ........................................ 18.00
Television Plate w/cup, 13 3/4" l.............. 180.00
Tumbler, 5 1/4" h ....................................... 25.00

## DUET ROSE PATTERN
Bowl, 5" d .................................................... 7.00
Canister, 6 1/2" h ..................................... 135.00
Plate, 6 1/2" d............................................. 6.00

## EL PATIO PATTERN
Bowl, 9" d, aqua ........................................ 30.00

**Carafe, 8 1/2" h, "El Patio" pattern, turquoise glaze, wood handle, $65.**

Chop Plate, 12" d, lt yellow.........................................20.00
Cup and Saucer, aqua..............................................15.00
Platter, 13" l, matte pink.........................................39.00
Teapot, aqua..........................................................95.00

**FIVE FRUITS PATTERN**
Creamer, 4 1/2" h ...................................................50.00

**FORGET-ME-NOT PATTERN**
Cereal Bowl ...........................................................40.00
Cup and Saucer ......................................................30.00
Fruit Bowl ..............................................................30.00
Plate
    8" d................................................................50.00
    10 3/4" d..........................................................47.00

**FRESH FRUIT PATTERN**
Bowl, 9" d .............................................................48.00
Cereal Bowl, 6" d....................................................18.00
Fruit Bowl, 5 1/4" d .................................................15.00
Plate
    6 1/2" d.............................................................8.00
    10 1/2" d..........................................................30.00
Platter, 14 1/2" l ....................................................80.00

**FRUIT PATTERN**
Cereal Bowl ...........................................................15.00
Cup and Saucer ......................................................15.00
Plate
    6 3/8" d............................................................12.00
    10 1/2" d..........................................................15.00

**HACIENDA PATTERN**
Cereal Bowl, 5 1/4" d.................................................7.00
Creamer .................................................................7.00
Plate
    8 1/4" d.............................................................5.00
    10 1/2" d............................................................7.00
Platter, 13" l .........................................................10.00
Soup Bowl, 6 1/4" d ..................................................8.00
Sugar Bowl, Cov.......................................................12.00

**HAWAII PATTERN**
Berry Bowl, 5" d.......................................................3.00
Creamer, 3 3/4" h ....................................................3.00
Cup and Saucer ........................................................5.00
Plate
    6" d..................................................................5.00
    10" d.................................................................6.00

**IVY PATTERN**
Bowl, 8" d .............................................................25.00
Cereal Bowl ...........................................................25.00
Coffeepot.............................................................260.00
Cup and Saucer ......................................................26.00
Gravy Boat with Liner ...............................................72.00
Pitcher, 8" h .........................................................100.00
Plate
    6 1/2" d............................................................12.00
    10" d...............................................................25.00
Platter, 11 1/4" l .....................................................65.00
Salad Bowl
    7" d................................................................49.00

11" d............................................................... 125.00
Shakers, leaf, pr....................................................30.00
Sugar Bowl, Cov .....................................................45.00
Teapot ................................................................310.00
Vegetable Bowl, 8" d...............................................60.00

**MARIPOSA PATTERN**
Cup and Saucer ......................................................95.00
Plate
    6" d .................................................................35.00
    8 1/2" d.............................................................70.00
    9 1/2" d.............................................................75.00
    10 1/2" d............................................................95.00

**MEADOW ROSE PATTERN**
Cereal Bowl, 5 1/2" d..............................................15.00
Cup and Saucer ......................................................13.00

**METROPOLITAN PATTERN**
Cup and Saucer, Demitasse
    Ivory...............................................................35.00
    Ivory and coral ..................................................40.00

**MISCELLANEOUS**
Vase, 11" h, bulbous body, short, flared neck and rim,
    oxblood red.....................................................975.00

**OCTOBER PATTERN**
Cereal Bowl...........................................................15.00
Plate
    8" d.................................................................20.00
    10 7/8" d............................................................30.00
Shakers, pr............................................................45.00

**PLATINUM BAND PATTERN**
Cup and Saucer ......................................................25.00
Plate
    6 3/8" d.............................................................15.00
    8 1/4" d.............................................................20.00

**POPPY PATTERN**
Butter Dish, Cov .....................................................80.00
Chop Plate, 12" d ....................................................75.00
Creamer ................................................................50.00
Cup and Saucer ......................................................40.00
Gravy Boat w/underplate............................................82.00

Cereal Bowl,
7" d, "October"
pattern, $16.

Plate

| | |
|---|---|
| 6 1/2" d | 15.00 |
| 10 1/2" d | 32.00 |

Sugar Bowl ........................................ 30.00

## REFLECTIONS PATTERN
Platter, 14" l, silver gray ............................. 40.00

## RIDGEWOOD PATTERN
Cup and Saucer, Demitasse ........................ 25.00

## ROSSMORE PATTERN
Cup and Saucer ...................................... 20.00

Plate

| | |
|---|---|
| 6 1/2" d | 18.00 |
| 9 1/2" d | 25.00 |
| 10 1/2" d | 30.00 |

## STARBURST PATTERN
Bowl, 8" l, oval ...................................... 22.00
Butter, Cov ........................................... 60.00
Creamer .............................................. 25.00
Cup and Saucer ...................................... 10.00

Platter

| | |
|---|---|
| 13" l | 48.00 |
| 15" l | 40.00 |

Relish Tray, 9" lx 6 1/2" w, 3 section ............. 65.00
Shakers, 4" h, pr .................................... 50.00
Sugar Bowl, Cov ...................................... 35.00
Syrup Pitcher, 5 3/4" h ............................. 65.00
Water Pitcher, 10" h ................................ 130.00

## STRAWBERRY TIME PATTERN
Cup and Saucer ...................................... 15.00
Plate, 10 3/4" d ..................................... 15.00

## TIEMPO PATTERN
Casserole, Cov, 11" H-H, olive green ............. 25.00
Cup and Saucer, olive green ....................... 10.00
Vegetable Bowl, 10" sq, olive green .............. 20.00

## TRIO PATTERN
Cup and Saucer ....................................... 9.00

Plate

| | |
|---|---|
| 6" sq | 6.00 |
| 8" sq | 8.00 |
| 9 1/2" sq | 12.00 |

**Casserole, Cov, 11" H-H, "Tiempo" pattern, dk green glaze, $50.**

## TULIP TIME PATTERN
Cup and Saucer ....................................... 3.00
Plate, 10 3/4" d ...................................... 5.00

## TWILIGHT ROSE PATTERN
Cup and Saucer ...................................... 15.00

## WESTWOOD PATTERN
Bowl, 6" d ........................................... 38.00
Creamer, 3" h ........................................ 42.00
Cup and Saucer ...................................... 45.00

Plate

| | |
|---|---|
| 6" d | 38.00 |
| 7" d | 24.00 |
| 10" d | 45.00 |

## WHEAT PATTERN
Cup and Saucer, Harvest Brown .................... 24.00
Plate, 10" d, Harvest Brown ....................... 28.00
Platter, 12" d, Summer Tan ...................... 40.00

# Gonder Ceramic Arts, Inc.

## South Zanesville, Ohio
## 1941-1957

**History:** Lawton Gonder purchased the former Zane Pottery Company after Florence Pottery burned in 1941. He started his pottery with many of the Rum Rill molds he purchased and brought with him from Florence, where he was manager.

After World War II, Gonder was able to make a higher priced art pottery, and he hired excellent sculptors and artists to design his pieces. Gonder is also known for numerous innovations in pottery making at his establishment. He developed flambe glazes for commercial use. He was the first to make a gold crackle glaze. He also used the Chinese crackle glazes on his pottery that he duplicated from old Chinese patterns. He developed "Volcanic Glazes" where two glazes were utilized with one melting over the other for unusual effects.

With the increasing demands for pottery after the war, Gonder put on two additions to his building in 1946. He opened a separate plant to make ceramic lamp bases that was called Elgee Pottery. They operated for eight years and then were destroyed by fire. He put on another addition after the fire and moved all operations to South Zanesvile. Gonder shipped most of his lamps to the Bradley Lamp Company in Chicago where they were assembled and sold with the Bradley label.

When foreign imports started to hurt the pottery business, Gonder converted to the production of ceramic tile in 1955. After two years, he sold the company but continued to work as a consultant to Allied Tile Company before he retired.

Gonder's art pottery figures included elephants, cats, and panthers, in addition to an assortment of vases and ginger jars with Chinese glazes and shapes. Other glazes used were Mother of Pearl, Coral, Ebony Green, Royal Purple, Wine Brown, Red Flambe on vases and such, and Gold Crackle on figures and vases.

Additionally he made cookie jars, candleholders, bookends, ewers, ashtrays, planters, and figural lamp bases.

During the early '50s, a line of dinnerware called "La Gonda" was introduced with square shaped pieces. Gonder designed this line, and the handles were shaped like Gs.

Many Gonder examples had the double glaze with a pink interior. Most pieces were marked "GONDER" or "GONDER USA" in a variety of ways. Some pieces also had paper labels. Most examples also were numbered.

**References:** Ron Hoopes, *The Collector's Guide and History of Gonder Pottery*, L-W Book Sales, 1992.

**Collectors' Club:** Gonder Collectors, Carol Boshears, 917 Hurl Drive, Pittsburgh, PA 15236-3636, quarterly newsletter, $10 per year; Gonder Newsletter, P.O. Box 4263, N. Myrtle Beach, SC 29597, quarterly newsletter, $8.

Basket, 8" h, figural conch shell base, overhead handle, brown over yellow glaze, #674.................10.00
Bowl, 8" d, lobed body, closed rim, blue-green ext, peach int, #H-29 .............................................. 10.00
Creamer, 3 1/2" h, brown drip, yellow ground, #P-33...30.00
Ewer
    5 3/4" h, lobed body, lt blue glaze ........................... 10.00
    11" h, gold finish, #J-25.........................30.00
    14" h, figural seashell, starfish on base, cream, #508
    ..................................................................65.00
Figure
    5 1/2" h, kneeling coolie, yellow, Kongeling Peron ..45.00
    8" h, standing Chinese man, brown glaze
    ..................................................................15.00
    19" l, reclining panther, green, #210 ......................200.00
Ginger Jar, Cov, 8" h, turquoise crackle glaze, pink int
    ..................................................................95.00
Lamp, 12" h x 10" w, lavender blue figural seagulls, matte white frame ......................................... 110.00
Mug, 5" h, La Gonda, green volcanic glaze, unmkd.....10.00

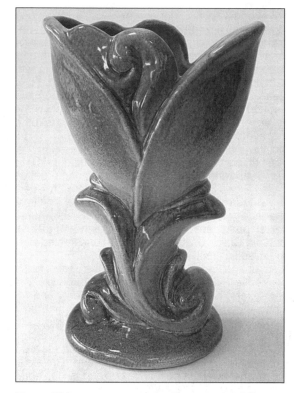

**Vase, 9" h, green ground w/brown speckling, salmon int, #H-68, $65.**

Pitcher, 7 1/2" h, gold crackle glaze, #H-73 .................50.00
Planter
    4 1/2" h, sq shape and ft, maroon glaze w/cream border drip ......................................................... 15.00
    6 1/2" h x 8 1/4" w, figural basket w/overhead handle, relief molded leaves on body, orchid glaze, #H-39
    ..................................................................15.00
Teapot, 7" h, streamline shape, gloss brown and blue-green spatter finish, #P-31.................................25.00
Tea Set, pot, 6 1/2" h, creamer, 4" h, cov sugar bowl, 4" h, aqua ground, brown speckle and brush finish ....... 100.00
Vase
    5 1/2" h, figural swimming swan, gray ext, pink int, #E-44.....................................................35.00
    6" h
        Fluted panel shape w/molded ivy vase, yellow glaze w/pink spray, pink int, #E-66 ......................... 18.00
        Twisted shape, lavender glaze, #E-64 ............... 30.00
    6 1/2" h, baluster base, flared top, molded leaf scroll handles, caramel drip ext, pink int. #E-67 ................ 45.00
    7" h
        Figural seashell fan, gray ext, pink int, #E-5 ....... 40.00
        Narrow waist, flared and lobed top, gray with turquoise flecks, pink int, #E-6 ................................ 25.00
    8" h
        Rect, relief of standing flamingo, gray ext, pink int
        ..............................................................33.00
        Swan shape, green ext, pink int.........................55.00
    8 1/2" h
        Lobed, flared body, offset bamboo type handles, circ base, gold crackle glaze ............................. 52.00
        Molded overlapping leaves, 2 sm curled handles, purple glaze, #H-17 ........................................ 50.00
        Squat base, tapered neck, twist handles from rim to base, brown over pink glaze......................... 30.00
        Triple loop handles, dk green ext, pink int, #H-75
        ..............................................................40.00
    9" h
        Bottle shape, black striated glaze over white ground, #1210....................................................... 70.00
        Dbl twisted loop handles, pink luster ext, pink int, #H-5 50.00
        Rect, relief molded crane and reeds on side, white glaze ........................................................ 10.00
        Trumpet shape
            Triple loop handles at sides, aqua ext w/yellow, green, and pink blended shades, pink int, #H-81 65.00
            Two handles, relief molded flowers and leaves, white........................................................ 60.00
    9 1/4" h, trumpet shape w/leaf molded base, pink glaze, #J-64 ..................................................50.00
    9 1/2" h
        Figural butterfly, pearlized gloss gray ext, pink/gray int 180.00
        Stylized intertwined leaves, blended chartreuse
        ..............................................................30.00
    11 1/2" h
        Fan shape, molded overlapping peacock feathers, mauve glaze, #K-15......................................30.00
Overlapped wings, pink int, blue ext with pink splashes, pr ....................................................... 45.00

# Griffen, Smith and Hill

## Phoenixville, Pennsylvania
## 1879-1889

**History:** In 1879, Beerbower and Griffen became Griffen, Smith and Hill and specialized in majolica. The two Griffen brothers were technicians, Smith did designs and glazes, and Hill was the master potter. The following year the factory closed for a short time due to a worker's strike, and Hill left. Though they became Griffen, Smith and Company, they still maintained the GSH monogram and marked their pieces in that manner.

Many European artisans were employed at the factory to produce their Etruscan majolica examples. At the World's Industrial and Cotton Centennial Exposition in New Orleans in 1884 and 85, they exhibited approximately 150 examples including their most famous Shell and Seaweed pattern. With their success at the exposition, they received numerous new orders and expanded their operations. George Hartford of the Great Atlantic and Pacific Tea Company decided to give majolica as a premium with purchases of baking powder. He became GSH's largest customer. Another firm gave GSH examples with the purchase of tea.

By 1886, the financial picture had changed. The high cost of all the hand decorating and the low prices that GSH charged in the bulk sale to Hartford caused the firm to be less profitable. There was also less demand for majolica examples. In 1889, Smith withdrew from the concern and J. Stuart Love became a partner in Griffen, Love and Company.

Griffen, Smith and Hill's Etruscan majolica designs reflected the Victorian interest in marine and plant life. Begonia, maple, and oak leaves, ferns, vegetables, fruits, and a wide assortment of flowers all appeared on majolica pieces. Shell and Seaweed, their most famous pattern, was done in shades of pink, brown, gray and blue with green seaweed accents. Shells and dolphins also appeared on examples. Oriental motifs included thorns, bamboo and bird designs. Some human and mythological figures were used.

All sorts of shapes were employed including butter pats, compotes, napkin plates, bowls, humidors, cheese bells, paperweights, sardine boxes, syrup jugs, cuspidors, umbrella stands, and a variety of pitchers. Interiors of hollow ware pieces usually were pink, but some were pale blue or green. Dinner, tea, and coffee services were made in Cauliflower, Bamboo, and Shell and Seaweed patterns.

"GSH" was the earliest mark used. By 1880, some pieces were marked "GSH" with two concentric circles and "Etruscan Majolica" between them. Other marks also were used.

**References:** Marilyn G. Karmason with Joan B. Stacke, *Majolica*, Harry N. Abrams, 1989; M. Charles Rebert, *American Majolica, 1850-1900*, Wallace-Homestead, 1981.

**Museums:** Chester County Historical Society, West Chester, PA; Historical Society of Phoenixville, PA; Philadelphia Museum of Art, PA.

**Reproduction Alert:** 20th century reproductions using "Etruscan Majolica" marks are available in the marketplace.

Bread Tray, 13 3/4" l, shell and seaweed design, brown, cream, pink, and green, rim repair, (A) .................. 600.00
Butter Pat
    Geranium pattern ..................................................... 70.00
    Shell and seaweed pattern ................................... 275.00

Compote, 10" d, classical design, lt tan glaze ........... 350.00
Creamer, 4 1/4
    Corn design, yellow and green, (A) ...................... 250.00
    Hawthorne design, pink and green, (A) ................ 225.00
Cup and Saucer
    Albino shell and seaweed pattern, (A) .................... 50.00
    Bamboo design, brown, green, and yellow, pink int, (A)
    .................................................................... 175.00
    Cauliflower design, green and cream, (A) ............ 170.00
    Shell and seaweed design, green, brown, and pink, (A)
    .................................................................... 150.00
Dish
    8 3/4" l, figural Begonia leaf, green center, tan border with red splashes ..................................................... 165.00
    12 1/4" l, leaf shape, green leaf w/yellow edge, pink rim, brown branch handle, imp mk ........................... 235.00
Jug, 7 3/4" h, relief molded baseball or soccer designs, gray-brown monochrome, rim and spout repair, (A)
.................................................................... 150.00
Mug, 3 1/2" h, Pink Int
    Pineapple design, green and yellow, (A) ............... 325.00
    Water lily design, green and yellow, (A) ................... 50.00
Mustache Cup and Saucer, shell and seaweed, brown, pink and green, (A) ..................................................... 200.00
Pickle Dish, 8 1/2" l, daisy design, yellow, pink, and green, rim chip, (A) ......................................................... 125.00
Pitcher
    4 1/2" h, bamboo pattern ....................................... 135.00
    6" h, shell and seaweed design, imp mk ............... 195.00
    6 3/4" h, coral design, green, pewter lid, (A) .......... 325.00
    7" h, fern design, green ferns, cream ground, pink int, (A)
    .................................................................... 750.00
    8" h
        Green, pink, and tan molded leaves, grapevines, and flowers, molded green branch handle, dk pink int, imp mk ........................................................... 525.00
        Sunflower design, yellow flower, cobalt ground, pewter lid, (A) ........................................................... 450.00
        Wild rose design, butterfly spout, (A) ............... 225.00
Plate
    6" d, shell and coral design, brown, pink, and green, mkd, pr, (A) ......................................................... 185.00
    7 7/8" d, pink outlined green leaf in center, tan basketweave border, imp mk ................................. 255.00
    8" d
        Cauliflower design, green and cream, (A) ......... 375.00
        Pond lily design, green and yellow, (A) ............. 275.00

**Teapot, 7" h, green, brown, and yellow designs, white ground, imp mk, $695.**

Relief of classical figures in center, raised border of squares, maroon, imp mk ............... 50.00

8 1/4" d, shell and seaweed design, tan, gray, and pink, imp mk ............... 240.00

9" d, green maple leaves, pink ground, (A) ........... 275.00

Pink outlined tan star in center, green leaf border, imp mk ............... 425.00

9 1/4" d, shell and seaweed design, green, brown, and pink, (A) ............... 200.00

Salad Comport, 5" h x 9" d, daisy design, yellow and pink flowers, lavender ground, (A) ............... 375.00

Tea Set

Pot, 5 1/2" h, creamer, cov sugar bowl, majolica, green and yellow cauliflower pattern, stains and chips, (A) ............... 550.00

Pot, 6 1/2" h, creamer, 3 1/4" h, cov sugar bowl, 5 1/2" h, majolica, albino shell and seaweed pattern, (A) ............... 100.00

Tray, 8" l, green maple leaf, pink border, cobalt handle, (A) ............... 225.00

1907-1911

# Grueby Pottery

## Boston, Massachusetts
## 1897-1921

**History:** W.H. Grueby worked at Low Art Tile Works from 1880-90, when he started a plant in Revere, Massachusetts to make architectural faience. In 1894, Grueby-Faience Company formed to make glazed bricks, tiles, and architectural terra cotta.

In 1897, Grueby-Faience was incorporated to make art pottery. Grueby made the glazes and was general manager. William Graves was the business manager, and George Kendrick was the designer and craftsman of the early artware designs. They won medals for their thrown artwares with excellent shapes and unique glazes in Paris, St. Petersburg, and St. Louis.

Grueby used a lot of flower and leaf designs that were done freehand. Pieces were modeled by hand. The veining of the leaf was added as a thin piece of clay to the body of a vase. Cucumber Grueby green was the most successful of the matte glazes, but blue, yellow, brown, gray, and ivory were also used. The Grueby green was imitated by Van Briggle, Rookwood, Hampshire, Teco, and Pewabic to name a few. Grueby also made lamp bases for other companies.

The business was divided into architectural faience and art pottery. In 1907, the Grueby Pottery Company was incorporated in Massachusetts. The Grueby Faience and Tile Company was organized in 1909 for production of architectural wares that utilized Grueby's glazes and methods. Graves became head of Grueby when Grueby returned to

architectural faience, but the last artwares were made in 1911.

After the pottery burned in 1913, Grueby Faience and Tile was rebuilt to continue architectural faience. James Curley joined the firm in 1919 and improved its economic position. The company was sold to C. Pardee Works of Perth Amboy, New Jersey, and Pardee moved Grueby to New Jersey in 1921.

Grueby's artwares were marked, but sometimes the marks were obscured by the heavy glaze. Paper labels were used with the company's lotus trademark. Pieces after 1905 were marked Grueby Pottery.

**References:** Dr. Susan Montgomery, *The Ceramics of William H. Grueby*, The Arts and Crafts Quarterly Press, 1993.

**Museums:** Museum of Fine Arts, Boston, MA; New Orleans Museum of Art, LA; The Newark Museum, NJ.

Bookend, 6" h, brown, green, and blue pine trees in landscape cuenca tile end, hammered copper frame, pr, (A) ............... 8,800.00

Bowl

3 3/4" h x 4 3/4" d, coupe shape, ftd, mottled matte green ext, gloss int, (A) ............... 495.00

5" d, flared rim, sculpted and applied leaves on ext, matte green and lt green glaze, imp mk, (A) ............... 4675.00

6" h x 8 1/4" d, squat shape, applied leaves alternating with buds, matte green glaze, Florence Liley, (A) ............... 5,500.00

7" d , flared floriform shape, tooled flower buds, curdled matte green glaze, gloss green int, Ruth Erickson, (A) ............... 2,750.00

Cabinet Vase, 3" h, squat shape, leathery matte oatmeal glaze, base altered, (A) ............... 825.00

Candlestick, 8 1/2" h, corset shape, bulbous top, tooled and applied leaves, textured blue-green matte glaze, paper label, (A) ............... 2,530.00

Floor Vase

15 1/2" h, bulbous, sm flared rim, tooled and applied leaves alternating w/yellow buds, textured matte green glaze, "incised WP" mk, (A) ............... 66,000.00

23 1/4" h, stovepipe neck, tooled and applied yellow outlined green leaves on body, yellow and green buds on neck, (A) ............... 27,500.00

Jardiniere, 5 3/4" h, curdled matte green glaze, "stamped Grueby Pottery" mk, (A) ............... 1,760.00

Paperweight, Scarab Shape

3" l, French blue matte glaze, chips, (A) ............... 660.00

4" l, white curdled glaze, (A) ............... 880.00

Vase

4 1/2" h, wide base, narrow rim, curdled matte green glaze, gloss brown int glaze, "imp Grueby Pottery Boston USA 170" mk, (A) ............... 880.00

5 1/2" h, bulbous shape and ribbed, collar neck, frothy matte green glaze, (A) ............... 1,430.00

7" h

Bulbous base, flared neck and rim, thick, leathery matte green glaze, (A) ............... 1,870.00

Tapered shape w/2 open handles, green and blue gloss glaze, stamped mk, (A) ............... 578.00

7 1/2" h, bulbous shape

Applied round leaves on base, celadon semi-matte glaze, (A) ............... 1,980.00

Curled leaves and tall buds, dk green textured glaze, restored rim chip, (A) ............... 2,420.00

**Vase, 12 1/2" h, incised design, matte green glaze, imp mk, (A), $27,500.**

Lobed opening, tooled and applied leaves w/alternating buds, matte blue-green glaze, restored rim chip, (A) .................................................. 1,980.00

Three sculpted and applied leaves on sides, matte green glaze, mkd, (A) ............................... 2,310.00

Swollen cylinder shape w/5 alternating leaf and bud motifs, matte green glaze, Gertrude Priest, "Grueby Faience Boston, U.S.A." mk, c1905, restored chips, (A) ............................................................. 1,955.00

7 3/4" h, floriform rim, tooled and applied broad leaves, textured matte green glaze, (A) ...................... 2,640.00

8" h, swollen cylinder shape, long sculpted and applied leaves, matte green glaze, imp mk, (A) .......... 4,125.00

8 3/4" h, matte green tooled leaves, mustard ground, Ruth Erikson, "incised RE/9/22/37" mk, (A) .... 5,500.00

9" h

Bottle shape, tooled and applied leaves, matte med green glaze, (A) ...................................... 11,000.00

Ovoid, floriform rim, tooled and applied yellow iris in green leaves, matte green ground, Ruth Erikson, chips, (A) ...................................................... 9,900.00

9 1/2" h, bulbous base, long flared neck, sculpted and applied leaves on base, tooled stems, buds at top, matte green glaze, imp mk, (A) ...................... 4,675.00

10" h, ovoid shape, tooled and applied leaves, curdled ochre glaze, chips, mkd, (A) ........................... 3,850.00

11 1/4" h

Scrolled handles on shoulder, tooled and applied leaves, curdled matte green glaze, (A) ...... 2,420.00

Swollen cylinder shape, everted rim, tooled and ochre centered applied yellow, red, and green daffodils, leathery matte green glaze, "Grueby Pottery" mark, restored chips, (A) ................................... 11,000.00

11 1/2" h, ovoid, tooled and applied leaves and daffodils, leathery matte green glaze, Marie Seaman, (A) ................................................................... 7,150.00

12" h, gourd shape, smaller rim, tooled and applied leaves, matte green glaze, G.P. Kendrick, restored rim chips, (A) ...................................................... 22,000.00

12 7/8" h, bulbous oviform w/flared rim, tooled and applied daffodil blooms, buds, and leaves, mottled matte green glaze, "imp Grueby Faience Company, Boston, U.S.A.," c1904, (A) ......................... 10,350.00

13" h, sculpted and tooled overlapping leaves on base, tooled vert stems w/open blossoms, matte green glaze, sgd "W. Post," (A) ............................... 8,800.00

13 3/4" h, bottle shape, leathery matte green glaze, rim chip, (A) ....................................................... 4,675.00

20" h, bulbous shape, carved yellow and red water lily blossoms and curled leaves, thick matte green glaze, (A) ........................................................... 22,000.00

Vessel

4 1/2" h, curdled beige-ochre glazed, (A) ............. 660.00

7" h, squat shape, tooled and applied leaves w/alternating yellow buds, pulled matte green glaze, chips, "Grueby Faience" mk, (A) ............................... 9,350.00

8 1/4" h, ball shaped body, flared rim, horiz ridges, matte green glaze, restored rim chip, (A) ................ 3,850.00

1941

# Haeger Pottery

### Dundee, Illinois
### Macomb, Illinois
### 1871-Present

**History:** For four generations, Haeger Pottery has remained a family owned business. It was started in Dundee, Illinois by David Haeger, who made bricks and tiles in 1871. Edmund, his son, took over in 1900 and introduced art pottery in 1914. Haeger hired Martin Stangl, who had helped create Fulper Pottery in Flemington, New Jersey. By 1918, Stangl returned to Fulper and eventually bought the pottery.

Haeger claims to be the world's largest art pottery. The first piece was the Classic Greek Vase Design #1. Haeger pottery is characterized by lustrous glazes, bright colors, and soft glowing pastel colors. For the 1934 Chicago World's Fair, Edmund built a complete working ceramic factory for exhibit.

Joseph Estes, the son-in-law, became general manager in 1938 and expanded and diversified the product line. He introduced the Royal Haeger line of artwares and lamp bases. A second factory was opened in Macomb, Illinois that still produces a ceramic line for florists.

Royal Arden Hickman was the chief designer from 1938-1944, and he was hired to design the Royal Haeger line. His designs were flamboyant and sensual. There was a tremendous variety of pieces made since there was a huge demand for these pieces. There were pitchers, vases, figurines, planters, lamps, candleholders, jardinieres, bowls, leaf plates, ashtrays, and such. The panther from 1941 came in three sizes in a hi-gloss ebony finish. Hickman's pieces bore the "Royal Haeger by Royal Hickman" mark until he left in 1944 to start his own pottery.

In 1939, the Royal Haeger Lamp Company was established for the production of a wide variety of lamps, and this proved very successful. Royal Haeger figurines were used for the lamps with the styling carried through in the design of the lamp shades and finials. Many of these lamps and shades were designed by Hickman. They were made at the Dundee location from 1939-69, and then moved to Macomb in 1969 when they took over the Western stoneware plant. Both figural and non-figural lamps and TV lamps were made with only a paper label.

During the 1930s and 40s, there was a wide variety of finishes on Royal Haeger pieces. There were the brilliant high gloss glazes as well as other glazes, and a wide variety of colors. "Stick ups" were used which were small handmade flowers and leaves appliquéd to the body of pieces with liquid slip.

Eric Olsen became the chief designer for The Haeger Potteries, Inc. in 1947 and stayed until 1972. He designed ninety percent of the Haeger artware and lamps. His creations were lifelike and graceful. One of his most famous designs was the red bull in ebony and Haeger red from 1955.

Royal Haeger examples were numbered with an R-1 for the first piece done by Royal Hickman. The lower the number, the older the design. A wide variety of marks was used over the long years of production.

The Studio Haeger line started in 1947-8 period had a variety of different finishes. There pieces were marked with an "S" prefix in addition to the number.

Joseph Estes became president of the pottery in 1954. The Royal Garden Flower-ware line with a body called "porceramic" resembled porcelain more than pottery. The line was designed by Elsa Ken Haeger from 1954-63. The examples had soft matte finishes and muted glazes. Marks had an "RG" prefix and started with #1. Vases, planters, low bowls, candlesticks, figurines, and jardinieres were made.

In 1979, the fourth generation of the family took over at Haeger. Nicholas became president of Royal Haeger Lamp Company in Macomb, and Alexandra became president of Haeger Potteries of Dundee. By 1984, Nicholas was president of Haeger Potteries of Macomb, and Alexandra was president of Haeger Industries, Inc. and on the Board of Directors.

Dinnerware at Haeger was made as early as 1919 with hexagonal plates, salad bowls with matching plates, and mayonnaise bowls. An assortment of teawares was made along with children's feeding bowls, plates, and mugs. From 1929-33, Haeger dinnerwares were done in blue, yellow and green.

Rare examples of Royal Haeger included the Portable Electric Fountains from 1941, a line of music boxes, and clocks.

**References:** David D. Dilley, *Haeger Potteries Through the Years*, L-W Books Sales, 1999; Lee Garman and Doris Frizzell, *Collecting Royal Haeger*, Collector Books, 1989; Joe & Joyce Paradis, *The House of Haeger 1914-1944: The Revitalization of American Art Pottery*, Schiffer Publishing Ltd.1999.

**Collectors' Club:** Haeger Pottery Collectors Club of America, Lanette Clarke, 5021 Toyon Way, Antioch, CA 94509

**Museums:** Haeger Museum, Dundee, IL.

Ashtray, 13 1/2" l, oval, green drip glaze, Royal Haeger ........................................................................15.00

Bowl, 14" l, molded overlapping leaves, brown agate blended glaze, #R988, Royal Haeger ......................35.00

Bud Vase
    10" h, lt brown drip over dk brown body...................10.00
    15" h, brown, lime green, and yellow volcanic glaze ........................................................................60.00

Console Set, bowl, 18" l, shell form, 2 vases with kneeling nudes holding cornucopia, ivory, Royal Haeger ........................................................................165.00

Dish, 18 1/4" l, 3 section, fish shape, peach glaze, "863-HUSA" mk ................................................................40.00

Figure
    4 3/4" h, mouse, brown .............................................38.00
    5" l, snail, brown.......................................................38.00
    7" h, standing horse, white with foamy mottling, #R103, Royal Haeger .................................................30.00

Planter, 7 1/4" h, yellow glaze, $120.

Planter, 5" h, white raised letters and figures, pink ground, $25.

12" l, panther, chartreuse.........................................35.00
15 1/2" h, seated cat, Mandarin orange.................135.00
20" h, "Rendezvous," pale salmon pink, white base ........................................................................82.00
20" l, crouching fox, matte white glaze ...................65.00
Flower Holder, 7 1/2" h, figural young girl, opening at waist, lt blue ........................................................................15.00
Lamp
    8" h x 11" l, figural gazelle, dk green.....................65.00
    10" h x 11" w, figural dancing harlequins, dk green . 75.00
Pitcher, 18 1/2" h, ebony cascade, #408.....................85.00
Planter
    4" h
        Paneled body, flared circle at top, yellow glaze, #3764 ........................................................................18.00
        Seated Teddy bear, tan .....................................20.00
    6 1/2" h, leaping gazelle, green .............................35.00
    11" h x 16" l, donkey, gray, gold-brown accents.......50.00
Vase
    6" h, rect shape, volcanic glaze, #4083 ..................35.00
    6 1/2" h
        Fan shape, scalloped rim, turquoise ground, silver overlay ......................................................295.00
        Grecian urn shape, matte ivory glaze ................10.00
    7" h, lobed body, raised circle design, green glaze, #3480 ........................................................................20.00
    7 1/2" h, bulbous base, flared slender neck, Fern agate, green and brown agate .....................................20.00
    8" h
        Hourglass shape, flared rim, frosted matte green glaze ......................................................125.00
        Sunflower, mustard yellow base shaded to brown, R647 ........................................................................35.00
    21 1/2" h, pebble white glaze, #R1743....................65.00

**Vase, 6" h, matte black glaze, $40.00.**

**Planter, 8 1/2" h, turquoise glaze, "Royal Haeger R386" mk, $85.**

# Hall China Company

## East Liverpool, Ohio
## 1903-Present

**History:** Robert Hall established the Hall China Company in 1903, when the East Liverpool Potteries Company was dissolved. Robert Taggert Hall, his son, took over when Hall died one year later. Mostly toilet sets, whiteware, and jugs were made.

Robert Hall was experimenting continuously to perfect a non-lead glazed china with a single fire process that was economical to produce. He was successful in 1911, when he made whiteware that was strong, non-porous, and craze-proof. At first they concentrated on institutional wares, and then made their Gold Decorated Teapot line.

By 1930, they needed a new plant which then required numerous expansions during the 1930s and '40s. Hall introduced decal dinnerwares, kitchenwares, refrigerator wares, teapots, and coffeepots. The company is still in business. Decorating was done either by hand painting or transferring decals or prints. A wide variety of marks was used on Hall china. Most pieces had identifying back stamps.

Hall began decal pattern dinnerware in 1936 with its Autumn Leaf breakfast set. Many different patterns and several shapes were used during the years of Hall's production. Autumn Leaf was first used in 1933 on mixing bowls and other kitchenwares. It was developed as a premium line for the Jewel Tea Company. New items were added and older pieces discontinued until 1976. A large assortment of kitchenwares, accessory pieces, and even a clock was made. Other companies using Autumn Leaf decals included Columbia, Crown, Harker, American Limoges, Paden City, and Vernon. Autumn Leaf dinnerware was made into the mid-1970s.

Blue Bonnet was made for Standard Coffee Company from the early 1950s until the mid 1960s, Crocus started in the mid-1930s, Mums dated from the late 1930s, Orange Poppy was made for the Great American Tea Company from 1933 to the 1950s, Pastel Morning Glory dates from the late 1930s, Red Poppy was a premium for Grand Union Tea Company from the mid-1930s to the mid-1950s, and Silhouette had an all black decal from the 1930s and was made for Cook Coffee and Standard Coffee. Taylor, Smith, and Taylor and Harker also used the silhouette decals.

J. Palin Thorely designed Monticello and Mount Vernon for the Sears Harmony House label from 1941-1959. Eva Zeisel designed the Hallcraft Line for Hall China in the early 1950s. She also designed kitchenwares.

The Medallion Kitchenware line was introduced in 1932 in ivory and lettuce. Other colors and shapes were added as were decals. Hall continued to introduce numerous kitchenware lines during the following twenty years.

For Refrigerator Ware, Hall made lines for retail sales, as well as exclusive designs for General Electric, Sears, Hotpoint, Montgomery Ward, and Westinghouse. Water bottles or servers, leftovers or refrigerator boxes, and covered butters were made, plus additional shapes for the retail market.

Hall's first teapots were part of its institutional line. The most popular ones are from the Gold Decorated Line. A wide assortment of teapots was made in all sorts of shapes. Novelty teapots from 1938 were made in automobile, basket, birdcage, donut, football, and basketball shapes. Aladdin dates from 1939. Coffeepots also were made in numerous shapes. Some were sold to Enterprise, Tricolator, and Westinghouse. Hall made the coffeepot bodies for the Drip-O-Lator by the Enterprise Aluminum Company.

Additional wares included beer sets, punch sets, Tom and Jerry sets, watering cans, advertising and promotional items, some items for hotels and restaurants, and china bodies for lamps.

**References:** Jo Cunningham, *The Autumn Leaf Story*, Hafa-Production, 1976; Harvey Duke, *Superior Quality Hall China*, ELO Books, 1977; _____ *Hall 2*, ELO Books, 1985; Margaret and Kenn Whitmyer, *The Collector's Encyclopedia of Hall China, Second Edition*, Collector Books, 1997.

W. A. Woodard Memorial Library

**Collectors' Clubs:** Hall Collectors Club, Virginia Lee, P.O. Box 360488, Cleveland, OH 44136; Eva Zeisel Collectors Club, 22781 Flamingo Street, Woodland Hills, CA 91364.

**Newsletter:** *Hall China Connection*, P.O. Box 401, Pollock Pines, CA 95726; *Hall China Encore*, quarterly, Kim Boss, editor, 317 North Pleasant Street, No. YP, Oberlin, OH 44074-1113.

### BLUE BOUQUET PATTERN
French Baker, 7 3/4" d ................................................. 15.00

### BROWN EYED SUSAN PATTERN-E-STYLE
Cup and Saucer .............................................................. 12.00
Fruit Bowl, 5 1/4" d ........................................................ 7.00
Plate, 9 1/4" d .............................................................. 12.00
Platter, 13 1/2" l ........................................................... 20.00
Salad Bowl, 9" d ............................................................ 25.00
Vegetable Bowl, 9" d ...................................................... 25.00

### CAMEO ROSE PATTERN
Creamer ...................................................................... 12.00
Cup and Saucer .............................................................. 12.00
Plate
    7 1/4" d ................................................................. 8.00
    8" d .................................................................... 9.00
    9" d .................................................................... 9.00
    10" d .................................................................. 12.00
Platter, 11 1/2" l ........................................................... 25.00
Sugar Bowl, Cov ............................................................ 20.00
Vegetable Bowl, 10 1/2" l ................................................ 30.00

Coffeepot, 8 1/2" h, "Target" shape, red and black Dutch decal, white ground, "The Enterprise Aluminum Company, Massillon Ohio" mk, $75.

Mixing Bowl, 9" d, "Crocus" pattern, $22.

### CROCUS PATTERN
Berry Bowl, 5 1/2" d ....................................................... 5.00
Bowl
    6" d .................................................................... 28.00
    7 1/2" d ................................................................ 35.00
    8 5/8" d ................................................................ 40.00
    9 1/4" d ................................................................ 45.00
Coffeepot, "Medallion" .................................................... 79.00
Creamer, 3 1/2" h .......................................................... 50.00
Cup and Saucer .............................................................. 25.00
French Baker, 8" d .......................................................... 88.00
Jug, 6 1/2" h, #3 Ball ................................................... 235.00
Plate
    8 1/4" d ................................................................ 20.00
    9 1/4" d ................................................................. 8.00
    9" d .................................................................... 25.00
Platter
    11 1/2" l ............................................................... 25.00
    13 3/4" l ............................................................... 30.00
Soup Plate, 8 1/2" d ....................................................... 25.00
Soup Tureen, Cov, 9" H-H ............................................... 475.00
Sugar Bowl, Cov, 5" h ..................................................... 75.00

### DRIP-O-LATOR COFFEEPOTS
Meltdown design, red bottom, silver stripes, w/strainer
................................................................................ 59.00
Rounded Terrace, 7 1/2" h, "Pasture Rose" decal
................................................................................ 25.00
Viking, 8" h, "Flamingo" decal ........................................ 30.00
Waverly design .............................................................. 70.00

### FLORAL LATTICE PATTERN
Batter Bowl, 6 3/4" d ...................................................... 80.00
Pitcher, 4 1/2" h ............................................................ 45.00

### HEATHER ROSE PATTERN
Salad Bowl, 9 1/8" d ....................................................... 30.00

### KITCHENWARE
Canister Set, 7 1/2" h, "Radiance," "Flour, Tea, Coffee, Sugar," cobalt ground, set of 4 ............................. 475.00
Casserole, 7 1/4" d, Blue Willow pattern ....................... 10.00
Jug, 5" h, "Five Band," green ........................................ 45.00

### MONTICELLO PATTERN
Cup and Saucer .............................................................. 6.00
Gravy Boat, w/undertray ................................................ 16.00
Plate, 6 3/8" d ............................................................... 8.00
Platter, 13 1/2" l ........................................................... 20.00
Soup Plate, 9 3/4" d ....................................................... 10.00
Vegetable Bowl, 9 1/4" l ................................................ 12.00

### MOUNT VERNON PATTERN
Berry Bowl, 5" d ............................................................ 7.00
Bowl, 9 1/4" l ............................................................... 24.00
Creamer ...................................................................... 15.00
Cup and Saucer .............................................................. 11.00
Plate
    6" d .................................................................... 4.00
    10" d .................................................................. 11.00
Platter, 13" l ............................................................... 19.00

Soup Plate, 7 3/4" d......................................................14.00
Sugar Bowl, Cov............................................................15.00
Vegetable Bowl, 9" l.....................................................13.00

**ORANGE POPPY PATTERN**
Berry Bowl, 5 1/2" d........................................................3.00
Casserole, Cov, 9 1/2" H-H, oval...............................40.00
Creamer .........................................................................25.00
Cup and Saucer ............................................................25.00
Custard.............................................................................8.00
Jug
   6 1/2" h, #3 Ball.....................................................125.00
   Radiance.................................................................45.00
Mixing Bowl
   7 1/4" d...................................................................45.00
   8" d.........................................................................45.00
   8 3/4" d, Radiance ...............................................48.00
Plate, 7" d......................................................................10.00
Platter, 13" l...................................................................15.00
Pretzel Jar......................................................................35.00
Teapot
   6 1/4" h...................................................................95.00
   8" h, donut...........................................................395.00
Sugar Bowl .....................................................................35.00
Vegetable Bowl, 9" d....................................................15.00

**PASTEL TULIP PATTERN**
Bowl, 10 1/4" l................................................................39.00
Cup and Saucer ............................................................22.00
French Baker, 9" d........................................................39.00
Plate
   6" d...........................................................................5.00
   9" d.........................................................................22.00

**PINK MORNING GLORY-PATTERN**
Gravy Boat .....................................................................45.00
Mixing Bowl, Radiance
   7 1/4" d...................................................................25.00
   8 1/4" d...................................................................39.00
Plate
   7" d.........................................................................22.00
   8" d.........................................................................25.00
   9" d.........................................................................25.00

**Refrigerator Ware-Casserole, Cov, 9" l, Westinghouse, yellow, $40.**

**PINK MUMS PATTERN**
Berry Bowl, 5 1/2" d......................................................12.00
Cereal Bowl, 6" d..........................................................29.00
Creamer
   Medallion style ....................................................40.00
   New York style .....................................................40.00
Cup and Saucer ............................................................25.00
Plate
   6" d...........................................................................7.00
   7" d.........................................................................22.00
   9" d.........................................................................25.00
Platter, 13" l...................................................................45.00
Soup Plate, 9" d............................................................29.00
Vegetable Bowl, 9 1/4" d.............................................45.00

**POLKA DOT PATTERN**
Casserole, Cov
   6" d.........................................................................20.00
   8 3/4" d...................................................................20.00
   10" H-H, 28.00
Pitcher, 5 1/4" h.............................................................68.00

**REFRIGERATOR WARE**
**General Electric**
   Leftover, 5 3/4" d x 3 1/4" h, gray ext,
     yellow int ..........................................................17.00
   Water Server, blue..............................................75.00

**Hotpoint**
   Dish, Cov
     4" sq, orange.....................................................25.00
     4 3/4" sq, dk gray .............................................30.00
     5 3/4" sq, green.................................................27.00
     6 3/4" d, green...................................................28.00
     7 3/4" d, maroon................................................32.00
     8 3/4" d, yellow..................................................35.00
     9" w x 3 1/4" h, dk yellow, "Made Exclusively By Hall China Co. For Hotpoint Refrigerators" mk
     ...........................................................................45.00
   Water Server, cork stopper, blue ......................90.00

**Montgomery Ward**
   Leftover, Cov, 8 1/2" l x 4 1/2" h, gray.............35.00
   Water Server, blue..............................................80.00

**Westinghouse**
   Butter Dish, Cov,
     7" l, "Hercules," oval, green..........................20.00
     7 1/2" l x 4" h, "Hercules," rect, yellow
     ...........................................................................40.00
   Casserole, Cov
     Plain, delphinium..............................................40.00
   Casserole, Open, ribbed, yellow........................30.00
     Ribbed, yellow...................................................40.00
   Leftover
     7 1/2" l x 4" h, "General," orange..................40.00
     "Hercules," oval, ivory .....................................35.00
   Water Bottle, 9 1/2" h, "General," delphinium .........75.00

**RED POPPY PATTERN**
Berry Bowl, 5" d............................................................11.00
Coffeepot, 8" h..............................................................40.00
Cream Pitcher, 4 3/8" h................................................12.00

**Pitcher, 8 1/2" h, "Rose Parade" pattern, blue body, $75.**

Mixing Bowl, 6 1/4" d, "Silhouette" pattern, $10.

Cup and Saucer ........................................................ 18.00
Dish, Cov, 4 3/4" h ................................................. 45.00
Mixing Bowl, 6 1/8" d, 7 3/4" d, 9" d, set of 3 ............... 95.00
Pitcher, 6 1/2" h ..................................................... 45.00
Plate
    7" d ..................................................................... 18.00
    9" d ..................................................................... 20.00
Salad Bowl, 9" d ..................................................... 24.00
Soup Plate, 8 1/2" d ............................................... 18.00
Sugar Bowl, Cov ..................................................... 25.00
Vegetable Bowl, 9" d .............................................. 25.00

**ROSE PARADE PATTERN**
Casserole, Cov, 10" H-H, tab handles ........................ 34.00
Custard, 3 1/2" h .................................................... 70.00
Jug, 5 1/2" h .......................................................... 45.00
Mixing Bowl
    6 1/8" d ............................................................... 15.00
    9" d ..................................................................... 20.00
Pitcher, 5" h .......................................................... 43.00
Shakers, Pr ........................................................... 45.00
Teapot, 6" h .......................................................... 95.00

**ROSE WHITE PATTERN**
Bowl, 6 1/4" d ......................................................... 28.00
Grease Jar, Cov, 6" H-H ......................................... 35.00
Jug, 7 1/2" h .......................................................... 95.00
Teapot, 5 1/2" h ..................................................... 92.00

**ROYAL ROSE PATTERN**
Bowl, 9" d .............................................................. 35.00
Drip Jar, Cov, 5 3/4" d ............................................ 40.00
Pitcher, 7 3/4" h ................................................... 125.00

**SERENADE PATTERN**
Berry Bowl, 5" d ...................................................... 6.00
Coffeepot, Step Down ............................................. 49.00
French Baker, 9" d .................................................. 29.00
Gravy Boat ............................................................ 29.00
Plate, 9" d ............................................................. 15.00
Platter, 13" l .......................................................... 32.00

**SHAGGY TULIP PATTERN**
Bean Pot .............................................................. 275.00

**SILHOUETTE PATTERN**
Baker, 8" d, fluted .................................................. 65.00
Bowl, 9" d .............................................................. 35.00

Plate, 9 1/8" d, "Springtime" pattern, $9.

Fruit Bowl, 5 1/2" d .................................................. 12.00
Jug
    5" h, #3 Medallion ................................................. 25.00
    6 1/2" h, #3 Ball ................................................. 195.00
    8" h, Simplicity ................................................... 235.00
Mixing Bowl, Medallion
    6 1/4" d ............................................................... 10.00
    7 1/2" d ............................................................... 20.00
    8 1/2" d ............................................................... 22.00
Mug, 4 1/4" h .......................................................... 25.00
Shakers, Pr, bulbous .............................................. 65.00

**SPRINGTIME PATTERN**
Berry Bowl, 5 1/2" d .................................................. 6.00
Cup and Saucer ..................................................... 12.00
Creamer ............................................................... 12.00
Gravy Boat ............................................................ 24.00
Jug, 6 1/2" h, #3 Ball ............................................ 115.00
Plate
    6" d ..................................................................... 5.00
    7" d ..................................................................... 7.00
    9 1/4" d ............................................................... 10.00
Platter, 13 1/4" l ..................................................... 24.00
Soup Bowl, 8 1/4" d ................................................ 15.00
Sugar Bowl, Cov ..................................................... 20.00
Vegetable Bowl, 10 1/2" l ........................................ 22.00

## TEAPOTS

Airflow
  6 cup, Indian red ..................................... 195.00
  8 cup, warm yellow and gold.......................95.00
Aladdin
  Black and gold, oval infusor .......................... 95.00
  Canary and gold, round infusor............................ 75.00
  Maroon and gold, round infusor ..................... 95.00
Albany, emerald and gold ................................. 50.00
Automobile
  Canary ...................................................... 600.00
  Maroon......................................................625.00
Baltimore, maroon and gold ............................... 55.00
Basketball, canary ........................................... 750.00
Bellevue, 2 cup, delphinium ................................ 65.00
Boston
  3 cup, yellow and gold .................................. 45.00
  6 cup, maroon and gold ................................ 125.00
Cleveland, mustard with gold butterflies.....................75.00
Donut, canary ................................................. 350.00
Hollywood, ivory and gold .................................. 35.00
McCormick, maroon, with infusor ........................ 40.00
Melody, 6 cup, ivory.....................................225.00
Parade, canary and gold .................................... 35.00
Philadelphia, 6 cup
  Turquoise and gold ...................................... 55.00
  Warm yellow and gold................................... 60.00
Star, emerald ................................................... 85.00
Surfside, emerald and gold ................................ 165.00
Twinspout
  Black and gold ........................................... 110.00
  Canary and gold.......................................... 110.00
Windshield, Camelia
  Gold dots ................................................... 75.00
  Gold trim ................................................... 35.00

## TRI-CO-LATOR COFFEEPOTS
Coffee Queen, 7 1/2" h, green....................25.00

## TULIP PATTERN
Casserole, Cov, 9" d.....................................60.00

## WILDFIRE PATTERN
Creamer ......................................................... 20.00
Cup and Saucer ................................................ 18.00
Gravy Boat ...................................................... 38.00
Mixing Bowl
  5 1/2" d....................................................... 15.00
  7 1/2" d........................................................32.00
  9" d ............................................................ 24.00
Plate
  7" d ............................................................ 18.00
  9" d ............................................................ 18.00
Platter
  11" l ........................................................... 32.00
  13" l ...........................................................38.00
Soup Bowl, 8 1/2" d ......................................... 15.00
Sugar Bowl, Cov..............................................29.00
Tid-Bit, 3 tier ..................................................55.00

Vegetable Bowl
  9 1/4" d ....................................................... 38.00
  10 1/4" l ...................................................... 45.00

## WILD ROSE PATTERN
Casserole, Cov, 11 1/2" d.................................45.00
Pitcher, 7 1/2" h ............................................... 95.00

## EVA ZIESEL DESIGNS
### Arizona Pattern
  Platter, 17" l ................................................. 50.00
  Salad Bowl, 14 1/2" d ..................................... 36.00

### Bouquet Pattern-Classic Shape
  Ashtray ....................................................... 10.00
  Creamer........................................................22.00
  Gravy Boat ................................................... 49.00
  Platter, 13" l, lug handle ................................. 30.00
  Salad Bowl, 14 1/2" d ..................................... 49.00
  Teapot, 6 cup .............................................. 155.00
  Vegetable Bowl, 8 3/4" sq................................ 29.00

### Buckingham Pattern
  Bowl, 12 3/4" d.............................................. 33.00
  Creamer ...................................................... 15.00
  Soup Bowl, 9" d ............................................ 19.00
  Sugar Bowl, Cov ........................................... 25.00
  Vegetable Bowl, 8 3/4" sq................................ 33.00

### Caprice Pattern
  Creamer........................................................17.00
  Fruit Bowl, 5 3/4" d .......................................... 8.00
  Platter, 12 1/4" l ............................................ 32.00

### Century Fern Pattern
  Plate, 6" d ..................................................... 5.00
  Sugar Bowl, Cov, 4 1/2" h................................ 25.00
  Vegetable Bowl, 11 1/4" l x 8 1/4" w, divided .......... 40.00

### Fantasy Pattern
  Bowl, 6" d..................................................... 20.00
  Cup and Saucer............................................. 10.00
  Plate
    6 1/2" d...................................................... 5.00
    8 1/2" d...................................................... 6.00
    11" d ......................................................... 11.00
  Platter
    15" l x 10" w, lug handle ................................ 30.00
    17 1/2"l x 1" w, lug handle ................................ 35.00

### Harlequin Pattern
  Berry Bowl, 5 3/4" d .......................................... 8.00
  Cereal Bowl, 6" d ........................................... 15.00
  Creamer........................................................26.00
  Cup and Saucer............................................. 12.00
  Plate
    6" d .......................................................... 6.00
    8 1/2" d ..................................................... 12.00
    11" d ......................................................... 22.00
  Platter, 15" l ................................................. 40.00

### Parfait Pattern
  Cereal Bowl, 6" d ............................................. 8.00

**Pinecone Pattern**

    Bowl, 14" l x 10 1/2" w .............................................39.00
    Cup and Saucer, Demitasse ..................................55.00
    Gravy Boat, 6" h.....................................................36.00
    Platter, 15" l x 9 3/4" w .........................................39.00

**Spring Pattern**

    Platter, 13" l ............................................................25.00

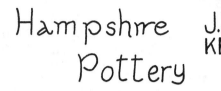

Bowl, 5 1/2" d, molded floral design on shoulder, matte green glaze, (A), $210.

# Hampshire Pottery

## Keene, New Hampshire
## 1871-1923

**History:** James Taft and James Burnap established the pottery to make flower pots. Before they started, there was a fire, and they rebuilt. In 1874, they acquired another pottery that they used to make redware. One pottery was used for jugs, pitchers, churns, spittoons, water kegs, and such, while the other made earthenware hanging vases, flower pots, cuspidors, florist's ware, and Rockingham teapots.

Thomas Stanley joined the pottery from England in 1879 and introduced a majolica type ware for pitchers, tea sets, mugs, and vases. The corn pattern was one of their most popular patterns. Under the direction of Wallace King in 1882, they produced a line of Royal Worcester type ware with a muted ivory ground on souvenir and specialty ware such as plates, rose bowls, pitchers, bonbon dishes and such. Some items were decorated in the underglaze technique being used for Rookwood's Standard ware.

When Cadmon Robertson joined Hampshire in 1904, he was responsible for a huge variety of matte glazes including their matte green glaze used on a line of art pottery examples such as vases, bowls, flower holders, candlesticks, clock cases, and lamp bases.

After King retired and Robertson died, Taft stopped production in 1914 and sold the firm to George Morton from Grueby in 1916. Morton expanded the business, but closed it in 1917 due to the war, and he returned to Grueby. After the war he made white china for hotels and restaurants. From 1919-21 he made mosaic floor tiles. Due to competition, the pottery closed in 1923.

Some Hampshire pieces were marked, and some paper labels were used.

**References:** Marilyn G. Karmason with Joan B. Stacke, *Majolica*, Harry Abrams, 1989; Joan Pappas and Kendall Harold, *Hampshire Pottery Manufactured by J.S. Taft and Company, Keene, New Hampshire*, Crown Publishers, 1971.

**Museums:** Chrysler Museum, Norfolk, VA; Colony House Museum, Keene, NH; National Museum of History and Technology, Smithsonian Institution, Washington, DC; New Orleans Museum of Art, LA.

Bowl

    4" d, emb panels of overlapped artichoke leaves, matte mottled brown, sage green, and olive glazes, (A) .............................................................413.00

    10 1/2" d, flat shape, matte green w/raised lt green flowerhead, "imp Hampshire Pottery and M" mk .............................................................750.00

Bud Vase, 6 1/4" h, serpent handles, matte green glaze, (A) .............................................................303.00

Candlestick

    5 1/2" h, handled, matte lavender-pink glaze w/gray streaks, "incised Hampshire Pottery, M/78" mk, (A) .............................................................495.00

    7 3/4" h, chamber stick shape, matte green glaze .............................................................410.00

Creamer, 4" h, side pour spout, matte green glaze, "imp Hampshire" mk, (A)....................................130.00

Dresser Tray, 8" l x 6 1/2" w, pink florals, gold trim, cream ground, "gold Mt. Mansfield," "Hampshire Pottery, Keene, N.H." mk .............................................................110.00

Inkwell, 3" h x 4" d, 3 circ openings, dk matte green glaze, unmkd, (A) .............................................................220.00

Ewer

    5 1/2" h, transfer printed view of Longfellow's home, lt yellow ground w/black and brown running accents, (A) 35.00

    9 1/2" h, wide base, matte green glaze, (A)..........550.00

    10" h, relief molded flowerheads, matte blue glaze .............................................................795.00

Mug, 5 1/4" h, multicolored transfer print of windmill, emb leaves, beige ground, (A) .......................................20.00

Pitcher

    4" h, side pour, loop handle, matte green glaze, "raised Hampshire, M 60" mk, (A) .................................187.00

    6" h, bulbous body, pedestal base, curved handle, dk matte green glaze, "imp JST & Co. Keene NH" mk, (A) .............................................................275.00

    7 1/2" h, emb band of leaves on rim, matte green glaze, (A) .............................................................150.00

    8 1/4" h, emb stylized leaf design, curled stem handle, matte cerulean glaze w/aqua and steel blue mottling, "incised Hampshire Pottery, M 86" mk, (A) .............................................................1,210.00

    9 1/2" h, tapered cylinder shape, emb stylized palm trees on sides, matte green glaze, "incised Hampshire Pottery, M 81" mk, (A).............................................467.00

Plate, 6 1/2" d, Royal Worcester style, oyster white center, green border, gilt edge................................................50.00

Tankard, 9" h, raised horiz ribbing top and base, applied handle w/thumblift, matte green glaze, (A) ...........143.00

Teapot, 4 1/2" h, w/insert, HP florals, lt pink ground, black borders, handle, and knob, "imp Hampshire" mk, (A) .............................................................605.00

Toothpick Holder, 2" h, figural emb ear of corn, gloss caramel glaze, "imp JST & Co." mk, (A) ......................330.00

**Vase, 6" h, matte green glaze, (A), $350.**

Vase

2 7/8" h, flattened sq shape w/inverted rim, brown over matte green curdled glaze, "imp M circle" mk, (A) .................................................................... 288.00

3 1/2" h, swollen tapered body w/shoulder, matte green glaze, imp mk, (A) ............................................. 275.00

5" h, swollen body, short collar, molded Greek key design on shoulder, matte green glaze, (A) ................... 413.00

5 1/8" h, melon shape, maroon, salmon-pink, and yellow roses, gold accented green shaded stems and leaves, matte ivory ground, "stamped Hampshire/JS Taft/Pottery" mk, (A) ......................................................... 193.00

5 1/2" h, bulbous base, flared neck and rim, matte blue glaze, imp mk, (A) ............................................... 286.00

5 3/4" h, baluster form w/flared lip, relief molded corn and husks on sides, matte dk green glaze, (A) .................................................................... 770.00

6 3/4" h, ovoid, closed rim, emb broad leaves, green and blue glaze, "incised *Hampshire Pottery*" mk, (A) .................................................................... 825.00

7" h

Molded vert leaves and stems and buds, matte green glaze, (A) ....................................................... 715.00

Ovoid shape, incised vert panels, cerulean blue mottled glaze, gray streaks, "incised Hampshire Pottery, M/157" mk, (A) ........................................ 660.00

Shouldered form, matte green glaze, (A) .......... 357.00

8" h, cylinder shape, rolled rim, matte yellow glaze .................................................................... 900.00

8 3/4" h

Emb floral design on neck, oblong panels, volcanic style mottled sea green glaze w/cobalt accents on cerulean-steel blue ground, "incised Hampshire Pottery, M 68" mk, (A) ................................. 3,300.00

Ovoid, short neck, relief of stylized tulips and stems, matte teal green glaze w/drip, "incised Hampshire Pottery, M 8" mk, (A) ..................................... 935.00

9" h, squat base, straight neck, flared rim, matte green and blue glaze, (A) ......................................... 1,210.00

9 3/4" h, trumpet shape, matte cocoa brown glaze, mottled base, "incised Hampshire Pottery, M/107" mk, (A) .................................................................... 413.00

10 1/2" h, urn shape, rect handles, matte green glaze, (A) .................................................................... 880.00

11" h, figural bag w/figural bow at pinched neck, matte green glaze, "imp Hampshire, M" mk, (A) ......... 770.00

12" h, tapered cylinder shape, short, flared rim, matte blue and green glaze w/black and white accents, (A) .................................................................... 660.00

14" h, slender neck, flared crimped rim, matte green glaze .................................................................... 600.00

Vessel, 5 1/4" d, squat shape, emb swirls, matte brown glaze, "imp Hampshire" mk, (A) ........................ 230.00

# Harker Pottery Company

**East Liverpool Ohio**
**1840-1930**

**Chester, West Virginia**
**1931-1972**

**History:** Harker Pottery Company started in East Liverpool, Ohio in 1840 to make everyday wares. When Benjamin Harker Senior came from England, he first sold his clay to James Bennett and other potteries. He decided to use his own clay and make pottery, and that was the beginning of the oldest continually run pottery in the United States. For more than one hundred years, the Harker and Boyce families were involved with pottery in East Liverpool, Ohio and much later, in Chester, West Virginia.

John Goodwin was hired to run the pottery and teach Harker's sons, George S. and Benjamin, Jr. the pottery business. When Ben Sr. retired, he sold the property to his sons. Over a period of years, many American potters worked at Harker for a time and eventually opened their own establishments.

From 1840-46, there was no recorded name for the firm, and they made yellowwares and Rockingham pieces. In 1846 and until 1851, the Harker sons were joined by James Taylor as a partner and made yellowwares and Rockingham ware that were impressed and embossed with their marks. The firm was Harker, Taylor, and Company. For a time the firm was called Etruria Pottery, and pieces were so marked.

From 1851-1877, there was a confusing collection of partners and firm names when the brothers split up and rejoined. Artisans continued to come from England to work at the factory. When George died in 1864, David Boyce, his brother-in-law, ran the pottery until George's sons were old enough to take over. During this period, they continued the utilitarian yellowwares that were either glazed or decorated with colored bands or sponging. Mugs, bowls, nappies, milk and baking pans, plates, and such were made. Rockingham ware examples were hound-handled pitchers, Toby mugs, spaniel dogs, ewers, spittoons, mugs, and basins.

In 1877, all interests were sold to George's sons by W.W. Harker and his brother Hal. By 1881, they began to make whiteware table, cooking, and sanitary wares with clay imported from other areas instead of the yellowwares and Rockingham with their own buff-burning clay.

Utilitarian everyday wares continued to be Harker's strong point. Early shapes were given names such as Bedford, Dixie, Cable, Waverly, Lorain, Fairfax, and such. Sanitary wares consisted of ewers, basins, toothbrush holders, shaving mugs, feeders for invalids and infants, and such. Transfer printing was used to decorate the early whitewares, while colored and metallic embellishments followed later.

The George S. Harker Company was incorporated as Harker Pottery in 1898. Before this time there had been a series of floods when the Ohio River was too high, and transportation problems when the river was too low. When they needed to expand, they purchased the National China plant and a Homer Laughlin factory. When more room was needed, they looked across the river in Chester, West Virginia where conditions were more ideal since they were safe from floods and had more expansion room. Many other factories had already left East Liverpool. In 1931 Harker purchased the old Knowles pottery but retained the East Liverpool address and mark. They had also created the Columbia China Company one year earlier with its trademark Statue of Liberty in color and monochrome.

During the Depression years, Harker tried to keep its workers busy as best they could. Their wares were sold in department stores and used as premiums for businesses. Columbia survived until 1955. Its most famous pattern was Autumn Leaf for the Jewel Tea Company.

Harker usually applied its decals over the glaze. Since the best decals came from Germany and were sold through catalogs, other potteries sometimes duplicated Harker patterns. Some decals were exclusive for Harker.

A tremendous amount of souvenir pieces, as well as advertising giveaways, were made at Harker. Ashtrays were some of the favorite souvenir pieces. Plates were frequent advertising pieces, as well as pitchers, refrigerator jugs, jars, and plaques. Numerous giftwares were also made.

Harker continued to expand after World War II and kept introducing new shapes. Sales were excellent in the early '50s, but it was possible to see problems ahead. The production and personnel costs continued to rise. Plastics were increasingly popular. Cheaper imports were forcing American potteries to struggle for market share, and lower Japanese tariffs helped to kill the American dinnerware industry.

Harker kitchenwares that were introduced in 1926 with the HotOven line, Bakerite in 1935 and SunGlow in 1937, were very popular with collectors. With the expansion into dinnerwares, there were floral designs, and Colonial Lady, the silhouette pattern. Harker's Gadroon from 1949 was the most versatile and recognized shape with its rope-like pattern on the edge of pieces.

What Harker is best known for is the patented intaglio process that George Bauer brought from Europe. The white design appeared to be carved out of the colored surface. Bauer came to Harker in 1939 and patented his process in 1941. At first this process was used on blue and white called Cameoware with the Dainty Blue pattern. The process was expanded to include other colors, decorations, and shapes, and was used on dinnerwares, too. Dainty Flower was used on almost every Harker shape. Pink and yellow were made, but were less popular. White Rose was made for Montgomery Ward and marked "Karv-Kraft." Other intaglio lines included Wild Rice, Vine, Wheat, Engraved Rooster, and Cock-o-the Morn.

Paul Pinney worked at Harker from 1940 until its closing and supervised the colors for Cameo and the other intaglio

lines made. During the 1950s Russel Wright made his first patterned dinnerware line for Harker called White Clover that came in four colors.

Stone china was introduced in the '50s and '60s. The heavy gray stoneware body was dipped in solid color pastels and white. Stone china also was used with the intaglio process and with decals for decoration.

Harker Pottery was sold to the Jeanette Glass Company in 1969. To revitalize the company they tried a revival of the Rockingham wares and made hound handle pitchers, Rebekah-at-the Well teapots, and Toby mugs.

In 1972, Harker Pottery closed. For a time the plant was used by Ohio Valley Stoneware, but burned down in 1975.

**References:** Neva W. Colbert, *The Collector's Guide to Harker Pottery U.S.A.*, Collector Books, 1993; William C. Gates and Dana E. Ormerod, *The East Liverpool Ohio Pottery District: Identification of Manufacturers and Marks*, Ann Arbor, 1982.

**Museums:** Museum of Ceramics, East Liverpool, OH.

## AMY PATTERN

| | |
|---|---|
| Bowl, 5" d | 16.00 |
| Cake Plate, 11" H-H | 10.00 |
| Cup and Saucer | 10.00 |
| Custard Cup, 2" h x 3 1/4" d | 5.00 |
| Fruit Dish, 6" d | 5.00 |
| Jug, 6 1/2" h, "Hotoven-Carnivale" pattern, green, gold, and rust, white ground, black trim | 50.00 |
| Pie Plate | 12.00 |

Plate

| | |
|---|---|
| 7" d | 4.00 |
| 9" d | 4.00 |

## BAMBOO PATTERN-TAN

Plate

| | |
|---|---|
| 7 1/4" d | 3.00 |
| 10 1/4" d | 5.00 |
| Platter, 11 1/2" l | 8.00 |

## BERMUDA PATTERN-ROYAL GADROON SHAPE

| | |
|---|---|
| Creamer | 6.00 |
| Cup and Saucer | 5.00 |
| Gravy Boat | 8.00 |

Plate

| | |
|---|---|
| 6 1/4" d | 5.00 |
| 8" sq | 8.00 |
| Platter, 12 1/4" l | 15.00 |
| Sugar Bowl, Cov | 8.00 |

## BIRDS AND FLOWERS PATTERN

| | |
|---|---|
| Platter, 10 5/8" H-H | 10.00 |

## BRIDAL ROSE PATTERN

| | |
|---|---|
| Creamer | 6.00 |
| Cup and Saucer | 12.00 |

Plate

| | |
|---|---|
| 8 1/4" sq | 6.00 |
| 10 1/2" d | 7.00 |

Platter

| | |
|---|---|
| 12 1/4" l | 20.00 |
| 16" l | 20.00 |
| Serving Bowl, 9" d | 15.00 |
| Sugar Bowl, Cov | 6.00 |

## CALICO TULIP PATTERN
Batter Bowl, 9 1/2" d.................................50.00
Casserole, Cov, 8 1/2" d...........................10.00
Crock, 2 1/2" h.......................................10.00
Pitcher, Cov, 4 1/2" h..............................40.00
Plate, 8" d............................................20.00
Serving Plate, 12" H-H ...........................18.00

## CHESTERTON PATTERN-GADROON SHAPE
Bowl, 6 5/8" d, gray ...............................3.00
Creamer, 2 5/8" h, gray ..........................6.00
Gravy Boat, gray ...................................15.00
Plate
    6 1/2" d, gray................................2.00
    9 1/2" d, teal, set of 4 ....................16.00
    10" d, gray.....................................8.00
Platter, 11" H-H, gray.............................8.00
Shakers, Pr, gray ..................................10.00
Sugar Bowl, Cov, 4 3/4" h, gray...............8.00
Teapot, 6 1/2" h, gray, Royal Gadroon .......59.00

## COLONIAL LADY PATTERN
Cake Plate, 12" H-H ..............................10.00
Custard, 2 1/2" h x 3 1/2" d......................8.00
Gravy Dish............................................20.00
Pie Plate, 9" d.......................................8.00
Plate, 10" d...........................................5.00
Platter, 11 1/2" l ...................................10.00

## CORINTHIAN PATTERN
Vegetable Bowl, 8 3/4" d ........................10.00

## COTTAGE PATTERN
Teapot...................................................89.00

## COUNTRY COUSINS PATTERN
Platter, 11 1/4" l, tan .............................8.00
Tid-Bit Dish, 10 1/4" d, tan......................7.00

## DAINTY FLOWER PATTERN
Cake Plate, 12" H-H, blue and white...........28.00
Casserole, Cov, 9" d
    Blue and white .................................40.00
    Pink and white..................................50.00
Custard, 2" h, blue and white ..................8.00
Pitcher, Cov
    6 1/2" h, blue and white ...................78.00
    6 3/4" h, pink and white....................98.00
    8" h, pink and white..........................100.00
Plate
    6" d, blue and white, Swirl shape.........5.00
    8" d, blue and white .........................12.00
Platter
    10 3/4" H-H, pink and white ..............25.00
    13 7/8" l
        Pink and white ...........................28.00
        Swirl mold, blue and white............20.00
Rolling Pin, blue and white .....................100.00
Teapot, 7" h, blue and white ...................85.00
Trivet, 6 1/2" d, blue and white ...............68.00
Vegetable Bowl, 9" d, swirl mold, blue and white .........35.00

Vegetable Bowl, 9 3/8" H-H, "Deco Dahlia" pattern, red and black, $6.

## DECO DAHLIA PATTERN
Cake Plate, 12" H-H................................24.00
Cake Server ..........................................20.00
Custard Cup, 2" h, set of 6 ......................25.00
Plate, 9" d.............................................8.00
Platter, 11" l.........................................25.00
Relish Tray, 8 1/4" l................................50.00

## DOGWOOD PATTERN
Cake Set, master plate, 11" H-H, 6 plates, 6" d ..........25.00
Plate, 10" d............................................4.00
Platter, 11 1/2" l .....................................6.00

## GODEY PATTERN
Berry Bowl, 5 1/2" d................................8.00
Cereal Bowl, 6 1/4" d..............................12.00
Creamer ................................................16.00
Cup and Saucer ....................................12.00
Plate
    6 1/4" d ..........................................8.00
    8" sq..............................................14.00
    10 1/4" d .........................................15.00
Platter, 12" l..........................................22.00
Serving Bowl, 9 1/2" l..............................12.00
Soup Plate, 8 1/2" d................................15.00
Sugar Bowl, Cov ....................................26.00
Vegetable Bowl, 9" d...............................24.00

## IVY PATTERN-INTAGLIO
Plate
    7 1/4" d ..........................................7.00
    10" d ..............................................9.00

## IVY PATTERN-ROYAL GADROON SHAPE
Bowl, 6 3/4" H-H.....................................20.00
Platter
    13 1/2" l...........................................20.00
    15 3/4" l...........................................30.00

## LISA PATTERN
Bowl, 11 1/4" d ......................................45.00

## MALLOW PATTERN
Cake Plate, 12" d, w/lifter .......................48.00
Casserole, Cov, 6 1/2" d..........................65.00
Cereal Bowl, 6 1/2" d...............................18.00

Cup and Saucer .................................................... 12.00
Custard Cup, 2" h ............................................... 15.00
Fruit Bowl, 5 1/2" d ............................................. 12.00
Plate
    6" d ................................................................ 6.00
    7" d .............................................................. 10.00
    8 1/2" sq ...................................................... 19.00
    9 1/8" d ......................................................... 8.00

## MODERN TULIP PATTERN
Cake Lifter ........................................................... 15.00
Creamer, 4" h ........................................................ 5.00
Custard Cup, 4" d ................................................... 9.00
Mixing Bowls, 3 1/4" d, 4" d, 5" d, 6" d, set of 4 ........... 15.00
Pie Plate, 9" d, "Bake Rite" ................................... 20.00
Pitcher, 7 1/2" h .................................................. 25.00
Plate
    6 5/8" sq ........................................................ 3.00
    11 1/2" d ...................................................... 20.00
Platter, 13 1/2" l ................................................. 24.00
Refrigerator Jug, 8" h ........................................... 30.00
Tray, 7 1/2" l ...................................................... 20.00

## MONTEREY PATTERN
Cake Plate, 12" H-H ............................................. 38.00

## ORIENTAL POPPY PATTERN
Cake Lifter ........................................................... 29.00
Casserole, Cov, 6 1/2" d ........................................ 25.00
Plate, 9" d ........................................................... 15.00

## PETIT POINT PATTERN
Berry Bowl, 5 1/2" d ............................................... 5.00
Bowl, 9" d, rose design .......................................... 12.00
Cake Plate, 11 1/2" d ............................................ 25.00
Carafe, Cov, 6" h .................................................. 35.00
Casserole, Cov, 9" d ............................................. 26.00
Cup and Saucer ..................................................... 8.00
Pie Plate
    8" d, rose design ............................................ 12.00
    10" d, rose design .......................................... 20.00
Pitcher, Cov, 8" h ................................................. 62.00
Plate
    9" d ................................................................ 5.00
    10" d ............................................................. 15.00
Platter, 11 5/8" l ................................................. 15.00

## PROVINCIAL TULIP PATTERN
Tidbit, 10 1/4" d, white intaglio design, lt green ground
.......................................................................... 18.00

## RED APPLE PATTERN
Cake Plate, 12" H-H, Apple II ................................. 30.00
Casserole, Cov, 9 1/2" d, Apple II .......................... 40.00
Cake Lifter, Apple II ............................................. 34.00
Mixing Bowl, 9" d .................................................. 32.00
Pie Plate, 10" d, Apple II ....................................... 25.00
Pitcher, Cov, 10" h, Apple II, red loop knob
.......................................................................... 98.00
Platter, 12" l, Apple II .......................................... 22.00
Teapot, 6 3/4" h, Apple II ....................................... 60.00
Tray, 12 1/4" H-H, Apple I ...................................... 35.00

## REFRIGERATOR WARE
Pitcher, 4 3/4" h x 10 1/4" l, black Kelvinator transfer, white
    ground .......................................................... 78.00

## ROCAILLE PATTERN
Plate
    6" d ................................................................ 3.00
    10" ................................................................. 4.00

## ROCKINGHAM DESIGNS
Mug
    4 1/2" h, Jolly Roger, blue-green ...................... 29.00
    4 3/4" h, Davy Crocket, brown .......................... 30.00
    5" h, hound handled, dk brown .......................... 35.00
Pitcher, 8 1/4" h, hound handle, dk brown .............. 50.00
Teapot, 8 1/4" h, Rebecca at the Well .................... 40.00

## ROLLING PINS
15" l
    Amy pattern .................................................. 90.00
    Apple II pattern ........................................... 140.00
    Cottage pattern ........................................... 175.00
    Dainty Flower pattern, blue and white cameo...... 100.00
    Deco Dahlia pattern, red ................................ 158.00
    English Ivy pattern ....................................... 148.00
    Ivy pattern .................................................. 135.00
    Kelvinator pattern ........................................ 175.00
    Modern Tulip pattern ..................................... 120.00
    Monterey pattern .......................................... 168.00
    Pansy pattern .............................................. 185.00
    Pastel Tulip pattern ...................................... 145.00
    Petit Point Rose pattern, blue and white ........... 132.00
    Shaggy Tulip pattern ..................................... 132.00
    Taverne pattern ........................................... 175.00

## ROOSTER PATTERN
Plate
    7" d ................................................................ 5.00
    10" d .............................................................. 5.00
Platter, 11 1/4" l .................................................. 15.00

## SEA FARE PATTERN
Cup and Saucer ..................................................... 6.00
Plate
    6" d ................................................................ 4.00
    7" d ................................................................ 6.00
    10" d .............................................................. 8.00

## SHADOW ROSE PATTERN
Cake Lifter ........................................................... 25.00
Plate, 7" sq ........................................................... 5.00

## SHAGGY TULIP PATTERN
Bowl, 6 1/2" d, ftd ................................................ 20.00
Dish, Cov, 7" d ..................................................... 50.00
Plate, 6 1/2" sq .................................................... 12.00
Serving Bowl, 11" d ............................................... 55.00

## SHELL PINK
Cup and Saucer ..................................................... 15.00
Plate, 10" d .......................................................... 18.00

## SPRING TIME PATTERN
Cereal Bowl, 6" d .................................................... 2.00

**Platter, 13 1/2" l x 11 1/2" w, "Springtime" pattern, tan ground, $18.**

| | |
|---|---|
| Cup and Saucer | 3.00 |
| Plate | |
| 7 1/4" d | 6.00 |
| 10" d | 8.00 |
| Platter | |
| 11 1/4" l | 7.00 |
| 13 1/2" l | 10.00 |

### WILD ROSE PATTERN

| | |
|---|---|
| Bowl | |
| 6" d | 12.00 |
| 7 1/2" d | 6.00 |
| Cake Lifter | 18.00 |
| Creamer, 5" d | 8.00 |
| Cup and Saucer | 6.00 |
| Plate | |
| 6" d | 3.00 |
| 8 1/2" sq | 11.00 |
| 10 3/8" d | 6.00 |
| Platter, 12" H-H | 15.00 |
| Serving Bowl, 8 1/2" d | 12.00 |
| Sugar Bowl, Cov, 5" d | 8.00 |
| Tray, 9" l | 12.00 |

# Head Vases

### Late 1940s-1960s

**History:** Ceramic head vase planters were made in America from the late 1940s until the late 1960s by a variety of companies. The lady heads were the most popular and well known. They featured designs inspired by fashion magazines, retail catalogues, and important women from the various time periods.

None of the designs were copyrighted so the designs were copied by other companies. In addition to being used for flowers and plants, some were perfume atomizers, candleholders, and pin cushions. They came in singles, as well as pairs. Some examples had hands and were decorated with rhinestones and 22K gold trim.

American head vases were made before their Japanese counterparts. The majority of American examples dates prior to the mid 1950s when wages and production costs were still low in America. After World War II, most of the ceramic head vases were Japanese made since they were much less costly to produce. Then they were imported by numerous American china novelty companies.

There were a variety of US makers. **Florence Ceramics** of California made full figure flower containers and head vase planters known as "Violet" and "Fern." **Hull Pottery** of Crooksville, Ohio made head vase planters with religious themes from the 1950s-1970s. **McCoy Pottery** of Roseville, Ohio made an Uncle Sam vase and a Lady Head wall pocket. **Shawnee Pottery** of Zanesville, Ohio made three head vase planters, two of a girl with ragdoll and a Polynesian planter girl.

**Spaulding China Company** including **Royal Copley and Royal Windsor** made a pirate head planter, two Blackamoor planters, and an oriental boy and oriental girl. **Stanford Art Pottery** from Sebring, Ohio made the Scottish twins Jean and Sandy, and a Nubian head planter. Even the **Van Briggle Pottery** from Colorado Springs, Colorado made head vase planters.

Some of the most distinct American head vase planters were made by **Betty Lou Nichols Ceramics** of La Habra, California. She started in 1945 when no imports were available and used underglaze hand painted marks on bases of her pieces or the company's ink stamp mark. Since her designs were never copyrighted, many companies copied her lines including cover girls, Gay Nineties girls, santas, Fantasia figurines for Disney, and Flora-Dorables. The company closed in 1962 due to the competition from Japan.

The **Ceramic Arts Studio** from Madison, Wisconsin started making head vases in 1940 until the company was sold and moved to Japan. They made African Man and African Woman head vases.

**References:** Kathleen Cole, *Encyclopedia of Head Vases with Price Guide*, Schiffer Publishing Ltd. 1996; _____, *Head Vases, Identification & Values*, Collector Books, 1998; Mike Posgay & Ian Warner, *The World of Head Vase Planters*, Antique Publications; Mary Zavada, *Lady Head Vases*, Schiffer Publishing Ltd, 1995.

**Collectors' Club:** Maddy Gordon, *Head Hunters Newsletter,* P.O. Box 83H, Scarsdale, NY 10583.

| | |
|---|---|
| 3 3/8" h, little girl wearing green boater hat, brown side ponytails, yellow dress, Peter Pan collar, bisque, unmkd | 45.00 |
| 3 1/2" h, "Demi-Dorable," yellow dress, Betty Lou Nichols | 85.00 |

**Vase, 7 1/2" h, blue loop and flowers on dress, white ground, c1930s, $45.**

3 3/4" h, tilted lady's head, blue dress w/white and blue blouse, red-brown hair, white hat w/blue designs and red-brown puffy flower, unmkd ...................................... 25.00

4" h

Little girl w/open mouth, closed eyes, orange head scarf, blue dress w/white puffy sleeves ......................... 55.00

Pink face w/freckles, blond hair, "California Clemensons Hand Painted" mk ........................................... 50.00

5" h

Betty Lou Nichols type, lg black hat, lg blond bun on neck, dk green dress w/white diamonds ........... 150.00

Blond child praying, dk red robe, bisque ................. 85.00

"Mei-ling," turquoise, white, and black, Ceramic Arts Studio .................................................................. 130.00

5 1/8" h, "Becky," brown hair, Ceramic Arts Studio ................................................................ 125.00

5 1/4" h

Blond woman wearing blue straw hat w/pink daisies, blue polka dot bow under chin .................................... 95.00

Peach frock w/multicolored corsage, hat w/yellow rose, unmkd ..................................................................... 20.00

5 1/2" h, 1940s style, upswept hair, white w/red dotted flower on front ......................................................... 30.00

6" h

Happy child head, white, "USA 408" mark ............... 40.00

Polynesian girl, tan, yellow, and green, Shawnee.... 70.00

Seated baby, red hair, yellow rattle, pink britches, flowered bib .............................................................. 75.00

6 1/2" h, "Ermintrude," green dress, Betty Lou Nichols .................................................................. 100.00

7" h, peasant woman w/hands next to face, white, Catalina Pottery.................................................................... 195.00

7 1/2" h

"Manchu," Ceramic Arts Studio............................. 170.00

"Mary Lou," blond hair, black and white dress and hat, Betty Lou Nichols ............................................... 300.00

7 7/8" h, "Lotus," cream and black, Ceramic Arts Studio .................................................................. 175.00

8 1/2" h, "Marilyn Monroe," Clay Art ........................... 165.00

9" h, bust of woman with head tilted back, large flat brimmed hat, white.................................................................. 150.00

10" h, woman wearing lg hat, bow under chin, white glaze, Haeger ....................................................................... 20.00

12" h, "Flora Belle," green and yellow, Betty Lou Nichols .................................................................. 500.00

# Hull Pottery Company

## Crooksville, Ohio

### 1905-1986

**History:** A.E. Hull, W.A. Watts, and J.D. Young left the Globe Stoneware Company and founded the A.E. Hull Pottery Company in 1905 and concentrated on stonewares. They purchased the Acme Pottery Company of Crooksville,

a semi-porcelain dinnerware firm. Hull made pottery that was sold to gift shops and florists all over the country. Hull Art in matte and high gloss finishes was molded in relief, decorated in bright colors, and was very popular. Hull made art wares, lamp bases, novelties, blue band kitchenware, Zane Grey kitchenware, and stoneware.

After World War I, they made toilet, kitchen, and luster-wares in addition to stonewares. Hull imported earthenware china and pottery from Europe from 1921-1929. In 1927 they started to make tiles in matte, gloss, and stippled finishes. They only made tiles until 1933 since they were too expensive to be profitable.

A.E. Hull Jr. took over in 1930 when his father died. Stoneware, kitchenware, garden ware and florist ware were the Hull products. In 1937, Hull left to manage the Shawnee Pottery Company, and Gerald Watts, William's son, took over. From 1937-44, they made shaving mugs and other toiletry items for Shulton.

Art pottery lines at Hull from the late 1930s included Tulip, Orchid, Calla Lily, Thistle, and Pinecone. Matte art pottery wares continued to flourish during the 1940s with patterns such as Iris, Dogwood, Poppy, Rose, Magnolia, Wildflower, Water Lily, Granada, Bowknot, and Woodland. Many of these art lines were marked by the decorator on the bottom, since each decorator had a number and/or letter. Two high gloss lines from the period included Rosella and Magnolia.

Kitchenware and novelty items were made in the early 1940s; 1943 saw the introduction of the Red Riding Hood cookie jar blanks by Louise Bauer. These pieces were sent to the Royal China and Novelty Company of Chicago for decoration.

A major fire struck the plant in 1950. J.B. Hull took over in 1952 when the new plant was built. The name was changed to The Hull Pottery Company. Louise Bauer became the designer for the art lines at Hull. New lines included Parchment and Pine, Sunglow, Ebb Tide, Classic, Blossom Flite, Butterfly, Serenade, Royal Woodland, Fiesta, and such.

Numerous novelty items included swans, banks, dogs, cats, and the kitchenwares. In the 1960s, the focus changed from art lines to House 'n Garden serving ware that was made until the factory closed, and Crestone, a casual serving ware in turquoise with a white edge.

J.B. Hull died in 1978, and several presidents were involved until the factory closed in 1986. They were subjected to union strikes and competition from inexpensive foreign made wares. Until 1985, they made several dinnerware lines such as Heartland, Blue Belle, the Ridge Collection, and the House 'n Garden line.

A wide assortment of marks was used on the different type of Hull pieces. Paper labels also were used.

**References:** Barbara Loveless Gick-Burke, *A Guide to Hull Pottery Company: The Dinnerware Lines*, Collector Books, 1993; Pamela Coates, *Hull*, available from author, 1974; Joan Gray Hull, *Hull, The Heavenly Pottery*, 6th edition, 1999; Brenda Roberts, *The Collector's Encyclopedia of Hull Pottery*, Collector Books, 1999; _____*Ultimate Encyclopedia of Hull Pottery and The Companion Guide to Ultimate Encyclopedia of Hull Pottery*, Walsworth Publishing, 1992; Mark E. Supnick, *Collecting Hull Pottery's Little Red Riding Hood: A Pictorial Reference and Price Guide*, L-W Book Sales, 1998.

**Collectors' Clubs:** Dan and Kimberly Pfaff, 466 Foreston Place, Webster Groves, MO 63119, $20 per year, monthly newsletter; Hull Pottery Association, 4 Hilltop Road, Council Bluffs, IA 51503, $10 per year.

**Newsletter:** Barbara Burke, 4213 Sandhurst Drive, Orlando, FL 32817, "Hull Dinnerware Collectors Newsletter," $10 per year, bimonthly.

**Reproduction Alert:** The Hull Orchid pattern vase is being reproduced in the original colors and it has markings like the original piece. Other reproductions include: Mermaid and Shell planter, Magnolia Matte large vases, and BowKnot shapes. Original pieces are used as models to cast new molds from which the reproductions are made.

### BLOSSOM FLITE
Basket
6" h, #T-2 ................................................. 35.00
8 1/4" h, #T-8 ........................................ 175.00
10" l, cream and pink with gold flowers ................. 100.00
Candlestick, 3 3/4" h, #T-11, pr ................................. 125.00
Flower Bowl Planter, 10 1/2" l, #T-12 ........................ 135.00
Honey Jug, #T-1 ........................................................ 25.00
Pitcher, 8 1/2" h, #T-3 .............................................. 135.00
Teapot, 8" h, #T-14 .................................................. 140.00

### BOW KNOT
Basket, 12" h, pink and blue, #B-29 ...................... 19,995.00
Cornucopia
7 1/2" h, blue, #B-5 ............................................ 120.00
13" w, dbl, #B-13 ............................................... 295.00
Jardiniere, 5 3/4" h, pink and blue, #B-18 ................. 200.00
Pitcher
5 1/2" h, #B-1 .................................................... 185.00
6" h, blue, #B-26 ............................................... 225.00
Vase
5" h, #B-2 .......................................................... 165.00
5 1/2" h, #B-4 .................................................... 250.00
8 1/2" h
#B-7 ............................................................. 275.00
Blue, #B-9 ................................................... 190.00

**Vase, 15" h, "Continental" pattern, persimmon, $150.**

10 1/2" h
#B-10 ........................................................... 550.00
Pink and blue, #B-11 ................................. 429.00
12 1/2" h, #B-14 ..................................................... 995.00

### BUTTERFLY
Cornucopia, 10 1/2" h, #B-12 ..................................... 40.00
Teapot, 8 1/2" h ....................................................... 140.00
Vase, 7" h, #B-10 ....................................................... 40.00
Window Box, 12 3/4" l, B-8 .......................................... 30.00

### CALLA LILY
Vase, 13" h ............................................................... 185.00

### CONTINENTAL
Basket, 12 1/2" h, green, #C55 ................................. 190.00
Candy Dish, 8 1/4" h, #C62 ......................................... 45.00
Pitcher, 12 1/2" h, #C56 ........................................... 175.00
Vase, 15" h, #C59 ...................................................... 60.00

### CRESTONE
Casserole, 6 1/4" l ..................................................... 25.00
Coffeepot, 10" h ......................................................... 75.00
Creamer, 4 1/8" h ....................................................... 20.00
Sugar Bowl, Cov, 3 1/2" h ........................................... 20.00
Teapot, 5 3/4" h ......................................................... 55.00

### DOGWOOD
Ewer, 4 3/4" h ............................................................ 85.00
Pitcher
4 3/4" h, cream and blue, #520-4-3/4 ................... 125.00
7" h, #505-7 ...................................................... 250.00
Teapot, 5 1/2" h, #507 .............................................. 280.00

**Planter, 11" l x 9" h, "Capri" goose, white, $32.**

### EBB TIDE
Basket, 16 1/2" h, lt green ext, salmon int, gold trim .. 270.00
Console Set, bowl, 15 3/4" l, candleholders, pr, #E-12, #E-13 ..................................................................... 190.00
Vase, 14 1/2" h ......................................................... 150.00

### GRANADA/MARDI GRAS
Basket, 10" h, #66 .................................................... 150.00
Vase, 9" h, pink and blue, #49-9 ................................. 50.00

### HERITAGE WARE
Bowl, Azure Blue
6 1/2" d .............................................................. 10.00
8 1/2" d .............................................................. 25.00

**Tea Set, pot, 8 1/2" h, "Butterfly" pattern, pink, turquoise, yellow, and black, white ground, $195.**

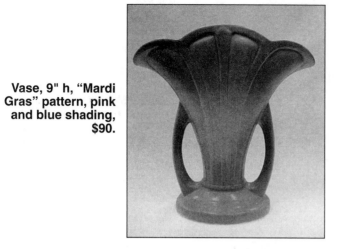

Vase, 9" h, "Mardi Gras" pattern, pink and blue shading, $90.

Bank, 8 1/2" h, Little Red Riding Hood, $2,495.

## HOUSE 'N GARDEN
Ashtray, 8" d, emb deer in center, mirror brown .......... 18.00
Casserole, Cov, 8" h, hen on nest, "Bake & Serve," mirror
    brown ........................................................................ 58.00
Fruit Bowl, 5 1/4" d, brown drip ....................................... 5.00
Gingerbread Server, 10" l, brown drip ......................... 25.00
Plate, 10 1/4" d, mirror brown ........................................ 5.00
Vegetable Bowl, 10 3/4" l, divided, mirror brown .......... 15.00

## HULL ART
Vase, 6 1/4" h, molded flowerhead, blue ground, wing
    handles ..................................................................... 89.00

## IRIS
Vase, 7" h, matte pink, #407 ......................................... 80.00

## LITTLE RED RIDING HOOD
Batter Jug, 6 3/4" h ..................................................... 450.00
Canister, 9 1/2" h, Cereal ......................................... 1,350.00
Cracker Jar, 8 1/2" h, unmkd .................................... 950.00
Grease Jar, 6 1/2" h, wolf, red base ...................... 1,250.00
Hanging Bank, 9" h ................................................. 3,000.00
Lamp, 8" h ............................................................... 2100.00
Milk Pitcher, 8" h ....................................................... 395.00
Shakers
    3 1/2" h, pr ........................................................ 120.00
    4 1/2" h, pr ..................................................... 1,260.00
Spice Jar, 4 3/4" h
    Allspice ............................................................. 775.00
    Ginger ............................................................... 775.00
Standing Bank, 6 3/4" h ............................................ 850.00
String Holder ......................................................... 2,600.00

## MAGNOLIA
Cornucopia, dbl, 7 1/2" h, yellow and green on cream and
    brown ..................................................................... 190.00
Creamer, 3 3/4" h, matte, #24 ...................................... 55.00
Ewer, 13 1/2" h, gloss, #H-19 .................................... 245.00
Vase
    6 1/2" h, pink and blue ........................................ 85.00
    8 1/2" h, matte, #2 ............................................. 135.00
    10 1/2" h, matte finish ....................................... 160.00
    12 1/2" h, matte pink and blue, #22 .................. 325.00

## MISCELLANEOUS
Clock, Bluebird ......................................................... 300.00
Console Bowl, 13" l, matte mint green, "151" mark
    ............................................................................... 36.00

Match Box, 6" h, Little Red Riding Hood, $995.

Liquor Bottle, Leeds Pig, blue, tan, and red ................ 55.00
Planter
    5 1/2" h, dog and yarn ball, green and brown .......... 38.00
    7" h
        Praying Madonna, yellow, gold trim ................... 52.00
        Twin geese, teal w/lt green accents ................... 40.00
    8" h, standing figural poodle, #114 ........................ 25.00
    8 3/4" h x 10 3/4" l, figural swan, white, #23 ........... 32.00
    10 3/4" d, figural flying duck, green with maroon accents
    ............................................................................... 75.00

## NULINE
Batter Jug, 6" h, diamond quilt, ivory .......................... 60.00
Mixing Bowl, 6" d, drape and panel pattern, lt blue
    ............................................................................... 35.00

## OPEN ROSE
Ewer, 13 1/4" h, #106-13-1/4 ..................................... 650.00
Pitcher, 10 1/2" h, #140-10-1/2 ............................... 1,100.00
Vase, 6 1/2" h, swan, rose and cream, #118
    ............................................................................. 135.00

## PARCHMENT & PINE
Console Bowl, 16" d, #S-9 .......................................... 80.00
Cornucopia
    8" h, #S-2 ............................................................. 38.00
    12" h ................................................................... 175.00

Pitcher, 13 1/2" h ..................................................57.00
Teapot, 8" l ...........................................................80.00
Vase, 6" h ............................................................45.00

**PINE CONE**
Vase, 6 1/2" h, pink, #55 ...............................125.00

**ROSELLA**
Basket, 7" h, pink, #R12 .................................330.00
Vase, 8 1/2" h, floral on cream, #R14 ...........88.00

**ROYAL**
Vase, 6 11/2" h, turquoise, #W4 ....................20.00

**SERENADE**
Candlesticks, 6 1/2" h, #516, pr .....................45.00
Fruit Bowl, 11 1/2" d, ftd, #515 .......................70.00
Pitcher, 13 1/2" h, #S13 .................................350.00
Teapot, 6 cup .................................................135.00
Vase, 10 1/2" h, blue, #S11 ...........................125.00

**SUN GLOW**
Basket, 6 1/2" h, pink.......................................55.00
Wall Pocket
    5 1/2" h, figural whisk broom #81 ..........65.00
    6" h, figural iron .......................................35.00

**THISTLE**
Vase, 6 1/2" h, blue, #54-6-1/2 ......................125.00

**TOKAY**
Basket
    8" h, white, #6 ...........................................55.00
    10 1/2" h, moon shape, white, #11 ...........50.00
Cornucopia, 10 1/2" l, white, #10...................45.00
Consolette, 15 3/4" l, #14 ...............................75.00
Vase, 12" h, #12 ..............................................75.00

**TULIP**
Vase
    6 1/2" h ....................................................110.00
    8" h, pink and blue, #105-33 ...................195.00

**WATER LILY**
Basket, 10 1/2" h, tan and brown, #L-14
    .................................................................350.00
Candlesticks, 4" h, pink and turquoise, #L-22, pr .......150.00
Cornucopia, 12" l, dbl, pink and turquoise,
    #L-27 .......................................................225.00
Jardiniere, 5 1/2" h, #L-23 ...............................79.00
Pitcher, 5 1/2" h, pink and turquoise, #L-3 .........95.00
Teapot, 6" h, #L-17 .........................................200.00
Vase
    5 1/2" h, #L-2 .............................................30.00
    6 1/2" h, matte finish ................................75.00
    10 1/2" h, pink and turquoise, #L-12 ......200.00

**WILDFLOWER**
Basket, 10 1/2" h yellow and pale rose, #W-16 .........250.00
Floor Vase, 15" h, pink and blue, #W-20 ....600.00
Vase
    8 1/2" h, #67 ............................................250.00
    10 1/2" h, fan shape, rose and yellow,
    #W-15-10 1/2 ..........................................175.00

**WOODLAND**
Basket, 10 1/2" h, gloss, #W-22 ...................185.00
Cornucopia, 11" l, pink, #W-10, pr ...............120.00
Ewer, 13 1/2" h, gloss pink and green, twig handle....250.00
Pitcher
    6 1/2" h, gloss, #W-6 ...............................55.00
    13 1/2" h, gloss, #W-24 ...........................140.00

# Iroquois China Company

### Syracuse, New York
### 1905-1969

**History:** From 1905-1939, George Bowman controlled the Iroquois China Company, where he made semi-porcelains. In 1939, the firm was sold from the bank to Earl Crane who made hotel wares until 1946. Iroquois China introduced "Casual China" designed by Russel Wright in a wide assortment of colors in 1946. In 1953-54, they added a mottled glaze effect to Casual China called "Raindrop." Decorations were added in 1959 that were mostly floral. Cookwares also were made in this pattern. Two important lines designed by Ben Seibel were "Informal" and "Impromptu." During the late '50s or early '60s, Iroquois dropped hotel wares and concentrated on these three popular lines.

In 1947, Iroquois built a plant in Puerto Rico and manufactured under the name Crane China Company. The plant was acquired by the Sterling China Company in the early 1950s, and the name was changed to Caribe China. This plant closed in 1977.

Financial problems during the late 1960s caused Iroquois to go in and out of production, but it stopped completely in 1969. Its plant was sold to a wood working company in 1971. A wide variety of marks was used by Iroquois.

**CARRERA MODERN PATTERN**
Cup and Saucer, dk gray...............................15.00
Serving Bowl, 10" d, white.............................33.00

**CHATHAM PATTERN**
Berry Bowl, 5 3/8" d........................................3.00
Cereal Bowl, 6 1/4" d.......................................5.00
Cup and Saucer ...............................................5.00
Plate
    7 1/4" d ......................................................6.00
    9" d ............................................................8.00
Platter, 12 1/2" l .............................................15.00
Vegetable Bowl, 10" l .....................................15.00

**CLIFF DWELLER DESIGNS-PETER MAX**
Ashtray, 7" d .................................................110.00
Bowl, 7" d .......................................................18.00
Plate, 10" d .....................................................38.00

**IMPROMPTU**
Creamer
    Garland pattern..........................................17.00
    Grapes pattern............................................16.00
    Vision pattern, blue and pink .....................8.00
Cup and Saucer
    Bridal white ................................................12.00

Stellar pattern................................................ 10.00
Gravy Boat, 9 1/2" l, Grapes pattern .......................... 25.00
Plate
    6 1/2" d, Vision pattern, blue and pink ...................... 3.00
    10" d, Stellar pattern ................................................ 12.00
Platter, 11" l, Vision pattern, blue and pink
    .................................................................................. 15.00
Salad Bowl, 7 1/4" l, Stellar pattern ........................... 10.00
Serving Bowl, 9 5/8" l, Stellar pattern ........................ 45.00
Shakers, Pr, Grapes pattern ....................................... 18.00
Sugar Bowl, Cov, 6" d, Grapes pattern ........................ 20.00

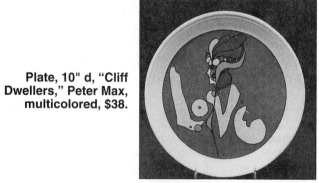

**Vegetable Bowl, 9 7/8" l x 8 1/4" w, "Stellar" pattern, Ben Seibel, $10.**

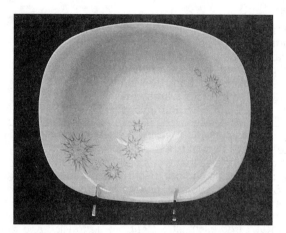

**Plate, 10" d, "Cliff Dwellers," Peter Max, multicolored, $38.**

**Pitcher, 12" h, "Impromptu-Pins and Beads" pattern, Ben Seibel, $14.**

## INFORMAL

Berry Bowl, 5" d, Bombay ............................................. 3.00
Bowl, Cov, 10 1/2" d, Pins and Beads ........................ 40.00
Coffee Set, pot, creamer, sugar bowl, Harvest Time.... 55.00
Creamer, 5 3/4" h, Harvest Time ................................. 17.00
Cup and Saucer
    Blue Diamonds ...................................................... 10.00
    Harvest Time ......................................................... 12.00
Milk Pitcher, 9" h, Lazy Daisy .................................... 45.00
Platter
    12" l
        Blue Diamond.................................................. 25.00
        Harvest Time ................................................... 29.00
    15" l
        Blue Diamond.................................................. 25.00
        Harvest Time ................................................... 29.00
        Lazy Daisy....................................................... 30.00
Serving Bowl, 10 1/2" l
    Blue Diamond ........................................................ 18.00
    Harvest Time ......................................................... 22.00
    Lazy Daisy............................................................. 27.00
Sugar Bowl, Cov
    Bombay .................................................................. 10.00
    Lazy Daisy............................................................. 18.00

## INTAGLIO

Cereal Bowl, 6 1/4" d, Woodale pattern ........................ 5.00
Creamer, 3 1/2" h, Woodale pattern ............................. 8.00
Cup and Saucer, Woodale pattern ................................ 7.00
Plate
    8 1/2" d, Woodale pattern ....................................... 6.00
    10 5/8" d, Woodale pattern ..................................... 7.00
Serving Bowl, 7 5/8" d, Woodale pattern ...................... 8.00

**Plate, 6 1/2" d, "Impromptu-Diamonds" pattern, Ben Seibel, $8.**

**Vegetable Bowl, 10" l, "Chatham" pattern, $15.**

# Josef Originals

## California
## 1945-1985

**History:** Muriel Joseph George's first designs were produced in California from 1945-1962. To remain competitive, economics forced a move to manufacturers in Japan after that. Muriel sold her company to George Good when she retired in 1982. He continued production of Josef Originals until 1985 when the company was sold to Southland Corporation.

The figures illustrate a love of family from motherhood through the wonders of childhood. The appreciation of nature is a recurring theme using flowers and ecology. Figures were also designed for Christmas, Valentine's day, and birthdays.

Muriel designed the figures and workers painted them. All were hand painted so no two are exactly alike. They also came in a variety of colors. Molds for the more popular figures were used for a long time, as much as fifteen to twenty years.

Since there was a glut of copies imported from various Japanese factories, the Katayama Company built a new factory in 1959 to produce Josef Originals designs. This allowed Muriel more time to concentrate on new designs instead of worrying about production.

Functional pieces also were made including pin boxes and trays, soap dishes, lipstick holders, mugs, salt and pepper shakers, nightlights, planters, vases, head vases, jam jars, cookie jars, ashtrays, cotton dispensers, stamp boxes, rosary holders, and music boxes. Holiday designs included examples for Christmas, Valentine's day, and Mother's day. There was also a "Professions" series from 1960-62. Numerous animal figurals were made too.

Figurals made from 1982-1985 have the Josef Originals name but were not designed by Muriel since she retired in 1982. George Good continued to use her designs but changed the eye color from black to brown. Additional designers were employed, but never captured the Muriel look. George sold the company in 1985, and the name is currently owned by Applause.

Marks labels with "California" were used from 1945-1962. Labels for pieces made in Japan date 1959-1985. Korea and Taiwan labels date 1982-1985 on Applause examples. There are also incised or ink marks on California pieces.

**References:** Dee Harris, Jim and Kaye Whitaker, *Josef Originals: Charming Figurines*, Schiffer Publishing Ltd. 1999; Jim & Kaye Whitaker, *Josef Originals: A Second Look*, Schiffer Publishing Ltd. 1996; _____, *Josef Originals Figurines of Muriel Joseph George*, Schiffer Publishing Ltd. 2000.

**Collectors' Club:** Josef Original, P.O. Box 475, Lynnwood, WA 98046. Quarterly newsletter, $10.

Ash Receiver, 5 3/4" h, figural outhouse, yellow-brown siding, red roof.............................................................15.00
Ash Tray, 4 5/8" d, raised Santa Claus or candle and holly, red trim, white ground, pr.........................................28.00
Figure
  2 3/4" h
    "Doc," mouse with stethoscope, white coat.........25.00
    Mouse blowing bubblegum..................................25.00
  3" l, puppy, tan and brown......................................10.00
  3 1/2" h, seated bear cub, brown, fuzzy body...........8.00

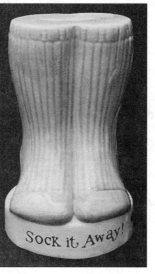

**Bank, 5" h, pink socks, yellow toes, diamond designs on sides, white base, $46.**

3 1/2" l, Pomeranian dog, brown .............................25.00
3 3/4" h, February, amethyst stone, pink gown........20.00
3 3/4" l, locomotive, black ground w/blue and rose applied flowers, gold trim ...................................70.00
4" h
  Girl Graduate, pink dress ....................................25.00
  Little Pet series, girl w/dog .................................35.00
  November, topaz stones, peach gown ...............20.00
4 1/2" h
  Little Girl with Big Dog, "Big Sisters & Little Sisters" series ...........................................................130.00
  Standing rabbit holding orange carrot w/green top ........................................................................15.00
5 1/2" h
  Simone, "Morning, Noon, and Night" series ......100.00
  Teddy, blue ........................................................45.00
5 1/2" l, German Shepherd dog lying, brown and tan ........................................................................45.00
5 3/4" h, girl cutting rose, "Morning, Noon, and Night" series................................................................75.00
6" h
  "Jacques," lt purple suit, blue vest, gold trim ........................................................................40.00
  Lady in lavender gown with parasol ...................75.00
6 1/2" h
  Horse, gloss brown, black mane and tail ...........75.00
  Girl in lavender dress w/roses...........................95.00
7" h, "17th Century French" series, Marie.............125.00
8" h
  "New Hat," green dress w/gold trim, hat box in hand ........................................................................70.00
  "The Courtship-Romance Series," blue.............100.00
8 1/2" h, "Tanya," ballerina on toes, lt blue w/gold trim ........................................................................100.00
9 1/2" h, Adelaide, "Colonial Days" series ............225.00
Black Eyed Birthday Girl
  4 1/4" h, #6......................................................35.00
  5" h, #9............................................................35.00
Brown Eyed Birthday Girl
  3" h, #1, baby ..................................................10.00
  3 1/4" h, #2......................................................12.00

3 1/2" h, #5 .............................................. 13.00
3 3/4" h, #6 .............................................. 14.00
5 1/2" h, #10 ............................................ 18.00
6 1/4" h, #15 ............................................ 22.00
6 1/2" h, #19 ............................................ 24.00

Music Box

4 1/2" h, girl seated at piano, pink dress ................ 75.00
6 1/4" h, "Three Coins in a Fountain," young girl and fountain ................................................ 95.00

Napkin Ring, 5" h, figural owl on branch, brown and tan shades ........................................................ 30.00

Night Light, 5 3/4" h, figural seated cat, white w/pink and brown accents, purple bow .............................. 50.00

Rosary Holder, 5" h, singing nun, black, gold trim
.............................................................. 40.00

# Jugtown Pottery

## Seagrove, North Carolina
## Early 1920s-Present

**History:** Jugtown Pottery was established by Jacques and Juliana Busbee in Moore County, near Seagrove, North Carolina about 1921. Early wares were sold in their tea and sales room in Greenwich Village in New York City.

From 1922-1947, Jugtown examples were produced by Ben Owen and supervised by Jacques. All types of traditional utilitarian pottery pieces were made including vases, candlesticks, flower bowls, and table accessories in an assortment of glazes from salt glaze to heavy glazes. Chinese style pieces also were made, with Chinese blue being the most popular color. Other colors included cream, orange, white, black, green, and brownish orange with black areas.

When Jacques died in 1947, Juliana continued to operate the pottery with Owen. When she signed two deeds, there were complications in the sale, and the pottery closed for one year. It was reopened in 1960. Ben Owen established his own pottery close by and made similar wares. He marked his pieces "Ben Owen, Master Potter."

John Mare managed Jugtown from 1960 until the nonprofit corporation Country Road, Inc. purchased it, and Nancy Sweezy operated it for them. Vernon Owens purchased the pottery in 1982 since he had been chief potter since 1960. Through all these years the same shapes and glazes were made.

The pieces were marked "Jugtown Pottery" in a circular die-stamped mark.

**References:** Charles G. Zug III, *Turners and Burners: The Folk Potters of North Carolina*, University of North Carolina Press.

**Museums:** Chrysler Museum, Norfolk, VA; Cleveland Museum of Art, OH; Museum of North Carolina Traditional Pottery, Seagrove, NC; National Museum of History and Technology, Smithsonian Institution, Washington, DC; St. Johns Art Gallery, Wilmington, NC.

Bank, 7" h, beehive shape, knob top, speckled orange glaze, (A) ........................................................ 45.00

Bean Pot, 5 1/2" h, cord handles, orange clear glaze w/overall black dots, (A) ...................................... 132.00

Bowl

5 1/2" d, dk brown glaze .............................. 50.00

6" d, flared shape, ftd, blue "lead free" glaze, orange clear glaze on base, dk brown rim, (A) ...................... 44.00

7 1/4" d, flat rim, "Chinese Blue" glaze, (A) .......... 825.00

8" d, ruffled rim, mottled green and gray glaze, mkd, (A)
.............................................................. 77.00

13" d, redware w/yellow slip design chicken, "imp Jugtown" mk, (A) ...................................... 165.00

Bowl, Cov

2" h x 5 1/2" d, mottled blue and lavender glaze, (A)
.............................................................. 30.00

4" h x 5 1/4" d, orange glaze, c1930, (A) ................ 60.00

Cabinet Vase, 4" h, closed top, "Chinese Blue" glaze, (A)
.............................................................. 825.00

Candlestick

7 1/2" h, orange glaze, "imp Jugtown" mk, (A)
.............................................................. 20.00

11 1/2" h, cup bobiche, flared base, semi-matte blue glaze, pr, (A) ...................................... 123.00

Chalice, 3 1/2" h, blue glaze, (A) .............................. 45.00

Charger, 15 1/2" H-H, applied handles, orange-brown glaze
.............................................................. 75.00

Egg Cup, 3" h, dk orange glaze .............................. 20.00

Figure

1 1/2" h, pinch style chicken, cinnamon glaze w/blue glazed wing and tail feathers, (A) .................. 22.00

7 1/2" h, hen, mottled brown and ochre glaze, salt glaze finish, chips, (A) ...................................... 56.00

Jar, 8 3/4" h, red clay, brown Albany slip, 4 applied handles, "imp Jugtown" mk, (A) ...................................... 28.00

Jar, Cov, 5 1/2" h, brown textured body, central cobalt band w/incised zigzags ...................................... 60.00

Jug

4 1/8" h, 2 incised lines on shoulder, "frogskin" glaze, "imp Jugtown Ware and jug" mk, (A) .................. 192.00

10" h, w/stopper, 3 incised lines on shoulder, flat ribbon handle, clear glaze, (A) .................................. 88.00

10 1/4" h, salt glaze w/scattered cobalt stylized flowerheads ........................................................ 65.00

11 5/8" h, ring shape, flat base, 4 cobalt brushed florals, salt glaze, (A) ...................................... 100.00

Mug

4 1/2" h, blue glaze, mkd .............................. 50.00

4 3/4" h

Horiz ribbing, green ...................................... 75.00

Taupe glaze ...................................... 80.00

Pitcher

5 1/2" h, "tobacco spit" brown glaze .................. 70.00

8 1/2" h, gray salt glaze, brown accents, "imp Jugtown" mk, (A) ........................................................ 25.00

9 1/8" h, "Han" style, squared horiz handles, variegated turquoise over black glaze w/white base glaze, (A)
.............................................................. 1,870.00

9 1/4, h, squat base, incised horiz lines, "Chinese Blue" glaze, black-green Albany glaze int, chips, (A)
.............................................................. 1,650.00

Pitcher, Cov, 6" h, orange clear glaze, finger brace on handle, (A) ........................................................ 192.00

Plate, 8 1/2" d, orange glaze, "imp Jugtown" mk, (A) ... 25.00

Soup Bowl, 7" H-H, tab handles, dk brown glaze ........ 25.00

Urn, 7" h, bulbous shape, 2 sm loop handles on shoulder, red "Chinese Blue" glaze, "stamped JUGTOWN WARE" mk, (A) ........................................................ 3,850.00

**Pitcher, 5" h, pitcher, 3 1/2" h, cov jar, 3 1/2" h, orange to brown glaze, red clay, (A), $40.**

Vase

    4" h, ball shape, frog skin finish ................................ 65.00
    5 1/4" h, ovoid, "Chinese Blue" glaze, mkd, (A)
    ............................................................................ 770.00
    6 1/2" h, ovoid, closed rim, dripping semi-matte white glaze, brown clay body, (A) .............................. 495.00
    7" h, swollen shape, olive green glaze................... 165.00
    7 1/4" h, bulbous base, flared neck and rim, mottled semi-matte ice white and celadon green glazes, (A) .235.00
    14 1/2" h, milk can shape, emb medallions on shoulder, mottled semi-matte white glaze, hairlines, "stamped Jugtown Ware" mk, (A).................................... 1,100.00

# Brad Keeler

## Los Angeles, California
## 1939-1953

**History:** Brad Keeler worked as a modeler for Philips Bronze and Brass before he started a ceramics studio in his parents' garage in Glendale, California in 1939. The naturalistic, hand-decorated birds he made were a big success. Needing additional space, he leased part of Evan K. Shaw's American Pottery in Los Angeles.

Shaw added Keeler's birds to the ceramic giftware he represented. More than fifty different models were made there. Keeler's birds had the color applied to the bisque ware with an airbrush. Then, hand-painted details such as beaks and eyes were done. A transparent glaze was then sprayed on. Although Keeler's flamingoes were the most popular, he also modeled seagulls, blue jays, swans, ducks, chickens, herons, cockatoos, pheasants, canaries, parrots, and parakeets. Most were done in male-female sets though some were combined figures.

After a fire in Shaw's plant, Keeler moved in 1946 to larger space. He started making Shaw's line of Walt Disney figurines. Freelance designers were added to produce additional lines. Fred Kaye was the favored designer who worked on birds, the "Exotic Series," and a variety of animals called the "Pryde and Joy" line.

Working with Andrew Malinovsky Jr., Keeler developed one of the first true red glazes called Ming Dragon Blood that was used on an extensive collection of Chinese Modern housewares which also utilized high gloss black. Included in the Ming line were vases, ginger jars, low bowls, candleholders, planters, cigarette boxes, and ashtrays. There was also a buffet line of serving dishes with lobster handles.

Brad Keeler also made plain and decorated wares in the form of bowls and teasets.

Even though Japanese imports were threatening his business, Keeler felt the need for a larger building. In the midst of construction on a new factory, Keeler died of a heart attack in 1952 at age 39. The new plant was sold in 1953.

Marks used included an incised "Brad Keeler" plus the model number with an American Pottery paper label. After 1946, a new paper label was used in conjunction with the original recessed mark. Stamped marks were used on small items or works of outside designers.

**References:** Jack Chipman, *Collector's Encyclopedia of California Pottery*, Collector Books, 1992; _____2nd Edition, Collector Books, 1999; Mike Schneider, *California Potteries*, Schiffer Books, 1995.

Bowl

    10 1/2" d, white figural molded scallop shells, airbrushed black rim, mkd.................................................. 100.00
    12" d, 2 red figural lobsters on rim, green shell body
    ............................................................................ 400.00
Charger, 11" d, turquoise shaded fish, 2 yellow fishing flies
    ............................................................................ 150.00
Dish

    6 1/2" l x 5 1/2" w, figural pear, yellow and red, green and dk red stem and leaves...................................... 25.00
    7" l x 6" w, figural plums, 3 sectioned, dk red plums, green leaves........................................................ 35.00
    9" l, figural lobster claw, gray and red, #3............... 25.00
    14" d, divided, figural lobster ................................... 70.00
Figure

    4" h, "Pryde n' Joy-Little Miss Muffet" ..................... 85.00
    4 1/2" h, standing rooster, yellow, tan, dk red, and green
    .............................................................................. 25.00

**Figure, 12 1/2" h, rose-pink, black and green, $195.**

**Planter, 8 1/4" x 8 1/2" l, red Santa, green sleigh, tan bag, $75.**

5" h, "Wee Willie Winkle," white gown w/blue accents, holding lantern ....................................................160.00

6" h, canary on branch, yellow, rose head, green accents, "Brad Keeler No. 17" mk......................70.00

6 1/8" h, "Exotic Pheasant," yellow, rose, and green ........................................................................60.00

7" l, 8" l, kittens, black w/gray accents, pr..............140.00

7 1/2" h

    Bird on branch, apricot and black, "incised Brad Keeler No. 39" mk .........................................75.00

    Female flamingo, #3.........................................135.00

7 1/2" l, kitten lying on back, lt brown shades ..........50.00

8 1/2" h, standing flamingo and chicks, pink, c1940s ........................................................................45.00

8 3/4" h, cockatoo, #34 .........................................125.00

9 5/8" h, bluejay, #19.............................................62.00

10" h, rooster, bisque, black with red comb, pr ........................................................................150.00

10 1/2" h, egret, yellow w/black accents, "Brad Keeler No. 713" mk .....................................................125.00

12" h, standing male flamingo, #1......................200.00

12 1/4" l, pheasant, yellow, red, and brown, cream base ........................................................................75.00

Planter

    6" h, "Pryde n' Joy" figural little boy, yellow, green, and black............................................................60.00

    7 1/4" h, figural swan, cream ground w/gray and pink accents .......................................................65.00

    8 1/2" l, figural swan, cream, pink accents, "Brad Keeler 818 Made in USA" mk ..........................70.00

Relish Dish, 9" d, 3 section, figural red lobster handle, green leaf base ...............................................40.00

Shaker, 4" h, fish standing on tail, turquoise and beige, pr ........................................................................125.00

Tray

    9" l, red tomato on lettuce leaf ..................25.00

    14" d, red pepper on lettuce leaf............................40.00

# Edwin M. Knowles China Company

## Chester and Newell, West Virginia
## 1900-1963

**History:** Edwin Knowles and several others started the Knowles China Company in Chester, West Virginia in 1900. They used the East Liverpool address for their offices. A new plant was built in Newell, West Virginia in 1913. Both plants operated until 1931, when the Chester plant was sold to the Harker Pottery Company, and all operations moved to the Newell plant.

Semi-vitreous dinner services, toilet wares, cuspidors, and covered jars were made in a tremendous variety of shapes and patterns. By 1940, Edwin M. Knowles was the third largest producer in the United States. A series of marks was used during the long history of the company.

The company closed in 1963 due to competition from the inexpensive foreign imports that were produced with low labor costs.

### APPLE BLOSSOM PATTERN
Cereal Bowl, 6" d, tab handle.........................................2.00
Creamer ...........................................................................3.00
Cup and Saucer ...............................................................3.00
Plate
    6 1/4" d ....................................................................3.00
    10 1/4" d ..................................................................4.00
Sugar Bowl, Cov .............................................................4.00

### BLOSSOM TIME PATTERN
Berry Bowl, 5 1/4" d.........................................................3.00
Plate
    6" d ..........................................................................3.00
    10" d ........................................................................4.00
Platter, 11" l ..................................................................45.00

### BLUEBELLS PATTERN
Creamer ...........................................................................5.00
Cup and Saucer ...............................................................3.00
Gravy Boat .......................................................................5.00
Plate
    6 1/4" d ....................................................................3.00
    7 1/2" d ....................................................................3.00
    10 1/4" d ..................................................................4.00
Platter, 12 1/2" l ..............................................................7.00

### BLUE LAUREL PATTERN
Plate
    6" d ..........................................................................3.00
    7 1/4" d ....................................................................3.00
    9" d ..........................................................................4.00
Serving Bowl, 8 1/2" d......................................................4.00
Soup Bowl, 7 1/2" d..........................................................3.00

## BRIDAL FLORAL PATTERN
Plate, 9" sq ................................................. 3.00
Soup Plate, 7 1/2" sq ...................................... 5.00

## BUTTERCUP PATTERN
Berry Bowl, 5 1/2" d ....................................... 4.00
Bowl, 9" d .................................................. 8.00
Cereal Bowl, 6" d .......................................... 5.00
Plate, 10" d ............................................... 3.00

## CHALET PATTERN
Bowl, 5" d ................................................. 3.00
Plate
    6 1/4" d ......................................... 2.00
    10" d .............................................. 4.00
Soup Bowl, 8" d ............................................ 4.00

## CONCORD PATTERN
Plate 6 3/8" d ............................................. 3.00

## COTTON BLOSSOM PATTERN
Cup and Saucer ............................................ 3.00
Gravy Boat, 8" l ........................................... 12.00
Plate
    6 3/4" d ........................................... 2.00
    7 1/4" d ........................................... 3.00
    9" d ............................................... 5.00
Serving Bowl, 9" d ........................................ 6.00

## DAMASK ROSE PATTERN
Cup and Saucer ............................................ 4.00
Fruit Bowl, 5 1/2" d ....................................... 3.00
Plate
    6 1/4" d ........................................... 3.00
    10 1/4" d .......................................... 6.00
Platter, 12 1/2" l ......................................... 12.00

## DUBARRY PATTERN
Berry Bowl, 5 1/4" d ....................................... 4.00
Plate
    8 1/4" d ........................................... 4.00
    10" d .............................................. 5.00

## EBONETTE PATTERN
Plate
    6" d ............................................... 3.00
    10 1/2" d .......................................... 6.00

## FORSYTHIA PATTERN
Berry Bowl, 5 1/2" d ....................................... 3.00
Creamer ................................................... 5.00
Cup and Saucer ............................................ 3.00
Plate
    6" d ............................................... 3.00
    10" d .............................................. 6.00
Platter
    8 1/2" l ........................................... 6.00
    12 1/2" l .......................................... 6.00
Soup Bowl, 7 3/4" d ....................................... 5.00
Sugar Bowl, Cov ........................................... 5.00

## FRUITS PATTERN
Cake Plate, 10" H-H ....................................... 38.00

Utility Ware, "Fruits" pattern, cov jug, $50; bowl,
2 1/4" h x 4" d, $12.

Pitcher, Cov, 7 1/2" h ..................................... 48.00
Syrup, Cov, 6 3/4" h ....................................... 20.00

## GALA PATTERN
Creamer ................................................... 5.00
Plate, 10" d ............................................... 5.00
Soup Bowl, 7 3/4" d ....................................... 3.00

## GLORIA PATTERN
Fruit Bowl, 5" sq .......................................... 5.00
Plate, 7" sq ............................................... 3.00
Soup Bowl, 7 3/4" sq ...................................... 4.00

## GODEY PRINTS DESIGN
Plate, 7 1/8" d, set of 4 .................................. 30.00

## GOLDEN WHEAT PATTERN
Cereal Bowl, 7 1/2" d ...................................... 6.00
Cup and Saucer ............................................ 6.00
Fruit Bowl, 5 1/2" d ....................................... 8.00
Plate
    7 1/2" d ........................................... 8.00
    9 1/4" d ........................................... 10.00
    10" d .............................................. 15.00

## GRAPEVINE PATTERN
Creamer, 3 1/4" h ......................................... 4.00
Cup and Saucer ............................................ 3.00
Fruit Dish, 5 1/2" d ....................................... 2.00
Plate, 10 1/4" d ........................................... 10.00
Platter, 12" l ............................................. 10.00
Soup Bowl, 8" d ........................................... 6.00
Sugar Bowl, Cov, 4" h ..................................... 6.00
Vegetable Bowl, 8 3/4" d .................................. 8.00

## HOSTESS PATTERN
Bowl, 9" d ................................................. 5.00
Fruit Bowl, 5 1/2" d ....................................... 4.00
Gravy Boat, 8 1/2" l ...................................... 6.00

## MONTICELLO PATTERN
Fruit Bowl, 5 1/2" d ....................................... 2.00
Plate
    6 1/4" d ........................................... 2.00
    10 1/4" d .......................................... 5.00

Soup Bowl, 7 3/4" d..............................................3.00
Vegetable Bowl, 8 1/2" d......................................7.00

## PASADENA PLAID PATTERN
Platter, 14" l....................................................14.00
Shakers, Pr........................................................8.00
Sugar Bowl, Cov.................................................8.00
Teapot.............................................................25.00

## PENTHOUSE PATTERN
Plate
  7" d...................................................9.00
  10 1/2" d...........................................10.00
Platter, 11" d...................................................15.00

## ROSE TREE PATTERN
Plate
  6" sq..................................................3.00
  10 1/4" sq............................................4.00

## SLEEPING MEXICAN PATTERN
Berry Bowl, 5 1/4" d............................................5.00
Bowl 8 3/4" d....................................................38.00
Plate
  6 1/2" d..............................................4.00
  9 1/4" d.............................................15.00
  11 1/2" d.............................................8.00

## SUNLIGHT PATTERN
Cup and Saucer ...............................................12.00
Plate
  6" d.................................................12.00
  10" d................................................12.00
Sugar Bowl, Cov..............................................22.00

## SWEETBRIAR PATTERN
Plate, 10 1/4" d.................................................5.00

## TEA ROSE PATTERN
Cup and Saucer ...............................................3.00
Plate
  6 1/8" d..............................................4.00
  10 1/8" d.............................................5.00
Platter, 12" l...................................................10.00

## TIA JUANA PATTERN
Berry Bowl, 5 1/4" d............................................7.00
Bowl, 9 1/2" d..................................................15.00
Cake Plate, 6 1/2" d, red rim ................................6.00
Creamer, 3 1/2" h.............................................18.00
Plate
  6" d...................................................4.00
  7 1/2" d.............................................14.00
  9 1/4" d.............................................18.00
Platter
  11" H-H.............................................10.00
  13 3/4" l.............................................40.00
Soup Plate, 8" d...............................................15.00
Sugar Bowl, Cov..............................................40.00

## TULIP TIME PATTERN
Bowl, 6 1/4" d ...................................................4.00
Cup and Saucer ...............................................5.00

**Vegetable Bowl, Cov, 10" H-H, "Wild Rose" pattern, $15.**

**Bowl, 10" d, "Yorktown" pattern, burnt orange, "Edwin M. Knowles China Co." mk, $38.**

Plate
  9" d...................................................5.00
  10 1/2" d.............................................6.00
Platter, 10 1/2" H-H............................................8.00

## WEATHERVANE PATTERN
Creamer, 7" h...................................................5.00
Cup and Saucer ...............................................2.00
Fruit Bowl, 5 1/2" d.............................................3.00
Plate, 6 1/4" d..................................................2.00
Platter, 13" l....................................................8.00

## WILD ROSE PATTERN
Dessert Dish, 5 1/4" d ........................................4.00
Soup Bowl, 7 1/2" d............................................5.00
Vegetable Bowl, Cov, 10 1/2" H-H...........................15.00

## YORKTOWN PATTERN
Cup and Saucer, yellow .......................................5.00
Plate
  6 1/2" d, maroon.....................................5.00
  9 1/2" d, yellow.......................................6.00

1890s          c.1878-1885

# Knowles, Taylor, and Knowles

## East Liverpool, Ohio
## 1870-1929

**History:** Isaac Watts Knowles started his business in 1854, but incorporated in 1870 when John N. Taylor, his son-in-law, and Homer S. Knowles, his son joined the company as Knowles, Taylor, and Knowles. In the 1860s and early 1870s, they made yellow earthenware and Rockingham wares. White ironstone for hotel china was begun in 1872, and the other wares were discontinued. Ironstone tea sets, dinner services, toilet wares, cooking wares, accessories, and pitchers were made.

In 1888, they built a new plant to make porcelain. Joshua Poole, a Belleek manager from Ireland, supervised the production of the thin, creamy, eggshell porcelain based on the Irish examples in 1889. This was the first pottery in the Midwest to develop the Belleek porcelains. After only nine months, the factory burned and had to be rebuilt.

When the new factory was ready, they did not return to the production of Belleek, but decided to make a new translucent bone china body to compete with the Belleek being made at the Trenton firms. The new line was Lotus Ware: an excellent quality porcelain comparable to examples from England and Europe.

The white Lotus Ware body was adorned with flowers, leaves, filigree, and lace-like work that was all done entirely by hand. Colored bodies such as olive and celadon green also were used. Patterns had names such as Arcanian, Cremonian, Etruscan, Parmian, Thebian, and Umbrian. A wide assortment of designs was made of this very ornamental, delicate ware. It proved to be too expensive since it required so much handwork and was discontinued in 1897.

Production of semi-porcelain continued after Lotus Ware was stopped. Hotel china, hospital wares, and electrical porcelains were made. The firm continued through several managerial changes, but business declined in the mid 1920s. The pottery closed its doors in 1929.

A wide variety of marks was used on Knowles, Taylor, and Knowles examples. Many Lotus Ware pieces had the company's initials with a star and crescent shape printed inside a circle with "Lotus Ware" printed underneath.

**References:** Mary Frank Gaston, *American Belleek*, Collector Books, 1984; William C. Gates, Jr. and Dana E. Ormerod, *The East Liverpool, Ohio, Pottery District: Identification of Manufacturers and Marks*, The Society for Historical Archaeology, 1982; Timothy J. Kearns, *Knowles, Taylor & Knowles: American Bone China*, Schiffer Publishing Ltd. 1994.

**Museums:** Museum of Ceramics at East Liverpool, OH; National Museum of History and Technology, Smithsonian Institution, Washington, DC.

## LOTUS WARE
Ewer, 7 1/4" h, HP purple clematis, lt blue and white ground, encrusted gold accents, (A) .................................. 440.00
Jar, Cov, 6 3/4" h, lobed, reticulated body, cov, and knob, repairs and hairline ............................................. 950.00

Plate, 8" d, portrait of "Madame Sans Gene," pink dress, red hair, gold "Pittsburgh Commandery No. 1 KT 28th Triennial Louisville 1901 Kentucky," cobalt border w/gold overlay and molded florals, $95.

Pitcher, 5 1/4" h, cream body, molded handle, (A) ..... 275.00
Vase
  8" h, bulbous base, sm bulbous neck, 2 fancy handles, HP thistles, encrusted gold, white and lt green shaded ground, (A) ........................................................ 577.00
  9" h
    HP purple florals and green leaves, shaded ground, gilt handles .................................................. 260.00
    Tapered bulbous body, scalloped rim, 2 gilt scrolled handles on shoulder, gilt accented and pink roses and leaves in panels, pea green ground .... 1200.00

### BLUEBIRD DESIGNS
Berry Dish, 4 1/4" d ...................................................... 5.00
Gravy Boat, 8" l, bluebird design ................................ 55.00
Plate
  8" d .......................................................................... 7.00
  9" d ........................................................................ 15.00
  9 3/4" d, "K.T.K-S..V China V.E.G." mk .................... 20.00
Relish Tray, 9 3/8" H-H, lg and sm bluebirds on border
  ................................................................................ 25.00
Soup Plate, 7 1/2" d .................................................. 25.00
Vegetable Bowl, 8 1/4" l, bluebird design ................... 20.00

### IVY PATTERN
Bowl, 10" d .................................................................. 8.00
Creamer, 3" h .............................................................. 5.00
Plate
  8" d .......................................................................... 4.00
  10" d ........................................................................ 5.00
Platter, 14 1/2" l ........................................................ 10.00
Soup Bowl, 7 3/4" d ..................................................... 5.00
Sugar Bowl, Cov, 3 1/2" h ........................................... 6.00

### MISCELLANEOUS
Bowl
  9" l, multicolored bird of paradise design, "K.T.K.S...V" Ivory" mk ............................................................... 10.00
  10 1/4" d, lobed body, white granite ware, c1900 .... 10.00
Casserole, Cov, 11 1/4" H-H, gold handles, knob, and bands w/leaves on cov and body, "K.T.K. S.V" mk
  ................................................................................ 10.00

**Wash Set, pitcher, 12" h, bowl, 15 1/2" d, toothbrush holder, 4 5/8" h, slop basin, 15" h, cov soap dish, 5 1/4" d, cov chamber pot, 12" d, peach and blue flowers w/green leaves, raised designs, gold dusting, $550.**

Gravy Boat, 7" l, center band of multicolored florals and pheasants ...................................................... 10.00
Plate, 9 1/4" d, "Ramona," bust of brown haired woman wearing blue gown w/rose on breast, gold lined inner and outer rim, mkd .......................................................... 50.00
Platter
    13" l, white ironstone, scalloped rim ......................... 7.00
    15 3/4" l, white ground, gold border bands ............... 7.00
Pitcher, Cov, 8 1/2" h, paneled, scattered red and yellow garden flowers, green leaves and stems ................. 20.00
Vegetable Dish, Cov, 12" H-H, Nasturtium pattern ....... 23.00
Wash Set, basin, 17" d, waste jar, 14 1/2" h, cov chamber pot, 12 1/2" d, cov soap dish w/drain, 5 1/2" d, mug, 3 1/2" h, rose pattern w/gilt trim ......................... 360.00
    Whiskey Jug, 7 1/2" h, green "Meredith's Diamond Club Rye Whiskey," white ground .......................... 145.00

# Lamberton Scammell China Company

## Trenton, New Jersey
## 1924-1954

**History:** D. William Scammell had been working with the Maddocks from Maddock Pottery Company in the Old Lamberton Works in 1901 and eventually bought out their interests in the Lamberton Works. Shortly after that he purchased the remaining stock in Maddock Pottery Company and formed the Scammell China Company in 1924 to make hotel and railroad china.

In 1939, a fine translucent china for the home was introduced with a porcelain body in a ivory tone that was called Lamberton China in a wide variety of tablewares. Decora-

tions were molded, painted, modeled, transfer printed, and gilded. Scammell made its own decalcomania for transfer printing. The Lamberton mark is "Lamberton Ivory China Made in America" in a square.

Scammell also made blue china for the Baltimore and Ohio Railroad for about twenty five years. Scenes included "Cumberland Narrows," "Indian Creek," "Thomas Viaduct," "Potomac Valley," "Harper's Ferry," and such.

Scammell used a wide assortment of marks.

Bowl, 5 3/4" d, stylized red and blue offset flowerheads w/yellow center streak, brown and yellow striped border ...................................................... 4.00
Butter Dish, 7" l, platinum blue glaze ........................... 5.00
Butter Pat, 4 1/4" l, w/tab handle, int blue border band of florals and leaves ................................................... 8.00
Celery Dish, 9 1/2" l, inner band of fruit and flowers and banding, floral bunches and red border w/stars ......... 5.00
Chop Plate, 10 1/2" d, central village scene w/bridge and pond, flowerhead border, brown transfer ............... 10.00
Creamer
    2 1/2" h, band of multicolored garden flowers between gold bands ...................................................... 15.00
    3 1/4" h, multicolored floral bouquet on sides, gold lined rim and handle ................................................... 10.00
Cup and saucer, red and blue bird of paradise on front, yellow-centered blue and red flowerheads w/green leaves on borders, blue lined rims ............................... 15.00
Dish, 5 1/2" d, stylized red and blue offset flowerheads w/yellow center streak, brown and yellow striped border ...................................................... 3.00
Figure
    4 1/4" h, Art Deco style bust of woman w/head raised, "stamped LAMBERTON SCAMMELL SCULPTURED BY GEZA DE VEGH," gloss beige glaze, (A) ...... 45.00
    8" h, Art Deco kneeling holding flower bouquet, gloss white glaze, "LAMBERTON SCAMMELL SCULPTED BY GEZA DE VEGH" mk, (A) ........................... 200.00
    10 1/2" h, bust of Art Deco woman w/short, curly hair, sq base, gloss white glaze, "LAMBERTON SCAMMELL SCULPTED BY GEZA DE VEGH" mk, (A) ....... 140.00
    11 3/4" h, bust of Art Deco woman w/ribbon, sq base, gloss white glaze, "LAMBERTON SCAMMELL SCULPTURED BY GEZA DE VEGH" mk, (A) .. 370.00
Gravy Boat
    6 1/2" l, platinum blue glaze, Lamberton Scammell ...................................................... 5.00
    9" l, multicolored sailing ship on side ...................... 10.00
Plate
    4 3/4" d, "Indian Tree" pattern ................................. 3.00
    6" d, border band of pink roses and green leaves, gold rim ...................................................... 6.00
    7 1/4" d, 2 multicolored geese landing in marsh, gold and inner outer band, Lamberton Scammell ............. 10.00
    7 1/4" H-H, hanging pink rose garlands, gold rim, Lamberton Scammell ................................................ 10.00
    7 1/2" d, "Puritan" pattern, blue w/gold trim .............. 5.00
    8 1/4" d, border band of brown urns, green flowers, band of brown leaves, green and white dots ................ 10.00
    8 1/2" d, floral bunches on border separated by red swirl and dot pattern ..................................................... 7.00
    9" d
        Classic garden and buildings in center, border band of garden flowers, blue transfer ........................... 7.00

SCAMMELL'S TRENTON CHINA

**Plate, 7 1/4" d, multicolored, $25.**

"DuParquet" pattern, bird and butterfly design ...... 7.00
9 1/2" d, border of blue, red, and yellow-gold flower sprays, dk blue inner border band ...................... 15.00
10 1/2" d, "Puritan" pattern ......................................... 5.00
Platter
10 1/2" l, border band of blue urns, fruit bowls, and curlicues ............................................................... 7.00
14" l, "Dorthea" pattern ............................................ 25.00
14 1/4" l, "Moss Rose" pattern, gold trim ................. 15.00
Soup Plate, 7 1/2" d, multicolored exotic birds in center, floral sprays on rim ...................................................... 20.00
Vegetable Bowl
9 3/4" l, border band of blue urns, fruit bowls, and curlicues ...................................................................... 10.00
10" l, dogwood design, Lamberton Scammell .......... 12.00

**REVERIE PATTERN**
Cream Soup, 6 1/8" H-H, w/underplate ........................ 20.00
Cup and Saucer ........................................................... 10.00
Plate
6 3/8" d ................................................................. 8.00
7 5/8" d ................................................................. 8.00
10 3/8" d ............................................................... 15.00

# The Homer Laughlin China Company

## East Liverpool, Ohio 1871-1929
## Newell, West Virginia, 1929-Present

**History:** The Homer Laughlin China Company was founded by Homer and Shakespeare Laughlin in East Liverpool, Ohio in 1871. Homer bought out Shakespeare in 1877 and

continued until he sold the company in 1897 to a group headed by Louis Aaron, his sons Marcus and Charles, and W.E. Wells. The company still operates with these two families in control.

The early years started with white granite ware in 1872. They won an award for whiteware at the Centennial Exposition in 1876. Dinnerwares and commercial china became the mainstay of this company, and eventually they became the largest potter in the world. Expansion was continuous; new plants were added in Newell in 1907, and by 1929, they moved their entire operation across the river to Newell, West Virginia.

Dr. Albert Bleininger joined the company in 1920 as ceramics engineer and was responsible for the clays and glazes. In 1934, Harry Thiemecke worked with him. Frederick Rhead became art director in 1927 and introduced many new designs that were less imitative of European potteries.

Shapes created by Rhead included Liberty in 1928, with a gadroon edge on all pieces, Virginia Rose in 1929, Century in 1931, Fiesta in 1935, Nautilus in 1935 with a sculptured-shell motif, Harlequin in 1936, Brittany in 1936, Eggshell Nautilus and Eggshell Georgian in 1937, Swing in 1938, and Theme made to commemorate the World's Fair in 1939.

After Rhead died in 1942, Don Schreckengost became art director in 1945 and was responsible for the Jubilee, Debutante, Rhythm and Cavalier shapes which were more modern in concept.

In 1959, the company diversified into hotel, restaurant, and institutional china, and by the 1970s, it was producing more of these wares than china for home use. It remains the largest manufacturer in the United States today.

Homer Laughlin wares were sold through large mail-order firms and department stores, were distributed as premiums with soaps, breakfast foods, and other household products, and through coupon programs by grocery stores. The company named each of the shapes it produced, but only named some of the patterns since some were named by the companies that sold the wares to the public. There was a tremendous amount of shapes produced during its years of production.

Virginia Rose, the most popular shape made from 1929 until the early 1970s, was used for more than a dozen dinnerware patterns that were either decaled or embossed. Pale pink roses were used most often. After the shape was discontinued for home use, it was adopted by the hotel china division for institutional use.

Eggshell wares were lighter in weight and had a tremendous diversity of patterns. Jubilee had a solid color glaze and was made to commemorate the 75th anniversary of the company. The Rhythm shape from the late 1940s was the first to be put on the automatic jigger equipment.

Introduced in 1936, Fiesta was designed by Frederick Rhead in vivid colors with a simple design motif. Concentric bands of rings were the only decorative elements aside from the bright, original colors of red, blue, green, yellow, and ivory. Turquoise was added one year later. Numerous pieces were made in all of these colors until 1943 when "Fiesta red went to war" since the uranium oxide for the red glaze was no longer available.

In 1944, the colors produced were turquoise, green, blue, yellow, and ivory, and the 1946 and 1948 price lists indicated the same colors. In 1951, light green, dark blue, and old ivory were retired and replaced by forest green, rose, chartreuse, and gray, along with turquoise and yellow. These colors continued in production until 1959, when Fiesta red returned. Turquoise, yellow, and medium green were continued, while rose, gray, chartreuse, and dark green were discontinued. These colors continued through the 1960s until 1969, when Fiesta was restyled and only the original red continued to be made.

The restyled Fiesta was called Fiesta Ironstone in 1969. Antique gold and turf green were utilized with the red, now called mango red until 1972 when Fiesta red was discontinued, and one year later all Fiesta dinnerware came to an end.

Fiesta Kitchen Kraft was a bake and serve line introduced in 1939 with utilitarian items in red, yellow, green, and blue which was in production until sometime during World War II.

Fiesta was reintroduced in 1986 after a thirteen-year absence. Colors made included cobalt blue, rose, white, apricot, and black with additions of gray and yellow. A vitrified body was used for the "new" Fiesta which was denser and did not absorb moisture. This Fiesta was more appealing to the restaurant trade in addition to being used in private homes. Four additional colors have been added including turquoise, pale yellow, periwinkle blue and sea mist green. Molded hollowware forms are identical to the original Fiesta since the original molds were used. Sizes vary among the other pieces since some are smaller while others are larger. The variety of forms continues to expand in new Fiesta along with new colors every few years.

Harlequin was also designed by Rhead as a less expensive dinnerware to be sold through Woolworth's without the trademark. Yellow, green, red, and blue were used along with bands of rings for decoration. Styling was the Art Deco format used for Fiesta. Additional Fiesta colors were added, and the last piece was made in 1964. Although Woolworth's requested a reissue of Harlequin in 1979, it was only made for a few additional years. Harlequin animals were also sold through Woolworth's from the late 1930s into the early 1940s in six animal forms and four colors.

In 1938, Riviera was introduced and sold by the Murphy Company. It was lighter and less expensive than the other colored dinnerwares. Mauve blue, red, yellow, light green and ivory were the colors used, and the line was discontinued prior to 1950.

From 1900 to the present, Homer Laughlin coded almost all of the production ware with the month, year, and plant of manufacture.

**References:** Jo Cunningham, *Homer Laughlin China: "A Giant Among Dishes" 1873-1937*, Schiffer Publishing Ltd. 1998; Sharon and Bob Huxford, *The Collector's Encyclopedia of Fiesta, Eighth Edition*, Collector Books, 1998; Joanne Jasper, *The Collector's Encyclopedia of Homer Laughlin China*, Collector Books, 1997; Darlene Nossaman, *Homer Laughlin China: An Identification Guide*, Privately Published, 1992; Richard G. Racheter, *Collector's Guide to Homer Laughlin's Virginia Rose*, Collector Books, 1997; Jeffrey B. Snyder, *Fiesta: Homer Laughlin China Company's Colorful Dinnerware, 2nd Edition*, Schiffer Publishing Ltd. 1999.

**Collectors' Clubs:** Fiesta Club of America, Ronald E. Kay, P.O. Box 15383, Machesney Park, IL 61115-5383; quarterly newsletter, $20 per year; The Fiesta Collector's Quarterly, Virginia Lee, P.O. Box 471, Valley City, OH 44280, 4 newsletters, $12 per year; Homer Laughlin China Collectors Association, P.O. Box 26021, Crystal City, VA 22215.

**Museums:** Museum of Ceramics, East Liverpool, OH.

## ART POTTERY

Bowl, 12" H-H, lobed body, Currant pattern, orange-brown ext ............................................................... 165.00
Mug, 4 3/4" h, monk playing violin, brown shades, figural antler handle .......................................... 85.00
Pitcher, 12" h, Gibson girl portrait in colors .............. 135.00
Vase
  7" h, 3 handles, "White Pets" design ..................... 100.00
  8" h, handled, "White Pets" design ...................... 100.00

Gravy Boat, 8 1/2" l, "Dogwood" pattern, $20.

## AMERICANA SHAPE
### Blue Willow Pattern
Creamer ................................................................ 32.00
Cup and Saucer .................................................... 14.00
Fruit Bowl ............................................................. 8.00
Gravy Boat ........................................................... 48.00
Plate
  6" d .................................................................. 8.00
  8" d .................................................................. 12.00
  9 7/8" d ............................................................ 15.00
Platter
  11" l ................................................................. 28.00
  13" l ................................................................. 38.00
Sugar Bowl, Cov ................................................... 45.00
Vegetable Bowl, 10" l, oval .................................. 25.00

### Currier and Ives Pattern
Gravy, "Preparing for Market & Harvest" ............... 55.00
Plate
  6 1/4" d, "Hudson River-Crow Nest" .................... 12.00
  9 7/8" d, "Home Sweet Home" ........................... 32.00
Platter
  11 1/2" l, "View of Harpers Ferry" ...................... 55.00
  13" l, "Suspension Bridge, Niagara Falls" ........ 115.00

### Early American Homes Pattern
Nappy, 8 1/2" d .................................................... 12.00
Plate, 6 1/4" d ...................................................... 12.00
Platter, 11 1/2" l ................................................... 55.00

## CAVALIER SHAPE
### Persian Garden Pattern
Fruit Bowl, 5" d ..................................................... 8.00
Pie Plate, 7" d ....................................................... 7.00
Plate
  6" d .................................................................. 7.00
  10" d ................................................................ 7.00
Soup Plate, 8" d .................................................... 8.00

### Pink Rose Pattern
Berry Bowl ............................................................ 8.00
Plate
  6" d .................................................................. 8.00
  7" d .................................................................. 10.00
  10" d ................................................................ 15.00
Platter, 12" l ......................................................... 22.00

## CENTURY SHAPE
### Conchita Pattern
Pie Plate
    9" d, Daisy Chain, blue edge ............................. 45.00
    10" d, Oven Serve Daisy Chain .......................... 38.00
Soup Plate, 7 3/4" sq ............................................. 26.00

### Mexicana Pattern
Casserole, Cov, 8" d, Kitchen Kraft ..................... 125.00
Chop Plate, 10 5/8" d .......................................... 28.00
Cup and Saucer ..................................................... 15.00
Plate
    8" d .............................................................. 15.00
    9" d .............................................................. 20.00
    10" d ............................................................ 35.00
Platter, 11" H-H ................................................... 68.00
Vegetable Bowl, 8 1/2" d ..................................... 45.00

## EGGSHELL NAUTILUS SHAPE
### Ferndale Pattern
Berry Bowl, 5 1/4" d ................................................ 5.00
Cup and Saucer ....................................................... 5.00
Plate
    8" d ................................................................ 5.00
    10" d .............................................................. 5.00
Platter
    11 1/2" l ....................................................... 20.00
    14" d ............................................................ 28.00
Serving Bowl, 9 1/2" d .......................................... 28.00

### Lexington Pattern
Creamer ................................................................ 16.00
Cup and Saucer ..................................................... 12.00
Nappy .................................................................... 22.00
Plate
    6" d ................................................................ 6.00
    10" d ............................................................ 12.00
Platter, 13" d ....................................................... 35.00
Sugar Bowl, Cov ................................................... 22.00

### Priscilla Pattern
Creamer ................................................................ 16.00
Cup and Saucer ..................................................... 12.00
Gravy Boat ............................................................ 32.00
Kitchen Kraft
  Mixing Bowl
    6" d, without gold trim .............................. 30.00
    10" d, gold trim ........................................ 42.00
Plate
    6" d ................................................................ 8.00
    8" d .............................................................. 10.00
    9" d .............................................................. 12.00
Platter, 13 5/8" d ................................................. 35.00
Sugar Bowl, Cov ................................................... 28.00
Teapot ................................................................... 85.00

### Rose Petit Point Pattern
Creamer ................................................................ 20.00
Cup and Saucer ..................................................... 15.00
Sugar Bowl, Cov ................................................... 32.00

**Water Pitcher, 7 3/4" h, "Fiesta" pattern, turquoise, $130.**

### Tulip Pattern
Bowl, 8 1/4" d ......................................................... 4.00
Plate, 10" d ............................................................ 8.00
Soup Bowl, 8 1/4" d .............................................. 10.00

## EPICURE
Ashtray
    Charcoal Gray ........................................... 310.00
    Dawn Pink ................................................. 300.00
Coffee Cup and Saucer
    Charcoal Gray ............................................. 30.00
    Snow White ................................................. 33.00
Coffeepot
    Dawn Pink ................................................. 290.00
    Turquoise Blue .......................................... 297.00
Creamer, Turquoise Blue ...................................... 20.00
Gravy Bowl
    Snow White ................................................. 28.00
    Charcoal Gray ............................................. 30.00
Gravy Ladle, Charcoal Gray ............................... 250.00
Nappie, Turquoise Blue ........................................ 45.00
Plate
  6" d
    Dawn Pink .................................................... 5.00
    Snow White ................................................... 6.00
    Turquoise Blue .............................................. 8.00
  8" d
    Snow White ................................................. 18.00
    Turquoise Blue ............................................ 18.00
  10" d
    Charcoal Gray ............................................. 22.00
    Dawn Pink ................................................... 20.00
    Snow White ................................................. 21.00
    Turquoise Blue ............................................ 22.00
Shakers, Pr
    Charcoal Gray ............................................. 15.00
    Snow White ................................................. 13.00
Sugar Bowl, Dawn Pink ........................................ 32.00

## FIESTA
Ashtray
    Chartreuse .................................................. 72.00
    Cobalt ......................................................... 67.00
    Forest Green ............................................... 83.00
    Red ............................................................. 64.00
    Turquoise .................................................... 44.00
    Yellow ......................................................... 41.00

Bowl
  4 3/4" d
    Cobalt ................................................. 35.00
    Ivory .................................................. 31.00
    Med Green ....................................... 680.00
    Yellow ................................................ 25.00
  5 1/2" d
    Forest Green ..................................... 39.00
    Med Green .......................................... 77.00
    Red ..................................................... 30.00
    Turquoise ........................................... 25.00
  11 3/4" d
    Cobalt ............................................... 335.00
    Ivory ................................................. 325.00
    Red .................................................. 340.00
    Yellow ............................................... 295.00
Bud Vase
  Ivory .................................................. 135.00
  Red ................................................... 130.00
  Turquoise ........................................... 115.00
Candle Holder
  Bulb
    Cobalt ............................................... 125.00
    Ivory ................................................. 120.00
    Red ................................................... 103.00
  Tripod
    Ivory ................................................. 775.00
    Red ................................................... 900.00
    Turquoise ........................................... 740.00
    Yellow ............................................... 500.00
Carafe
  Cobalt ............................................... 280.00
  Red ................................................... 370.00
  Turquoise ........................................... 275.00
Chop Plate
  13" d
    Chartreuse .......................................... 95.00
    Gray ................................................. 100.00
    Red ..................................................... 65.00
  15" d
    Cobalt ............................................... 115.00
    Ivory ................................................. 100.00
Comport, 12" d
  Cobalt, (A) ......................................... 180.00
  Turquoise, (A) .................................... 160.00
Cream Soup
  Chartreuse ........................................... 61.00
  Cobalt ................................................. 45.00
  Forest Green ....................................... 62.00
  Ivory .................................................. 58.00
  Med green, (A) ................................ 4,000.00
  Red ..................................................... 57.00
  Rose ................................................... 66.00
  Turquoise ............................................ 47.00
Dessert Bowl, 6" d
  Red ..................................................... 50.00
  Turquoise ............................................ 40.00

Divided Plate
  10 1/2" d
    Cobalt, (A) .......................................... 30.00
    Ivory, (A) ............................................ 38.00
    Lt green, (A) ........................................ 40.00
  12" d
    Ivory, (A) ............................................ 25.00
    Red, (A) .............................................. 90.00
    Yellow, (A) ........................................... 50.00
Fruit Bowl, 5 1/2" d
  Chartreuse, (A) .................................... 28.00
  Med green, (A) ..................................... 70.00
  Rose, (A) ............................................. 20.00
Kitchen Kraft
  Cov Jar Lg
    Red, (A) ............................................. 275.00
    Yellow, (A) ......................................... 250.00
  Med, red, (A) ...................................... 250.00
  Sm, red, (A) ........................................ 275.00
Mixing Bowl
  #1
    Green ................................................ 250.00
    Red ................................................... 325.00
    Turquoise ........................................... 300.00
  #3
    Ivory ................................................. 155.00
    Yellow ............................................... 135.00
    Turquoise ........................................... 145.00
  #4
    Cobalt ............................................... 210.00
    Green ................................................ 125.00
    Ivory ................................................. 175.00
    Red ................................................... 215.00
  #5
    Green ................................................ 255.00
    Ivory ................................................. 265.00
    Red ................................................... 260.00
  #6, turquoise ...................................... 350.00
  #7
    Cobalt ............................................... 610.00
    Ivory ................................................. 635.00
    Red ................................................... 700.00
Nappy
  8 1/2" d
    Chartreuse .......................................... 56.00
    Cobalt ................................................. 55.00
    Forest Green ....................................... 58.00
    Med Green ......................................... 180.00
    Red ..................................................... 65.00
  9 1/2" d
    Cobalt ................................................. 60.00
    Ivory ................................................... 58.00
    Red ..................................................... 60.00
    Turquoise ............................................ 45.00
Onion Soup, Cov
  Cobalt ............................................... 745.00
  Lt green ............................................. 800.00
  Med green, (A) ............................... 10,000.00

Red .......................................................... 755.00
Turquoise ............................................... 3,287.00
Yellow ..................................................... 815.00
Pitcher
  Disk Juice
    Red .......................................................... 600.00
    Yellow ...................................................... 35.00
  Disk Water
    Chartreuse ............................................... 265.00
    Forest Green ............................................ 270.00
    Ivory ........................................................ 100.00
    Red .......................................................... 175.00
    Turquoise ................................................. 115.00
  Ice Lip
    Cobalt ...................................................... 145.00
    Turquoise ................................................. 125.00
Plate
  6" d
    Cobalt ...................................................... 6.00
    Ivory ........................................................ 8.00
    Med Green ............................................... 30.00
  7" d
    Chartreuse ............................................... 10.00
    Cobalt ...................................................... 10.00
    Red .......................................................... 12.00
  9" d
    Chartreuse ............................................... 18.00
    Forest Green ............................................ 25.00
    Red .......................................................... 18.00
    Rose ........................................................ 25.00
    Turquoise ................................................. 12.00
    Yellow ...................................................... 13.00
  10" d
    Chartreuse ............................................... 50.00
    Cobalt ...................................................... 45.00
    Gray ........................................................ 48.00
    Ivory ........................................................ 45.00
    Med Green ............................................... 175.00
    Turquoise ................................................. 45.00
Vase
  8" h
    Cobalt ...................................................... 800.00
    Green ...................................................... 660.00
    Red .......................................................... 735.00
  10" h
    Green ...................................................... 1,100.00
    Yellow ...................................................... 750.00
  12" h
    Cobalt ...................................................... 1,400.00
    Ivory ........................................................ 1,350.00
    Turquoise ................................................. 1,000.00

## GEORGIAN EGGSHELL SHAPE

### Blue Chateau Pattern
  Chop Plate, 14" d ..................................... 48.00
  Cup and Saucer ........................................ 12.00
  Plate
    6" d .......................................................... 8.00

Teapot, 7 1/4" h, "Harlequin" pattern, blue, $165.

    9" d .......................................................... 12.00
    10" d ........................................................ 18.00
  Platter
    11 3/4" l .................................................... 24.00
    13 1/4" l .................................................... 35.00
  Soup Plate ................................................ 15.00
  Vegetable Bowl, 8 1/2" d ........................... 24.00

### Cotillion Pattern
  Cup and Saucer ........................................ 8.00
  Fruit Bowl, 5 1/4" d ................................... 8.00
  Plate
    6 1/4" d .................................................... 6.00
    10" d ........................................................ 12.00

### Norway Rose Pattern
  Creamer .................................................... 16.00
  Cup and Saucer ........................................ 12.00
  Plate
    7" d .......................................................... 6.00
    10" d ........................................................ 15.00
  Platter, 11 3/4" l ....................................... 24.00
  Soup plate ................................................ 15.00
  Sugar Bowl, Cov ....................................... 26.00

### Pink Chateau Pattern
  Platter
    11 3/4" l .................................................... 24.00
    13" l ......................................................... 35.00
  Soup Plate ................................................ 15.00

### HARLEQUIN
Cereal Bowl, 6 1/2" d
    Rose ........................................................ 16.00
    Turquoise ................................................. 10.00
Creamer, yellow ............................................ 15.00
Cup and Saucer
    Gray ........................................................ 15.00
    Yellow ...................................................... 11.00
Figure
  Cat
    Maroon .................................................... 225.00
    Spruce ..................................................... 225.00
  Donkey, yellow ......................................... 225.00

Duck
  Spruce ............................................. 225.00
  Turquoise, (A) ................................ 3,000.00
Penguin
  Spruce ............................................. 225.00
  Yellow .............................................. 200.00
Fruit Bowl, 5 1/2" d
  Gray ................................................... 10.00
  Pink ..................................................... 8.00
  Yellow .................................................. 8.00
Gravy Boat, maroon ................................. 46.00
Plate
  6" d
    Dk green ............................................ 6.00
    Turquoise ........................................... 2.00
  7 1/4" d, mauve blue ............................. 5.00
  9" d, gray ............................................ 14.00
  10" d, turquoise .................................. 20.00
Platter, 13" l x 10" w, turquoise ............... 18.00
Sugar Bowl, Cov, rose ............................ 26.00

## JUBILEE SHAPE
Chop Plate, 15" d, Shell Pink ................... 45.00
Coffeepot
  Mist Gray ........................................... 55.00
  Shell Pink ........................................... 55.00
Creamer, Celadon Green ......................... 14.00
Cup and Saucer, Celadon Green .............. 12.00
Plate
  6" d, Mist Gray ..................................... 8.00
  7 3/8" d
    Cream Beige .................................... 10.00
    Mist Gray ........................................ 10.00
  9" d
    Celadon Green ................................. 12.00
    Cream Beige .................................... 12.00
Platter, 11" l
  Cream Beige ....................................... 22.00
  Shell Pink ........................................... 22.00
Sugar Bowl, Cov, Celadon Green ............. 20.00
Teapot, Shell Pink .................................. 75.00

## KITCHEN KRAFT
Mixing Bowl, 10" d
  "Conchita," Fiesta blank ...................... 65.00
  "Petit Point" ....................................... 20.00
Pie Plate, 9" d, "Sun Porch" ................... 95.00

## MISCELLANEOUS
Bowl, 8 3/4" d, multicolored decal of courting couple on int,
  maroon int border band with gold overlay ............... 15.00
Dish, 7" l, bluebird pattern ..................... 30.00
Plate, 9" d, bluebird pattern ................... 15.00

## RHYTHM SHAPE
### DuBarry Pattern
  Berry Bowl, 5 1/4" d .............................. 8.00
  Plate, 7 1/4" d ...................................... 8.00
  Platter, 11 1/2" l ................................ 10.00
  Serving Bowl, 9" d ............................... 10.00
  Soup Bowl, 8 1/4" d ............................... 5.00

Plate, 10" d, "Rhythm" shape, #M54N5 pattern, red-pink and green, $8.

### Lotus Hai Pattern
  Cereal Bowl, 5 1/2" d, ftd ...................... 15.00
  Creamer ............................................. 14.00
  Cup and Saucer .................................. 12.00
  Plate
    6" d ................................................. 8.00
    10" d .............................................. 12.00
  Platter
    13 1/2" l .......................................... 32.00
    15 1/4" l .......................................... 38.00

## Solid Colors
  Creamer, chartreuse ............................ 12.00
  Cup and Saucer, yellow ........................ 15.00
  Gravy Boat, maroon ............................. 22.00
  Nappy, 9" d
    Chartreuse ...................................... 18.00
    Gray ................................................ 18.00
  Plate
    6 1/4" d, yellow .................................. 8.00
    9" d, gray ........................................ 18.00
  Platter, 11" l, forest green .................. 18.00

## RIVIERA-CENTURY SHAPE
Fruit Bowl, 5 1/8" d
  Orange ............................................... 12.00
  Yellow ................................................ 12.00
Plate
  6" d, green ........................................... 8.00
  9" d, green ......................................... 16.00

## VIRGINIA ROSE SHAPE
### Meadow Goldenrod Pattern
  Creamer ............................................. 16.00
  Cup and Saucer .................................. 12.00
  Nappy, 8 1/2" d .................................. 20.00
  Plate
    9" d ................................................ 10.00
    10" d .............................................. 15.00
  Platter, 13" l ..................................... 35.00
  Soup Plate ......................................... 15.00

## Moss Rose JJ59 Pattern

| | |
|---|---|
| Butter Dish, Cov | 175.00 |
| Cereal Bowl | 18.00 |
| Creamer | 20.00 |
| Cup and Saucer | 15.00 |
| Gravy Boat and Stand | 65.00 |
| Nappy, 8" d | 28.00 |
| Pie Baker, 9 1/2" d | 48.00 |

Plate

| | |
|---|---|
| 6" d | 8.00 |
| 7" d | 12.00 |
| 8" d | 35.00 |
| 9 3/8" d | 15.00 |
| 10" d | 22.00 |

Platter

| | |
|---|---|
| 11 1/2" l | 22.00 |
| 13 1/4" l | 38.00 |
| Sugar Bowl, Cov | 35.00 |
| Vegetable Bowl, 9" l | 20.00 |

## WELLS ART

| | |
|---|---|
| Bowl, 8" d, rust | 12.00 |
| Plate, 6" d, pink | 5.00 |
| Sauce Boat, rust | 30.00 |

# Lenox, Inc.

## Trenton, New Jersey
## 1889-Present

**History:** Jonanthan Coxon Senior and Walter Scott Lenox founded the Ceramic Art Company in Trenton, New Jersey in 1889 after they had both worked at Ott and Brewer. Lenox had apprenticed there and at Willets, and had been art director at Ott and Brewer. They worked together until Lenox bought out his partner in 1894 and became sole owner. The Ceramic Art Company made table items, vases, thimbles, inkstands, and parasol handles.

At first Lenox concentrated on Belleek wares, and he imported two potters from Ireland. Lenox was anxious to improve American ceramics to compete with or exceed European standards. Americans were purchasing their fine china from European firms since there was nothing comparable being made in America.

Despite Lenox's blindness and paralysis which occurred in 1895, he continued to work every day. In 1906, the company's name was changed to Lenox, Inc. Harry Brown assisted Lenox in all phases of the company.

Lenox discovered that superior table services could be made from Belleek ware. Before that time, mostly ornamental wares were made. From 1889-1918, the main production of Lenox was decorative pieces. When dinnerware exceeded sales of decorative pieces, it became the mainstay of Lenox production.

Tiffany and Company in New York displayed Lenox's first complete set of dinnerware in 1917. In that year, President Wilson ordered a 1,700-piece dinner set for the White House, designed by Frank G. Holmes. Other Presidential sets were later made for Franklin Delano Roosevelt in 1932, Harry S. Truman in 1951, and Ronald Reagan in 1981.

The company was well established by the time Lenox died in 1920. Several important patterns had been introduced before his death, including Lenox Tradition in 1914 and Autumn China in 1919. William Morley was a noted artist who designed beautiful plates with landscapes, birds, horses, ships, game, and flowers. Most were done in series of twelve hand-painted examples.

By the 1930s, Lenox was a major force in the American market. Frank Holmes was another Lenox designer responsible for modern styles on ivory grounds. Lenox made translucent, ivory toned fine china, translucent fine white bone china, and a casual line with the strength of stoneware.

During World War II, when imports from Europe were cut off, Lenox continued to expand and supply fine china for the increasing American market.

Major growth took place during the 1960s when Lenox acquired companies which produced silver, crystal, and casual wares. Additional plants were built in North Carolina in the 1980s and 1991. Today there is a new plant in Pomona, New Jersey.

Lenox continued to introduce new patterns all during its history. Only 24 karat gold and platinum were used for the trims. A line of figurines as well as Toby mugs, ring boxes, salt and pepper shakers, cosmetic bottles, and lamp bases all were made by Lenox.

Originally palette marks were used which were followed by the wreath marks.

**References:** Mark Frank Gaston, *American Belleek*, Collector Books, 1984; Richard E. Morin, *Lenox Collectibles*, Sixty Ninth Street Zoo, 1993.

## CERAMIC ART COMPANY BELLEEK

Bowl, Cov, 7 1/2" d, painted Art Nouveau bust of woman in gilt medallion on cov, lustered green ground, sgd "Florence M. Brooks," dtd 1904, (A) ............ 345.00

Bud Vase, 9 1/4" h, silver overlay of oriental style cherry blossoms and baskets, ivory ground, silver neck, white mk, c1889 ............ 265.00

Cider Pitcher, 6" h

Green and purple grapes, lt cream ground, green molded handle, "CAC" mk ............ 650.00

HP yellow roses, green foliage, shaded brown ground, "CAC" mk ............ 375.00

Inkwell, 4" sq, multicolored garden flowers, shaded lavender ground, sgd "Morley," "CAC" mk, (A) ............ 125.00

Mug

5" h, HP blackberries and cherry blossoms, dtd 1904, "CAC" mk, (A) ............ 45.00

5 5/8" h, brown monk drinking in tavern, gold rim ............ 160.00

5 3/4" h, lt purple grapes, green leaves, cream to lt purple ground, brown-gold handle, "CAC Belleek" mk. 250.00

7" h, painted frieze of parading roosters, pink and mirrored black ground, Lenox Belleek stamp, (A) ............ 165.00

Pass Cup, 8" h, 3 handles, HP purple and red roses, green leaves, shaded green ground, gold tracery, pink handles, "purple CAC palette" mk ............ 350.00

Pitcher

6" h, ball shape, painted bust of woman wearing brown drape hat, shaded green ground, c1889, "CAC Belleek" mk ............ 950.00

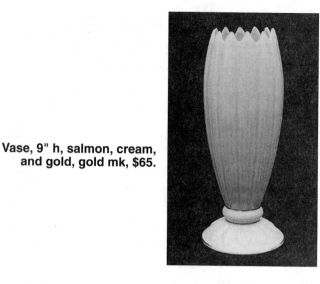

Vase, 9" h, salmon, cream, and gold, gold mk, $65.

Vase, 11 1/2" h, Belleek, multicolored maiden, pink and green floral bkd, "CAC" mk, c1904-24, $875.

8" h, orange berries, green ground, c1890, palette mk ........................................................................ 195.00

Spoon Warmer, 7" h x 6" l, gold impasto and polychrome apple blossoms on ivory ground, "lavender CAC BEL-LEEK" mk, (A) ...................................................... 420.00

Tankard

5 3/4" h, blue and white monk drinking in wine cellar ........................................................................ 395.00

6" h

Art Nouveau style yellow tulips and jonquils, green leaves, silvered ground, brown handle, c1900 ........................................................................ 265.00

Painted Indian head wearing white war bonnet, dk blue to brown ground, sgd "M. Crilley," dtd 1903 ........................................................................ 395.00

"Salmagundi," blue and white abstracts, grotesques, and faces, "1911, No.8, L.Belleek" mk, (A) ... 385.00

7 1/4" h, black panels with silver leaves, grapes, and lines, salmon accents, sgd "Robinson," "CAC Lenox Belleek" mk................................................ 195.00

14 1/2" h, painted standing nude female w/grape arbor and gold chalice in landscape, sgd "E.I. Beck," palette mk, (A) ...................................................... 605.00

Vase

4 1/2" h x 7" d, squat shape, orange and white nasturtium, gold and black ground, "C.A.C." mk, (A)... 110.00

10" h, tapered form, flared rim, blue, tan, brown, and red painted Arts and Craft landscape design, "green CAC BELLEEK" mk, (A)...................................... 895.00

11" h, cylinder shape, silver overlay of vines and trellis fencing, ivory ground, "L and palette Belleek" mk ........................................................................ 750.00

11 1/4" h, bottle shape, sm flared rim, HP orange and green trumpet flowers, "CAC" mk, (A) .............. 330.00

11 1/2" h, cylinder shape

Black wreath and ribbons, black banded rim and base, ivory ground, "CAC" mk ................................ 450.00

Multicolored standing maiden, pink and green floral bkd, "CAC" mk, c1906-24 ............................ 875.00

12 1/2" h, bulbous base, slender flared neck and rim, HP yellow and amber roses, sgd "Henrietta Wright," lavender CAC mk, (A) ...................................... 295.00

16 1/4" h, cylinder shape, painted polychrome, lake scene w/trees and swans, sgd "R. Petger," dtd 1911, palette mk, (A) ...................................................... 375.00

## AUTUMN PATTERN

Cake Stand, 8 3/4" d x 2 3/4" h, (A) ........................... 77.00
Cup and Saucer ....................................................... 15.00
Plate
7 1/2" d ............................................................. 14.00
8 1/2" d ............................................................. 15.00
9" d ................................................................... 16.00
10 1/2" d ........................................................... 20.00

## BELVEDERE PATTERN

Cup and Saucer ....................................................... 45.00
Platter, 17" l........................................................... 235.00

## BLUE TREE PATTERN

Plate, 10 1/2" d, set of 10......................................... 60.00

## CARLBEE PATTERN

Plate, 10 1/2" d........................................................ 55.00

## CHARLESTON PATTERN

Cup and Saucer ....................................................... 15.00
Plate
6 1/2" d ............................................................. 12.00
8" d ................................................................... 15.00
10 3/4" d ........................................................... 20.00

## CRETAN PATTERN

Coffeepot................................................................ 165.00
Creamer ................................................................. 40.00
Gravy Boat, attached undertray ............................... 129.00
Platter
13 5/8" l............................................................. 95.00
17" l................................................................... 195.00

## DESIRE PATTERN

Plate, 10 5/8" d........................................................ 15.00

## ETERNAL PATTERN

Cup and Saucer ....................................................... 23.00
Platter, 16 1/2" l....................................................... 110.00

## FALL BOUNTY PATTERN

Berry Bowl, 4 3/4" d.................................................. 3.00

Bowl, Cov

    4 1/4" d..............................................5.00

    5" d..................................................6.00

Creamer, 4" h .........................................3.00

Cup and Saucer ......................................4.00

Plate

    6 1/2" ..............................................4.00

    10 1/2" d..........................................5.00

Soup Bowl, 6" d......................................4.00

## GOLDEN WREATH PATTERN
Cup and Saucer ....................................30.00

## HARVEST PATTERN
Cup and Saucer ....................................75.00

Plate

    6 1/4" d..............................................8.00

    8 3/4" d..............................................8.00

    10 1/2" d..........................................12.00

## IMPERIAL PATTERN
Cup and Saucer ......................................8.00

Plate, 6 1/4" d .........................................8.00

## LAURENT PATTERN
Creamer ...............................................60.00

Platter, 16" l, oval...............................165.00

Vegetable Bowl, 9 1/2" l.....................145.00

## MING PATTERN
Bowl, 9 3/4" d ....................................175.00

Butter Tub, 4 1/2" d..............................75.00

Compote, 8 7/8" d..............................100.00

Creamer, 3 1/2" h ................................70.00

Cup and Saucer ....................................35.00

Cup and Saucer, Demitasse..................18.00

Dessert Plate, Coup, 7" d .....................25.00

Jam Jar, 3 3/4" d................................135.00

Plate

    6 3/8" d............................................16.00

    8 1/4" d............................................28.00

    Plate, 9" d ........................................32.00

    10 1/2" d..........................................40.00

Platter, 13 3/8" l..................................125.00

Soup Bowl, 7 1/4" d..............................45.00

Sugar Bowl, Cov, 3 5/8" h.....................80.00

Teapot, 4 1/2" h..................................150.00

Vegetable Bowl, 9 1/2" l........................75.00

## MISCELLANEOUS
Bud Vase

    8" h

        Bulbous body, flared ft and neck, 2 small handles, molded vert striping, white ..............48.00

        Tulips w/gold leaves, green mk ........125.00

    8 1/4" h, gold wheat design....................25.00

Candlestick, 3 3/4" h, "Greenfield" pattern, pr .............25.00

Dish, 5" l, leaf shape, brown and gray floral spray, silver rim ..................................................14.00

**Cup and Saucer, "Rose Manor" pattern, $35.**

Figure

    3 5/8" h, girl with pigtails and pin dress on block, (A) ....................................45.00

    5 1/4" h, rabbit seated on haunches, gloss white glaze, (A) ...................50.00

    9" h, bust of Art Deco woman, ivory .....................285.00

    13 1/2" h, Art Deco girl standing with greyhound at side, gloss ivory glaze, "imp LENOX/A.B.C.O. 37" mk, (A) ....................................467.00

    13 3/4" h, Art Deco standing girl holding hem of gown, gloss ivory glaze, "imp LENOX/A.B.C.O. 37" mk, (A) ....................................385.00

Lamp, 11" h, figural Leda and Swan, white, c1929, (A) ....................................187.00

Paperweight, 4 1/2" h, bisque, Art Deco bust of woman, (A) ....................................110.00

Pitcher, 5 1/4" h, swirl body, ivory.................45.00

Toby Jug, 6 3/4" h, half figure, cream.........125.00

Vase

    5" h, pastel blue ground w/gold nasturtium flowerheads, gold int.......................25.00

    7 1/2" h, bulbous shape, emb Greek key design on collar, 2 handles, ivory glaze, green wreath mk, (A)......70.00

    12" h, stepped cylinder shape, flared rim, stylized vert stiff leaf design, gold rim ......................95.00

## MOONSPUN PATTERN
Bowl, 10 1/2" l, oval............................145.00

Cup and Saucer ....................................20.00

Fruit Bowl, 5 1/4" d...............................45.00

Plate

    6 1/4" d............................................20.00

    8" d .................................................20.00

    10 1/2" d..........................................35.00

Platter, 17" l......................................225.00

## MYSTIC PATTERN
Cup and Saucer, Demitasse..................15.00

## OLYMPIA PATTERN
Plate, 10 1/2" d....................................12.00

Vegetable Bowl, 8 1/4" l............................................45.00

## ORLEANS PATTERN
Cup and Saucer ....................................................15.00

## PRINCESS PATTERN
Plate
6 1/4" d.............................................................5.00
7 3/4" d.............................................................8.00
10 3/8" d...........................................................10.00

## RHODORA PATTERN
Cup and Saucer ....................................................25.00
Fruit Bowl, 5 1/2" d...............................................25.00
Plate
6 1/4" d.............................................................25.00
8 1/4" d.............................................................30.00
10 1/2" d...........................................................35.00

## SOLITAIRE PATTERN
Plate
6 1/4" d.............................................................8.00
8" d....................................................................10.00
10 1/2" d...........................................................15.00
Soup Bowl, 7 5/8" d................................................30.00

## SPRINGDALE PATTERN
Cup and Saucer ....................................................40.00
Plate
8 1/4" d.............................................................30.00
10 1/4" d...........................................................35.00

## STARLIGHT PATTERN
Cereal Bowl, 6 1/4" d..............................................3.00
Cup and Saucer ....................................................3.00
Plate
8" d....................................................................3.00
10 1/4" d...........................................................5.00
Vegetable Bowl, 9 1/2" l...........................................25.00

## WEATHERLY PATTERN
Chop Plate, 12 3/4" d..............................................90.00

**Plate, 8" d, "Windsong" pattern, $15.**

Coffeepot, 7 3/4" h .................................................375.00
Cup and Saucer ....................................................36.00
Fruit Bowl, 5 1/2" d...............................................15.00
Plate
6 3/8" d.............................................................15.00
7 7/8" d.............................................................18.00
10 1/2" d...........................................................20.00
Teapot, 4 5/8" h....................................................375.00

## WHEAT PATTERN
Cup and Saucer ....................................................5.00
Plate
8 1/4" d.............................................................6.00
10 1/4" d...........................................................10.00

## WINDSONG PATTERN
Creamer 4" h........................................................125.00
Cup and Saucer ....................................................30.00
Fruit Bowl, 5 3/8" d................................................25.00
Plate
8" d....................................................................25.00
10 3/4" d...........................................................25.00
Sugar Bowl, Cov ...................................................135.00
Vegetable Bowl, 10" l..............................................165.00

# Limoges China Company
## 1900-1949

# American Limoges China Company

### Sebring, Ohio
### 1949-1955

**History:** The Limoges China Company was organized in 1900 by Frank and Frederick Sebring in Sebring, Ohio under the name of Sterling China Company. It made porcelain dinnerware, tea sets, chocolate, salad, fruit, and soup sets similar to the European wares for the American market. The name was changed to Limoges China Company. After a huge fire, porcelain was discontinued, and only semi-vitreous china was made in a wide variety of patterns.

In a dispute with the Limoges China Company of France concerning overuse of the Limoges name, the company name was changed to the American Limoges China Company in 1949.

Limoges completely revolutionized the pottery industry when it developed the tunnel kiln which replaced the beehive type. They also used decalcomania transfers on dinnerwares. Victor Schreckengost was an important designer for Limoges. A wide variety of marks was used. The company stayed in business until 1955.

**References:** Raymonde Limoges, *American Limoges*, Collector Books, 1996.

**Vegetable Bowl, Cov, 10 1/2" H-H, flowing blue border w/gold overlays, $225.**

## BEL CLARE PATTERN
Berry Bowl, 4" sq ................................................ 2.00
Cake Plate, 8 1/2" H-H ..................................... 10.00
Creamer, 3 1/2" h .............................................. 6.00
Cup and Saucer ................................................. 3.00
Plate
    6" sq ............................................................ 2.00
    7" sq ............................................................ 3.00
    9" sq ............................................................ 3.00
Platter
    8 1/2" l ...................................................... 10.00
    11 1/4" l .................................................... 10.00
    13 1/2" l .................................................... 12.00
Soup Bowl, 7 3/4" sq ......................................... 3.00
Sugar Bowl, Cov, 6 1/4" w ................................. 8.00
Vegetable Bowl, 9 3/8" l .................................. 10.00
Vegetable Bowl, Cov, 9" H-H .......................... 12.00

## BERMUDA PATTERN
Berry Bowl, 5 1/2" d .......................................... 3.00
Gravy Boat, 6 3/8" l ........................................... 8.00
Nappy, 8 3/4" d ................................................ 10.00
Plate
    6 1/4" d ...................................................... 3.00
    7" d ............................................................. 5.00
    10" d .......................................................... 10.00
Soup Bowl, 8 1/4" d ......................................... 10.00
Vegetable Bowl, 9" l .......................................... 3.00

## BLUEBIRD PATTERN
Soup Bowl, 8" d ............................................... 20.00

## BLUE WILLOW PATTERN
Bowl, 9" d ........................................................ 10.00
Plate, 6 1/4" d ................................................... 5.00

## BRIAR ROSE PATTERN
Plate, 9 1/2" d .................................................. 10.00

## CANDLE LIGHT PATTERN
Bowl, 8 1/2" d .................................................... 3.00
Plate
    6 1/2" d ...................................................... 3.00
    10" d ............................................................ 5.00
Platter, 15 3/4" l .............................................. 10.00

## CHINA D'OR PATTERN
Cereal Bowl, 6 1/8" d ........................................ 4.00
Cup and Saucer ................................................. 4.00
Plate
    7 1/4" d ...................................................... 5.00
    10 1/4" d .................................................... 8.00
Soup Bowl, 8 1/4" d ........................................... 5.00
Tray, 12" H-H .................................................. 10.00

## CORAL PINK PATTERN
Platter, 14" H-H ................................................ 5.00

## DELLA ROBBIA PATTERN
Platter, 16" l ................................................... 10.00
Serving Bowl, 9 1/2" d ....................................... 5.00

## FLOWER SHOP PATTERN
Gravy Boat, 8" l ............................................... 35.00

## FORTUNE PATTERN
Cup and Saucer ................................................. 4.00
Plate
    6 1/4" d ...................................................... 3.00
    7 1/2" d ...................................................... 4.00
    10" d ............................................................ 6.00
Platter, 8" l .................................................... 10.00
Soup Plate, 8 1/2" d .......................................... 4.00

## GARDENIA PATTERN
Plate, 10" d, set of 4 ....................................... 15.00

## GOOD HOUSEKEEPING LINE
Creamer, 3 1/4" h, pink floral spray, gold overlay .......... 8.00
Sugar Bowl, Cov, 5" h, ribbed, multicolored
    floral panel on int, gilt overlay ................................. 10.00

## GRAY BLOSSOM PATTERN
Fruit Bowl ......................................................... 8.00
Plate, 9 1/4" d ................................................ 12.00
Teacup and Saucer .......................................... 12.00

## HOLLYWOOD PATTERN
Bowl, 8 1/4" d .................................................... 3.00
Soup Plate, 8 1/4" d ........................................... 3.00

## KAREN PATTERN
Bowl, 8 1/2" d .................................................... 5.00
Creamer ............................................................. 3.00

## LACE BOUQUET PATTERN
Plate, 10 1/2" d ............................................... 12.00

## LA VERNE ROSE PATTERN
Bowl, 9 1/4" l x 7" w .......................................... 5.00

## LE FLEUR ROUGE PATTERN
Casserole, Cov, 8" d ........................................ 75.00
Cereal Bowl, 6 1/4" d ......................................... 3.00
Cup and Saucer ............................................... 10.00
Fruit Bowl, 5 1/4" d ........................................... 5.00
Plate
    6 1/2" d ...................................................... 5.00
    7 1/2" d ...................................................... 9.00
    10" d .......................................................... 10.00

Platter

  10" H-H ...............................................10.00

  12" H-H ...............................................15.00

Soup Bowl, 8" d ..........................................10.00

## LYRIC PATTERN

Berry Bowl, 5 1/4" d.......................................3.00

Bowl, Cov, 9" d ...........................................15.00

Cereal Bowl, 6" d .........................................3.00

Creamer ..................................................10.00

Cup and Saucer ...........................................15.00

Fruit Bowl, 5 1/4" d .......................................9.00

Plate

  6 1/4" d...............................................6.00

  9 1/2" d...............................................12.00

Platter

  11" l .................................................25.00

  13 1/2" H-H ...........................................15.00

Serving Plate

  8" H-H ................................................15.00

  10 1/2" H-H ...........................................15.00

Soup Plate, 8" d ..........................................5.00

Sugar Bowl, Cov...........................................15.00

Vegetable Bowl, 9" d ......................................27.00

## MISCELLANEOUS

Berry Bowl, 5 1/2" d, ridged blue border w/gold overlay
..........................................................29.00

Bowl, 12" l x 10" w, molded seashell shape, pink and turquoise flowers, green leaves, blue to white shaded
ground, gold lines, gilt rim ..............................37.00

Butter Dish, Cov, 8 1/2"H-H x 5 1/2" h, dome shape, ridged
blue border w/gold overlay...............................225.00

Plate, 9 1/2" d, flowing blue border w/raised design and gold
overlay .................................................10.00

Platter

  12 1/2" l, brown elk in center, scalloped rim, "LIMOGES
  CHINA CO." mk.........................................15.00

  14" l, oval, ridged blue border with gold overlay ......55.00

  15 1/2" l, oval, multicolored transfer of violets, daisies,
  and green leaves in center, cobalt scalloped border
  w/gold overlay, "LIMOGES CHINA" mk..............50.00

## OLD DUTCH PATTERN

Plate, 10" d .............................................10.00

Platter, 12" d ...........................................10.00

Tureen, Cov, 5" h x 10" l.................................50.00

## OLD VIRGINIA PATTERN

Cup and Saucer ...........................................3.00

Plate, 6" d ..............................................3.00

## POSEY SHOP PATTERN

Creamer, 3" h ............................................15.00

Plate

  6 1/4" d...............................................3.00

  9 1/2" d...............................................4.00

Platter

  11 1/2" l .............................................4.00

  13 3/4" l..............................................5.00

Sugar Bowl, 4 3/4" d .....................................15.00

## ROSALIE PATTERN

Berry Bowl ...............................................6.00

Creamer and Sugar Bowl....................................30.00

Plate

  6" d ..................................................6.00

  7 1/4" d...............................................5.00

  9 1/4" d...............................................12.00

  10" d .................................................6.00

Platter, 12" l ...........................................5.00

Teacup and Saucer ........................................12.00

## ROYAL MAZARINE PATTERN

Tea Service, pot, 8 3/4" l, creamer, cov sugar bowl, 4 plates,
8" d, cobalt ground, gold floral overlay, c1900.......395.00

## SERENADE PATTERN

Berry Bowl, 6 1/2" d......................................6.00

Bowl, 9" d ...............................................20.00

Creamer and Sugar Bowl....................................30.00

Plate

  6 1/2" d...............................................3.00

  7 1/4" d...............................................3.00

Platter

  12" H-H ...............................................24.00

  14" H-H ...............................................32.00

Soup Bowl, 6 1/4" d ......................................8.00

Teacup and Saucer ........................................12.00

## SHARON PATTERN

Cup and Saucer ...........................................8.00

Fruit Bowl, 5 1/4" d .....................................12.00

Plate

  6" d ..................................................9.00

  9" d ..................................................10.00

Vegetable Bowl, 5 1/4" d .................................7.00

## SILVER MOON PATTERN-PEACH BLOW

Berry Bowl, 5 3/4" d......................................4.00

Chop Plate, 11" d ........................................10.00

Cup and Saucer ...........................................10.00

Plate

  6 1/4" d...............................................5.00

  7 1/8" d...............................................5.00

  10" sq.................................................8.00

Platter, 11" l ...........................................20.00

Soup Bowl, 8 1/4" d.......................................6.00

## STARFLOWER PATTERN

Plate

  6 3/8" d...............................................2.00

  7 1/4" d...............................................3.00

Platter, 13 1/2" l........................................10.00

## SUNDALE PATTERN

Cup and Saucer ...........................................12.00

Plate

  6" d ..................................................6.00

  9" d ..................................................12.00

  10" d .................................................12.00

## TOLEDO DELIGHT PATTERN

Creamer, 2 3/4" h ........................................10.00

Gravy Boat, 3" h ................................................... 6.00
Plate
    6 1/4" d................................................... 10.00
    8 3/4" d................................................... 15.00
Platter, 11 1/4" l ................................................. 12.00

### TRILLIUM PATTERN-GLAMOUR SHAPE
Bowl, 8 1/2" d ................................................... 10.00
Fruit Bowl, 5 1/2" d ............................................. 3.00
Cake Plate, 11" H-H ......................................... 20.00
Cup and Saucer ................................................. 3.00
Plate, 10" d ........................................................ 8.00
Platter, 12 1/2" H-H ........................................ 15.00

### VERMILLION ROSE PATTERN
Bowl, 8 1/2" d ..................................................... 8.00
Cereal Bowl, 6 1/8" d........................................ 2.00
Chop Plate, 12 1/4" d ...................................... 10.00
Cup and Saucer ................................................. 7.00
Fruit Bowl, 5 1/2" d ............................................ 3.00
Plate
    6 1/2" d..................................................... 3.00
    7" d............................................................ 7.00
Platter, 11" l ..................................................... 15.00
Soup Plate, 8 1/4" d .......................................... 6.00
    Tray, 7 1/8" d, tab handles ....................... 20.00

# Maddock Pottery Company 1893-1923

# Thomas Maddock and Sons 1882-1929

# John Maddock and Sons 1895-1929

### Trenton, New Jersey

c.1904

**History:** Three separate Maddock family potteries were operating at approximately the same time in Trenton, New Jersey.

The Maddock Pottery Company operated from 1893-1923 in the old Lamberton Works that eventually became the home of Scammell China Company. "Lamberton China" was the name of the hotel china made by Maddock Pottery Company. They made white granite dinner sets, toilet sets, and plain and decorated odd dishes.

Thomas Maddock and Sons operated from 1882-1929. Thomas Maddock became the sole owner after he worked with Astbury from 1875-1882. He took his sons in as his partners. They made white earthenware, sanitary ware, decorated ware, souvenir and fraternal pieces. They purchased Glasgow Pottery in 1900 and made "American China."

John Maddock and Sons operated from 1895-1929 and made sanitary ware, sanitary specialties, and plumbers' ware.

They used a wide variety of marks on their wares from all three potteries.

Bowl, Cov, 5" d, band of blue curlicues and foliage on base and cov, loop knob, chips.......................... 10.00

**Pass Cup, 7 1/2" h, light and dark blue shades, "Thomas Maddock, Trenton, N.J." mk, $150.**

Butter Pat, center transfer of pink flower bouquet and green leaves, gold rim, set of 4........................................ 15.00
Compote, 4 1/2" h, lt pink and yellow flowers w/brown leaves and blue dots, sculpted gold rim, mkd.......... 10.00
Gravy Boat, 4 1/4" h, scattered pink tinted flowers, molded floral designs on spout, gilt accents........................ 10.00
Pitcher, 7" h, multicolored bouquets of garden flowers, gold trim, "MADDOCK LAMBERTON WORKS" mk ........ 20.00
Platter, 11 1/2" l, oval, green chain link pattern on rim, "MADDOCK CHINA AMERICAN" mk ................................ 5.00
Soup Bowl, 8 3/4" d, 3 groups of hanging stylized flowerheads, black transfer, black inner and outer banding
.......................................................................... 5.00

# Marblehead Pottery

### Marblehead, Massachusetts
### 1904-1936

c.1904-1936

**History:** Marblehead Pottery was actually started as part of a group industry called Handcraft Shops which were therapeutic workshops for recovering patients. The pottery proved too difficult and separated itself after the first year.

The pottery was founded by Herbert Hall, but was really controlled by supervisor Arthur Baggs. By 1908, they were making vases, jardinieres, lampstands, and tiles in simple form and matte glazes in gray, brown, blue, and yellow.

In 1912, they introduced a small line of tin-enameled faience in the form of teapots, mugs, children's sets, and small breakfast and luncheon sets. These were done in soft colors on cream, white, or gray grounds.

When Baggs became owner of the pottery in 1915, matte glazed wares were the mainstay of the operation in Marblehead blue, gray, wisteria, rose, yellow, and tobacco brown. Decorative jars, lamps, sculpture, and garden ornaments were added to the general line. Flowers, fruits, animals and sea motifs were used on the hand thrown pieces. Molds were only used for bookends and tiles.

Baggs continued to teach and became head of the Ceramic Art School at Ohio State University. He returned to work at Marblehead every summer until the pottery closed in 1936.

Marblehead won a series of awards for its pottery. Most examples were marked with the ship and "MP" cipher.

**Museums:** National Museum of History and Technology, Smithsonian Institution, Washington, DC; New Orleans Museum of Art, LA; The Newark Museum, NJ.

**Bowl, 7" d x 3 1/2" h, incised and painted dk brown stylized design, oatmeal ground, imp mk, (A), $5,500.**

**Vase, 5" h, incised and painted dk blue grapes, blue-green leaves, lavender ground, blue rim, hairlines, (A), $605.**

**Vase, 6 1/2" h, two-tone blue painted flowers and stems, slate gray ground, sgd "A.E. Baggs" and "Hanna Tutt," (A), $4,950.**

Bookend, 5 1/2" sq, blue and yellow painted and carved sailing ships at sea, pr, (A) ....................................... 3,575.00

Bowl

    4 1/2" d, spherical, dk brown speckled glaze over matte brown ground, "imp ship" mk, (A) ..................... 495.00

    6 1/2" d, closed form, matte blue glaze, (A) ........... 282.00

    8" d, flared rim, emb lotus design on ext, semi-matte dk blue ext glaze, semi-matte lt green int glaze, stamped ship mk, (A) ................................................. 357.00

    8 1/2" d, incised and painted black geometric design, matte green ground, imp mk, (A) ..................... 2,310.00

Bud Vase

    5 3/4" h, stick shape, black glaze w/blue speckling on base, "imp ship" mk, (A) .................................... 165.00

    6" h, squat base, tapered neck, matte brown glaze, (A) ...................................................................... 220.00

Cabinet Vase, 3 3/4" h, cylinder shape, flat rim, matte gray w/dk blue speckling, teal green int, hairline, "imp ship" mk, (A) ...................................................................... 247.00

Chamberstick, 8 1/2" h, loop handle, matte dk green glaze, imp mk, (A) .......................................................... 550.00

Flowerpot, 5" h, flared shape, dk blue glaze ............. 385.00

Pitcher, 5" h, emb medallions of tall ships, waves around neck, gray and blue semi-matte glaze, ochre ground, "imp ship" mk, (A) .......................................... 770.00

Vase

    3 1/2" h x 5 1/2" d, low, round form, yellow and brown matte glaze, imp mk, (A) .................................... 715.00

    3 3/4" h, gourd shape, 5 dk green relief molded abstracts, cobalt ground w/dk blue flecks, dk caramel brown int, Hannah Tutt, restored rim chip, (A) .................. 715.00

    4 1/8" d, tapered spherical shape, dk teal blue glaze, imp mk, (A) ...................................................... 173.00

    4 1/4" h, bulbous, red and purple stylized floral band on rim, pink semi-matte ground, (A) ...................... 880.00

4 1/2" h

    Short, cylinder shape, incised and painted green geometric design, blue ground, Arthur Baggs, hairline, (A) ............................................................... 1,045.00

    Tapered shape, band of incised and painted multicolored fruit on shoulder, blue and gray ground, Hannah Tutt, (A) .............................................. 1,540.00

4 3/4" h

    Bowl shape, squared shoulder, matte navy blue glaze, med blue int, chip on base, "imp ship" mk, (A) ................................................................. 385.00

    Cylinder shape, incised blue butterflies w/raised yellow dots, red and rose-pink flowers and green foliage, matte speckled lavender ground, "imp ship" mk, hairlines, (A) ...................................... 1,045.00

    Swollen cylinder shape, border band of red, blue, and tan raised flowers and leaves on speckled matte blue ground, imp mk, (A) ............................ 1,610.00

    Trumpet shape, flared rim, matte lavender glaze, imp mk, (A) ...................................................... 468.00

5" h x 7" w, short base, flared body, ext matte brown glaze, int med brown glaze, (A) ......................... 605.00

5 1/2" h, flared shape, matte dk blue glaze, (A) ..... 525.00

6" h, bag shape, flared rim, matte gray glaze, imp mk, (A) ...................................................................... 660.00

6 1/4" h, bulbous base, straight sides, brown incised stylized trees on border, speckled green ground, hairline, (A) ..................................................................... 3,575.00

6 1/2" h

    Bulbous base, tapered sides, incised dk brown flowerheads, stems, and horiz bands, lt brown ground, "imp ship" mk, (A) .......................................... 9,350.00

    Hourglass shape, matte lavender glaze, imp mk, (A) ................................................................. 550.00

    Trumpet shape, med lustered dk blue glaze, "imp ship" mk, (A) ...................................................... 247.00

7" h

    Blue-green stylized leaves and red berries on olive green vert stems, blue ground, imp mk, (A) ................................................................. 4,125.00

    Bulbous shape, incised dk brown panthers lt brown windows on border, lt green ground, "imp ship and HT" mk, (A) ....................................... 18,700.00

    Cylinder shape, matte green glaze, imp mk, (A) ................................................................. 660.00

    Ovoid shape, olive green stylized trees, dk blue ground, ship mk, (A) .................................. 3,575.00

Swollen base, flared neck, mottled matte blue, green, and gray toned glaze, imp mk, (A) ............... 990.00

7 1/2" h, bulbous body, flared rim, horiz lines, gloss blue glaze ................................................................. 285.00

8" h

Bag shape, flared rim, matte dk mustard yellow mottled glaze, speckled red-brown highlights, "imp ship" mk, (A) ...................................................... 715.00

Cylinder shape, flared rim, band of charcoal black stylized trees within incised and painted borders, matte green ground, Hannah Tutt, paper label, (A) ....................................................... 7,700.00

Tapered form, flared rim, matte dk blue glaze, (A) .............................................................. 990.00

8 1/2" h

Bell shape, frothy matte blue-green glaze, repaired base hole, "incised M and seagull" mk, (A) .............................................................. 990.00

Corset shape, incised vert ribs and checkered border bands top and base, matte brown and green shades, "imp ship" mk, (A) ...................... 36,300.00

Swollen, tapered shape, matte blue glaze, (A) ........................................................... 1,100.00

9" h, cylinder shape, rolled rim, matte blue glaze, imp mk, (A) ................................................................ 935.00

9 1/2" h, cylinder shape, tapered top, carved and painted stylized black floral design, matte green ground, hairline, (A) ....................................................... 1,650.00

11 1/8" h, hourglass shape, emb and incised dk gray arts and crafts from rim to base, matte green ground w/gray speckling, gloss caramel brown int, Hannah Tutt, "imp ship" mark, hairlines, (A) ................ 1,870.00

Vessel, 3" h x 4 1/4" d, ribbed body, matte green and charcoal glaze, "incised winged M" mk, (A) ................................................................ 440.00

# Mayer China Company

## Beaver Falls, Pennsylvania
## 1881-1985

MAYER
CHINA
BEAVER FALLS. PA
U. S. A.
SHASTA
160

**History:** Joseph Mayer came from England and organized Mayer Potteries Company, Ltd. with his brother in 1881. They later incorporated as Mayer China Company.

During its history, the company made a variety of products. Tea leaf white ironstone was an early ware. By the turn of the century, white granite, semi-porcelain, dinner sets, toilet sets, and odd dishes were made.

Mostly whitewares were being made by 1915. They produced hotel, restaurant, and institutional china at that time and gradually discontinued tableware for home use.

Shenango China Company of New Castle, Pennsylvania purchased Mayer China in 1964. Both companies were purchased by Interpace in 1968. In 1979, Shenango was sold to Anchor Hocking Corporation. Mayer China took over Walker China Company in 1980, and closed it one year later. Interpace sold Mayer in 1979 to investors who sold it to Syracuse China Company in 1985.

A wide variety of marks was used during the long history and various ownership changes of Mayer China Company.

Berry Bowl, 5 3/4" d, blue-green "Curtis" pattern, ........ 10.00

Butter Dish, 4" d, "Marion" pattern, blue-green .............. 5.00

Butter Pat, 3 1/4" d, "Tropic" pattern ............................ 3.00

**Platter, 12 1/4" l, "Indian Tree" pattern, $20.**

Cereal Bowl, 6 1/2" d, blue-green "Curtis" pattern ......... 4.00

Creamer

2 3/4" h, red floral blossoms and buds w/green foliage on shoulder, red striped rim ...................................... 10.00

3 1/2" h, wide blue band in center, gold banded rim ................................................................ 8.00

Cup and Saucer, flowing mauve, white int of cup .......... 5.00

Fruit Bowl, 4 1/2" d, "Mayan," dk red "Arrowhead" pattern ................................................................ 5.00

Gravy Boat

6 1/4" l, gray-green band of leaves and hanging flowerheads on border, mkd .................................... 5.00

9" l

"Mayan," band of brown curlicues on border ......... 6.00

White w/blue-green stripe ..................................... 5.00

Mug, 3 1/4" h, figural cobra handle, gold crown on side, gold border band ................................................................ 6.00

Pitcher, 5 1/2" h, tan and brown "Curtis" pattern ............ 5.00

Plate

5 1/4" d, yellow brown "Oak Leaf" pattern ................ 3.00

6" d, 2 pink flamingos in center w/ferns, green leaf rim, mkd .............................................................. 30.00

7" d, Mayan

Border band of dk brown curlicues ..................... 5.00

Dk red "Arrowhead" pattern ................................. 4.00

7 3/8" d, dk red border band of flowerheads and geometrics ................................................................ 5.00

8" d, chalet design w/flowerheads, blue shades, blue lined rim, mkd ................................................ 3.00

8 1/2" d, "Birkshire" pattern, gray and dk red ............ 8.00

9" d, "Saxony" pattern, border band of med brown leaf design and diag dashes ..................................... 5.00

10" d, "Doris" pattern, bouquets of anemones and hanging floral swags on border, center bouquet, green transfer ................................................................ 20.00

10" sq, white ironstone, relief molded border .......... 20.00

Platter

7 1/8" l, thick and thin green border bands ................ 5.00

12" l, "Lawson" pattern, multicolored florals .............. 7.00

12 1/4" l, lt brown "Curtis" pattern ........................... 8.00

Rosedale Pattern

Plate

5 1/2" d ................................................................. 4.00

7" d ....................................................................... 4.00

8 1/4" d ................................................................. 5.00

Serving Dish, 11" l, "Baltic" pattern, blue-green ............ 5.00

Soup Plate, 9" d, "Tremont" pattern, blue transfer ........ 10.00

Sugar Bowl, Cov, 4 1/2" h, band of black ric rac on
  borders .................................................. 6.00
Teapot, 5 1/2" h, stenciled dk pink stylized flower on side,
  dk pink lined rim ................................... 10.00

## J.W. McCoy

**1899-1911**

## Brush McCoy

**1911-1918**

## Nelson McCoy

**1910-1990**
**Roseville and Zanesville, Ohio**

**History:** James W. McCoy organized J.W. McCoy Pottery in Roseville, Ohio in 1899. At first he made utilitarian wares, and then made art wares such as pots, tankards, pitchers, mugs, and jardinieres with matching pedestals. Functional pieces included umbrella stands, a corn line, butter jars, and large amounts of cooking ware pieces.

Mount Pelee was made from 1902. It was a lava-type ware that was hand molded mostly in iridescent black. After a fire in 1903, different art lines were emphasized. Olympia and Rosewood were brown glazed with some diagonal orange streaks, Green Matt dates from 1906, and Loy-Nel-Art from 1908 was a brown ware with underglaze slip decoration similar to work done at Weller. Renaissance was a brown glaze ware with a flowing poppy in the Art Nouveau style.

Albert Cusick from Avon Faience worked for the factory from 1908. He became the principal design influence for more than thirty-five years. His first design was the Corn line of pitchers, mugs, and jars.

George S. Brush was appointed general manager in 1909 after having been at Owens Pottery from 1901-1905 and at his own Brush Pottery in 1907. He had acquired the molds of Union Pottery to make general kitchen wares, bowls, stoneware, and art pottery pieces. After fire destroyed Brush Pottery, he joined McCoy.

In 1911, the J.W. McCoy Pottery was changed to the Brush McCoy Pottery Company. The company made many lines of artware and utilitarian wares. The following year Brush McCoy purchased the A. Radford Pottery molds and equipment. With expansion of their operations, they moved to Zanesville where they concentrated on artwares and also retained the Roseville operation for the utilitarian wares.

Navarre was made for the Henri Deux line in matte green and white in 1912 with incised Art Nouveau figures. Other lines included Venetian, Basket Weave, and Green Woodland. Sylvan and Old Egypt were introduced in 1915.

Moss Green was made in 1915, while Vogue and Bon-Ton were made in 1916. After the Zanesville pottery burned in 1918, all work was continued at the enlarged Roseville plant. A huge number of lines were made.

Stoneware art lines produced at Brush McCoy's Roseville plant included Jetwood, Jewel, Florastone, Zuni-art, Panelart Kracklekraft, King Tut, and Stone Kraft from 1923-1928. These were basically unglazed but had squeeze bag glaze decorations applied.

In 1925, the name of the factory was changed to the Brush Pottery Company. During the 1930s, the company made planters, ashtrays, cookie jars, and an assortment of novelties. Brush Pottery had several different owners from 1978-1982 when it closed.

## NELSON MCCOY

**History:** Nelson McCoy, backed by his father J.W., established the Nelson McCoy Sanitary Stoneware Company in 1910 to manufacture utilitarian pieces such as jugs, churns, and crocks. By the mid 1920s, he expanded into molded art wares such as vases, jardinieres with matching pedestals, and pots.

In 1933, the name was changed to Nelson McCoy Pottery. During the early 1940s, he made numerous novelties including more than two hundred varieties of cookie jars. Kitchenwares, tablewares, garden and florist's ware, vases, industrial artware, cooking utensils, and heavy dinnerwares were made.

After Nelson died in 1945, the firm remained in the family. Nelson McCoy Jr. was the fourth generation in the family to be involved with pottery making. Nelson McCoy Pottery was purchased by Mount Clemens Pottery in 1967. A series of ownership changes followed. Nelson McCoy Jr. left the company in 1981. More changes followed and the plant finally closed in 1990.

Most of the McCoy pieces were not marked, except the impressed "Loy-Nel-Art" pieces. Some were marked "McCoy." "MITUSA," (Made in the United States of America) was the trademark used for ten years after being registered in 1915 and it was stamped on the bottom of the Brush McCoy wares. Very few pieces of Brush McCoy were marked except for the earliest ones. A variety of marks was used by Brush and Nelson McCoy potteries.

**References:** Bob Hanson, Craig Nissen & Margaret Hanson, *McCoy Pottery, Collector's Reference & Value Guide*, Collector Books, 1999; _____, *McCoy Pottery, Volume II*, Collector Books, 1999; Sharon and Bob Huxford, *The Collector's Encyclopedia of Brush-McCoy Pottery*, Collector Books, 1997;_____, *The Collectors Encyclopedia of Brush McCoy Pottery*, Collector Books, 1996; Martha and Steve Sanford, *The Guide to Brush McCoy Pottery*, published by author, 1989; _____, *Sanford's Guide to McCoy Pottery*, Adelmore Press, 1999; Jeffrey B. Snyder, *McCoy Pottery*, Schiffer Publishing Ltd. 1999.

**Newsletter:** Our McCoy Matters, Kathy Lynch, c/o McCoy Publications, P.O. Box 14255, Parkvile, MO 64152, $24. bimonthly.

**Museums:** Zanesville Art Center, OH.

**Additional Listings:** Cookie Jars.

## BLOSSOMTIME
Jardiniere, 5" h, sq shape, pink blossom, white ground
  ........................................................ 35.00
Vase, 6 1/2" h .......................................... 39.00

Vase, 8" h, green base, yellow flowers, brown trim, $125.

Planter, 6 5/8" l, white glaze, mkd, $12.

Vase, 8 1/4" h, green luster, "McCoy Made in USA" mk, $85.

## BUTTERFLY
Pitcher, 10" h, blue ......................................................75.00

## EL RANCHO
Food Warmer, brass wagon .....................................200.00
Mug .............................................................................40.00
Sombrero Serve-All, 12" h.......................................350.00
Tea Server ................................................................250.00

## FLORALINE
Jardiniere, 6 1/2" h, yellow w/gray flecks......................35.00

## IVY
Creamer, 3 1/2" h, Sugar Bowl, 3 1/2" h......................35.00

## KITCHENWARE
Bean Pot, Cov, 8" h, pink center band, 2 blue bands ...48.00
Mixing Bowl, 12" d, pink center band, 2 blue bands.....25.00

## LOY-NEL-ART
Vase
    3 1/2" h, leaf design, gloss brown ground................75.00
    4" h, painted cigars and matches, dk brown ground, (A)
    .......................................................................132.00

## MISCELLANEOUS
Candy Dish, 11 1/2" l, gondola shape, sm pink and white
    flowers, green leaves, gloss black ground ...............62.00
Console Bowl, 8" d, aqua, Nelson McCoy....................40.00
Jardiniere, 7 1/2" h, basketweave, aqua ......................80.00
Lamp, 6 1/2" h, figural cowboy boots, brown and cream
    .........................................................................98.00
Pitcher, 6" h, molded Angel Fish, med blue glaze ........85.00
Planter
    4 1/2" h, figural squirrel, med brown .......................25.00
    4 3/4" h x 6 1/2" l, oval shape, 3 feet, dk green glaze
    .........................................................................18.00
    5" h, figural tree stump, green...............................25.00
    6 1/4" h, deer and faun, brown and green ..............25.00
    6 1/2" h
        Black frog w/umbrella ........................................128.00
        Molded brown bamboo ext ..................................65.00
    6 3/4" l, oval, matte black glaze .............................16.00

7" h
    Figural wishing well, brown and green glaze ......24.00
    Quail, tan blend .................................................90.00
7 1/4" h, Spinning Wheel, brown and green ...........50.00
8" l
    Dbl shell, green .................................................30.00
    Scottie dogs, green and ivory w/brown spray .....45.00
9 3/8" l, rect dish-type, ribbed, off-white glaze, Nelson
    McCoy ...............................................................30.00
Vase
    6" h, squat base, flared neck, dbl handles on waist. 17.00
    7" h, 4 sm curled handles on rim, matte green glaze
    .........................................................................22.00
    7 5/8" h, lily leaf, white ...............................................85.00
    8" h
        Classic urn shape, sm handles at waist, white.... 29.00
        Flared sq shape, wavy side handles, green........35.00
    8 1/4" h, figural hand, matte white glaze.................45.00
    8 1/2" h
        Relief of bird, 2 sm handles, yellow.....................50.00
        Triple figural lily, gloss yellow .............................90.00
    9" h, raised wings on sides, ivory, c1941 ................45.00
    9 1/2" h, Ram head, black .....................................250.00
Watering Can, 10" l, figural turtle, green w/orange trim
    .........................................................................25.00

## NOVELTY
Dish, 10" l, pink figural bird, aqua dish base ...............50.00

## ONYX
Jardiniere, 7" h, swallow design ........................85.00

## SPRINGWOOD
Jardiniere, 8" h, green ...................................30.00

## BRUSH-McCOY

Bud vase, 10" h, Jewel ................................750.00
Butter Jar, 8 1/2" d, green daisy design.................300.00
Candleholder
    3" h, Amaryllis design .............................25.00
    4" h x 6 1/4" w, round with narrow round pedestal, swirl design, lt blue with gold speckles, "brush USA 927" mk ...............................................10.00
    7" h Jewel ........................................950.00
Casserole, Cov, 7" d, KolorKraft, green.................60.00
Figure, 8 1/2" h, squirrel, tan, #482 ...............68.00
Jardiniere
    5" h, Sylvan.......................................175.00
    10" h, Zuniart ..................................1,200.00
    12" h, Agean, green and white....................600.00
Jardiniere and Pedestal, Navarre Faience-forest green ...............................................4,500
Jug, Cov, 9 3/4" h, enameled bouquets of pink and white flowers, shaded matte khaki ground, unmkd, (A).....1,980
Mug, 4 3/4" h, Little Red Riding Hood, gold trim ..........25.00
Pitcher, 7" h
    "Amsterdam," blue Dutch boy and girl kissing, gray ground .............................................195.00
    "Old Mill," blue windmill and bush, gray ground .....395.00
Planter
    4 1/4" h, standing figural camel, tan...............35.00
    5 1/4" h, bear on log, brown and green, #205..........25.00
    5 1/2" h
        Pedestal base, fluted rim and base, lt and dk green, "Bush Quality USA #715" mk .............................15.00
        Raised fleur de lys design, yellow and white spotted design .........................................15.00
    6" l, standing bull "Ferdinand" lt brown spots, dk brown ground ...........................................30.00
    7" h, standing cow, med brown glaze .....................32.00
    10 5/8" h, bulbous base, pinched narrow neck, orange ...............................................20.00
Umbrella stand, 21" h, cocoa brown, #114..................375.00
Urn
    5" h, speckled green finish, #503 .........................30.00
    6" h x 8" H-H, onyx finish .........................65.00
Vase
    4" h
        Jewel, brown, dk brown, dk red, white jewels, #502 ...............................................250.00
        Onyx, squat shape, straight neck, brown ...........25.00
    4 3/4" h, tapered body, pinched handles, gloss mottled blue glaze, (A) .....................................60.00
    5" h, KolorKraft, bulbous base, ear handles, "Fawn," cobalt body with mottling ...................................72.00
    6" h, Brown Onyx, #50X................................40.00
    6 1/2" h, Brown Onyx, flat, bulbous base, tapered neck, streaked, brown onyx glaze................................45.00
    7" h, Rockraft, moss and gray, #805 ...................175.00

    8" h
        Bulbous shape, Chromart, cobalt sailboat and sunset ...............................................2,000.00
        Spread base, flared neck, Brown Onyx............. 165.00
        Vestal Duo-Tone, green and tan........................89.00
    8 1/2" h, Vellum, green .................................65.00
    9" h, paneled, Florastone........................2,800.00
    10" h, King Tut Scarab ...........................2,800.00
    10 1/8" h, Woodland, gloss green glaze, base chip, (A) ...............................................303.00
    10 1/2" h, tapered, Blue Onyx...............................250.00
    11 3/4" h, classic shape, stylized band of black outlined polychrome enameled scarabs and papyrus, semi-matte speckled green ground, (A)..................2,240.00
    12" h, Zuni Art, sand-colored body, #046 ...............3,000
    14" h, fan shape, cream glaze ................................40.00
Wall Pocket, 8" h, figural owl, green, gray and brown, (A) ...............................................110.00

c.1905-1920

# D.E. McNicol Pottery Company

### East Liverpool, Ohio; Clarksburg, West Virginia
### 1892-1954

**History:** The D.E. McNicol Pottery was formed from the former McNicol, Burton and Company in 1892 in East Liverpool, Ohio. Its first products were yellowware, Rockingham, and white ironstone called "semi-granite." In 1902, the pottery added a second plant for Rockingham and yellowware, and continued making ironstone in the original plant.

In 1914, it built a new plant in Clarksburg, West Virginia, and another in East Liverpool five years later. Products were expanded to include hotel, dinner, and toilet wares in semi-granite, semi-porcelain and cream colored wares. It continued to make yellowware until 1927.

Another specialty of McNicol was calendar and souvenir plates in a wide array of styles and decorative motifs. The West Virginia plant specialized in white and decorated vitrified china for hotels, railroads, hospitals, and restaurants.

It consolidated its operations in 1929 by closing the East Liverpool plants and concentrated on vitrified china in Clarksburg. The company stopped work in 1954. Numerous marks were used.

Bone Dish, 7 1/8" l, rect, black border band of flowerheads separated by cornucopia and swirls, set of 4........... 15.00
Bowl, 8 5/8" d, 3 pink roses in center, green leaves, hanging drops on border, Carnation mold ...........................10.00
Cereal Bowl
    6 1/2" d, "Dayton" pattern, dk red transfer .............. 10.00
    6 5/8" d, purple, yellow, and blue florals in center, single scattered florals on border, black lined rim............ 3.00
Cup and Saucer, bluebird design ................................... 8.00

**Bowl, 8 1/2" d, green and white lily of the valley, yellow border w/relief molded designs, "Carnation, D.E. McNichol" mk, $10.**

Cup and Saucer, Demitasse
　Black medallions and hanging swags on borders
　.......................................................................7.00
　Green hanging drape and tassel borders .................6.00
Dish, 8 1/4" l, "Beverly" pattern.....................................6.00
Gravy Boat
　9 1/2" l, lobed body, molded sawtooth border, green floral and leaf transfer on sides, Carnation mold
　.......................................................................10.00
　9 3/4" l, white ironstone.............................................6.00
Mug, 3 1/2" h, roses around int and ext border, gold rim and trimmed handle ...........................................................3.00
Pitcher, 6 1/4" h, white glaze, "McNichol China Clarksburg, W.Va." mk, (A) .........................................................10.00
Plate
　7" d, blue maple leaves on border ............................3.00
　7 1/4" d, border band of blue rachet designs.............5.00
　8 1/4" d, multicolored decal of Dutch boy and girl and saying, purple luster border w/gold swag inner border band ...........................................................10.00
　9" d
　　Border of classic black and blue cartouches w/pink roses, scattered florals between, blue inner and outer band.......................................................6.00
　　Bluebird border design ......................................15.00
　　Dk red rim band of compartments of curlicues and hanging urns, mkd .........................................10.00
　9 1/4" d, American flag in center, green luster border w/inner band of gold hanging swags ...................20.00
　9 3/8" d, multicolored bouquet in center, gold hanging swags from blue-pink border, mkd ......................5.00
　9 1/2" d, white, semi-vitreous, "McNichol Parkersburg, W.Va." mk .........................................................4.00
　9 3/4" d, "Dayton" pattern, dk red transfer ..............10.00
　10" d, lg mauve, pink, and white flowers, green leaves, brown and yellow shaded border, scalloped rim, Carnation mold...........................................................5.00
　11" d, pink to peach roses w/green leaves in center, mint green emb border..............................................10.00

Platter
　11" l, white granite ware...........................................15.00
　11 1/2" l, pink ground, black sawtooth and dot border
　.......................................................................5.00
　16" l, roses in corners, gold rim, mkd .....................25.00
　19" l, border bands of red roses and foliage, rim band of linked scalloped design .......................................20.00
Sauce Boat, 8 1/4" l, multicolored flower spray on side, blue stripe below rim ......................................................20.00
Serving Bowl, 9 3/4" d, pink and white roses in center, vert pink bands on border, 2 gold trim rings.....................5.00
Vegetable Bowl, Cov, 12" H-H, scattered floral bouquets on borders, Carnation mold..........................................25.00
Vegetable Dish, 9 3/4" l, tan, "Roloc" ..........................10.00

# Merrimac Pottery Company

### Newburyport, Massachusetts
### 1897-1908

**History:** Thomas Nickerson formed Merramic Ceramic Company in 1897 to make florist's ware and enameled tile. When W.G. Fisher joined a year later, they expanded the company.

In 1900, they shifted the focus to decorative and glazed artwares. The name was changed to Merrimac Pottery Company in 1902. The first artwares were vases and flower containers in matte green and yellow glazes.

By 1903, they expanded the range of glaze colors and added metallic luster, iridescence, and crackle glazes. Garden pottery was added to their product line. Arrhelian ware was another line that was based on redware from the Roman times. Their artwares won a silver medal at the St. Louis Exposition in 1904.

Pieces were mostly hand thrown. In 1908, a fire destroyed the pottery soon after Nickerson had sold to Frank Bray. Early wares were not marked. In 1900-01, they used a paper label. After that the mark was impressed or incised.

**Museums:** Boston Museum, MA; Worcester Art Museum, MA

Bud Vase, 4" h, squat base, trumpet neck and flared rim, curdled jade and hunter green glaze w/lustered black accents, (A) ...........................................................440.00
Chamberstick, 9" h, feathered matte green glaze ......400.00
Humidor, 7" h, 3 sm handles, mottled semi-matte green and gunmetal glazes, chips, (A) ...............................1,230.00
Jar, Cov, 5 1/4" h, speckled brown gloss glaze, paper label, (A) ...........................................................495.00
Umbrella Stand, 22 3/4" h, cylinder shape, tooled and applied leaves, leathery matte green glaze, crack and chips, (A) ...........................................................4,125.00
Vase
　4 1/4" h, swollen tapered shape, short collar, burnt orange and green speckled glaze, (A) .............880.00
　4 1/2" h, ovoid, blue and green drip over matte yellow body, mkd, (A) ...............................................1,100.00

Vase, 9 1/2" h, textured matte green glaze, imp mk, (A), $2,090.

Vase, 10" h, matte white finish, Romanelli, $275.

5" h, swollen cylinder shape, sm everted rim, matte dk blue-green glaze, hairline, (A) ...........................247.00

7" h, bulbous shape, flared rim, dripping crystalline mustard glaze over speckled matte mustard yellow glaze, mkd, (A) ...............................................................495.00

7 1/2" h, tooled and applied dogwood blossoms and leaves, textured matte green glaze, hairlines, (A) ................................................................................1,980.00

8" h, ovoid shape, closed rim, applied leaves, dk blue-green crystalline glaze, rim chip repair, (A) ....3,300.00

10" h, bulbous base, cylinder neck, green and mirrored black mottled glaze, unmkd, (A) .....................1,650.00

11 1/2" h, everted rim, applied stylized plants and leaves, textured semi-matte green glaze, hairline, restored chip, "stamped Merrimac" mk, (A) ...................1,980.00

Vessel, 4" h x 9" d, squat shape, short rim, matte green glaze, imp mk, (A) ..........................................1,320.00

# Metlox Pottery

## Manhattan Beach, California
## 1927-1989

**History:** T.C. Prouty and Willis, his son, established Metlox Pottery in Manhattan Beach, California in 1927 and made ceramic outdoor signs. The sign business declined during the Depression, and T.C. died in 1931. Willis converted the plant to dinnerware production.

In 1932, the first line of dishes was called California Pottery in bright colored glazes. Table and kitchenwares called Poppytrail were made in fifteen different colors starting in 1934 for an eight-year period. Poppytrail became the company's trademark in 1936 since the poppy is the California state flower. Talc was the major component of the body and metallic oxides were used in the glazes; these were native to California.

Carl Romanelli, the first artware designer at Metlox, started Metlox Miniatures in the late 1930s with small-scale animal figurines and other novelty pieces. Romanelli also designed Modern Masterpieces which included bookends, wall pockets, figural vases, figures, and such.

Very limited pottery was made during World War II, since the factory was converted to war production. After the war, it returned to dinnerware production. Evan Shaw purchased the business from Willis Prouty in 1946 and introduced the first decorated dinnerware line. California Ivy in 1946 was the first hand-painted pattern. Numerous patterns followed through the prosperous fifties.

In 1958, Metlox purchased the trade name and dinnerware molds from Vernon Kilns and developed a separate Vernon Ware branch. Artwares continued in the '50s and '60s with matte glaze examples and American Royal Horses and Nostalgia, scale model carriages.

Shaw also brought the Disney line with him to Metlox and Disney figures were made until 1956. During the '60s and '70s, Poppets by Poppytrail were stoneware flower holders and planters, Colorstax was solid color glaze dinnerware, and numerous cookie jars were made.

Evan Shaw died in 1980; his family was involved in the company until it closed in 1989. Numerous marks were used on Metlox examples.

**References:** Jack Chipman, *Collector's Encyclopedia of California Pottery, 2nd Edition*, Collector Books, 1998; Carl Gibbs, Jr., *Collector's Encyclopedia of Metlox Potteries*, Collector Books, 1995.

### ANTIQUE GRAPE PATTERN-TRADITIONAL SHAPE
Butter Dish, Cov ..........................................................60.00
Creamer ......................................................................20.00
Fruit Bowl, 6" d............................................................14.00
Gravy Boat with attached Liner ..................................35.00
Plate, 7" d....................................................................12.00
Sugar Bowl, Cov .........................................................25.00

### ART POTTERY
Figure
9" h, standing woman w/oil jar on shoulder, lt green glaze, Romanelli ...........................................................60.00
9 1/2" h, cowgirl, multicolored, Romanelli..............350.00
11" h, standing Indian brave, multicolored, Romanelli .................................................................................250.00

Vase
8 1/2" h, angelfish, lt blue, #1814, Romanelli ..........95.00
13 1/2" h, pillow shape, white nude design, blue ground, Romanelli .........................................................500.00

### CALIFORNIA IVY PATTERN-IVY SHAPE
Casserole, Cov, 11" H-H..............................................20.00

Vase, 12" h, seafoam green, $95.

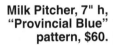

Milk Pitcher, 7" h, "Provincial Blue" pattern, $60.

Chop Plate, 13 1/4" d .................................................35.00
Cup and Saucer ...........................................................12.00
Fruit Bowl, 5 1/4" d .....................................................12.00
Plate
   8" d.........................................................................10.00
   10" d........................................................................13.00
Platter, 13" l ..................................................................35.00
Serving Bowl, Divided, 11" l.......................................40.00
Soup Bowl, 6 3/4" d ......................................................18.00
Teapot, 6 1/2" h ............................................................80.00
Vase, 6" h .....................................................................45.00
Vegetable Bowl, 9" d ...................................................35.00

### CALIFORNIA PEACH BLOSSOM PATTERN-BLOSSOM SHAPE
Butter Dish, Cov ...........................................................66.00
Celery Dish, 12 1/2" l....................................................45.00
Cup and Saucer ...........................................................14.00
Plate, 10" sq .................................................................18.00
Shakers, Pr....................................................................28.00

### CALIFORNIA PROVINCIAL PATTERN-PROVINCIAL SHAPE
Bowl
   6" d.........................................................................16.00
   7 1/4" d...................................................................10.00
Chop Plate, 12" d .........................................................40.00

Cup and Saucer ...........................................................15.00
Plate
   7 1/2" d ....................................................................4.00
   10" d..........................................................................8.00
Platter, 12" d.................................................................40.00

### COLONIAL HERITAGE PATTERN-PROVINCIAL SHAPE
Dish, 12" d, divided, handled........................................55.00

### FIGURES
POPPETS
   4 1/2" h, Dutch girl, turquoise jacket, yellow braids
   .....................................................................30.00
   6 1/2" h, Arnie, golfer .........................................60.00
   6 3/4" h, Nancy w/dog ........................................60.00
   7 5/8" h, Angelina ...............................................45.00

### HOMESTEAD PROVINCIAL PATTERN-PROVINCIAL SHAPE
Ashtray, 8 1/2" sq .........................................................28.00
Bowl
   5" d...........................................................................9.00
   9 1/2" H-H.............................................................43.00
Coffeepot.......................................................................68.00
Plate
   6 1/2" d ....................................................................9.00
   10" d........................................................................15.00
Serving Bowl, 10" d ......................................................40.00
Vegetable Bowl, 12" l, divided .....................................58.00

### LA MANCHA PATTERN
Cereal Bowl, 6 1/4" d, gold.............................................5.00
Plate
   6 1/2" d ....................................................................3.00
   10 3/4" d, gold........................................................5.00
Soup Plate, 8" d ..............................................................6.00

### LOTUS SHAPE
Bowl, 6 1/2" d..................................................................3.00
Cup and Saucer .............................................................3.00
Plate, 11" d .....................................................................5.00
Platter, 15" l, white........................................................45.00

### MISCELLANEOUS
Hen on Nest, 6" h x 6 1/2" l, green, chartreuse, and magenta hen, tan basket base ...............................................65.00

### NASTURTIUM PATTERN
Berry Bowl, 6" d..............................................................3.00
Cereal Bowl, 7" d............................................................3.00
Cup and Saucer .............................................................4.00
Plate
   7 1/2" d ....................................................................4.00
   8 3/4" d ....................................................................4.00
Platter, 13 1/2" l ...........................................................10.00
Vegetable Bowl, 9" d ......................................................8.00

### NAVAJO PATTERN
Bowl, 7" d .......................................................................6.00
Butter Dish, Cov ...........................................................10.00
Casserole, Cov, 8 3/4" d ...............................................50.00
Cup and Saucer .............................................................3.00
Plate
   7 1/2" d ....................................................................3.00

10" d.............................................................5.00
Platter, 14" l, rect ........................................10.00
Vegetable Bowl, 17" l, divided .................10.00

### PROVINCIAL FLOWER PATTERN-PROVINCIAL SHAPE
Dish, 12" d, divided, handled.......................45.00

### PROVINCIAL FRUIT PATTERN-PROVINCIAL SHAPE
Cereal Bowl, 7 1/4" d.................................10.00
Cup and Saucer ..........................................5.00
Fruit Bowl, 6 1/4" d .....................................8.00
Gravy Boat, 6" d........................................22.00
Plate
    6 1/2" d.................................................5.00
    7 1/2" d.................................................7.00
    10 1/2" d.............................................10.00
Platter, 13 1/2" l .......................................35.00
Serving Bowl, 10" d...................................40.00
Vegetable Bowl, 8 1/2" l, divided .............33.00

### RED ROOSTER PATTERN-PROVINCIAL SHAPE
Butter Dish, Cov ........................................50.00
Plate
    6 1/4" d.................................................7.00
    10" d.....................................................11.00
Shakers, Pr, 4" h, red ...............................18.00
Soup Bowl, Lug, 5" d.................................15.00
Vegetable Bowl
    10" d....................................................33.00
    12 " l, divided....................................40.00

**Chop Plate, 11" d,
"Wild Poppy"
pattern, $8.**

**Canister, 10 1/4" h, "Red
Rooster" pattern, wood
lid, "Flour," $48.**

### SAN FERNANDO PATTERN
Platter
    12" l......................................................10.00
    14" l......................................................12.00
Serving Bowl, 9" d.......................................6.00
Vegetable Bowl, 11 1/2" l, divided ...............8.00

### SCULPTURED DAISY PATTERN-PROVINCIAL SHAPE
Coffeepot...................................................75.00
Creamer .....................................................16.00
Cup and Saucer .........................................12.00
Platter, 14 1/4" l .........................................25.00
Sugar Bowl, Cov ........................................22.00
Vegetable Bowl, 9" H-H..............................26.00

### SCULPTURED GRAPE PATTERN-TRADITIONAL SHAPE
Creamer .....................................................18.00
Cup and saucer...........................................15.00
Plate, 7" d...................................................14.00
Vegetable Bowl, 9 1/2" d.............................32.00

### SCULPTURED ZINNIA PATTERN-TRADITIONAL SHAPE
Cereal Bowl, 7 3/8" d..................................15.00
Cup and Saucer ..........................................15.00
Plate
    6 1/4" d.................................................8.00
    7 1/2" d...............................................12.00
    10 1/2" d.............................................38.00
Shakers, Pr ................................................28.00

### TROPICANA
Tray, 16" l, jaw bone shape, white glaze ...................200.00
Vase, 16" h, bulbous base, tapered body, fish motif
..............................................................460.00

### VINTAGE PINK PATTERN-TRADITIONAL SHAPE
Cup and Saucer ..........................................10.00
Plate, 10 1/2" d...........................................10.00

### WOODLAND GOLD
Bowl, 9" d...................................................30.00
Creamer .....................................................20.00
Platter, 13" l................................................40.00

## Monmouth Pottery

### Monmouth, Illinois
### 1893-1906

MONMOUTH
POTTERY CO.
MONMOUTH, ILL.

**History:** In 1893, Banker William Hanna and his associates established Monmouth Pottery Company in Monmouth, Illinois to make stonewares. The factory sustained major fires in 1897 and 1905.

Monmouth stoneware examples were usually straight-sided pieces that were salt glazed or slipped in Albany or Bristol finishes. Frequently the only decoration was the stenciled capacity numbers within a circular motif.

Not all examples were plain. They also made blue sponged water coolers, crocks, and pitchers. Miniatures found form in crocks, jugs, chickens, pigs, dogs, and cows. Some were sponged, while others were Bristol glazed or had the Albany slip finish.

A large selection of other utilitarian wares included crocks, milk bowls, butter jars, churns, jugs, preserve jars, tobacco jars, cuspidors, chamber pots, and such.

The maple leaf was used as the company logo along with several other marks during their thirteen years of operation. Many pieces were marked MONMOUTH POTTERY CO. MONMOUTH, ILL.

In 1906, they merged with six other companies to form Western Stoneware. Many items continued to be made when Monmouth became Plant One of Western Stoneware. They stopped using the Monmouth Pottery Company logo at that time.

**References:** Jim Martin and Bette Cooper, *Monmouth-Western Stoneware*, Krause Publications, 1999.

**Collectors' Club:** Collectors of Illinois Pottery and Stoneware, David McGuire, 1527 East Converse Street, Springfield, IL 62703, $15 per year, newsletter.

Bean Pot
    5" h x 6" H-H, tan body, rose-pink cov, 2 sm handles ...................................................................... 10.00
    7 1/2" h x 9 1/2" H-H, dk brown top, cream base w/brown "BOSTON BAKED BEANS" on front ................... 10.00
Bowl
    6 1/4" d, Eva Zeisel design ..................................... 25.00
    8 1/2" d, green w/black flecks ................................. 5.00
    9 1/4" d, red and black cat-tails............................... 20.00
Bud Vase
    5" h, squat base, flared neck, black glaze ................. 5.00
    8" h, quilted body design, cream glaze ..................... 25.00
Canister, 5 1/2" h, dk brown top and cov, tan base w/"COFFEE" on front, mkd..................................................... 10.00
Chop Plate, 11 1/8" d, Eva Zeisel design ..................... 65.00
Custard Cup, 5" d, dk brown glaze................................. 5.00

**Vase, 12" h, gloss black glaze, stamped mk, $145.**

**Pitcher, 4 1/2" h, dk brown, raised leaf mk, $18.**

Jardiniere, 10 1/2" h, dk brown textured tree trunk design ...................................................................... 120.00
Milk Pitcher, 5 1/2" h, tapered shape, horiz ribbing, blue-gray glaze .................................................................. 15.00
Mixing Bowl, 8 1/4" d, cream ribbed ext, cobalt int....... 40.00
Mug, 5 1/2" h, blue belt w/"BULL AND ARROW" on side, "MONMOUTH USA" mk........................................... 30.00
Pitcher
    4 1/4" h, horiz rings, dk brown glaze........................ 18.00
    5 1/2" h, raised horiz ribs, tan glaze ....................... 30.00
    6" h, molded swirl body, sea green glaze ................ 45.00
    9 1/2" h, birdhouse and fence on side, white ground ...................................................................... 5.00
Planter, bust of Madonna wearing halo, white glaze.... 10.00
Serving Bowl, 8 1/2" d, pea green w/black flecks, mkd ...................................................................... 8.00
Tureen, Cov, 5 1/2" h, blue outlined rim and knob ...................................................................... 10.00
Vase
    5" h x 7" d, squat shape, triple loop handles, semi-matte yellow-gold glaze, "MONMOUTH POTTERY WILL NOT LEAK" mk ................................................... 50.00
    6" h, figural cabbage, 2 narrow handles, matte green glaze..................................................................... 30.00
    7" h, flared shape, molded horiz ribs, 2 sm handles, beige glaze..................................................................... 15.00
    7 1/4" h, urn shape, spread base, 2 stepped handles, turquoise glaze ....................................................... 30.00
    8" h
        Brush ware, relief molded leaf design, green wash ................................................................. 95.00
        Two sm handles on shoulder, raised vert panels, matte red-brown ground ......................................... 50.00
    12" h
        Corset shape, relief molded lotus design, gloss black glaze .......................................................... 180.00
        Jar shape, sm side handles from shoulder to rim, matte yellow glaze, c1937 .............................. 75.00
    16" h, tapered sides, wide shoulder, imp yellow arches on shoulder, blue glazed body, matte finish ................................................................. 395.00

**Vase, 11 3/4" h, turquoise glaze, $60.**

# Morton Pottery

## Morton, Illinois
## 1877-1976

**History:** Throughout the hundred years that there has been some form of Morton Pottery in Morton, Illinois, the Rapp sons and brothers and their descendants have been involved in the various concerns. Matthew Rapp and four sons established the first clay operation in 1877 with the primary emphasis on brick manufacturing and called it the Rapp Brothers Brick Company. Bricks were scarce at the time so it was a good business. Other Rapps joined, it became the Rapp Brothers Brick and Tile Company, and they added field drainage tile.

A second business was started called the Morton Pottery Works to make utilitarian items such as yellowware and Rockingham ware. All through the history there were a series of fires and rebuilding. In 1915-16, they separated the tile from the pottery works and named it Morton Earthenware Company. It was difficult to tell the newer products from the older ones since they used the same molds and glaze formulas. Sons and daughters of all six brothers were apprenticed to the tile works and the pottery.

Production was stopped from 1917-20 during World War I, since there were manpower and chemical shortages. From 1920-1940, several Rapp family members returned from the war and named their new pottery Cliftwood Art Potteries. Marks were not usually used, and paper labels were scarce. Items made included flower holders and inserts, bookends, planters, the Lorilei flower insert, candlesticks, bowls, various types of lamps, animals, bird figurines, and some human figures. Their special glaze was a chocolate brown drip. They were the first in America to use this glaze, and it was never made after Matthew's death in 1938 since he did not write down the formula. Jade Green and cobalt blue were added in the 20s. Cliftwood was sold through Morton Pottery as well as through showrooms in New York and Chicago. Vases were most prolific at Cliftwood Art Potteries.

After Matthew Rapp died, the sons were unwilling to continue work to the same degree so the pottery was sold in 1940. It became Midwest Pottery, but it was the shortest lived of all the potteries in Morton and only lasted from 1940-44. The Rapp brothers stayed in their positions and continued the Cliftwood line of wares but expanded figure production in the Art Deco style. They also expanded gold decorations. After a sale, a new manager, and the Rapps' departure, Midwest was destroyed by fire and finally moved to Wisconsin.

By 1946, the Rapp brothers were back in Morton and established their own American Art Potteries from 1947-1963. New designs included TV lamps, ceramic doll parts, figurines, and novelty planters. All the wares had foil labels. After a lot of financial problems, their pottery was auctioned off and purchased by the Morton Pottery Company.

The Morton Pottery Company was formed from Morton Pottery Works and Morton Earthenware Company from 1922-1976. Utilitarian items included kitchen ware, food storage containers, bakers, and flower pots. The Rapps were once again involved. Additional lines were Pilgrim Ware, Amish pottery, and steins for promotional advertising.

During the 1950s, they expanded the novelty items, along with flower containers, vases, lamps, holiday items, doll house accessories, planters, and bisque figures. Davy Crockett figural lamps also were made. Ceramic tiles and bathroom fixtures were added too. By 1966, Japanese competition impacted the tiles and novelty items since they could not match their prices. In addition to foreign competition, lower sales, profit losses, and attempts to unionize added to their problems. Several Rapps died and the company was sold, but continued to decline. The firm continued as a subsidiary of AKF Industries with cookie jars and inserts for Rival crock pots. After several additional sales, the pottery closed permanently in 1976.

**References:** Doris & Burdell Hall, *Morton Potteries: 99 Years, Vol. 2*, L-W Book Sales,1995.

Bean Pot, Cov, 8" h, ball shape w/horiz handles, streaked brown glaze ............................................................. 35.00
Candlestick, 5 1/4" h, 2 loop handles, spread base, matte green glaze, gray accents, Cliftwood mk ................. 25.00
Figure
  2 1/2" h, standing elephant w/raised trunk, raised "G.O.P." on side, reverse w/"McKeever," gloss gray glaze .................................................................. 15.00
  4" h x 6" l, standing cocker spaniel, brown .............. 15.00
  5 1/2" h x 8" l, standing Irish setter, dk brown ........ 200.00
  12" h, standing stylized horse, oval base, white glaze, Cliftwood ............................................................. 15.00
Flower Pot, W/Saucer
  3" h, vert ribbing, lt yellow ......................................... 5.00
  4 3/4" h, molded basketweave design, pink ........... 10.00
  5" h, patchwork design, dk reddish-pink .................. 15.00
Fountain, 8" h, leaping fish figure, blue ....................... 30.00
Lamp, 12" h, figural afghan hounds, gloss black glaze ............................................................................... 120.00
Mixing Bowl, 3 3/4" d, paneled, yellow ........................... 8.00
Pitcher
  3" h, emb grapes and leaves on sides, pink glaze ................................................................................. 15.00
  5" h, dbl spouts on sides, aqua "Woodland" glaze .. 25.00
  11 1/2" h, paneled, raised designs on sides, cobalt blue glaze .................................................................. 65.00
Planter
  3" l x 2 1/2" h, figural apple, dk red .......................... 10.00
  3 1/2" h, flower petal form, ftd, pink glaze, "MORTON USA" mk ............................................................... 10.00

**Wall pocket, 7 1/4" h, Love Birds, brown, turquoise, green and yellow, $35.**

4" h
  Figural squatting cat, yellow glaze ........................6.00
  Flared sq shape, relief molded open flowerhead in oval on sides, pink glaze................................15.00
  Seated bulldog, lt green glaze...........................20.00
4 1/2" h, figural turkey, brown glaze ........................15.00
5" h, figural seated camel, lt green glaze................20.00
6 3/4" h, singing seated figural cowboy playing guitar, red, brown, and cream, cactus in bkd ................30.00
7" l, figural flying bird, cream body w/red and blue accents ......................................................30.00
9" l, figural cat lying down, white...........................10.00
11" l x 5 3/4" h, 2 white calla lily flower bells w/raised blue-green leaves, dk green leaf tray .................20.00

Spoon Rest
  5" l, figural spoon, "SPOON" on bowl, seafoam green ......................................................................5.00
  5 5/8" l, figural fish, "SPOON" on body, med blue......5.00
Stein, 5" h, leaf design, Rockingham glaze ...................9.00

Vase
  5 1/4" h, swollen cylinder, rose red, blue flared rim .30.00
  6 1/4" h, flared, lobed form, rect base, dk brown w/lt brown drip on border .........................................10.00
  8" h, swollen cylinder shape, rose shaded to purple glaze ...........................................................40.00
  9 1/4" h, bulbous base, tapered neck, flared rim, rose red glaze......................................................70.00
  13" h, bulbous base, straight neck, handles from shoulder to rim, blue-mulberry red blended glaze, Cliftwood mk ...............................................................50.00

Wall Pocket
  6 1/2" h, vase shape, raised design, mottled green ................................................................34.00
  7 1/2" h, figure of sunbonnet girl and basket, cream ................................................................15.00

# Mount Clemens Pottery Company

### Mt. Clemens, Michigan
### 1914-1987

**History:** A group of businessmen started Mount Clemens Pottery in 1914 in Michigan. A year later, they produced dinnerware with decalcomania transfer patterns. They created a domestic market for their products during World War I. The S.S. Kresge Company was one of their major customers for open stock dinnerware.

After the war, there was increased competition. Kresge purchased the factory and provided the money to mass produce the dinnerwares, which were sold in their stores. Mount Clemens became a subsidiary of Kresge.

It made semi-porcelain dinnerware and a solid color ware in dark green, blue, and pink that was to compete with Homer Laughlin's Fiesta. Patterns included Flower Basket, Poppy, Robin, Rose Marie, Springtime, and Exotic Bird. A later pattern was Mildred made from 1934-1968.

The pottery was sold to David Chase in 1965, and the name was changed to Mount Clemens China Company one year later. During the 1970s, there was another reorganization. Mount Clemens was formed into a new company called Jamestown China in 1974, but the name was changed back to Mount Clemens in 1980.

MADE IN U.S.A.
535H
1935

The early pieces had the company backstamp with the initials of the company. Later pieces were backstamped U.S.A. in relief, though most pieces had no backstamp.

**BLUEBIRD PATTERN**
Bowl
  8" d ...............................................................10.00
  9" d ...............................................................15.00
Platter, 13 1/2" l...................................................25.00
Soup Plate, 9 1/2" d .............................................12.00

**BLUEBIRD IN WREATH PATTERN**
Bowl
  7 3/4" d ..........................................................6.00
  8" d ...............................................................15.00
Plate, 9" d...........................................................10.00

**CALIFORNIA POPPY PATTERN-TOULON SHAPE**
Platter, 11 1/4" l...................................................10.00

**MILDRED PATTERN**
Berry Bowl, 5" d....................................................5.00
Creamer ..............................................................3.00
Cup and Saucer ...................................................3.00
Plate
  6" d ...............................................................4.00
  9" d ...............................................................5.00
  10 1/4" d ........................................................5.00
Soup Bowl, 7 3/4" d..............................................6.00
Sugar Bowl, Cov ..................................................5.00
Vegetable Bowl, 8 3/8" d .....................................25.00

**OLD MEXICO PATTERN**
Plate, 9" d...........................................................10.00

**PETALWARE**
Cereal Bowl, 4 5/8" d, green .................................8.00
Plate
  7 1/2" d, green ................................................3.00
  9" d, maroon ...................................................5.00
Platter, 11" l, green ..............................................6.00
Sauce Boat, maroon ............................................12.00
Soup Bowl, 7 1/2" d..............................................6.00

**Plate, 9 1/8" d, robin in purple flower bower, $10.**

## POPPY PATTERN
Plate, 9 1/4" d ........................................................5.00
Soup Bowl, 8 1/4" d ..............................................6.00

## TOULON PATTERN
Bowl, 8" d, red ......................................................5.00
Plate, 9 1/4" d, red ..............................................5.00

## WILD BERRY PATTERN
Cup and Saucer ....................................................6.00
Plate
    7" d..........................................................................7.00
    10 1/4" d..............................................................8.00
Soup Bowl, 6 1/2" d ..............................................7.00

## WOODLAND PATTERN
Berry Dish, 5" d ....................................................2.00
Cup and Saucer ....................................................3.00
Plate
    6" d..........................................................................3.00
    9" d..........................................................................5.00
Platter, 11 1/2" l ....................................................6.00
Serving Bowl, 9" d ................................................6.00

# Muncie Pottery

### Muncie, Indiana
### 1922-1939

**History:** The Muncie Pottery was started next to the Gill Clay Pottery in 1922 with Charles Benham in charge. Boris Trifonoff was hired as designer and master mold maker to develop artistic pottery for Muncie. Although he only worked there for two years, he produced molds for many of the well-known Muncie shapes. Examples were carved with animal designs and also there were carved relief plaques.

James Willkins followed as head ceramist; he made molds and glazes for the "Artistic Pottery" line. He was responsible for most of Muncie's well known drip and matte glazes as well as the peachskin glaze. Over the years Muncie utilized forty-eight glazes. By 1926, they had made more than two hundred designs of vases, wall pockets, garden pottery, bird baths, baskets, candlesticks, juice and water sets, little brown jugs, breakfast and luncheon sets, bowls with flower frogs, and book ends in a variety of matte and glass glazes.

Muncie pottery examples had soft flowing glazes in quiet tones with the colors blended and shaded. This pottery had no surface paintings; instead the pottery was ribbed, pleated or sculptured. Many pieces had unusual handles.

Muncie also made lamp bases for Aladdin lamps and several other companies. They made more than forty styles of lamp bases where they utilized the same glazes as the art pottery line.

Reuben Haley did designs for Muncie that were similar to designs he did for Consolidated Glass. Styles included Martele from 1926, Florentine and Catalonian from 1927, and Ruba Rombic from 1928.

Munice Pottery examples were both marked and unmarked. Earlier pieces from 1922-1925 were unmarked. From about 1925, workers identified pieces with an assigned number or letter. In 1927, examples were stamped "MUNCIE" with letters and numbers.

They maintained a showroom in the Merchandise Mart in Chicago. The pottery was shut down in 1939 and the assets were transferred to the Gill Clay Pot Company. Muncie Pottery was liquidated in 1942.

**References:** Jon Rans & Mark Eckelman, *Collector's Encyclopedia of Muncie Pottery*, Collector Books, 1999.

**Reproduction Alert:** There is a reproduction of shape #306 in Muncie's 1929 catalog in the Ruba Rombic style. It is also lighter in weight than the original.

Bowl
    5" d, ftd, tab handles, blue drip over blue ground .... 75.00
    8" d x 2 1/2" h, flattened rolled shape, lt blue glaze
    ......................................................................... 90.00

Bud Vase
    6" h
        Bulbous shape, flared ft and rim, gloss blue glaze
        ......................................................................... 85.00
        Green drip, mauve ground, shape #109 .......... 125.00
    7" h, blended green over pink ground.................... 120.00

Chamberstick, 4 1/2" h, dk rose w/blue mottling ........ 150.00
Flower Holder, 11 1/4" l, w/frog, canoe shape, matte purple over green ground, "imp Muncie" mk, (A) .............. 247.00
Lamp Base, 12" h, flambe blue drip over green glaze, #418 .............................................................................. 275.00
Sugar Bowl, Cov, 3 1/2" h, rose pink........................... 15.00

Vase
    4" h
        Bag shape, crimped top, green over rose glaze
        ......................................................................... 95.00
        Bulbous shape, flared rim, vert ribbing, gloss black glaze ................................................................. 75.00
    4 1/4" "Ruba Rhomic" shape, green border over matte orange glaze, (A)................................................ 312.00
    4 1/2" h, swollen midsection, flared rim, narrow base, gloss black glaze................................................ 40.00
    5" h
        Fluted top, 2 handles, matte green drip, lavender ground .......................................................... 95.00
        Folded rim, green drip over orange ground, (A)
        ......................................................................... 165.00
    5 1/2" h, hat form, overlapped rim, green over purple glaze................................................................ 295.00
    5 7/8" h, rect, emb grasshoppers on stems, green border drip over matte orange glaze, "imp Muncie" mk, (A)
    ......................................................................... 330.00
    6" h
        Bag shape, ruffled rim, matte green and pumpkin orange, chips ................................................ 45.00
        Melon fluted, green drip, orange ground, shape #191
        ......................................................................... 190.00
        Trumpet shape, green to cream shading ........... 70.00
    6 1/4" h
        Bulbous base, flared top, cream drip over med red ground ......................................................... 180.00
        Tapered ball base, cylinder neck w/flared rim, airbrushed matte green over lilac glaze............ 130.00
    7" h
        Blue drip, aqua ground, shape #102 ................. 225.00
        Squat shape, 2 loop handles, matte blue airbrush over pink ground................................................ 40.00

**Vase, 6 1/4" h, shaded matte mauve to green ground, imp "MUNCIE" mk, $210.**

7 1/2" h

  Bulbous shape with trumpet neck, green drip, orange ground............................................................. 175.00
  Handles from base to rim, green drip, mauve ground, shape #143 ................................................... 290.00

9" h

  Hourglass shape, stylized flowers and vines, mauve and green, shape #266 ................................ 460.00
  Pillow shape, 2 sm loop handles, green drip, mauve ground, shape #192 ...................................... 250.00

9 1/4" h, melon fluted, sm loop handles, matte green, shape #192 .......................................................... 395.00

12 1/4" h, corset shape, purple top over matte pink ground, (A) ....................................................... 330.00

c.1895

# Newcomb Pottery

### New Orleans, Louisiana
### 1895-1940

**History:** In 1894, Mary Given Sheerer came to teach pottery and china decoration at H. Sophie Newcomb Memorial College for Women in New Orleans, Louisiana. Ellsworth Woodward, the founding dean, supervised the pottery-making operation which was founded in 1895 as an enterprise for Southern women "to provide useful and appropriate employment for women." Gabry came from France to do the heavy work, but was soon replaced by Joseph Mayer who worked at Newcomb from the early 1890s until 1927. He shaped all the pots for the decorators from the womens' drawings. By 1900, Newcomb Pottery won a bronze medal at the Paris International Exposition. This was the first of many medals that were to be won by this pottery, and showed recognition of the American art pottery movement in Europe. In 1901, Tulane provided a building for the pottery enterprise.

Both the English design schools and the Arts and Crafts movement influenced the designs on Newcomb Pottery. All the pottery was hand thrown; no two pieces were alike. Each was decorated individually by the artist/decorators working there. Southern flora and fauna were used for the subject matter. A range of cobalt blues and sage greens was the hallmark of Newcomb Pottery. Approximately ten to fifteen young women graduates of the college worked each year on the pottery designs.

Potters experimented with slip decoration and used underglaze painting into the 1930s. Some of the finest examples were made before 1910 and awarded numerous prizes at the various expositions. From 1903-07, pottery examples were made with deeply indented designs done on the wet clay. A red glaze was used from 1903-05, and yellow and orange were added from 1905-08.

Many fine designers worked at Newcomb over the years, but the mainstay group consisted of Sadie Irvine, Henrietta Bailey, and Anna Francis Simpson. When Paul Cox became technical director of Newcomb in 1910, matte glazes were developed. Cox had studied under Professor Binns at Alfred University.

From 1910-15, modeled designs largely replaced the incised ones, and the florals became more naturalistic rather than stylized. Sadie Irvine introduced the scenic oak trees with hanging moss and the moon shining through the trees. During this period the designs shifted away from the simplicity of the Arts and Crafts movement and reflected a more romantic feel. Blues and greens were still the main colors used, but matte glazes predominated.

In 1918, Paul Cox left Newcomb, the pottery left its Garden District campus and Newcomb College moved adjacent to Tulane's campus. Kenneth Smith took over Cox's job as ceramist and after Meyer's replacement left, he did both jobs.

During the 1920s, the wares became fairly standardized with bowls and vases having naturalistic flowers or the trees with moss designs. Some experimental works were still done. After Sheerer visited the Paris Exposition in 1925, some Art Deco designs found their way to Newcomb Pottery. Espanol was a new design motif that was influenced by a Spanish mantel and appeared in many variations throughout the 1930s.

When Ellsworth Woodward retired in 1931 after 46 years, and Mary Sheerer retired after 37 years, that was the end of an era for Newcomb Pottery. Though the pottery was being sold in many parts of the country, the stock was reduced in 1933. The three main decorators were spending more time teaching at the college than making pottery. During the 1930s, the trees and moss designs were continued along with newer abstract designs. By 1935, Smith and Irvine were left to carry on the pottery. Even during the Depression, they were still able to send out exhibitions.

In 1939, it was decided to continue the pottery school, but no longer conduct a commercial enterprise. The Newcomb Guild was established in 1941 to sell the works of the students and alumnae who were interested, but it was on a limited basis. A utilitarian line of simple vases, bowls, and ashtrays in muted colors or glazes was introduced in 1944, but the guild was finally closed down when Sadie Irvine retired in 1952.

Various marks were impressed, incised, or painted on Newcomb College Pottery. In 1901, a registration system was introduced, and in 1910 a number was assigned to the different shapes. Unacceptable pieces had an emery wheel through the mark.

**References:** Sally Main Spanola, *Newcomb Pottery: An Enterprise for Southern Women, 1895-1940*, Jessie Poesch Exhibition, Schiffer Publishing Ltd. 1984.

**Museums:** Howard-Tilton Library, Tulane University, New Orleans, Louisiana; Louisiana State Museum, New Orleans, Louisiana; Metropolitan Museum of Art, New York City; Museum of Fine Arts, Boston, Massachusetts; National Museum of History and Technology, Smithsonian Institution, Washington, DC; New Orleans Museum of Art, New Orleans, Louisiana; The Newark Museum, Newark, New Jersey.

**Reproduction Alert:** Reproductions of a high-glaze Newcomb Pottery are being sold by the Alumnae Association of Tulane University in New Orleans, Louisiana. The new Black-Eyed Susan pattern vase is being made by the Mottahedeh Company and does not have the weight or density of the original Newcomb Pottery. The pieces are marked as being made by Mottahedeh.

Bowl

    4 1/4" d, incised repeated green Deco design, recessed green beaded design on base, gloss dk brown glaze, "incised NC" mk, (A) ........................................... 385.00

    5 1/2" d, carved ivory flowers, green leaves, cobalt band, green ground, A.F. Simpson, "ink NC/FU99/AFS/JM" mk, (A) .......................................................... 1,760.00

    9" d, carved stylized blue, pink, and green flowers, matte blue ground, yellow int, hairline, "NC/NX38/313" mk, (A) ............................................................................ 990.00

    11 1/2" d, black swirls, gloss green and brown ground, Kenneth Smith, 1940, rim chips, (A) .................. 550.00

Bud Vase, 4 1/2" h, Transitional, sprigs of white flowers, blue-green ground, Henrietta Bailey, 1915, "imp NC/KB82/HB/212" mk, (A) .................................. 1,870.00

Candlestick, 6 1/2" h, carved white and yellow flowers, matte blue and green ground, Gertrude Maes, c1929, repairs, pr, (A) ......................................................... 990.00

Jar, 3" h, band of white flowers on shoulder, dk blue ground, A.F. Simpson, 1926, "imp NC/AFS/PF54/31" mk, (A) ............................................................................ 1,870.00

Milk Pitcher, 8" h, carved band of ivory flowers w/green leaves on cobalt ground shoulder, ivory and cobalt striped rim, cobalt handle, med blue textured body, Mazie Ryan, 1904, "NC/YY38/M.T.RYAN/JM" mk, (A) ............................................................................ 9,350.00

Mug, 4" h, stylized blue-green landscape, gloss overglaze, Desiree Roman and Marie Delavigne, 1901, "imp NC/DR/MD/G73X/Q/JM" mk, (A) ........................ 3,575.00

Pitcher

    5" h, Espanol pattern, matte dk blue ground, (A) ............................................................................ 1,320.00

**Vase, 6" h, green and blue swap lilies, gloss cream and blue bkd, Alice Urquhart, (A), $7,150.**

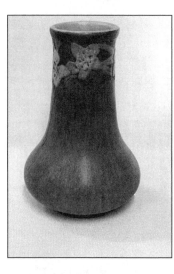

**Vase, 6" h, incised and painted pink flowers w/yellow centers, green leaves, multi-toned matte blue bkd, Henrietta Bailey, (A), $1,980.**

**Vase, 7" h, hand thrown, matte blue, brown, and green glaze, "imp JM" mk, (A), $523.**

    8" h, band of carved pink nasturtium, green leaves, matte blue ground, Sadie Irvine, 1924, "incised NC/SI/230/OB65" mk, (A) ............................... 2,310.00

Plaque, 6" h

    9 1/4" l, live oak tree, Spanish moss on riverbank, blue, cream, and yellow, A.F. Simpson, 1915, "AFS/HM7/263" mk, original frame, (A) ....................................... 7,150.00

    10" l, carved landscape of fishing boat, oak tree and Spanish moss, matte blue on white, Henrietta Bailey, 1922, "imp NC/HB/ML42" mk, (A) .................................................................. 13,200.00

Tea Set, pot, 6" h, creamer, cov sugar bowl, carved vert gold, green, cobalt and ivory floral designs, Henrietta Bailey, "NC/HB/JM/Q/BN99" mk, chips, (A) ...... 15,400.00

Toothpick Holder, 3 1/4" h, carved and painted floral design in blue shades, Juanita Gonzales, imp mk, (A) ..... 522.00

Trivet, 5 1/2" d, band of carved and painted pink flowers, green leaves, dk blue ground, A.F. Simpson, (A) .................................................................... 1,210.00

Vase

    2 1/2" h, multiple horiz ribbing, blue multi-tone glaze, (A) .................................................................... 330.00

    3" h, hand thrown, indentations at middle, gunmetal mahogany and green gloss glaze, (A) .............. 358.00

    3 1/2" h, bowl shape, white daffodils, green leaves, med blue ground, Sadie Irvine, "NC/271/KW46/S" mk, (A) .................................................................... 2,640.00

**Vase, 6" h, 3 handles, dk blue outlined lt blue daffodils, green leaves, cream ground, Harriet Jour, repair to handle, (A), $3,850.**

4" h

Bowl shape, band of incised and painted white and yellow crocuses, green and blue gloss ground, Marie Hoe LeBlanc, (A) ............................ 8,250.00

White, green, blue, and tan gloss glaze, (A) ..... 242.00

4 1/4" h, squat shape with short neck, blue outlined yellow sunflower petals and blue seeds, ivory ground, S. Massegali, "imp NC/P" mk, (A) ...................... 4,950.00

5" h, moonlit swamp scene, blue shades ........... 1,750.00

5 1/4" h, bulbous shape, flared rim, semi-matte raspberry glaze, periwinkle blue int, "stamped NC" mk, (A) ....................................................................... 440.00

5 1/2" h

Cylinder shape, short neck, carved white and yellow flowers, dk blue and blue-green ground, "stamped NC/AFS/JM/237/GP26/5/C" mk, (A) .......... 2,310.00

Jar shape, incised blue-green cactus plants w/lg yellow blossoms, Marie Ross, 1903, "stamped NC/MROSS/JM/X33" mk, rim chip, (A) .... 13,200.00

Tapered cylinder shape, sm straight neck, blue bell flowers, blue-green ground, Henrietta Bailey, 1915, "imp NC/HB/JM/HD21" mk, (A) .................. 1,980.00

5 3/4" h, incised band of sailboats, gloss blue, white, and green, Desiree Roman, "NC/W/D.R./X37/JM." mk, (A) ....................................................................... 13,750.00

6" h

Bulbous base, tapered neck, slightly flared rim, incised and painted matte cream, blue, and green, stylized floral design, #174, (A) ............................... 1,760.00

Cylinder shape, squat base, med purple narcissus, dk purple ground, A.F. Simpson, 1917, "imp NC/AFS/IN91/272/JM" mk, (A) .................. 2,200.00

Hourglass shape, carved and painted yellow flowers, green leaves, matte blue ground, Anna Francis Simpson, (A) ................................................. 1,870.00

Ovoid shape, carved blue shades oak trees and Spanish moss, Anna F. Simpson, 1930, "imp NC/AFS/JH/78/SG85" mk, (A) ................... 4,400.00

Tapered cylinder shape, short neck, carved and painted green and yellow flowers, dk purple and red overglaze over blue ground, Anna Francis Simpson, #HQ20, (A) ......................................... 1,650.00

7" h

Bulbous shape, carved cream and green butterflies and cotton blossoms, med blue ground, Sadie Irvine, 1926, "stamped NC/100/SI/JM/PE71," (A) ................................................................. 8,800.00

Swollen cylinder shape, incised and painted southern landscape w/blue trees and green moss, yellow moon, A. Arbo, (A) ...................................... 3,850.00

Tooled yellow flowerheads and celadon leaves, ivory ground, Esther H. Elliott, "stamped NC/EHE/BB10/Q/JM" mk, (A) ...............................24,750.00

7 1/2" h, incised blue-green stylized birch seed pods, ivory ground, Henrietta Bailey, 1904, "NC/PP71/HBaily/JM/Q" mk, (A) ............................................................... 15,400.00

8 1/2" h, ovoid, blue shaded oaks, Spanish moss, and moon, Anna Frances Simpson, 1920, "NC/133/LE74/AFS" mk, (A)................................................................. 5,500.00

9" h, tapered cylinder shape, small flared rim, blue outlined ivory and yellow blossoms, green ground, (A) ....................................................................... 6,600.00

9 1/2" h, cylinder shape, flared rim, Espanol pattern, Sadie Irvine, 1926, "stamped NC/229/SI/JM/PE95" mk, (A)............................................................... 7,150.00

Vessel

3 1/2" h, squat, dk blue carved oak trees, Spanish moss, and moon, med blue ground, Jonathan Hunt, 1932, (A) ...................................................... 3,190.00

(A) ................................................................. 742.00

4 1/4" h, spherical, white gladiola, green stems, blue ground, Sadie Irvine, "stamped NC/JM/SI/75/PK97" mk, (A) ...................................................... 2,640.00

5 3/4" h, spherical shape, carved pink chrysanthemums, matte blue ground, Henrietta Bailey, 1926, "stamped NC/HB/PG2/26" mk, (A) ............................... 1,320.00

Wall Pocket, 11" h, conical shape, bands of carved cobalt and green stylized trees, Leona Nicholson, c1904, (A) ................................................................. 9,350.00

# New Geneva and Greensboro Pottery

## Fayette and Greene Counties, Pennsylvania 1849-1917, 1810-early 20th century

**History:** Greensboro and New Geneva were two towns that were opposite from each other. Alexander and James Vance were the first Greensboro potters who made redware covered with brown slip in Greene County, Pennsylvania starting about 1810. They later used a white clay and made gray stonewares. There were numerous potters in the area after about 1860. James Hamilton is known for his stoneware pumps and enormous stoneware jars in 40-50 gallon sizes.

In 1849, George Debolt and Harry Atchison were making stoneware pottery in New Geneva in Fayette County, Pennsylvania. Some pieces made in New Geneva were salt glazed. During the years of operation, numerous potters worked there. Canning jars, whiskey jugs, crocks, and other wares were made. Some were not signed or decorated. The most desirable pieces were either decorated freehand or stenciled.

During the early years at New Geneva and Greensboro, potters used freehand designs of birds, leaves, flowers, fruit, straight and curved lines. Cut stenciled designs were fruit, turkeys, flowers, vines, plants, straight and curved lines. Painting could be done before or after the glaze. Blue was the most popular color for underglazing, while enamels were used for overglazing.

An assortment of vases, milk pitchers, water pitchers, doorstops, flower pots, banks, and large crocks that were 6-20 gallon sizes were made. With the coming of the age of glass, the pottery business slowly declined.

**References:** Dr. Carmen A. Guappone, *New Geneva and Greensboro Pottery, Illustrated and Priced*, Guappones' Publishers, 1975.

Bank, 6 1/2" h, gray-tan glaze w/dk brown Albany slip flowers, wear and chips, (A) ...................................... 1,870.00

Canning Jar, 9 3/4" h, blue stenciled "T.F. REPPERT, MANUFACTURER, GREENSBORO, PA." and diamond band on front................................................................ 125.00

Crock
8" h, applied handles, cobalt brushed stripes, "imp A. & W. BOUGHNER, GREENSBORO, PA. 2" on front, (A) ...........................................................................205.00
10" h, stenciled cobalt "HAMILTON & JONES" and swirls ................................................................................ 175.00

Flower Pot, Attached Underplate
5 1/2" h, finger crimped rims, 2 tone tan ground, dk brown slip on pot border and rim, chips, (A) ............... 125.00
7" h, redware body w/3 dk brown brushed slip lines, (A) ................................................................................ 165.00

Jar
10" h, cobalt stenciled "Hamilton & Jones, 2" and wavy lines, (A) ............................................................ 330.00
15" h
Applied shoulder handles, "cobalt stenciled and freehand T.F. REPPERT, SUCCESSOR TO JAS. HAMILTON & CO. GREENSBORO, PA. And 4," (A) ................................................................................220.00
Ovoid, cobalt brushed florals and "4," imp "Hamilton, Greensboro, PA. 4," applied shoulder handles, chips, (A)........................................................... 550.00
16" h
Cobalt stenciled "Williams & Reppert, Greensboro, PA. 5," applied handles, freehand lines, squiggles, and ferns top and base, (A) ................................. 500.00
Ovoid, cobalt stenciled "Hamilton & Jones, Greensboro, Green Co., Pa. 5" on front, hairline, (A) ................................................................................935.00

16 3/4" h, ovoid, applied shoulder handles, cobalt stylized flowers, dashes, and "6," stenciled "HAMILTON & JONES, GREENSBORO, PA." on front, (A)...... 660.00

Jug
14" h, ovoid, cobalt stenciled and freehand "WILLIAMS & REPPERT, GREENSBORO, PA. 2," (A) ........... 330.00
14 1/2" h, cobalt stenciled "HAMILTON & JONES, GREENSBORO, PA." and cobalt and red trim ................................................................................ 350.00

Pitcher
5 1/4" h, dk brown Albany slip floral and scalloped design, tan clay, strap handle, (A) ................................. 880.00
6 5/8" h, tan body, dk brown slip floral design, band of dots on shoulder, base, and handle, lobed slip rim, (A) ................................................................................ 358.00
7" h
Black slip freehand floral design ...................... 330.00
Brown slip stenciled floral design, (A) .............. 193.00
7 1/8" h, freehand brown slip floral bud and leaves, scalloped band on shoulder, banded rim and base, rim chips, (A) ...................................................... 165.00
7 1/2" h, gray body, black slip dashes, rim repair, (A) ................................................................................ 165.00
8" h, brown Albany slip stylized leaf and flowerbuds, orange-brown ground........................................ 600.00

Preserve Jar
9 1/2" h, red-brown slip freehand floral design, spout chips, (A) ................................................................ 193.00
10" h, "blue stenciled HAMILTON & JONES GREENSBORO, PA. and leaves" on front, c1870, hairline, (A) ................................................................................ 77.00
11" h, "cobalt stenciled flowers and JAS HAMILTON & CO. 2," hairlines, (A) ......................................... 248.00

Spooner, 4" h, dk blue stylized flowers and leaves, imp mk ................................................................................ 10.00

Storage Jar, 16" h, top to bottom blue stylized florals, leaves, and wavy lines, blue "5" on lower section, c1860,

**Jar, 12" h, blue design and "WILLIAM AND REPPERT GREENSBORO, PA," $375.**

# Niloak Pottery Company

## Benton, Arkansas
## 1910-1947

**History:** Charles Dean Hyten of Hyten Pottery, later known as Eagle Pottery, formed Niloak Pottery with a group of investors in 1911. At first he made ordinary stonewares in the form of crocks, churns, and jugs as his family had before him, but when demand decreased for these ordinary wares, Hyten set out to create a unique art pottery.

Niloak is kaolin spelled backwards. Hyten mixed the colored, native Arkansas clays into a swirled mixture. This marbleized design of two or more colors was then placed on the potter's wheel to form the vases and bowls called "Mission Swirl" and marketed under the Niloak name. Colors were brown, blue, and cream for the most part, but green, pink, and white also were used. The pottery was quite successful, due to a good distribution system, and it was popular with tourists.

Early swirl pieces had a rough texture and dull exterior. A clear interior glaze was used to make the pieces waterproof. With the increased popularity of Niloak, other shapes were made which included lamps, umbrella stands, pitchers, tankards, candlesticks, clock cases, and the like. By the 1920s, there was more mass production to meet the demand for pieces. Shapes became more standardized.

Hyten did many demonstrations and exhibits of the Niloak technique. In 1925, he got a trademark for his wares, and received his patent on the swirl pottery technique in 1928. That same year the company was incorporated as the Niloak Pottery and Tile Company.

By 1929, there was a large, new showroom on Military Road. With the Depression looming ahead, there were heavy expenses and decreased sales. In 1931, Hyten developed a line of molded wares in matte, semi-matte, gloss and dip glazes called Hywood art pottery. M. Stoin from Weller worked on this line before the fire of 1932. When Howard Lewis came to help in 1932, this new glazed ware was called Hywood by Niloak to capitalize on the Niloak name. Some hand thrown pieces were made along with the castware. When Rudy Ganz designed the molds for the casted pieces, these became dominant since they were less expensive and easier to produce. In 1933, Niloak exhibited as the Chicago Century of Progress Exposition. Ganz left in 1933 and Lewis left in 1934.

In 1934, Winburn and his associates purchased Niloak, and the company concentrated on industrial castwares in an attempt to increase sales. By 1937, castware was called Niloak. At the end of the 1930s, there were improved sales in all aspects of the pottery; stonewares, castware, and some swirl pieces. Winburn was in total control, and Hyten became a castware salesman. He finally resigned in 1940 and moved on to Camark Pottery.

Just prior to World War II, Niloak was quite prosperous. They continued to produce an abundance of castwares, in addition to stonewares, flower pots, a new line of novelties, and a small number of swirl examples. However, by 1942, the pottery was mostly converted to war production, especially clay pigeons for military training.

After a fire in 1945, the company filled numerous back orders for castwares, but there were not many new sales. Postwar glazes were primarily glossy on whatever pieces were made. By 1947, Niloak was no longer functioning as a pottery. Winburn formed the Winborn Tile Company with his brother.

A variety of impressed die-stamp marks was used on the Mission Swirl pieces. Raised mold marks were used on later pieces. Ink stamp markings on Hywood Art Pottery were introduced in 1931.

**References:** David Edwin Gifford, *Collector's Encyclopedia of Niloak*, Collector Books, 1993.

**Museums:** Chrysler Museum, Norfolk, VA

**Collectors' Club:** Arkansas Pottery Collectors Society, 12 Normandy Road, Little Rock, AK 72007.

Bud Vase, 6 1/2" h, twisted sides, molded wing handles, yellow glaze, (A) ..........................................25.00
Cabinet Vase, 2 1/2" h, pitcher shape, Ozark Dawn II, Hywood................................................................30.00
Candlestick, 7" h, matte Lewis blue glaze, pr............100.00
Decanter Set, decanter, 8 3/4" h, 4 cups, black glaze, Hywood..............................................................200.00
Ewer
    6 3/4" h, matte blue glaze ....................................100.00
    9" h, peach glaze ....................................................10.00
    16 1/2" h, Ozark Dawn glaze ...............................150.00

Pitcher
    2 1/2" h, dimpled yellow glaze ...............................10.00
    7 1/4" h, "Bouquet" pattern, med blue, "imp NILOAK" mk ..................................................................................26.00
    10" h, relief molded bust of colonial woman on side, matte pink and blue glaze...................................35.00
Planter
    3 1/2" h, figural Scottie dog, blue glaze ..................26.00
    4 3/4" h, figural seal and bowl, tan w/dk brown accents ..................................................................................18.00
    5" l x 3 1/2" h, figural walking bear, lt brown w/black accents................................................................36.00
    6" h, figural squirrel, pink .........................................60.00
    6 1/2" h, figural swan, matte green glaze ...............65.00
    7" l x 5" h, figural seated fox, speckled red, orange, and gray glaze............................................................35.00
    7 1/2" h, "Peter Pan" figure seated on flower lobed bowl, Ozark Dawn II .....................................................35.00
    8 1/2" l, figural swimming fish, lt blue glaze ............20.00
Shakers, Pr, 2 3/4" h, figural penguins, matte blue ......75.00
Strawberry Jar, 7" h, matte ivory .................................28.00
Vase
    2 3/4" h, castware, lobed bowl shape w/scalloped rim, matte dk red glaze...............................................55.00
    3 1/4" h, cornucopia shape, matte green and brown shades................................................................ 15.00
    3 5/8" h, swollen middle, spread ft and rim, molded handles, matte rose glaze, Hywood .........................45.00
    4 1/2" h, urn shape, 2 sm handles, matte dk yellow glaze ..................................................................................20.00
    5 1/2" d x 2 3/4" h, ball shape, lobed body, matte wine red ..................................................................................55.00
    5 1/2" h, leaf form, Ozark Dawn II glaze, rose and blue ..................................................................................50.00
    5 3/4" h, circus elephant, figural elephant standing on platform, matte yellow glaze, (A)........................82.00
    5 7/8" h, side handles, Ozark Dawn II .....................35.00
    6" h, folded, fluted top, circ base, matte green glaze ..................................................................................10.00
    6 1/2" h, bulbous shape, free form rim, matte green glaze, Hywood ...............................................................60.00
    6 3/4" h
        Five openings w/leaf design, lt blue ...................35.00
        Flared neck, matte blue.....................................100.00
    7 1/2" h, winged handles, pink glaze ......................24.00

**Vase, 4 5/8" h, mission swirl ware, tan, dk brown, cream, and turquoise swirl, imp mk, $100.**

8" h
    Bulbous body, disk ft, scroll handles, celadon green glaze ............................................................. 38.00
    "Peacock," Ozark Dawn glaze ........................... 35.00

**MISSION SWIRL**
Bottle, 7 1/2" h, blue, red, and tan, (A) ...................... 357.00
Bowl
    6" d, blue, brown, cream, and terra cotta
    .............................................................................. 150.00
    10" d, w/flower frog, tan, brown, and dk brown, (A)
    .............................................................................. 264.00
Candlestick, 8" h, flared base, brown, blue, sand, and terra cotta swirls, "stamped Niloak" mk, pr, (A)
    .............................................................................. 330.00
Cigarette Holder, 3 1/2" h, cylinder shape, blue and dk brown, (A) ............................................................ 88.00
Cup, 2" h, tan, dk brown, and green swirl ................... 265.00
Humidor, 6 1/2" h, blue, cream, and med brown swirl, "imp Niloak" mk ............................................................ 800.00
Lamp, 13 1/2" h, tan, med brown, dk brown, and red, (A)
    .............................................................................. 467.00
Mug, 4 3/8" h, red, tan, green, and brown swirl .......... 450.00
Pitcher, 10 1/2" h, tan, blue, and dk brown, (A) ......... 660.00
Toothpick Holder, 1 3/4" h, tan and taupe .................... 85.00
Tumbler, 4" h, brown and blue swirls ........................... 35.00
Tumble Up, 7 1/2" h, red, blue, tan, med brown, and dk brown, (A) ........................................................... 522.00
Vase
    4 1/2" h
        Red, blue, gray, and cream .................................. 75.00
        Tan, brown, and blue ........................................ 150.00
    5" d, closed rim, pierced for flowers on border, blue, tan, and dk brown, (A) ............................................. 297.00
    5" h
        Ball shape, swirled blue, brown, and red, (A) .... 210.00
        Turned in rim, blue, brown, tan, taupe, and terra cotta .............................................................. 160.00
    5 1/2" h, cylinder shape, blue, tan, and dk brown, (A)
        .............................................................................. 176.00
    5 3/4" h
        Spherical shape, closed in rim, brown, blue, sand, and terra cotta swirl, (A) ................................... 247.00
        Tapered cylinder shape, blue, red, yellow, and brown swirl ....................................................... 240.00
    6" h, blue, tan, and terra cotta ............................... 175.00
    6 1/2" h, tan, med brown, and dk brown, (A) ......... 209.00
    8" h
        Corset shape, tan, red, blue, and dk brown, (A)
        .............................................................................. 154.00
        Tapered body, flared rim, yellow, med brown, dk brown, (A) ....................................................... 522.00
    8 1/2" h, trumpet shape, flared ft, brown, blue, and terra cotta swirl, "stamped Niloak" mk, (A) ................. 165.00
    9" h, cylinder shape, blue, red, and med brown, (A)
        .............................................................................. 264.00
    9 1/2" h
        Ball base, flared neck, brown, blue, purple, and terra cotta swirls, (A) ........................................... 357.00
        Baluster shape, brown, blue, sand, and terra cotta swirls, (A) ...................................................... 297.00

9 3/4" h, pear shape, brown, blue, sand, and terra cotta swirls, (A) ........................................................... 385.00
10" h
    Cylinder shape, brown, blue, and terra cotta swirls, (A)
    .............................................................................. 385.00
    Hourglass shape, brown, blue, and terra cotta swirl, (A) .................................................................... 220.00
    Tan and taupe ...................................................... 375.00
10 1/2" h, swollen base, flared rim, slate blue, brown, and tan ........................................................................ 180.00
12" h, swollen shape, everted rim, brown, ivory, and terra cotta swirls, (A) ..................................................... 495.00
12 1/4" h, hourglass shape, brown, blue, purple, and terra cotta swirls, (A) ................................................... 330.00
14" h, tapered cylinder shape, rolled rim, brown, blue, purple, and terra cotta swirls, (A) ..................... 880.00
18" h, tapered shape, flared rim, blue, tan, red, med brown, and dk brown, (A) ............................. 2,970.00
Vessel, 6" h x 8" d, bowl shape, brown, beige, and terra cotta swirls, "stamped Niloak" mk, (A) .............. 440.00

# North Dakota School of Mines

### University of North Dakota
### Grand Forks, North Dakota
### 1910-1963

**History:** In 1910, Earle Babcock persuaded the University of North Dakota to establish a Ceramics Department to work with North Dakota clay. Margaret Cable, who studied with Charles Binns and Frederick H. Rhead, taught at the North Dakota School of Mines in Grand Forks from 1910-1949.

Pottery examples made at the school included vases, figurines, cookie jars, lamp bases, ashtrays, tea sets, plaques, and such. Almost all of the pieces were made from molds, though a few were hand thrown by Margaret Cable. Pottery was sometimes decorated with designs carved in low relief or hand painted with colored glazes. Native themes included flowers and animals. Some pieces were done in Art Nouveau and Art Deco styles.

Other artists working there with the native clays were Flora Huckfield, Agnes Dollahan, Frieda Hammers, Margaret Pachl, and Julia E. Mattson. Only a limited amount of pieces were sold to the general public. Some pottery was marked "U.N.D., Grand Forks, N.D.," while others had an incised mark in a circle in cobalt blue under the glaze "University of North Dakota Grank Forks, N.D. Made at School of Mines of N.D. Clay."

**References:** Margaret Barr, Donald Miller, and Robert Barr, *University of North Dakota Pottery, The Cable Years*, Knight Publishing Company, 1977; Donald Miller, *University of North Dakota Pottery, The Cable Years, Second Edition*, 1999.

**Collectors' Club:** North Dakota Pottery Collectors' Society, Sandy Short, Box 14, Beach, North Dakota 58621, quarterly newsletter, $15 per year.

Bookend, 5 1/2" h, brown w/incised windmill design dk brown streaked bkd, (A) ....................................... 220.00
Bowl
    4" d, dk blue glaze, (A) ............................................. 55.00

4 1/4" h x 9" d, ext carved matte green and white heart-shaped leaves, (A) ............................................. 495.00

6 1/4" d x 3 1/2" h, "Meadow Lark" design, carved band of birds, matte olive green glaze ........................ 1,495.00

6 1/2" d, low form, HP and tooled scene of oxen, covered wagons on prairie, blue sky, brown ground, mkd, (A) .................................................................... 1,045.00

8" d, carved leaf design on int, green glaze, (A) .... 385.00

8 1/2" d, closed rim, ivory ext, green int, (A) .......... 115.00

Charger, 9 3/4" d, border design of dk brown flowers on burnt sienna ground, dk brown center, Margaret Cable, 1932, (A) ................................................................. 990.00

Coaster, 3 1/2" d, emb prairie rose design, white, (A) .. 55.00

Figure

3" h, seated chicken, orange-brown glaze, (A) ......................................................................... 220.00

3" l, dog, ivory ground, blue accents, (A) ............... 165.00

3 1/2" h, seated coyote, gloss green and brown glaze, (A) ......................................................................... 165.00

4 1/2" h, Bentonite cowboy, brick red, black, and gold glazes, "incised JH/13/UND" mark, (A) ............. 715.00

Jug, 3" h, gloss dk brown glaze, (A) .......................... 88.00

Lamp Base, 13" h, spread ft, matte dk tobacco brown glaze, dtd March 1926, (A) ...................................... 880.00

Pitcher, 5" h, squat shape, emb frieze of "Red River Ox Carts," gloss ivory glaze, (A) ................................ 990.00

Plaque, 7 1/2" l x 4 1/2" w, rect, emb design of farmer w/oxcart, brown glaze, (A) .................................. 220.00

Plate, 5" d, painted border of green leaves, vines, and 4 red dot flowerheads, tan ground, (A) .......................... 200.00

Trivet, 5" d, carved green and ochre swimming fish, cream ground, "stamped JM58" mk, (A) ......................... 275.00

Vase

2 1/2" h, hand built, ivory ground, green indented vert loops on shoulder, (A) ........................................ 138.00

3 1/4" h, green horiz stripes, mustard body, mkd, (A) ......................................................................... 357.00

4" h

Bulging body, closed rim, gloss turquoise glaze, chip, (A) ...................................................................... 50.00

Carved leaf design at rim, tan, sgd "Cable" ......................................................................... 250.00

Tan w/carved leaf design, sgd "Cable" .............. 240.00

Tapered shape, imp horiz ribbing, shaded lustered green to blue glaze, aqua int ......................... 375.00

5" h

Bulbous, flared rim, emb prairie roses, mottled green crystalline glaze, "incised Steen-Huck-1100" mk, (A) ...................................................................... 1,320.00

Tapered body w/wide shoulder, short rim, black and yellow Native American design on dk red ground, (A) ......................................................................... 625.00

5 1/2" h, Bulbous Shape

Closed rim, mustard yellow carved hanging lanterns on shoulder, vert stripes and squares, gloss charcoal blue glaze, circ mk, (A) ...................... 5,500.00

"Prairie Rose," carved band of coral stylized flowers and green leaves, sand ground, (A) ............. 990.00

5 3/4" h, bulbous shape, emb frieze of Souix Indians on horseback, dk brown matte glaze, Flora Huckfield, (A) .................................................................... 1,980.00

6" w, black and yellow Native American design on red ground, (A) ......................................................... 605.00

6 1/8" h, swollen shape, border band of blue slip decorated thistles on tan ground, blue body, (A) ... 1,650.00

6 3/4" h, flared shape from base to wide shoulder, sm rim, frieze of bronco riders, brown to green matte glaze, Julia Mattson, "incised J.M./133," (A) ............. 2,310.00

7" h, incised stylized turquoise blossoms, beige ground, stamped mk, (A) .............................................. 1,430.00

7 1/4" h, tapered cylinder shape, "N. D. Rodeo," emb cowboy scene under matte chocolate brown glaze, (A) .................................................................... 1,650.00

8" h, carved daffodils, matte mahogany glaze, circ mk, "incised McCosh," (A) ..................................... 1,210.00

8 1/4" h, cylinder shape, incised horiz banding, lime green luster glaze ............................................ 425.00

8 7/8" h, ball shaped base, cylinder neck, horiz ribbing, white glazed base, brown neck, aqua int .......... 395.00

9" h, carved mocha-brown narcissus, dk brown ground, "incised F. Cunningham" (A) .......................... 1,100.00

10" h, ovoid, short collar, carved wheat sheaths, matte purple-brown glaze, F. Huckfield, (A) ............ 1,430.00

Vase, 7 1/2" h, incised brown leaves, blue ground, "J. Mattson" stamped mk, (A), $715.

**Vase, 4" h, gloss brown glaze, blue stamp mk, $225.**

Vessel

    4" h x 4 1/2" d, squat shape, closed rim, carved band of leaves on border, gloss blue glaze, (A) ............ 165.00

    4 1/4" h, jar shape w/shouldered collar, Bentonite, yellow and black Native American style birds and geometrics, dk red ground, "incised Armstrong/1948" mk, (A) ........................................................ 1,010.00

    5 1/4" h, emb frieze of bison on shoulder, ochre and brown matte glaze, Margaret Cable, (A) ........ 1,980.00

    6 1/4" h, emb frieze of "Covered Wagon" on shoulder, matte brown glaze, Margaret Cable, (A) ........2,530.00

G. E. OHR,
BILOXI.

# George Ohr/Biloxi Art Pottery

### Biloxi, Mississippi
### 1883-1906

**History:** George Ohr's pottery was established in Biloxi, Mississippi in 1883, where he first made pitchers, cooking pots, water coolers, and chimney pots that he sold at local and regional fairs. By the late 1880s, he had discontinued molded wares and started throwing his pottery.

Known as "the mad potter of Biloxi," Ohr's technique involved twisting, denting, folding, pinching, squeezing, and generally "torturing" the white and red burning local clays he used into art pottery wares with extremely thin walls.

A tremendous variety of pieces was made including vases, teapots, jugs, bowls, and pitchers. No two pieces made by Ohr were alike in shape or decoration. Many pieces showed Art Nouveau influences. Some were made with marbleized clay. Pieces were also decorated with modeled snakes and lizards. Vases could have ruffles or applied loop handles.

Ohr did outstanding work with glazes that were bright, luster, or matte finishes. Tortoiseshell, mottled, metallic, monochromatic, or transparent lead glazes were used. Some unglazed pieces were made. He won a medal at the St. Louis Exposition in 1904.

Although Ohr received some assistance from Leo, his son, with the clays, his was essentially a one-man operation. Ohr's pottery closed in 1906. His pieces were usually signed and "Biloxi" was most often incised or impressed.

**References:** Robert W. Blasberg, *The Unknown Ohr*, Peaceable Press, 1986; Garth Clark, Robert A. Ellison, Jr., Dr. Eugene Hecht, *The Mad Potter of Biloxi: The Art and Life of George E. Ohr* Abbeyville Press, 1989; *The Biloxi Art Pottery of George E. Ohr*, Mississippi State Historical Museum, privately printed, 1978.

**Museums:** George E. Ohr Arts & Cultural Center, Biloxi, MS; Mississippi Museum of Art/Gulf Coast, Biloxi, MS; National Museum of History and Technology, Smithsonian Institution, Washington, DC; State Historical Society, Madison, WI.

Bottle, 14 3/4" h, tapered form, dk brown glaze, script mk, (A) ................................................................. 4,200.00

Cabinet Vase, bulbous, mid body twist, cupped rim, gunmetal glaze, "stamped G.E.OHR, Biloxi" mk, (A) ........................................................................ 1,540.00

Candlestick, 4 1/2" h, gunmetal glaze, mkd, (A) ........ 413.00

Chamberstick, 4" h, molded twisted base, ribbon handle, gunmetal and green ext, matte ochre int, "incised G.E.OHR." mk, (A) .............................................. 2,310.00

Cup

    3" h, flared with vert dimples, gloss green and purple ext, matte red int, "black LG606." mk, (A) ............. 2,860.00

    3 1/2" h, tapered, horiz ribbing, mahogany ext w/mirror surface, dk ochre int w/brown speckling, "G.E.Ohr/Biloxi, Miss." mk, (A) ......................... 385.00

Inkwell

    2 3/4" w x 3 3/4" l, artist palette shape, green lustered glaze, repairs, "stamped G.E.OHR/Biloxi" mk, (A) ................................................................. 4,125.00

    3" h x 4 1/2" w, figural cabin shape, gloss green glaze, "stamped GEO.OHR/BILOXI, MISS." mk, (A) ................................................................. 2,310.00

Mug, 5" h, ribbed top, applied snake, mottled gunmetal brown glaze, (A) ................................................. 3,575.00

Pitcher

    4" h

        Applied rosette on front, angular ribbon handle, mirrored umber and gunmetal mottled glaze, clay price tag, "imp G.E.OHR Biloxi, Miss." mk, (A) ................................................................. 2,970.00

        Pinched and lobed body, cut-out handle, mottled cobalt glaze, restored rim chip, "stamped G.E.OHR, Biloxi, Miss." mk, (A) ................................. 1,980.00

    6" h, gourd shape, ribbed body, blue and green mottled glaze, "imp G.E.OHR Biloxi, Miss." mk, (A) ................................................................. 1,320.00

    6 1/2" h, ribbon handle, pink, green, red, and white sponged matte glaze, "imp G.E.OHR/Biloxi, Miss." mk, (A) ................................................................. 7,700.00

**Vase, 5" h, charcoal and mustard speckled glaze, lt red clay, (A), $2,100.**

8 3/4" h, tapered shape, sponged umber and green bands, clear gloss glaze, "stamped GEO. E. OHR, BILOXI, MISS." mk, (A) ...................................5,500.00

Puzzle Mug

3 1/2" h, tooled body, gunmetal and green glaze, rect handle, "stamped G.E.OHR/Biloxi, Miss." mk, (A) ............................................................1,320.00

4" h, in twist, rabbit handle, dk brown glaze, "incised Cloister/JR/HE/6-10-95," "stamped G.E.Ohr BILOXI MISS." mk, (A)...............................................2,420.00

Teapot

4" h, bulbous shape, sponged brown, green, and black design on khaki ground, "stamped GEO.OHR/BILOXI, MISS." mk, (A)............................................6,050.00

6" h, chartreuse volcanic glaze, "stamped G.E. OHR/Biloxi, Miss." mk, (A)...........................13,440.00

7 1/2" h, Cadogan, ear shaped handle, long spout, hammered ground, dk brown glaze, (A) ...............9,350.00

Vase

4" h, bottle shape, squat base, gunmetal, raspberry, and green frothy glaze, (A)...................................3,300.00

4 1/2" h, bulbous, w/triangular, 3 lobed top, speckled olive green glaze, "stamped G.E.OHR, Biloxi, Miss." mk, (A) ............................................................2,420.00

4 3/4" h, bulbous, folded rim, speckled ochre and green glaze, "imp G.E.OHR Biloxi, Miss." mk, (A) ............................................................2,640.00

5" h, ftd, twisted waist and top, green and purple gloss glaze, gunmetal accents, imp mk, (A) ............8,250.00

5 1/2" h
Body twist, dk red gloss glaze, "stamped G.E.OHR/Biloxi, Miss." mk, (A) .................6,600.00
Sculptured shape, pulled lip, green and gunmetal mottled glaze, restored pulls on base, (A) ............................................................1,650.00

6" h, pear shape, folded rim, raspberry, green, blue, and gray sponged glaze, "stamped G.E.OHR/Biloxi, Miss." mk, (A).............................................4,400.00

**Vase, 6" h, applied snake, green spotted glaze, incised mk, (A), $468.**

6 1/2" h, baluster shape, ochre, red, and gunmetal sponged ground, "imp G.E.OHR Biloxi, Miss" mk, (A) ............................................................1,980.00

9 1/2" h, ftd, dbl gourd shape, twisted top, brown, gunmetal, green, and gloss glazes, imp mk, (A) ............................................................16,500.00

10" h, full length dimples, folded neck, green, pink, red, and gunmetal lustered glaze, restored, "stamped G.E. OHR/Biloxi, Miss." mk, (A) ............................................................14,300.00

Vessel

2 3/4" h, squat shape, pink, purple, red, and green sponged glaze, "stamped G.E.OHR/Biloxi, Miss" mk, (A) ............................................................1,870.00

5" h, 2 pinched and folded lobes, 2 incised lines on shoulder, bisque scrolled clay, script mk, (A) ............................................................2,090.00

5 1/4" h, spherical w/pinched sides, ruffled top, pink volcanic glaze, green, black, and white sponged accents, "stamped G.E.OHR/Biloxi, Miss." mk, (A) ............................................................5,500.00

6" h, bulbous shape, in body twist and folds, bisque, script mk, (A) ...............................................1,650.00

# Old Sleepy Eye Stoneware and Pottery

## Monmouth, Illinois
## Weir Pottery Company 1899-1905
## Western Stoneware Company 1906-1937

**History:** Sleepy Eye, Minnesota and the Sleepy Eye Milling Company were named for the Sioux Indian chief from Brown County. In business from 1883-1921, the Sleepy Eye Milling Company used the Indian's bust as its advertising trademark. Premiums given away by this company were made by the Weir Pottery Company and Western Stoneware Company in Monmouth, Illinois.

The Weir Pottery Company was the original manufacturer of the Old Sleepy Eye premiums: the butter crock, bowl, tankard, and vase made from 1899-1905 in the molded Flemish blue and gray stoneware. Weir received a contract to make 500,000 pieces of this stoneware. The vase pictured the trademark head used by Sleepy Eye Milling Company and had "Old Sleepy Eye" embossed under the bust. The background texture of the vase resembled an orange peel. The reverse side had the cattails, dragonfly, and frog. The salt crock, tankard, and bowl had a smooth finish. Pieces were put into sacks of flour as a premium until the government made the company stop that practice. They also made a cobalt and white pitcher with the Indian's head.

The merger of seven potteries in 1906, including Weir, formed the Western Stoneware Company. Western was the last producer of Sleepy Eye premiums from 1906-1937. Pitchers were made by Western Stoneware in cobalt blue and white in five sizes: half pint, pint, quart, half gallon, and gallon. These pieces all had the same shape, had the Indian profile in a war bonnet, and had wigwams, trees, or a crouching Indian on the reverse side.

In addition to the pitchers, Western made steins in two sizes, a sugar bowl, a hot plate or trivet, jar, bowl, vase, and three sizes of mugs. Many pieces were unmarked, but some had a backstamp WSCO Monmouth, Illinois in a diamond shape in blue or black under the glaze. Additional colors included brown on white, green on white, brown on yellow and some solid colors. These pieces were made until 1937.

Molds were redesigned in 1952 for steins in two sizes. The Indian bust had a different profile, and the glaze was chestnut brown. The pieces were marked with a raised maple leaf and "W." They were not embossed "Old Sleepy Eye." The Indian head was still molded on the handle, and the reverse scene resembled the earlier steins.

Commemorative steins in blue and buff color were made by Western from 1968-1973 for members of the Board of Directors and such. They were not available to the general public.

**References:** Jim Martin and Bette Cooper, *Monmouth-Western Stoneware*, Wallace-Homestead, 1983; Elinor Meugniot, *Old Sleepy Eye*, Delos L. Hill and Ozella I. Hill, 1979.

**Collectors' Club:** Old Sleepy Eye Collectors' Club of America, Inc. P.O. Box 12, Monmouth, IL 61462-0012, newsletter five times per year, $10.

**Reproduction Alert:** The Sleepy Eye examples made by Western Stoneware from 1906 until 1937 are being reproduced. Reproduction pitchers are cast as one piece to speed up production leaving a hole on the inside of the pitcher, and the new handles are hollow. New pitchers are also lighter in weight and have a raised ridge running around the lip. There are also salt and peppers and toothpicks being made which were not made originally, along with a curved sugar bowl shape.

Bowl, 4" h, cobalt and gray, hairlines, (A)................... 198.00
Butter Crock, 5" h x 6 1/4" d, c1903 ........................ 1,200.00
Mug, 4 1/2" h, cobalt and white, unmkd ..................... 220.00

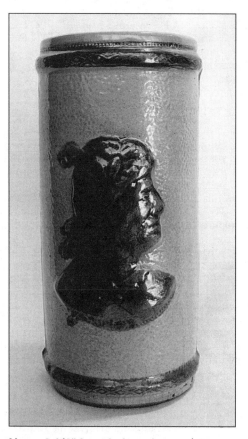

**Vase, 8 3/4" h, cobalt and gray, $575.**

Pitcher
  4" h, cobalt and white, #1 size
    Blue rim .................................................... 530.00
    Plain rim ................................................... 70.00
  5 1/4" h, cobalt and white, #2 ............................. 475.00
  6 1/2" h, cobalt and white, #3 size ........................ 325.00
  8" h, blue and white, "WS Co. Monmouth, Ill." mark, stains and hairline, (A) ..................................... 110.00
  9" h, blue and white, #5
    Blue rim .................................................... 325.00
    Plain rim ................................................... 225.00
Stein
  5 1/2" h, brown, 22oz, Western Stoneware .......... 250.00
  7 1/2" h, blue, gray ground .................................. 650.00
Sugar Bowl, 3 1/4" h, cobalt and white...................... 750.00
  Vase, 9" h, Flemish, cat-tails, blue and gray.......... 295.00

# Ott and Brewer

## Trenton, New Jersey
## 1863-1892

**History:** Etruria Pottery was established by Joseph Ott and others. He was joined by John Brewer in 1865, and the pottery was called Ott and Brewer. Until 1875, they mostly made white granite and cream colored wares.

Isaac Broome was the first American artist to work in parian, and he worked at Ott and Brewer from 1873-1878. He did portrait busts of historical figures such as his famous Cleopatra. He is best known for his pair of baseball vases in parian made in 1876 when they were displayed at the Centennial Exposition.

In 1882, William Bromley, Jr. came from the Belleek factory in Ireland, along with William, his father, and John, his brother, to perfect an American Belleek formula utilizing American clays at the Ott and Brewer operation. They became known for their tete-a-tete sets that were as delicate as the Irish Belleek counterparts. Many Irish patterns were copied at Ott and Brewer. Royal Worcester type designs were also used on the Belleek body. Influences of oriental art were reflected in American Belleek examples using dark colors as matte grounds for metallic designs on the cream Belleek body.

In 1892, Ott and Brewer sold to C. Cook and Company, and the Bromleys went to work for Willets Manufacturing Company. Ott and Brewer used five different marks on their Belleek porcelains.

**References:** Mark Frank Gaston, *American Belleek*, Collector Books, 1984.

**Museums:** New Jersey State Museum, Trenton, NJ.

Bouillon Cup, w/underplate, shell ribbed ext, gold rim, gold acorns on branch handles, cream ground ............ 195.00
Cake Plate, 8" sq, pedestal base, painted multicolored hummingbird over orchid, gilt edge ruffled rim, "pink stamped BELLEEK/O&B/TRENTON NJ" mk, chip on rim, (A)
............................................................................ 1,000.00

Cracker Jar, 8" h, flowing blue acorn pattern, white ground w/gilt accents, dk blue handles and finial, mkd, (A)130.00

Cup and Saucer, Demitasse, eggshell, gold impasto bamboo, "stamped BELLEEK/O&B" mk, (A) .................. 56.00

Dish, 5 1/2" w, shell shape, 2 sm shell feet ............... 375.00

Figure, 6 1/4" h, bust of Rutherford Hayes .............. 1,600.00

Pitcher

3 1/4" h, scalloped rim, yellow glaze, gold accents, mkd .................................................................. 120.00

5 3/4" h, flattened shape, imp stylized leaves on sides, gilt painted dandelions on front, mkd ............. 1,000.00

6 1/2" h, ironstone, wide blue center band w/narrow gold stripes, emb foliate scrolls .................................. 35.00

Vase

4" h, free form, 3 scalloped openings, emb blue and red forget-me-nots, mkd, (A) .................................. 825.00

4 1/2" h x 10 1/2" l, figural horn of plenty, painted gold, pink, and blue chrysanthemums, mkd ........... 1,250.00

5" h, tree trunk shape w/molded stumps, multicolored transfer of florals and buds, white ground, gold ruffled rim, (A)................................................................ 495.00

# Overbeck Pottery

## Cambridge City, Indiana
## 1911-1955

1911

**History:** Overbeck Pottery was established by four sisters: Margaret, Hannah, Elizabeth, and Mary Francis in the family home in Cambridge City, Indiana in 1911. Margaret died during the first year of operation; Hannah, an invalid, supplied designs for decorations of the pottery until her death in 1931; and Elizabeth developed the glazes, clay mixtures and threw the pieces until she died in 1937. Mary continued to make pottery by herself until she died in 1955.

Mary Francis was involved with the artistic side of the works. Two methods of decoration were used on the thrown pottery examples: glaze inlay and carving. Glazes used on the vases, bowls, candlesticks, flower frogs, tea sets, and tiles included hyacinth, turquoise, and creamy yellow in matte finishes in the beginning. Brighter glaze colors were added. Most designs were based on nature and pictured insects or flowers.

Ceramic sculpture was started before Elizabeth died. In the studio period beginning in 1936, mostly small figurines were made of cats, dogs, and birds. Live animals were used as models to make them more lifelike. The colors used to paint them were as natural as possible.

When Mary died in 1955, the pottery closed. The mark usually was the OBK cipher. Before 1937 it also included the initial of the sister who decorated and/or made the piece. Studio pieces were marked with the MF cipher.

**References:** Kathleen R. Postle, *The Chronicle of the Overbeck Pottery*, Indiana Historical Society, 1978.

**Museums:** Art Association of Richmond, IN; Art Gallery, Ball State University, Muncie, IN; Indianapolis Museum of Art, IN; Postle Collection, Cambridge City Library, IN; Wayne County Historical Society Museum, Richmond, IN.

Bud Vase, 2 5/8" h, figural girl in hooped dress holding flower basket, red and green stripes and flowered skirt on gray clay ground, repaired chips, (A) .................... 770.00

Cabinet Vase, 3" h, tapered shape, short collar, 3 panels of matte pastel Japanese lady, hairline, "OBK,E,F" mk, (A) ................................................................................. 1,210.00

Figure

1 1/4" h x 2 1/4" l, frog, yellow, brown, and lt blue-green, (A) ..................................................................... 303.00

1 1/2" h

Seated spaniel dog, dk brown with red and white accents, "imp OBK" mk, (A) .......................... 248.00

Squirrel eating corn, brown shades, "stamped OBK" mk, (A) ......................................................... 175.00

2 1/4" h x 3 1/4" l, fanciful dog, green body with black polka-dots, pink webbed feet, (A) ..................... 413.00

2 1/2" h, fanciful woodpecker, brown, red, white, and lt blue, "imp OBK" mk, (A) .................................. 385.00

2 3/4" h, photographer and camera, blue jacket, gray slacks, yellow camera, black hood, Mary Overbeck, (A) ....................................................................... 880.00

4" h x 7" l, white elephant w/pink accents, blue eyes, (A) .................................................................... 1,430.00

5" h

Bride and Groom in 19th C southern clothes, red, blue, and yellow, "stamped OBK" mks, pr, (A) .................................................................. 440.00

Farm scene, 2 children, calf, and fence, polychrome, "imp OBK" mk, (A) ..................................... 1,430.00

5 1/2" h, postman, brown uniform, yellow mail sack, "imp OBK" mk, (A) ..................................................... 193.00

**Vase, 5 1/2" h, dull green cutback and painted birds in panels, lt rose ground, initialed "E.H," (A), $3,850.**

Vase, 5 1/2" h, swollen shape, tapered collar, 3 excised panels of stylized birds, dk pink on mauve ground, "incised OBK, FM" mk, (A) ............................ 3,080.00

# J.B. Owens Pottery

## Zanesville, Ohio
## 1891-c1928

**History:** John B. Owens incorporated as J.B. Owens Pottery Company in 1891 and moved to Zanesville, Ohio the following year. At first he made flower pots, and then Rockingham-type glaze jardinieres and teapots.

In 1897, he introduced his slip-painted underglaze decorated artwares. The first of his famous lines was Utopian which was decorated with flowers, animal and human figures, and some Indians in both high gloss and matte finishes. Owens employed many talented artists during the decade in which he made art pottery. Several went on to open their own potteries at a later date.

A rivalry existed among the Zanesville potters: Owens, Weller, and Roseville. They each offered a large number of lines, many of which were imitations of each others works. Owens introduced more new lines than any of the other potters during this period.

Within a short period of time, Owens made Lotus, Alpine, Henri Deux, Corona, Cyrano, Venetian, Feroza Faience, Gun Metal, Mission, Wedgwood Jasper, Rustic, Opalesce, Utopian Opalesce, Art Vellum, Red Flame, Aborigine, and Sunburst lines. In 1905, Owens won four gold medals for artwares at the Lewis and Clark Exposition in Portland, Oregon.

In addition to the tremendous amount of art pottery, Owens had a commercial line by 1902. Up to that time, there were continuous additions to his plant to accommodate all the work being done. A huge fire destroyed his plant in 1902, but it was rebuilt quickly. In 1905, Owens devoted much of his time to the production of tiles. With expansion of the plant for the tile operation, this portion of his business was called the Zanesville Tile Company. Although the art pottery was continued, the less expensive, mass produced lines were stopped.

Owens concentrated on the high quality artwares called Owensart. When F. Ferrel joined with Owens, additional lines were introduced such as Soudanese, Aqua Verdi, and three new versions of Lotus.

The Tile Manufacturers Association took over the Zanesville Tile Company part of Owens and closed it. The art pottery worked stopped soon after that. Several years later Owens began tile work again at a new Zanesville location.

Much of Owens' pottery was marked with one of the several ciphers used by the company. Some pieces were artist signed.

**References:** Frank L. Hahn, *Collector's Guide to Owens Pottery*, Golden Era Publications, 1996; Kristy & Rick McKibben, Jeanette & Marvin Stofft, *Owens Pottery Unearthened*, available from authors.

**Museums:** National Museum of History and Technology, Smithsonian Institution, Washington, DC; Zane Grey Museum of Ohio Historical Society, Zanesville, OH; Zanesville Art Center, OH.

Bottle, 10 1/2" h, blue, green and white dripping flambe glazes over matte brown ground, stamped "OWENS 1110" mk, (A) ............................ 660.00
Box, 3" h, Oriental, red and white beading, dk blue ground, (A) ............................ 165.00
Bud Vase
    4 1/4" h, Utopian
        Sq sides, flowers on sides ............................ 175.00
        Squat shape, 2 handles, wild roses on shaded brown ground, (A) ............................ 143.00
    12 1/4" h, Malachite Opalesce Utopian, orange-red nasturtiums, gold leaves, "imp Owens Utopian 1068" mk, (A) ............................ 357.00
Candlestick, 6" h, Utopian, oak leaf design, dk brown-black glaze ............................ 125.00
Cruet
    4 3/4" h, matte cream and gray glazes, "Owens 1216" mk, (A) ............................ 165.00
    5 3/8" h, Lightweight, yellow nasturtiums, green leaves, glass brown ground, (A) ............................ 220.00
Ewer, 9 1/2" h, floral design, brown ground, loop handle, "Utopia #981m" mk ............................ 350.00
Humidor, 4 3/8" h, Aborigine, incised and painted design, glazed int, (A) ............................ 330.00
Jardiniere
    6 3/8" h, Lotus, blue lotus blossoms, (A) ............................ 413.00
    6 3/4" h, Majolica, cream emb flowers and birds in center, dk blue base, green-shaped rim, "J.B.Owens shield" mk, (A) ............................ 165.00
    8 7/8" h, Art Nouveau, spittoon shape, red zigzags, cream comma-shaped swirls, olive ground, (A) ............................ 412.00
Jug
    5 1/8" h, Aborigine, painted and slip trail decorated, "imp Owens 31 1864, incised JBO" mk, (A) ............................ 137.00
    6 1/2" w, painted tulip design, sgd "Tot Steele," (A) ............................ 231.00
    7 1/2" h, overhead handle, yellow corn, sage green husk, gloss brown glaze, "imp Owens/1266" mk, (A) . 275.00
Lamp Base, 10 1/2" h, Utopian, pansy design, (A) ............................ 110.00
Mug
    3 7/8" h, matte green, imp combed design, "imp Owens 46" mk, (A) ............................ 220.00
    4 1/2" h, Utopian, flowers and leaves design ............................ 250.00
    5" h, Utopian, painted apples and leaves, dk brown ground, #1035 ............................ 295.00
    5 1/8" h Utopian, brown and ivory cherries, folded leaves, med brown to dk brown gloss ground, "imp Owenszart/Utopia/1035," mk, set of 4, (A) ............................ 412.00
Paperweight, 3 7/8" l x 2 3/8" w, rect, Majolica, "raised elk head, EDMISTON HORNEY COMPANY ZANESVILLE OHIO" on top, matte green glaze, "Made by the J.B.Owens Pottery Co." on reverse, (A) ............................ 82.00
Pitcher, 9" h, Lotus, water bird and water lily, restored, (A) ............................ 165.00
Tankard
    12" h, Utopian, bearded wheat design ............................ 350.00
    12 1/2" h, painted orange-red tulips, green leaves, brown-blue shaded ground, (A) ............................ 319.00

Vase

3" h

Aborigine, black swastikas, brown and terra cotta ground......................................................220.00

Squat shape, orange roses, green leaves, Utopian glaze, shape #1050 .....................................250.00

4" h, squat shape, narrow base, short collar, Soudaneze, white pansies, glass black ground, "imp Owens 202" mk, (A)..................................................330.00

4 1/4" h, ftd pillow shape, Cyrano, squeezebag dk green flowers, ivory swags, brown ground, "stamped OW" mk, (A)................................................155.00

4 3/8" h, twisted bottle shape, Utopian, brown shaded floral design, "3 7 Owens Utopian 120" mk, (A) ........................................................ 110.00

4 1/2" h, squat shape, loop handles, lt yellow trumpet flowers, green leaves, Utopian glaze ...............260.00

4 5/8" h, Utopian, floral design, orange to brown shaded ground ........................................................200.00

5" h, twisted shape, sq base, coralene Opalesce-Utopian, brown and yellow painted gooseberries on textured green and gold ground, "stamped Owens Utopian" mk, (A)..................................................120.00

5 1/4" h, Utopian, pillow shape, scalloped rim, 4 sm feet, white, burnt orange and mustard yellow raised daisies, dk brown to ochre shaded ground w/speckling, "imp Owens Utopian 821" mk, (A)............................275.00

5 3/8" h, Aborigine, slip train design around collar and shoulder, "imp Owens 29, incised JBO" mks, (A) ........................................................165.00

5 1/2" h

Aborigine, black, red and buff geometrics, (A) ........................................................209.00

Bottle shape, orange roses, green leaves, Utopian glaze, shape #1048 .....................................250.00

5 3/4" h, pillow, Oriental, white and blue beading, dk blue ground, unmkd, (A) ......................................55.00

5 7/8" h bulbous shape w/4 buttressed feet, matte green, (A) ......................................................275.00

6" h

Corset shape w/broad shoulder, Lotus, painted cream mushrooms, shaded cream to dk green glaze, "imp Owensart torch" mk, (A) .............................467.00

Swollen Shape, rolled rim, Arts & Crafts, imp center band of rectangles, matte green glaze, "Owens 218" mk, (A)................................................330.00

6 1/2" h, matte green, reticulated top, 2 handles, (A) ........................................................770.00

6 3/4" h

Cyrano, raised blue and white banded beading ........................................................250.00

Matte Utopian, HP iris design, turquoise to brown shading ........................................................325.00

7" h, Matte Utopian, peach, cream and blue carved tulips and leaves, (A) ......................................440.00

8" h

Matte Utopian

Bottle shape, slip relief design of wild roses, shaded ground, "stamped OWENS" mk, (A) ........350.00

Fall leaf decoration, (A) ...............................275.00

Squat base, swollen neck, Utopian, clover design, (A) ........................................................176.00

Trumpet shape, Utopian, floral design, (A) .......165.00

10 1/2" h

Hourglass shape with rolled rim, green holly, red berries, Utopian glaze......................................325.00

Straight sides, short neck, Utopian, painted fall leaves, (A)................................................413.00

10 3/4" h, ovoid, matte Lotus, slip design of lt yellow jonquils, green leaves under crackle glaze, "imp Owensart torch" mk, (A) ...........................................275.00

12" h, bulbous shape, short, rolled rim, Utopian, portrait of Native American, "High Bear Sioux," (A)....8,250.00

12 1/2" h, squat body, stick neck, multicolored painted leaves, (A) ........................................................275.00

**Vase, 6" h, "Sunburst" pattern, brown streaks, c1907, $95.**

**Vase, 6" h, carved and painted florals, cream, lt green, and olive glazes, incised mk, (A), $3,250.**

12 3/4" h, bottle shape, Matte Utopian, painted rose on shaded brown and green ground, "stamped Owens" mk, (A).............................................................200.00
13" h

Ball base, slender neck, Matte Utopian, cherry design, (A).............................................................467.00

Lighthouse shape, Metal Deposit, incised iris and leaf design, "imp Owens 123" mk, (A)................440.00

13 1/2" h, squat shape, tall, slender neck, orange flowers, green leaves, Utopian glaze, shape #1068.......425.00

14" h, lamp shape, Soudaneze, red and gold cherries, glass black ground, gold trim, (A)......................880.00

15" h, ovoid shape, brown and French blue gooseberry branch, restored chips, (A)..............................815.00

17" h, swollen cylinder shape, Utopian, "Jack Red Cloud, A Sioux Indian," (A).........................................5,040.00

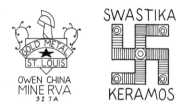

# Owens China Company/Minerva

**Minerva, Ohio**
**1906-1932**

**History:** Owens China Company was founded by Ted Owens in Minerva, Ohio in 1906. Semi-porcelain and hotel china were made with the local clay, along with tea and dinner services with underglaze and overglaze decorations.

Swastika Keramos was first exhibited in 1906 as the art pottery line with metallic lusters in shades of bronze, brass, and copper with scenic decorations on a white clay body. The line was only made for several years.

Despite being a successful company, it could not survive the economic hardships caused by the Depression and closed its doors. The mark on the Swastika Keramos pieces were an inmold raised seal. Some pieces were unmarked.

Bowl, 11 3/4"d, red hanging cherries w/green leaves in center, raised disc and dot border w/blue-green accents, mkd ..................................................................10.00

Gravy Boat, center band of pink and blue flowerheads and geometrics, gilt rim......................................10.00

Plate, 9" d, girl in blue Victorian bathing suit standing by sea, gold drops on border..................................20.00

Platter, 13 1/2" l, multicolored scene of steepled farm house, sailing ship and boy and woman on road, dk red inner border band................................................10.00

Tankard

5" h, standing Victorian woman holding fruit bowl on hip, gray-brown ground, gold gargoyle handle, Owen Minerva mk.............................................................30.00

10 3/8" h, Art Nouveau style, black outlined dk red flowerheads and leaves, gold ground, Swastika Keramos, (A)..............................................................303.00

Vase

7 3/4" h, ball base, tapered neck above notched middle, green and gold crystalline glaze, "Swastika Keramos" mk..............................................................250.00

8" h, tapered shape, short, collar, metallic floral design, mkd, (A)...........................................................253.00

**Vase, 6 1/2" h, decal bust of woman in white bonnet, blue dress, pink splashes, cream ground, swastika mk, $135.**

11" h, scenic trees, matte metallic luster glaze, Swastika Keramos mark......................................................375.00

Vegetable Bowl, Cov, 11" H-H, border bands of pink and blue flowerheads and geometrics, gold outlined handles and knob......................................................20.00

# Paden City Pottery

**Sisterville, West Virginia**
**1914-1963**

**History:** Paden City Pottery was started near Sisterville, West Virginia in 1914 and made semi-porcelain dinnerware. The company perfected underglaze decals which would not change color in the gloss firing.

*Shenandoah* PASTELS MADE IN U.S.A.

"Bakserv" was its kitchenware line in solid colors and decals from 1931. The Shenandoah line had six different decorations in solid colors and decals that were intended to resemble hand painting.

The Elite shape from 1936 was plain and round with shell-like handles, finials, and feet. One year later they added shell-like embossing and called it the Shellcrest shape. The Caliente line from 1936 utilized bright colors on the Elite/Shellcrest shape. Decals also were used. A Blue Willow pattern was started in 1937. Sears sold the Nasturtium pattern about 1940. Highlight from 1951-1953 was designed by Russel Wright and made for a short time in five colors.

Paden City closed in 1963. A variety of back stamps was used.

**AMERICAN ROSE PATTERN**

Berry Bowl, 5 1/4" d......................................................2.00
Cup and Saucer ............................................................6.00
Plate

6 1/2" d ...............................................................3.00
9" d .....................................................................5.00

## BLOSSOMS PATTERN-SHELL KREST SHAPE
Platter, 14 1/4" H-H..................................................8.00

## CALENTE PATTERN
Creamer, blue..........................................................8.00

## COSMOS PATTERN
Cup and Saucer .....................................................10.00
Plate, 9 3/8" d .......................................................10.00
Tray, 11 5/8" l, band of blue and red cosmos w/green leaves
    on border, Shenandoah Ware.................................12.00

## DUCHESS PATTERN
Cup and Saucer .......................................................3.00
Fruit Bowl, 5 1/8" d ..................................................3.00
Plate
    6 3/8" d................................................................4.00
    8" sq..................................................................5.00
    10 1/4" d.............................................................5.00
Soup Bowl, 7 7/8" d .................................................6.00

## EDEN ROSE PATTERN
Berry Bowl, 5" d .......................................................5.00
Cup and Saucer .......................................................5.00
Plate
    6" d ...................................................................4.00
    9" d ...................................................................6.00

## FAR EAST PATTERN
Bowl, 6 1/2" d ..........................................................5.00
Creamer, 3" h ........................................................10.00
Cup and Saucer .......................................................5.00
Fruit Bowl, 5 1/4" d ..................................................5.00
Plate, 8 1/2" d .........................................................5.00
Platter
    12" l...................................................................12.00
    14 1/2" l..............................................................15.00
Sugar Bowl, Cov ....................................................15.00

## IVY PATTERN
Cup and Saucer .....................................................12.00
Dessert Dish, 5 3/8" d................................................4.00
Plate
    6 1/4" d................................................................6.00
    9 1/2" d..............................................................12.00
    10" sq................................................................15.00
Platter, 13 3/4" l .....................................................35.00

## JONQUIL PATTERN-REGINA SHAPE
Bowl, 8 1/2" sq ......................................................10.00

## MODERN ORCHID PATTERN
Bowl, 5 1/4" d ..........................................................4.00
Creamer, round shape............................................14.00
Cup and Saucer .......................................................6.00
Plate
    5 1/4" d, round shape............................................4.00
    6 1/2" d, round shape............................................5.00
    7 1/2" d................................................................5.00
    9 1/2" d, round shape............................................9.00
Platter, 11 3/4" l ....................................................20.00
Sugar Bowl, Cov.....................................................10.00

## MORNING GLORY PATTERN
Platter, 13 3/4" l ....................................................15.00

Plate, 9 1/2" d, "Morning Glory" pattern, red, blue, and green, $10.

## NASTURTIUM PATTERN
Berry Bowl, 5 1/2" d..................................................4.00
Bowl, 8" H-H............................................................8.00
Pie Plate, 10" d.........................................................8.00
Plate, 7 1/4" d..........................................................5.00
Platter
    11 3/4" l..............................................................20.00
    13 3/4" l..............................................................32.00

## PATIO PATTERN
Plate, 9 1/2" d.........................................................20.00
Platter, 14" l...........................................................35.00

## POPPY PATTERN
Bowl, 8 3/4" d ..........................................................5.00
Plate
    6 1/4" d................................................................5.00
    8 3/8" d................................................................5.00
    9 1/4" d..............................................................10.00
Platter, 13 3/4" l, Shenandoah Ware .........................28.00

## RED ROSE PATTERN
Platter, 14" l...........................................................10.00
Teapot ...................................................................10.00

## ROSALEE PATTERN
Berry Bowl, 5 1/4" d..................................................3.00
Cup and Saucer .......................................................4.00
Plate
    6 1/2" d ...............................................................3.00
    10" d ...................................................................6.00
Serving Bowl, 9 1/4" H-H............................................8.00
Soup Bowl, 8 1/4" d ..................................................4.00

## TULIP PATTERN
Service Plate, 13 3/4" d, maroon border, gold overlay
    ...........................................................................38.00

## WILD ROSE PATTERN
Bowl, 5 1/4" d ..........................................................8.00
Cereal Bowl, 7 3/8" d.................................................8.00
Cup and Saucer .......................................................6.00
Plate
    5 3/4" d ...............................................................2.00

| | |
|---|---|
| 6 3/8" d | 2.00 |
| 8" d | 3.00 |
| 9 1/4" d | 5.00 |
| Platter, 11 1/4" l, oval | 5.00 |
| Serving Bowl, 8 1/2" d | 7.00 |

**YELLOW ROSE PATTERN**

| | |
|---|---|
| Cup and Saucer | 4.00 |
| Plate | |
| 6 1/2" d | 4.00 |
| 7" sq | 4.00 |
| 9" sq | 6.00 |

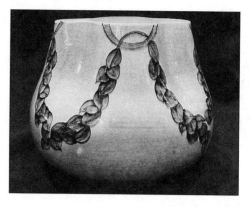

Vase, 6 1/2" h, yellow and brown hanging seeds, shaded yellow ground, crackle, c1900, $695.

1888-1909

# Pauline Pottery

**Chicago, Illinois**
**1882-1888**

**Edgerton, Wisconsin**
**1888-1909**

**History:** Pauline Pottery was established by Pauline Jacobus in Chicago, Illinois. At first she did china painting in her home, and then studied art pottery with Maria Nichols of Rookwood.

By 1883, artwares were begun utilizing Ohio clays for the yellow earthenware body decorated with monochrome glazes or underglaze decorations. Redwares also were made. By 1886 a second plant was needed due to the company's success.

A new pottery was built in Edgerton, Wisconsin in 1888 when a closer source for clay was located there. An assortment of wares including vases, tea sets, candlesticks, fireplace tiles, ewers, and such were made mostly decorated by brush with clear glazes on the cream ground. Pauline often drew the floral and geometric patterns.

Oscar Jacobus had founded a separate plant for commercial wares, but when he died in 1893 that business decreased and closed. In 1894 Pauline sold her pottery, and Edgerton Pottery was organized to take over. This new company failed in 1902.

A thin black outline around the designs characterized many Pauline examples. Pauline experimented with a variety of glazes and also produced a majolica-type ware. After 1902 she used a blending of glazes, notably a peacock color that merged deep blue and dark green. Some examples had three color combinations. Pieces often were crazed and were not always waterproof.

Pauline started working at home again after reassembling her kiln and establishing herself as a studio potter. Students produced forms in the summer workshops, and Pauline and her daughter decorated them during the winter months. A sale to close the pottery was held in 1909. The home and studio burned in 1911.

Not all pieces were marked. Early marks were either incised or impressed, while later ones were incised or imprinted beneath the glaze. The Pauline name and trade-

mark were used from 1902-09. The most common mark was the crown with the P and reverse P on either side.

**References:** *Sharon S. Darling, Chicago Ceramics and Glass: An Illustrated History from 1871 to 1933,* Chicago Historical Society, 1979.

**Museums:** City Art Museum, St. Louis, MO; Neville Public Museum, Green Bay, WI; State Historical Society, Madison, WI.

Ashtray, 4" h x 7" l, figural seated dog on rim, brown shades, mkd ........................................................... 150.00

Jug, 8" h, bulbous, barbotine style brown and black monk on front, gloss cream ground, imp mk, (A) .................. 725.00

Vase

3 3/4" h, squat shape, short collar, stepped handles, irid pink glaze, "incised Pauline," ........................... 200.00

7 1/2" h, teardrop shape w/wavy rim, dk red sun and star overlays, "PAULINE" mk ..................................... 20.00

8" h, bulbous body, flared ft and rim, gold outlined cream and brown painted florals in 3 panels, yellow ground w/gold accents, (A) ........................................... 187.00

# Pennsbury Pottery

**Morrisville, Pennsylvania**
**1950-1970**

**History:** Pennsbury Pottery was started by Henry and Lee Below, German immigrants who were both associated with Stangl Pottery in Trenton, New Jersey before founding their own pottery in 1950.

Pennsbury Pottery Morrisville Pa.

Their first products at Pennsbury were birds that were similar to those made by Stangl in many respects, though they made fewer varieties. They stopped making birds during the mid-1950s. The largest birds were the rooster and the hen. Birds were made in a variety of color combinations and were numbered. A small number of birds were done in all white or ivory glaze, and these are quite rare.

"Slick-chick" was made after the birds. This was a small bird that was perched on top of a hollowed out gourd. "Slick-bunny" also was made. These examples were not always marked.

The finish on Pennsbury Pottery required two firings. The background color varies from a light tan to a dark brown. The earthenware used was fired at a high temperature.

The first Pennsbury dinnerware line was the Black Rooster, followed by Red Rooster and then the Folkart line in brown finishes. Folkart was also made on white with cobalt blue decorations and called Blue Dowry.

During the 1960s, Folkart was changed to Brown Dowry. Toleware was dark brown with red and white fruit. When made in white with a blue ground and blue fruit decoration, it was called Delft Toleware.

Most of the dinnerware lines at Pennsbury were done with the brown background color. Red and Black Rooster were made in full dinner sets. Other dinnerware patterns included Folkart, and two versions of the Hex. One had small heart like designs between teardrop shape decoration, and Pennsylvania Hex did not have the hearts.

The most popular and sought after examples were decorative pieces with sayings. Other popular pieces were the Amish designs with figures and scenes. These artware examples were made in a small number of shapes, not complete sets. There were quite a few Amish decorated lines. Other desirable pieces included Barber Shop Quartet, Gay Nineties, Eagle, and Fisherman. There was a line of ashtrays and hanging plaques with clever sayings that were quite collectible.

1970 saw the Pennsbury Christmas plate Stumar Angel made only for one year. Additional Christmas merchandise was made on a commissioned basis.

A limited number of pieces were molded in high relief instead of the carved designs. Railroad plaques and trays featured different locomotives, and Ships detailed eight sailing ships. During the early 1950s, Pennsbury made commemorative merchandise that customers ordered for Christmas, weddings, ashtrays, beer mugs, coasters, etc. Associations and businesses also ordered pieces for their groups. They made a wide variety of novelties in the form of bread plates, oil and vinegar bottles with sayings, pottery pie pans, banks, salt and pepper shakers, tiles, figural candle holders, and the like.

After Henry died, Lee and Ernst, her son, operated the pottery until the late 1960s when sales decreased due to the heavy competition from Europe and Japan since those ceramics were coming into the country at a much cheaper price. In 1970, they were forced to file for bankruptcy and production ceased. The pottery was destroyed by fire in 1971.

The earliest pieces were signed by hand when they were decorated in blue, brown, or black. Some marks were hand incised or stamped, and some pieces were not marked at all.

**References:** Lucile Henzke, *Pennsbury Pottery*, Schiffer Publishing Ltd. 1990.

## AMISH DESIGN
Cake Stand, 4 1/2" h x 11" d ........................ 125.00
Jug
    2 1/2" h, man ........................................ 25.00
    5" h, man ............................................. 35.00
Oil and Vinegar, 7" h, pr ............................. 85.00
Plaque, 4" d .............................................. 25.00
Pretzel Bowl, 12" l x 8" w ........................... 55.00
Shakers, Pr .............................................. 35.00

## BARBER SHOP QUARTET DESIGN
Mug, 5" h ................................................. 35.00
Pretzel Bowl, 12" l x 8" w ........................... 60.00

## BLACK ROOSTER DESIGN
Baker, 6 1/2" d, crimped ............................. 25.00

Charger, 14" d .......................................... 25.00
Coffeepot, 8" h ......................................... 95.00
Cookie Jar ............................................... 175.00
Cup and Saucer ........................................ 10.00
Pitcher, 4 1/2" h, tan and brown ................... 25.00
Plate
    6 1/4" d ............................................. 10.00
    10" d ................................................. 20.00
Salad Bowl, 11" d ...................................... 60.00
Vegetable Bowl, 9 1/2" l, divided, rect ........... 20.00

## EAGLE DESIGN
Beer Mug, 4 3/4" h, (A) ............................... 10.00
Pitcher, 7 1/2" h ........................................ 65.00

## FIGURES
3" h, 3" l, Redstart, blue and yellow, #113 ...... 80.00
3 1/2" h
    Hummingbird ...................................... 250.00
    Nuthatch, blue and gray-blue, #110 ......... 75.00
5 1/2" h, Slick-Chick, yellow ........................ 52.00
6 1/2" h, Barn Swallow, blue ........................ 300.00
10 1/2", 11 1/2" h, rooster and hen, multicolored, pr .. 375.00

## GAY NINETY
Mug, 4 3/4" h, "Hears Looking at You," .......... 24.00
Pitcher, 7 1/4" h ........................................ 85.00

## HARVEST DESIGN
Plate, 11" d .............................................. 75.00

## HEX DESIGN
Ashtray, 7 1/2" d ....................................... 23.00
Creamer, 4" h ........................................... 30.00
Pitcher, 6 1/2" h ........................................ 75.00
Plate
    8 1/8" d ............................................. 28.00
    10" d ................................................. 75.00
Sugar Bowl, 3 1/2" h ................................... 40.00
Teapot, 5 3/4" h ........................................ 60.00

## MISCELLANEOUS
Bowl, 9" d, Dutch Talk design ...................... 25.00
Bread Plate, 7 3/4" d, "Give us this day our daily bread" and wheat shaft tops, green and brown ........ 35.00
Candy Dish, 6" w x 5 3/4" l, heart shape, "Bird Over Heart" design ..................................... 45.00
Chamberstick, 5 1/4" d, "Tulip" design ........... 55.00
Charger, 11 1/2" d, Amish family ................... 70.00
Mug, 4 1/2" h, relief of shield and owl ............ 40.00
Pie Plate, 9" d, "Picking Apples" .................. 105.00
Plaque
    4 1/4" d
        "It Is Whole Empty," mother and child .. 10.00
        "Its Makin Down" ............................. 10.00
    7 3/4" l x 5 3/4" w, "Western and Atlantic Railroad" ...................................... 15.00
Wall Pocket, 6 1/4" sq, green clown w/yo yo, tan ground ...................................... 95.00

## RED BARN DESIGN
Creamer, 2 3/4" h ...................................... 15.00
Pitcher, 6" h ............................................. 100.00

Plate, 13 3/4" d, "Red Rooster" pattern, yellow, red, green, and brown, $195.

Pitcher, 5 1/4" h, "Red Rooster" pattern, $40.

## RED ROOSTER DESIGN

Beer Mug, 5" h................................................28.00
Casserole, Cov, 6 1/4" d................................55.00
Coffee Mug......................................................15.00
Creamer, 4" h..................................................22.00
Egg Cup, 4" h..................................................10.00
Pitcher, 5" h....................................................15.00
Plate, 10" d.....................................................40.00
Vase, 5" h, cylinder shape.............................28.00

# Peters and Reed Pottery/Zane Pottery Company

## Zanesville, Ohio
## 1898-1941

ZANE WARE
MADE IN U S A
c.1921

**History:** John Peters and Adam Reed started a pottery in 1898, making red earthenware flower pots and gardenwares in Zanesville, Ohio. From 1903-06, they added cooking wares with a white lining. When they enlarged their plant in 1907, they added additional garden wares and some inexpensive hand painted jardinieres in matte and high gloss glazes.

When designer Frank Ferrel joined Peters and Reed from Weller in 1912, they started their artware lines. Ferrel recreated his Pine Cone design and others for Moss Aztec with the molded designs in relief and sprayed with green. Other artwares included Pereco, Landsun, Chromal, Persian, and Montene.

With Peters retirement, Reed became president and changed the pottery's name to Zane Pottery Company in 1921. Reed retired one year later, and Harry McClelland who had worked at Peters and Reed since 1903 took over. He continued the current lines in addition to the new artware lines of Sheen, Powder Blue, Crystaline, and Drip. The clay body was changed from reddish brown clay to white in 1926.

McClelland died in 1931 and his family carried on until 1941 when they sold to Gonder Ceramic Art Pottery Company. Peters and Reed examples were usually not marked, while Zane Pottery was marked with an impressed mark.

**References:** Jeffrey, Sherrie, and Barry Hershone, *The Peters and Reed and Zane Pottery Experience*, privately printed, 1990.

Bowl
    4" d, Landsun, blue, green, cream, and tan, Peters and Reed...............................................120.00
    4 1/2" d, Moss Aztec, dragonflies, Peters and Reed
    ..........................................................120.00
    5" d, Pereco, emb dragonfly design, dk blue glaze, (A)
    ..........................................................65.00
    5 1/2" d
        Floral and leaf design, matte tan and green, Peters and Reed......................................45.00
        Molded handles on shoulder to rim, matte deep rose glaze, Peters and Reed.................50.00
    6" d, Pereco, relief molded classic design, green speckling on cream ground.........................25.00
    6 3/4" d, ftd, relief design of flowering vine, dk green over brown glaze, early 20th C, unmkd....................250.00
    7" d, 4 buttresses on rim w/geometric designs, matte green glaze, (A)................................99.00
    9"d, molded organic design on ext, matte green glaze, Zane Ware, (A).................................220.00
Bud Vase
    7" h, Pereco, tapered, 4 sided, med blue glaze, (A) 45.00
    8 1/2" h, squat base, flared neck and rim, ear handles, blue, "ZPCo" mk..............................95.00
Ewer, 12 1/2" h, Brownware, serpent handle............230.00
Jardiniere, 9" h, Moss Aztec Pompeiian design, dancing women, brown, Peters and Reed.........................455.00
Jug
    4 3/4" h, band of raised green, yellow, and tan grapes and leaves w/lion head in center, gloss brown glaze, Peters and Reed..............................150.00
    7 1/2" h, pinched body, raised yellow bust of cavalier, pink and green raised florals, gloss streaked dk brown ground, Peters and Reed................................250.00
    9" h, Brownware, emb grape design, Peters and Reed
    ..........................................................85.00
Lamp Base, 7" h x 8" w, dbl handles, Arts and Crafts style flower and leaf design, matte green glaze, Zane Ware
    ..........................................................225.00
Mug, 5 3/4" h, emb purple grapes, tan leaves, gloss brown ground, Peters and Reed..........................115.00
Pitcher, 4 1/2" h, raised green flowerheads, gloss brown ground, Peters and Reed..........................30.00
Planter, 6" d x 7" h, relief band of vert geometrics, rose glaze
    ..........................................................75.00
Sand Jar, 23 1/2" h, brown, blue, tan and green marbled glazes, (A)........................................770.00
Tankard, 12" h, Brownware, emb green grapes and leaves, brown ground, Peters and Reed..................245.00

**Vase, 4 3/4" h, dk blue frothy glaze, $55.**

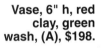

**Vase, 6" h, red clay, green wash, (A), $198.**

Trophy Cup, 6 1/2" h, 3 handles, raised green and tan lute and florals, gloss streaked brown glaze, Peters and Reed .................................................................................250.00
Umbrella Stand, 22 1/2" h, corset shape, Moss Aztec, stylized grape clusters, Frank Ferrell, (A)....................320.00
Vase
    2 3/4" h x 5 1/4" d, squat form, emb cream flowers, gloss brown ground, Peters and Reed .........................65.00
    3" h, shouldered form, streaked blue, green, and brown flambe glaze, Zane Ware, (A)..............................50.00
    5" h, squat jar shape, band of relief molded geometrics, matte green glaze, Zaneware, (A)........................66.00
    6" h
        Bottle form, brown sprigging, standard glaze, Peters and Reed .....................................................160.00
        Bulbous body, straight collar, matte brown and green glaze over cream ground, Zaneware, (A) ................................................................................220.00
        Moss Aztec, relief molded flowerheads, stems, and leaves, brick red ground, (A) ........................150.00
        Peasant pottery, conc horiz molded rings, flat ring handles, brown, Zane Ware ..............................175.00
        Squat base, cylinder neck, rolled rim, matte green glaze, Zane Ware..........................................180.00
    6 3/4" h, tapered body, flared rim, Chromal, base chip, (A) ...................................................................120.00

8" h
    Cylinder shape w/flared rim, Moss Aztec, Peters and Reed ...........................................................250.00
    Deco style ribbed design, scrolled rim w/matte tan drip over cobalt ground......................................125.00
    Moss Aztec, blackberries and leaves, Peters and Reed ...........................................................190.00
8 1/8" h, Moss Aztec, relief of blackberries, cream body, tan accents, "Zane Ware" mk, (A) ......................82.00
9" h, urn shape, dbl rope handles, crystalline cucumber green glaze ...............................................115.00
9 1/2" h
    Brownware, ball shape, 2 side handles on shoulder, cream bust of Lincoln-type figure ................245.00
9 5/8" h, bag shape, flared rim, mottled matte brown and tan glazes, "imp Zane Ware" mk, (A) ...............192.00
10 1/4" h, ovoid shape, short collar, black drips and slanted bands, ochre ground, (A)......................240.00
10 1/2" h, Pretzel, green and yellow molded floral design, dk brown ground, (A)............................148.00
11" h, marbleized blue, brown, green, yellow, and black on terra cotta ground, Peters and Reed
    ................................................................................220.00
12" h
    Corset shape, tobacco brown accented relief molded leaf and vine, ivory ground, Zane Ware, (A) . 176.00
    Cylinder shape w/flared rim, green, yellow, and blue marbleized glazes over umber ground, Peters and Reed ............................................................170.00
    Moss Aztec, matte glaze, Peters and Reed......175.00
13" h, Chromal, brown, green, and blue pastoral scene, unmkd, (A)...................................................... 1,210.00
Vessel, 6" d, ftd, emb floral band on shoulder, dk brown glaze, Peters and Reed, (A) ...................................55.00
Wall Pocket, 8" h
    Egyptian design, green glaze, (A) ......................192.00
    Moss Aztec, grape design, sgd "Ferrell"...............135.00

# Pewabic Pottery

### Detroit, Michigan
### 1903-Present

**History:** Mary Chase Perry, a china decorator, started Pewabic Pottery in 1903 with James Caulkins in Detroit, Michigan. "Pewabic" in Chippewa meant "clay with copper color." Mary developed the forms and glazes, and James worked with the clay.

    Early artwares had a dark matte green glaze on the bowls, jars, and vases. Sometimes these pieces had carved or applied stylized leaf or floral designs on the simple thrown shapes. At the St. Louis Exposition in 1904, they showed pieces with yellow, buff, and brown matte glazes. Her Egyptian blue glaze was perfected in 1911.

A new English Tudor pottery building was constructed for Pewabic in 1907, and later Mary Perry married the architect William Stratton at age 51. She was working with many glazes and also added iridescent and luster glazes.

Pewabic also became famous with its decorative tiles and murals used in large churches throughout the country. They did extensive ceramic mosaics for the Detroit Library, The Detroit Institute of Arts, and buildings in New York City, Omaha, and San Francisco. Tiles were made for churches in Detroit, Pittsburgh, Evanston, St. Paul, Philadelphia, and Washington, D.C.

Despite hardships during the 1930s, the firm continued and survived making artwares until the death of Mary Perry Stratten in 1961 at age 94. In 1968, the pottery was reopened by Michigan State University as a school and studio with the Pewabic name. The building was placed on the National Register as a historic site in 1971. In 1981, the Pewabic Society bought the building from Michigan State University and operated it as a non-profit ceramics learning center and gallery. Today the Pewabic Society is producing architectural tiles, vases, and small vessel ware.

Pewabic art pottery was marked, but heavy glazes sometimes covered the impressed mark. Paper labels also were used.

**References:** Lillian Myers Pear, *The Pewabic Pottery: A History of the Products and Its People,* Wallace-Homestead Books, 1976.

**Museums:** Detroit Institute of Art, MI; Fine Arts Gallery of San Diego, CA: Freer Gallery of Art, Smithsonian Institution, Washington, DC; Henry Ford Museum and Greenfield Village, Dearborn, MI: Pewabic Society, Detroit, MI.

Bowl
  4" d, flared shape, mottled irid celadon, purple, and gold glaze, (A) ..................330.00
  8 1/2" d, low form, closed rim, figural lily pad ring handles, flowing matte green glaze, "imp PEWABIC" mk, (A) ..................3,300.00

Cabinet Vase
  2" h, ball shape, flared rim, Persian blue crackled glaze, (A) ..................247.00
  2 1/2" h, tapered shape, shouldered collar, lustered green and red glaze, "stamped PEWABIC DETROIT" mk, (A) ..................560.00
  2 1/2" h
    Ball shape, thick pink, gold, and blue luster drip glaze, "stamped circ Pewabic/Detroit/PP." mk, (A) ..................1,320.00
    Cylinder shape, turquoise, green, and blue luster drip glaze, "stamped circ Pewabic/Detroit" mk, (A) ..................467.00
    Swollen body, short collar, celadon and oxblood luster glaze, mkd, (A) ..................385.00
  3 3/4" h, irid cobalt glaze, imp mk, (A) ..................385.00
  4 1/2" h, bottle shape, thick turquoise drip over gold ground, "stamped PEWABIC DETROIT" mk, (A) ..................1120.00

Candlestick
  6" h
    Mottled irid white and green glaze, imp mk and paper label, (A) ..................165.00
    Stepped shaft, matte green glaze, imp mk, (A) .385.00
  9" h, matte orange and yellow, imp mk, (A) ..........252.00
Plate, 10 3/4" d, blue slip dragonflies on border to center, white crackle ground, chip on ft, "stamped PEWABIC" mk, (A) ..................1,100.00

**Vase, 4" h, platinum and purple metallic glaze w/irid highlights, imp mk, (A), $358.**

Vase
  1 1/2" h, flared, squat base, short neck, blue, gold, and green metallic glaze, (A) ..................100.00
  3" h, short ft, bulbous body, short rim, volcanic pink, gold, and blue metallic glaze, (A)..................138.00
  3 1/2" h
    Squat body, short, flared neck and rim, blue, gold, and green metallic glaze, (A)..................72.00
    Wide, straight neck, blue, gold, and green metallic glaze, (A) ..................75.00
  3 3/4" h, swollen shape, turquoise and purple luster dripping glaze, (A) ..................660.00
  4" h, bulbous base, flared neck and rim, blue, gold, and green metallic glaze, (A) ..................85.00
  4 5/8" h, bulbous middle, narrow base, lt blue-green wave over dk blue-green wave on base ..................695.00
  4 3/4" h, bulbous body
    Flared rim, lustered celadon and purple glaze, mkd, (A)..................550.00
    Mirrored gold glaze drip over gloss blue ground, chip on base, (A)..................1,210.00
  5" h, wide center, flared neck and base, purple mirror glaze, (A)..................770.00
  5 1/2" h
    Bulbous, flared ft and rim, splashed lustered turquoise and taupe glaze, (A) ..................715.00
    Horiz ridging, blue, red, and gray metallic glaze, imp mk, (A) ..................660.00
  7" h
    Blue drip rim ..................675.00
    Tapered shape, sloped shoulder, matte brown, green, and drip glazes, "stamped PEWABIC" mk, chip, (A) ..................660.00
  8" h, amphora shape, flared ft and rim, lustered dk blue glaze, (A)..................825.00
  8 1/2" h, ovoid shape, flowing fire orange and green glaze, mkd, (A)..................1,980.00
  9 3/4" h, bottle shape, thick fire orange and green glaze, mkd, (A)..................2,090.00
  10 1/2" h, flared shape w/horiz bands, ivory crackle glaze, "incised Pewabic/1935" mk, (A)..........1,120.00
Vessel, Squat shape
  3 3/4" h, semi-matte blue, green, and mauve glaze, mkd, (A) ..................660.00
  4 3/4" h, flat shoulder, lustered, volcanic cobalt and celadon glaze, mkd, (A)..................5,320.00

Salad Bowl, 11" l x 5" h, "Country Time" pattern, Ben Seibel, gray leaves and pears on int, flower on ext, yellow ground, $65.

# Pfaltzgraff Pottery Company

## York, Pennsylvania
## 1811-Present

**History:** German immigrant George Pfaltzgraff and other family members made redware and stoneware for well over one hundred years in York, Pennsylvania. Pfaltzgraff is one of the oldest makers in the United States. Their entire family has been involved in stoneware and related products.

Crocks, jugs, pots, and such were their products from 1811-1913. Food storage was the primary purpose for these stoneware pieces with gray salt glaze and blue decoration. Red clay flower pots were made from 1913-1942 when they returned to stoneware production. Art pottery was made from 1931-1937. Kitchenwares were introduced in the 1930s.

A group of character mugs and tumblers marked "Muggsie" started in the 1940s and became very popular. Derby Dan, Cockeyed Charlie, Handsome Herman, Flirty Girty, Myrtle, Sleepy Sam, Pickled Pete, Burnie, and others were made.

Pfaltzgraff first made dinnerware in 1940. Patterns included Gourmet, Heritage, Yorktowne, and Village for the stoneware dinnerwares. Their plants expanded to meet the production needs for these useful and decorative dinnerwares.

Utilitarian pieces included mixing bowls, custard cups, planters, cookie jars, ashtrays, and other kitchenwares.

Their trademark shows the castle outline in a variety of different marks.

**Collectors' Club:** Pfaltzgraff "America" Club, 401 South Walnut Street, P.O. Box 50, Pinckneyville, IL 62274, quarterly newsletter, $8.

## AMERICA PATTERN
Ashtray, 6 1/2" d ........................................................ 7.00
Baker, 10" l ............................................................... 12.00
Berry Bowl, 4 1/2" d ................................................. 5.00
Bread Tray, 12" l ..................................................... 13.00
Candlestick, 3 1/4" h, pr ........................................ 21.00
Cereal Bowl, 5 1/2" d .............................................. 4.00
Cup and Saucer ....................................................... 8.00
Custard Cup ............................................................. 4.00
Pie Plate, 9" d ....................................................... 12.00
Plate
    7" d ...................................................................... 3.00
    8 1/2" d .............................................................. 8.00
    10" d .................................................................... 8.00
Platter, 14" l .......................................................... 23.00
Soup Plate, 8 1/2" d ................................................ 8.00
Vegetable Bowl, 8 1/2" d ...................................... 16.00

## AURA PATTERN
Cereal Bowl, 6" d ..................................................... 3.00
Cup and Saucer ....................................................... 3.00
Plate
    7" d ...................................................................... 2.00
    10" d .................................................................... 4.00
Platter, 14" l .......................................................... 10.00
Vegetable Bowl, 8 1/2" d ...................................... 10.00

## FILIGREE PATTERN
Plate, 10" d .............................................................. 5.00

## FOLK ART PATTERN
Bowl
    7 1/4" d .............................................................. 15.00
    12" d .................................................................. 30.00
Mixing Bowl, 10 1/4" d .......................................... 25.00
Mug, 4 3/4" h ............................................................ 8.00
Plate
    6 3/4" d ................................................................ 8.00
    8 1/4" d ................................................................ 9.00
    10 1/4" d ............................................................ 12.00
Soup Plate, 8 1/4" d ................................................ 8.00

## GARDEN PARTY PATTERN
Plate, 10 1/2" d ....................................................... 6.00

## GOURMET PATTERN-BROWN DRIP
Bowl, 5 1/2" d ........................................................... 4.00
Cup and Saucer ....................................................... 2.00
Egg Dish, 6" d ........................................................ 12.00
Mixing Bowl
    8" d .................................................................... 12.00
    10" d .................................................................. 20.00
Vegetable Bowl, 9" d ............................................ 12.00

## HEIRLOOM PATTERN
Cereal Bowl, 6" d ..................................................... 5.00
Cup and Saucer ....................................................... 4.00
Fruit Bowl, 5" d ......................................................... 5.00
Plate
    9" d ...................................................................... 8.00
    10 1/2" d .............................................................. 8.00
Platter, 14 1/2" l .................................................... 12.00
Vegetable Bowl, 8 3/4" d ...................................... 10.00

## HERITAGE PATTERN
Platter, 14 1/2" l, York White .......................................... 10.00
Teapot, 6 1/2" h ..........................................................42.00

## MAZARINE PATTERN
Cup and Saucer ............................................................ 5.00
Plate, 11" d .................................................................. 5.00

## MISCELLANEOUS
Flower Pot, 4 3/4" h, attached saucer, ribbed body, salmon
    pink w/gold speckles, "PFALTZGRAFF USA" mark . 25.00
Vase
    5 1/2" h, stepped lobes, pink to matte green glaze
    .....................................................................60.00
    8 1/4" h, swollen shape, 2 arched handles on shoulder,
    matte pink to green shaded glaze ....................... 95.00
    8 1/2" h, 2 handles, orange glaze, c1936 .............. 180.00

## MONTAGE PATTERN
Coffee Mug and Saucer................................................. 12.00
Plate
    8 1/4" d............................................................... 8.00
    10 1/2" d............................................................ 10.00
Soup Plate, 9" d .......................................................... 10.00

## OCEAN BREEZE PATTERN
Cup and Saucer ............................................................ 5.00
Plate
    6 3/4" d............................................................... 4.00
    10" d.................................................................... 6.00

## POETRY PATTERN
Cereal Bowl, 6" d........................................................... 5.00
Mug, 3 3/4" h ............................................................... 6.00
Plate
    7 1/4" d............................................................... 4.00
    10 1/2" d............................................................ 13.00

## REMEMBRANCE PATTERN
Cereal Bowl, 6" d........................................................... 8.00
Cup and Saucer ............................................................ 5.00
Gravy Boat ................................................................. 12.00
Plate
    7 1/4" d............................................................... 6.00
    10 1/4" d............................................................ 10.00
Platter, 14 1/2" l .......................................................... 15.00
Salad Bowl, 12 1/8" d ................................................... 20.00

## SKY PATTERN
Bowl, 5 3/4" d ............................................................... 5.00
Platter, 14" l .............................................................. 12.00
Vegetable Bowl, 8 1/2" d ................................................ 8.00

## SNOW VILLAGE PATTERN
Cereal Bowl, 6 1/4" d...................................................... 8.00
Cup and Saucer .......................................................... 10.00
Plate, 11" d ............................................................... 12.00

## SPRING SONG PATTERN
Plate, 10" d ............................................................... 12.00

## TEA ROSE PATTERN
Bread Tray, 12 1/2" l..................................................... 10.00
Coffee Cup and Saucer.................................................... 3.00

Plate, 7" d, "Village" pattern, brown and tan, $5.

Creamer ...................................................................... 5.00
Plate
    7 1/2" d ............................................................... 3.00
    10 1/2" d .............................................................. 5.00
Platter, 14 3/4" l........................................................... 10.00
Serving Bowl, 10" l ......................................................... 8.00
Shakers, Pr .................................................................. 5.00
Soup Bowl, 9" d ............................................................. 5.00
Sugar Bowl, Cov ............................................................ 7.00

## VILLAGE PATTERN
Baker, 10" l................................................................. 20.00
Butter Dish, Cov ........................................................... 18.00
Creamer .................................................................... 12.00
Cup and Saucer ........................................................... 10.00
Goblet, 5" h .................................................................. 5.00
Platter, 14" l ............................................................... 22.00
Shakers, Pr ................................................................. 20.00
Sugar Bowl, Cov ........................................................... 18.00

## WYNDHAM PATTERN
Cup and Saucer ............................................................ 3.00

## YORKTOWNE PATTERN
Butter Dish, Cov, 4 1/2" h x 7" d ................................... 15.00
Cereal Bowl, 6" d............................................................ 5.00
Cup and Saucer ........................................................... 10.00
Plate, 7" d ................................................................... 3.00
    Platter, 12" l, gray w/blue trim................................... 7.00

# Pickard China

## Chicago and Antioch, Illinois
## 1894-Present

**History:** Pickard China was
founded by Wilder Pickard in Chicago in 1894 as a decorating firm
that did painted and gold decorations on table china blanks made by
other companies. Decorations
included hand painted fruit, florals,
birds, portraits, and scenics. Most of

the blanks came from Europe. Many artists from The Art Institute of Chicago worked there.

By 1908, Pickard made more than one thousand shapes and designs. Vases, tablewares, dresser sets, tea sets, and dessert sets were all made. Figural type patterns included Dutch Decoration on a bisque-like surface, and Praying Mohammedan on vases and framed wall plaques. Conventionalized designs included Cornflower Conventional from 1908, Aura Argenta Linear in gold and silver from 1910, and Pink Enamel Flower. Tea sets, hot chocolate sets, and after-dinner coffee services increased in number in 1910.

Gold encrusted and gold etched china were introduced in 1911 and became Pickard's most popular lines. Patterns included Bordure Antique, Honeysuckle, Deserted Garden, Antique Chinese Enamels, Encrusted Linear, Italian Garden, and others. Gold decorated wares are still being made.

A 1913 allover scenic design called Wildwood was introduced that was awarded first prize at the Chicago Ceramic Exhibition that year. Four new patterns from 1916 included Secret Garden, Columbine, Rosabelle, and Mauresque. Many top artists worked at Pickard from 1905-1919 and signed their works. Edward S. Challinor was noted for his floral, fruit, bird, and scenic designs. He came to Pickard in 1902 and remained until his death in 1952.

After World War I, the concentration of gold-encrusted and etched pieces continued. The designs were transferred to a specially prepared tissue paper by means of a press and then transferred to the china. The back stamp mark was changed to reflect this with "Pickard Etched China" in a black border along with the foreign blank mark in 1920.

The company incorporated in 1925 and became Pickard Studios, Inc., and the first lion trademark appeared. Blanks used were mostly Bavarian after the war. A gold tracery decoration was also used in the 1920s in a snowflake-like pattern of fine gold lines.

Around 1935, they decided to make their own china after Austin, Wilder's son, joined the firm. They built a plant in Antioch, Illinois after they developed a formula for fine translucent china. By 1938, they had a completely vitrified, translucent, thin, light product with excellent glaze. Many outstanding decorators worked at Pickard. The first china both made and decorated at Pickard was introduced at Marshall Field in Chicago in 1938. The name of the company was changed to Pickard, Inc.

By 1941, the entire Pickard operation had moved from Chicago to Antioch. During World War II, they made china for the navy to obtain fuel oil to remain in operation.

During the transition period from 1942-1952 when Challinor was art director, simpler dinnerware patterns were becoming a larger part of their business. Various forms of gold decoration were still used. Decalcomania decorations from Challinor originals were employed. Some hand painted patterns were made including Botany, Chinese Seasons, Bouquet, Field Flowers, Aurora, Challinor Rose, and Camellia. All over gold etched art pieces were still made in large numbers for coffee sets, cake plates, bonbon dishes, vases, salts and peppers, ash trays, and cigarette boxes.

After Challinor died in 1952, hand painting was just about finished. The costs were exceptionally high, and it was also difficult to find qualified artists. New designs in 1955 included Gossamer, Blue Skies, and Silver Twilight. Austin's son Pete joined the business and designed new shapes and decorations. Crescent, a popular modern pattern was his design. Monogrammed ware was brought back along with a new art line called Accent with a gold or platinum line.

Pickard started limited edition commemorative plates and bells in 1970. The following year, they were selected by the U.S. Department of State to make official china for use in embassies and diplomatic missions.

When Pickard only decorated china, two marks may be found: one for Pickard and one for the company who made the china blanks. They used a variety of marks when they made their own china.

**References:** Sharon Darling, *Chicago Ceramics and Glass: An Illustrated History from 1871 to 1933*, Chicago Historical Society, 1979; Dorothy Pickard Platt, *The Story of Pickard*, published privately, 1970; Alan B. Reed, *Collector's Encyclopedia of Pickard China*, Collector Books, 1995.

**Collectors' Club:** Pickard Collectors' Club, Jackie Pope, 300 E. Grove St., Bloomington, IL 61701, quarterly newsletter, $20 per year.

Bowl
  7 1/4" d, ftd, painted berries and plums on border, gold handles............................................................. 225.00
  9 1/4" d, ftd, "Peaches Linear" design, orange peaches, green foliage, sm purple flowers, gold lines, sgd "Beutlich"............................................................. 240.00
  9 1/2" d, "Gifford Poppies," orange-red, black, and gold, sgd "Gifford" ....................................................... 200.00
  10" d, "White Poppy and Daisy" design, sgd "Gasper" ......................................................................... 250.00

Cake Plate
  10 1/2" d, "Classic Ruins by Moonlight" design ......................................................................... 275.00

  11" H-H
    Oct, multicolored waterfalls, dk blue and mauve accents, gold trim, sgd "Marker" ................... 450.00
    Rose and daisy design, gold trim ...................... 110.00
Candlestick, 9" h, flared sq base, overall gold finish w/etched designs, pr............................................ 275.00
Chocolate Cup and Saucer, "Raised Gold Daisy" pattern, sgd "Vobar" ................................................................. 60.00
Cider Pitcher, 8" h, "Arabian" pattern, red, lt green, pink, and gold panels, gold bamboo handle, (A)................ 1,760.00
Condiment Bowl, 6 1/2" l x 5 1/2" w, HP fall scene, sgd "E.Challinor," .......................................................... 295.00
Creamer and Cov Sugar Bowl, "Golden Orchid" pattern, Stouffer ................................................................. 210.00
Cup and Saucer
  "Cornflower" pattern, blue flowers, gold stems and rims .. 10.00
  "Nocturne" pattern, silver lined black borders .......... 25.00

**Pitcher, 7 3/8" h, red fruit, gold border and handle, tan to brown ground, "Pickard" and "J & C. Germany" mks, c1905, $840.**

Dinner Service

Cinderella Pattern

Cup and Saucer .................................................6.00

Plate

6 1/2" d..................................................8.00

8 1/4" d..................................................8.00

10 5/8" d................................................10.00

Horizon Pattern

Cup and Saucer .................................................5.00

Creamer ........................................................10.00

Plate

6 1/2" ...................................................4.00

8 1/4" d..................................................5.00

10 1/2" d.................................................5.00

Platter, 15 1/4" l ....................................30.00

Serving Bowl, 9" d ...................................20.00

Soup Plate, 8" d .......................................9.00

Sugar Bowl, Cov........................................15.00

Nocturne Pattern

Plate

8 1/4" d..................................................35.00

10 3/4" d.................................................85.00

Dish

5 1/2" d, 3 HP poinsettias, green leaves, gold scalloped rim, sgd "H.Tolley" .............................40.00

8 1/2" l, boat shape, grape clusters, autumn leaves, gold leaf border, sgd "Beutlich" ...............500.00

Lemonade Pitcher, 6" h, HP fruits on sides ................695.00

Nut Set, master dish, 8" l, 6 side dishes, 4 1/2" l, leaf shape, HP brown shade nuts, gold wavy rims ..................350.00

Plate

5 1/2" d, HP poinsettias, green leaves, gold scalloped rim, sgd "H. Tolley," ...........................37.00

6" d, lg red strawberries, sgd "Haag," c1905-10 .....................................................65.00

7 1/2" d, white daisies w/green leaves, shaded tan to cream gold, gold rim, Florence James ...............70.00

**Vase, 7 7/8" h, red, green, and orange flowers and stems, MOP luster ground, gold border and trim, sgd "Menges," Pickard, R. & C. Germany mks, $650.**

8 1/4" d, gooseberry design w/leaves and branches, blended green to yellow to amber ground, gold scalloped rim, sgd "Challinor" ...................135.00

8 3/8" d, multicolored "Classic Ruins" design, sgd "Harriet Corey," c1912-18............................300.00

8 1/2" d, multicolored Fall scene, sgd "Marker," ..................................................................495.00

8 5/8" d, gloss pink and white poppy cluster, scalloped rim, sgd "E. Challinor" ...........................500.00

8 3/4" d, painted white and yellow tulips, green leaves, sm purple flowerheads on border......................225.00

9" d, hanging bunches of red cherries and green leaves, gold border........................................75.00

10 1/12" d, Indian Tree pattern ..........................125.00

11" d, multicolored formal garden setting in center, cream border w/gold floral baskets and rim, Challinor . 360.00

Platter, 12" l, oval, painted strawberries, gold whiplash ..................................................................1,195.00

Punch Bowl

13" d, red currents and leaves, maroon to yellow shaded ground, gold trim, sgd "Vokral," (A) ...............3,960.00

14" d, "Strawberry Sprays" design, sgd "LeRoy" 2,200.00

Shakers, 2 1/2" h, "Rose and Daisy" design, etched gold, pr ..................................................................25.00

Sugar Bowl, Cov, Deco gold panels w/silver stylized flowers and lines, off white ground, sgd "Vobor" ...............150.00

Tankard, 13 3/4" h, multicolored scene of monk pealing turnip, flowers on base, grapes, blossoms, and branches on border, gold trim, sgd "P.Gasper," c1905-10, (A) 3,190.00

Tray

13" l, fluted, enameled tulip pattern, gold trim .... 1,095.00

16" d, 3 multicolored hunting dogs in green meadow, sgd "Farrington," 1903 .......................................2,895.00

Vase

3 1/2" h, squat shape, gold outlined red shaded poinsettias w/jeweled centers, black and cream ground, sgd "Loh".............................................................295.00

5 1/2" h, fan shape, mint green leaf silhouettes, gold rim, gold mk, c1930-38.............................................220.00

6" h, multicolored Deco style florals, lemon yellow ground, sgd "Marker"........................................250.00

6 1/4" h, HP violets, gold trim ..................................95.00

7" h

Gold water lilies and green leaves, ivory ground ..................................................................135.00

Tapered shape w/wide shoulder and flared rim, gold stylized florals, leaves, and curlicues on gold ground on upper portion, pearl white lower section ..................................................................95.00

Trumpet shape, circ base, overall gold floral design, lt green int..............................................70.00

Two handles, "Fruit Basket" medallion, aqua ground w/gold tracery, sgd "Klipp" .........................1,000.00

7 1/4" h, multicolored landscape w/cattle and mountains, gold rim, sgd "Kubash," c1903-05, (A) ...........3,850.00

10" h, multicolored waterfall scene, sgd "Marker," ..................................................................695.00

10 1/8" h, tapered shape, 2 sm handles, painted pheasant, blue upper section, etched gold morning glory designs on lower section, Challinor...................650.00

14" h, multicolored standing peacock on black bottom, gold upper half ground, sgd "E. Challinor," c1925-30, (A) ..................................................................1,870.00

# Howard Pierce

**LaVerne, California
1941-1968**

**HOWARD
PIERCE**

**Joshua Tree, California
1968-Present**

**History:** Howard Pierce started
work at William Marker's plant before he started his own studio in La Verne, California in 1941. At first he worked in pewter, and then did defense work during the war. In 1945, he returned to ceramics and started production with his wife. Pierce made figurines in a porcelain material called nepheline syenite. He supervised almost every step of production himself.

The 1950s were the peak years of production. Pierce made porcelain sculptures of animals, birds, and human subjects that were sold in fine gift shops and department stores. They were mostly sold in sets of two or three.

The earliest glaze was a satin matte white, which was followed by a brown and white combination that was a preferred finish for nearly fifteen years. Additional satin colors included black on white, all black, and all gray. High-gloss colors were brown agate, slate gray, and sandstone. Many experimental colors were also used.

In 1956, Howard Pierce tried a version of Wedgwood's jasper with raised cameos that were cast as an integral part of objects with background colors of brown, green and blue. These efforts were not too successful.

High glazed vases and lamps with open centers containing miniature animals and plant forms in white porcelain bisque were more popular.

Pierce and his wife moved to Joshua Tree in 1968 near Palm Springs in semi-retirement. He still creates new designs and glazes.

Marks utilized included a stamped mark of the full name in block letters. In the 1950s, they used "Howard Pierce Porcelain" or "Pierce Porcelain." Some pieces have incised signatures with "Claremont, Calif." Smaller items of a set were often unmarked.

**References:** Jack Chipman, *Collector's Encyclopedia of California Pottery, 2nd Edition*, Collector Books, 1998; Darlene Hurst Dommel, *Collector's Encyclopedia of Howard Pierce Porcelain*, Collector Books, 1998.

Bowl
8" d, ftd, shaded brown to white ............................... 45.00
9 1/2" d, lobed, brown leopard glazed int, brown ext
.................................................................................. 70.00

Figure
2" l, baby bear, dk brown ........................................ 45.00
3" h x 6 1/2" l, mother bear, dk brown and tan ......... 50.00
3 3/4" h, sparrow, white ........................................... 50.00
4" h, seated rabbit, dk brown and gray .................... 40.00
4 1/2" h
   Beaver, brown .................................................. 55.00
   Robin, orange-red breast .................................... 80.00
   Seated dove, cream with brown accents ............. 45.00
   Stylized angel and lamb, blue-gray ..................... 75.00
5" h
   Owl, gloss brown .............................................. 70.00
   Standing chipmunk, brown and white, pr ........... 80.00
5 1/2" h
   "Quail Family", black and gray, "Howard Pierce," mks, set of 3 ........................................................ 95.00

Seated deer, tan and white ................................. 65.00
6" h, elephant w/trunk raised, gray shades ........... 125.00
6 1/2" h, quail on branch, white and tan ................. 85.00
7" h, pelican, mottled brown ................................. 90.00
8 1/2" h, cat, brown and white ............................. 125.00
8 1/2" l, raccoon, tan and brown .......................... 115.00
9" h
   Peasant girl, brown and gray ........................... 110.00
   Standing girl holding pot, 2 jugs on rect base, tan-brown glaze .................................................. 75.00
9" l, Road Runner, tan and brown .......................... 58.00
9 1/2" l, running dachshund, metallic black .......... 115.00
9 5/8" h, seated deer, matte black finish ................. 78.00
11 1/2", 9 1/2" h, 5 1/2" h, giraffe family, set of 3 ... 185.00
12" h, St. Francis of Assisi holding bird, gray shades
.................................................................................. 195.00
13 1/2" h, Madonna and child, gold ........................ 75.00
Flower Frog, 8" h, figural quail, gold glaze ................. 20.00
Flower Pot, 4" h x 6" l, figural turtle, brown and white .. 32.00
Planter, 2 1/4" h x 3 5/8" sq, maroon ext, pea green int, pr
.................................................................................. 15.00

Vase
3 1/2" h, squat base, slanted opening, blue-green striated body w/cobalt drip .................................. 40.00
7" h, white vert rect body, white Bonsai tree support, black rect base ................................................. 22.00

**Figure, 7" h x 7" l, brown and tan shades, $65.**

**Figure, 8" h, brown and white, $82.**

# Pigeon Forge Pottery

## Pigeon Forge, Tennessee
## 1946-Present

**History:** Douglas Ferguson started the Pigeon Forge Pottery in Tennessee with Ernest Wilson, his father-in-law, in an old tobacco barn and made high-fired stoneware. They used red or gray clay found in the area. When fired, the fine textured clay resulted in a speckled gray body.

*The Pigeon Forge POTTERY Pigeon Forge Tenn.*

Shapes were both functional and decorative in nature. Many examples were sculptured. Examples included vases, bowls, pitchers, teapots, wall pockets, and such. Delicate and subdued tone glazes were utilized on the hard stoneware pieces. Tourist pieces, such as the black bear figurines were added to the factory's output. These were some of the most popular items made by the pottery. They built a new building in 1957, after a fire destroyed the pottery.

Jane Ferguson, Douglas' daughter, continues at the pottery and makes one-of-a-kind hand-thrown utilitarian and architectural forms in the high fired stoneware and porcelain.

Most pieces were marked with the full name either stamped or incised on the base.

Figure, 7 3/4" h, textured gray-black, white face, $45.

Figure, 5 5/8" l, gray speckled body, brown eyes, black accents, $75.

Bowl
   3 1/2" d, gloss Chinese orange glaze ..................... 15.00
   4 3/4" d, brown glaze, cream band on int and ext
   ................................................................... 100.00
   5 1/2" d
      Closed rim, emb green, white, and brown flowers and stems on ext border, dk pink ground, (A) ........ 33.00
      Red clay body w/brown and white mottled glaze, green swirls on int ......................................... 50.00
   8" d x 5 3/4" h, curved freeform top and base, conc ring pattern, lt green, mkd ...................................... 10.00
Candlestick, 3 3/4" h, swollen middle, flared base and rim, tan glaze ................................................................ 12.00
Coaster, 3 3/4" d, incised swan, grasses, and water ripples, blue-gray, set of 6 ................................................... 18.00
Dish, 5" d, ruffled shape, celadon green glaze ............. 10.00
Figure
   2 1/4" h x 3 1/2" l, bird, matte blue body, black beak and eyes ..................................................................... 27.00
   3 3/4" h, chipmunk seated on haunches, tan shades ..................................................................... 20.00
   4 1/4" h, seated bear cub, black face, gray body ..... 15.00
   6" h, 2 bear cubs standing together, semi-gloss black glaze, mkd ....................................................... 45.00
   7 3/4" h, owl, textured gray-black, white face ......... 45.00
Mug
   3" h, blue stylized deer on side, white ground ......... 15.00
   4 1/2" h, brown incised pine tree on side, matte green bkd, (A) ............................................................... 297.00
Pitcher, 4 1/2" h
   Matte gray-brown ext, chartreuse int ...................... 10.00
   White dogwood blossoms on side, matte gray-brown ground, gloss lt yellow int ................................. 10.00
Planter, 3 1/8" h x 8 1/4" l, free-form, 4 sm feet, textured tan ext, gloss yellow int .............................................. 16.00

Sugar Bowl, 3" h, white dogwood blossom, green leaves, matte brown glaze, cream int .................................... 5.00
Trivet, 5" d, relief molded lt brown 4 sectioned leaf, cream ground ................................................................. 25.00
Vase
   2 1/4" h x 3 1/4" d, bowl shape, horiz ribbing, textured brown surface .................................................... 20.00
   4" h
      Bulbous body, straight neck, matte olive green glaze, imp mk, (A) ..................................................... 15.00
      Rect shape w/ruffled rim, brown drip over green luster body w/white flecks ......................................... 65.00
   4 1/2" h, beige textured ball shape base, dk brown flared neck and rim, artist sgd .................................... 15.00
   5" h, cylinder base w/raised rows of dashes, flared neck and rim, olive green glaze, Ferguson .................. 40.00
   5 1/2" h
      Bulbous base, trumpet neck, blended red, burgundy, purple, and brown glazes .............................. 15.00
      "Harmony," textured steel blue ext, cream int
      ............................................................... 25.00
   7" h
      Corset shape, textured brown body, (A) ............. 15.00
      Wedding, textured steel blue surface ................. 25.00
   7 3/4" h, flat, triangle shape, tan bubbles over pink ground, sgd "Douglas Ferguson" ....................... 125.00
   9" h
      Bulbous shape, med blue w/speckles shaded to shaded brown top .......................................... 125.00

Bud Vase, 5" h, mustard yellow, brown, and orange drip, tan base, "Pigeon Forge Pottery Tenn. Douglas Ferguson" mk, $45.

Paneled fan shape, curled loop handles, blended ochre and green glaze ....................................15.00
Wall Pocket, 4" h, painted dogwood blossom and branch .........................................................5.00

# Polia Pillin

### Los Angeles, California
### 1948-1992

**History:** Polia Pillin came to the United States from Poland in 1924. She was educated at the Jewish People's Institute and studied pottery for only six weeks at Hull House in Chicago. She was mostly self taught in ceramics after being influenced by oriental pottery.

Polia and William, her husband, established a pottery studio in their garage studio in Los Angeles, California. William prepared the clay and glazes, and was responsible for the casting and firing. Polia was a painter first and used color heavily on her ceramics pieces. Polia painted on her pottery with colored slips to which she added various oxides to derive pigments of varying tones and intensity. She also used the techniques of sponging, sgraffito, and banding to achieve a variety of textures on her pottery. Many of her painting styles carried over to her pottery. Some pieces exhibit the "Byzantine" quality from her paintings.

Pillin's works were signed "Pillin," "W & P Pillin," or "Polia Pillin." Pillin died in 1992.

**Museums:** Dallas Art Museum, TX; Everson Museum of Art, Syracuse, NY; Long Beach Museum, CA; Otis Art Institute, Los Angeles, CA.

Beverage Set, decanter, 15" h, painted w/3 women and birds, 5 goblets painted w/woman, gray and pink streaked ground, sgd "*Pillin*," (A) ........................1065.00

Bottle
  6 1/2" h, teal blue portrait of woman, figure of woman, and bird, indigo ground, (A).............................500.00
  11" h, bulbous shape, painted birds on green, blue, and gray ground, sgd "*Pillin*," (A) ...........................785.00
Bowl
  5" d, painted rooster, dk green ground, mkd..........150.00
  6 1/2" d, low profile, painted harlequin and horse, yellow ground, sgd "*Pillin*," (A) .....................................390.00
  8" l, free form, painted cats, gray streaked ground, sgd "*Pillin*," (A) .......................................................500.00
Box, 4" d, woman holding black cat on lid, chips, (A) ..........................................................................330.00
Bud Vase
  4 1/4" h, bottle shape, painted woman and birds, pink and gray ground, sgd "*Pillin*," (A) .............................450.00
  4 1/2" h, squat base, short neck, 3 chickens, blue-gray ground, "incised PILLIN" mk, (A).......................412.00
  6" h
    Bottle shape, circus woman and 2 horses, lt blue ground, "Pillin" mk...........................................625.00
    Ovoid shape, sm opening, green and turquoise microcrystalline glaze, mkd, (A) ...........................275.00
  6 1/4" h, squat base, elongated pastel woman, mustard ground, sgd "*Pillin*," rim chip, (A).....................385.00
  6 1/2" h, bulbous base, short, flared neck and rim, streaked blue glaze .........................................100.00
  8 1/2" h, bulbous base, short, narrow neck, charcoal and yellow gloss glaze, incised mk, (A) ..................825.00
  8 5/8" h, bottle shape, bright red gloss glaze, "Pillin" mk ....................................................................425.00
Dish
  6 1/2" l
    Free form, painted woman and rooster, green ground, sgd "*Pillin*," (A) .............................................280.00
    Kidney shape, 2 women bathing, polychrome, "incised *Pillin*" mk, restored chips, (A).......................495.00
  8" l,
    Almond shape, 3 running horses, blue streaked ground, sgd "*Pillin*," (A)................................450.00
    Free form, pastel painted swimming fish, gray ground, sgd "*Pillin*," (A) ...........................................475.00
  9" sq, blue, dk and lt blue horses in center, painted mk, (A) ..............................................................1,210.00
Plaque, 5 1/2" h, triangle shape, multicolored pastel woman w/blue bird, shaded magenta ground .........................................................................750.00

Plate, 8 3/4" d, tan, dk red, white, and black, $595.

**Vase, 9" h, blue, green, dk pink striping, white, $1,950.**

7 1/2" h, 3 sided bullet shape, multicolored woman, horse, and chicken, (A) ...................................... 715.00

8 3/4" h, tapered shape, polychrome painting of 2 women, white ground, chips, (A)...................... 728.00

9" h, cylinder shape, band of women, rooster, and bird, upper and lower brown bands, sgd "*Pillin*," (A) . 896.00

11 3/4" h, bottle shape, bust of woman and horse in brown shades, black ground, "incised *Pillin*" mk, (A) ...................................................................... 1,650.00

12" h, swollen cylinder shape, trumpet neck, matte yellow-green crystalline drip on shoulder over yellow crystalline ground, "WTP Pillin" mk, (A) ............ 275.00

12 1/4" h, hourglass shape, bulbous base, standing young girls, pink, blue, and tan pastels .......... 2,750.00

20" h, cylinder shape, multicolored scene of woman holding flowers, lady and horse on reverse, (A)....... 825.00

Vessel

3" d, squat shape, painted fish, blue ground, mkd, (A) ...................................................................... 250.00

6 3/4" h, cup shape, short stem base, multicolored scene of 2 women, horse, and birds in tree, tan textured ground, chip on base, (A) ................................. 385.00

# Pisgah Forest Pottery

### Arden, North Carolina
### 1920s-Present

**History:** Walter B. Stephen founded Pisgah Forest Pottery in the 1920s in Arden, North Carolina. He continued the work he had started at Nonconnah Pottery in Skylark, North Carolina.

His best works were the cameo ware scenes of American pioneer life that were done using the pate-sur-pate technique in white or dark blue matte, dark green, brown, and other colors. Crystalline glazes were developed in the mid 1920s, and often two or three colors were used. Various colored glazes included turquoise, ivory, pink, and wine. Shapes used for the artwares were vases, teapots, mugs, pitchers, candlesticks, cups and saucers, creamers and sugar bowls, and miniature pieces.

Every piece of Pisgah Forest was hand made. Most pieces were signed with an impressed mark either "Pisgah Forest" or "Stephen." Dating began in 1926. After 1961, the date was omitted from the mark.

Stephen died in 1961, and the pottery was taken over by Tom Case and Grady Ledbetter. They continued to use the colored glazes, but all cameo ware and crystalline glazes were discontinued.

**Museums:** Chrysler Museum, Norfolk, VA.

Bowl, 8" d, rolled rim, gloss dk plum glaze, matte ivory int, 1934, (A) .................................................. 110.00

Cereal Bowl, 5 1/2" d, white cameo of mountains and cabin on brown ground, pink int, (A) ............................ 110.00

## Vase

2 3/4" h, squat shape, flat base, short neck, multicolored birds, med blue ground, mkd ............................ 425.00

4 1/2" h, cylinder shape, young girl holding balloons, horse head on reverse, pastel colors, blue crackle ground, "*Pillin*" mk ............................................... 895.00

5" h

Bulbous, multicolored woman, horses, and birds, charcoal gray ground ........................................... 695.00

Triangle shape, painted w/3 roosters, beige streaked ground, sgd "*Pillin*," (A) ................................. 335.00

5 1/4" h

Bowl shape, sm spread ft, swimming fish, blue and pink streaked ground ................................... 800.00

Cylinder shape, painted woman, horse, and bird, blue streaked ground, sgd "*Pillin*," (A) ................... 365.00

Pillow shape, painted prancing horses, yellow ground, sgd "*Pillin*," (A) ............................................. 448.00

6" h

Bottle shape, multicolored circus lady on 2 horses, lt blue ground.................................................... 625.00

Spherical shape, multicolored painting of 4 prancing horses on banded pink, coral, and turquoise ground, (A) ................................................... 728.00

6 1/4" h, bulbous shape, circ base, blue lady, bird, and horse designs, blue shaded ground, mkd ......... 635.00

6 1/2" h

Bottle shape, polychrome woman and birds and woman and horse, "incised PILLIN" mk, (A) . 605.00

Cylinder shape, painted w/2 women and birds, brown and pink streaked ground, sgd "*Pillin*," (A).... 615.00

Tumbler shape, pastel girl playing lute, girl in red skirt on reverse, brown ground, chips on base..... 350.00

6 3/4" h, squat bottle shape, cranberry red glaze, mkd, (A)...................................................................... 385.00

7" h, cylinder shape, rooster design, blue ground.. 495.00

7 1/4" h, flared shape, painted w/4 women and trees in dk green shades, sgd "*Pillin*," (A) ...................... 1,680.00

Pitcher, 4 1/2" h, blue and cream glaze w/red accents, (A), $20.

Creamer, 4" h, pink glaze ............................20.00
Cup, 2 3/4" h, gloss brown glaze, pumpkin int, (A)
................................................................33.00
Dresser Jar, 4" h, aqua glaze, pink int, dtd 1935........125.00
Ewer, 8 1/2" h, maroon crackle glaze, sgd "Stephen"
................................................................195.00
Jar
    3 1/2" h, ball shape, mottled aqua glaze, lt brown int, dtd 1941 ....................................200.00
    7 1/2" h, baluster shape, flared rim, amber flambe glaze w/scattered blue crystals, (A) ............523.00
Jar, Cov, 4" h, aqua glaze, pink int, dtd 1935 ............125.00
Jug, 5" h, turquoise drip over purple body................75.00
Mug, 3 1/2" h, white cameo of cabin in mountains, teal blue ground, mkd, (A) ...............................300.00
Pitcher
    4" h, turquoise crackle glaze..................................60.00
    4 1/8" h, aqua ext, lt pink int.................................22.00
    5 1/2" h, rope twist handle, turquoise ext, brown int
................................................................35.00
    6 1/2" h, olive green glaze ....................................85.00
Plate, 9 1/4" d, rose glaze, crazed, WBJ Stephen........60.00
Tea Set, pot, 5 1/4" h, creamer, cov sugar bowl, white cameo band of wagons and landscape, dk matte green ground, dtd 1943, chips, (A)................770.00
Vase
    3 1/2" h, squat shape, short rim, gloss pink glaze, (A)
................................................................88.00
    3 3/4" h, trumpet shape, turquoise blue glaze ........50.00
    4" h x 5 1/2" d, bowl shape, white and blue crystalline glaze, 1948, (A) ..........................605.00
    4 1/2" h, flared shape, gray and ivory crystalline glaze, dtd 1946, (A)......................................253.00
    5" h
        Bulbous shape, white and amber glaze w/blue crystals, dtd 1940, (A) .............................357.00
        Corset shape, flared rim, gloss purple glaze, (A)
................................................................100.00
        Grecian urn shape w/side handles, flared ft, raised leaf design, green crystalline glaze, caramel brown ground, (A)........................................330.00
    5 1/4" h, turquoise top, dk maroon on middle and base
................................................................150.00
    5 3/8" h, bulbous middle, flared top, turquoise top shaded to brown base ..................................65.00

5 1/2" h
    Ball shape, crackled turquoise glaze, sgd "Stephen"
................................................................150.00
    Hourglass shape, turquoise drip over maroon ground, sgd "Stephen"....................................115.00
    Swollen cylinder shape, flared rim, white cameo band of wagon train w/oxen, med blue body, sgd "Stephen"....................................................250.00
5 5/8" h, bowl shape, turquoise glaze, "Stephen 1951" mk
................................................................225.00
6" h, crackled turquoise glaze, sgd "Stephen" .......150.00
6 1/8" h, classic shape, rose int, camel brown glaze w/green-blue crystals, (A) ...............................302.00
6 1/2" h
    Corset shape, amber glaze w/gray crystals, (A)
................................................................413.00
    Swollen body, flared rim, amber glaze w/white and blue crystals, dtd 1940, (A)........................660.00
    Swollen shoulder, flared rim, gloss black glaze... 85.00
6 3/4" h, bottle shape, camel brown ground w/long green-black stripes and blue crystals, (A) ..................302.00
7" h, bulbous, straight neck, brown and amber flambe glaze w/lg blue crystal clusters, (A)..................523.00
7 3/4" h, bulbous middle, spread ft and rim, blue, green, and white crystalline glaze, (A) ......................495.00
8" h, bottle shape, white glaze w/white crystals, dtd 1941, (A) .....................................................715.00
8 1/2" h, white cameo of dancing couples, violin and guitar players on matte green ground, (A) ..........1,210.00
10" h
    Classical shape, celadon, mauve, and ivory crystalline glaze, lg blooming crystals, mkd, (A).........1,320.00
    White cameo of wagon train on brown banded collar, mottled blue body, (A)..................................512.00
Vessel, Bowl Shape
    3 3/4" h x 4 1/2" d, amber flambe glaze w/celadon crystals, Stephen mk, (A)....................................303.00
    5" h x 5 3/4" d, amber glaze w/blue and white crystals, dtd 1947, "raised Stephen and date" mk, (A)....385.00

c.1910

# Pope-Gosser China Company

## Coshocton, Ohio
## 1902-1958

**History:** The Pope-Gosser China Company was organized in 1902 by Charles Gosser and Bentley Pope in Coshocton, Ohio. Pope had worked at Trenton and Knowles, Taylor, and Knowles. The company made a high quality, highly vitrified translucent china body for vases and such.

In 1904, Pope-Gosser won a Silver medal for superior semi-porcelain at the St. Louis Louisiana Purchase Exposition, and also won other awards for their wares. Despite the awards, these wares were not profitable, and they switched their production to dinnerware.

Pope-Gosser joined with eight companies in 1929 to form the American China Corporation. After the corporation broke up, Pope-Gosser was reorganized by Frank Judge in 1932. It continued to make semi-porcelain until closing in 1958.

Rosepoint was used on a variety of bodies from 1934 until the factory closed. It had a raised design of trailing roses in white with a rose finial on covered pieces. Decals were added the following year. Candlewick was introduced in 1936.

Steubenville Pottery bought the molds for Rosepoint, and then Canonsburg bought Steubenville and the molds. Rosepoint that was marked made by Steubenville was made at Canonsburg after 1959.

Pope-Gosser closed in 1958 due to foreign competition. A variety of marks was used.

### BLUE BELLE PATTERN

| | |
|---|---|
| Berry Bowl, 5 3/4" d | 3.00 |
| Cup and Saucer | 10.00 |
| Plate | |
| 6" d | 10.00 |
| 7 3/8" d | 10.00 |
| 9" d | 10.00 |
| 10 1/8" d | 15.00 |
| Platter, 13 3/4" l | 15.00 |

Creamer, 3 3/4" h, Cov Sugar Bowl, 3 3/4" h, "Sharon" pattern, "Futura" shape, black, mauve, and silver, $10.

Platter, 11 1/4" l, "Dogwood" pattern, $10.

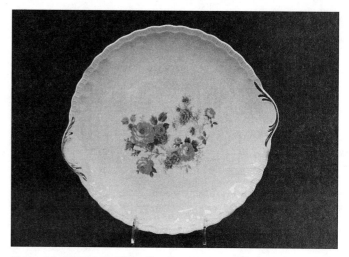

Tray, 11 3/8" H-H, "Sterling" pattern, gold trimmed handles, $10.

| | |
|---|---|
| Relish Tray, 8 3/4" H-H | 15.00 |
| Serving Bowl, 8 1/2" d | 10.00 |
| Soup Bowl, 7" H-H | 6.00 |
| Sugar Bowl, Cov | 15.00 |
| Vegetable Bowl, 9 3/4" l | 18.00 |

### BRIAR ROSE PATTERN

| | |
|---|---|
| Platter, 11 1/4" l | 15.00 |

### CLEMENTINE PATTERN

| | |
|---|---|
| Berry Bowl, 5 1/8" d | 3.00 |
| Plate | |
| 7 1/4" d | 4.00 |
| 10" d | 12.00 |

### FLORENCE PATTERN

| | |
|---|---|
| Creamer | 40.00 |
| Cup and Saucer | 8.00 |
| Dessert Dish, 5 5/8" d | 10.00 |
| Plate | |
| 6" d | 6.00 |
| 7 1/4" d | 9.00 |
| 8 1/4" d | 8.00 |
| 9" d | 8.00 |
| 10" d | 10.00 |
| Platter | |
| 11" l | 25.00 |
| 13" l | 15.00 |
| 15" l | 20.00 |
| Serving Bowl | |
| 8" d | 30.00 |
| 9" d | 30.00 |
| Sugar Bowl, Cov | 45.00 |

### FUTURA PATTERN

| | |
|---|---|
| Bowl, 8 1/4" d | 4.00 |
| Gravy Boat | 8.00 |
| Vegetable Bowl, 8 1/4" l, divided | 5.00 |

### JEAN PATTERN

| | |
|---|---|
| Berry Dish, 5 3/4" d | 3.00 |

Figure, 8 1/4″ h, Florence, "Blossom"
and "Lantern Boy," pr, $150.

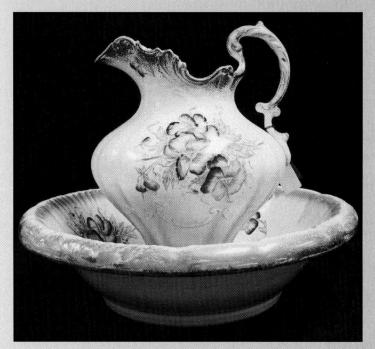

Wash Set, pitcher, 13″ h, bowl, 17″ d,
Limoges China, $295.

Vase, 11″ h, Van Briggle, "Lady of the Lily," 1902,
"incised AA VAN BRIGGLE 1902 III" mk, (A), $41,250.
Photograph Courtesy of David Rago Auctions.

Beverage Set, pitcher, 10 1/2″ h,
6 mugs, 4″ h, Warwick, $650.

Pitcher, 5 3/4″ h, Ott and Brewer, $1,100.

Vase, 5 1/2″ h, Niloak,
Mission Swirl, (A), $110.

Tankard, 11″ h, Pickard, $795.

Bud Vase, 6 1/4″ h, Pillin, $750.

Coffeepot, 7″ h, Griffin Smith
and Hill, Etruscan, $1,100.

Coffeepot, 10 1/4″ h, Hall,
"Silhouette" pattern, $90.

Teapot, 7″ h, Red Wing and
Rumrill, "Village" pattern, $32.

Carafe, 8 1/2″ h, Vernon Kilns,
"Organdie" pattern, $68.

Pitcher, 11 1/2″ h, Vernon
Kilns, "Tam O' Shanter"
pattern, $60.

Pretzel Bowl, 12″ l, Pennsbury,
"Amish" pattern, $130.

Vase, 5″ h, Clifton, $350.

Pretzel Jar, 7 1/4″ h, Hall, $350.

Bean Pot, 6 1/2″ h, Robinson-Ransbottom,
stoneware, $125.

Planter, 10 1/4″ l, McCoy, $69.

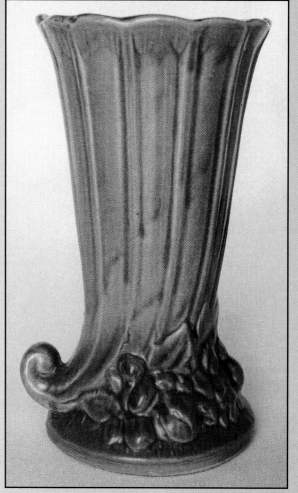

Vase, 8″ h, Nelson McCoy, $58.

Planter, 6 1/4″ h, Roseville,
"Water Lily" pattern, $75.

Planter, 5 1/4″ h x 6 3/8″ sq,
Shawnee, $20.

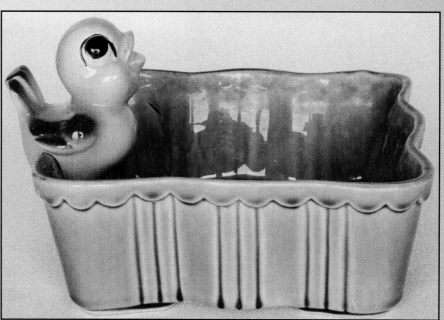

Vase, 10″ h, Clewell, (A), $290.

Vase, 7 1/2″ d, J.B. Owens, (A), $210.

Vase, 8 3/4″ h, "UC 1913 TD" mk, University City, (A), $13,200. Photograph Courtesy of David Rago Auctions.

Vase, 11 1/2″ h, #2482, dated 1924, Rookwood, (A), $880.

Vase, 11″ h, Grueby, 3 white daffodils, (A), $9,900.

Vase, 4 1/2″ h, Hampshire, (A), $200.

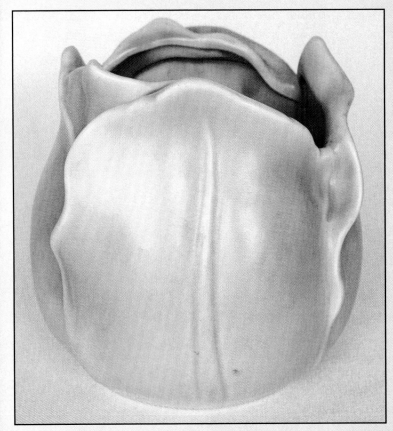

Vase, 5 1/2″ h, Stangl, cabbage, $95.

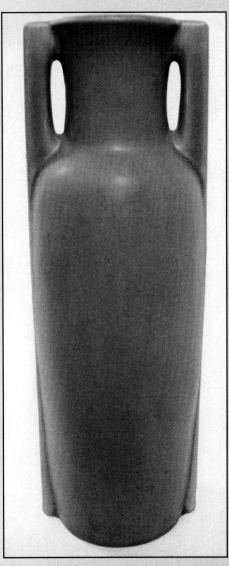

Vase, 11 1/2″ h, repaired chip, Teco, (A), $1,100.

Vase, 9″ h, raised vert mk,
Fulper, (A), $523.

Lamp, 18″ h x 16″ d, rect mk, Fulper, (A), $12,100.
Photograph Courtesy of David Rago Auctions.

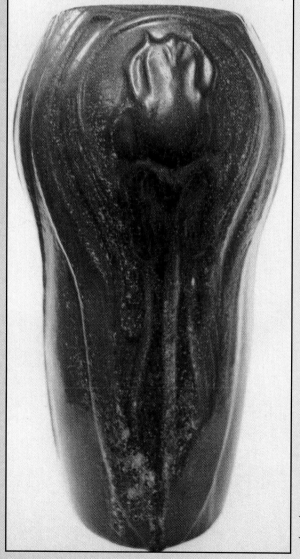

Vase, 6″ d, dated 1915, Van Briggle, (A), $770.

Vase, 15″ h, c1903, incised mks,
Van Briggle, (A), $18,700.

Figure, 11″ h, Bennington, $325.

Cookie jar, Josef Originals, $40.

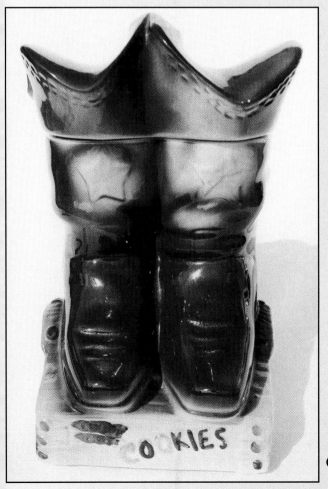

Figures, 8 1/2″ h, 6 1/4″ h, Kay Finch,
"Butch" and "Biddy," $285.

Cookie jar, McCoy, $400.

Plate, 8 1/2″ d, Dedham, $225.

Plate, 10 5/8″ d, Gladding McBean-Franciscan, "Fresh Fruit" pattern, $30.

Plate, 10 3/4″ d, Gladding McBean-Franciscan, "Cafe Royal" pattern, $14.

Oyster Plate, 9 1/2″ d, Union Porcelain, $995.

Platter, 11 5/8″ H-H, Crooksville, "Southern Belle" pattern, $24.

Plate, 8″ d, Knowles, Taylor, Knowles, $125.

Plate, 8 3/8″ d, Southern Potteries-Blue Ridge, "County Fair" pattern, "Colonial" shape, $14.

Dish, 7 1/8″ l, stenciled air-brushed design, Restaurant China, Jackson mk, $15.

Chamberstick, 8″ d, Jugtown, $175.

Jug, 9 1/2″ h, Jugtown, $250.

Vase, 5 1/2″ h, Pisgah Forest, (A), $90.

Vase, 7 1/2″ h, Pisgah Forest, $1,000.

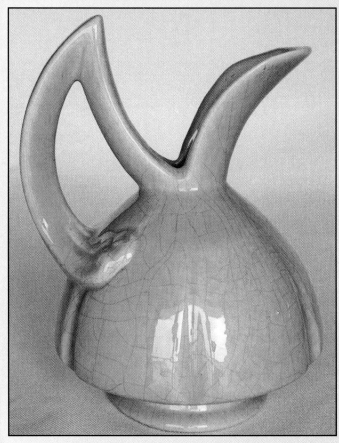

Pitcher, 7 3/8″ h, Gonder, $32.

Jar, Cov, 7″ h, hand-built form, Newcomb College, Sadie Irvine, imp mk, (A), $1,100.

Pitcher, 6" h, Newcomb College, Henrietta Bailey, (A), $2,200.

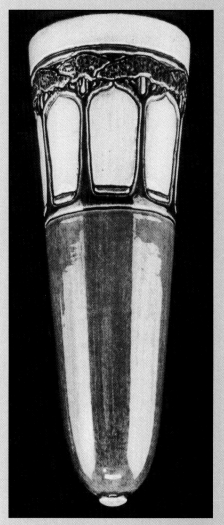

Wall Pocket, 11″ h, Newcomb College, (A), $9,350.

Vase, 8 1/2″ h, California-Faience, $500.

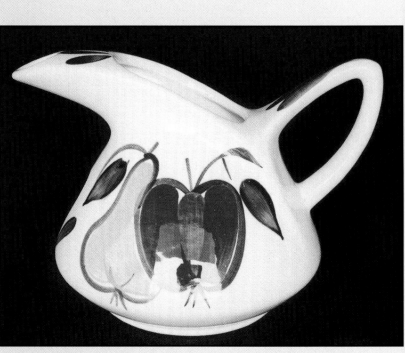

Dutch Jug, 6″ h, Purinton, "Fruit" pattern, $40.

Tankard, 5 3/4″ h, Willets, snake mk, $225.

Teapot, 7″ h, Purinton, "Fruit" pattern, 4 cup, $50.

Vase, 5″ w, Muncie, (A), $200.

Pitcher, 7″ h, script signature,
George Ohr, (A), $3,850.

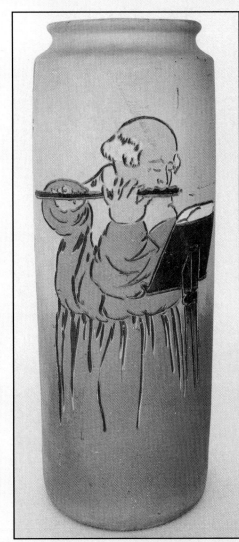

Vase, 10 1/4″ h, Weller,
Dickensware, $395.

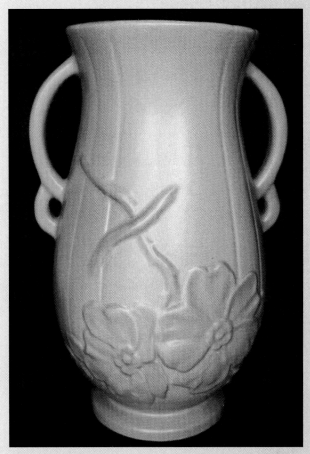

Vase, 13″ h, Weller, "Wild Rose" pattern, $195.

Vase, 5″ h, Batchelder, (A), $495.

Vase, 7″ h, Peters and Reed, Zane mk, $175.

Console Set, center bowl, 6″ h x 9 1/2″ l, 2 candleholders,
5 1/4″ l, imp mks, Cowan, $400.

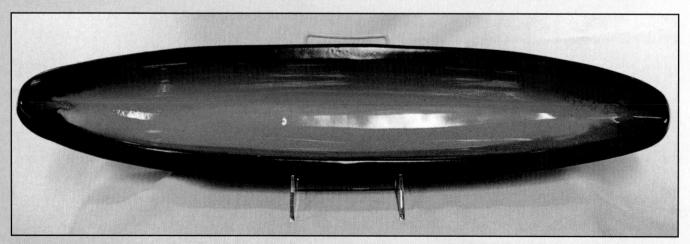

Bowl, 24″ l, Russell Wright, Bauer, (A), $1,540.

Casserole, Cov, 7 1/2" d..................................10.00
Cup and Saucer ...............................................5.00
Plate
    6" d................................................................3.00
    8" d................................................................4.00
    10" d..............................................................6.00
Platter
    11 1/2" l........................................................12.00
    15 1/4" l........................................................15.00
Soup Bowl, 7 3/4" d...........................................5.00
Vegetable Bowl, 9" l........................................10.00

## LA BELLE PATTERN
Berry Bowl, 5" d.................................................3.00
Cereal Bowl, 7" H-H ..........................................5.00
Plate
    6 1/8" d..........................................................4.00
    10" d..............................................................8.00
Teapot, 9 1/8" h...............................................25.00
Vegetable Bowl
    9 5/8" l..........................................................10.00
    10 3/8" l........................................................12.00

## LARGO ROSE PATTERN
Gravy Boat .......................................................18.00
Plate
    8 1/4" d..........................................................9.00
    9 1/2" d..........................................................9.00
    10" d............................................................10.00
Teacup and Saucer ........................................12.00
Vegetable Bowl, 8 1/2" d ................................18.00

## MADISON PATTERN
Creamer, 3" h ....................................................5.00

## MADRID PATTERN
Creamer ............................................................8.00
Gravy Boat, 8" l, w/attached undertray.........20.00
Serving Bowl, 10 1/4" d ..................................15.00
Sugar Bowl, Cov..............................................12.00

## MARCHETA PATTERN
Cup and Saucer ...............................................5.00

## MELROSE PATTERN
Berry Bowl, 5" d.................................................3.00
Cup and Saucer ................................................4.00
Gravy Boat w/undertray.....................................5.00
Plate
    6 1/4" d..........................................................6.00
    10" d..............................................................7.00
Platter, 13 1/4" l...............................................10.00
Vegetable Bowl, 8 1/4" d ..................................8.00

## MILAN PATTERN
Plate, 10 1/8" d..................................................4.00
Platter, 15 1/4" l...............................................10.00

## MISCELLANEOUS
Plate, 7 1/4" d, "I chatter, chatter, I flow...Tennyson" decal of
    waterfall and flowers in center, pink and green shading
    ........................................................................12.00

## PINAFORE PATTERN
Berry Bowl, 5 1/2" d...........................................5.00
Butter Dish, Cov, 7 1/2" l.................................55.00
Cup and Saucer ................................................7.00
Gravy Boat, 8 1/2" l, attached undertray .......28.00
Plate
    6 1/4" d..........................................................5.00
    8 1/4" d..........................................................6.00
    9" d................................................................6.00
    10" d............................................................15.00
Platter, 13 1/2" l...............................................25.00
Relish Dish, 9" l...............................................10.00
Serving Bowl, 9" d...........................................15.00
Soup Bowl, Lug, 7 1/4" H-H .............................10.00

## ROSE POINT PATTERN
Bowl, 7 3/4" d ....................................................5.00
Cake Plate, 11 1/2" d.......................................40.00
Creamer, 3 1/2" h.............................................10.00
Cream Soup w/underplate ...............................10.00
Gravy Boat, attached undertray ......................32.00
Plate
    6 1/2" d, plain border ....................................8.00
    7 1/2" d, plain rim..........................................8.00
    10" d, plain rim.............................................10.00
Platter, 13" l, gold rim .....................................25.00
Sugar Bowl, Cov..............................................15.00
Vegetable Bowl, 9 1/2" d, plain border ..........15.00
Vegetable Bowl, Cov, 9" l................................45.00

## SILVER DAWN PATTERN
Butter Dish, Cov, 8 1/2" l...................................4.00
Cereal Bowl, 7" d...............................................3.00
Creamer .............................................................4.00
Gravy Boat, 8" l, w/attached undertray...........10.00
Sugar Bowl, Cov.................................................5.00
Vegetable Bowl, 10" l.......................................10.00

## WHEATLAND PATTERN
Creamer ............................................................16.00
Plate
    6" d................................................................6.00
    10" d.............................................................12.00
    Teapot..........................................................48.00

# Purinton Pottery

## Shippenville, Pennsylvania
## 1936-1959

**History:** Bernard Purinton was general manager at East Liverpool Potteries Company when it closed in the early 1930s. He founded Purinton Pottery in a small plant in Wellsville, Ohio in 1936. He developed a mechanical casting process for rapid manufacture of pottery on a production line.

The first products made were coffee, tea, and salad sets and other hand-painted decorative pieces in a folk art style in the "Peasant Ware" line. This line included Peasant Garden, Cactus Flower, Sun Flower and Desert Scene. After a short time Purinton outgrew its plant and moved to Shipppenville, Pennsylvania in 1941.

There was a large demand for American dinnerware and pottery since imports were severly restricted due to World War II. In 1940, Purinton got a patent for his unique casting process where a group of molds were immersed completely into a body of slip. Twenty to forty molds were done at one time. Handles and spouts were cast along with the main body. Teapot lids were also part of the molds.

Dorothy Purinton and William Blair, her brother, designed the patterns utilized on the wares and trained the decorators. The pottery was decorated free hand using mineral dyed slip, glazed with white glaze and then fired. All the pieces were hand painted with free brush patterns.

Patterns included: Apple, Chartreuse, Maywood, Palm Tree, Provincial Fruit, Fruit, Harmony, Ming Tree, Sarabond, Seaform, Heather Plaid, Intaglio, Normandy Plaid, Pennsylvania Dutch, and Tea Rose. Some of the patterns were named by the company, while others were named by authors and collectors. All pieces of dinnerware were made in these patterns along with a tremendous variety of accessory pieces.

Purinton pottery was made in canister sets, oil and vinegar bottles, teapots, cruets, candleholders, range sets, coffee pots, bean pots, vases, covered casseroles, divided relish dishes, and candy dishes. Identifying shape names were given to jugs such as Dutch, Kent, Rebecca, Oasis, and Honey.

Apple was the most popular pattern designed by William Brair in the 1940s. Intaglio was an incised design from 1950 that was done on a brown or blue-green background. A few artist signed one of a kind pieces were done by William and Dorothy.

Purinton cookie jars such as the pig with corn cob, Humpty Dumpty, and rooster are rare.

Purinton made pottery under contract for other companies such as Esmond Industries, National Pottery Company of Cleveland, Rubel Company, and Taylor, Smith, and Taylor.

In 1948, a second plant opened in Tionesta, Pennsylvania. By 1958, there were financial problems due to post war imports now coming to the US after the war restrictions were lifted.

Taylor, Smith, and Taylor bought stock in the company, but the plant closed in 1959.

There is a characteristic look to Purinton pottery with its hand painted designs, its simplicity, and original forms. Many pieces are not marked. Marked pottery usually had "Purinton Slipware," or "Purinton Slipware Hand Painted" in brown, or "Purinton Pottery" in teal.

**References:** Jamie Bero-Johnson & Jamie Johnson, *Purinton Pottery*, Schiffer Publishing Ltd. 1997; Susan Morris, *Purinton Pottery: An Identification & Value Guide*, Collector Books, 1994.

**Collectors' Club:** Purinton Pottery Convention, Lori Hinterleiter, P.O. Box 9394, Arlington, VA 22219, quarterly newsletter, $10; Purinton Pastimes, 20401 Ivy Bridge Court, Gaithersburg, MD 20879.

## APPLE SERIES
Chop Plate, 12" d, scalloped rim ................................. 58.00
Creamer, 4 1/2" h ........................................................ 20.00
Pitcher
    5 3/4" h, 2 pt.................................................... 50.00
    7" h .................................................................. 165.00
Plate, 9 1/2" d ............................................................. 35.00

Relish, 10" d, 3 section, center ring............................. 40.00
Shakers, 4 1/2" h, pr.................................................... 60.00
Sugar Bowl, Cov, 5 1/2" h ........................................... 25.00
Tea and Toast Set, 8 1/2" l .......................................... 15.00
Tray, 11 3/4" d ............................................................. 45.00
Tumbler, 5" h ............................................................... 25.00

## BLUE PANSY SERIES
Basket Planter, 6 1/2" h................................................ 55.00

## CHERRIES SERIES
Teapot, 5 3/4" h, 6 cup ................................................ 85.00

## CRESCENT FLOWER SERIES
Teapot, 6" h ................................................................. 90.00

## DAISY SERIES
Canister, 9" h, red trim................................................. 60.00
Rebecca Jug, 7 1/2" h .................................................. 60.00

## FRUIT SERIES
Bud Vase, 8" h............................................................. 95.00
Canister Set, 7" h, straight sides, revolving wood base
     ................................................................... 110.00
Creamer, 3 1/4" h ......................................................... 45.00
Grease Jar, 5 1/2" h ..................................................... 65.00
Pitcher
    5 1/2" h .............................................................. 32.00
    7" h .................................................................... 98.00
Teapot, 4 1/2" h ........................................................... 75.00
Tumbler, 3" h ............................................................... 20.00
Vinegar and Oil, 5" h, pr............................................... 65.00

## HALF BLOSSOM SERIES
Vase, 6 1/2" h ............................................................... 18.00

## HEATHER PLAID SERIES
Platter, 12 1/2" l............................................................ 25.00

## INTAGLIO SERIES
Butter Dish, 6 3/4" l, brown.......................................... 55.00
Cereal Bowl, 5" d, brown.............................................. 8.00
Cup and Saucer, brown................................................ 10.00
Mug, 4" h, paneled, brown ........................................... 30.00
Plate, 9 3/4" l, brown.................................................... 15.00
Tea and Toast Set, 8 1/2" l, dk brown.......................... 15.00

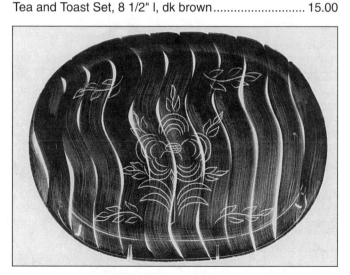

Tray, 12 1/2" l x 9 3/8" w, brown "Intaglio" pattern, $30.

Teapot, 7" h, brown.................................25.00
Tumbler, 5" h, brown, set of 4..................150.00
Vinegar Cruet, 5" h, brown .........................15.00

## IVY SERIES
Coffeepot, 7 3/4" h, red blossoms .............30.00
Dutch Jug, 5 3/4" h, red blossom ................30.00
Honey Jug, 6" h, red blossoms.....................35.00
Kent Jug, 4 3/4" h, red blossoms.................35.00
Teapot, red blossom
    5" h, 4 cup ..............................................40.00
    6" h, 6 cup ..............................................30.00

## MAYWOOD PATTERN
Chop Plate, 12" d ......................................70.00
Plate, 9 3/4" d..............................................5.00

## MING TREE PATTERN
Plate, 6 7/8" d.............................................55.00

## MISCELLANEOUS
Candleholder, 10" h, figural peasant lady, pr...........1,250.00
Shakers, 3" h, figural sailor and wife, blue and red trim, pr
.........................................................165.00
Vase, 6" h, cornucopia, ftd, blue flower ........25.00

## MORNING GLORY SERIES
Honey Jug, 6 1/4" h......................................55.00

## MOUNTAIN ROSE SERIES
Basket Planter, 6 1/2" h..............................30.00
Bud Vase, 6 1/4" h, dbl, handled .................35.00
Shakers, Range, pr.....................................80.00
Teapot, 4 1/2" h .........................................50.00
Vase, 6 1/4" h, bulbous shape, squared ends.............25.00

## NORMANDY PLAID SERIES
Bowl, 12" d ...............................................20.00
Cup and Saucer ........................................18.00
Grease Jar, Cov, 5 1/2" h............................45.00
Plate, 9" d.................................................20.00
Platter, 12" l..............................................52.00
Salad Bowl, 11" d ......................................90.00
Teapot, 6" h, 6 cup.....................................40.00
Vegetable Bowl
    8 1/2" d................................................40.00
    10 1/2" l, divided .................................50.00

## PALM TREE SERIES
Honey Jug, 6 3/4" h...................................225.00

## PENNSYLVANIA DUTCH SERIES
Jam, 5 1/2" l.............................................200.00
Kent Jug, 4 1/2" h ....................................330.00
Plate, 9 1/2" l.............................................25.00
Platter, 11" l..............................................45.00

## SEAFORM SERIES
Shakers, 3" h, pr........................................20.00
Teapot, 4 1/2" h, 2 cup, green and rose red design, made for
    Ming Tea Company.................................30.00
Vase, 6" h, cornucopia shape, brown, red and blue stylized
    floral design on side, cream ground.........32.00

## SHOOTING STAR SERIES
Honey Jug, 6" h .........................................40.00
    Vase, 5" h ............................................30.00

# Railroad China

**History:** China made for railroad dining cars was usually a basic, heavyweight, institutional grade ware that was also used for hospitals and restaurants. There were an endless variety of sizes, shapes, and patterns that were selected by each railroad. Pieces usually had heavy rolled edges, stout bottom rims, and were thick. Colorful company heralds were used to identify the railroad. Dining car china was also used as a promotional or advertising item to create interest in the railroad.

At first dining car china came from England and France, but the American manufacturers took over. More than sixty different factories made railroad china at some time. Many railroads did not have patterns especially designed for them. They would take a stock pattern from a manufacturer and customize it to suit their needs. The railroad name or logo would be placed on the top surface of a stock pattern example, usually below the border at the top of the piece. The border transfer would also be broken and the railroad name applied in the middle. Some patterns had the logo placed in the center of a piece. Sometimes the railroad had a backstamp applied to show the ownership of the stock pattern piece.

One of the most prolific manufacturers of railroad china was Buffalo China. Many examples were dated, but the date was when a pattern was designed or copyrighted. The Chesapeake and Ohio Railroad was one of its largest clients. In 1932, they created a set to celebrate the bicentennial of George Washington's birthday. Buffalo produced the Chessie cat for a train called "The Sportsman." Other Buffalo patterns included Flora of the South, Susquehanna, DeWitt Clinton, and Platinum Blue.

Syracuse China was a major manufacturer of railroad dining car china. The company started as Onondaga Pottery in the 1870s. Patterns included Adobe, Mimbreno, Chuck Wagon, DeWitt Clinton, Stampede, Berkshire, Chessie, Silhouette, Glory of the West, Wild Rose, to name just a few of the numerous patterns they made.

Hall China made numerous serving pieces for railroads. Shenango China in New Castle, Pennsylvania was another major manufacturer. McKinley, Flambeau, El Reno, Yellowstone, Mountain Laurel, Feather River, and such were some of Shenango's patterns.

Additional companies included Sterling, Warwick, Lenox, Scammell, Knowles, Taylor, Knowles, McNicol, Homer Laughlin, Fraunfelter, Iroquois, Mayer, and others.

**References:** Stanley L. Baker, *Railroad Collectibles: An Illustrated Value Guide, Fourth Edition*, Collector Books, 1990; Douglas W. McIntyre, *The Official Guide to Railroad Dining Car China*, published by author, 1990.

**Collectors' Clubs:** Railroadiana Collectors Association, Inc. Bob Chase, RCAI Memberships, 550 Veronica Place, Escondido, CA 92027. $15 per year, quarterly newsletter, *The Express;* Key, Lock and Lantern, P.O. Box 15, Spencerport, NY, quarterly newsletter.

**Museums:** Baltimore and Ohio Railroad, Baltimore, MD; California State Railroad Museum, Sacramento, CA; Charleston Railroad Artifacts Museum, SC; Mid-Continent Railway Historical Society, North Freedom, WI; Museum of

Transportation, Boston, MA; National Museum of Transport, St. Louis, MO; National Railroad Museum, Green Bay WI; New York Museum of Transportation, Albany, NY; Railroad Museum, Galveston Island, TX; Railroad Museum of Pennsylvania, Strasburg, PA.

**Reproduction Alert:** Museums, the railroads, and private corporations have all reproduced popular railroad china patterns. Some had paper stickers at one time, and some are identified on the back. Patterns being reproduced include AT&SF Mimbreno, B&O Centerary, and Pullman Indian Tree.

Fakes known as fantasy pieces may have a railroad name or logo and the look of railroad china, but are not identical in design to any pattern ever used by a railroad. Makers of these pieces are not reproducing original designs, but inventing new ones.

Hall, Homer Laughlin, and Sterling made reproductions in addition to making authentic period railroad china.

### ATCHISON TOPEKA SANTA FE
Bowl, 6" d, Mimbreno pattern w/rabbit......................... 100.00
Butter Pat
    Dk pink hummingbird design.................................... 75.00
    California Poppy pattern, Syracuse mk..................... 35.00
    Mimbreno Bird pattern .............................................. 60.00
Candy Dish, 6" d, California Poppy pattern
    .................................................................................... 150.00
Dish, Handled, 5 3/4" d, Black Chain pattern
    .................................................................................... 175.00
Plate
    7 1/2" d, Black Chain pattern ................................. 225.00
    8" d, California Poppy design, orange flowers, Syracuse
    .................................................................................... 58.00
Platter, 9 1/2" l, Black Chain pattern........................... 225.00

### ATLANTIC COAST LINE
Flora of the South pattern
    Compote, 2 1/2" h x 6 1/2" d................................. 110.00
    Plate, 7 7/8" d ......................................................... 85.00
Plate, 7 3/4" d, Carolina pattern, gray stripes, Sterling
    .................................................................................... 10.00

Plate, 7 5/8" d, "Indian Tree" pattern, black "PULLMAN" on top, Syracuse mk, $80.

### BALTIMORE AND OHIO
Compote, 6 3/4" d, ftd, Centennial pattern, blue ........ 100.00
Cup and Saucer, Demitasse, 1927 Centennial .......... 110.00
Plate, 10" d, Centennial pattern, blue, Shenango mk
    .................................................................................... 125.00
Vegetable Dish, 5 3/4" l, Centennial pattern, blue........ 50.00

### CHESAPEAKE & OHIO
Cup and Saucer, multicolored bust of George Washington
    on border w/gold bands, (A) ................................... 120.00
Plate, 9" d, multicolored bust of George Washington on border w/gold banding, (A) ........................................ 135.00

### CHICAGO BURLINGTON & QUINCY
Butter Pat, Violets and Daisies pattern, purple, white, and
    yellow...................................................................... 25.00
Platter, 12" l, Violets and Daisies pattern, purple, white, and
    yellow, Shenango ................................................... 35.00

### CHICAGO MILWAUKEE ST. PAUL & PACIFIC
Platter, 10" l x 8" w, Traveler pattern, pink and black ... 85.00

### DENVER AND RIO GRANDE
Cup and Saucer, blue center logo and border stripes
    .................................................................................... 50.00

### FRED HARVEY
Egg Cup, Dbl, black chain pattern, Shenango mk ..... 100.00
El Tovar Hotel design, med blue
    Cup and Saucer, Syracuse...................................... 65.00
    Plate
        6 1/8" d............................................................. 35.00
        7" d.................................................................... 45.00
    Platter, 13 1/2" l, Syracuse .................................... 95.00

### GREAT NORTHERN
Ashtray, 4" d, mountain w/goat and evergreens, green and
    gray........................................................................... 75.00
Plate
    6 1/2" d, Mountain and Flowers pattern, yellow, gold, and
        red .................................................................... 55.00
    7" d, Glory of the West pattern, green and gray, Syracuse
    .................................................................................... 75.00
    7 1/4" d, Mountain and Flowers pattern, yellow, gold, and
        red, Syracuse.................................................. 65.00
Platter, 9" l, Mountain and Flowers pattern, yellow, gold, and
    red, Syracuse ......................................................... 225.00
Sauce Dish, Mountain and Flowers pattern ................. 95.00
Soup Bowl, 6 1/4" d, Glory of the West pattern, green and
    gray........................................................................... 75.00

### NEW GEORGIA
Plate, 9 3/4" d, red trim and logo, Shenango mark ...... 40.00

### NEW YORK CENTRAL
Celery Dish, 10" l, Mercury design, brown, Syracuse mk
    .................................................................................... 100.00
Plate, 9" d, Mercury design, brown, Syracuse mk........ 80.00
Tray, 8 1/4" l, DeWitt Clinton design, blue, Buffalo mk
    .................................................................................... 225.00

### NORTHERN PACIFIC
Plate, 7 1/2" d, Yellowstone Park Line, red and black logo on
    border, green and orange stripes ........................... 70.00

## PENNSYLVANIA

Celery Dish, 9" l, Keystone, logo, and pinstripe pattern, War-
  wick mk ................................................................... 115.00

Plate

  7 1/4" d, dk brown Keystone and stripes on border,
    Scammell................................................................. 45.00

  8 3/4" d, red Keystone and stripes on border .......... 50.00

  10" d, Purple Laurel design...................................... 40.00

Platter, 11" l, Keystone logo, pinstripe border, Syracuse
  ................................................................................. 100.00

## PULLMAN

Dish, 7 1/2" H-H, Calumet design, Syracuse............. 250.00

## SOUTHERN PACIFIC

Bowl, 6 1/2" l, Sunset pattern, Syracuse mk ............. 140.00

Butter Pat, Sunset pattern, Buffalo Pottery mk.......... 225.00

Cup, California Poppy, orange flowers ......................... 35.00

Plate

  7 1/2" d, Prairie Mountain Wildflowers, red, yellow, and
    blue shades, black stripe..................................... 75.00

  10 1/4" d, Sunset design on border, Buffalo pottery
    ............................................................................. 150.00

Platter

  9" l, Sunset pattern, leaf border, green .................. 145.00

  12 1/2" l, "Golden State" and oranges design, green
    striped rim, Syracuse............................................ 90.00

## UNION PACIFIC

Bouillon Cup, Harriman Blue ........................................ 35.00

Bowl

  4 3/4" d, Streamliner pattern, Sterling.................... 20.00

  5 1/4" d, Challenger pattern, Syracuse mk
    ............................................................................... 35.00

  6" d, Harriman Blue.................................................. 25.00

  6 1/2" d, Streamliner pattern, Scammell ................ 35.00

Butter Pat, Challenger pattern...................................... 20.00

Child's Serving Plate, 8" d, Circus Series-multicolored clown
  ................................................................................. 140.00

Plate

  6 1/2" d, Challenger pattern, blue and red lettering and
    stripes.................................................................... 45.00

  7" d

    Harriman Blue drape on rim, Scammell .............. 48.00

    Streamliner pattern, Sterling mk.......................... 45.00

  8 5/8" d, Streamliner pattern, Trenton mk
    ............................................................................... 30.00

  10 3/4" d, Streamliner pattern, Sterling mk ............. 75.00

Platter

  8" l, Desert Flower pattern green shades, Syracuse
    ............................................................................... 65.00

  8 1/4" l, Streamliner pattern, Scammell ................... 40.00

  9" l, Harriman Blue ................................................... 50.00

  11" l, Harriman Blue ................................................. 70.00

Serving Bowl, 8" l, Harriman Blue, Maddock mk ........ 140.00

Sherbet Bowl, 4 5/8" d, Streamliner pattern ................ 30.00

Soup Bowl, 7 1/2" d, Streamliner pattern, Scammell.... 45.00

## WESTERN PACIFIC

  Plate, 7 1/2" d, Feather River Route, red and black letter-
    ing, tan ground ..................................................... 75.00

# Red Cliff Pottery

## Chicago, Illinois
## 1950-1980

**History:** Red Cliff Pottery in Chicago, Illinois was a decorating and distributing company that decorated many ironstone
pieces utilizing the old patterns and shapes.

Red Cliff sent original pieces of English Tea Leaf Ironstone China to Hall China for them to copy for Red Cliff. Hall
China made these Tea Leaf wares for Red Cliff in the 1950s
and 1960s. All of them were clearly marked.

Some of the flatware Tea Leaf pieces were made for Red
Cliff by the Walker China Company of Bedford Heights,
Ohio. All of the hollow ware and molded Tea Leaf pieces
were made by Hall China.

Bowl, 9 1/2" d, "Heirloom" pattern ............................... 20.00

Candelabrum, 11 1/2" l x 7" h, 3 light, relief molded grape
  design, pr................................................................ 75.00

Casserole, Cov, 13 1/2" H-H, grapes and leaves pattern
  ................................................................................... 60.00

Cereal Bowl, 6" H-H ........................................................ 8.00

Coffeepot, 10" h, tapered paneled body....................... 75.00

Creamer, Sugar Bowl, and Tray, leaf pattern ............ 125.00

Cup and Saucer

  Copper tea leaf design .......................................... 15.00

  "Heirloom" pattern.................................................. 10.00

Gravy Boat, 4" h, w/undertray, 12" H-H, ladle, squat shape
  w/raised leaves on base ........................................ 35.00

**Tureen, 14 1/2" h, white ironstone, $165.**

Milk Pitcher, 7 3/4" h, lobed body, relief of wheat on sides
................................................................................30.00
Pitcher
    5 1/2" h, leaf pattern......................................................30.00
    6 1/2" h, ribbed, emb grapes and leaves on sides...70.00
    6 3/4" h, paneled.........................................................25.00
    10" h, beaded design on base, fancy handle w/thumb rest
    ................................................................................35.00
Pitcher and Bowl Set, pitcher, 3 1/4" h, bowl, 4 5/8" d, molded hanging grapes around base of pitcher.......25.00
Plate
    8 3/4" d, "Heirloom" pattern.....................................18.00
    10 1/4" d, relief of blue-purple grapes, green leaves on border..................................................................12.00
    11" d, "Heirloom" pattern.........................................20.00
Serving Bowl, 9" d, lobed body, molded grape pattern.20.00
Soup Plate
    9" d, grapes and leaves pattern..............................10.00
    9 1/2" d, "Heirloom" pattern.....................................20.00
Teapot
    10" h, grapes and leaves pattern..........................100.00
    10 1/2" h, leaf pattern.............................................125.00
Tureen, Cov, 12" H-H
    11" h, w/ladle, lobed body.........................................60.00
    12" h
        Oct, molded center band of grape clusters, figural grapes and stem knob.....................................50.00
        W/underplate and ladle, relief molded wheat pattern
        ................................................................100.00
    15 3/4" H-H x 10 1/4" h, w/undertray and ladle, scalloped rib design...........................................................85.00
Vegetable Bowl, 9" l, relief grape design on border, (A)
................................................................................25.00
    Vegetable Bowl, Cov, 10 1/2" H-H, ftd, paneled body, fruit knob..........................................................................56.00

# Redware

## East, Midwest, South
## 17th Century-early 20th Century

**History:** Redware was made in all the colonies to meet the utilitarian needs for food preparation and all types of storage vessels. Most redware was thrown on a wheel; handles and spouts were formed separately and then attached. Pie plates and platters were drape molded. Not many pieces were made by press molding or slip casting.

Redware pieces were seldom marked. Similar forms were made over long periods of time in many different areas. A tremendous variety of forms was produced by American redware potters. The vast majority of pieces were not decorated at all. They had a basic glaze of lead and silica which fired to a clear, shiny finish. Pieces could be glazed by dipping, or glaze could be poured in or painted on. The bottoms and sometimes the rims were left unfinished since they would fuse together in the kiln.

The clear glaze was used most of the time, but three basic colorants also were used. Iron oxide produced a range of browns, copper oxide produced green, and manganese dioxide resulted in brown to jet black finishes. Colored glazes could completely cover a piece or be applied to some areas with a sponge or brush.

White slip was either trailed or brushed on pieces as a decorative element or as a background for additional deco-

ration. With sgraffito decoration, pieces were covered with thick white slip and then designs were scratched through to reveal the redware body underneath. Green, yellow, brown, or black were used to highlight the piece.

Most decorations were done freehand, but some pieces were done with a paper pattern. Decorated pieces usually were intended for display or gifts. Some early redware pieces were dated and signed by the potters. Redware was very fragile, and pieces were usually sold in the immediate area where it was made.

During the 18th and 19th centuries, most of the items made were to meet domestic needs. Tablewares made included bowls in many sizes, platters, porringers, cups, mugs, beakers, goblets, and serving dishes such as compotes, bread baskets, divided vegetable bowls, tureens, and cake stands. Trivets, eggcups, teapots, coffeepots, sugar bowls, salts, pitchers in sizes from 1/2 pint creamers to 2 gallon ciders, puzzle jugs, and beer pitchers were all made. Cooking and baking utensils found form in bean pots, stew pots, pipkins in 1 pint to 1 gallon size, pudding pans, bakers, nappys, roasting pans and skillets, pie plates, cake and jelly molds, milk pans, cream and butter pots, and churns.

Jugs, jars, pots, and crocks were made for food and drink storage along with water coolers, flasks and bottles. Pitchers and wash bowls, barber bowls, shaving mugs, soap dishes, spittoons, chamber pots, bed pans, pap boats and hot water bottles also were made in redware. Fat lamps, candlesticks, fishing lamps, candle molds, and match holders also were made along with toys and miniatures including salesmens' samples. Some figural pieces were made for mantel decorations. By 1900, flower pots, decorative terra cotta for builders, and many novelty items were made for promotional purposes.

Glass, tin, and iron gradually replaced redware storage and utilitarian pieces when they became available. Redware dishes were standard until that time since pewter was expensive and difficult to get, and wood was hard to clean. By the mid 19th century, European imports and later American ironstone replaced redware dishes.

The majority of the early New England redware potters came from Massachusetts where they followed the British traditions. The other eastern states of New Hampshire, Vermont, Connecticut, Rhode Island, and Maine all had potters working on redwares. In New York State, redwares were made from the 1650s until 1942.

Pennsylvania became the most important American redware center. From the 17th until the 20th centuries, their designs showed the English and German influences. More sgraffito designs pieces were made there. Many of these artistic pieces were marked.

In the South, North Carolina was best known for redware pottery, while some was made in other mid Atlantic and southern states. Some redwares were made in the midwest, and very little was done in the south and west.

**References:** William C. Ketchum, Jr. *American Redware*, Henry Holt and Company, 1991; Kevin McConnell, *Redware: America's Folk Art Pottery, 2nd Edition*, Schiffer Publishing Ltd.1999.

**Museums:** Bennington Museum, VT; Brooklyn Museum, NY; Henry Ford Museum and Greenfield Village, Dearborn, MI; Henry Frances du Pont Winterthur, DE; Shelburne Museum, VT; Wadsworth Atheneum, Hartford, CT.

Apple Butter, Jar, 5" h, applied handle, tooled lines, brown splotches, dk orange ground, (A).........................578.00
Bean Pot, 9" h, incised wavy line on shoulder, ear handles, Pennsylvania.......................................................200.00
Bowl
    5 1/4" d, ftd, brown spots on orange ground, (A)...303.00

6 3/4" d, mottled green glaze with brown specks and amber spots, white slip ext rim, (A) .................. 275.00

8 5/8" d, wavy and straight yellow slip lines, (A) ....275.00

9" d, yellow slip and red design, applied finger crimped rim, hairlines, (A) ............................................... 330.00

14 3/4" d, white slip curlicues and squiggles, dk brown glaze, rim chips, (A)........................................ 1,980.00

Butter Tub, 9 1/4" l, vert twisted handles, orange-brown glaze w/overall manganese spots, sgd "John Bell, Waynesboro," chips and hairlines, (A) ................ 1,400.00

Charger, 11 3/4" d, yellow slip curved lines, hairline ..985.00

Chicken Feeder, 7" h, dome-shaped, flat knob, unglazed ext, (A) ..................................................................... 25.00

**Bottle, 8 3/4" h, red-brown body w/black flecks, c1860, $280.**

Creamer

2 1/8" h, cup shape, applied handle, reeded base, green and mottled brown glaze on orange ground, chips, (A) ...................................................................... 303.00

3" h, applied handle, brown fleck glaze, (A) .......... 110.00

Crock, 7 1/4" h, ovoid shape, dk brown glaze, sgd "John Bell, Waynesboro," (A)........................................... 120.00

Dish

4" d, orange glazed ground w/yellow slip crow's ft design, coggle rim, (A)...................................................... 700.00

6 1/2" d, brown daubs, salmon ground, chips, (A) ............................................................................. 82.00

7 1/2" d

Orange glazed int, black patina on ext and rim, hairlines, (A) ...................................................... 303.00

Yellow slip pinwheel design, rim chips, (A)........ 138.00

11 3/4" l, brown and green spots, orange ground, (A) ............................................................................. 660.00

Doorstop, 10 1/4" h, cast figural seated dog, unglazed, "imp Superior Uhrichsville, O." (A)................................. 385.00

Figure

4" h, standing Uncle Sam, polychrome accents, (A) ............................................................................. 275.00

10" h, molded and tooled bust of man w/full period wig, brown glaze, (A)................................................. 770.00

Flask

7" h, dk brown splotch, dk orange ground, (A) ...... 385.00

8 1/2" h, red-yellow glaze, c1830, (A) ................. 132.00

Flower Pot, 5" h, attached saucer, yellow slip and brown glaze, mottled orange, cream, and brown finish, hairlines, (A) ....................................................................... 358.00

Food Mold

5 1/2" d, Turk's head................................................ 60.00

8" d, Turk's head, fluted, brown daubing, chips, (A) ............................................................................. 85.00

Grease Lamp, 4" h, green-amber glaze w/brown flecks, chips and rim damage, (A).................................... 193.00

Jar

6 3/8" h, dk brown streaks, orange brown ground, hairline, (A)............................................................... 275.00

7 1/2" h, ovoid, dk red glaze, "imp JOHN BELL, WAYNESBORO," hairline, (A)........................... 275.00

8 5/8" h, greenish glaze w/amber spots and brown brushed spirals, chips, (A)............................... 853.00

12 1/2" h, ovoid, applied shoulder handles, tooled lines, dk brown glaze w/brown flecks, (A)............... 2,420.00

Jar, Cov

7 1/2" h, gallery lip, dk brown next pattern, burnt orange ground, chips, (A)............................................... 523.00

8" h, mottled amber, yellow and green w/dk brown daubs on greenish glazed ground, (A)...................... 1,485.00

Jug, Ovoid Shape

3 5/8" h, ribbed strap handle and tooled lines, brown splotches and green mottled glaze on amber ground, (A) ................................................................. 4,510.00

7 1/4" h, applied ribbed handle, brown flecks on metallic amber ground, rim chips, (A)........................... 193.00

8 1/2" h, mottled green glaze, strap handle, (A) ...... 82.00

8 3/4" h, applied strap handle, black splotches on dk brown ground, (A) .............................................. 302.00

9 1/4" h, green-amber glaze, brown flecks, (A) ..... 138.00

11" h, ribbed strap handle, dk brown glaze, (A)..... 138.00

**Plate, 8 1/2" d, yellow slip designs, beaded rim, rim chips, c1860, $375.**

**Loaf Pan**

14" l, 3 sets of 3 parallel yellow wavy yellow lines, yellow vert slip designs between, coggled rim, (A).......715.00

14 1/4" l, 4 yellow slip lines, coggled rim, chips and wear, (A)............................................................770.00

17" l, 3 wavy yellow slip lines, coggled rim, (A) .....715.00

**Milk Bowl**, 11" d, wavy and straight brown and yellow slip lines, chips and hairlines, (A)................................385.00

**Mug**

3 1/2" h, applied handle, flared rim, dk brown splotches, burnt orange ground, chips, (A).........................138.00

3 5/8" h, applied handle, tooled horiz bands, dk brown glaze, (A) ......................................................121.00

4 7/8" h, applied ribbed handle, tooled bands w/dk burnt orange and brown streaks, chips, (A)................138.00

6 3/8" h, applied ribbed handle, brown splashes on green-orange ground, chips and hairlines, (A) ..330.00

**Mush Cup**, 3 3/4" h, applied handle, dk brown amber glaze, crazing, (A)........................................................194.00

**Pie Plate**

7 7/8" d

Coggled rim, brown and green accented yellow slip designs, gray-amber ground, (A)..................550.00

Yellow slip splashes.........................................550.00

8" d, 3 line yellow slip design, coggled rim, hairline, (A) ......................................................................385.00

8 1/8" d, brown splotches, salmon ground, wear and crazing, (A) .........................................................220.00

8 1/4" d

Brown daubs, orange ground, (A) ..................1,155.00

Three wavy yellow slip lines, chips, (A).............275.00

8 3/8" d, wavy white slip lines, dk brown and green flecked glaze, (A)............................................550.00

8 1/2" d, wavy yellow slip lines, straight brown lines, coggled rim, (A) ..............................................412.00

9" d, splashed yellow slip dots, coggled rim, chips and hairline, (A) ..........................................................150.00

10" d

Three wavy, intersecting yellow slip lines, coggled rim, chips, (A).......................................................468.00

Yellow slip bird on branch, coggled rim, hairlines, (A) ......................................................................3,410.00

10 1/2" d, yellow slip seaweed design, coggled rim, hairlines and chips, (A)........................................1,622.00

11" d, 2 yellow slip lines, coggled rim, chips, (A) ...192.00

**Pitcher**

6 3/4" h, ribbed strap handle, brown splotches, lt brown ground, (A) .......................................................220.00

8 5/8" h, arched handle, applied rosebud and leaves under spout w/curved stem w/roses and leaves, dk brown glaze, (A) .................................................200.00

11" h, ribbed strap handle, molded lip, dk brown splotches, orange ground, (A) .........................495.00

**Pitcher, Cov**, 10 3/4" h, yellow slip daubs, brown and green accents, clear mottled green glaze, brown glazed int, ribbed strap handle, wood lid, (A) .......................9,900.00

**Pot**, 5 1/2" h, ovoid, strap handle, mottled amber and tan w/brown flecks, (A)..............................................165.00

**Pot, Cov**, 6 1/2" h, dk brown vert splotches, strap handle, spout, and lid, (A)...................................................138.00

**Pudding Jar**, 6 3/8" h, Albany slip glaze ......................39.00

**Sugar Bowl, Cov**, 5 3/4" h, dk blue glaze, "incised Made by I.S. Stahl, July 6, 1939" label, (A) ......................220.00

**Teapot**, 7" h, yellow slip and sgraffito swirled design, cat's head finial and yellow, blue, and green dots, chips, (A) .............................................................................. 358.00

# Red Wing Potteries

**Red Wing, Minnesota**
**1877-1967**

# RumRill Pottery

**Little Rock, Arkansas**
**1930s-1942**

**History:** The Red Wing Stoneware Company operated in Red Wing, Minnesota from 1877-1906. David Hallum, who originally used the Goodhue clay for utilitary stonewares, was the chief engineer. The clay was a light tan/gray that retained its original color. Decorations on the utilitarian stoneware examples were done by the slip cup method. The Red Wing area potters did not use brushes to decorate their pieces. The early works were hand drawn.

Various types of glazes were used, such as salt glaze and Bristol glaze. Albany slip coated the inside of the crocks. Not all pieces were marked. Some stoneware examples had a stamp on the crock front indicating "Red Wing Stoneware Company." By 1888, the Red Wing Stoneware Company was the biggest producer of stoneware in America. At that time, everything was stored in stonewares. The more complicated designs and cruder pottery pieces indicate earlier examples. The butterfly was the first trademark, and the leaf was the second one used by Red Wing.

Red Wing decorated its utilitarian stoneware with drawings of animals, flowers, birds, or geometric designs in blue made from cobalt oxide. Examples included water jars, crocks in all sizes, meat jars with covers, butter jars, churns, and the like. Many pieces were used by companies to advertise their wares and had a square or picture on the front with the company's name and address on fruit jars, honey jars, cheese crocks, mixing bowls, and whiskey or druggists' chemical jugs. Pottery from Red Wing had heavy, rounded rims, ear handles, and good uniformity of color and smoothness of the salt glaze.

**Minnesota Stoneware Company 1883-1906**

These pieces had raised letters from a pressing mold on the bottoms of their stonewares in a circle or double circle. The early examples had "Red Wing" after "Minnesota Stoneware." They added "Minn." to Red Wing when they started to ship out of state.

**North Star Stoneware Company 1892-1896**

This stoneware company was only operating for a four year period. They used a star on the bottom of all the early pieces. Some examples were marked "North" in the star points.

## Union Stoneware Company 1894-1906

The Union Stoneware Company was formed as a selling agency of the three large potteries: Red Wing, North Star, and Minnesota Stoneware Company. North Star was bought out by the other two companies in 1896.

## Red Wing Union Stoneware Company 1906-1936

In 1906, the three companies merged into a single company called the Red Wing Union Stoneware Company. Utilitarian stonewares continued to be made. About 1912, they added a red wing as a trademark on their products.

## Red Wing Potteries, Inc. 1936-1967

In 1936, the legal name of the potteries was changed to Red Wing Potteries, Inc. In 1947, it stopped making stonewares.

Red Wing made art pottery from about 1929 until it closed in 1967. Primarily vases were made, but it added planters, figurines, candleholders, bowls, compotes, ashtrays, and what-nots. They were offered in a wide range of styles, shapes, and glazes, but they were still only a small part of the company's output. The company's "Brushed Ware" was a stoneware clay with the body stained green with the highlights brushed to expose the natural clay. By 1931, the company expanded its offerings to include 130 Glazed Ware and 74 Brushed Ware pieces.

It also produced "kitchen ware" including cookie jars, teapots, coffee servers, water pitchers, mugs, casseroles, bowls, and serving plates.

Red Wing produced art pottery for the mass market at affordable prices in about 1930, with smooth glazes and classical forms. Its art pottery was made for four decades. More than two thousand different styles or shapes were made. Each was assigned a unique number, but sometimes the numbers were repeated. In 1953, Red Wing celebrated its 75th anniversary with the introduction of some specialty glazes. It used over-lay glazes and a glaze called "fleck." From the late 1930s until the end of production in 1967, Red Wing made approximately 84 different patterns of dinnerware. The most popular hand painted lines were Bob White from 1956 and Round Up from 1958. Solid color dinnerwares were also popular lines. Foreign competition, a decaying physical plant, and a factory workers strike finally forced the pottery to close in 1967.

**References:** Stan Bougie and David Newkirk, *Red Wing Dinnerwares*, available from authors, 1981; Dan and Gail DePasquale & Larry Peterson, *Red Wing Collectibles*, Collector Books, 1997; _____, *Red Wing Stoneware*, Collector Books, 1997; B.L. & R.L. Dollen, *Red Wing Art Pottery Books I & II*, Collector Books, 1997, 1998; Ray Reiss, *Red Wing Art Pottery*, Property, 1996; _____, *Red Wing Art Pottery #2*, 2000; Bonnie Tefft, *Red Wing Potters and Their Wares*, Locust Enterprises, 1981; Lyndon C. Viel, *The Clay Giants: The Stoneware of Red Wing, Goodhue County, Minnesota, Book 3*, Wallace-Homestead, 1987.

**Collectors' Clubs:** Red Wing Collectors Society, Inc. John & Kim Key, P.O. Box 50, Red Wing, MN 55066, bimonthly newsletter, $20.

**Museums:** Goodhue County Historical Society Museum, Red Wing, MN; Kenosha Public Museum, WI.

# RumRill

**History:** The RumRill Pottery Company was originally founded in 1930 in Little Rock, Arkansas as the Arkansas Products Company which was a distributing and selling company for Camark in 1932. In the early 1930s, George RumRill contracted with Red Wing pottery to produce RumRill pottery for George to sell and distribute through his RumRill Pottery Company. Wares were often called "RumRill by Red Wing."

Belle Kogan was one of the Red Wing artists who designed figures for RumRill. Some have the letter "B" before the Red Wing mark. Figures included Bird, Oriental Man, Oriental Goddess, Cowboy, Cowgirl, Dancing Girl, Man playing accordion, Tom Sawyer lad, and such.

Other pieces made were ashtrays, cookie, jars, jardinieres, mugs, candlesticks, trays, bowls, and other items. Impressed marks were used on artwares, as well as silver paper labels. A variety of glazes included soft velvety matte, matte, and gloss. Different colored glazes were used on the outside and inside of pieces. One popular line in soft ivory matte glaze had brown color sprayed on and then lightly rubbed off.

George RumRill broke with Red Wing in 1939 and moved production of RumRill to Florence Pottery of Mt. Gilead, Ohio after having it made at the Bates Company in Chicago for a short time. Some pieces were designed by RumRill family members. Flower containers and vases were the main products. By 1939, Florence Pottery made the entire RumRill line. Between 1939-1943, George Rumrill and Lawton Gonder had a marketing relationship for pottery since Gonder was general manager at Florence. Wares were also made at Shawnee Pottery Company in Zanesville, Ohio after being made at Florence.

Florence was destroyed by fire in 1941, and RumRill's entire stock and molds were destroyed. With no inventory, no factory, and the start of World War II restricting access to raw materials, the RumRill Company closed in 1943.

Some pieces were inkstamped "RumRill." Many pieces made at Red Wing had paper labels. Often examples were unmarked. Pieces made at other factories than Red Wing usually had "Made in USA" in the mark.

**Reference:** Dolores Simon, *Red Wing Pottery with RumRill*, Collector Books, 1980.

**Collectors' Club:** RumRill Society, Francesca Malone-Gern, P.O. Box 2161, Hudson, OH 44235, newsletter.

## ART POTTERY
Bowl
    6 3/4" d, pointed spikes, turquoise ground w/black speckles ..................................................................... 16.00
    7" d, Brushware, raised cranes design on ext, green ext w/brown accents, green int, "RED WING UNION STONE WARE" mk ........................................... 75.00
Console Bowl
    9" d, shell shape, speckled turquoise glaze ............ 45.00
    12" l, dk yellow ext, dk green int, "RED WING USA B 2015" mark ...................................................... 26.00
    13" l, free form, rolled edge, burgundy ext, gray int, #1304 .................................................................... 30.00
Dish, 7 1/4" d, leaf shape, magenta glaze .................... 42.00
Figure
    5" h, seated frog, green ......................................... 225.00
    8 3/4" h, School Girl, red-brown, blue, white, and green, #1121 ................................................................ 650.00
Planter
    3" h
        9 5/8" l, rect, yellow bamboo ext, dk green int, "RED WING USA 431" mark ................................... 34.00
        11" l, blue ground, black speckles, #M1495 ........ 22.00

5"w x 10 1/4" l, tapered rect shape, indented sides, white ext, turquoise int, "RED WING USA 1265" mk ..................................................................28.00

14 1/2" h, figural violin, rust......................80.00

15" h, figural banjo, white........................80.00

Vase

6 1/2" h, Brushware, squat shape, 2 loop handles, relief molded overlapped leaves, gray-brown ext, green int ...........................................................285.00

7" h, 2 handles, imp leaves and acorns, green and tan ground, chip on base, (A) ....................231.00

7 1/4" h, figural fawn and leaves on flared body, blue and lavender, #1120 ....................................58.00

7 1/2" h

Brushware, raised brown floral and starfish design and scales, green int..............................85.00

**Pitcher, 6 1/2" h, RumRill, orange, $55.**

Elephant handles, cobalt..................................195.00

7 5/8" h, flattened center w/raised stylized flower, horiz banded rolled ends, copper, #765......................62.00

8" h

Cylinder shape, sm handles on each side, raised bust of woman and deer, tan glaze, turquoise int .....................................................110.00

Prismatique line, celadon ext, orange int ...........32.00

Urn shape, turquoise glaze, #763 .....................35.00

9 1/2" h, trophy shape, rect handles, 4 vert panels of yellow raised trees, dk green body, (A).................220.00

10" h, cornucopia shape, emb flowerheads on base, yellow ext, red-brown int, "RED WING USA 1290" mk ..................................................................38.00

10 1/2" h, figural woman in turquoise gown, 2 ribbed gray engobe ribbed cylinders at sides, glazed magenta ints .....................................................600.00

12" h, gladiolus, 5 tube, gloss blue glaze w/gold flecks, #416, (A) ....................................................115.00

12 1/4" h, trophy shape, 2 rect handles, gloss yellow panels of woodland scenes, matte brown body, "imp Red Wing Union Stoneware Co. Red Wing, Minn. 163" mk, (A) .................................................................302.00

12 1/2" h, architectural handles, lt blue, #155........110.00

14 1/2" h, bottle shape, applied stylized figures, beads, and geometrics, green and yellow crystalline glaze, #M3103, (A) .......................................................660.00

### ARDENNES PATTERN-PROVINCIAL SHAPE
Chop Plate, 14" d ...........................................45.00

### BLOSSOM TIME PATTERN-CONCORD SHAPE
Bowl, 7 1/2" sq ..............................................5.00
Serving Bowl, 8 1/2" sq ..................................15.00

### BOB WHITE PATTERN-CASUAL SHAPE
Casserole, Cov, 13" H-H x 8" h ....................................65.00
Creamer .................................................................28.00
Cup and Saucer ......................................................8.00
Lazy Susan, 12" d ...............................................250.00
Pitcher, 12" h .......................................................55.00
Plate
6 1/2" d ..................................................................4.00
10 1/2" d ................................................................8.00

**Vase, 10 1/2" h, yellow ext, brown int, "RED WING USA 1290" mk, $38.**

**Pitcher, 6 1/4" h, "Sponge Band," rust and blue banding, tan ground, blue circ "Made in Red Wing" mk, hairline, $75.**

Platter, 12" l ....................................................35.00
Shakers, Pr
    2" h, mushroom shape...............................35.00
    6" h.............................................................30.00
Sugar Bowl, Cov....................................................28.00
Tumbler, 4" h, set of 4.........................................105.00
Vegetable Bowl, 14" l, divided ..............................50.00
Water Pitcher, 11 3/4" h........................................59.00

### BRITTANY PATTERN-PROVINCIAL SHAPE
Plate, 10 1/4" d ....................................................19.00
Teapot, 6 1/4" h.....................................................65.00

### CAPISTRANO PATTERN-ANNIVERSARY SHAPE
Bowl
    5 1/2" d............................................................10.00
    8" d.................................................................28.00
Buffet Bowl, 9" d....................................................30.00
Cake plate, 6 1/2" d..................................................9.00
Creamer ..................................................................15.00
Cup and Saucer ....................................................10.00
Nappy, 8" d.............................................................15.00
Plate
    6" d...................................................................5.00
    8" d...................................................................8.00
    11" d...............................................................20.00
Platter
    13" l................................................................25.00
    15" l................................................................25.00
Sugar Bowl, Cov....................................................20.00

### COUNTRY GARDEN PATTERN-ANNIVERSARY SHAPE
Platter, 15" l ..........................................................30.00

### DRIFTWOOD PATTERN-ANNIVERSARY SHAPE
Gravy Boat .............................................................25.00
Plate, 10 1/2" d ......................................................12.00

**Plate, 10 1/2" sq, "Lotus" pattern, "Concord" shape, $10.**

### FRUIT PATTERN-CONCORD SHAPE
Deviled Egg Plate...............................................135.00

### GRANADA PATTERN
Bowl, 8 1/2" d .........................................................15.00
Plate, 10 3/8" d .......................................................10.00
Platter, 15" l ...........................................................30.00
Vegetable Bowl, 11 1/2" d ......................................30.00

### LANTERNS PATTERN-CONCORD SHAPE
Cereal Bowl, 7 1/2" d...............................................4.00
Egg Tray, Cov........................................................235.00
Plate
    6 1/2" d.............................................................3.00
    10 1/2" d...........................................................5.00

### LEXINGTON PATTERN-CONCORD SHAPE
Creamer ...................................................................8.00
Cup and Saucer ....................................................10.00
Plate
    6 1/2" d...........................................................10.00
    7 1/2" d...........................................................12.00
Sugar Bowl, Cov....................................................12.00

### LOTUS PATTERN-CONCORD SHAPE
Berry Bowl, 5 1/4" sq...............................................5.00
Beverage Server, 12" h ..........................................20.00
Bowl, 8 1/2" sq..........................................................8.00
Casserole, Cov.......................................................20.00
Creamer and Cov Sugar Bowl ...............................12.00
Cup and Saucer ......................................................6.00
Plate
    6 1/2" sq...........................................................4.00
    10 1/2" sq.......................................................10.00
Relish Dish, 8 1/2" l ...............................................10.00
Shakers, pr...............................................................6.00
Tidbit, 11" h, 2 tier.................................................35.00

### LUTE SONG PATTERN
Cup and Saucer ......................................................8.00
Platter, 12 1/2" l .....................................................15.00
Salad Bowl, 11 1/4" d .............................................65.00
Serving Bowl, 8 3/4" d ...........................................25.00

### MAGNOLIA PATTERN-CONCORD SHAPE
Console Bowl, 12" d..............................................115.00
Cup and Saucer .....................................................10.00
Soup Plate, 10 1/2" d ...............................................9.00

### MISCELLANEOUS
Bowl
    6 3/4" d, Saffron, blue bands .................................35.00
    10" d, sponge band..............................................165.00
Butter Jar, 4 7/8" h, brown glaze, imp mk....................40.00
Canning Jar, 6 1/4" h, black transfer printed "STONE, MASON-FRUIT JAR, UNION STONEWARE CO. RED WING, MINN." zinc lid, (A)....................................275.00
Chicken Feeder, 11" h, "blue Ko-Rec Feeder Red Wing Union Stoneware Co." on front ............................250.00
Churn, 18 1/2" h, 5 gallon, 2 blue leaves and "UNION STONEWARE CO. RED WING, MINN." in oval .... 525.00
Cov Dish, 8" l x 6" h, figural rooster, yellow.................45.00

Crock

    2 3/4" h, red wing and blue oval "RED WING STONE-WARE CO. RED WING MN" on front .................. 20.00

    5" h, 4 birch leaves, "cobalt oval RED WING STONE-WARE CO. RED WING, MN, 35" ........................ 35.00

    13 1/2" h, "blue 5," red wing, "blue Patent Dec. 21, 1915" ...................................................................... 50.00

    24" h, "blue 30," red wing, "blue Red Wing Union Stone-ware Co." on front ........................ 165.00

Custard Cup, 2 1/2" h, sponge band ........................ 190.00

Jar, 15" h, ball lock, red wing and blue "3" on front .... 175.00

Jug

    14 1/4" h, beehive shape, 5 gallon, single red wing ........................................................................ 385.00

    19 " h, straight sides, "blue 5," large red wing ........ 150.00

Koverwate Dish, 10 1/4" d, #5, gray and blue ........... 250.00

Mixing Bowl

    7 1/8" d, white ground, wide blue band and 2 narrow blue stripes ........................................................ 95.00

    9" d, blue sponged rim ........................................ 50.00

Pitcher

    7 5/8" h, sponge band ........................................ 100.00

    Cherry Band

        6" h ............................................................ 295.00

        8 1/2" h ...................................................... 350.00

Pitcher and Bowl, pitcher, 10 3/4" h, bowl, 15 7/8" d, relief tulip design, shaded blue ground ........................ 950.00

Sand Jar, 15" h x 12" d, brown highlighted molded elk in woodland scene, beige ground, unmkd, (A) .......... 413.00

Soda Fountain Crock, 18" h, red wing and blue "15" on front, spigot on base ........................ 260.00

Toothpick Holder, 1 3/4" h, stoneware, red wing on side, cream glaze ........................................................ 12.00

Water Cooler, 11" h, stoneware, "blue Water Cooler," single red wing mark, "blue oval Red Wing Union Stoneware Co. Red Wing, Mn." ........................ 350.00

## MORNING GLORY PATTERN-CONCORD SHAPE

Cup and Saucer, blue ................................................ 6.00

Plate, 10 1/2" d, blue .................................................. 7.00

## PEPE PATTERN-DUO TONE SHAPE

Beverage Server, 13" h ............................................ 90.00

Bowl, 6" d ................................................................ 12.00

Casserole, Cov, 9" d ................................................ 65.00

Cup and Saucer ...................................................... 10.00

Plate

    6" d ...................................................................... 6.00

    7" d .................................................................... 10.00

    10 1/2" d ............................................................ 12.00

Platter

    13" l .................................................................. 30.00

    15 1/2" l ............................................................ 35.00

Serving Bowl, 8" d .................................................. 15.00

Sugar Bowl, Cov ...................................................... 28.00

## PROVINCIAL PATTERN-VILLAGE GREEN SHAPE

Creamer .................................................................. 12.00

Cup and Saucer ...................................................... 10.00

Plate

    6" d ...................................................................... 4.00

    10" d .................................................................. 10.00

## RANDOM HARVEST PATTERN-FUTURA SHAPE

Creamer, 3" h .......................................................... 7.00

Cup and Saucer ...................................................... 18.00

Gravy Boat w/undertray .......................................... 35.00

Plate

    8 1/2" d .............................................................. 15.00

    10 1/2" d ............................................................ 18.00

Salad Bowl, 12" d .................................................... 85.00

## ROUND-UP PATTERN-CASUAL SHAPE

Cereal Bowl ............................................................ 46.00

Creamer .......................................................... 7" h 45.00

Fruit Dish ................................................................ 40.00

Platter, 20" l .......................................................... 200.00

## RUMRILL

Bud Vase

    4 1/4" h, squat base, flared sq neck, floral rim, orange and brown streaking over yellow ........................ 15.00

    8" h, squat base, stick neck, matte ivory glaze w/speckled ochre base, #510, (A) .................................... 50.00

Ewer, 7 1/2" h, orange glaze .................................... 55.00

Pitcher, 8" h, ball shape, green haze over pink ground ...................................................................... 155.00

Planter

    6" h, figural wishing well, blended tan glaze over green ground, "RUMRILL MADE IN USA" mark .......... 60.00

    8" d, 3 molded handles, molded horiz ribbing, mottled blue glaze, #304 ................................ 85.00

    9" l x 5 1/2" h, diamond shape, pedestal base, imp lines on body, white ext, turquoise int ........................ 68.00

Vase

    4 3/4" h, lobed, flowerform top, molded leaf body, green glaze, paper label ........................................ 25.00

    5" h, paneled bulbous base, paneled trumpet neck and rim, blue-green over pumpkin orange body ........ 25.00

    5 1/2" h, ball shape, 3 openings, orange glaze ...... 195.00

    5 3/4" h

        Ball shape, 2 loop handles, orange-red ground .. 65.00

        Sm loop handles on shoulder, matte green glaze, #318 .......................................................... 55.00

    6" d

        Sylvan, relief of leaves, white, #514-6 .............. 75.00

        Two molded handles, flared rim, tan ext, turquoise int, #636 .......................................................... 75.00

    6 1/2" h, ball shape, molded elephant head handles, gunmetal glaze .................................................. 300.00

    7" h

        Mandarin shape, matte cream glaze, #311-7 ...... 65.00

        Two handles, squat middle, flared ft, shaded pink glaze .......................................................... 58.00

    7 5/8" h, trophy shape, steel blue, #705 ................ 65.00

    8" w, blue stippled glaze, #501 ............................ 95.00

    8 1/2" h, "Victory," figural "V" and Morse code, white glaze ...................................................................... 55.00

    9 1/2" h, Athena, figural girl and vase, semi-matte ivory glaze, #576 ............................................ 750.00

    11" h, Deco style, diamond fan shape, emb graduated overlapping leaves, lime green glaze w/mottled ochre accents, (A) ...................................... 88.00

    12" h, relief of grapes, turquoise ext, peach int, #620 ...................................................................... 75.00

## SMART SET-CASUAL SHAPE
Pitcher
    11 3/4" h...............................................85.00
    15" h.................................................140.00
Plate ......................................................13.00
Platter, 14" l.........................................48.00

## TAMPICO PATTERN-FUTURA SHAPE
Cup and Saucer .................................10.00
Plate, 10 1/2" d..................................20.00
Vegetable Bowl, 9 1/4" l.....................10.00

## TIP-TOE PATTERN-CASUAL SHAPE
Cup and Saucer .................................15.00
Pitcher, 6" h.......................................32.00
Plate
    7 1/2" d.........................................15.00
    10 1/2" d.......................................12.00
Sugar Bowl, Cov.................................22.00

## TOWN AND COUNTRY PATTERN-EVA ZEISEL
Casserole, Cov, 11 1/2" H-H, brown ext, green int.......20.00
Cup and Saucer, rust...........................22.00
Platter, 11" l, peach.............................60.00
Relish Dish, 5" d, gray.........................28.00
Sauce Dish, 7" l, dk green....................40.00

## VILLAGE GREEN PATTERN
    Bean Pot, 6" h...............................75.00

# Regal China Corporation

### Antioch, Illinois
### 1938-Present

PEEK·A·BOO
Van Tellingen
©

**History:** Regal China Corporation of Antioch, Illinois was founded in 1938 and bought by Royal China and Novelty Company, a distributing and sales organization, in the 1940s as the manufacturer of its contract and premium business.

Regal made Snuggle Hugs designed by Ruth Van Tellingen Bendel in 1948. Bunnies, bears, pigs, Dutch Boy and Girl, and such were the subjects. Ruth Van Tellingen Bendel also designed the Peek-a-Boo bears in pajamas in large and small shaker sets and cookie jars.

Regal makes decorative or art wares on a contract basis only. It has sold nothing to the retail trade since 1968. Products made for other companies include a cookie jar for Quaker Oats in 1976, a milk pitcher for Ovaltine, a ship decanter and coffee mug for Old Spice in 1983, lamp bases for Lamplight Farms, products for Marshall Burns, and vases for Soovia Janis in 1985. Regal is owned by Jim Beam Distilleries as a wholly owned subsidiary and makes its Jim Beam bottles.

Regal marks include the name of the product.

### GENERAL
Compote, 3 1/2" h x 5 1/2" d, piecrust rim w/green trim on rim and ft................................................10.00
Planter
    10" l
        4 1/2" h, pink lobed flower head body, green molded leaf base ......................................10.00

Figural cornucopia, green shaded to white .........10.00
Shakers
    Figural fish, clear glaze, pr.......................22.00
    Humpty Dumpty, pr.................................90.00
Vase, 13" h, white fluted vert column w/green and white figural doe and fawn on molded green grass base, "REGAL USA" mk .................................................45.00

## OLD MACDONALD PATTERN
Canister
    5 1/2" h, Allspice, blond haired girl .........80.00
    9 1/2" h, red ribbed body
        Cereal, blond haired girl..................175.00

**Shakers, 3 1/2" h, 4 1/8" h, Old McDonald Farm, boy w/orange hat, brown hair, girl w/yellow hair and red-brown bows, pr, $85.**

**Teapot, 8 1/2" h, Old McDonald Farm, red cap, green bandana, yellow-brown body, $425.**

| | |
|---|---|
| Coffee, horse head | 275.00 |
| Four, mother's head | 275.00 |
| Salt, farmer head | 275.00 |
| Tea, boy's head | 250.00 |
| Creamer 6" h, rooster | 150.00 |
| Shakers, churns, pr | 50.00 |
| Sugar Bowl, Cov, hen | 175.00 |

## VAN TELLINGEN DESIGNS
Salt and Pepper

| | |
|---|---|
| Bears, green | 45.00 |
| Black Boy and Dog | 90.00 |
| Bunnies, green | 30.00 |
| Ducks | 35.00 |
| Dutch Boy and Girl | 49.00 |
| Mary and Lamb | 65.00 |
| Pigs, huggers | 150.00 |
| Sailor and Mermaid | 185.00 |

# Restaurant China

## c1920s-1970s

**History:** Restaurant china has been produced from the 1920s until the 1970s by a wide variety of companies. Characteristic of restaurant wares are glazes that are formulated to resist utensil scratching, food staining, harsh detergents, and thermal shock. Wares usually had a rolled, welted or beaded rim that was designed to be break and chip resistant.

Before 1900, American dining wares used products of Union Porcelain Works, Onondaga Pottery, and Maddock Pottery since they made fully vitrified china beginning in the 1890s, or they utilized non-vitrified ware or European porcelain for restaurant ware. By the 1920s, American commercial china in heavy or medium heavy gauge was made by many potteries.

**Buffalo China** from Buffalo, New York began making restaurant wares in 1915, but they are better known for their railroad china examples.

**H.F. Coors China Company** from Inglewood, California made restaurant china from 1925 until the present time. The company was founded by Herman Coors and products included Alox, Chefsware, and Coorsite.

**Iroquois China Company** from Syracuse, New York worked from 1905-1969. Pieces usually were white, deep ivory, or tan with a rolled edge and were decorated with lines, bands, decals, and transfer prints.

**Jackson China** from Falls Creek, Pennsylvania worked from 1917-1987 and made wares in blue, pink, tan, ivory, and white bodies with an assortment of names.

**Homer Laughlin China Company** has been in Newell, West Virginia since 1907 but in business from 1873 to the present. The largest volume of commercial china in the United States was made here in a wide variety of shapes.

**Mayer China Company** from Beaver Falls, Pennsylvania had a succession of owners in its history from 1888-1984. They used off white, ivory, and tan bodies and a variety of decorating methods.

**McNicol** in Clarksburg, West Virginia was in several different locations from 1892-1969 and used blue, pink, tan, and off-white bodies.

**Scammell China Company, Lamberton Works** was located in Trenton, New Jersey from 1924-1954 and then Sterling purchased their rights and molds. Their Lamberton and Trenton lines used decals and transfer prints.

**Shenango Pottery Company** had several different names changes from 1901-1954 and eventually became a division of Syracuse China. At one time Wallace and Mayer were both a part of Shenango. They made china in tan, ivory, and white bodies with assorted decorations.

**Sterling China** from Wellsville, Ohio worked from 1917 until the present. They purchased Scammell's molds, engravings, lithos, decals, and rights to the Lamberton and Trenton trade name in 1954. Their off-white, ivory, tan, blue, and pink bodies had a variety of decorations. Sterling purchased Wellsville China in 1959.

**Onondaga Pottery Company** from Syracuse, New York worked from 1871-1966 until it became part of Syracuse from 1966 until the present. Syracuse purchased both Mayer and Shenango in the 1980s. Their off-white, ivory (Old Ivory) and tan (Adobe Ware) had a variety of decorations.

**Tepco** of El Cerrito, California from 1918-1968 made popular Western patterns including "Western Traveler," "Broken Wagon Wheel," "Early California," "Ox Head," and "Branding Iron."

**Bailey-Walker China Company** from Bedford Heights, Ohio was in business from 1923-1942 and became **Walker China** from 1942-1981. Their bodies were off-white, ivory, and tan. Mayer purchased Walker in 1980.

**Wallace China** from Huntington Park, California from 1931-1964 had its "Westward Ho" patterns designed by Till Goodan. China made included "Rodeo," "Little Buckaroo," "Boots 'n Saddle," "Longhorn," "Pioneer Trails," "49er," and "Chuck Wagon." Some grounds were off-white but most were tan. Two of Wallace's Westward Ho patterns, "Little Buckaroo" and "Rodeo" have been recently reproduced by True West, of Comanche, Texas and marked with the Westward Ho mark.

Each of these companies utilized a wide variety of marks on their restaurant wares.

**References:** Barbara J. Conroy, *Restaurant China, Volume I*, Collector Books, 1998; _____ *Restaurant China, Volume 2*, Collector Books, 1999.

Berry Bowl
  5" d
    Black formal urn and ribbon drape border, Lamberton Scammell .......................................... 5.00
    Brown wavy border design on ext, white ground, Sterling mk .............................................. 4.00
Bouillon Cup, 4 1/4" d, 2 green bands, Mayer ............... 5.00
Bowl
  5" d, stenciled airbrushed brown leaping deer and trees, white ground, Syracuse .................................... 20.00
  6 3/8" d, airbrushed sky blue half border, Sterling ..... 6.00
  6 3/4" d, "blue Schweizer's" design, white ground, Mayer mk ................................................................ 5.00
Cereal Bowl
  5" d, stenciled airbrushed red-brown wave design on ext border, Sterling ................................................ 5.00

5 1/8" d, maroon stripes, pink ground, Sterling mk .... 4.00

6" d, gray stenciled airbrush border of pagodas and oriental themes, unmkd ....................................... 6.00

8" d, ftd, green stenciled airbrush flowerheads and leaves on border, Sterling
.............................................................................. 20.00

9" d, "Whitfield Gardenia" pattern, Syracuse
.............................................................................. 10.00

Chili Bowl

4 1/2" d, dk brown cattle brands, tan ground, Jackson
.............................................................................. 25.00

5" d, "SanTan," ext red transfer of florals, curlicues, and hatching, Wellsville ............................... 12.00

5 3/4" d, dk red band of x's around ext, Shenango
.............................................................................. 10.00

Creamer

2" h

Airbrushed gray border drip, Shenango
.................................................................. 5.00

Black and orange stripes ................................... 4.00

"Lune" line, lt blue, Buffalo ............................... 5.00

2 1/2" h, "Gold Rush" pattern, brown transfer, Sterling
.............................................................................. 15.00

3" h

Blue airbrushed oak leaf, Syracuse .................... 10.00

Orange-red, Hall ............................................ 32.00

White .............................................................. 6.00

3 1/4" h, cylinder shape

Burgundy scattered flowerheads and bouquets on border, burgundy lined rim, Mayer ..................... 10.00

Red "Sharon" pattern, Mayer ............................ 8.00

4" h, band of dk red flowerheads around border, Shenango ............................................. 12.00

Creamer and Cov Sugar Bowl, creamer, 4 1/2" h, sugar bowl, 3 1/2" h, green stenciled airbrush border design of waves, Jackson ............................................. 25.00

Cup and Saucer

Airbrushed blue tulips, blue trimmed handle and rims, Syracuse ............................................. 10.00

Border bands of green hanging hearts and flowers, Jackson ............................................................ 4.00

Green and white shadowleaf design, Wallace ......... 15.00

Red, gold, black, and green retro design, Syracuse ............................................................ 5.00

Rust red and white magnolia design, Wallace ......... 10.00

Stenciled airbrushed white dogwood and green leaves, Syracuse ............................................. 8.00

Turquoise and brown intertwined border bands, "Laurence Ware, Shenango" mk ............................... 6.00

Wide band of red flowerheads, buds, and leaves, Syracuse ............................................................ 5.00

Wide green border bands, gold lined trim, McNicol, set of 6 ......................................................... 10.00

Custard Cup

2 1/2" h, 2 red stripes, Mayer, set of 6 ..................... 16.00

2 3/4" h, black transfer of 3 dancing nudes in half wreath, wide and narrow black border bands ..................... 6.00

Dessert Dish, 6 1/2" d, russet brown "Poppies" pattern, Wallace ............................................................ 10.00

Dish

4 1/4" d, "brown *Mirabelle* and fruit" in center, brown rim, Mayer ......................................................... 8.00

9" l, blue Hilton Hotel symbol at top, blue lined swirls on border, Shenango.............................................. 20.00

10 1/2" l, red floral border band, rolled rim, Shenango mk
.............................................................................. 8.00

Egg Cup, 3 3/4" h, stenciled airbrushed yellow rose, dk green ground, Syracuse ...................................... 7.00

Grill Plate

9 1/4" d

Blue Willow pattern, "St. Louis Grill Carr China" mk
.............................................................................. 10.00

Border of green leaves and scrolling, "Shenango China" mk ....................................................... 10.00

9 1/2" d, pink and red sheet floral design, Wallace
.............................................................................. 20.00

9 5/8" d, brown stylized florals and birds on border, Sterling.............................................................. 6.00

10" d

"Gold HANNA CLUB" on border, white ground ... 18.00

Green Willow pattern, Buffalo ............................. 10.00

10 1/4" d

Brick red inner stripe, tan ground, Shenango Inca Ware ............................................................ 12.00

Green Willow design, "Jackson Vitrified China" mk
.............................................................................. 55.00

14" d, brown bucking bronco and branding irons, tan ground, Tepco ................................................. 98.00

Jam Jar, 2 3/4" h, bulbous shape, brown striped lobes at top, tan body, "Desert Ware Wallace China" mk ............ 12.00

Mug, 3 1/4" h, green flower and leaf design, white ground, Shenango ............................................................ 4.00

Mustard Jar, Cov, 3 1/4" h, stenciled airbrushed green wave rim, green cov and knob ...................................... 20.00

Pitcher, 6" h, brown stripe on Desert Tan ground, Wallace
.............................................................................. 15.00

Plate

5 1/4" d, red-brown oak leaves on border, shaped rim, Mayer, set of 4................................................... 10.00

**Plate, 8 1/4" d, stenciled airbrushed black design, Buffalo mk, $10.**

5 1/2" d

Stenciled Airbrushed

Blue swimming fish in center, pink to gray-green shaded border ground, Syracuse .............. 20.00

Gray shaded and pink oriental flower and stem, "Jackson China Falls Creek, Pa V3" mk..... 10.00

White rooster, med blue ground, Jackson ...... 10.00

Red "Linden" pattern, Mayer ................................. 6.00

Turquoise lined shaped rim, Buffalo .................... 5.00

6 1/4" d

Shaded dk red border, McNicol ........................... 2.00

Stenciled airbrushed green "Montrose" pattern, Syracuse ...................................................... 10.00

7" d

Blue and burgundy flower and green leaf border, Mayer ............................................................... 5.00

Border of aqua green and brown design of feathers and urns, Shenango ......................... 4.00

7 1/4" d

Dk maroon geometric curls on border, tan ground, "Curtis Restaurant," Mayer ............................. 8.00

Stenciled airbrushed green palm trees and ocean, Jackson............................................. 25.00

8 1/4" d, tan ground, emb border, Syracuse ............. 3.00

9" d

Blue bellflower border, Syracuse.................... 6.00

Bob's Big Boy design .......................................... 50.00

Gray band of roses on inner and outer border, Walker .............................................................. 8.00

Green airbrushed racing horse........................... 12.00

Green floral band border, red "POINSEITT CLUB," Sterling........................................................... 15.00

Indented green wave border, McNicol ................. 5.00

Red-brown airbrushed Indian on horseback ..... 100.00

Red "TOSI'S" at top, red and green character crushing grapes and "VIVERE," green sprayed border, Homer Laughlin ............................................. 5.00

Red Willow pattern, Wallace china ..................... 12.00

"Sears Coffee House" design, green and brown, Syracuse ...................................................... 10.00

Stenciled airbrushed orange and pink tulips, green stems, tan ground, Syracuse ......................... 10.00

9 1/8" d, brown "MARTIN'S" and walking hobo chicken, dk brown striped border, tan ground, Iroquois..... 25.00

9 1/2" d

"American Rose" pattern, red, Homer Laughlin..... 5.00

Blue dahlia pattern, Wallace............................... 30.00

Stenciled airbrushed gray interlocking leaf border, Sterling............................................................. 8.00

9 3/4" d

Blue hummingbird and flowers in center, flower wreaths on border, Jackson........................... 10.00

"Dresden" pattern, scattered multicolored floral sprays, Shenango ......................................... 5.00

"Gold KCC" on green border band, white ground, McNicol mk .................................................. 8.00

"Ye Tavern Club" w/period dining scene in center, border of inns, dk brown transfers, lt brown ground, Shenango ................................................... 12.00

9 7/8" d, "red Howard Johnson" logo on border, white ground, Syracuse mk ...................................... 7.00

**Plate, 9 3/4" d, stenciled airbrushed brown design, black "Kalberer Hotel Supply Co." on reverse, Jackson mk, $30.**

10" d

"Sambo's" w/palm tree, "Jackson China Falls Creek, Pa T6" mk ...................................................... 10.00

Stenciled airbrushed white rose, gray shaded leaves, Jackson ...................................................... 5.00

11" d, Red Willow pattern, Jackson ......................... 25.00

Platter

6 7/8" l, oval, stenciled airbrushed green and white polo cap, saddle, and mallet ..................................... 10.00

9 1/2" l

Brown scalloped design on border, Syracuse ....... 5.00

"Ravenna" design, wide and narrow green stripes on inner and outer rim ..................................... 10.00

9 3/4" l

Green, red, yellow, and black "Chicken in the Rough" on border, tan ground, Syracuse ................... 60.00

Red Howard Johnson design and stripe on border, Walker China ............................................... 28.00

10 3/8" l, "MM" intertwined w/brown stripes on border, Lamberton Scammell ..................................... 12.00

11" d, red and pink swirls in center, red and pink floral banding and swirls on border, Shenango........... 23.00

11 1/4" l, red and black border stripes, Sterling ........ 5.00

11 1/2" l, stenciled airbrushed green dogwood flowers in center, green border, Syracuse ..................... 10.00

11 3/4" l, Oval

Border band of white dogwood blossoms, green leaves, brown stems, shaped rim, Syracuse ................................................................. 20.00

Inner and outer green bands, McNicol ................. 5.00

12" l, oval, border band of black triangles, Coors China ................................................................. 10.00

13" l

Border of white flowers and green leaves, Shenango ................................................................. 5.00

Wide dk blue border, Shenango ......................... 5.00

13 3/8" l, red stenciled airbrushed lobster .............. 65.00

## Relish Dish

7 1/4" l, gilt line and magenta stripe on border, white ground, Shenango ...............................................8.00

8 3/4" l, green leaf pattern border, Buffalo mk............ 4.00

9" l, red Howard Johnson restaurants on border ....... 9.00

9 1/2" l

Overall brown glaze, raised Buffalo mk ................. 8.00

Red floral fan and shell border, white ground, Sterling mk .................................................................. 7.00

Sauce Boat, 6 3/8" l, pink plumed crowned crest over "CH," maroon stripe, Sterling................................ 10.00

Sauce Dish, 4" d, red Willow pattern, Jackson............ 10.00

## Soup Bowl

7" d, black inner stripe, dk red shaded border ...........5.00

8 3/4" d, 3 rust-red ext rings, desert tan body, Sterling ..................................................................................3.00

9" d, Mayfair pattern, blue transfer, "O.P.Co. Syracuse China" mk .................................................. 10.00

## Soup Plate

8 3/4" d, green "Sea Shell Inn" and stripes on border, "D.E. McNicol" mk ........................................... 20.00

9 1/4" d, pink and gray banded rim, Shenango..........8.00

## Sugar Bowl, Cov

3" h, "Rod's Steak House," Wallace .........................55.00

4" h, black stripe w/brown stripes, tan ground, "Sterling China" mk .................................................. 6.00

4 1/4" h, yellow and gray striping, Iroquois ............. 18.00

4 1/2" h, dk blue rim bands of lambrequins and sawtooth designs ................................................................... 25.00

Teapot, 5 1/2" h, gray airbrushed swirl design............. 20.00

Toothpick Holder, 2 3/4" h, blue band of curlicues and urns below blue band, Scammell ...................................... 16.00

Vegetable Bowl, 7 3/4" l, green and beige wreath w/letter "H" on int border, black and yellow striped rim, Thomas Maddock .................................................................. 12.00

## Robinson-Ransbottom Pottery

### Roseville, Ohio
### 1901-Present

**History:** Frank Ransbottom purchased the Oval Ware and Brick Company in Roseville, Ohio with his three brothers. It was called the Ransbottom Brothers Pottery for eight years and produced stoneware jars.

By 1920, it merged with Robinson Clay Products. Since stoneware jars were declining in popularity, it shifted its production to garden wares such as planters, urns, and bird baths. The company still make these today along with crocks, water coolers, milk churns, and water pitchers.

Old Colony was made from the mid-1930s until 1940, while Rustic Ware was made from the mid-1930s until the 1960s. Both functional and decorative pieces were hand decorated under the glaze in various color combinations that were sold under the Crown Pottery brand.

Other wares were jardinieres, flower pots, figurines, vases, teapots, plates, casseroles, baby shoe planters, and commemorative cups and mugs. About twenty five different cookie jars were made, with the figural ones being the most desirable. Both stoneware and white body characters cookie jars were available into the 1960s. The company no longer makes character cookie jars or whiteware jars since they are too expensive to produce.

Much of the pottery is marked. Most examples include "R.R.P.Co., Roseville, O." or some variation of that mark. Some also had the five-point crown symbol in several marks. Paper labels also were used.

**References:** "R.R.P.Co.-Roseville's Other Pottery Survives," *Antique Weekly*, July 20, 1992.

**Museums:** The Pot Shop, Roseville, OH.

Bean Pot, 5" h, tan base, dk brown top and cov, mkd.... 8.00

Bowl

5 3/8" d, "Rustic" pattern, mauve dash flowers w/green, tan, and blue dashes................................................ 7.00

6" d, closed rim, green body w/brown drip on border .......................................................................... 10.00

6 1/4" d, relief molded wave design w/vert ribbing, brown-pink glaze ......................................................... 15.00

7" d, incised design, matte brown finish, mkd.......... 15.00

11 3/8" d x 23/4" h, yellowware, sloped sides, "RRP Co ROSEVILLE, OHIO #051" mk, (A) ...................... 50.00

11 1/4" d, "Rustic" pattern, dk red, med blue, and green stylized florals and streaks, mkd ........................ 85.00

12" d, vert banded body, overlapping rings on rim, brick red .............................................................................. 45.00

15" d, blue sponging, cream ground........................ 75.00

Butter Crock, Cov, 7" d, stoneware, blue relief molded vines on side, blue lined rims, "The Robinson Clay Products Co. Akron, Ohio" mk, (A) ...................................... 138.00

Console Bowl, 10" l, mottled green ground, gold drip rim, mkd ................................................................................ 10.00

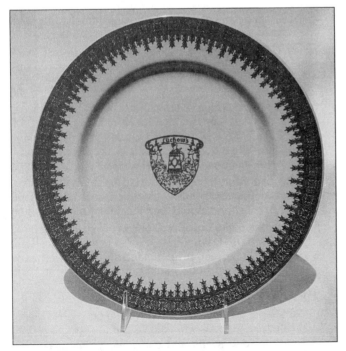

**Service Plate, 11" d, blue transfer, Sterling china, $60.**

**Dish, 10 3/8" d, "Rustic Ware," med blue flowers, red centers, green leaves, brown inner band, dk red outer band, $8.**

Cooler, 11 3/4" h, blue washed relief of woman at wishing well in oval cartouche, bundles of flowers on sides, nickel spout, "The Robinson Clay Products Co. Akron, Ohio" mk, (A) ................................................................260.00
Cream Pitcher, 8 1/2" h, blue sponging, cream ground
....................................................................................75.00
Creamer, 4 1/4" h, "Rustic" pattern, dk red and turquoise swirls ............................................................................6.00
Crock, 5 1/2" h, gray stoneware w/2 dk blue bands .....25.00
Floor Vase, 14" h, relief molded shells on side, figural deer head handles, maroon glaze............................35.00
Garden Vase, classic shape, mottled crystalline drip over matte beige ground, chips, (A)................................99.00
Jar, 19" h, figural swan head handles, yellow.............195.00
Jar, Cov, 4" h, brown glaze, cream drip........................10.00
Jardiniere
    4 3/8" h, relief molded starbursts, aqua glaze..........35.00
    5 5/8" h, raised stylized leaves, brown, green, and cream drip, mkd..................................................................40.00
Jardiniere and Pedestal, 21 1/2" h, raised fern fronds, green and brown glazes, chip on ft, (A) ...........................121.00
Jug, 12" h, dk brown top, Bristol glaze on lower section w/"CHR. HANSEN'S RENNET EXTRACT BUTTER COLOR CHEESE COLOR LITTLE FALLS, NY USA"
....................................................................................85.00
Lawn Figure, 14" l, figural elf reclining on tree stump, blue trousers and cap, olive green shirt, white beard ......76.00
Milk Pitcher, 6" h, tan drip over gloss brown ground, mkd
....................................................................................10.00
Mixing Bowl, 6"d, 8"d, 10 1/2" d, blue flowers, green leaves, magenta dots, brown lines, yellow ground, set of 3.80.00
Pie Plate, blue wheat stalk in center, blue sponged border.....................................................................10.00
Pitcher
    4 3/4" h, indented yellow diamonds and geometrics, cream ground ................................................................15.00
    6 1/8" h, dk burgundy center and thin dk blue outer banding...........................................................................5.00
    6 1/4" h
        Dk brown top, tan base ......................................15.00

**Pitcher, 4 3/4" h, yellow indentations, cream ground, $15.**

    Two horiz blue bands around base, white ground
    ..............................................................................12.00
    6 1/2" h, wide dk red and 2 narrow blue bands on base
    ................................................................................8.00
    8 1/2" h
        Blue wheat spears on sides, white ground, blue sponged rim..................................................35.00
        Relief molded arches w/figures, sawtooth borders, white glaze................................................15.00
    9" h, pink diamond imp, yellow ground, "EMBASSY HOTEL PITTSBURGH" on side .........................45.00
Pitcher and Bowl, pitcher, 8 5/8" h, bowl, 11 1/2" d, dk brown ground w/cream and brown border drips, mkd ........15.00
Planter
    4" h
        Bowl shape, relief molded hanging ribbons, lt yellow glaze, mkd ......................................................10.00
        Sq shape w/molded leaves, circ base, brown glaze w/cream drip over rim ...................................10.00
    4 1/2" h, figural baby shoes on sq base, gloss blue glaze
    ..............................................................................10.00
    5" h, pot shape, 3 legs, 2 sm handles, satin black glaze
    ................................................................................8.00
    5 3/8" h, sq shape, pink ground w/scattered dk pink stylized flowerheads ..............................................15.00
    5 1/2" h, brown sponging on yellow body ...............10.00
    5 3/4" h, flared sq shape, flared sq base, molded overlapped leaf design, yellow glaze .........................7.00
    6" h x 7 1/2" l, flared shape, vert fluting, lt green .....15.00
    6 1/2" h, figural bird house w/2 blue, yellow, and red birds perched on roof ......................................10.00
    6 1/2" l x 4 1/2" w, rect, relief molded stylized flowerheads in center, raised horiz ribbing on body and rim, pink glaze...................................................................10.00
    7" h
        Jar shape, relief molded florals, satin gray-white glaze, mkd................................................................10.00
        Relief molded swirls and curlicues, yellow glaze w/lt green trim on rim, mkd.....................................15.00

**Vase, 6 3/4" h, ivory glaze, imp mk and #298, $20.**

7 1/4" l, figural cricket, matte yellow w/gray, tan, and black accents.........................................45.00

10" l x 4" h, bowl shape, incised overlapped curved lines, spread ft, green glaze.........................10.00

10" w, bowl shape, closed rim, brown body, green and beige drip on rim...............................10.00

11 3/4" l, tab handles, black speckling on yellow ground, mkd..................................................10.00

Serving Dish, 10" H-H, oval, white glaze.......................4.00

Spaghetti Bowl, 14 1/2" d, "Rustic" ware, lt blue and green swirls, dk red-brown inner and outer borders...........35.00

Sugar Bowl, 3 1/2" h, red and blue stripes on base, open wing handles..................................................5.00

Urn, 14 3/4" h, relief molded daisy chain above waist, vert loops on waist, fluted ft, green glaze.....................150.00

Vase

    5 1/2" h, bulbous middle, sq base and collar, 2 sm flower-head handles, white dogwood blossoms, green leaves, brown branches, pink ground, mkd.........10.00

    7 1/2" h, fluted flared body and ft, chain at base of body, dk orange glaze.......................................5.00

    7 5/8" h, flared, fluted body and ft, beaded band above ft, matte white glaze ...............................18.00

    7 3/4" h, cylinder shape w/ribbed molding and leaf design, shaded rust to tan glaze, #160/5 ...........25.00

    8" h

        Flared base and top, green ribs w/brown drip at top, mkd...........................................20.00

        Tapered, relief molded design of 2 parakeets on side, yellow.....................................15.00

    8 1/4" h, bulbous middle, flared rim and base, emb anchor design in circle on sides, 2 sm handles, yellow glaze.............................................20.00

    9 1/4" h, cylinder shape, flared rim, green ground w/cream drip......................................10.00

    10" h, Grecian urn shape, 2 sm handles on shoulder, mottled blue glaze, (A) ........................45.00

    12 3/4" h, bulbous base, flared neck and rim, 2 wishbone handles, med blue, hairlines, pr .........................50.00

# Rookwood Pottery Company

## Cincinnati, Ohio
## 1880-1967

**History:** Maria Longworth Nichols founded her pottery in an old schoolhouse and named it "Rookwood" after her father's estate. She designed the first art pottery wares. From 1880-1884, they used a variety of glazes and clay bodies with decorations that were carved, printed or painted underglaze. A lot of gold was used over the glaze. Numerous shapes were made, and each year additional ones were added to the line.

Albert Valentien was the first full-time decorator at Rookwood and came in 1881. He worked with Laura Fry and many other decorators. W.W. Taylor became manager in 1883 and introduced the *Rookwood Shape Record Book*.

Standard Ware was started in 1883 with underglaze slip painting applied to a white or yellow body with a glossy, yellow-tinted glaze combined with atomized grounds. The glaze was perfected by Laura Fry who patented this method in 1889. Decorations were often fish, fruit, portraits, or native flowers. Background colors included dark browns, reds, orange, and yellow under the yellow-tinted glaze. Standard Ware characterized much of Rookwood's production through the 1890s.

After Mrs. Nichol's husband died in 1885, she married Bellamy Storer the next year. When she retired in 1890, Taylor became president and took over her interests in the pottery. The Japanese artist Kataro Shirayamadani brought a strong Japanese influence to Rookwood pottery in 1887 and stayed until 1948, except for a ten-year period in Japan.

The Tiger Eye glaze was developed by accident in 1884 and was the first of the crystalline glazes produced. In 1889, Rookwood won a Gold Medal at the Exposition Universelle in Paris for Tiger Eye and dark wares. The Rookwood pottery continued to grow and expand. A new plant was built in 1892 and enlarged several times after that. New shapes were added every year, too.

In 1894, the Iris line was created by changing the background colors to soft pastels from the dark colors and decorated with slip painting and a gloss glaze. Aerial Blue had a light ground with blue decorations and a gloss glaze, but this line was not produced. Sea Green was introduced in the same year with aquatic life decorations on a white body with a high gloss lead glaze.

By 1900, Rookwood was experiencing the competition from J.B. Owens, Roseville, Weller, and other area potteries who were imitating Rookwood's Standard glaze on their pottery.

Rookwood sent many of its artists to study in Europe to improve their techniques. By 1904, Rookwood's high glazed wares were being phased out in favor of matte finishes with stylized decorations.

A variety of matte glazes was introduced. There were matte glazed examples with floral subjects that were decorated in reds, yellows, greens, and blues. Some pieces had black outlined designs with flat decorations. Incised matte glazed pieces had incised geometric designs. Modeled matte glazed pieces were decorated with sculpted subjects in high relief with the matte finish.

Vellum ware was developed by Stanley Burt in 1904 as a cross between a transparent glaze and a matte finish. The glaze was developed in the kiln at the same time as the decoration, thus affording a greater variety of decoration themes including scenes, plants, fish, birds, and landscape subjects. Vellum also accepted tints such as Green Vellum and Yellow Vellum.

Large architectural projects were undertaken about 1907, when Rookwood produced murals of Rookwood faience and wall plaques. Tiles were made for theaters, railroad stations, clubs, restaurants, homes, schools, and office buildings.

For its 30th anniversary in 1910, Rookwood introduced a matte glazed line called Ombroso, which was used on modeled objects such as bookends and paperweights. When Taylor died in 1913, Joseph Gest became president.

Rookwood introduced a soft porcelain line in 1915 with both gloss and matte glazes on flower bowls, vases, paperweights, and flower frogs. Jewel porcelain followed in 1920 and was made until the closing days of the pottery.

During the 1920s, a wide variety of finishes was used on Rookwood examples. Ornamental wares were cast in molds since they were less expensive to produce. Vases, paperweights, bookends, candlesticks, bowls, ashtrays, and tea sets were made by this method. Some were artist signed in the master mold, but were not individual artist signed Rookwood pieces.

John D. Wareham became president in 1934 when the company was experiencing financial difficulties. Many decorators had been laid off. The Depression had taken its toll and equipment was outdated. Very little pottery was made in 1935, and architectural wares shut down in 1936. When the company filed for bankruptcy in 1941, it was purchased by a group consisting of Walter Schott, Marge, his wife, and others.

When the United States entered World War II, Rookwood was forced to curtail production due to lack of supplies. Part of the plant was used for war work, and pottery was made on a limited scale. In 1941, the Schott group transferred ownership to the Institution Divi Thomae Foundation under the jurisdiction of the Roman Catholic Archdiocese of Cincinnati. The commercial operations was transferred to Sperti, Inc., with Wareham guiding the pottery production. After World War II they planned to expand, but sales were not going well. By 1948, most of the decorators were laid off. Production of signed decorated pieces decreased.

Edgar Heltman took over direction of Rookwood in 1954, and they made simple shapes and commercial wares. The following year, production just about stopped and Sperti sold in 1956. By 1959, Herschede Hall Clock Company bought Rookwood and moved the following year to Starksville, Missouri. Some pottery was made in about sixty different shapes and nine glazes, but there was not much appeal for buyers. By 1967, Rookwood Pottery was suspended.

The Rookwood marking system was based on numbers, letters, and symbols. Hand-decorated pieces were signed by the artist. Systematic dating began in 1886, and pieces after that time are dated. The letter "P" with the reversed "R" was used in 1886. Until 1900, a flame point was added to this monogram. In 1901, Roman numerals were added below the monogram. This system was used until the pottery closed. In all, there are more than 120 artists or decorators at Rookwood Pottery in its 87 years of operation.

**References**: Cincinnati Art Galleries, *The Glover Collection of Rookwood Pottery*, L-W Books, 1993; Virginia Raymond Cummins, *Rookwood Pottery Potpourri*, published by author, 1979; Anita J. Ellis, *Rookwood Pottery: The Glorious Gamble*, Rizzoli International Publications, Inc.1992; _____, *Rookwood Pottery, The Glaze Lines*, Schiffer Publishing Ltd. 1995; Herbert Peck, *The Book of Rookwood Pottery*, Crown Publishers, Inc. 1968; _____, *The Second Book of Rookwood Pottery*, published by author, 1985; Kenneth R. Trapp, *Ode to Nature: Flowers and Landscapes of the Rookwood Pottery 1880-1940*, Jordan-Volpe Gallery, 1980; _____ *Toward the Modern Style Rookwood Pottery: The Later Years 1915-1950*, Jordan-Volpe Gallery, l983; Neil Wood, editor, *A Price Guide to Rookwood*, L-W Book Sales, 1999.

**Museums**: Brooklyn Museum, NY; Chrysler Museum, Norfolk, VA; Cincinnati Art Gallery, OH; Cincinnati Art Museum, OH; Cooper-Hewitt Museum, NYC; J.B. Speed Art Museum, Louisville, KY; Milwaukee Public Museum, WI; Museum of Fine Arts, Boston, MA; Museum of History and Technology, Smithsonian Institution, Washington, DC; Newark Museum, NJ; New Orleans Museum of Art, LA; Philadelphia Museum of Art, PA; St. Louis Art Museum, MO; Western Reserve Historical Society, Cleveland, OH.

**Reproduction Alert:** A Michigan couple bought the remains of the original Rookwood company and are making pieces from original molds limiting production to 500 of each mold number. They have made at least thirty different pieces. All new pieces are glazed only; no hand decorating is applied. The new pieces are dated in Arabic numbers, not Roman numerals. The dates are ground into the glaze. New Rookwood is all stark white porcelain.

Ashtray, 5 1/2" d, harp shape, lt green gloss glaze, dtd 1927 ................................................................ 195.00

Bookend, 5 3/8" h, figural rook, dk blue, William P. McDonald, dtd 1934, pr, (A) .................................. 440.00

Bowl
   6" d, ftd, matte med blue emb water lily design, shape #1351, dtd 1919 ............................................... 155.00
   13" d, black ext, pink int, dtd 1913 ......................... 395.00

Bud Vase, 7 1/4" h, Wax Matte, blue flowers, green leaves, burgundy butterfat ground, "imp flame HM/XXII/2546F" mk, (A) .................................................... 715.00

Cabinet Vase, 5 1/2" h, Black Iris, stylized lt pink apple blossoms, black ground, Fred Rothenbush, "flame, 785L/FR" mk, 1900, (A) ...................................................... 1430.00

**Bookend, 7 1/2" h, turquoise, dtd 1945, pr, $795.**

Candle Holders

    3" h, matte pink glaze, shape #2282, dtd 1940, pr ................................................................235.00

    11 3/4" h, figural dolphin base, twisted shaft, flared bobiche, gunmetal glaze, "flame XXI/2464" mk, pr, (A) ................................................................715.00

Centerpiece Bowl, 13" d, Jewel Porcelain, polychrome abstract bird on blossoming branch, E.T. Hurley, "flame XXIX/2574C/E.T.H." mk, (A)...............................1,430.00

Ewer

    5 1/2" h, Standard Glaze, red cosmos, Edward Abel, 1893 .................................................................725.00

    11 1/2" h, Standard Glaze, wild flowers and leaves, shaded green to brown ground, K. Shirayamadani, dtd 1890, (A).........................................1,540.00

Mug, 5 1/2" h, incised geometric design, shaded matte green glaze, #1071, dtd 1906, (A) .........................358.00

Pitcher

    5" h, Standard Glaze, yellow flower design, Harriet Wilcox, shape #87, dtd 1888 ................................450.00

    6" h, slip painted white and black butterflies and bamboo, gray and white ground, gilt accents and rim, dtd 1883, (A)...................................................660.00

    7 1/2" h, Standard Glaze, yellow flowers, shaded gold to brown ground, silver overlay, Josephine Zettel, dtd 1893, (A) ...............................................2,310.00

    12 1/4" h, Standard Glaze, wild rose design, Harriet Wilcox, shape #540, dtd 1890 ...........................1,950.00

Pitcher, Cov, 8 3/4" h, cameo design of white narcissus, salmon pink ground, (A).........................................440.00

Plaque, Scenic Vellum

    7" h x 10" l, snow scene of birches at dawn, Sallie Coyne, 1899, framed, (A) ...........................................4,075.00

    11" h x 13" l, multicolored autumn scene of birch trees and pond, E.T. Hurley, original frame, paper label, (A) ...............................................................11,000.00

Ring Tray, 4" h, yellow, black, and purple seated figure of clown at edge of tray, Sallie Toohey, dtd 1929, (A) ................................................................320.00

Trivet, 5 5/8" d, matte aqua and white gull design, shape #2351, dtd 1918....................................................325.00

**Vase, 18" h, Standard glaze, yellow and brown shades, Kataro Shirayamadani, (A), $3,750.**

Urn, 9 1/4" h, horiz handles, Standard Glaze, portrait of young man, shaded green to brown ground, Mathew Daly, "flame, 584E, W.MAD" mk, (A) ..................2,200.00

Vase

    5" h

        Flared shape, Jewel Porcelain, pink tulips, shaded gray ground, M.H. McDonald, "flame XLIII/6305/MHM" mk, (A) ...............................................................715.00

        Matte pink glaze, shape #2090, dtd 1932 ...........95.00

        Squat shape, Standard Glaze, gold and brown pansies, brown ground, E.T. Hurley, dtd 1898, (A) ...............................................................660.00

    5 1/4" h, flared shape, ivory and pink gloss glaze, shape #2236, dtd 1916 ................................................375.00

    5 1/2" h, bulbous, Jewel Porcelain, burgundy and brown stylized flowers, taupe ground, Lorinda Eply, (A) ...............................................................605.00

    6" h

        Bulbous base, flared neck, Sea Green, white hydrangea, opalescent blue and green ground, Sara Sax, 1902, (A) ..............................................5,225.00

        Carved Iris, spherical shape, white dogwood blossoms and branches, silver gray ground, E.T.Hurley, dtd 1900, (A)...............................................4,675.00

        Corset shape, Vellum, garlands of blue and yellow flowers, turquoise ground, Ed Diers, "imp flame XXII/ED/1358F" mk, 1922, (A)...................1,045.00

        Cylinder shape, Iris Glaze, lavender wisteria, black to gray shaded ground, Katherine Van Horne, "imp flame VII/KVH/931W" mk, 1907, (A) ...............................................................1,760.00

        Jewel Porcelain, white and brown fish, cobalt ground, Jens Jensen, "imp flame XXXIII/JJ/S" mk, 1933, (A) ...............................................................3,300.00

    6 1/2" h

        Flared shape, quilted body, gloss yellow glaze, #6174, dtd 1938......................................................195.00

        Ovoid

            Iris Glaze, yellow crocuses, shaded ivory to gray ground, Clara Lindeman, "imp flame VI/C.C.L./30F" mk, 1906, (A)...............................................1,650.00

            Jewel Porcelain, slip painted yellow pears, brown leaves, gray ground, Elizabeth Barrett, "flame XLV/6644E/3125" mk, pr, (A) ................1,045.00

            Scenic Vellum, green, purple, and ivory snowy landscape, Elizabeth McDermott, "imp flame XVIII/EHM/913E" mk, 1918, (A) ...........1,100.00

    6 3/4" h, Iris Glaze, white and gray waterlilies, shaded gray ground, Constance Baker, 1904, "flame IV/C.A.B./922/D." mk, crazing, (A) .................2,420.00

    7" h

        Cylinder shape, rolled shoulder, Iris Glaze, lt pink apple blossoms, shaded gray to pink ground, E.D.Diers, "flame V/ED/951E" mk, 1905, (A) ...............................................................1,430.00

        Squat base, cylinder neck, flared rim, Jewel Porcelain, brown horses and dogs, pink ground, Jens Jensen, "imp flame XXXIII/JJ/S" mk, 1933, restored chip, (A)...............................................................605.00

        Wax Matte, red flowers, pink ground, Catherine Covalenco, 1930, (A) .........................................770.00

    7 1/2" h

        Art Deco design on neck, matte green glaze, shape #2324, dtd 1916............................................239.00

Bottle shape, Wax Matte, pink, mauve, and green gooseberries and leaves, turquoise and blue ground, Margaret Helen McDonald, "flame XXVI/2936/HMH" mk, (A).............990.00

Iris Glaze, yellow nasturtium, black to gray shaded ground, Sallie Coyne, "flameIV/SEC/505" mk, (A) ............3,575.00

Ovoid shape, Wax Matte, blue carnations, green leaves, blue and claret ground, 1925, "flame XXV/233/cipher" mk, (A) ............1,210.00

8" h

Sm base, bulbous body, short neck, med blue raised leaping deer and foliage, "flame XLV 6053" mk ............435.00

Tapered cylinder shape, sm spread rim, Iris Glaze, band of white cherry blossoms and branches on ivory ground, blue-gray body, Lenore Asbury, "flame X/90 DL.A." mk, (A)............1,540.00

Wax Matte, orange and yellow tulips, green leaves, raspberry and ivory ground, Kataro Shirayamadani, 1936, (A) ............1,870.00

8 1/2" h

Carved Matte, blue band of Chinese junks on shoulder, brown and green ground, William Hentschel, "imp flame XI/614E/WEH" mk, 1911, (A) ...1,210.00

Iris Glaze, painted white hydrangea, shaded lavender ground, Rose Fescheimer, crazing, "flame III/R.F./922C" mk, (A) ............2,090.00

8 3/4" h, cylinder shape, Iris Glaze, band of purple irises, ivory ground, lavender body, Lenore Asbury, "imp flame IX/L.A./952" mk, 1909, (A) ............1,980.00

9" h

Corset shape, Vellum, red, blue, and green stylized daisies, ivory and dk blue ground, Katherine Van Horne, "imp flame XVI/1358D/V/KVH/R/VII" mk, 1916, (A) ............770.00

Cylinder shape, Scenic Vellum, birch trees, pastel sky, matte green top and base, Kataro Shirayamadani, 1911 ............5,400.00

Iris Glaze, lavender cyclamen, shaded gray ground, crazing, John D. Wareham, "imp flame III/935C/JDW" mk, 1903, (A)............2,530.00

Three attached amphora-shaped vessels, Standard Glaze, amber and cobalt star flowers, shaded brown to gold ground, (A) ............770.00

Vellum, purple carnations, shaded celadon ground, Carl Schmidt, "imp flame XI/CS/954D?V" mk, 1911, (A) ............1,980.00

Wax Matte, yellow and red tulips, shaded yellow to green ground, "flame XXXVII/892C/MHM" mk, 1937, pr, (A) ............2,400.00

9 1/4" h

Iris Glaze, purple irises, shaded green ground, Sara Sax, "imp flame VI/907DDsx" mk, 1906, (A) ............4,225.00

Scenic Vellum, blue and scene of tall pines in winter landscape, Sallie Coyne, flame XVIII/SEC/1356D mk, (A) ............3,080.00

Wax Matte, purple orchids, dk green leaves, green ground, Jens Jensen, "flame XXIX/132, cipher" mk, 1929, (A) ............1,540.00

9 1/2" h

Scenic Vellum, blue landscape, Lenore Asbury, 1914 ............3,500.00

Sung Plum, carved clusters of blue wisteria and green leaves, shaded celadon to burgundy ground, K. Shirayamadani, dtd 1917, "flame XXII/120" mk, (A) ............14,300.00

Vellum, hanging blue wisteria, beige ground, E.T. Hurley, "imp flame/E.T.H./XXV/2745" mk, 1925, (A) ............990.00

10" h, Iris Glaze, golden rod flowers, shaded gray ground, Rose Fesscheimer, "imp flame II/814A/V/R.F." mk, 1902, (A)............4,400.00

10 1/4" h

Matte, emb roses, stems, shaded pink and beige ground, "imp flame, XVII/1709" mk, 1917, (A) ............605.00

Wax Matte, polychrome elm trees in landscape, Mary Helen McDonald, "imp flame XXXVIII/892C/MHM" mk, 1938, (A) ............3,850.00

10 3/4" h, Scenic Vellum, banded blue, green, yellow and purple misty landscape, Lenore Asbury, "flame XXXIII/900B/L.A." mk, (A) ............2,750.00

11 3/4" h

Iris Glaze, purple irises, shaded green ground, A.R. Valentien, "imp flame III/901V/A.R. Valentien" mk, 1903, repaired hairline, (A) ............5,225.00

Vellum, lavender and white magnolias, lt purple to blue shaded ground, Lenore Asbury, "imp flame 827 XXVII" mk, 1927, (A) ............6,050.00

12" h, Wax Matte, blue and red morning glories, green leaves, pumpkin orange butterfat ground, Sallie Coyne, "imp flame/sc/XXIV/2790" mk, restored rim chip, (A) ............1,320.00

15" h, Wax Matte, blue iris, green leaves, pink ground, Sallie Coyne, "flame, XXV/1369B/SEC." mk, 1925, (A) ............3,575.00

21" h, squat base, cylinder neck, flared rim, Carved Matte, green leaves, yellow and blue chrysanthemums, mottled blue and purple ground, Charles S. Todd, 1915, hairline, (A) ............3,300.00

26" h, Matte, emb stylized band on neck, frothy matte green glaze, "flame XVI/306" mk, 1916, (A)...3,575.00

Wall Sconce, 11 1/4" h, emb pr of owls, brown and green matte glaze, "flame X/1688" mk, 1910, (A) ............660.00

Whiskey Jug, 9 1/2" h, Standard Glaze, corn and husk design, Anna Valentein, shape 512B, dtd 1898 ............895.00

# Roselane Pottery

## Pasadena, California
## 1939-1977

**History:** William (Doc) Fields and Georgia, his wife, started Roselane Pottery at home in Pasadena, California in 1938. William was the designer and Georgia was in charge of production. They sold the figurines they made to local florists.

Their operation moved to a factory in 1940. Wares were displayed at gift shows and shipped all over the country, and to Alaska and South America. The Chinese Modern line included vases, bowls, figurines, candle holders, and wall pockets in high gloss colors and combinations. Aqua Marine was a buffet serving line.

They made a series of small abstract ceramic sculptures of animals mounted on walnut bases that were modified with attached eyes to make them more realistic. Their best known and most recognized product were the Sparklers series of animals that were started in 1952. The airbrush decorated semi-porcelain animals and birds were finished with colored rhinestone eyes which were later changed to plastic eyes.

Roselane also made flower bowls, vases, ashtrays, covered boxes, and other decorated housewares. The factory moved in 1968 until 1974.

William died in 1973, and the business was sold to Prather Engineering Corporation and moved to Long Beach. Roselane production stopped in 1977.

Roselane used a series of incised and stamped marks. Most used Roselane, but some state Made in California or Made in U.S.A. From 1965-67, Hagen-Renaker distributed the Roselane line.

**References:** Jack Chipman, *Collector's Encyclopedia of California Pottery*, Collector Books, 1992; _____*Collector's Encyclopedia of California Pottery, 2nd Edition*, Collector Books, 1999; Mike Scheider, *California Potteries*, Schiffer Publishing Ltd. 1995.

**Reproduction Alert:** Beware of unmarked sparklers. Copies were made in Japan and imported by American importers; i.e. Napco-National Potteries Company.

Bookend, 5" h, seated oriental figure leaning against wall, pr ........................................................................ 110.00
Bowl
    4" h x 6 1/4" l, ftd, wave form, lt aqua glaze w/pink accent ........................................................................ 10.00
    12" l x 5" w, dk gray and pink .................................. 35.00
Candleholder
    2 3/4" h x 4 1/4" sq, relief molded geometric design on bobiche, sea green top, gray ftd base ................ 15.00
    3 1/4" h, cut out ovals on base, med blue w/charcoal shading, pr................................................................. 40.00
    10" h, open, abstract shape, lt brown glaze, pr........ 22.00
Candy Dish, 8" d, ftd, raised stylized flowers, yellow glaze ............................................................................. 22.00
Console Bowl, 12" l, lobed body, incised geometric ends, maroon glaze ........................................................ 20.00

Figure
  Sparkler
    3 1/2" h, owl, green-gold body, black accents, red eyes ........................................................................ 10.00
    3 3/4" h, Hound, brown and tan ......................... 25.00
    4" h, Scottie Dog, seated, black .......................... 35.00
    4" l, resting fawn................................................ 20.00
    5" h, prancing horse, green w/red-brown accents ...................................................................... 15.00
    5 3/4" h, Siamese Cat, brown and tan ............... 36.00
    6 1/2" h, Siamese Cat sitting, tan and brown ...... 38.00
    7" h, seated Chihuahua, tan............................... 78.00
  5 1/2" h
    Standing doe and fawn, semi-matte blue glaze ...................................................................... 25.00
    Stylized standing cowboy, tan w/brown accents, blue eyes ............................................................. 15.00
  6" h, Borzoi dog, white.......................................... 125.00
  6 1/2" h, deer, brown............................................ 22.00
  6 3/4" l, swimming duck, gold-yellow body, blue and maroon loops on body, black bill ......................... 28.00
  7" h, robed Oriental figure holding bottle, dove gray glaze, tan accents .............................................. 25.00
  8" h, rearing horse, lt green w/lt brown tail, mane, and hooves, mkd...................................................... 15.00
  8 1/2" h, cockatoo w/spread wings, gray ................ 98.00
  10" h
    Country man or woman dancing, lt gray glaze, pr ...................................................................... 20.00
    Tufted crane on perch, white w/red-brown accents ...................................................................... 25.00
  11" h, Bali dancing man, gray glaze ...................... 35.00
Planter
  5 1/2" d, bowl shape w/imp geometrics, 4 spread feet, pea green ........................................................... 15.00
  12 1/2" l x 5" w, scalloped base, lt brown ext, green int ...................................................................... 25.00
Salad Bowl, 14" d, w/serving spoon and fork, turquoise ground w/incised leaping fish ................................ 115.00

**Bowl, 11 1/2" d, imp gray designs, pink int, gray ext, "ROSELANE PASADENA CALIF" mk, $35.**

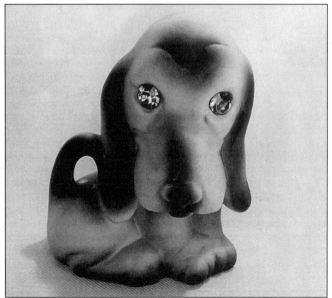

**Figure, 4" h, tan and brown, blue-green glass eyes, $15.**

Teapot, 8" h, flat triangle shape, yellow side panels w/incised fruit, olive green body ............................... 50.00

Vase

6 3/4" h, swollen tube shape, sq base, green glaze, pr ........................................................................ 30.00

9" h, figural flowerhead, individual openings, chartreuse ........................................................................ 55.00

10" h

Painted brown and green pine cones, green needles, yellow-green ground ........................................ 20.00

Sq shape, swollen base, flared neck and rim, vert lines on base, brown .............................................. 15.00

10 1/2" h, oval cylinder shape, wavy rim, brown pine cones, green needles, white ground .................. 25.00

11" d, wavy freeform, gray impressed lines and dots pattern, pink ground, pink int, "Roselane China, Pasadena, Calif" mk ................................................... 38.00

# Rosemeade/Wahpeton Pottery Company

### Wahpeton, North Dakota
### 1940-1961

**History:** Laura Taylor and Robert Hughes established and owned the Wahpeton Pottery Company in Wahpeton, North Dakota in 1940. Laura designed the original models for the pottery they called Rosemeade which was made from North Dakota clay. The pieces were hand modeled in clay, plaster molds were made, and then the pieces were made by slip casting.

Rosemeade pottery was successful from the start, and there were huge demands for the pieces made there. After several years, Laura and Robert married, moved their factory, and soon added an addition. Howard Lewis came from the Niloak Pottery and joined them as plant manager and partner in 1944 to increase their production. He was responsible for formulation of the glazes and also introduced the swirl clay from Niloak.

Laura's designs were inspired from the earth and nature in her surroundings in North Dakota. She excelled in designing figures of birds, animals, and other wildlife. Her most successful examples were pheasants and mallards. Her first pheasant was made in 1942; she made nineteen different designs of pheasants. Animal shaped salt and pepper sets were quite popular. Other items included bookends, tea bells, vases, candleholders, creamer and sugar sets, planters, plaques, miniatures, figurines, ashtrays, TV lamps, and commemorative wares. More than two hundred designs of Rosemeade pottery were made. Many pieces had advertising information.

There were many experiments with color. Her Harvest Gold was a mixture of red and amber. High gloss glazes, dark bronze, and softly shaded matte finishes were utilized on Rosemeade pieces.

Most Rosemeade examples have a paper sticker and/or are marked ROSEMEADE in black or blue lettering. The paper sticker has the wild prairie rose and ROSEMEADE on it.

In 1956, Howard Lewis sold his interest to the Hughes, and Joe McLaughlin came from Red Wing. Laura died in 1959, and the factory closed in 1961.

Rosemeade
NORTH DAKOTA

**References:** Shirley L. Sampson and Irene J. Harris, *Beautiful Rosemeade*, privately published, 1986.

**Collectors' Club:** North Dakota Pottery Collectors Society, Sandy Short, Box 14, Beach, ND, 58621, $10 per year.

**Museums:** Richland County Historical Museum, Wahpeton, ND.

Ash Receiver, 2 3/4" h, figural standing elephant, pink and blue ........................................................................ 30.00

Bell, 3 1/2" h, figural tulip, red flower, green stem handle ........................................................................ 90.00

Bowl, 6" d, pinched rim, rose pink ............................... 30.00

Bud Vase

4 3/4" h, brown glaze ............................................... 50.00

7 1/2" h, bulbous base, flared neck, maroon ........... 18.00

Butter Pat, 4" d, figural pansy flower, yellow petals w/brown accents ...................................................................... 150.00

Candleholder, 2 3/4" h, figural bird on perch, turquoise w/pink accents ......................................................... 20.00

Cream Pitcher

3 1/4" h, blue-green glaze ......................................... 25.00

6" l, figural turkey, brown w/yellow and red accents ........................................................................ 135.00

Figure

2" l x 1 3/4" l, lying brown striped orange tiger ....... 300.00

2 1/2" h, goose, blue w/orange feet and beak ......... 25.00

3 3/4" h, pelican, yellow bill and feet, cream body ... 75.00

**Sprinkling Can, 4 1/2" h, turquoise glaze, $135.**

**Vase, 6 1/4" h, purple glaze, 1930s, $34.**

7 1/2" h, standing deer, irid finish w/copper accents ............................................................ 50.00

Flower Frog, 3 3/8" h, figural bird on stump, 6 holes, med blue ................................................ 22.00

Mug

3 3/4" h, relief molded wheat on sides, chartreuse glaze .......................................... 30.00

4" h, incised prairie rose design ........................ 50.00

Paperweight, 4" d, "Theodore Roosevelt Centennial 1858-1958," orange ..................................... 52.00

Pitcher

5 1/2" h, bulbous, relief design of horse on side, dk brown ............................................... 35.00

6" h, twist handle, matte beige glaze, sticker ........ 125.00

8 1/2" h, corset shape, gloss black .................... 50.00

Planter

8" l x 4" h, folded wave design, med purple glaze ... 55.00

8 1/2" w, frog, 7" h, gloss black dish, white egret flower frog w/tan and black accents ............................ 50.00

Plaque, 6" l, raised figure of bass ............................ 225.00

Shakers, Pr

Black bears w/tan faces ........................................ 30.00

Brussels sprouts .................................................... 20.00

Buffalo ................................................................. 125.00

Bulldogs, brown ................................................... 100.00

Chihuahuas ........................................................... 550.00

Chow Dog .............................................................. 95.00

Dalmatians ........................................................... 150.00

Fox Terrier ............................................................. 85.00

Leaping deer .......................................................... 95.00

Moccasin ................................................................ 50.00

Mountain Goats .................................................... 150.00

Pheasants, tail up .................................................. 45.00

Pointers .............................................................. 1,900.00

Puma ................................................................. 1,200.00

Quail ...................................................................... 55.00

Tulip ...................................................................... 50.00

Vase

3" h, rose bowl shape, matte lavender pink to gray-aqua glaze .............................................. 20.00

3 1/2" h, brown, tan, and blue swirl ...................... 325.00

4" h, swollen base, flared neck and rim, rose pink glaze ................................................... 20.00

4 3/4" h, figural swan, pink-gray .......................... 110.00

7" h, figural boot, gloss black glaze ...................... 165.00

# Roseville Pottery Company

**Zanesville, Ohio**
**1892-1954**

*Roseville U.S.A. 470-5"*

**History:** Roseville Pottery Company was incorporated in 1892 with George Young as the general manager. He had been making stoneware and purchased the J.B. Owens Pottery in Roseville to make flower pots, cuspidors, cooking utensils, and umbrella stands.

The company expanded in 1898 with the purchase of the Midland Pottery plant in Roseville. They moved the main office to Zanesville, purchased the Peters and Reed plant, and acquired the Muskingun Stoneware plant in 1901.

George Young hired Ross Purdy to develop Roseville's first artware line to compete with the other art potteries such as Weller, Owens, and Rookwood. The first line was called Rozane which also became the general name for all of the artwares or prestige lines. The original Rozane had a high gloss glaze of dark blended colors and was decorated with underglaze slip painting. Subjects included nature studies, florals, animals, portraits, and American Indians on the vases, bowls, floor vases, and such.

In 1902, they introduced the Azurean line in blue and white underglaze decoration on blue ground, and the renamed Rozane Royal with pastel shades including grays, blues, greens, rose shades, and ivory with the underglaze slip painting. Rozane Egypto came in 1904 with a matte glaze in soft green. The new lines were always competing with the lines being introduced at Weller. John Herold created the Rozane Mongol in 1904, a high gloss ox blood line that used typical Chinese vase forms. Herold also designed Rozane Mara in 1904 that was a metallic luster line from deep magenta to rose with embossed designs.

The Japanese artist Gazo Fudji worked for Roseville and introduced the oriental art style of decoration for his 1905 line of Rozane Woodland that had outlined naturalistic flowers and leaves incised in the clay. These decorations were colored with glossy enamel, while the grounds remained in the bisque state. A crystalline glaze was used for Rozane Crystalis in 1906.

The most famous Roseville artline was Della Robbia from 1906 that was designed by Frederick Hurten Rhead who was art director at Roseville from 1904-1908. His vases, tankards, bowls, and urns were made with the sgraffito process. Seventy-two different forms were offered in 1906. The motifs were both naturalistic and stylized with fruits, flowers, geometrics, animals, warriors, gladiators, and such being featured.

Rozane Olympic from 1905 resembled Greek red figure ware with Greek key designs. Artwares continued to be made until 1919, but there was declining interest before that date.

John Herold established the commercial artware department in 1903 with stein sets, smoker sets, dresser sets, tea sets, juvenile wares, banks, pitchers, and such with the decalcomania transfers in a large number of patterns.

Harry Rhead replaced Frederick, his brother in 1908 as art director. In 1914, he introduced the Pauleo line of luster and marbleized effects on eighteen different shapes. His Aztec design from 1915 was a slipware line, and his Donatello line from the same year featured one hundred shapes.

Two Roseville locations closed in 1910, and one plant had a fire in 1917. With one location left in 1918, they expanded the remaining plant. When George Young retired that year, Russell, his son, took over. Frank Ferrel replaced Harry Rhead in that same year and remained as art director until 1954 when the pottery closed.

With Ferrel's arrival, Roseville really shifted its attention to industrial artwares since Ferrel was responsible for more than eighty lines during his tenure. Sylvan was his first design with a bisque ground resembling tree bark and enameled decoration of leaves, foxes, owls, and grapes. Dogwood had matte glazed floral designs. At least two new lines were introduced each year when Ferrel was director.

In 1932, the firm became Roseville Pottery, Inc. Ferrel designed Pine Cone in 1935 and that became the most popular line at Roseville. It was made for fifteen years in seventy-five different shapes in brown, blue, and green. He had utilized a similar design previously at other potteries where he worked.

After World War II, there was a decline in sales due to inexpensive imports and the introduction of plastics. Several additional utilitarian lines were introduced such as a high gloss Mayfair and Artwood. In 1952, an oven-to-table dinnerware called Raymor was not too successful. In 1954, the Roseville plant was sold to the Mosaic Tile Company.

During the long years of operation, a wide variety of marks was used. Some examples originally had paper labels, while some were not marked at all.

**References:** Mark Bassett, *Introducing Roseville Pottery*, Schiffer Publishing Ltd. 1999; Jack and Nancy Bomm, *Roseville In All Its Splendor with Price Guide*, L-W Books,1998; Sharon and Bob Huxford, *The Collector's Encyclopedia of Roseville Pottery, First Series*, Collector Books, 1997; *Second Series*, 1997; _____,*The Roseville Pottery Price Guide*, Collector Books, 1997; Dr. James Jenkins, *Roseville Art Pottery 1999 1/2 Price Guide, Vol III*, LW Books, 1999; Randall Monsen, *Collectible Compendium Roseville Pottery, Volume I And Volume II*, Monsen & Baer, 1995, 1997.

**Collectors' Clubs:** Roseville's of the Past Pottery Club, P.O. Box 656, Clarcona, FL 32710-0656, bimonthly newsletter, $19.95.

**Museums:** American Ceramic Society, Columbus, OH; Chrysler Museum, Norfolk, VA; National Museum of History and Technology, Smithsonian Institution, Washington, DC; National Road, Norwich, OH; New Orleans Museum of Art, LA; Zanesville Art Center, OH.

**Reproduction Alert:** Copies of Roseville art pottery vases marked like originals include Magnolia and La Rose. They were made in China with a paper label but also have the raised lettering that appears on the originals. Two Roseville wall pockets have also been reproduced also with Roseville dealer signs. Additional reproductions include Clematis candleholders, Jonquil vases, Luffa vase, Water Lily vase, Zephyr Lily vase, sugar, creamer, and ewer, Magnolia vases, and a watering can. In all, over one hundred new Roseville shapes are being made in China. The new Roseville is made from molds taken primarily from old originals and include original appearing marks and shape numbers.

## APPLE BLOSSOM
Basket, 10" d, blue ................................................. 300.00
Bud Vase, 7 1/4" h, (A) ........................................... 132.00
Candlestick, 4 1/2" h, green, pr, (A) ..................... 165.00
Console Bowl, 15" l, (a) ......................................... 253.00
Ewer, 8" h, (A) ....................................................... 187.00
Planter, 2 1/2" h, brown, (A) ................................. 140.00
Tea Set, pot, creamer, sugar bowl ........................ 360.00
Vase
    7" h, green ......................................................... 168.00
    15 1/2" h, green ................................................. 525.00
Wall Pocket, 8 1/2" h,
    Blue ................................................................... 475.00
    Green .................................................................. 450.00

## ARTCRAFT
Jardiniere and Pedestal, 19 1/2" h, (A) .............. 1,760.00

## BANEDA
Console Bowl, 12" d, 6 sides, green, #237-12 ........ 1,595.00
Jardiniere and Pedestal, 19 1/2" h, (A) ............... 2,090.00
Urn, 5" h, green, #235-5 ......................................... 695.00
Vase
    4" h, green, #587-4 ............................................. 550.00

4 1/2" h, pink, #603-4 ............................................. 595.00
6" h, 2 handles, ftd, pink, #602-6 ........................... 595.00
8" h, 2 handles, green, #595-8 ............................ 1,450.00
9" h, green, #596-9 .............................................. 1,450.00

## BITTERSWEET
Wall Pocket, 7 1/2" h, gray, #866-7 ........................ 395.00

## BLACKBERRY
Console Bowl, 8" d, 6 sides, #277-8 ...................... 850.00
Jardiniere, 4"h, #623-4 ........................................... 595.00
Jardiniere and Pedestal, 29" h, chip, (A) .............. 3,425.00
Vase
    4" h, #576-4 ........................................................ 595.00
    5" h
        Volcano, #569-5 ............................................ 895.00
        #570-5, gold label ......................................... 650.00
    6" h, #572-6 ........................................................ 700.00
    8" h, #576-8 ........................................................ 995.00
    10" h, #577-10 .................................................. 1,795.00
Wall Pocket, 8 1/2" h, (A) .................................... 1,430.00

## BLEEDING HEART
Basket, 10" h, #360-10 ........................................... 250.00
Console Bowl, 14" d, #384-14, blue ....................... 325.00
Floor Vase, 15" h, blue, #976-15 ............................ 950.00
Vase, 7" h, (A) ........................................................ 176.00

## BURMESE
Bookend, 8" h, blue-green, pr, (A) .......................... 242.00
Wall Pocket, 7 1/2" h, blue ..................................... 385.00

## BURNTWOOD
Jardiniere, 10" d x 8" h, scene of sheep, (A) .......... 3,851.00

## BUSHBERRY
Bookend, 5 1/4" h, blue, pr, (A) .............................. 192.00
Cider Set, pitcher, rust, 2 mugs, rust, 2 mugs, green,
    2 mugs, blue ...................................................... 850.00
Ewer, 10" h, russet brown, #2-10 ........................... 325.00
Wall Pocket, 8" h, blue, #1291-8 ............................ 695.00

## CAMEO
Jardiniere, 11" h, cream, amber, and green frolicking girls,
    hairlines ............................................................. 450.00

## CARNELIAN I
Ewer, 12" h, dk blue drip over lt blue ground ............. 500.00
Wall Pocket, 8" h, gray drip, pink ground, #1251-8
................................................................................ 495.00

## CARNELIAN II
Vase, 8" h, green drip, blue body, #334-8 ................ 475.00

## CHERRY BLOSSOM
Jardiniere, 8" w x 6 1/4" h, brown ........................... 550.00
Jug Vase, 4" h, brown ............................................. 345.00
Vase
    5" h, brown ......................................................... 595.00
    6" h, brown ......................................................... 450.00
    8 1/2" h, blue .................................................... 1,100.00

## CLEMANA
Urn, 9 1/2" h ........................................................... 398.00

**CLEMATIS**
Basket, 7" h, green ....................................230.00
Bookend, 5" h, pr, (A) ..............................220.00
Bud Vase, 5" h, triple, green, (A) ................88.00
Ewer, 6" h, (A) ........................................ 110.00
Vase, 8 3/4" h, blue ..................................210.00

**COLONIAL**
Pitcher, 11" h, green .................................200.00

**COLUMBINE**
Ewer, 7" h, blue, #18-7 .............................315.00
Vase, 6" h, brown, (A) .................................99.00
Wall Pocket, 8 1/2" h, blue, #1290-8 ..........750.00

**CORINTHIAN**
Vase
    8 1/2" h ..............................................160.00
    10" h .................................................450.00

**COSMOS**
Console Bowl, 15 1/2" d, green, #374-14
    ........................................................595.00
Vase
    4" h, green, #944-4 ..............................155.00
    8" h, green to tan, #950-8 .....................475.00
    10" h, green, #954-10 ...........................235.00

**DAHLROSE**
Bud Vase, 6" h, triple, #76-6 .....................345.00
Candlestick, 3 1/2" h, pr, (A) .....................198.00
Jardiniere and Pedestal, 30 1/4" h, (A).....1,475.00
Vase
    8" h, #367-8 .......................................339.00
    12 1/2" h, (A) ......................................357.00
Wall Pocket, 9" h, #1258-8 ........................495.00

**DOGWOOD II**
Basket, 9" h, green with white flowers.........350.00
Bud Vase, 8" h, green with white flowers ....250.00
Jardiniere and Pedestal, 33" h, (A)...........1,870.00

**DONATELLO**
Bowl, 8" d ............................................... 148.00
Bud Vase, 7" h, dbl, (A) ........................... 150.00
Candlestick, 6 1/2" h..................................265.00
Jardiniere, 8" h ........................................200.00
Jardiniere and Pedestal, 28" h, (A)............385.00
Vase, 10" h ..............................................200.00
Wall Pocket, 10" h, #212 ..........................330.00

**DUTCH**
Mug, 5" h, ftd ............................................75.00
Tankard, 11 1/2" h, Dutch ladies ................285.00

**EARLAM**
Vase, 4 1/2" h, handled, blue, green, and tan crystalline
    glaze, #516-4 1/2 ................................265.00

**EGYPTO**
Pitcher, 5" h, matte green, Rozane Ware seal, #E33-5
    ........................................................495.00

**FALLINE**
Vase, 6" h, blue, #644-6 ........................1,495.00

**FLORANE**
Bowl, 8" d, tan, #62-8 .................................50.00
Bud Vase, 7" h, green and tan, #79-7 ...........40.00

**FLORENTINE**
Jardiniere, 8" h, lt tan and green ................475.00
Vase, 6" h ................................................185.00

**FOXGLOVE**
Bookend, 6" h, blue, pr, (A) .......................495.00
Bud Vase, 4 1/2" h, dbl, blue, #160-4 .........175.00
Conch Shell, 6" w, blue .............................200.00
Jardiniere and Pedestal, 26 1/4" h, (A) ....1320.00

**FREESIA**
Bowl, 12" l, brown, chips, (A) ......................99.00
Candlestick, 4 1/2" h, brown, chips, pr, (A) .....33.00
Cornucopia, 6" h, dk green, #197-6 ............145.00
Vase
    7" h, dk green (A)................................. 110.00
    12" h, dbl handles, pink, #45-7 .............. 115.00
Wall Pocket, 8 1/2" h, blue, #1296-8 ..........350.00

**FUDJI**
Vase, 9" h, Rozane Ware, slip decorated, bisque ground
    .....................................................1,650.00

**FUCHSIA**
Basket, 8" h, green, attached flower frog, #350-8 ......695.00
Jardiniere, 3" h, green, #645 .....................160.00
Pitcher, 8" h, ice lip, blue, #1322 ...............895.00
Pot, 5" h, c1939 ...................................... 165.00
Vase
    6" h, blue, lg handles, #893-6 ................350.00
    8" h, blue, #898-8 ...............................475.00
    12" h, green, #903 ..............................630.00
Wall Pocket, 8 1/2" h, blue, #128-8 .........1,195.00

**FUTURA**
Bottle, 8 1/2" h, squat shape, green, brown, and orange
    geometrics, (A) ...............................1,200.00
Jardiniere, 6" h, pink and gray, #616-7 ........750.00
Vase
    3 1/2" h, "Box" style, blue, #190-3 1/2-6 ..............495.00
    7 1/2" h, "Bamboo Ball Leaf," #387-7 .....1,450.00
    8" h, "Jukebox," pink and gray, #386-8 ....1,095.00

Vase, 8 1/4" h, "Futura" pattern, pink and lt green, $1,500.

8 1/2" h, 3 sided geometric, lt and dk blue, (A) ...... 605.00
10" h, green, c1924.................................................795.00
14" h, "The Arches," tan and green, #411-14......3,800.00
Wall Pocket, 8" h, tan, #1261-8 ..................................895.00

## GARDENIA
Ewer, 15" h..........................................................295.00
Vase, 7" d, 2 sm handles, green, (A) ..........................121.00

## HOLLAND
Pitcher and Bowl, pitcher, 10" h, bowl, 15" d, Dutch boys and girls, ivory ground, green rim ......................1,200.00

## IRIS
Basket, 9 1/2" h, pink, #355-10 .................................495.00
Cornucopia Vase, 5" h, (A) .........................................77.00

## IXIA
Bowl, 9" h, blue............................................................200.00

## JONQUIL
Jardiniere, 5 1/2" h, "551" ........................................395.00
Vase, 6 1/2" h............................................................275.00

## LAROSE
Wall Pocket, 8 3/4" h ..................................................270.00

## LAUREL
Console Bowl, 6 1/2" d x 3 1/2" h, green, #253-6 1/2
.................................................................................495.00
Vase
    6" h, matte green, #668-6 ....................................495.00
    7" h, green, #670-7 1/4 ........................................595.00

## LOTUS
Candlestick, 2 1/2" h, pr, (A).........................................55.00

## MAGNOLIA
Basket, 8" h x 10" w, matte.......................................275.00
Candlestick, 2 1/4" h, pr, (A)......................................187.00
Vase
    8" h, brown, #91-8.................................................200.00
    9" h........................................................................325.00

## MING TREE
Bowl, 9" d, #985 .........................................................135.00
Ewer, 10" h, white......................................................150.00
Planter, 5" h, green, (A) ...............................................80.00
Vase, 8" h, green, (A) .................................................150.00
Wall Pocket, 8 1/2" h, green, #566-8 .........................395.00

## MOCK ORANGE
Vase
    4" h, (A)...................................................................88.00
    6 1/2" h, (A)..............................................................77.00

## MORNING GLORY
Candlestick, 5" h, green, #1102-4 1/2, pr ...................895.00
Pillow Vase, 7" h, green, #120-7 ................................695.00
Vase
    4" h, bulbous shape, green, #268-4 ......................725.00
    6" h, white handles, #269-6 ..................................795.00
    8" h, green .............................................................725.00

## MOSS ROSE
Vase, 7" h, fan shape ...............................................410.00

**Vase, 10" h, "Mostique" pattern, green stems, yellow flowerheads, dk blue triangles, gray textured ground, (A), $330.**

**Planter, 9 3/4" l x 6 1/4" h, "Peony" pattern, raised "ROSEVILLE USA 426" mk, $275.**

## MOSTIQUE
Bowl, 7" d, yellow, blue, and green incised stylized floral design, textured gray ground, (A) ........................198.00
Jardiniere, 10" h, green, red, yellow, and blue stylized flowerheads and bands, gray textured ground, drilled base, (A)........................................................................660.00
Vase
    10" h, corset shape, gray, #164-10 .......................375.00
    15" h, corset shape, (A) ........................................715.00
Wall Pocket, 10" h .....................................................600.00

## PANEL
Vase, 8" h, brown w/orange pumpkins ......................295.00
Wall Pocket, 9" h, brown w/pansies ..........................325.00

## PEONY
Tea Set, pot, 8" h, (A) ................................................165.00

## PINECONE
Basket, 6" h, brown, #408-6 ......................................425.00
Bud Vase, 7 1/2" h, green, (A)....................................180.00
Floor Vase, 18" h, blue, #918-18 .............................3,500.00
Jardiniere and Pedestal
    24 3/4" h, green .................................................2,200.00
    27" h, green ......................................................1,985.00
Vase, 12" h, brown, #712-12 .....................................475.00

Pot, 7" h, "Pinecone" pattern, blue, $535.

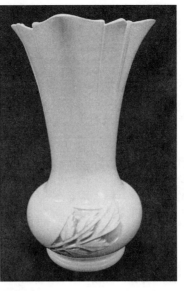

Vase, 14 1/2" h, "Silhouette" pattern, lt green relief bkd, white body, #789-14, $375.

Vase, 12" h, "Rozane Della Robbia" pattern, carved and cutback yellow daffodils, dk green stems and leaves, lt green to med green shaded ground, reticulated neck, Rozane ware seal, (A), $13,200.

## PRIMROSE
Jardiniere, 4 1/2" h, 2 handles, salmon, "Roseville 284-4" mk, chips ............................................................... 90.00

## RAYMOR
Bean Pot, Cov, 7" h, Beach Gray, Ben Seibel design
.................................................................................. 120.00
Celery Dish, 15 1/4" l, blue, #177 .............................. 225.00
Cup and saucer, Matte Avocado ................................. 25.00
Gravy Boat, Matte Avocado ........................................ 35.00
Plate
    8 1/2" d, Matte Avocado......................................... 20.00
    10 1/2" d, Matte Avocado....................................... 28.00
Ramekin, Cov, 6" h, Beach Gray, #156 ...................... 45.00

## ROSECRAFT-PANEL
Vase, 8" h, fan shape, white nude panels, green ground
.................................................................................. 995.00
Wall Pocket, 7" h, white nude panels, green ground
.................................................................................. 950.00

## ROZANE
Paperweight, 4" w, clover design, sgd "B. Myers," (A)
.................................................................................. 252.00
Vase
    5" h, brown and green glaze w/Art Nouveau silver flower
        overlay, (A) ...................................................... 605.00
    6 1/2" h.................................................................. 95.00

## RUSSCO
Vase, 8 1/2" h, dbl loop handles, (A) ......................... 154.00

## SILHOUETTE
Planter, 9" h, dbl, white florals on green ground, white body,
    (A) ........................................................................ 66.00
Vase, 7" h, fan shape, white w/nude, #783 ............... 300.00

## SNOWBERRY
Basket, 8" h, #1BK-8 ................................................. 195.00
Ewer, 5" h, green ...................................................... 130.00
Tea Set, pot, creamer, sugar bowl, pink .................... 325.00
Vase, 8" h, rim handles, blue..................................... 125.00

## STEIN SET
Pitcher, 11 1/2" h, 6 mugs, 5" h, "Elks" design ........ 1,500.00

## SUNFLOWER
Candlestick, 4 1/2" h, dk blue base, pr.................... 1,695.00
Urn, 5" h .................................................................. 1,395.00
Vase
    4 1/2" h, 2 sm handles ......................................... 785.00
    5" h, #486-5 ........................................................ 1,395.00
    8" h, green, yellow, and red, #490-8 .................. 1,795.00
    10" h .................................................................... 2,100.00

## TOPEO
Bowl, 9" w, blue ........................................................ 250.00

## TOURMALINE
Vase
    6" h, blue.............................................................. 135.00
    10" h .................................................................... 275.00

## TUSCANY
Candleholders, 3 1/2" h, pr........................................ 65.00

## VISTA
Vase, 8 1/2" h, multicolored molded landscape, (A)
.................................................................................. 358.00

## WATER LILY
Basket, 8" h, (A) ....................................................... 130.00
Bookend, 5" h, pr, (A) ............................................... 385.00
Cornucopia Vase, 6" h, (A)........................................ 66.00

Vase
  4" h, (A) ...................................................... 66.00
  6" h, brown, (A) ........................................... 99.00

**WILD ROSE**
Pitcher, 9" h .................................................. 195.00

**WINCRAFT**
Basket, 8" h, chartreuse, #208-8 ............................... 145.00
Bookend, 6 1/4" h, blue, pr, (A) ............................... 176.00
Candlestick, 4 1/2" h, pr, (A) ................................. 260.00
Coffeepot, 9 1/2" h, chartreuse, (A) ........................... 143.00
Console Bowl, 132 1/2" l, brown, (A) ........................... 165.00
Ewer, 18" h, chartreuse, (A) ................................... 440.00
Tea Set, pot, 9 12" w, creamer, sugar bowl, chartreuse, (A)
  ............................................................. 165.00
Vase, 6" h, hi-glaze, (A) ...................................... 90.00

**WINDSOR**
Vase, 7" h, trumpet shape, slender handles, mottled blue,
  #-548-7 ..................................................... 895.00

**WISTERIA**
Candlestick, 4" h, dk blue, #1091-4, pr .................... 1,250.00
Vase
  7" h, blue, #634-7 ........................................ 1,195.00
  8" h, blue, #633-8 ........................................ 1,595.00
  8 1/2" h, tan, #638-9 ..................................... 1,650.00

**WOODLAND**
Vase, 8" h, Rozane Ware, Golden Cyclamen flowers and
  green leaves, bisque ground, c1905 ........................ 1,495.00

**ZEPHYR LILY**
Basket, 5" h, hanging style, w/insert, (A) ..................... 143.00
Bookend, 6" h, pr, (A) ......................................... 264.00
  Vase, 7 1/2" h, (A) .......................................... 88.00

DOGWOOD

UNDERGLAZE
BY ROYAL SEBRING, OHIO
PAT. PEND.

# Royal China Company

## Sebring, Ohio
## 1933-1986

**History:** The Royal China Company took over the E.H. Sebring China Company plant in 1933. For several years, the factory was not used after the collapse of the conglomerate American Chinaware Corporation formed in 1929. By 1939, the plant was remodeled and working.

Royal China made semi-vitreous dinnerware, baking, and cooking ware, tea sets, premiums, and artware. Some of the major patterns included Colonial Homestead dating 1950-52 and advertised by Sears through the 1960s, Old Curiosity Shop, a 1950s pattern, Bluebell, Blue and Pink Willow, and Royal Oven Ware, all from the 1940s. One of the most popular patterns was the Currier and Ives drawings in green or cobalt blue from 1949. Royal operated the W.S. George Pottery in East Palestine, Ohio, but Jeanette closed it when they purchased Royal in 1969. Royal purchased the French-

Saxon Company in 1964 and operated it as a subsidiary. Royal China had a major fire in 1970, but the pottery was rebuilt. Both Jeanette and Royal were purchased by Coca Cola Bottling Company of New York in 1976.

Royal was sold again in 1981 to investors J. Corporation of Boston. Another change of ownership occurred in 1984 when Royal was sold to Nordic Capitol of New York City. Through all of these changes, Royal kept its name, and new lines were always being made. The last year of production was 1986.

Numerous marks were used during the long history of Royal China.

**References:** William C. Gates, Jr. and Dana E. Ormerod, *The East Liverpool, Ohio, Pottery District: Identification of Manufacturers and Marks*, The Society for Historical Archaeology, 1982.

**Collectors' Club:** Currier & Ives Dinnerware Collectors, Eldon R. Aupperle, 29470 Saxon Road, Toulon, IL 61483, quarterly newsletter, $15.

**BLUE HEAVEN PATTERN**
Coffeepot, 8 1/2" h ......................................... 10.00
Cup and Saucer ............................................. 6.00
Fruit Bowl, 5 1/2" d ....................................... 3.00
Plate
  6" d ..................................................... 3.00
  10" d .................................................... 6.00
Platter, 11 1/2" H-H ....................................... 14.00
Serving Bowl, 11 1/2" H-H .................................. 12.00
Soup Bowl, 8" d ............................................ 7.00
Sugar Bowl, cov ............................................ 10.00

**BLUE WILLOW PATTERN**
Chop Plate, 12 1/4" d ...................................... 10.00
Fruit Bowl, 5 1/2" d ....................................... 5.00
Plate
  7 1/4" d ................................................. 5.00
  9 1/4" d ................................................. 8.00
  11 1/4" d, divided ....................................... 8.00
Soup Bowl, 8 1/4" d ........................................ 8.00

**BUCKS COUNTY PATTERN**
Berry Bowl, 5 1/2" d ....................................... 3.00
Cereal Bowl, 6 1/4" d ...................................... 4.00
Creamer .................................................... 5.00
Grill Plate, 11" d ......................................... 25.00

**Bowl, 10 1/4" d, red "Willow" pattern, "Royal Willow Ware" mk, $35.**

Plate
 7 1/2" d........................................................12.00
 10" d............................................................13.00
Platter
 11 1/4" H-H, tab handles ..................................10.00
 12 1/4" l........................................................12.00
 13" l..............................................................15.00
Serving Bowl, 9" d...........................................10.00
Soup Plate, 8 1/2" d..........................................3.00

## CHIPPENDALE PATTERN
Platter, 12 1/2" d.............................................10.00

## COLONIAL HOMESTEAD PATTERN
Cereal Bowl, 6 1/4" d.........................................7.00
Chop Plate, 12" d............................................28.00
Creamer ............................................................6.00
Plate
 6 1/2" d............................................................3.00
 9" d..................................................................9.00
 10" d............................................................12.00
Platter, 11 3/4" d.............................................12.00
Soup Plate, 8 1/4" d..........................................4.00
Teapot.............................................................90.00
Vegetable Bowl, 9" d.......................................15.00

## CURRIER AND IVES PATTERN
Blue
 Ashtray, 5 1/4" d.............................................15.00
 Bowl
  5 1/2" d...........................................................4.00
  8 1/2" d.........................................................14.00
 Chop Plate, 12 1/4" d......................................35.00
 Coffee Cup and Saucer ...................................25.00
 Coffee Mug .....................................................35.00
 Cup and Saucer ................................................3.00
 Dessert Bowl....................................................8.00
 Gravy Ladle.....................................................75.00
 Gravy Boat w/undertray ...................................55.00
 Pie Baker, 10" d..............................................20.00
 Plate
  7" d................................................................18.00
  10" d................................................................9.00
 Platter, 13" l....................................................45.00
 Shakers, Pr .....................................................45.00
 Soup Plate, 8 1/2" d.........................................10.00
 Sugar Bowl, Cov .............................................18.00
 Vegetable Bowl, 9" d.......................................28.00
Pink
 Chop Plate, 12" d............................................65.00
 Creamer ............................................................8.00
 Cup and Saucer ..............................................10.00
 Plate, 10" d.....................................................18.00
 Platter, 13" l....................................................45.00

## DAISY ANN PATTERN
Plate
 6 3/8" d............................................................2.00
 7 1/4" d............................................................2.00
Serving Bowl, 9 1/4" d........................................6.00

## FAIR OAKS PATTERN
Creamer ..........................................................16.00
Gravy Boat, w/underplate.................................35.00
Plate
 6" d..................................................................8.00
 7" d................................................................12.00
 10" d..............................................................12.00
Platter, 13" l....................................................38.00
Soup Bowl, 8 1/4" d..........................................15.00
Vegetable Bowl
 9" d................................................................26.00
 10" d..............................................................28.00

## FALLING LEAVES PATTERN
Cup and Saucer ................................................3.00
Plate
 6 1/2" d............................................................3.00
 7" d..................................................................4.00
 10" d................................................................6.00

## GREENBRIAR PATTERN
Plate, 9" d..........................................................5.00

## GREEN PLAID PATTERN
Cup and Saucer ................................................2.00
Plate
 7 1/4" d............................................................2.00
 10" d................................................................4.00

## HABANA PATTERN
Bowl, 8" d..........................................................5.00
Cup and Saucer ................................................4.00
Plate
 6" d..................................................................4.00
 10" d................................................................5.00

## LAMAR PATTERN
Bowl, 8 1/2" d.....................................................8.00
Plate, 9" d..........................................................4.00
Soup Bowl, 7 3/4" d............................................3.00

## MEMORY LANE PATTERN
Ashtray ...........................................................12.00
Casserole, Cov, 10 1/4" H-H ...........................40.00
Cereal Bowl, 6" d...............................................6.00

**Bowl, 9" d, "Pink Orchid" pattern, $6.**

Chop Plate, 12" d ........................................30.00
Coffee Mug ................................................38.00
Cup and Saucer .........................................12.00
Butter Dish, Cov, 8" l ................................25.00
Plate
    6 1/2" d ..........................................8.00
    7 1/4" d ........................................18.00
    10" ..................................................9.00
Platter, 10 1/2" H-H ..................................12.00
Soup Bowl, 8 1/2" d ..................................15.00
Sugar Bowl, Cov. .....................................15.00
Teapot ....................................................145.00
Vegetable Bowl
    9" d ................................................16.00
    15" d ..............................................20.00

## MEXACALI PATTERN
Cake Plate, 9 1/2" d, wide red rim ...........10.00
Platter, 11 1/2" H-H, wide red rim ............15.00

## OLD CURIOSITY SHOP
Platter, 12" l .............................................25.00
Tray, 10 1/4 H-H .......................................24.00
Vegetable Bowl
    9" d ................................................15.00
    10" d ..............................................25.00

## PARK LANE PATTERN
Cake Plate, 11 1/2" H-H ...........................20.00

## PINK ORCHID PATTERN
Berry Bowl, 5 1/4" d ....................................3.00
Cereal Bowl, 5" d ........................................3.00
Chop Plate, 12 1/4" d ..................................8.00
Creamer, 2 1/2" h ........................................3.00
Plate
    6 1/2" d ..........................................4.00
    9 1/2" d ..........................................6.00
Platter, 11 1/2" H-H ..................................10.00
Shakers, Pr. ................................................8.00

## PRINCESS PATTERN
Plate, 10" d .................................................4.00
Platter, 13 1/2" l, oval ...............................10.00
Soup Bowl, 8" d ...........................................3.00

## QUBAN PATTERN
Cereal Bowl, 6 1/4" d ..................................3.00
Creamer, 6 1/4" l .........................................5.00
Plate
    6 1/4" d ..........................................3.00
    7 1/4" d ..........................................3.00
    10 1/4" d ........................................4.00
Platter, 14" l ..............................................18.00
Serving Bowl, 9" d .....................................10.00

## ROSEMARY PATTERN
Casserole, Cov, 10" H-H ...........................15.00
Cereal Bowl, 6" d ........................................3.00
Fruit Bowl, 5" d ...........................................2.00
Platter
    11 1/4" l .........................................13.00
    13" l ...............................................15.00

Relish Tray, 8 1/4" l ....................................8.00
Serving Bowl, 9" l ......................................10.00
Soup Bowl, 8" d ...........................................3.00
Teapot, 8 1/4" h .........................................20.00

## SONJA PATTERN
Dessert Bowl, 5 1/2" d .................................3.00
Plate
    6 1/4" d ..........................................3.00
    10" d ................................................5.00
Soup Bowl, 8 1/2" d ....................................4.00

## STAR GLOW PATTERN
Berry Bowl, 5 5/8" d ....................................2.00
Butter Dish, Cov, 7 1/2" l ..........................15.00
Dessert Dish, 7 1/8" d .................................2.00
Plate, 10 1/8" d ...........................................3.00
Platter
    7 1/2" H-H .......................................8.00
    11 1/2" H-H ...................................10.00

# Salem China Company

### Salem, Ohio
### 1898-Present

**History:** Salem China Company was founded in 1898 in Salem, Ohio. First it made white granite ware, then earthenware, kitchen articles, and semi-porcelain. The company had financial troubles and was purchased by F.A. Sebring in 1918, and was successful after that.

Many of the shapes and patterns were designed by Viktor Schreckengost during the 1930s and '40s. The company made fine dinnerware until 1967. Salem used a lot of 22K gold trim on its wares.

A wide variety of marks was used. Some marks included a date code. In 1968, it became a sales and service organization.

**Plate, 6 1/4" d, "Hopscotch" pattern, $5.**

## AMERICAN TRADITION
Tray, 11 3/4" l, "Nantucket" pattern ..............17.00

## AUTUMN LEAVES PATTERN
Fruit Bowl, 5 1/4" d ..........................................2.00
Plate, 10" d ......................................................4.00

## BISCAYNE PATTERN
Cake Plate, 11 1/2" H-H ................................10.00
Creamer, 4 3/4" h .............................................3.00
Cup and Saucer ................................................4.00
Dessert Bowl, 5 1/4" d .....................................3.00
Plate
    6" d ..............................................................4.00
    7 1/4" d ........................................................3.00
    9 1/4" d ......................................................10.00
Soup Bowl, 6 1/4" d ..........................................3.00
Vegetable Bowl, 9 1/4" H-H ..........................10.00

## BLUEBIRD PATTERN
Berry Bowl, 5" d .............................................10.00
Bowl, 8" d .......................................................20.00
Cup and Saucer ..............................................35.00
Plate
    7" d ............................................................12.00
    9" d ............................................................20.00
Platter, 11 1/2" l .............................................30.00

## BOUNTIFUL PATTERN
Casserole, Cov, 9" d .......................................10.00
Creamer .............................................................8.00
Cup and Saucer ................................................6.00

## BRIAR ROSE PATTERN
Cup and Saucer ..............................................10.00

## CASTLEWOOD PATTERN
Berry Bowl, 5 1/2" d ..........................................2.00
Creamer .............................................................4.00
Cup and Saucer ................................................6.00
Plate, 10" d ......................................................4.00
Sugar Bowl, Cov ...............................................5.00

## CENTURY PATTERN
Berry Bowl, 5 1/4" d ..........................................2.00
Cereal Bowl, 6 1/8" d ........................................3.00
Cup and Saucer ................................................3.00
Plate
    6 1/4" d ........................................................3.00
    7" d ..............................................................4.00
    9 1/8" d ........................................................5.00
Platter
    8 3/4" l .......................................................10.00
    11 1/2" l .....................................................15.00
    13 3/4" l .....................................................15.00
Soup Bowl, 7 1/4" d ..........................................3.00

## COCK O' THE WALK PATTERN
Plate
    6" d ..............................................................3.00
    10" d ............................................................4.00

## COMMODORE PATTERN
Creamer .............................................................8.00
Cup and Saucer ................................................6.00
Fruit Bowl, 5 3/8" d ...........................................3.00
Plate, 9 1/4" d ..................................................6.00
Sugar Bowl, Cov ...............................................8.00

## DOGWOOD PATTERN
Cup and Saucer ..............................................12.00
Plate
    6" d ..............................................................6.00
    7" d ..............................................................8.00
    9" d ............................................................12.00
Teapot .............................................................48.00

## DUTCH PETIT POINT PATTERN-TRICORN SHAPE
Creamer ...........................................................12.00
Plate, 9" d ........................................................8.00
Sugar Bowl, Cov .............................................20.00

## ENGLISH VILLAGE PATTERN
Cup and Saucer ..............................................10.00

## FAR EAST PATTERN
Cup and Saucer ................................................4.00
Plate
    6 1/4" d ........................................................3.00
    9 1/4" d ........................................................4.00
Serving Bowl, 8 1/2" d ......................................5.00

## FREEDOM HOPSCOTCH PATTERN
Cup and Saucer ..............................................35.00
Fruit Bowl, 5 3/8" d ...........................................5.00
Plate
    6" d ............................................................12.00
    10" d ..........................................................12.00
Platter, 13" l, lug handle ................................95.00
Vegetable Bowl, 9 1/4" H-H, divided ............35.00

**Plate, 10" d, "Briarcliff" pattern, $40**

## GODEY PRINT PATTERN
Coffee Service, pot, 10" h, creamer, 3" h, cov sugar bowl,
    5" h, 5 cups and saucers ..........................................65.00

## GOLDEN MAIZE PATTERN
Pitcher, 7" h ..............................................................45.00

## HEIRLOOM PATTERN
Gravy Boat w/undertray, 9 1/2" l.................................20.00
Plate, 10" d ................................................................8.00
Platter, 11" l .............................................................15.00
Soup Bowl, 8" d ..........................................................3.00
Vegetable Dish, 9 1/2" l............................................20.00

## INDIAN TREE PATTERN
Berry Bowl, 5 1/2" d....................................................2.00
Cake Plate, 10" H-H ..................................................10.00
Cereal Bowl, 6" d.........................................................3.00
Cup and Saucer .........................................................15.00
Plate
    6" d.......................................................................2.00
    10" d....................................................................15.00
Platter
    11 1/2" l ...............................................................8.00
    13 1/2" H-H .........................................................10.00
    14" l ...................................................................12.00
Soup Plate, 8 1/4" d..................................................10.00
Sugar Bowl, Cov, 5" h................................................50.00
Vegetable Bowl, 9" d .................................................10.00

## JAMAICA PATTERN
Berry Bowl, 5 1/2" d....................................................2.00
Casserole, Cov, 10" d ................................................10.00
Creamer, 3 1/2" h ........................................................3.00
Plate
    6 1/2" d.................................................................3.00
    7 1/2" d.................................................................4.00
    10" d......................................................................4.00
Platter
    12" H-H .................................................................5.00
    14" H-H .................................................................8.00

## MANDARIN PATTERN
Pitcher, 8 1/4" h ..........................................................5.00
Plate, 7 1/4" d..............................................................3.00
Platter, 13 1/4" H-H.....................................................20.00

## MAPLE LEAF PATTERN
Cereal Bowl, 6 1/8" d....................................................3.00
Gravy Boat, 7 3/4" l .....................................................7.00
Plate
    6 1/8" d.................................................................2.00
    7 1/4" d.................................................................3.00
    9 1/8" d.................................................................4.00
Platter, 13 1/4" l ........................................................24.00
Serving Bowl, 9" d ......................................................10.00
Serving Plate, 10 1/2" H-H .........................................10.00

## MISCELLANEOUS
Plate, 10 1/2" d, General MacArthur............................40.00
Service Plate, 11" d
    Godey print, cobalt border w/gold overlay ..............12.00
    Multicolored floral bouquet in center, cream border w/gold
        overlay .............................................................8.00

Purple plum and fruit ................................................10.00

## NORTH STAR PATTERN
Cake Plate, 11 1/2" H-H ...............................................5.00
Casserole, Cov, 9  " d, turquoise cov white bowl..........20.00
Cup and Saucer ...........................................................6.00
Gravy Boat, 7 3/4" l ...................................................20.00
Milk Pitcher, 5" h........................................................20.00
Plate
    7" d ......................................................................6.00
    9" d ......................................................................5.00
Platter, 11 1/2" H-H....................................................15.00
Serving Bowl, 9" d ......................................................10.00
Tidbit Tray, 9" h, 2 shelves .........................................65.00

## PETIT POINT BASKET PATTERN
Coffeepot, 9" h ............................................................5.00
Creamer, 2 1/4" h .........................................................3.00
Fruit Bowl, 5 1/2" d.......................................................3.00
Plate
    6 1/2" d.................................................................5.00
    7" d ......................................................................3.00
    9 1/2" d.................................................................6.00
Platter
    11 3/4" H-H .........................................................10.00
    13" l ...................................................................10.00
Serving Bowl, 8 1/2" d ................................................10.00
Serving Plate, 8 1/4" H-H .............................................8.00
Soup Bowl, 6 1/2" d......................................................5.00
Sugar Bowl, 2 1/4" h....................................................4.00

## SERENADE PATTERN
Cup and Saucer ...........................................................3.00
Plate
    7  " d....................................................................5.00
    10" d......................................................................6.00

## SILVER ELEGANCE PATTERN
Berry Bowl, 5 1/4" d......................................................4.00

**Platter, 13 1/2" l, "Symphony" pattern, sm pink roses, blue flowers, yellow border, gold rim, $10.**

Plate, 10" d ........................................................5.00

**SIMPLICITY PATTERN**
Cake Plate, 11" H-H ........................................6.00

**SOUTH SEAS PATTERN**
Platter, 11 3/4" l ..............................................5.00

**STARLIGHT PATTERN**
Platter
    11 1/2" H-H.............................................15.00
    12 3/4" H-H.............................................18.00

**SYMPHONY PATTERN**
Serving Bowl, 8 3/4" d ...................................10.00

**TALISMAN PATTERN**
Tennis Set, 9" d ..............................................8.00

**TULIPTIME PATTERN**
    Platter, 11 1/2" H-H ................................10.00

# Saturday Evening Girls/Paul Revere Pottery

**Boston, Massachusetts**
**1906-1915**

**Brighton, Massachusetts**
**1915-1942**

**History:** In 1906, the Saturday Evening Girls club was started with Mrs. James Storrow as patron to improve conditions for underprivileged working girls with craft and ceramic activities. Edith Brown was hired to supervise their work in all aspects of the creation and decoration of pottery examples. They moved to the Library Club House near the Old North Church which provided the inspiration for the Paul Revere name. It was also called the "Bowl Shop" until 1915.

The pottery moved to a new building in Brighton in 1915. All sorts of tablewares and accessories were made including plain and decorated vases, dinner services, breakfast and tea sets, bookends, inkwells, paperweights, and tiles detailing the story of Paul Revere's ride. Most popular were the children's breakfast sets with a pitcher, bowl, and plate decorated with chicks, rabbits, roosters, ducks, nursery rhymes, and such. Flowers, trees, boats, and the horse and rider were also used for P.R.P. examples.

Pieces were hand decorated with mineral colors. Some utilized the incised technique with the design outlined in black and painted with flat colors. The matte glaze palette included blue, green, gray, white, brown, and yellow. Some high-glaze pieces were made.

Paul Revere Pottery was never a successful venture in terms of making money and always required some additional financial backing from supporters. Edith Brown died in 1932, and the pottery closed in 1941.

Some paper labels were used with "Bowl Shop" prior to 1915, in addition to the impressed or imprinted mark with Paul Revere on horseback. Some pieces had P.R.P. or S.E.G. painted on the base.

Jar, Cov, 5" h, yellow and black banded design and rim, cream ground, sgd "E.G.," (A), $440.

**Museums:** Society for the Preservation of New England Antiquities, Boston, MA.

Bowl
    4 1/2" d, green and blue landscape on ext border, tan to ivory ground, (A)...............................................715.00
    5 1/2" d, ext border band of black outlined incised stylized white lotus blossoms, med blue accents and ext, white int, "SEG/AM/11" mark, (A) ...............................770.00
    6 3/4" d, cuerda seca ext band of trees and blue sky on matte moss green ground, "S.E.G./4-15/S.G." mk, (A) .................................................................2,970.00
    7 3/4" d, ftd, ext border band of black lined med blue lotus flowers, gloss teal blue ext, int w/teal blue streaks on ochre ground, Paul Revere, (A) .......................220.00
    8 1/4" d, low design, cuerda seca band of green, blue and gray landscape ext border, (A) .......................1,650.00
    9" d, closed form, semi-gloss green glaze, mkd, (A) .................................................................100.00
    10 3/4" d, flared rim, border band of black outlined white orchids and green leaves on blue band, white body, Paul Revere, (A)................................................880.00
Candlestick, 8 1/2" h, gloss blue glaze, Paul Revere paper label, pr......................................................375.00
Bud Vase, 4 1/8" h, bulging base, tapered cylinder neck, satin mocha brown glaze, speckled tan int, Sarah Galner, "SEG/1913/SG" mark, (A)....................................357.00
Cabinet Vase, 4 1/2" h, bag shape, flared rim, cuerda seca brown and blue Greek key pattern on border, green ground, (A)...........................................................825.00
Centerpiece Bowl, 10" d, inner border of black outlined yellow stylized tulips and green leaves, dk blue int, med blue rim and ext, Paul Revere, hairlines, (A)................825.00

Vase, 4 1/2" h, mustard yellow, imp horse and rider mk, Paul Revere, $350.

**Cereal Bowl**

5" d, blue stylized trees, ivory sky, blue-green ground on ext, ivory int, blue-green rim band, "S.E.G./R.H./83-2-11" mark, (A) .................................................. 1,100.00

5 1/2" d, band of cuerda seca of brown and ivory dancing rabbits on ext, (A) ..........................................2,310.00

**Charger**, 12 1/2" d, border band of green trees and blue sky, ivory ground, "S.E.G./E.T./5-17" mark, (A) ............. 660.00

**Creamer**

2" h, band of black outlined stylized white lotus on yellow ground, white ground, "SEG/10-20/LM" mark, rim hairline, (A) ................................................................. 137.00

3 1/2" h, band of black outlined seated squirrels w/blue oblong panels above, ivory-white glazed body, "SEG/2-7-12" mark, rim chip, (A) ...................... 385.00

**Cup and Saucer**, black outlined ivory band borders, sage green bodies, "SEG/1913/1915/EG" marks, (A) .... 110.00

**Egg Cup**, 1 3/4" h, black outlined white chick, blue glazed ground, (A) ....................................................... 275.00

**Inkwell**, 3" sq, w/liner, incised band of brown and green trees in landscape, steel blue, yellow, tan, and white accents, steel blue body, "SEG/9-17/AM" mark, (A) ................................................................. 1,870.00

**Jar, Cov**, 4" d, yellow and blue shaded painted sailing ship on cov, blue body, Paul Revere, (A)...................... 495.00

**Milk Pitcher**, 4 1/4" h, cuerda seca black outlined band of white rabbits and tortoise on green band w/"Slow but Sure," blue-gray body, (A) ................................... 1,650.00

**Paperweight**, 2 1/2" d, oct

Black outlined incised yellow and brown sailing ship, yellow ground, "SEG/JG/3-15" mark, (A) ............... 385.00

Matt finished incised black outlined brown windmill on dk blue landscape ground, med blue body, "SEG/9-20/EW" mark, (A)................................................. 513.00

**Pitcher**, 5" h, incised band of green trees, brown trunks, mocha brown ground, med blue sky around rim, speckled sage green body, restored spout, "SEG/1-11-11/FL" mark, (A) ............................................................. 605.00

**Pitcher, Cov**, 5" h, black outlined lotus flower band on white ground, steel blue body and cov, Tillie Block and Fannie Levine, dtd 1912, (A)............................................. 550.00

**Plate**

6 1/4" d

Border band of black outlined brown shaded pinecones, green needles, and black stems, ivory ground, Eva Geneco, "SEG/6-17/EG" mark, (A) ............................................................. 247.00

Yellow center w/brown inner stripe, incised border band of "bears," brown cottages, plants, and trees, cream rim, Fannie Levine, 1914, "SEG/6-14/FL" mk, (A) ...................................................... 2,420.00

7 1/2" d, incised black outlined tan Greek key design on blue banded border, sage green center and rim, Sarah Galner, "SEG 2-16/SG" mark, (A)...................... 385.00

7 3/4" d, "black Nancy.Pierce.Her.Plate" and rosettes on black outlined ivory ground, dk blue rim and inner band, ivory center, "SEG/9-21/FL" mark, (A) ................................................................. 303.00

91/2"d,"black   Eate.Thy.Breade.In.Joye.And.Thankfulness" on white border band, black monogram in center, satin rose pink body and rim, Lillie Shapiro, "Paul Revere Pottery/9-36/LS" mark, (A).................................. 495.00

10" d, center w/black outlined incised green trees, blue pond, dk blue, white, and yellow skyline, dk blue inner

border, white-blue outer border, Paul Revere, dtd 1926, (A) .................................................. 1,430.00

**Trinket Holder**, 1 1/2" h x 3" d, cylinder shape, black outlined stylized yellow tulips and green leaves, khaki green border, ivory ground, "SEG/4-8-14/JG" mark, (A) ....... 193.00

**Trivet**, 5 14" sq, black outlined center green square, black outlined blue or mocha brown rect borders, white rim, "SEG/6-16/TB" mk, (A) ......................................... 550.00

**Vase**

4" h, rolled top, black outlined dk green geometric border, med green ground, (A) ...................................... 605.00

4 1/4" h, rolled top, black outlined green landscape band, blue-gray body, Paul Revere, (A) ...................... 935.00

5" h, bulbous body, flared rim, iced white glaze, paper label, Paul Revere, (A) ...................................... 155.00

5 1/4" h, ovoid, closed top, abstract green trees and white sky, dk gray ground, "3-22/S.E.G./E.G." mk, (A) ................................................................. 1,540.00

5 1/2" h, ovoid body, flared rim, aqua blue speckles and spatters on med gray ground, Paul Revere, (A) ................................................................. 193.00

6" h, narrow base, swollen shoulder, black, gray, and brown leopard skin glaze, artist sgd, (A) ........... 495.00

7 1/8" h, bulbous base, elongated neck, speckled dk blue gloss glaze, "SEG 5. 24 M" mk, (A)................... 345.00

13" h, shouldered form, black and blue gloss glaze, Paul Revere, (A)....................................................... 495.00

# Edwin and Mary Scheier

## University of New Hampshire 1938-1950

## Green Valley, Arizona At Present Time

**History:** Edwin and Mary Scheier are studio potters who taught at the University of New Hampshire from 1938-1950. They made both utilitarian and expressive wheel thrown pottery. Sculptural pottery bowls, vases, jars, and platters were made. Their work was influenced by African and pre-Columbian motifs and contemporary painters of the 1940s period.

They moved to Oaxaca, Mexico in 1950 and operated a pottery there. They returned to the states in 1978 and still operate a pottery in Green Valley, Arizona. The marks used are the Scheier name incised on the pieces.

**Reference:** Michael K. Komanecky, *American Potters: Mary & Edwin Scheier*, 1994.

**Museum:** Everson Museum of Art, Syracuse, NY.

**Bottle**

5 1/2" h, squat shape, incised primitive figures, mottled matte beige and brown ground, (A)............... 2,016.00

7 1/2" h, bulbous shape, incised interlocking primitive figures, mottled gloss mauve and blue ground, "incised Scheier" mk, (A) ............................................. 1,064.00

9 1/4" h, ovoid shape, wide gunmetal band of sgraffito abstract faces, mottled matte brown body, "incised Scheier" mk, (A) ............................................. 1,230.00

18" h, emb child-animal figures, unglazed brown body, unmkd, (A)......................................................... 990.00

**Vase, 5" h x 8" w, brown, blue, and cream glazes, incised mk, (A), $385.**

**Vessel, 17" h, blue, black, and metallic bronze, repairs, $1,000.**

Bowl

  4 1/2" d

    Sgraffito stylized horse design on blue int center, white-beige ribbed body, "incised Scheier" mk, (A) .................................................................. 110.00

    Spherical shape w/ext circ base, stylized fish or figural motifs, olive green over gloss blue glaze, "inscribed Scheier" mk.................................................. 400.00

  6" d, int center design of stylized deer and ornaments, ivory-tan ext glaze w/cobalt, chartreuse, and dk brown flecks, "incised Scheier" mk, (A)........................ 165.00

  6 1/2" d, incised abstract faces, thick dk brown, cobalt, and buff flambe, mahogany brown ground, "incised Scheier" mk, (A) .................................................. 275.00

  7" d x 6" h, ftd, coupe shape, center band of incised fish and primitive figures on shaded blue ground, mottled gray and matte blue body, "incised Scheier" mk, (A) ..................................................................... 785.00

  7 3/4" d x 5 1/2" h, flared, folded shape, semi-matte mottled sand and brown glaze, "incised Scheier" mk, (A) ..................................................................... 275.00

  8 1/4" d, incised interlocking primitive figures of men and women, gloss blue and semi-matte brown glaze, "incised Scheier" mk, (A).................................... 672.00

  9" d

    Buff yellow glaze w/green speckling on int, "incised Scheier" mk, (A)............................................ 220.00

    Ftd, gloss dk brown glaze w/abstract designs and mirror accents and drips, mahogany, blue, and caramel flecks, "incised Scheier" mk, (A) ............ 357.00

  11" d, flared shape, incised stylized fish, celadon crystalline glaze over dk brown clay, "incised Scheier" mk, hairline, (A)...................................................... 1,680.00

Bowl, Cov, 9" d x 10 1/4" h, knob of 3 stylized sculptured birds, textured matte turquoise glaze, "*Scheier*" mk .................................................................................. 700.00

Charger

  12 1/2" d, line design of amoeba forms, dk brown sandy ground, "incised *Scheier*" mk, (A)...................... 935.00

  14 1/4" d, ivory sgraffito primitive fish, matte dk brown ground, "incised Scheier" mk, (A)................... 1,540.00

  15" d, man and woman holding toothed fish, volcanic blue, green, purple, and off white, bubbled border .................................................................................. 835.00

Figure

  4" h, Amish man or woman, polychrome, "incised M. Scheier" mk, pr, (A) ........................................... 137.00

  9 3/4" h, 2 women holding child aloft, unglazed gray earthenware, matte blue flower caps on each figure, "incised *Scheier*" mk, chips, (A) ..................... 1,045.00

Lamp Base, 14 1/4" h, 4 sided w/emb faces, matte purple and med blue glaze, "incised Scheier" mk............. 990.00

Mug

  5 1/4" h, brown stylized bird, ivory ground, c1940s .................................................................................. 90.00

  5 1/2" h, black stylized llama, ivory ground, 1945 .................................................................................. 92.00

Planter, 4 1/8" h, ftd, brown glaze w/gold flecks......... 195.00

Pot

  6 1/2" h x 7" d, dk brown raised stylized human figures, mottled blue ground glaze................................ 700.00

  14" h, pale blue and dk brown relief molded band of stylized human figures w/arms raised, med blue textured ground ........................................................... 1,895.00

Tea Service, Part, pot, 6 1/4" h, 5 demitasse cups and saucers, sage green drip glaze w/teal green and brown accents, rope knob, "incised Scheier" mks, (A) .................................................................................. 275.00

Vase

  7 1/4" h, cylinder shape, short ft, metallic black accented incised vert lines, frothy brown ext ground w/white spatter, swirled multi-glazed int, "incised Scheier" mk, (A) .................................................................. 330.00

  8" h, tapered shape, sgraffito design of abstract figures, matte gunmetal glaze, "incised Scheier" mk, hairlines, (A) .................................................................. 450.00

  8 3/4" h, flared, teardrop base, flared neck and rim, sgraffito design of man in fish and sun rays, speckled bronze-gold metallic glaze w/gold dust speckles, "incised Scheier" mk, (A).................................... 330.00

  17" h, multilevel, incised blue head design on black crater glaze, hairlines, (A) ......................................... 357.00

Vessel, 7 1/2" h, chalice shape, short, stem base, carved primitive figures and medallions, gunmetal glaze, "incised *Scheier*" mk, (A)................................... 605.00

## Hedi Schoop Art Creations

### North Hollywood, California
### 1940-1958

**History:** Hedi Schoop was born in Switzerland and studied fashion design, sculpture and other arts. She fled Nazi Germany and settled in California in 1933. After her fashion designs were discovered, Schoop was advised to turn her attention to ceramics, and she designed and molded painted slip-cast figures.

Needing additional space, Schoop opened her factory in North Hollywood, California in 1940 and incorporated in 1942. Her figures were decorated by approximately fifty decorators employed by the studio. During the peak years of post-war production, 30,000 hand painted pieces were made.

Schoop designed and modeled figures utilized a tinted clay, had high glazes and a gold or platinum overglaze. Many of the figures incorporated a planter or flower holder. Young women in the form of ballet or flamingo dancers, mermaids, international figures and peasant type characters were designed by Schoop. Often they were made in pairs such as the Dutch boy and girl and oriental couples. Console bowls were also modeled with figures.

Schoop's figures had distinctive facial features such as heart shaped lips, and characteristic eyes they were often demurely closed. The hair was often sharply incised. Some figures were produced with varying decorations such as different colors or applied florals or incised decorations. Many of Schoop's figures resembled mannequins from her fashion design background.

Schoop also produced animals, vases, wall plaques, planters, candlesticks, covered boxes, ashtrays, snack sets, and dinnerware. In the fifties she made a series of TV lamps. A fire destroyed her factory in 1958, and Schoop elected not to rebuild. After doing some free-lance work for several other California potteries, Schoop retired from full time pottery in the early 1960s.

A variety of marks included an incised or underglaze painted "Hedi Schoop" or "California," "Hollywood California," or "No. Hollywood Cal." Unmarked examples are very unusual.

There are many imitations of Hedi Schoop ceramics. Two former employees Kim Ward and Yona Ceramics started their own companies and imitated the Schoop wares.

**References:** Jack Chipman, *Collector's Encyclopedia of California Pottery*, Collector Books, 1992; _____ *Collector's Encyclopedia of California Pottery, 2nd Edition*, Collector Books, 1999; Tina Richey, "California Dreamin" Hedi Schoop Pottery, *Antiques and Collecting Magazine*, December, 1999; Mike Schneider, *California Pottery, The Complete Book*, Schiffer Publishing Ltd. 1995.

Bowl
    8" d, ftd, horiz ribbing, gunmetal glaze, wavy gold rims ........................................................................85.00
    13 1/2" l, lg pink dogwood blossoms, green leaves, textured gray ext, pink int ......................................45.00
Box, Cov, 8" l, free form, dk pink cov, gray wave handle w/gold flecks, gold flecked sides..............................45.00

Candlestick
    8" h, dbl arm, twisted stems w/bowls on top, polychrome ....................................................................65.00
    12 1/2" h, dbl sides figural female, blue and olive striped dress ............................................................170.00
Console Bowl, 12" l, oval, vert pink or white stripes, gold flecks and rim ..........................................................15.00
Dish
    8" w, figural butterfly, green w/gold and white accents ....................................................................10.00
    10" w, figural flowerhead, green and mauve...........35.00
Figure
    6" h, stylized owl seated on gnarled branch, brown ....................................................................65.00
    8" h, shy cat, white w/pink bow, yellow bell ..........145.00
    8 1/2" h, woman in pink gown, red sash and hem, black fan ................................................................30.00
    9 1/2" h
        Dancing girl, turquoise and pink swirled skirt......80.00
        Girl w/pony tail, blue skirt, gray poodle.............145.00
    10 1/2" h, woman with arms spread at sides, gray gown with brown circles...............................................100.00
    10 3/4" h, 11 1/4" h, Dutch boy w/yoke and 2 buckets, Dutch girl holding apron, brown vests, yellow hair, white and beige, pr...........................................125.00
    11 1/4" h, standing oriental woman with open fan . 150.00
    12" h, oriental woman, white hair, black and gray gown ....................................................................67.00
    12 1/2" h, young woman holding bucket under arm, another at side, green blouse, white apron with red flowers and greens............................................130.00

Figure, 8 1/4" h, brown hair, white dress, blue trim, yellow pot and underdress, "incised HS 1700-L" mk, $85.

Flower Bowl, 11" d x 8 1/2" h, cream ground, med blue flowers w/yellow centers, brown leaves, blue dress and hair trim, blue edge, cream hair, "Heidi Schoop Hollywood" mk, $140.

13 1/2" h, girl holding bowl over head, tan, blue, and cream ................................................. 220.00
Lamp, 12 1/2" h, oriental lady, white w/green accents . 40.00
Planter

5" h x 7 1/2" l, figural duck, green body w/gold wings, bill, and comb................................................ 25.00

7 1/4" h, smiling white cat, yellow bells around neck, green bow planter.................................... 35.00

8 1/2" h, bust of brown skinned angel, white wings and hair ............................................................ 75.00

9 1/8" h, figural lady holding book, green, cream, and red .................................................................... 95.00

Plate, 7 1/2" sq, HP black Scottie Dog, black streaked border.................................................................... 100.00
Vase

4 1/2" h x 8 1/4" w, dbl, 2 flower forms, rose red w/purple accents, "HEDI SCHOOP CALIFORNIA 480" mk .................................................................. 40.00

6" h, tapered cylinder shape, ftd, HP white flowers and buds, green cactus branches, white needles, mottled dk gray ground, shaded green int........................ 20.00

6 1/2" h, bulbous base, flared neck and rim, gray or yellow vert panels, platinum sparkle trim, "HEDI SCHOOP CALIFORNIA" mk ............................. 50.00

7" h, bust of man on front, woman on reverse, green lobed inner frame, white body ............................ 55.00

9" h, figural kneeling girl holding leaves, black, pink, gray, and gold, pr .................................................. 195.00

12" h, female figure w/white curls and gold bow, rose dress w/blue flowers, gold accents, umbrella flower holder ............................................................ 175.00

13" h, standing girl holding edge of green flowered dress, bowl on head, "Hedi Schoop" mk ...................... 220.00

# Sebring Pottery Company

**East Liverpool, Ohio**
**1881-1898**

**Sebring, Ohio**
**1898-1940s**

**History:** The Sebring Pottery Company was formed when five Sebring brothers established a partnership with George Ashbaugh and Sampson Turnbull in 1887. They purchased a plant that needed to be remodeled and made white granite ware. After two years, the brothers bought out their partners.

In the 1890s, the Sebring brothers added three potteries and also made semi-vitreous porcelain. In 1893, they leased the plant of the former East Palestine Pottery Company. In 1896, they built the Ohio China Company in East Palestine. Two years later, they gave up on East Palestine and built a new pottery called "Klondike" in East Liverpool. Wares included plain and decorated semi-porcelain, ironstone dinner and toilet sets, commemorative plates, and accessory pieces.

They laid out the town of Sebring, Ohio and moved their East Liverpool operations there. Other potteries established during the early 20th century included the Oliver China Company, Strong Manufacturing Company, Limoges China Company, Saxon China Company, E.H. Sebring China Company, and Sebring China Company.

During these early 20th century years, Sebring Pottery made numerous organizational changes, formed holding companies and corporations with many potteries. They continued to produce semi-vitreous dinnerware. In 1940, the company was absorbed by Limoges China Company, which continued the Sebring China line until 1948. With all of these changes, there were numerous marks used during the history of Sebring Pottery.

**References:** William C. Gates, Jr. and Dana E. Ormerod, *The East Liverpool, Ohio, Pottery District: Identification of Manufacturers and Marks*, The Society for Historical Archaeology, 1982.

**BLUEBIRD PATTERN**
Berry Bowl, 5" d............................................................ 10.00
Cup and Saucer ......................................................... 18.00
Plate

6" d ....................................................................... 18.00
8" d ....................................................................... 18.00
Platter, 11 1/2" l, "S.P.Co. S-V Sebring, O." mk ........... 20.00

**CHANTILLY PATTERN**
Berry Bowl, 5 3/8" d......................................................... 4.00
Cup and Saucer ........................................................... 3.00
Plate

6 1/4" d .................................................................... 3.00
9 1/2" d .................................................................... 4.00
Platter, 13 3/4" H-H ...................................................... 20.00
Serving Bowl, 8 3/4" l..................................................... 9.00
Soup Bowl, 8 1/4" d........................................................ 5.00

**CHATEAU-MINUET PINK PATTERN**
Bowl, 8 1/2" d ................................................................. 5.00
Cup and Saucer ............................................................. 7.00
Fruit Bowl, 5 1/4" d ......................................................... 5.00

**Plate, 11" d, "Celestial" pattern, "Jubilee" shape, $15.**

Plate
    6 1/8" d.................................................5.00
    9" d.....................................................10.00
Platter, 11 1/2" l..........................................5.00

## CHINA BOUQUET PATTERN
Plate, 6 1/4" d..............................................2.00
Platter
    12" H-H.............................................4.00
    13 3/4" H-H........................................5.00

## FLORENTINE PATTERN
Platter, 12" d..............................................10.00

## FORTUNE PATTERN
Dessert Bowl, 5 1/4" d...................................2.00
Plate
    6 1/4" d..............................................3.00
    9 3/4" d..............................................4.00
Platter, 10 3/4" H-H.....................................10.00
Serving Bowl, 9" d......................................10.00
Vegetable Bowl, 9 1/4" H-H..........................10.00

## GOLDEN MAIZE GLAZE
Basket, 6 3/4" d..........................................10.00
Dish
    6 3/8" d..............................................5.00
    8 1/2" l x 6 3/4" w...............................22.00

## MARTHA WASHINGTON
Berry Bowl, 5" d..........................................3.00
Cup and Saucer ..........................................3.00
Platter, 12" H-H..........................................10.00
Vegetable Bowl, Cov, 10" H-H......................20.00

## MINUET PATTERN
Creamer ....................................................3.00
Plate
    6" d...................................................2.00
    9 1/2" d..............................................3.00

**Platter, 12" l, "Fortune" pattern, $10.**

Soup Plate, 8" d...........................................4.00
Sugar Bowl, Cov...........................................4.00

## MISCELLANEOUS
Bowl, multicolored decal of cottage and garden in center, flowing blue border w/gold ganging swags, shaped rim
.................................................................10.00
Creamer, 3" h x 5 3/4" w, "Floral Krest" pattern, silver trim
...................................................................7.00

## PROMENADE PATTERN
Plate, 10" d................................................4.00

## ROSE BOWER PATTERN
Plate, 10 1/4" d............................................4.00
Platter, 11 1/2" H-H.....................................12.00
Serving Bowl, 8 3/4" d...................................6.00

## ROYAL DELIGHT PATTERN
Berry Bowl, 5 1/8" d.....................................3.00
Cup and Saucer ..........................................3.00
Plate
    6 1/4" d..............................................4.00
    9 1/8" d..............................................8.00
Soup Bowl, 8 1/4" d......................................5.00

## SAHARA ROSE PATTERN
Plate
    6" d...................................................3..0
    7" d...................................................3.00
    9" d...................................................4.00

## SERENADE PATTERN
Plate
    7" d...................................................5.00
    10" d.................................................10.00

## THE POPPY PATTERN-GOLDEN MAIZE
Berry Bowl, 5 1/4" d.....................................3.00
Bowl, 6 1/4" d.............................................4.00
Creamer ...................................................10.00
Cup and Saucer .........................................10.00
Plate
    6 1/4" d..............................................5.00
    7" d...................................................4.00
    9" d...................................................6.00
    9 3/4" d..............................................5.00
Platter
    8 1/2" l...............................................8.00
    11 1/2" l.............................................10.00
    14" l..................................................10.00
Serving Bowl, 8 1/2" d...................................6.00
Soup Bowl, 8" d...........................................3.00
Sugar Bowl, Cov.........................................15.00
Vegetable Bowl, 9 1/2" l...............................15.00

## TOLEDO DELIGHT PATTERN
Berry Bowl, 5 1/4" d.....................................3.00
Cup and Saucer .........................................15.00
Plate
    6" d...................................................3.00
    9" d...................................................5.00
Vegetable Bowl, 9" d...................................20.00

**VERMILLION ROSE PATTERN**

| | |
|---|---|
| Cereal Bowl, 4 1/2" d | 5.00 |
| Cup and Saucer | 4.00 |
| Fruit Bowl, 5 1/2" d | 3.00 |
| Plate | |
| 7" d | 4.00 |
| 8 1/2" d | 5.00 |
| 9 1/2" d | 5.00 |
| Platter, 11 1/2" l | 10.00 |
| Soup Plate, 8 1/2" d | 5.00 |
| Vegetable Bowl, Cov, 9" d | 15.00 |

# Sevres China Company

### East Liverpool, Ohio
### 1900-1908

1900-1908

**History:** In 1900, a group purchased the former Sebring Pottery and it became the Sevres China Company. It made semi-porcelain dinnerware, hotel ware, toilet, and tea sets. The company did not do well, and several owners forming the group dropped out.

J.R. Warner joined the group in 1908 and changed the name of the company to Warner-Keffer China Company, but the pottery closed in 1911. Various marks had the fleur-de-lys with names such as Geneva, Berlin, Melton, and Sevres underneath. Their hotel china was marked as such.

Bowl, 9 1/2" H-H, blue windmill and canal scene in center, gold dusted border and shaped rim .......................... 7.00

Cake Plate, 10 1/2" H-H, 2 bouquets of pink roses, molded bows and dots on border, shaded green and yellow border ground.............................. 84.00

Creamer, 5 1/2" h, figural robin, orange-red breast, gray body ........................................................ 50.00

Mug, 4 1/4" h, multicolored monk reading newspaper, brown shaded ground.......................................... 40.00

Plate, 10 1/2" d

Multicolored Dutch mother and children, raised lilies and dots, gold trimmed scalloped rim, mkd................ 15.00

**Bowl, 9" d, hanging red cherries, green leaves, molded vert ribs, gold dust rim, $10.**

**Beverage Set, pitcher, 16" h, 4 mugs, 5 3/8" h, purple grapes, purple tendrils, yellow shaded ground, shaded green top, gold trim, $175.**

Pink rose bouquet and foliage in center, molded shell border w/gold floral swags, shaped rim.................... 20.00

Platter

13" l, 3 groups of red cherries and green leaves, green shaded border, mkd ............................................. 12.00

15" l, multicolored peacocks in forest ...................... 35.00

Punch Bowl, 12" d x 7 1/2" h, green ground w/hp cherries on int and ext ............................................ 225.00

Serving Dish, 12" l x 8" w, kidney shape, blackberries, green leaves, brown stems, vert fluted border, gold dust rim, mkd ........................................................ 20.00

Tankard, 7 5/8" h, lg red roses on sides .................. 20.00

# Sewer Pipe Art

### Indiana, Ohio, Pennsylvania, West Virginia
### 1880s-1930s

**History:** The same clay that was used to make sewer tile was also utilized to make an assortment of folk art objects. Workers in the various factories used their spare time to make planters, vases, figures, and such for their own use. Some pieces were molded, while others were made freehand. They were not sold for profit. These pieces are now called "sewer tile art" or "sewer pipe art."

In addition to being made at sewer tile factories, these pieces were made at any factory where they used low-grade fireclay, such as roofing tile and chimney top factories. Many of these factories were located in Ohio.

The first clay works factory was started in 1883 by James and Frank Maurio. Factories continued to be developed in the 1900-1925 period. There was a great deal of business for these factories until the Depression. Additionally, the introduction of plastic caused many clay works factories to close.

Most of the sewer pipe art examples were made during the 1920s and 1930s. Tree-stump planters were the most commonly produced items made. Some were quite ornate, and others were more simple in design. They were used for planters and headstones. Other examples made included figures such as dogs, lions, and frogs, lamps, ashtrays, dog dishes, plaques, pipes, and yard ornaments. Examples that were made freehand are more desirable than those pieces made from molds.

Additional clay works factories were located in Indiana, West Virginia, and Pennsylvania.

**References:** Jack E. Adamson, *Illustrated Handbook of Ohio Sewer Pipe Folk Art*, privately printed, 1973; Susan Mellish, "Factory Workers Formed Fireclay into Folk Art," *Antique Week*, September 14, 1992.

Ashtray, 4" h, figural lion head, stamped "Carl Vera" and "Vera," (A) ............................................................ 120.00
Bank
  4 1/2" h, figural boy's head, chip, (A) ..................... 302.00
  9" h, seated pig, green-amber glaze, (A) ............... 605.00
  10 1/4" h, seated spaniel dog, (A) .......................... 154.00
Figure
  4 1/2" h
    Child seated on top hat, chips, (A) .................... 165.00
    Seated spaniel, brown-amber glaze, (A) .......... 198.00
  5" l, lying lion, head turned, rect base, Ohio, (A) ... 385.00
  6 3/4" h, squirrel eating nut, (A) ............................ 220.00
  7" d, sleeping curled cat, chips, (A) ..................... 125.00
  8 1/4" l, crawling turtle w/tooling, (A) ..................... 124.00
  10 1/2" l, crouching lion, scalloped edge, sgd "Antonini," (A)............................................................. 413.00
  12 1/2" h, seated dog, "imp Superior Clay Corp. Uhrichsville, Ohio, Handcrafted by Walter Smith," firing cracks, (A) ..................................................................... 330.00
  14" l, basset hound, (A) ..................................... 1,540.00
  16" l, crouching lion w/tree stump, shaped base, chips, (A) ................................................................. 110.00
  17" h, owl on perch, open top, (A) ........................ 660.00
  19 1/4" l, locomotive and tender, "imp Superior Clay Corp. Uhrichsville, Ohio, Handcrafted by Walter Smith," (A) ..................................................................... 660.00
Jar, 2 1/4" h, hex shape, incised bird, leaf, and house design, (A)................................................................ 25.00
Lawn Tile, 8" w x 7 1/2" h, molded sunburst design, chips, set of 28, (A) ........................................................ 275.00

**Figure, 9" h x 12" l, brown, Ohio Sewer Tile, $150.**

Pitcher
  6 1/2" h, tooled bark design, tooled face spout, "incised Jamie Stasser" on base, (A)............................. 150.00
  7 3/4" h, incised tree bark design, molded woman's head spout, relief of man smoking pipe in front, red-brown glaze, (A) ........................................................... 303.00
Planter, 15" h, figural tree stump w/8 branch openings, tooled bark, chips, (A) ....................................... 330.00

# Shawnee Pottery

### Zanesville, Ohio
### 1937-1961

**History:** Addis E. Hull, Jr. came from the Hull Pottery Company of Crooksville, Ohio and with Robert C. Shilling, along with some others, started the Shawnee Pottery Company in 1937. They took its name from an Indian tribe that inhabited the area and utilized the Shawnee Indian with an arrowhead as its trademark.

Shawnee manufactured earthenware products that were inexpensive, but were of high quality. They acquired the American Encaustic Tiling Company plant in Zanesville. Both kitchen and utilitarian wares were made along with decorative art pottery pieces such as ashtrays, bookends, trays, paperweights, wall pockets, jardinieres, lamp bases, and such.

They used glazes in varying textures and both bright and pastel colors. Overglaze and underglaze decorations were done. Shawnee utilized a unique glazing method which required only one firing by using new methods of drying the pottery so they could fire only once. This greatly reduced costs while producing a good product.

From 1937-1942, Shawnee supplied decorated pottery for inexpensive stores such as Kresge Company, Kress Company, Woolworth Company, and Sears, Roebuck and Company. Mostly flower pots, dishes, vases, and figurines were made for these chain stores. For Sears, they also made dinnerware and kitchenware which was called the Valencia line. Sears promoted this line by giving away a set free with any refrigerator purchase.

Rudy Ganz was hired in 1938 and designed some of the most popular cookie jars such as Jack and Jill, Sailor Boy, Smiley, and Puss'n Boots.

During the war period, production slowed down since the factory was mainly used for war contracts. Decorative pottery was made for RumRill from their own designs. Additionally, premiums were made, for it was the most recognizable line that Shawnee had produced. He also introduced a Pennsylvania Dutch line of small figurines, salt and pepper sets, planters, and vases.

After Hull left Shawnee in 1950, Albert P. Braid became president. There were financial losses during the early 1950s since the market was flooded with novelty pottery.

When John Bonistall took over in 1954, he changed the emphasis of the company from kitchenware to decorative items. He introduced new lines and increased sales. To cut costs, he eliminated hand decorating and substituted the spray gun method of decoration.

Kenwood Ceramics was a new division he introduced to make kitchenwares. The glaze on King Corn was changed to darker green and lighter yellow, was renamed Queen Corn, and sold in prepackaged sets. Touche was one of the most successful art lines. Others included Liana, Chantilly, Petit Point, Cameo, Fairywood, Fernwood, and Elegance. The pottery became one of the largest and most successful in the country under Bonistall's management. When the pottery closed in 1961, Bonistall purchased the molds and started Terrace Ceramics in Marietta, Ohio.

Many examples were marked with a number only. Some were marked with a number and U.S.A. A different range of numbers was used on different lines. Paper labels also were used for different lines.

**References:** Pam Curran, *Shawnee Pottery: The Full Encyclopedia*, Schiffer Publishing Ltd. 1995; Jim & Bev Mangus, *Shawnee Pottery*, Collector Books, 1998; Mark E. Supnick, *Collecting Shawnee Pottery*, L-W Books, 2000; Duane and Janice Vanderbilt, *The Collector's Guide to Shawnee Pottery*, Collector Books, 1998.

**Museums:** Har-Ber Village, near Grove, OK.

**Collectors' Club:** Shawnee Pottery Collectors, Dept. NR, P.O. Box 713, New Smyrna Beach, FL 32170-0713, ten newsletters, $25; *Shawnee News,* Kathleen Moloney, 211 W. 92nd Street, Box 42, New York, NY 10025.

**Reproduction Alert:** The #73 corn ware casserole and the #70 cream pitcher are being reproduced and both pieces are marked the same as original pieces. The original paper label had an arrowhead trademark in the upper left hand corner, and the new one has a tomahawk trademark.

## KING CORN
Bowl
| | |
|---|---|
| 6" d, #50 | 50.00 |
| 8" d | 65.00 |
| Casserole, Cov, 12 1/2" l | 60.00 |
| Corn Holder, 8 1/4" l, #79 | 32.00 |
| Creamer | 25.00 |
| Cup and Saucer | 80.00 |
| Dish, Cov, 11 1/2" l, #74 | 85.00 |
| Fruit Bowl, 6" d | 45.00 |
| Mixing Bowl, 6 1/2" d | 32.00 |

**Shakers, 5 1/2" h, yellow and green, $50.**

**Pitcher, 4 3/4" h, blue bib, yellow body, $85.**

**Teapot, 7 1/2" h, raised dk pink rose, green leaves, gold trim, $50.**

Pitcher
| | |
|---|---|
| 4 3/4" h | 45.00 |
| 11" h | 75.00 |
| Plate | |
| 7 1/2" l | 27.00 |
| 10" l, #68 | 60.00 |
| Platter, 12" l, #96 | 35.00 |
| Teapot, 7 1/2" h | 195.00 |
| Sugar Bowl, Cov | 54.00 |
| Vegetable Bowl, 9" l | 45.00 |

## KITCHENWARE-FIGURAL
Creamer
| | |
|---|---|
| 4 1/2" h, elephant, maroon trim | 35.00 |
| 5 1/2" h, Puss'n Boots, red tie | 55.00 |
| Milk Pitcher | |
| 7 5/8" h, Charlie Chicken, green, maroon, and brown accents | 90.00 |
| 7 3/4" h, Bo Peep, blue hat, red jacket | 265.00 |
| Shakers, Pr | |
| Puss & Boots, 3 1/2" h, red bows | 35.00 |
| Smiley Pig | |
| 3 1/8" h, blue bib | 55.00 |
| 5 1/4" h | |
|     Green bib | 125.00 |
|     Peach bib | 95.00 |
| Teapot | |
| 5" h, Tom, Tom, blue patches | 55.00 |

8 3/4" h, Granny Ann
Green apron, gold lace trim.............................235.00
Orange apron .............................................175.00
Purple apron, green trim................................150.00

## LOBSTER DESIGN
Cream Pitcher, 4 1/2" h, lobster handle, gray glaze
.....................................................................35.00
Dish, Cov, 8 1/2" l, handled, set of 4 .........................150.00
French Casserole, 11 1/4" l ........................................70.00
Shakers, Pr
Claw shape ..............................................95.00
Full body .................................................165.00
Sugar Bowl, Cov......................................................65.00

## MISCELLANEOUS
Bank, 5 3/4" h, standing Smiley Pig, blue bow............25.00
Bud Vase, 5" h, figural overlapped leaves, ribbed, magenta
.......................................................................8.00
Figural, 3" l, swan, matte white glaze............................5.00
Planter
4" h
Figural butterfly on log, brown, #524 ...................15.00
Figural pixie, gold trim, #586 .........................35.00
4 1/2" h
8" l, figural lying spaniel, burgundy glaze ...........40.00
Boy and dog, red, white, and yellow...................13.00
5 1/4" h, dancing couple, tan and red .....................14.00
5 1/2" h
13" l, pink-gray textured ext, gloss pink int..........34.00
Colonial lady, turquoise and red ..........................28.00
Smiley Pig, blue overalls, yellow trim .................26.00
6" l, overlapping shells, green glaze .......................16.00
6 1/4" h, boy at pump, tan, blue, and brown ...........22.00
6 1/2" h, figural 2 lovebirds, blue-green glaze.........15.00
7" l, figural pig, red bow ........................................20.00
8 1/2" l, wishing well, khaki green well and base, brown,
chartreuse, and cream boy and girl figures ........27.00
11 1/4" l, "Touche" wing design, blue and pink speckled
ext, pink int ..............................................10.00
14" l x 5" w, rect, blue-gray w/white threading .........20.00
Teapot
6 1/2" h, emb flower design, blue..............................60.00
Vase
4 3/4" h
Chain of Flowers design, lug handles .................22.00
Yellow wheat, blue-green accents ......................22.00
5 1/2" h, bulbous base, flared neck, long, straight handles, horiz ribbing, turquoise green ....................12.00
6" h, cornucopia shape, ribbed, lt blue glaze ..........22.00
7" h, flared top, handles on waist, med blue glaze ..16.00
8 1/2" h, indented sides, turquoise ground w/black speckling..........................................................25.00
9" h, dove, gloss yellow .........................................40.00
9 1/2" h, ball base, fan shaped body, yellow glaze, #890
.....................................................................15.00
9 5/8" h, figural hand, yellow glaze .........................33.00
11" h, figural giraffe head, brown glaze...................85.00

## QUEEN CORN
Creamer ...............................................................30.00

Dish, 6 1/8" l, #92 ..................................................45.00
Fruit Bowl, 6" l, #92 ...............................................45.00
Mixing Bowl, 6 1/2" d, #6 .......................................35.00
Mug, #69 ..............................................................37.00
Plate, 7 1/8" l, #93 .................................................32.00
Sugar Bowl, Cov, 4 1/2" h ......................................69.00
Teapot, 6 1/2" h ...................................................169.00

# Shearwater Pottery

## Ocean Springs, Mississippi
## 1928-Present

**History:** Peter Anderson established Shearwater Pottery in 1928 and worked with Jim, his son. Both wheel thrown and molded pieces were made. He worked in partnership with Walter, his brother, who was an expert with glazes. Figures, utilitarian, and decorative articles were made. When his brother died, his family assisted him in the pottery. Their wares were sold in their own showroom.

Bowl, 5 3/4" d, freeform, irid center and border, rust and blue
inner circles .........................................20.00
Figure
5 1/4" h, stylized bird on pedestal, gray w/turquoise and
blue accents....................................................35.00
6" h, pirate holding bottle, blue hat, yellow clothes, green
boots ..............................................................70.00
6 1/4" h, pirate holding 2 rum barrels, blue striped shirt,
yellow pants, pink hat.......................................75.00
12 1/2" h, stylized standing horse, turquoise glaze, imp
mk ................................................................395.00
Goblet, 4 1/2" h, ftd, tan and green flambe ..............130.00
Pitcher
5 1/2" h, blue drip over orange-red ground, imp mk
.....................................................................32.00
7 1/4" h, dbl handle, matte green castware body, black
metallic glaze, mkd, (A)....................................55.00

**Beverage Set,** pitcher, 5 1/2" h, 4 cups, 3 1/2" h, mottled
turquoise ground, brown rims, $135.

**Figure, 6 1/2" h, yellow and green striped cape, lt brown boots, blue tricorn hat, $75.**

# Shenango Pottery Company/Castleton China, Inc.

### New Castle, Pennsylvania
### 1901-Present

**History:** The Shenango China Company was incorporated in New Castle, Pennsylvania in 1901 and made semi-vitreous hotel and home dinnerware, and toilet sets. After financial difficulties, it reorganized as the Shenango Pottery Company. Additional difficulties led to a takeover by new management. It purchased the plant of New Castle Pottery Company and moved there in 1913.

Through the years of the Depression, it continued making hotel wares and railroad china. William Haviland from the Theodore Haviland Company of Limoges, France came to Shenango when he was looking for a company to make Haviland China in America. From 1936-1958, Shenango Pottery Company made china for the Theodore Haviland Company of France using its formula, blocks, cases, decals and such. These wares were marked "Haviland, New York."

The American representative for Rosenthal China of Germany, Louis Hellman also sought out Shenango in 1939 and arranged for them to make Rosenthal shapes and patterns. In 1940, the first Castleton China from Rosenthal designs was made by Castleton China, Inc. Shenango invested in this company. Shenango purchased Castleton stock and took over the sales and manufacture of Castleton China in 1951. It made a fine dinnerware line until c1970.

The company desired to create a fine china line with European craftsmanship utilizing the American technology. Contemporary designs were used for these tablewares in shape and decoration. Artists were hired to create these new designs. Eva Zeisel designed the Castleton "Museum" shape, which was the first freeform modern shape in fine china that was entirely hand crafted.

In 1955, Castleton made gold service plates for the White House State Dining Room that were ordered by Mamie Eisenhower. It also created a special design for Eisenhower's first birthday in the White House. In 1968, a Castleton set by Shenango was made for the Johnson administration for a state service. Dinnerware sets were also made for foreign heads of state. During the 1950s, Castleton made a series of game plates and a line of everyday china.

The name of the company was changed back to Shenango China, Inc. in 1954. Two years later, it developed a "Fast-Fire" kiln which revolutionized the vitrified china industry by reducing the glost fire time to one hour and ten minutes from 36-40 hours.

In 1959, Shenango bought Wallace China in California, and it was operated as a wholly owned subsidiary. Two years later, the assets of Shenango were transferred to Shenango Ceramics, Inc., which was held by the Sobiloffs who had purchased all the shares in 1959. They purchased Mayer China Company of Beaver Falls, Pennsylvania in 1964 and liquidated Wallace China. All assets of Shenango

Soup Bowl, 4 1/2" l, lug handle, swirled green glaze.... 10.00
Teapot, 6" h x 9" w, green glaze w/dk brown and blue drips, Peter Anderson ....................................................... 55.00
Vase

   2 1/4" h, miniature, ball base, straight neck, shaded brown glazes ...................................................... 40.00

   2 1/2" h, miniature, lustered green glaze ................. 25.00

   3" h, bulbous base, straight neck, gloss purple glaze, (A) ..................................................................... 45.00

   4" h, bulbous shape, lt green glaze w/gunmetal streaks ....................................................................... 35.00

   4 1/2" h, goblet shape, tan and green flambe ........ 130.00

   5" h

      Ball shape, sm handles, turquoise .................... 250.00

      Trumpet shape, lt blue, hairlines ......................... 10.00

   5 1/2" h, corset shape, rolled rim, turquoise glaze... 75.00

   6" h

      Bulbous body, flared rim, mottled brown to gray glaze, (A) ............................................................... 110.00

      Dk aqua glaze ................................................. 240.00

   6 1/2" h, trumpet shape, lt green ground with metallic silver shading ...................................................... 265.00

   9 1/2" h, flared shape w/rolled rim, multi-shaded blue drip glaze over green ground, imp mk, (A) .............. 286.00

   11" h, bulbous shape with short cylinder neck, blue crystalline emb dancing figures and stylized grapevines, gunmetal ground, unmkd, (A) ........................ 4,400.00

   12" h, cylinder shape, hand thrown, lt green glaze ....................................................................... 125.00

including Castleton and Mayer were sold by the Sobiloffs to Interpace Corporation which made Fransciscan earthenware and fine china in 1968.

Shenango was taken over by Anchor Hocking Corporation in 1979, and it continue to make hotel, restaurant, and institutional ware. Marks with "Castleton China" date from 1940-1968. Interpace marks date from 1968-1979. A tremendous amount of marks was used. The Shenango Indian was the trademark of Shenango China.

## CASTLETON

### Caprice Pattern
Bread and Butter Plate............................................10.00
Cup and Saucer........................................................13.00
Dinner Plate.............................................................15.00
Salad Plate...............................................................11.00

### Carlton Pattern
Creamer....................................................................45.00
Cup and Saucer........................................................36.00
Gravy w/stand........................................................110.00

### Castleton Manor Pattern
Cup and Saucer........................................................20.00
Plate
   8 3/8" d...............................................................10.00
   10 3/4" d.............................................................15.00

### Dolly Madison Pattern
Creamer, 2 5/8" h.....................................................50.00
Cup and Saucer........................................................35.00
Fruit Bowl, 5 5/8" d...................................................30.00
Gravy Boat and Stand............................................110.00
Plate
   6 1/2" d...............................................................15.00
   8" d.....................................................................25.00
   10 3/4" d.............................................................35.00
Platter
   13 3/8" l..............................................................98.00
   15 7/8" l............................................................125.00
Serving Dish, 10" l....................................................50.00
Soup Bowl, 8" d........................................................45.00
Sugar Bowl, Cov, 2 3/4" h.........................................70.00

**Plate, 10 5/8" d, "Jade" pattern, "Castleton Studios" mk, $18.**

### Flair Pattern
Cup and Saucer..........................................................8.00
Plate, 6 1/2" d..........................................................15.00

### Gloria Pattern
Cup and Saucer........................................................36.00
Cup and Saucer, Demitasse.....................................35.00
Plate
   6 1/2" d...............................................................15.00
   8" d.....................................................................25.00
   10 3/4" d.............................................................35.00
Platter, 16" l.............................................................85.00
Sauce Dish, 5 5/8" d...................................................7.00
Vegetable Bowl, 11 1/4" l.........................................95.00

### Golden Meadow Pattern
Bowl, 8" d...................................................................5.00
Vegetable Bowl
   9" l........................................................................7.00
   11" l......................................................................9.00

### Golden Scroll Pattern
Vegetable Bowl, 10 1/2" l.........................................25.00

### Jubilee Pattern
Cup and Saucer........................................................10.00

### June Pattern
Cream Soup, 4 3/4" d................................................10.00
Cup and Saucer........................................................22.00
Fruit Bowl, 5 1/2" d...................................................10.00
Plate
   6 1/4" d...............................................................12.00
   8 3/8" d...............................................................18.00
   9" d.....................................................................20.00
   10 5/8" d.............................................................22.00
Platter, 13 1/8" l......................................................35.00
Vegetable Bowl, 11" l...............................................35.00

### Lace Pattern
Cup and Saucer........................................................30.00
Plate, 10 5/8" d........................................................35.00

### Lyric Pattern
Cup and Saucer........................................................35.00
Plate
   6 1/4" d...............................................................12.00
   8 1/2" d...............................................................12.00
   10 1/2" d.............................................................15.00

### Mandalay Pattern
Cup and Saucer..........................................................8.00
Plate
   6" d.......................................................................6.00
   8" d.......................................................................8.00
   10 3/4" d.............................................................10.00
Vegetable Bowl, Cov, 10" d......................................25.00

### Mayfair Pattern
Cup and Saucer........................................................10.00
Plate
   6 1/4" d.................................................................5.00
   8 1/2" d.................................................................6.00
Platter, 13 1/4" l......................................................35.00

Tea Set, pot, 7" h, creamer, 3 1/2" h, cov sugar bowl, 5 1/2" h, "Sunnybrooke" pattern, $70.

## Peony Pattern
Plate, 9 1/4" d ........................................................ 15.00

## Rose Pattern
Cup and Saucer .................................................... 10.00

## Sunnybrooke Pattern
Cream Soup, 5" d, w/underplate ........................... 50.00
Cup and Saucer .................................................... 20.00
Plate
  6 1/4" d ............................................................. 20.00
  8 1/2" d ............................................................. 25.00
  10 3/4" d ........................................................... 30.00
Platter
  13 1/8" l ............................................................ 75.00
  18 1/2" l .......................................................... 100.00
Vegetable Bowl
  10" l ................................................................. 60.00
  11 1/4" l ............................................................ 75.00

## Sunnyvale Pattern
Creamer ............................................................... 30.00
Plate
  5" d .................................................................. 14.00
  10 1/2" d ........................................................... 28.00
Teapot ................................................................ 225.00
Vegetable Bowl, 11" d ...........................:............. 60.00

## SHENANGO

### Inca Ware
Bowl
  5" d ................................................................... 5.00
  10 1/4" d ........................................................... 20.00
Butter Pat, 4" d, set of 4 ......................................... 6.00
Cup and Saucer ..................................................... 3.00
Gravy Boat ........................................................... 10.00
Platter
  12 1/2" l ............................................................ 10.00
  15" l ................................................................. 16.00

## MISCELLANEOUS
Cup and Saucer, Willow pattern, blue ....................... 5.00
Mug, 4 7/8" h, brown branding irons and long horn steers on rim ................................................................... 38.00
Plate
  6 3/4" d, Indian Tree pattern .................................. 5.00

10 3/4" d, drunken Shriner w/bandage on head in
  center, multicolored .......................................... 45.00
Platter, 12" l, oval, emb vert ribbed border, ivory glaze
  ......................................................................... 5.00

# Southern Potteries, Inc. Blue Ridge Dinnerware

## Erwin Tennessee
## 1938-1957

**History:** Southern Potteries was incorporated in 1920, with E.J. Owens from the Owens China Company as president. Charles W. Foreman purchased the pottery in the early 1920s and completely changed the pottery made there by introducing the technique of hand painting under the glaze. By 1938, Blue Ridge dinnerware began with full freehand painting. This process was a great success since so many other companies were using decal decorations. No two pieces were exactly alike since they were all hand painted.

With World War II, dinnerware imports were cut off, which allowed U.S. potteries to expand. The peak years for Southern Potteries were the mid-1940s until the early 1950s. After that, imports became prominent again, and plastics also came to the forefront. In 1951, Southern Potteries was the largest hand painting pottery in the United States. The patterns were sold at major department stores and other retail outlets. Most of the patterns were done freehand, with the decorators copying from a master pattern piece.

Lena Watts was the chief designer for Blue Ridge Pottery. She later moved to Stetson China Company. By 1951, there were more than four hundred patterns in open stock. Most were designed by a chief designer, while some were created by buyers from major department stores who worked along with the designers.

There were eleven different shapes of Blue Ridge dinnerware such as Candlewick with a beaded edge, Colonial with fluted shapes, Piecrust with a crimped edge, Clinchfield with a wide, flat rim, Trailway with wide painted borders and numerous others. Some of the patterns were done on several shapes. Patterns usually were numbered consecutively: 3000 numbers in the 1940s, 4000 numbers in the 1950s. Most Blue Ridge patterns were not named at the factory, only numbered. Sometimes they acquired a name when they were advertised either by the pottery or the store that was selling them. Many patterns acquired a name in the *Blue Ridge Dinnerware* book by Betty and Bill Newbound. The majority of patterns showed an assortment of florals, fruits, farm scenes, roosters, leaves, peasant figures, and such.

A line of about forty pieces of vitreous chinaware specialty items was introduced about 1945 that included decorative pitchers, shakers, creamers and sugars, chocolate pots, teapots, vases, relishes, and character jugs. No dinnerware sets were made in chinaware. Teapots were made in both earthenware to match dinnerware sets and in china. A small line of ovenware also was made.

Premiums were made for Avon, Quaker Oats, Stanley Home Products, and also for trading stamp companies and Montgomery Wards. During the mid-1950s, a line of table lamp bases was introduced, as was a line of china character jugs. The subjects were Pioneer Woman, Daniel Boone, Paul Revere, and the Indian. Artist signed pieces from the mid-1940s included scenic and wildlife plates and platters on earthenware blanks.

Labor costs continued to rise and the pottery business decreased. In the later years, when designs were stamped on the pottery and filled in by hand, sales declined. Southern Potteries tried cutting operating time in half, but eventually closed in 1957.

Nine different marks were used on Blue Ridge pottery. Some marks were used concurrently. Some pieces have jobbers' marks from supermarkets and trading stamp companies.

**References:** Winnie Keillor, *Dishes, What Else? Blue Ridge Of Course!* Privately Printed, 1983; Betty & Bill Newbound, *Blue Ridge Dinnerware, Revised Third Edition*, Collector Books, 1999; _____, *Collector's Encyclopedia of Blue Ridge Dinnerware, Volume II*, Collector Books, 1998; Betty Newbound, *Southern Potteries, Inc. Blue Ridge Dinnerware, Revised 3rd Edition*, Collector Books, 1989; values updated 1993; Frances & John Ruffin, *Blue Ridge China Today*, Schiffer Publishing Ltd.1997; _____*Blue Ridge China Traditions*, Schiffer Publishing Ltd. 1999.

**Collectors' Clubs:** Blue Ridge Collectors Club, Phyllis Ledford, 245 Seater Road, Erwin, TN 37650-3925, dues $5.

**Newsletters:** *The Blue Ridge Beacon*, 7091 S. Main Street, Helen, GA 30545, bimonthly; *National Blue Ridge Newsletter*, Norma Lilly, 144 Highland Drive, Blountville, TN 37617-5404, bimonthly, $15.

**Museums:** Unicoi Heritage Museum, near Erwin, TN.

## ASTOR SHAPE
Corsage Pattern
  Plate
    9" d................................................16.00
    10 1/4" d..........................................22.00
Cumberland Pattern
  Fruit Bowl, 5" d....................................6.00
Freedom Ring Pattern
  Plate, 10 1/4" d...................................22.00
Fruit Cocktail Pattern
  Salad Plate, 8" d.................................22.00
Hopscotch Pattern
  Plate, 9" d.........................................45.00
Roseanna Pattern
  Egg Cup.............................................40.00
  Platter, 17" l......................................75.00

## CANDLEWICK SHAPE
Blue Bell Bouquet Pattern
  Creamer.............................................15.00
  Cup and Saucer...................................15.00
  Plate
    7" d................................................20.00
    10 1/4" d..........................................30.00
  Platter, 13" l......................................35.00
  Sugar Bowl, Cov..................................22.00
  Vegetable Bowl, 9" d...........................20.00

Carnival Pattern
  Plate
    6 1/4" d............................................6.00
    9 1/4" d............................................8.00
Cherry Cherry Pattern
  Platter, 12" l......................................18.00
Dahlia Pattern
  Cup and Saucer...................................30.00
  Plate, 10 1/4" d...................................30.00
  Vegetable Bowl, 9 1/4" l........................40.00
Green Lanterns Pattern
  Plate, 6 1/4" d......................................5.00
  Platter
    11 1/2" l...........................................12.00
    13" l................................................15.00
Highland Posy Pattern
  Cup and Saucer...................................15.00
  Dessert Bowl, 5" d.................................5.00
  Plate
    6 1/4" d............................................7.00
    9 1/4" d............................................10.00
Hilda Pattern
  Plate
    7" d.................................................4.00
    9 1/4" d.............................................6.00
Honolulu Pattern
  Plate, 8" d
    Apples.............................................25.00
    Cherries...........................................22.00
Mountain Ivy Pattern
  Plate, 6 1/4" d......................................5.00
  Platter, 13 3/4" l.................................15.00
  Serving Bowl, 9" l...............................10.00
Mountain Nosegay Pattern
  Plate
    6 1/4" d............................................5.00
    9 1/4" d............................................25.00
  Platter, 11 1/2" l.................................25.00
Plum Duff Pattern
  Plate, 8" d.........................................18.00
Pom Pom Pattern
  Platter, 9" l.......................................18.00
Quaker Apple Pattern
  Bowl
    5 3/8" d............................................8.00
    6" d.................................................8.00
    8" d.................................................8.00
    9" d.................................................9.00
  Creamer, 2 3/4" h...............................25.00
  Plate
    6 1/4"...............................................7.00
    7" d................................................15.00
  Platter, 13 1/4" l.................................30.00
  Sugar Bowl, Cov, 3 1/2" h....................25.00
Spindrift Pattern
  Plate, 9" d..........................................7.00
Sweet Clover Pattern
  Plate, 10 1/4" d...................................22.00

Bowl, 9" d, "Crab Apple" pattern, "Colonial" shape, $12.

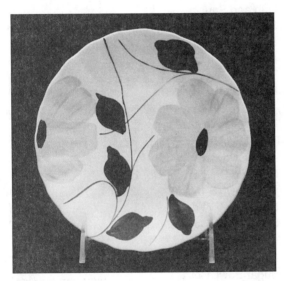

Plate, 6 3/8" d, "Ridge Daisy" pattern, "Colonial" shape, $8.

Platter, 14" l ...................................................40.00
Sungold I Pattern
    Gravy Boat .............................................18.00
Sunshine Pattern
    Plate, 9" d .............................................18.00
Tricolor Pattern
    Fruit Bowl, 5" d .......................................6.00
Tulip Time Pattern
    Bowl, 8" d ..............................................8.00

## CLINCHFIELD SHAPE
Fairmede Fruit Pattern
    Platter, 14 1/2" l ....................................65.00
Lyonnaise Pattern
    Chop Plate, 11 1/4" d..............................150.00
    Coaster, 4" d...........................................45.00
    Platter
        13 1/2" l...........................................275.00
        17 1/4" l...........................................425.00

## COLONIAL SHAPE
Apple Trio Pattern
    Cup and Saucer .....................................10.00
    Plate
        6" d .................................................3.00
        9 1/2" d ............................................5.00
Autumn Apple Pattern
    Creamer ................................................15.00
Beaded Apple Pattern
    Plate, 10" d............................................18.00
Becky Pattern
    Plate
        8" d .................................................8.00
        10" d ...............................................12.00
Big Apple Pattern
    Creamer and Cov Sugar Bowl ................10.00
    Plate
        6" d .................................................2.00
        7" d .................................................3.00
        9 1/2" d ............................................4.00
Cherry Bounce Pattern
    Plate
        7" sq...............................................25.00
        9" sq...............................................18.00
Chintz Pattern
    Plate, 10" d............................................28.00
Chrysanthemum Pattern
    Platter, 15" l ..........................................65.00
    Vegetable Bowl, 9" d ..............................40.00
County Fair Pattern
    Bowl, 10" d.............................................45.00
    Plate, 8" d, plums .................................25.00
Crab Apple Pattern
    Bowl, 9" d...............................................30.00
    Creamer, 3" h ........................................15.00
    Plate
        6" d .................................................5.00
        7 1/2" sq..........................................20.00
        9 1/2" d ...........................................12.00
Day Dreams Pattern
    Platter, 13 1/2" l .....................................65.00
    Vegetable Bowl, 9" d ..............................48.00
Dazzle Pattern
    Plate, 9 1/2" d .......................................18.00
Edgemont Pattern
    Platter, 13" l...........................................25.00
Fairy Bells Pattern
    Plate, 9 1/2" d .......................................28.00
Flower Bowl Pattern
    Cake Plate, 12" d ...................................85.00
    Plate, 7" d..............................................22.00
French Peasant Pattern
    Bowl, 9 1/4" d .......................................110.00
    Chocolate Pot........................................650.00
    Cup and Saucer, Demitasse ..................50.00
    Fruit Bowl, 4 1/2" d ................................45.00
    Pitcher, 5" h, Antique shape...................385.00

Plate

6" d................................................45.00

8" d................................................85.00

10" d..............................................115.00

Platter, 13 1/2" l.....................................325.00

Soup Plate, 8" d.....................................95.00

Fruit Punch Pattern

Plate, 9 1/2" d.......................................12.00

Jubilee Fruit Pattern

Plate, 8" d, pomegranate.........................25.00

Laurie Pattern

Plate, 10" d..........................................30.00

Nocturne Pattern

Bowl, 5" d............................................8.00

Cake Plate...........................................30.00

Plate, 9 1/2" d.......................................14.00

Platter, 11" l.........................................25.00

Poinsettia Pattern

Creamer...............................................25.00

Cup and Saucer.....................................25.00

Plate, 10" d..........................................32.00

Red Willow Pattern

Plate, 9 1/2" d.......................................45.00

Rugoa Pattern

Butter Dish, Cov, 7 1/2" l.........................80.00

Cereal Bowl, 6 1/4" d..............................9.00

Plate

6" d................................................7.00

8 " d...............................................12.00

Teapot, 6 1/4" h.....................................100.00

Savannah Pattern

Plate, 8 1/4" d.......................................25.00

Vegetable Bowl, 9" d...............................45.00

Serapta Pattern

Berry Bowl, 5 1/4" d................................8.00

Plate, 9 1/2" d.......................................15.00

Sherry Pattern

Plate, 6" d............................................5.00

Sunbright Pattern

Cake Plate, 10 1/2" d..............................28.00

Sunflower Pattern

Bowl, 5 1/4" d........................................5.00

Plate

9 1/2" d...........................................10.00

10 1/4" d..........................................14.00

Sungold #2 Pattern

Plate, 6" d............................................5.00

Platter, 13" l.........................................15.00

Tess Pattern

Berry Bowl, 5" d.....................................6.00

Triple Treat Pattern

Platter, 14" l.........................................35.00

Wildflower Pattern

Fruit Bowl, 5" d......................................10.00

Plate, 9 1/2" d.......................................15.00

Vegetable Bowl, 9" d...............................36.00

Wild Rose Pattern

Creamer...............................................10.00

Sugar Bowl, Cov.....................................15.00

Wild Strawberry Pattern

Plate

7" d................................................15.00

9 1/2" d...........................................22.00

Wildwood Flower Pattern

Creamer...............................................30.00

Fruit Bowl, 5" d......................................12.00

Plate

9 1/2" d...........................................35.00

10" d..............................................35.00

Platter

12" l................................................65.00

15" l................................................75.00

Sugar Bowl, Cov.....................................35.00

Wrinkled Rose Pattern

Cup and Saucer.....................................22.00

Eggcup................................................55.00

Plate, 9 1/2" d.......................................18.00

Platter, 12" l.........................................48.00

## MISCELLANEOUS

Vase, 5 1/2" h, pink and red hibiscus..........95.00

## PIECRUST SHAPE

Anemone Pattern

Cup and Saucer.....................................17.00

Fruit Bowl, 5 1/4" d.................................10.00

Soup Bowl, 7" d.....................................15.00

Sugar Bowl, Cov.....................................25.00

Daffodil Pattern

Plate, 10" d..........................................22.00

Sugar Bowl, Cov.....................................25.00

Green Briar Pattern

Berry Bowl, 5 1/4" d................................5.00

Cereal Bowl, 6 1/4" d..............................5.00

Creamer...............................................15.00

Cup and Saucer.....................................6.00

Plate

6" d................................................10.00

9 1/4" d...........................................10.00

Platter, 14" l.........................................25.00

Sugar Bowl, Cov.....................................20.00

Highland Ivy Pattern

Creamer...............................................10.00

Cup and Saucer.....................................6.00

Gravy Boat............................................12.00

Plate

6" d................................................6.00

9 1/4" d...........................................8.00

10" d..............................................12.00

Sugar Bowl, Cov.....................................15.00

Ring-O-Roses Pattern

Vegetable Bowl, 9" d...............................55.00

Spray Pattern
Plate
6" d............................................................3.00
9 1/2" d..................................................... 12.00
Whirligig Pattern
Bowl
6" d............................................................8.00
9 1/2" d..................................................... 18.00
Cup and Saucer, Demitasse............................65.00
Plate, 10" d................................................... 25.00
Wild Cherry #3
Bowl, 5 1/4" d .................................................5.00
Creamer ........................................................ 15.00
Cup and Saucer ............................................. 15.00
Plate
6" d............................................................8.00
7" d............................................................7.00
9 1/2" d..................................................... 10.00
10 1/2" d................................................... 22.00
Sugar Bowl, Cov............................................. 22.00
Vegetable Bowl, 9 1/2" d ................................ 20.00

**PITCHERS**
5" h, Romance, Antique .......................................... 125.00
6 1/2" h, Alice shape
Fruit Basket ...................................................... 95.00
Opulance ......................................................... 225.00
7" h, Tralee Rose, Spiral shape ............................... 60.00
7 1/4" h, Sculptured Fruit Pattern............................ 185.00
8 1/4" h, "Betsy," brick red trim.............................. 235.00

**SKYLINE SHAPE**
Apple Jack Pattern
Vegetable Bowl, 9" d ......................................... 18.00
Arlington Apple Pattern
Cup and Saucer .................................................... 15.00
Plate
7 1/2" d..................................................... 12.00
9 1/2" d..................................................... 15.00
Platter, 11 1/2" l ............................................... 25.00
Bright Eyes Pattern
Creamer ............................................................... 15.00
Cup and Saucer .................................................. 12.00

**Tray, 11 3/4" H-H, "Gingham Fruit" pattern, "Trailway" shape, $8.**

Sugar Bowl, Cov ............................................. 20.00
Cheerio Pattern
Cup and Saucer ............................................. 10.00
Plate, 10 1/2" d............................................. 18.00
Darcy Pattern
Berry Bowl, 5" d .............................................. 6.00
Dessert Flower Pattern
Plate, 9 1/2" d............................................... 12.00
Festive Skyline Pattern
Plate, 10" d................................................... 15.00
French Knots Pattern
Plate
7 1/2" d..................................................... 5.00
10 1/2" d................................................... 6.00
Soup Bowl, 7" d.............................................. 6.00
Green Eyes Pattern
Plate, 6" d..................................................... 4.00
Green Plaid Pattern
Cup and Saucer ............................................. 15.00
Half Penny Pattern
Plate, 9 1/2" d............................................... 20.00
Hops Pattern
Berry Bowl, 5 1/2" d ........................................ 5.00
Mayflower Pattern
Cup and Saucer ............................................. 3.00
Berry Bowl, 5 1/2" d ........................................ 3.00
Plate, 9 1/2" d............................................... 4.00
Platter, 12" l................................................... 6.00
Petal Point Pattern
Bowl, 9" d ..................................................... 28.00
Creamer ........................................................ 12.00
Cup and Saucer ............................................. 10.00
Plate
6" d............................................................ 6.00
9 1/2" d..................................................... 10.00
Pinkie Pattern
Berry Bowl, 5 1/2" d ........................................ 5.00
Cereal Bowl, 6 1/2" d ...................................... 5.00
Cup and Saucer ............................................. 10.00
Plate, 9 1/2" d............................................... 10.00
Platter
11 3/4" l..................................................... 10.00
13" l.......................................................... 18.00
Plantation Ivy Pattern
Berry Bowl, 5 1/2" d ........................................ 8.00
Creamer ........................................................ 15.00
Cup and Saucer ............................................. 15.00
Plate
6 1/2" d..................................................... 5.00
9 1/2" d..................................................... 15.00
Vegetable Bowl, 8 7/8" d ................................ 20.00
Poinsettia Pattern
Bowl
5 1/2" d..................................................... 3.00
6" d............................................................ 7.00
Red Barn Pattern
Cup and Saucer ............................................. 9.00

Fruit Bowl, 5 1/2" d ......................................... 15.00
Plate, 9 1/2" d .................................................. 30.00
Rustic Plaid Pattern
    Cup and Saucer .......................................... 8.00
    Dessert Bowl, 5 1/2" d ............................... 5.00
    Plate
        6" d ........................................................ 5.00
        9 1/2" d ................................................ 12.00
    Platter, 13 3/4" l ........................................ 15.00
Shadow Fruit Pattern
    Platter, 11 1/2" l ........................................ 15.00
Silhouette Pattern
    Cereal Bowl, 7" H-H, pink ......................... 7.00
    Creamer, pink ............................................ 12.00
    Cup and Saucer, pink ................................ 12.00
    Plate
        6" d, pink .............................................. 7.00
        10 3/8" d, pink ...................................... 12.00
    Sugar Bowl, Cov, pink .............................. 18.00
Spiderweb Pattern
    Plate, 10" d ............................................... 18.00
Stanhome Ivy Pattern
    Berry Bowl, 5 1/2" d ................................... 7.00
    Cup and Saucer ........................................ 12.00
    Plate
        6 3/8" d ................................................. 7.00
        9 1/2" d ................................................ 12.00
Strawberry Sundae Pattern
    Platter, 11 3/4" l ........................................ 25.00
Sunny Spray Pattern
    Cup and Saucer ........................................ 12.00
    Plate, 9 1/2" d ........................................... 18.00
Tropical Pattern
    Plate, 9 1/2" d ........................................... 12.00
Weathervane Pattern
    Cup and Saucer ........................................ 39.00
    Plate
        6" d ........................................................ 12.00
        7" d ........................................................ 15.00
        9 1/2" d ................................................ 35.00
    10 1/4" d ..................................................... 39.00

# Spaulding China Company

**Sebring, Ohio**
**1942-1957**

*Royal*
## COPLEY

c1947

**History:** The Spaulding China Company began production in 1942 in Sebring, Ohio under the direction of Morris Feinberg as president. Its motto, "gift shop merchandise at chain store prices," emphasized its concern for design and quality. Eighty-five percent of its production was Royal Copley merchandise, which was sold in chain stores. Woolworth was its biggest customer.

Mass-produced Royal Copley examples included figures of all kinds, planters, vases, and wall planters in many colors that were applied with an air brush. The first items in the line were decal bud vases and pitchers with decals of pink and blue flowers on a cream ground.

More birds were made than any other single item since they were the biggest sellers. Other very successful pieces were piggy banks, roosters, large ducks, and oriental boy and girl wall pockets. Tony Priolo was the primary artist for the Spaulding firm.

Many items were marked with either a green or gold stamp, and some were marked with raised letters. Most only had the paper labels, which soon disappeared.

Pieces made for the Royal Windsor and Spaulding lines were very similar in design to the Royal Copley examples. Royal Windsor and Spaulding were sold to jobbers and distributors who sold the articles to department stores, florists, and gift shops. Planters made for the florist trade included the "Books of Remembrance" pieces. Lamp bases were made under the Spaulding label.

During the mid-1950s, there was strong competition from the inexpensive Japanese imports that were flooding the U.S. market. With ever-increasing labor costs driving the prices for U.S. goods higher, Feinberg retired in 1957 and ceased operations at the Sebring plant. Orders continued to be filled for two years by the China Craft Company.

**References:** Joe Devine, *Royal Copley, Book 1*, Collector Books, 1999; Mike Schneider, *Royal Copley: Identification and Price Guide*, Schiffer Publishing Ltd.; Leslie C. and Marjorie A. Wolfe, *Royal Copley*, Collector Books, 1992;_____, *More About Royal Copley*, Collector Books, 1992.

**Collectors' Newsletter:** Dan Benton, 1639 N. Catalina Street, Burbank, CA 91505, *The Copley Courier,* bimonthly, $15.

Creamer, 5 1/2" l, figural pig, pink and cream, blue hat and tail .................................................................. 35.00
Figure
    4 1/2" h, pig, pink ..................................... 20.00
    4 1/2" l, pheasant, tan, red, and gray ....... 25.00
    7 1/2" h, pr of parakeets on branch, blue .. 25.00
Planter, 7 1/2" h, figural elephant w/ft on ball, gunmetal and yellow ...................................................... 10.00
Vase
    5 1/4" h, figural boot, red and green florals .............. 28.00
    8 1/4" h, floral
        "Barbara" decal ..................................... 45.00
        "Betty" decal .......................................... 10.00

**ROYAL COPLEY LINE**
Bank
    6" h, pink pig, blue bow ............................. 30.00

Planter, 7 7/8" h, pink, brown, cream, and gray, $65.

Vase, 8" h, black leaf and vine, pink ground, cream int, $26.

Vase, 9 1/2" h, brown shades, $23.

7" h, rooster, blue tail ...................................... 59.00
Creamer and Sugar Bowl, 3" h, yellow .......................... 40.00
Figure
    5" h, Cocker Spaniel head, brown ......................... 25.00
    6 1/2" h, Airedale, brown ................................ 25.00
    8" h, cat, pink bow, green eyes ........................ 45.00
Pitcher, 8" h
    Pink and yellow daffodil design ........................ 25.00
    Raised yellow daisies, pink ground .................... 15.00
Planter
    3 1/4" h x 6" l figural coach ......................... 15.00
    3 3/4" h, black floral and stem design, pink ground
    ........................................................ 22.00
    3 1/2" h x 5" w, flared triangle shape, white vert fluting, yellow lobed corners and ends ........................ 10.00
    4" h
        Green philodendron, 3 brown feet ................... 12.00
        Joyce decal, "COPLEY CHINA" mk ................... 10.00
    4 1/2" h
        Harmony, molded leaves, green w/brown edging
        ..................................................... 25.00

Oval shape, blue-green ext w/raised bird tracks, pink int.................................................... 10.00
5" h, figural bluebird on rim pink and blue bowl ....... 15.00
5 1/2" h, Nuthatch on stump ................................. 15.00
6" l, swimming fish, black and plum ........................ 25.00
6 1/4" h, girl leaning on brown bucket, dk green and rose clothes .................................................. 10.00
6 1/2" h
    Coolie, blue, white, brown, and black ................. 14.00
    Finch with large apple ................................. 29.00
    Ram's head, brown ..................................... 55.00
6 3/4" w, figural tulip, lt pink and yellow, blue base .. 20.00
7" h, sq shape, raised brown doe and faun on front, cream ground, green base ............................... 15.00
7 1/2" h
    Bear w/concertina, brown shades, cream and red
    ....................................................... 115.00
    Figural elephant w/ball, yellow and gray-brown .. 25.00
7 3/4" h
    Figural Mallard duck ................................... 30.00
    Parrot, white body, yellow head and beak, blue, red, and yellow wings, brown base ...................... 28.00
    Standing coolie girl, black hat, holding 2 buckets
    ....................................................... 18.00
8" h, figural seated black and white cat .................. 20.00
8 1/4" h
    Standing clown, yellow, white, and black ........... 95.00
    Tony, blue-green hat ................................... 55.00
8 3/4" h, dog w/mailbox, yellow box, green base, tan and brown dog ............................................. 22.00
9 1/4" h, figural deer head and fawn, tan and brown
................................................................ 38.00
Razor Blade Receptacle, 6 1/4" h, figural barber pole
.................................................................... 75.00
Vase
    5 1/2" h
        Marine, green and gray ............................ 25.00
        Oriental dragon design, blue and red ............ 25.00
    6" h
        Harmony, overlapped leaves, chartreuse green w/brown accents ................................. 12.00
        Rose and beige leaves, beige ground ............ 24.00
    6 1/4" h, classical shape, 2 handles, pink glaze ........ 5.00
    7" h
        "Carol's Corsage," lg blue flowerheads, pink ground
        ................................................... 20.00
        Green ivy, off-white body, black base ............ 18.00
    7 3/4" h, "Hardy Stem," white on black ................... 15.00
    8" h, molded yellow sunflowers, dk to lt green shaded ground ............................................... 30.00
    8 1/4" h, cylinder shape, relief of swimming fish, tan-black ground w/green accents .......................... 25.00
    8 1/2" h
        Figural horse head and foal, tan, brown, and black
        ................................................... 85.00
        Stem and leaf design, black and white ............ 10.00
Wall Pocket
    5 1/2" h, figural red apple, green leaves ................. 45.00
    7" d, red, yellow, and green raised fruit .................. 40.00
    8" h, figural angel, blue ................................... 70.00

**ROYAL WINDSOR**
Figure
>    5 1/2" h, 6" h, #1 hen and rooster, pr ......................75.00
>    8 3/4" h, 9 1/4" h, Mallard, green, tan, and cream, pr
>    ........................................................................55.00

Planter
>    6 3/4" h, ribbed figural star planter and candleholder, gold
>    trim ..............................................................50.00
>    7" h, erect white poodle, green planter ...................45.00
>    7" l x 3 1/2" w, rect, "Rex," rose and ivory ...............10.00

# Spongeware

## New Jersey and Midwest
## c1850s-1960s

**History:** Spongeware is a decorating technique used on several different clay bodies at various times: white earthenware, stoneware, and yellowware. Probably sponge decoration was used first on whiteware. Much of the sponge decoration was used on a coarse stoneware body that was first covered with opaque white Bristol slip. Sponged stoneware bodies tended to be simpler than the sponged earthenware examples.

The spongeware decoration shows a mottled design effect that varies from object to object. Much of the decoration seems to be randomly placed blotches or dots, but some pieces show repeats of a specific shape or pattern. Some sponge design is combined with solid color bands. Sometimes the decoration appears to form a net pattern or is arranged in rows.

Some early blue sponged white earthenware was found from New Jersey, Pennsylvania, and Ohio in the 1850-70 period. International Pottery Company and Etruria Pottery from New Jersey made early examples on white earthenwares. James Bennett was probably the earliest maker in Ohio to make blue sponged wares.

By the time spongeware was being made in larger quantities, potteries were using stoneware and yellowware clay bodies and producing mostly utilitarian pieces in the 1880-1940s period.

Red Wing, Minnesota was the source for large amounts of American spongewares. At first it was made at the Minnesota Stoneware Company where stoneware was covered with white Bristol slip glaze for the bail handled jugs and pipkins that were marked. When they merged with the Red Wing Union Stoneware Company from 1906-1936, many more examples were made including spittoons, covered chamberpots. covered slop jars, and umbrella stands. Sponge designs were blue on white, brown on white, or red and blue on white. Pieces were marked.

During the early 1930s, they also used yellowwares for sponge designs. Examples included pitchers, mixing bowls, covered bowls, casseroles, baking dishes, bean pots, butter crocks with tops, beater jars, and small handled jugs. Sponge colors were blue or brown on white, red and blue on white, and brown and green on yellow. A variety of marks was used such as RED WING SAFFRON WARE, RED WING OVENWARE, REDWING U.S.A., and MADE IN REDWING. In 1936 until 1967, they became Red Wing Potteries and still made spongewares until after World War II. A large amount of advertising spongewares also was made.

In Illinois, the Western Stoneware Company in Monmouth was the largest stoneware producer from 1910-1940, but made less spongeware than Red Wing. It made sponged water coolers, mixing bowls, and spittoons in 1906 that were marked WESTERN STONEWARE CO. or WESTERN STONEWARE COMPANY/MONMOUTH, ILLINOIS. Its examples were heavier and cruder than those from Red Wing. From 1893-1906, until it was purchased by Western, Monmouth Pottery made marked spongeware water coolers in two to ten gallon sizes and miniature water coolers.

Many smaller makers produced spongeware examples at various times in their history. Fulper Pottery in Flemington, New Jersey made pitchers, spittoons, vases, and jardinieres designed by J.M. Stangl on stoneware bodies. They still make sponged pieces on a white earthenware body. Robinson Ransbottom in Ohio still produces spongeware too.

A tremendous assortment of utilitarian pieces was made in spongeware with bowls being the most common examples. Mixing bowls in many sizes as well as "shoulder bowls" and nappies ranging in sizes from 4"-12" in diameter were made. Capped bowls were often used for advertising premiums.

Pitchers in a variety of sizes and shapes were made with the all over blue sponging being the most popular type. Storage vessels such as shoulder jugs, bail handled jugs, water coolers, covered butter crocks, and kitchen storage jars all were made.

In cooking utensils, there were pie plates from 6"-12" in diameter, custard cups, beater jars, colanders, measuring cups, funnels, casseroles, bean pots, and stew pans. Tablewares included plates, mugs, teapots, mush cups and saucers, platters, gravy boats, and covered sugar bowls. Toilet sets, cuspidors, umbrella stands, vases, and jardinieres all found form in spongeware. Miniatures were used for gift items and advertising pieces.

**References:** William C. Ketchum, Jr. *American Country Pottery, Yellowware and Spongeware*, Alfred A. Knopf, 1987; Kevin McConnell, *Spongeware and Spatterware, 2nd Edition*, Schiffer Publishing Ltd.1999; Earl F. and Ada Robacker, *Spatterware and Sponge*, A.S. Barnes & Co. 1978.

Batter Pitcher, Cov, 5 1/4" h, green sponging, yellowware body..................................................................75.00
Bean Pot, Cov, 7 1/2" h, mottled brown sponging w/blue and rust accents ......................................................300.00
Beater Jar, 5 1/2" h, green and brown sponging ..........15.00
Bowl
>    5 1/2" d, blue and white sponging, (A).....................45.00
>    6" d, red sponging, hairline .....................................25.00
>    7 1/2" d
>    >    Blue sponging, yellow ground, wavy rim ............65.00
>    >    Brown sponging, yellow ground ........................75.00
>    8" d, yellowware, green sponging, stains and wear, (A)
>    ..................................................................50.00
>    9 1/2" d, stepped, tan, green, and brown sponging
>    ..................................................................60.00
>    10" d, basin shape, blue and white, chips, (A).........55.00
>    11" l, oval, blue sponging, yellowware body, (A)......65.00
>    12 1/4" d, blue and white sponging on border and base, (A) ..................................................................385.00
Butter Crock, 4 1/2" d, blue "BUTTER" on front, blue and white sponging, (A)..............................................58.00
Butter Pat, 4" d, blue and white sponging, (A) .............18.00
Casserole, Cov
>    9 1/2" d, tan, green, and brown sponging, tan int
>    ..................................................................78.00

**Jar, 5 3/8" h x 5" d, brown sponging, yellow body, $38.**

11" d, cobalt sponging ....................................... 100.00
Cereal Bowl, 5" d, brown sponging, yellow ground ...... 25.00
Chamber Pot, 8 3/4" d, blue sponged border and base, center blue stripes and band, chips, (A) ........................ 83.00
Crock, 7 1/2" d x 4 1/2" h, blue sponging, gray ground, (A) ................................................................................ 138.00
Crock, Cov, 6 3/4" h, bail handle, blue sponging, c1880, (A) ................................................................................ 358.00
Cup, 3" h, ovoid w/molded ribbing, applied handle, mottled green glaze and brown sponging on orange ground, (A) ................................................................................ 275.00
Cup and Saucer, blue and white, set of 8, (A) ........... 220.00
Dish
    6 1/2" d, redware body, orange ground, brown sponged rim, (A) .......................................................................... 440.00
    8 1/2" l, brown and green sponging, (A) ................ 193.00
Egg Cup, 3" h, black sponging, redware body, (A) ..... PRICE
Food Mold, 7 1/2" w, Turk's head, redware, dk brown sponged int and ext border, (A) ................................. 68.00
Jar, 6" h, ovoid, applied strap handle and tooled bands, burnt orange ground w/brown sponging, (A) .......... 165.00
Jar, Cov, 2 ear handles, vert ribbing, blue, red, and brown sponged center band, yellowware body, (A) .......... 220.00
Jug
    6 1/2" h, bulbous shape, overhead handle, blue and brown sponging, (A) .............................................. 90.00
    8" h, blue, red, and brown sponging, yellowware body, (A) ............................................................................. 220.00
Mixing Bowls, 3 3/4", 4 3/4", 5 3/4", 6 3/4", 7 3/4" d, paneled, brown sponging, set of 5 ................................. 88.00
Pie Plate
    8 1/4" d, brown sponging, redware body, hairline and chips, (A) .......................................................... 138.00
    9 3/4" d, Bennington style tan and brown sponging ................................................................................ 105.00
Pitcher
    4 1/2" h, ribbed, brown sponging w/lt green areas, yellow body ...................................................... 55.00
    5 1/2" h
        Blue and white sponging, (A) .......................... 195.00
        Ribbed, green and brown sponging ................... 55.00
    6" h, Bristol glaze, brown sponging, "Lowell Pottery Co." mark .......................................................... 3500.00
    6 5/8" h, molded bands top and base, blue sponging w/2 narrow blue stripes, c1900-20, hairlines and chips, (A) ................................................................................ 125.00

6 3/4" h, green and white sponging, blue border stripes, (A) .............................................................................. 165.00
7 1/2" h, blue sponging, white ground, (A) ............ 192.00
8 1/4" h, gray-white glaze, blue sponged shoulder and spout, hairlines, (A) ......................................... 121.00
8 1/2" h, bulbous, lt blue sponging on upper half, crazing, c1880, (A) ......................................................... 187.00
9" h
    Cylinder shape, blue sponging, white ground ... 485.00
    Tankard shape, emb flower design, molded rim, blue sponging, white ground ................................ 375.00
11 1/2" h, bulbous shape, blue and white sponging, (A) ................................................................................ 990.00
Pitcher, Cov, 9" h, redware, brown sponging, red ground, clear glaze, ribbed strap handle, (A) ..................... 522.00
Pitcher and Bowl
    Pitcher, 11 3/4" h, bowl, 15" d, overall blue and white sponging, (A) ................................................. 275.00
    Pitcher, 14" h, bowl, 16" d, blue sponging, center blue stripes on bowl ext and pitcher, repairs, c1880, (A) ................................................................................ 523.00
Plate, blue and white sponging
    7 5/8" d, molded rim, (A) .................................... 50.00
    9" d, (A) ............................................................... 53.00
    10 1/4" d, plain rim, (A) ........................................ 80.00
Platter, 9 1/2" l, blue and white, molded and shaped rim, (A) ................................................................................ 150.00
Soup Plate, 9 1/2" d, molded rim, blue and white sponging, (A) ............................................................................... 65.00
Spittoon
    5" h x 7 3/4" d, blue sponged stoneware ................ 40.00
    5 1/4" h x 8 1/4" d, overall blue sponging, blue accent stripes, hairline, c1880, (A) .............................. 110.00
Teapot, 8 1/4" h, blue and green sponging, (A) ......... 220.00
Vase
    4" h, bulbous center, spread ft and rim, cobalt sponging, c1890, (A) ............................................................ 88.00
    7 1/4" h, conical shape, flared rim, yellowware, blue and white, repaired chip, (A) ................................. 78.00
Vegetable Bowl
    8 1/4" l, rect, dk brown sponging, molded beaded rim, redware, (A) ................................................... 385.00
    9 7/8" l, oval, blue and white sponging, (A) ............ 42.00

# Stangl Pottery

## Flemington and Trenton, New Jersey
## 1929-1978

### (See Fulper for early history)

**History:** In 1926, Fulper purchased the Anchor Pottery in Trenton, New Jersey where the dinnerwares were made. The Flemington Pottery burned in 1929 and manufacturing moved temporarily to Trenton, while Flemington was rebuilt at a different site. Martin Stangl acquired Fulper in 1930.

Both art pottery and dinnerwares were made, but by the late 1930s, it concentrated on dinnerware, low-cost artware and utilitarian wares. Colonial and Americana were the most popular shapes. The red body replaced the white body in 1942 for dinnerware that was hand carved. The slip was cut through to reveal the red clay underneath. The artists hand painted with bright colors underglaze between the carved lines. There are almost 100 of the hand painted and carved dinnerware lines, the majority of which are fruit or floral motifs.

During World War II, Fulper curtailed its regular lines due to a shortage of raw materials. Stangl decided to produce a line of pottery birds inspired by Audubon prints of American birds. The birds were made of a fine clay body. Auguste Jacob designed and created the models for the pottery bird molds that were hand painted by various decorators in high gloss glazes. Each bird was signed on the bottom with the decorator's initials in addition to the number of the bird and Stangl Pottery.

Due to the scarcity of European and Japanese imports from World War II, eventually over one hundred varieties of birds were produced to fill this void. The twelve different porcelain birds were more elaborate than the pottery ones with more intricate decorations, life-like colors, fine molded details, and more leaves and flowers.

Birds with a "F" under the glaze were decorated at Flemington. Paper tags marked the birds with their name and number. Both the Fulper and Stangl names were utilized on the bird's tags until about 1955 when the company name was changed to Stangl. Birds continued in production until 1978.

Other lines included Kiddieware made from c1942 until the 1970s with hand painted, hand carved subjects including nursery rhymes and "wild west" decors. Later dinnerwares included Indian Summer, Maize-Ware, and numerous other lines.

In the late 1950s, a popular art line called "Antique Gold" was made by hand brushing 22 karat gold over matte green glaze. "Granada Gold" was gold over turquoise, "Black Gold" was brushed over black, and "Platinum" was a silver brushed finish.

Many Stangl items with the exception of dinnerware have an impressed mark in the mold with "Stangl" or "Stangl USA" and a shape number. Some hand painted dinnerware have the name or initial of the decorator painted on the bottom of the piece. Some pieces have a stamped mark under the glaze. Stangl also used a back stamp mark with the oval trademark and pattern name.

Martin Stangl died in 1972 and Frank Wheaton Jr. bought the pottery. When he sold out to Pfaltzgraff Pottery Company in 1978, production was stopped since they wanted the real estate to utilize the Flemington location as an outlet shop for Pfaltzgraff products.

**References:** Harvey Duke, *Stangl Pottery*, Wallace-Homestead, 1993; Joan Dworkin and Martha Horman, *A Guide to Stangl Pottery Birds*, Willow Pond Books, Inc. 1977; Norma Rehl, *The Collectors Handbook of Stangl Pottery*, Democrat Press, 1982; Rob Runge Jr., *Collector's Encyclopedia of Stangl Dinnerware*, Collector Books, 1999; Mike Schneider, *Stangl and Pennsbury Birds: Identification and Price Guide*, Schiffer Publishing Ltd., 1995.

**Collectors' Club:** Stangl Bird Collectors Association, Lynn A. Davis, POB 3146, Patchoque, NY 11772, $25 per year, quarterly newsletter; Stangl/Fulper Collectors Club, P.O. Box 538, Flemington, NJ 08822, quarterly newsletter, $25 per year.

**Planter, 9 1/2" l, "Antique Gold," #2064, $25.**

### AMBER GLO PATTERN
Pitcher, 5" h .................................................................. 10.00
Salad Bowl, 10" d ......................................................... 20.00

### APPLE DELIGHT PATTERN
Cup and Saucer ............................................................. 6.00
Hostess Set, 10" l, w/cup .......................................... 18.00
Pan, 9 1/2" l ................................................................. 35.00
Plate, 10" d ................................................................... 10.00
Platter, 15" l ................................................................. 45.00

### BACHELOR BUTTON PATTERN
Bowl
    8 1/2" d ................................................................ 12.00
    10" d ..................................................................... 25.00

### BITTERSWEET PATTERN
Plate, 10 1/2" d ........................................................... 12.00
Tidbit Tray, 10" d ........................................................ 45.00
Tray, 13 1/2" l .............................................................. 28.00

### BLUEBERRY PATTERN
Bowl, 8" d .................................................................... 35.00
Cake Plate, 12 1/2" d .................................................. 25.00
Cup and Saucer ........................................................... 10.00
Lug Soup, 5 1/2" H-H .................................................. 10.00
Plate
    8 1/4" d ................................................................ 15.00
    9 3/8" d ................................................................ 20.00
    10" d ..................................................................... 18.00
Shakers, Pr .................................................................. 22.00

### BLUE TULIP PATTERN
Plate, 6 1/4" d ............................................................... 5.00

**Pitcher, 6 1/4" h, "Country Garden" pattern, $95.**

## COUNTRY GARDEN PATTERN
Bowl, 5 1/2" d ....................................................... 15.00
Creamer ................................................................. 15.00
Cup and Saucer .................................................... 10.00
Plate
    8" d .................................................................. 8.00
    10" d ............................................................... 15.00
Sugar Bowl, Cov .................................................... 15.00

## COWBOY DESIGN
Charger, 12" d, matte green and yellow glaze, "stamped Stangl Pottery/Hand-Painted by MS" mk, hairlines, (A) ........................................................................ 330.00
Plate, 10" d, yellow, blue, and brown glaze, "stamped Stangl/Trenton" (A) ............................................ 330.00
Porringer, 6" H-H, yellow, blue, and brown glaze, "stamped Stangl/Trenton" mk ................................ 200.00

## DELLA WARE
Laurita Pattern
    Plate, 9" d, blue, red, and yellow triple flower, red and yellow rim .......................................................... 16.00

## FAIRLAWN PATTERN
Bread Tray, 15" l, cobalt, yellow, and brown flowers, white ground .................................................................... 45.00
Chop Plate, 12" d .................................................. 15.00

## FESTIVAL PATTERN
Chop Plate, 12 1/4" d ............................................ 75.00
Creamer ................................................................. 10.00
Plate
    8" d, fruit ....................................................... 12.00
    10" d, fruit ..................................................... 15.00
Sugar Bowl, Cov .................................................... 10.00

## FIGURES
3" h, Red-Faced Warbler, #3594 ........................... 45.00
3 1/8" h, Black-Throated Green Warbler, #3814 ........ 350.00
3 1/4" h, Quacking Ducks, Granada Gold, #3250A, 3250F, pr ..................................................................... 245.00
3 1/2" h
    Turkey, green and lt brown, #3275 .................. 450.00
    Wilson Warbler, #3597 ...................................... 55.00
4" h
    Black Hole Warbler, #3810, (A) ....................... 80.00
    Goldfinch, #3849 ............................................ 110.00
    Owl, #3407 ..................................................... 450.00
4 1/4" h
    Blue-Headed Vereo, #3448 .............................. 125.00
    Parula Warbler, #3583 ....................................... 71.00
4 1/2" h
    Blue Headed Vireo, #3448 ................................ 75.00
    Riefers Hummingbird, #3628 ........................... 150.00
4 3/4" h
    Gilded Wren .................................................... 50.00
    Gray Cardinal, #3596 ....................................... 55.00
5" h, Penguin, #3274, restored beak chip, (A) .......... 210.00
5 1/2" h
    Bird-of-Paradise, #3408 ................................. 147.00
    Dbl Oriole, #3402D ......................................... 125.00
    Triple Chicadees, #3581 ................................. 140.00

6" h, Broadtail Hummingbird, #3626 ...................... 150.00
6 1/4" h, Canary, blue flower, #3747 ...................... 250.00
6 3/4" h, Penguin, black, blue, yellow .................... 895.00
7 1/4" h x 15" l, Pheasant, #3457 .......................... 650.00
7 1/2" h, White Head Pigeons, #3518D ................... 795.00
8" h, Hummingbirds, #3599D ................................. 350.00
9" h
    Flying Duck, #3443 ......................................... 275.00
    Key West Quail Dove, wing up, #3454 ............. 165.00
    Redstarts, "STANGL #3490 RC F" mark ........... 230.00
9 1/4" h, Key West Dove, #3454, (A) ..................... 176.00
9 3/4" h, Parrots, recd, blue, green, and yellow, (A) ... 110.00
10" h, Bluejay and leaf, #3716 .............................. 495.00
10 1/2" h, Magpie Jay, #3358, (A) ......................... 775.00
11" h, Scissor-Tailed Flycatcher, #3757, (A) ........... 605.00
15" h, Bird-of-Paradise, #3626, (A) ..................... 1,525.00
18"l x 19" h, Passenger Pigeon, #3450 ............... 1,200.00

## FIRST LOVE PATTERN
Gravy Boat, 8 1/2" l ............................................... 30.00

## FRUIT AND FLOWERS PATTERN
Coup Soup, 7 1/2" d ............................................. 20.00
Plate
    6" d ............................................................... 10.00
    8" d ................................................................. 5.00
Sugar Bowl, Cov ...................................................... 5.00
Salad Bowl, 10" d .................................................. 35.00
Tidbit Server, 10 1/2" d ......................................... 15.00
Vegetable Bowl, 8" d ............................................. 10.00

## GARDEN FLOWER PATTERN
Chop Plate, 12 1/2" d ............................................ 35.00
Dish, 13 3/4" w ..................................................... 40.00
Platter
    12" d ............................................................... 32.00
    13 3/4" l ......................................................... 40.00
Salad Bowl, 10" d .................................................. 50.00

## GARLAND PATTERN
Bowl
    8" d ............................................................... 25.00
    12" d ............................................................... 45.00
Coffeepot, 9 1/2" h .............................................. 130.00
Cup and Saucer ..................................................... 12.00
Plate, 6" d .............................................................. 6.00

## GOLDEN BLOSSOM PATTERN
Bowl, 8 3/4" d ......................................................... 5.00
Cereal Bowl, 5 1/2" d .............................................. 4.00
Creamer and Cov Sugar Bowl ................................... 8.00
Cup and Saucer ....................................................... 8.00
Pitcher, 6" h .......................................................... 39.00
Plate
    6 1/4" d ........................................................... 3.00
    10" d ............................................................... 6.00
Platter, 12 1/2" d .................................................. 10.00
Shakers, Pr ........................................................... 10.00
Soup Bowl, 7 1/2" d ................................................ 4.00

Vegetable Bowl, 11" l, divided ...................................... 12.00

**GOLDEN GRAPE PATTERN**
Berry Bowl, 5 1/2" d .......................................... 6.00

**GOLDEN HARVEST PATTERN**
Bowl, 6" d, handled................................. 10.00
Bread Tray, 15" l........................................ 20.00
Chop Plate, 12 1/2" d ............................... 15.00
Creamer ...................................................... 10.00
Cup and Saucer ....................................... 10.00
Plate
    6" d............................................................5.00
    10" d........................................................ 12.00
Sugar Bowl, Cov.......................................... 12.00
Vegetable Bowl, 10 1/2" l............................ 8.00

**HOLLY PATTERN**
Platter, 12 1/2" d ..................................... 100.00
Serving Bowl, 10" d ................................... 75.00

**JEWELLED CHRISTMAS TREE PATTERN**
Cup and Saucer .......................................... 40.00
Plate
    6" d........................................................ 22.00
    10" d........................................................ 45.00

**LYRIC PATTERN**
Water Pitcher, 12 3/4" h............................ 100.00

**MAGNOLIA PATTERN**
Bowl, 6" d ..................................................... 6.00
Coffeepot, 5 1/2" h....................................... 35.00
Dish, Cov, 9 1/4" H-H ................................ 38.00
Lug Soup, 5 1/2" d....................................... 20.00
Plate
    6 1/2" d...................................................5.00
    8 1/2" d................................................. 10.00
Salad Bowl, 10" d ....................................... 38.00
Vegetable Bowl, 8" d ................................. 10.00

**MEDITERRANEAN PATTERN**
Coupe Soup, 7 1/2" d ................................ 18.00

Creamer ........................................................ 7.00
Fruit Dish, 5 1/2" d....................................... 10.00
Plate
    6" d........................................................8.00
    10" d....................................................... 22.00
Sugar Bowl, Cov ......................................... 12.00

**MISCELLANEOUS**
Ashtray
    9" sq, Mallard Duck................................50.00
    12" l, painted pheasant .........................40.00
Beverage Set, 9 1/2" h, w/aluminum stand, pitcher, matte cream glaze, 6 mugs, matte aqua glaze, ribbed designs, (A) ................................................................ 115.00
Bud Vase, 8" h, "Antique Gold" finish, "4050" mk........ 24.00
Dish, 7 1/2" l, pear shape, Antique Gold finish, #3783 ...................................................................... 18.00
Planter, 9" h x 9" l, figural French telephone, black w/gold ...................................................................... 175.00

Vase, 7 5/8" h, yellow glaze, $45.

Plate, 10" d, "Magnolia" pattern, $15.

Wig Stand, 15 1/4" h, brown hair, wood base, $595.

Vase

4 7/8" h, swirled ball shape, graduated ball handles, sq base, matte white glaze, c1930s .......................... 30.00

6" h, Terra Rose, tulip shape, blue ext, peach int .... 20.00

6 1/4" h, antique gold finish, #4002 .......................... 18.00

7" h

Cylinder shape, rolled top and base, 2 handles, orange, #3102 .................... 75.00

Tulip shape, med blue glaze, #3217 .................. 50.00

9" h, raised flowerhead and stalk on side, med blue matte glaze ........................ 35.00

9 1/4" h, ribbed, leaf shape, purple, Terra Rose #3441 ........................ 42.00

10" h, bulbous base, flared neck and rim, "Antique Gold" finish, #5028 .......................... 32.00

15" h, bottle shape, Pebblestone, #3999 ................ 80.00

Wig Stand, 10 1/2" h, brunette ......................... 335.00

**MOUNTAIN LAUREL PATTERN**
Charger, 12 1/2" d ............................ 110.00

**ORCHARD SONG PATTERN**
Bread Tray, 15" l ............................. 30.00
Cereal Bowl, 7 1/4" d ......................... 5.00
Coffeepot .................................... 72.00
Cup and Saucer ............................... 10.00
Plate

6" d .......................... 6.00
8" d .......................... 6.00
10" d ......................... 10.00
11" d ......................... 10.00

Serving Bowl

10" d ......................... 12.00
12" d ......................... 45.00

Sugar Bowl, Cov ............................. 10.00

**PAISLEY PATTERN**
Plate, 11 1/4" d ............................. 28.00

**PINK LILY PATTERN**
Chop Plate, 12 1/2" d ........................ 85.00

**PROVINCIAL PATTERN**
Bowl, 5 1/2" d .............................. 10.00
Plate

6" d .......................... 5.00
8" d .......................... 10.00
10" d ......................... 15.00

Tray, 11" l .................................. 35.00

**RUSTIC GARDEN PATTERN**
Cup and Saucer .............................. 5.00
Plate

8" d .......................... 4.00
10" d ......................... 5.00

**SCULPTURED FRUIT PATTERN**
Charger, 12" d .............................. 35.00

**STAR FLOWER**
Bowl

8" d .......................... 3.00
10" d ......................... 5.00

Cup and Saucer .............................. 3.00

Plate, 10" d ................................ 5.00
Shakers, Pr ................................. 20.00

**THISTLE PATTERN**
Bowl

8" d .......................... 30.00
10" d ......................... 30.00
12" d ......................... 35.00

Chop Plate, 12" d ........................... 25.00
Cup and Saucer .............................. 12.00
Egg Cup .................................... 15.00
Fruit Bowl, 5 1/2" d ........................ 4.00
Gravy Boat, 8 3/4" l ........................ 12.00
Pickle Dish, 10" l .......................... 15.00
Plate

6" d .......................... 6.00
8" d .......................... 14.00
10" d ......................... 15.00

Platter, 13 3/4" l .......................... 15.00
Sugar Bowl, Cov ............................. 22.00
Teapot, 6" h ................................ 40.00
Vegetable Bowl, 10 5/8" l, divided .......... 38.00

**TOWN & COUNTRY PATTERN**
Bowl, 6" d, green and white ................. 6.00
Chop Plate, 12" d, blue and white ........... 29.00
Creamer and Cov Sugar Bowl, green and white ......... 10.00
Flower Pot, 3 1/4" h, blue and white ........ 22.00
Pitcher and Bowl, pitcher, 10 1/2" h, bowl, 14 1/2" d, blue and white ........................ 162.00
Plate

6" d, blue .................... 6.00
8" d, blue .................... 20.00
10" d, blue ................... 8.00
10 3/4" d, green and white .... 8.00

**WHITE DOGWOOD PATTERN**
Cup and Saucer .............................. 7.00
Egg Cup .................................... 14.00
Plate

8" d .......................... 10.00
10" d ......................... 12.00

**WILD ROSE PATTERN**
Bowl, 8" d .................................. 25.00
Casserole, Cov, 8" d ........................ 45.00
Chop Plate, 12" d ........................... 29.00
Creamer .................................... 12.00
Cup and Saucer .............................. 12.00
Plate

6" d .......................... 10.00
10" d ......................... 10.00

Salad Bowl, 12" d ........................... 50.00
Soup Bowl, 7 3/4" d ......................... 8.00
Sugar Bowl, Cov ............................. 25.00

**YELLOW TULIP PATTERN**
Bowl

8" d .......................... 30.00
10" d ......................... 38.00
11" d ......................... 35.00

Casserole, Cov, 8" d.......................................40.00
Creamer ........................................................8.00
Cup and Saucer ...........................................12.00
Plate
   8" d.......................................................10.00
   10" d.....................................................15.00
   Platter, 14" l .........................................45.00

# Sterling China Company

### East Liverpool(Wellsville), Ohio
### 1917-Present

**History:** In 1917, a group founded the Sterling China Company in the former Patterson Brothers pottery in Wellsville, Ohio and made vitreous hotel china. The factory had numerous additions, and the product line continued to expand. During World War II, Sterling supplied most of the dinnerware used by the United States Armed Forces.

It used a wide variety of decorations on its hotel ware that usually was traditional in style and design. Sterling's commercial china was used by airlines, hotels, restaurants, railroads, and steamship companies. By 1949, it was one of the three largest producers of vitrified hotel and restaurant china in the world.

After World War II until 1950, Sterling had a non-traditional line of streamlined table ware designed by Russel Wright in Ivy Green, Straw Yellow, Suede Gray, and Cedar Brown. (see Russel Wright).

The company continued to expand. From 1951-1976, it operated a plant in Puerto Rico and made "Caribe China." In 1954, Sterling absorbed the Scammell China Company and now it produces the Lamberton China line.

A wide variety of marks was used by Sterling for its commercial wares. Though its pottery was actually in Wellsville, it preferred the East Liverpool address and used it to identify its company.

**MISCELLANEOUS**
Bowl, 9" d, "Blue Onion" design, mkd..........................10.00
Creamer
   3 1/4" h, dk red border bands, Desert Tan ground... 10.00
   3 3/4" h x 4" l, paneled, blue and gray cartouche w/red and gray stylized tulip head, blue line ..................8.00

**Jug, 9 1/4" h, multicolored Dutch children, gilt handle, $108.**

**Chocolate Pot, 10 1/2" h, multicolored transfers, shaded blue ground accents, gold trim, gold "RYTINA BAKING CO." "Sterling China and crown" mk, $600.**

**Plate, 9" d, gray-blue transfer, "Priscilla and John Alden" below, flowing blue border w/gold hanging wreaths, crown mk, $32.**

**Platter, 13 3/8" l, blue, brown, red, and green flowerheads, med brown striping, tan ground, "Sterling Desert Tan" mk, $7.**

3 7/8" h, shaded rose-pink ground, molded drape rim .................................................................................8.00
Custard Cup, 4" d, transfer of mauve flowers, set of 3. 10.00
Grease Jar, Cov
  5 1/2" h, red figural lobster handle ..........................20.00
  6" h, white ironstone, "Sterling Vitrified China Liverpool Ohio 1951" mk ..............................................12.00
Mug, 6" h, white ironstone, motto on side ......................5.00
Plate
  5 1/2" d, brown branch w/3 red cherries and green leaves, scalloped rim..............................................5.00
  6 1/2" d, wagon train in center, western tools on border, brown transfer, mkd..............................................12.00
  7 1/4" d
    Blue Willow pattern in center, "red ON LOCK SAM" on border, (A)......................................................20.00
    Brown Onion pattern, mkd..................................3.00
  7 1/2" d, rust red border band of thistles, ivy, and crests w/birds, scalloped rim ..............................3.00
  8" d, red lobster in center w/green seaweed, dk blue border w/raised designs and gold hanging swags....35.00
  9 1/4" d, 2 walking sandpipers in marsh, green shaded border, gold dusted rim......................................18.00
  9 1/2" d, border band of dk red leaves and dots ........4.00
  10" d, multicolored scene of inn and mill in center, flowing blue border w/raised designs and gold hanging swags .................................................................................12.00
Platter
  12 1/2" l, 2 multicolored pheasants in forest, cobalt border w/gold swag overlay, wavy rim, sgd "R K BECK" on front ...........................................................95.00
  12 3/4" l, relief molded geometric border, white glaze .................................................................................8.00
  13 1/4" l, oval, Berkshire pattern, red transfer ..........7.00
  13 1/2" l, oval, red lobster in center, green border w/gold hanging swags .................................................35.00
  15 1/2" l, oval, white ironstone, emb inner and outer borders, wavy rim ...............................................15.00

## SHELL PINK PATTERN
Bowl
  5 1/4" l.............................................................................4.00

5 3/4" d ...........................................................................4.00
Coffee Mug, 2 1/2" h .........................................................3.00
Gravy Boat, 7 1/4" l .......................................................13.00
Jam Jar, Cov, 3 1/2" h ....................................................10.00
Plate
  6 1/4" d ...........................................................................5.00
  7" d ..................................................................................8.00
  Platter, 11 1/2" l ............................................................5.00

# Stetson China Company

## Lincoln, Illinois
## 1919-1966

**History:** Stetson started as a decorating and distributing company in Chicago, Illinois in 1919. It purchased its blanks from Mount Clemens Pottery in the early years. To make sure it had a steady supply of blanks, it took over the Illinois China Company in Lincoln, Illinois in 1946 and changed the name to the Stetson China Company.

Stetson China made a lot of dinnerware, where it outlined the design and then filled it in with hand painting. This gave it a more uniform pattern without having to use a decal. These hand-painted dinnerwares were very popular with the public. Their wares were sold in department stores and specialty stores. Premium items were also made for the Procter and Gamble Company.

Many wares were made without marks and were confused with wares from Southern Potteries. The whole Stetson family was involved with the company. A wide assortment of patterns was made. Earthenwares were also made as well as premium orders decorated with decals for groceries.

Stetson eventually closed down since it could not compete with the inexpensive imports. Many different marks were used.

### AMERICAN BEAUTY PATTERN
Berry Bowl...........................................................................6.00
Coupe Soup
  7 1/2" d ..........................................................................12.00
  8" d .................................................................................12.00
Creamer ............................................................................12.00
Cup and Saucer ..................................................................6.00
Plate
  6" d ...................................................................................5.00
  7" d ...................................................................................8.00
  8 1/4" d .............................................................................9.00
  10 1/4" d .........................................................................10.00
Platter
  13 1/2" l .........................................................................25.00
  15/4" l ............................................................................30.00
Soup Plate, 8 1/4" d ...........................................................5.00
Sugar Bowl, Cov, 4" h ........................................................5.00
Syrup Pitcher, 5 1/2" h .....................................................25.00

Teacup and Saucer ................................................. 10.00
Vegetable Bowl
    9" d......................................................... 8.00
    9 1/2" l, oval .......................................... 18.00

## BAMBOO PATTERN
Serving Bowl, 9" d ............................................. 10.00

## BLUE PINE CONE PATTERN
Cereal Bowl, 7" d ................................................ 4.00
Dessert Bowl, 5 1/2" d ........................................ 3.00
Plate, 9 1/2" d .................................................... 4.00

## CYNTHIA PATTERN-IONIC SHAPE
Berry Bowl ......................................................... 3.00
Cup and Saucer ................................................. 4.00
Plate, 9 1/2" d .................................................... 3.00

## DIXIE DOGWOOD PATTERN
Creamer and Cov Sugar Bowl ............................ 18.00
Cup and Saucer ................................................. 3.00
Dessert Bowl, 5 1/4" d ........................................ 3.00
Plate
    6 1/4" d..................................................... 3.00
    9 1/2" d..................................................... 4.00
Platter, 12" l ..................................................... 6.00
Soup Bowl, 8 1/4" d ........................................... 4.00

## DUNCAN HINES PATTERN
Coupe Soup, 8 1/4" d .......................................... 8.00
Cup and Saucer ................................................. 3.00
Plate
    6 1/4" d..................................................... 4.00
    7" d......................................................... 4.00
Platter
    11 1/2" l................................................... 7.00
    13 1/2" l................................................... 8.00
Vegetable Bowl, 9" d ......................................... 12.00

## HIAWATHA PATTERN
Creamer ........................................................... 14.00
Cup and Saucer ................................................. 10.00
Plate
    7 1/2" d..................................................... 8.00
    10 1/2" d................................................... 12.00
Platter, 13 1/2" l ............................................... 18.00
Sugar Bowl, Cov................................................ 18.00

## LADY EVETTE PATTERN
Vegetable Bowl, Cov, 10 1/2" H-H........................ 25.00

## MADAME DUBARRY ROYAL BLUE PATTERN
Bowl, 9 1/2" d .................................................. 12.00
Platter, 13 1/2" l ................................................ 15.00

## MAGNOLIA PATTERN
Platter, 13 3/4" l ................................................ 15.00

## MILDRED PATTERN
Plate, 10" d........................................................ 3.00

## MISCELLANEOUS DINNERWARE
Cream Pitcher, 5 1/2" h, streamlined shape, gloss black
    .......................................................... 35.00

Lg red stylized tulip head, green leaves, long black stem
    Cup and Saucer...................................... 4.00
    Plate
        6 3/4" d............................................ 3.00
        9 1/2" d............................................ 7.00
Plate, 10 1/4" d, multicolored decal of Dutch girl and wind-
mill in center, gold overlay on border ...................... 10.00
Rust-brown border band w/hanging gold swag overlay
    Berry Bowl, 5" d ...................................... 4.00
    Plate
        7 1/4" d............................................ 5.00
        10" d............................................... 7.00
    Platter, 11 1/4" l..................................... 13.00
    Vegetable Bowl, 9 1/2" l........................... 8.00
    Vegetable Bowl, Cov, 11" H-H ................. 15.00

## PINE CONE PATTERN
Chop Plate, 11 3/4" d ......................................... 5.00

## OLD HOMESTEAD PATTERN
Fruit Bowl, 5 1/4" d............................................. 3.00
Platter, 10 1/2" H-H .......................................... 10.00
Serving Bowl, 9" d ............................................. 4.00

## QUEEN ANNE PATTERN
Platter
    9 3/4" l..................................................... 10.00
    13 3/8" l................................................... 12.00
    15 1/4" l................................................... 15.00

## RIO-ASSORTED PATTERNS
Bowl, 9" d .......................................................... 5.00
Cup and Saucer ................................................. 8.00
Dessert Bowl, 5 1/4" d......................................... 4.00
Plate
    6 1/4" d..................................................... 4.00
    9 1/2" d..................................................... 14.00
Platter
    10 1/2" d................................................... 8.00

**Plate, 9 1/2" d, "Rio" pattern, red, green, and black, $8.**

11 1/4" l ....................................................... 15.00
Soup Bowl, 8 1/4" d ........................................ 3.00
Tumbler, 5" h ............................................... 10.00

**SUSANNE PATTERN**
Berry Bowl, 5" d ............................................. 2.00
Plate
  6" d ............................................................ 2.00
  7" d ............................................................ 5.00
  Soup Bowl, 7 3/4" d ................................... 3.00

Steubenville
ROSE DAWN
1931

# Steubenville Pottery Company

## Steubenville, Ohio
## 1879-1959

**History:** A group of citizens opened Steubenville Pottery in 1879 in Steubenville, Ohio. They made dinner and toilet sets in semi-vitreous, cream colored wares, granite ware, and semi-porcelain.

American Modern designed in 1939 by Russel Wright came in a variety of colors. It was the most popular dinnerware in America in its time (see Russel Wright). Woodfield was a leaf pattern in solid colors of Salmon Pink, Tropic, Dove Gray, Rust, and Golden Fawn that was very popular. Steubenville was distributed to leading department stores in the United States.

The company experienced difficulties in the 1950s and closed in 1959. Canonsburg Pottery purchased Steubenville molds and continued to make some of the pottery.

A wide variety of marks was used.

**ADAM ANTIQUE-FLORAL PATTERN**
Bowl, 8 1/4" d ............................................... 10.00
Cereal Bowl, 7" H-H ...................................... 6.00
Creamer, 4" h ............................................... 8.00
Cup and Saucer ............................................ 8.00
Plate
  7 5/8" sq ................................................... 6.00
  9" d ............................................................ 8.00
Vegetable Bowl, 10 1/2" l, rect .................. 15.00
Vegetable Bowl, Cov, 10" H-H ................... 15.00

**BANDANA PATTERN**
Plate, 11 1/4" d ............................................. 5.00

**BLUEBIRD PATTERN**
Plate, 9" d ................................................... 20.00

**DOGWOOD PATTERN**
Cup and Saucer ............................................ 6.00
Platter, 13 1/2" l .......................................... 18.00

**Breakfast Service, teapot, 6 1/4" h, creamer, 3" h, cov butter dish, 7 3/4" d, cereal bowl, 7" H-H, plate, 7 1/2" d, plate, 8 1/4" d, sugar bowl, cup and saucer, lt blue design, white ground, $68.**

**FAIRLANE PATTERN**
Bowl
  6" d ............................................................ 3.00
  8" d ............................................................ 7.00
Butter Dish, Cov, 8" l ................................. 10.00
Egg Plate, 9" d, 12 wells ........................... 12.00
Plate, 10" d ................................................. 10.00
Platter, 14" H-H ........................................... 15.00

**HORIZON PATTERN**
Serving Bowl, 8 1/2" d .................................. 5.00

**MEISSEN ROSE PATTERN**
Platter, 11" l ............................................... 10.00

**Platter, 13" l x 9 3/4" w, "Adam Antique" pattern, multi-colored floral center, $10.**

## MISCELLANEOUS

Platter, 15" l, cavalier wearing feathered hat, brown shades, green luster border............................48.00

## MONTICELLO PATTERN

Berry Bowl, 5 1/2" d......................................3.00
Charger, 15 1/2" d .........................................10.00
Creamer ........................................................12.00
Cup and Saucer ............................................10.00
Plate
    6 1/4" d..................................................5.00
    8 1/2" d..................................................5.00
    10 1/2" d................................................6.00
Platter, 13 1/2" l ............................................15.00
Serving Bowl, 9 1/2" l ......................................8.00
Sugar Bowl, Cov.............................................15.00

## PEACOCK GARDENS PATTERN

Plate
    6" d......................................................3.00
    10" d....................................................3.00

## PROVINCETOWN

Platter, 14" l ..................................................5.00

## RAYMOR CONTEMPORA PATTERN

Plate, 7" d, textured charcoal surface..........15.00

## ROSE MINUET PATTERN

Cake Plate, 11 1/2" d......................................9.00

## ROSE POINT PATTERN

Plate
    7 3/4" sq...............................................6.00
    8 1/2" d................................................6.00

## SPRING BOUQUET PATTERN

Dish, Cov, 11" d ............................................10.00

## THE VIRGINIAN PATTERN

Creamer, 4 1/2" l.............................................5.00
Cup and Saucer ..............................................3.00
Fruit Bowl, 5 1/4" d .........................................4.00
Plate, 10" d....................................................5.00
Platter, 13 1/4" l ............................................10.00
Sugar Bowl, Cov.............................................10.00

## WILD ROSE PATTERN

Platter, 15" l ..................................................10.00

## WOODFIELD PATTERN

Ashtray, 4 1/2" d, chartreuse ..........................7.00
Bowl
    6" d, dk green.......................................9.00
    11" d, chartreuse................................15.00
Luncheon Set, 12 plates, 12 cups, 12 saucers, green, gray, chartreuse, and dusty rose ..................................150.00
Pitcher, 9 1/2" h, gray ....................................75.00
Plate
    6 1/2" d, gray.......................................5.00
    8 1/2" d, salmon pink ..........................5.00
    10 1/2" d, green .................................15.00

Platter, 13 3/4" l, turquoise blue ...................20.00
Relish, 9 1/2" l, gray ......................................38.00
Shakers, gray, pr .............................................18.00
Teapot, 11" l x 6" h, seafoam..........................50.00
Tidbit, 11" h, 2 levels, metal support, green ................38.00
Vegetable Bowl, 10 1/2" l ..............................15.00

# Stoneware

## Most of the United States
## 1630s-Present

**History:** Traditional stoneware had a ceramic body made of certain clays that when fired became vitrified, were non-porous and non-absorbent, and were exceptionally strong. They did not require a glaze to make them watertight, but the surface was very coarse and gritty. Most pieces were salt glazed to form a transparent shiny, pebbled finish that resembled orange peel to make the surface smoother. Salt glazing was the norm in the northeast and Midwest through the 19th century.

Albany slip was an alternative glaze used by 1800 that was a mixture of dark brown, finely grained clay with water that formed a smooth, opaque brown-colored glaze. It covered both the inside and outside of a piece, or could be used just on the inside, and the exterior could be salt glazed.

Alkaline glaze was used in the southeastern United States and produced a drippy olive or brown finish that was smoother and more uniform. Bristol glaze produced a white opaque finish that copied porcelain and white earthenwares. Started in the 1880s, this glaze provided a base for spongewares or was combined with Albany slip for brown-white wares.

The earliest stoneware examples prior to c1800 were based on English and German examples since the potters brought these traditions with them to America. Before the late 1800s, stoneware was thrown on the potter's wheel. Handles and spouts were applied separately. Eventually most stonewares were made by press molding, a little drape molding, and mostly by slip casting which dominated the stoneware production.

Since stonewares were designed with strict utilitarian purposes in mind, the forms were rather simple and limited in range. From the 18th through the 19th centuries, the shapes of the basic bowls, jugs, mugs, pots, chamber pots, and such remained the same. Ovoid forms eventually were replaced by straight sided examples.

Decoration was achieved in several different ways on the utilitarian stoneware examples. Most incised designs date prior to 1840 where the designs were scratched into the surface prior to firing. The decoration was then filled in with cobalt blue or manganese brown.

Impressed decorations had designs that were either stamped or impressed with a coggle wheel. Applied decorations were attached elements that were either hand shaped or formed in a press mold. Freehand slip decoration was usually done in cobalt blue and some manganese. Prior to 1850, decorations were the simple squiggles, tulips, trees and such.

After 1850, stylized birds, animals, humans, houses, ships, and scenes were used. Stencil decoration was in use c1870 picturing florals, figurals, geometrics such as circles, stars, and diamonds along with the company name of the pottery.

Slip-trailed decorations in cobalt blue on salt-glazed stonewares were primarily found in New England at Bennington, and in the Hudson River and Erie Canal areas of New York State. In western Pennsylvania and Ohio, brushed or painted cobalt blue decorations were found.

Stoneware potters mostly made items that were utilitarian in nature for the storage of foods and liquids. These pieces were extremely durable due to the nature of the material. Storage vessels found forms in jugs from 1/2 pint size to 20 gallon size in a variety of shapes, jars, pots for cream, crocks for preserving and storing foods, tobacco humidors, and water coolers. Bottles held beer and soft drinks, flasks were made in pint and half pint sizes, and canteens in pint and quart sizes often were used for advertising.

Simple mugs were made prior to 1850 by most potters, while some larger mugs and steins had pewter lids. Goblets, glasses, and pitchers in pint to two gallon sizes were made. Few tablewares were made. Punch bowls, covered and footed sugar bowls, salts, and bowls in 1/2 gallon to five gallon sizes were available.

Bean pots usually were brown and are still being made today. Teapots also were brown glazed. Household and dairy items such as churns and mortars, inkwells and bottles, chamberpots, spittoons, and hot water bottles were made. Flower pots and urns appeared after the 1860s. Toys, banks, whistles, and miniatures were made along with mantle pieces, doorstops, figural dogs, lions, and face jugs.

Vermont was one of the most important centers for stonewares. The Norton factory (see Bennington) and the Farrar family made important contributions. Many of the nation's earliest potters settled in New York since there were good sources for clay there. Noah White with his sons and grandsons in Utica from 1838-1907 made stonewares that are highly collectible today.

In New Jersey, David and John Henderson at the Jersey City Pottery made the first successful American mold made stonewares in 1828. Pitchers, spittoons, and soap dishes were marked. Abraham Fulper and his son in 1860 made blue decorated stonewares. All five of his sons were connected with the pottery business.

There was a vast stoneware industry in Pennsylvania, while Yorktown, Virginia had one of the nation's earlier stoneware kilns. Other important areas included North and South Carolina, many areas of Ohio, and the Midwestern states, especially Red Wing, Minnesota. (see Red Wing).

In the early 1900s, much blue and white utilitarian stoneware was made in a number of Ohio Valley potteries such as Brush-McCoy, Nelson McCoy, Burley, Uhl, and Logan. Many manufacturers of blue and white stonewares were unknown.

**References:** Georgeanna H. Greer, *American Stonewares: The Art and Craft of Utilitarian Potters*, Schiffer Publishing Ltd. 1999; Edith Harbin, *Blue and White Stoneware Pottery Crockery: Identification and Value Guide*, Collector Books, 1977; Kathryn McNerney, *Blue and White Stoneware*, Collector Books, 1996; Don and Carol Raycraft, *American Stoneware*, Krause Publications; _____, *Collector's Guide to Country Stoneware and Pottery*, 2nd Series, Collector Books, 1990; Terry Taylor and Terry & Kay Lawrence, *Collector's Encyclopedia of Salt Glaze Stoneware*, Collector Books, 1997.

**Collectors' Club:** Blue and White Pottery Club, 224 12th St., N.W., Cedar Rapids, IA 52405, $12 per year, quarterly newsletter; Collectors of Illinois Pottery and Stoneware, Norma Sams, 308 N. Jackson Street, Clinton, IL, quarterly newsletter, $15.

**Museums:** Bennington Museum, VT; Brooklyn Museum, NY; DAR Museum, Washington, DC; Henry Ford Museum and Greenfield Village, Dearborn, MI; Henry Francis DuPont Winterthur Museum, DE; Museum of Ceramics at East Liverpool, OH; Shelburne Museum, VT.

Apple Butter Jar, 6 3/4" h, "imp F.H. COWDEN, HARRISBURG", stains, (A) ................................................. 30.00
Bank
4 3/8" d, circ w/knob finial, brown, pebble glaze, "incised J.E.G." on base, (A) ........................................ 138.00
7" h, bottle shape w/stopper, applied relief of 2 men drinking, eating, windmill, and floral vines, applied floral leaf on stopper, "incised Ann Tye 1840," slot on side, c1840, (A) ..................................................... 413.00
7 1/2" h, figural fat man, Albany slip vest w/slot, blue collar, buttons, bow tie, and lapel, blue accented face and hair, restored hairlines, c1850, (A) ................ 8,250.00
10 1/8" h, jug shape, dbl ear loop handles, tapered knob finial and coin slot, dk brown Albany slip, (A).... 385.00
Batter Pail, 12" h, tin lid and bail handle, cinnamon clay, 2 gallon, c1891, (A) ............................................... 413.00
Batter Pitcher
7 1/2" h, bale handles, brush blue accents on spout, ears, and lug handle, c1860, chips and stains, (A) .... 176.00
9 1/2" h, brown.......................................................... 95.00
Bean Pot, 11 1/2" h, 2 loop handles, "incised *Tenth Reunion Sons and Daughters of Vermont 1883*," ............. 3,300.00
Bean Pot, Cov, 5 1/2" h, raised "blue BOSTON BAKED BEANS" on front, reverse w/2 figures making beans, gray textured ground, chips ........................................... 385.00
Beater Jar, 5" h, "blue WESSON OIL" and stripes ..... 125.00
Bottle
7 1/2" h, dk brown top, tan base w/oval of "DR. SWETT'S ORIGINAL ROOT BEER, ROOT BEER, REGISTERED, BOSTON, MASS." front ....................... 20.00
9 1/8" h, dk brown Albany slip w/matte finish, "imp *S. Routson, Wooster, O.*" label, (A) ...................... 605.00
9 1/4" h, mushroom lip, "imp cobalt enhanced HON. & WINNER, WEST NANTICOKE, PA." on shoulder, (A) ................................................................... 90.00
Bowl, 10 1/2" d, Albany slip covered, "incised for Mary Krohm" on bottom ................................................. 675.00
Butter Churn
13" h, blue dotted woven basket of flowers, "WEST TROY POTTERY," c1880, (A) ........................... 715.00
14" h, blue brush accents, "imp blue HENDERSON & RUDD WATERTOWN and 3," c1860, repaired chips, (A) ......................................................................... 143.00
16" h, w/original dasher, blue slip decorated dotted lily design, age cracks, c1880, (A).......................... 275.00
20" h, w/original dasher guide, blue dotted bird on flowering branches and 6, "imp oval J. BURGER JR. ROCHESTER, NY" on border, c1885, (A) ............... 4,400.00
Cake Crock, 7" h
Blue slip flower design, "EDMANDS & CO.," c1870, restored chip, (A)................................................. 187.00
Blue swag design, accented handles, "imp blue JOHN BELL WAYNESBORO and 2," c1860, (A)........ 550.00
Canning Jar
7 1/2" h, "blue stenciled G.W. Roberts & Co Dealers in general merchandise. Elizabeth, WVA," c1860, (A) ................................................................... 121.00
8 1/2" h, "brush cobalt W.P.H. and 1869," brush blue vine designs, c1869, (A) ......................................... 220.00
Chicken Water Crock, 7 1/2" h, domed top, chips........ 25.00

Churn

13 3/4" h, ovoid, cobalt quill flourish and "3," applied shoulder handles, (A) ...........................................82.00

15 1/2" h, cobalt quill squiggle and "3," applied shoulder handles, bubble glaze, (A)............................... 110.00

Cooler, Cov

15" h, blue stenciled grapes design, "F.T.WRIGHT & SON STONEWARE, TAUTON, MASS." on front, c1870, replaced lid, (A) ................................... 176.00

18 1/2" h, dbl ear handles, wood spout, cobalt "6" and floral splashes on shoulder and cov, (A) .............. 220.00

Cream Pot

8" h, blue triple flower design, "imp blue COWDEN & WILCOX, HARRISBURG, PA," c1870, hairline, (A) ...........................................................................385.00

9" h, ovoid, blue dotted and ribbed floral vine and "2," "blue imp N. CLARK JR. ATHENS, NY" on rim, c1850, hairlines, (A) ....................................................... 187.00

Crock

5 1/2" h x 6 5/8" d, "blue accented imp circ J.J. Heinz Co., Keystone Pickling & Preserving Works, Pittsburgh, Pa.," blue accented imp geometric designs on base and side and collar, chip, (A) ............................300.00

8" h, ovoid, "blue T.GOODWIN" on collar, c1830, (A) ...................................................................... 77.00

8 5/8" h, ear handles, cobalt painted spotted bird on scrolling ground, fan tree at side, "imp cobalt accented W.H. FARRAR & CO., GEDDES, N.Y." on border, "cobalt painted 2," chips and hairlines, (A) .....2,800.00

9" h

Cobalt quill flower and "2," imp "Burger," applied handles, hairlines, (A) ..............................82.00

Dk blue chicken pecking corn design, "imp BRADY & RYAN ELLENVILLE, NY," c1885, (A)...........770.00

Heavy cobalt crossed love birds and 2, "S.HART FULTON," c1875, repaired rim chip, (A).............523.00

**Crock, 9 1/2" h, blue accented "NEW YORK STONEWARE CO. FORT EDWARD, N.Y and 2" on front, tan ground, $275.**

9 1/4" h, blue bird on plume, "FULPER BROS., FLEMINGTON, NJ, 2" on front, c1870, (A)................ 633.00

9 1/2" h

Cobalt stenciled "JAS. BENJAMIN, STONEWARE DEPOT, CINCINNATI, O.," (A) .................... 138.00

Thick blue bulls eye design, "blue imp C.MILLER GROCERIES AND PROVISIONS FOREIGN & DOMESTIC LIQUORS, ROTTERDAM ST. SCHENECTADY, NY," 3 gallon, c1860, hairlines, (A)................................................... 1,320.00

10" h

Cobalt brushed flowers, imp "M. Woodruff Cortland 2," applied handles, (A).....................................275.00

Ear handles, "imp blue washed NEW YORK STONEWARE CO., FORT EDWARD,NY" on shoulder, 3 cobalt veined leaves and "3," hairlines, c1890 ................................................................................120.00

Ovoid

Blue triple tulip design, "W.H. FARRAR & CO.,GEDDES, NY" on rim, c1850, (A)..... 358.00

Thick blue stenciled snowflake design, blue accented ears, "imp F.H. COWDEN, HARRISBURG," c1890, hairline, (A) ....................176.00

10 1/4" h, applied handles, "imp J .FISHER, LYONS, N.Y.," cobalt quill dragonfly design and "3" on front, (A) ..............................................................................410.00

10 1/2" h, dk blue slip pear on branch design, "A.O.WHITTEMORE, HAVANA, NY, 4" on front, c1870, (A)550.00

11" h, "blue MANUFACTURED BY HERMANN & CO. MILWAUKEE," "blue 3,"........................................90.00

11 1/2" h

Blue dotted leaf design, "A.K.BALLARD, BURLINGTON, VT, 4," c1870, (A) ............................. 303.00

Blue hand holding cluster of grapes, flowers, and oranges and 5 on front, "imp WM. A MACQUOID & CO. NEW YORK LITTLE WEST 12TH STREET" on border, c1870, (A) ................................... 1,760.00

12 3/4" h, applied handles, tooled lines, cobalt quill tulip and "5," (A) ..................................................... 330.00

13" h

Blue bird on stump design, "imp blue J.A.&C.W. UNDERWOOD FORT EDWARD, NY and 6" on border, c1865, (A) ......................................... 1,155.00

Cobalt quill foliage and "5," applied handles, (A) ....................................................................................... 110.00

Slip cobalt dotted dog w/basket of flowers and "2," "imp blue A.P. COOK BROOKLYN MICH WHOLESALE & RETAIL DEALER IN DRY GOODS, HARDWARE, GROCERIES & C.," "S.HART FULTON" on reverse, restoration, (A)........................... 1,155.00

Thick blue dotted quail and cattails on front and "5," "imp blue JOHN BURGER, ROCHESTER" on rim, hairlines and chips, (A) ........................... 17,875.00

13 1/2" h, brush blue flowerheads, ribbed leaves, and plant, blue accents at handles, "J. MANTELL PENN YAN," c1860, hairline, (A)................................. 660.00

14" h, blue stylized flower, gray ground, "BACHELDER MENASHA, WI." on front, c1850, .................... 550.00

14 3/4" h, blue stylized flower and "6," "CHARLES HERMANN MILWAUKEE," c1850 ........................... 475.00

Custard Cup, 2 1/2" h, brown striping, tan ground ....... 20.00

Flask, 7 1/2" h, blue cross hatch on front and reverse, c1840, (A) ...................................................... 1,375.00

Inkwell, 2 1/4" h, figural bust of old woman w/bonnet, tan glaze w/brown accents, chips, (A) .........................275.00

**Jar**

7 1/2" h, cov, blue center flower design w/pine trees at sides, c1860, (A) .................................................440.00

9" h, "imp H. Nash Utica," c1838, staining, (A) ......132.00

9 1/2" h

Brush blue flower and accents at ears, "PENN YAN," (A) ................................................................330.00

Cov, blue stylized leaf design, 1 gallon, "EDMONDS & CO." mk, (A)....................................................187.00

10 1/4" h, ovoid, applied shoulder handles, cobalt brushed floral design w/tulip on one side, flowering tree on front, "imp S. BELL 1 1/2," chips, (A) .1,210.00

11" h, cov, ovoid, blue slip bird and flower, 2 gallon, "W.H. FARRAR & CO., GEDDES, NY" on shoulder, hairline and chips, (A) .................................................1,980.00

13" h

Cov, blue grape cluster, "SEYMOUR & BOSWORTH, HARTFORD, 3" on shoulder, c1875, (A).......165.00

Ovoid, cobalt splashed imp "I.M. Mead, Portage Co. Ohio and 3," applied shoulder handles, hairlines, (A) ................................................................138.00

14" h, applied shoulder handles, cobalt brushed tulip, "imp T. REED 3" on front, (A) ............................605.00

15" h, ovoid, applied shoulder handles, tooled bands, brushed cobalt vining floral design and "5," (A) ................................................................440.00

16" h, ovoid, applied shoulder handles, cobalt brushed and stenciled stylized flowers and "J.A. FRANZ, STAPLES & FANCY GROCERIES, POMEROY, OHIO 16 in center band," hairlines, (A) .........................3,410.00

**Jug, 10 1/2" h, salt glaze, brown "Turkey Drippings," tan textured ground, $160.**

**Jug**

3 3/4" h, dk brown Albany slip, (A).........................35.00

4" h, Albany slip glaze, "incised Little Brown Jug," ................................................................300.00

4 3/4" h, imp and blue "Con Keefe, 8 & 10 Cambridge, Boston, Mass." label, strap handle, (A).............110.00

6 1/2" h, Albany glaze, "incised Wood & Utley 103 N. Washington St. Rome, NY" c1880, (A) .............154.00

8 1/2" h, conical spout, filler hole, applied handle, cobalt slip "2" in scalloped edge circle, (A) ..................302.00

9 3/4" h, beehive shape, lustered brown glaze........18.00

10" d, canteen shape, ftd, metal bail handle, "raised cobalt BARDWELL'S ROOT BEER" and floral bulb on sides, leaves on shoulder.................................845.00

10 1/8" h, 1/2 gallon, "imp L.C. PAUL BLACKSTONE ST BOSTON" .........................................................145.00

10 1/2" h, brush blue leaf accent on shoulder, "W.H. FARRAR & CO.,GEDDES, NY" on shoulder, (A) .....302.00

10 3/4" h, Albany glaze w/sgraffito *Kauffman Lattimer Co. Wholesale Druggists, Columbus, Ohio* on front, chip on shoulder, (A) .....................................82.00

11" h

Bird w/feathers on triple flower, 1 gallon, c1860, restored handle, (A)....................................880.00

Cobalt quill leaf and polka dot design, strap handle, (A) ................................................................115.00

11 1/2" h, ovoid

Bristol base, lustered brown top, unmkd.............18.00

"C. CROLIUS MANUFACTURER MANHATTAN WELLS NEW YORK" on shoulder, c1800, (A) ..........2,640.00

Cobalt brushed flowerhead, strap handle, (A)...100.00

12" h, ovoid

Blue crossed love bird design and "2," "S.HART FULTON," c1870, (A) .........................................715.00

Cobalt band on neck, strap handle, (A)...............60.00

12 1/2" h

Ovoid, brush blue vine accents at handle and under "C.CROLUIS, NEW YORK," c1800, (A) .......522.00

"Raised blue H. BOSWORTH & SONS WHOLESALE DRUGGIST MILWAUKEE, WISC."...............265.00

13" h, blue winged eagle carrying banner design, "WME WARNER, WEST TROY," c1850, (A)..............688.00

13 1/4" h, brown Albany slip w/sgraffito *Stands and Kaiser, Col., O.* (A) ...............................................110.00

13 1/2" h

Brushed dbl blue flower, "blue imp Rossman & McKinstry Druggists 329 Warren St. Hudson, NY 1883," (A) ................................................................715.00

Lg blue dotted and stylized "2" on front, "imp TROY, NY POTTERY," c1885, (A) .........................358.00

Ovoid, gray-blue brushed tulip design, imp "2," strap handle, (A) ....................................................121.00

14" h

Blue stylized floral design, "WEST TROY POTTERY" above, *P.M.Carlisle Boston* below, c1880, (A) ................................................................330.00

Lg thick blue gooney bird w/long tail on floral leaf, "ROBERTS BINGHAMPTON, NY" on shoulder, c1860, restored spout chip, (A) ...................798.00

14 1/2" h, blue dotted snowflake on front, "imp blue "CLARK & CO., ROCHESTER" on shoulder, c1850, (A) ...................................................... 715.00

16" h, straight sides, blue painted "2" and stylized flower, c1890 ............................................................ 550.00

16 1/2" h, blue stylized swimming turtle design, "WEST TROY POTTERY" on neck, c1880, (A) ............ 633.00

17 3/4" h, lg cobalt floral design, imp "4," strap handle, (A) .............................................................. 330.00

Lamp, 5 3/4" h, saucer base with pan and wick spout, applied handle, greenish-tan glaze, (A) ................ 440.00

Matchholder, 3" h, tapered shape, quilted side, blue band on base .......................................................... 50.00

Milk Bowl, 11 1/2" d, cobalt brushed flowers around rim, "imp 1," (A) ....................................................... 440.00

Milk Crock, 9" h x 12" d, 3 incised lines and wave at ext center, streaked gloss glaze, (A) .................... 302.00

Milk Pitcher, 8" h, blue banding, c1900 ...................... 175.00

Mug

3 1/2" h, tooled and imp geometrics, dk brown metallic glaze ....................................................................... 75.00

5 1/8" h, cobalt bands top and base ........................ 35.00

5 1/2" h, "Windy City," blue accented relief of woman w/skirt blowing, gray ground, salt glaze, "stamped The Robinson Clay Product Co., Akron, OHIO" mk, (A) ........................................................................... 110.00

6 1/2" h, thick blue grapes, lg handle, c1860, (A) ..963.00

6 3/4" h, relief molded golfers and raised horiz banding, blue accents, lt blue ground, (A) .......................... 95.00

Oyster Jar

6" h, "imp blue T. DOWNINGS PICKLED OYSTERS #5 BROAD ST. NEW YORK" on front, c1850, (A)..550.00

8" h, "imp COWDEN & WILCOX," c1870, (A) ......... 88.00

Pail, 9" h, thick blue dancing flower design and "2," "imp blue HARRINGTON & BURGER, ROCHESTER" on rim, c1853, (A) ........................................................ 358.00

Pitcher

6" h, cobalt brushed floral decoration of branches, buds, and leaves, (A) ........................................... 285.00

8" h

Medallion w/2 raised cows grazing, blue and gray ........................................................................... 85.00

Raised hanging grapes and leaves on dk blue raised net ground ..................................................... 195.00

8 1/4" h

Blue raised butterfly design, gray body ................................................................................. 250.00

Relief of Indian head in circle, blue and white, (A) ................................................................................. 220.00

8 1/2" h, relief molded blue stork and flower, gray ground, chips ....................................................... 295.00

8 3/4" h, strap handle, sgraffito band and banner w/"N.H. Barber," (A) ............................................. 165.00

9" h, Relief Molded

Blue wild rose design, gray body ..................... 350.00

Vert cattails, blue accented borders, (A) ................................................................................. 248.00

10" h, incised and blue accented star design w/"1878" in center of star, c1878, (A) .............................. 1,705.00

10 1/2" h, brushed blue floral design, banded rim, c1860, (A) .................................................................... 688.00

11 1/2" h, "blue ONE and slashes," "N. CLARK & CO., MT. MORRIS," (A) ............................................... 853.00

12 1/2" h, dk blue bushy tailed bird on dotted plume design, dk blue squiggles under spout, c1880, chips, (A) ..................................................................... 1,072.00

13" h, cobalt brushed leaf design and "2," strap handle, hairline, (A) ......................................................... 170.00

13 1/2" h, cobalt stylized leaves from branches ................................................................................. 2,850.00

Pitcher and Bowl, pitcher, 13" h, bowl, 15" d, relief rose pattern, dk blue accents, salt glaze, c1880, (A).......... 413.00

Preserving Jar

7 1/4" h, ovoid, "imp T.J.S., T.T.I.F." label, (A) ......... 99.00

8" h, brushed cobalt wide stripes, (A) ................... 195.00

8 1/2" h, w/cov, "blue slip 4 QUARTS," c1860, (A) ................................................................................. 165.00

9" h, blue slip walking turtle design, "blue script 1/2 G," c1850, hairlines, (A) ......................................... 413.00

9 3/8" h, blue brush "coma" band, salt glaze, (A) ................................................................................. 65.00

9 1/2" h, clam shell design on front and back w/cobalt accents, "COMMERAWS STONEWARE" on front, c1790, staining, (A) ......................................... 3,080.00

9 3/4" h

Cobalt stenciled "A.P. Donagho, Parkersburg, W.Va.," (A).................................................................... 110.00

"Imp S. BELL & SON, STRASBERG, PA.," cobalt brushed commas on shoulder, (A)................ 248.00

10" h, blue swag designs, blue accented handles, "imp 1," dk clay, c1830, (A) ..................................... 303.00

10 3/4" h

Blue 5 ribbed leaf design and "2," "imp blue J. BURGER JR., ROCHESTER, NY" on neck, c1885, (A)..................................................................... 248.00

Streaked alkaline glaze, incised lines on shoulder, late 19th C, sgd "TR 1" on shoulder, Thomas Ritchie, hairline, (A) ................................................... 132.00

12" h, cobalt brushed and stenciled "From Handlan Ratcliff & Co.South W.Va. 2" and stylized leaves, (A) ................................................................................. 220.00

13" h, "imp Melcher & Co. Manufacturer's Louisville, KY 2" chips and hairline, (A) ................................ 110.00

Snuff Jar, 4" h, loop handle, raised cobalt curlicues, salt glaze finish........................................................... 325.00

Spittoon

5 3/4" h x 7 1/2" d, relief molded vert flowers and trees, blue wash, gray ground, c1880 ...................... 225.00

6" h x 10" d, blue swags and accented ears, "imp COWDEN & WILCOX, HARRISBURG, PA," c1870, (A) ..................................................................... 715.00

Storage Jar, Cov, 9" h, straight sides, brushed blue swag designs, blue accented handles, c1850, repairs, (A) ................................................................................. 220.00

Syrup Jug

9 1/2" h, Albany glaze, "incised Charles Hall Crockery, Springfield, Mass." c1880, (A) ......................... 110.00

12" h, squat shape, lg blue geometric sunflower design, carved wood stopper, c1860, restored spout chip, (A) ................................................................................. 358.00

12 1/2" h, squat shape, blue dbl bell flower design, "imp blue CORTLAND" on shoulder, c1860, (A) ....... 385.00

Water Cooler

16 3/8" h, ovoid shape, spread base, ear handles, incised facing birds on branches on front, cobalt petaled flowers above, "imp L. & B. C. CHASE, SOMERSET" under handle and "3," (A) ...............................3,000.00

19 1/2" h, Bristol glaze, relief of vines and florals, "incised blue Ice Water in label" on front, blue outlined bung hole, (A) ...............................................220.00

1895-1897

O.P. CO.
SYRACUSE
CHINA
1897-1920s

# Syracuse China/Onondaga Pottery Company

## Syracuse, New York
## 1871-Present

**History:** In 1871, the Onondaga Pottery Company bought out Empire Pottery and changed its name to Onondaga until 1966 when it became the Syracuse China Company of Syracuse, New York. Onondaga made white granite ware with the coat of arms of New York as its mark. High fired semi-vitreous wares were introduced in 1885 with a guarantee against cracking and crazing that was new to the chinaware industry.

"Imperial Geddo" from 1888 was a true vitrified china that was thin and translucent. It won an award at the Columbian Exposition in 1893. Onondaga had developed a full line of china by 1891. In 1893, it was making white granite, cream colored wares that were both plain and decorated, and dinner and toilet services. Semi-porcelain was made from 1886-1898.

The company continued to expand and added a new plant in 1921. It acquired Vandesa-Syracuse Ltd. of Quebec, a maker of hotel china, in 1959. In 1970, Syracuse discontinued chinaware for home use, having been forced out by the inexpensive imports. By the following year they were one of the largest producers of hotel, restaurant, airline, and commercial types of tablewares of excellent quality. All of its production was moved to one location in 1979, and it was no longer a privately owned company. In 1984, Syracuse purchased the Mayer China Company.

Its marks utilized a date code on the wide variety of marks used.

**References:** Cleota Reed & Stan Skoczen, *Syracuse China*, Syracuse University Press, 1997.

## ALLENDALE PATTERN
Platter, 14" l ...............................................75.00

## APPLE BLOSSOM PATTERN
Berry Bowl, 4 5/8" d...........................................7.00
Cup and Saucer .............................................15.00
Gravy Boat, 9" l ............................................20.00
Plate
  6 1/4" d.....................................................5.00
  8" d.............................................................8.00
Platter, 14" l ...............................................22.00
Serving Bowl, 8" d .........................................20.00

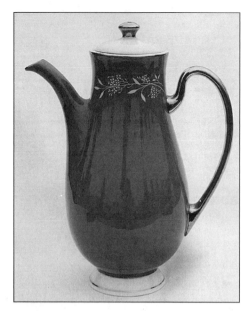

**Coffeepot, 9 1/4" h, "Candlelight" pattern, green, white, and silver, $50.**

## BAROQUE PATTERN
Cup and Saucer ...............................................5.00
Plate
  8" d .............................................................4.00
  10" d ...........................................................6.00
Soup Bowl, 8" d...............................................5.00

## BELMONT PATTERN
Plate, 6" d......................................................8.00
Sugar Bowl ....................................................12.00

## BLUE GRASS PATTERN
Cup and Saucer ...............................................6.00
Plate
  6 1/2" d ......................................................5.00
  8" d .............................................................5.00
  10" d ...........................................................6.00

## BOMBAY PATTERN
Berry Bowl, 5" d...............................................4.00
Creamer .........................................................8.00
Cup and Saucer ...............................................8.00
Fruit Cup, ftd .................................................8.00
Plate
  6 1/4" d ......................................................4.00
  8 3/4" d ......................................................6.00
  9 3/4" d ......................................................8.00
Soup Plate, 7 1/2" d.......................................10.00
Sugar Bowl, Cov ...........................................12.00
Teapot, 6" h ..................................................25.00

## BRACELET PATTERN
Cup and Saucer .............................................18.00
Fruit Bowl, 5" d .............................................10.00
Plate
  6 1/4" d ......................................................5.00
  9 3/4" d ....................................................15.00

10 1/4" d.................................................................18.00

## BRITTANY COTTAGE PATTERN
Berry Bowl, 4 5/8" d.................................18.00
Cereal Bowl, 6 1/2" d................................20.00
Cup and Saucer ........................................20.00
Plate
    7 3/8" d.............................................15.00
    9 1/2" d.............................................18.00

## CANDLELIGHT PATTERN
Coffeepot, 8 1/2" h....................................25.00

## CANTERBURY PATTERN
Cup and Saucer ..........................................3.00
Plate
    7" d...................................................4.00
    8" d...................................................4.00

## CARVEL PATTERN
Creamer .....................................................35.00
Cup and Saucer ........................................15.00
Dessert Bowl, 5" d....................................10.00
Plate
    6 1/2" d...............................................8.00
    10 1/2" d.............................................20.00
Sugar Bowl, Cov........................................40.00
Vegetable Bowl, 10 1/2" l.........................25.00

## CORABEL PATTERN
Casserole, Cov, 10" H-H ...........................65.00
Creamer .....................................................15.00
Cup and Saucer ..........................................8.00
Fruit Bowl, 5" d..........................................12.00
Gravy Boat, 9 5/8" l, w/attached undertray.................10.00
Plate
    6 1/4" d...............................................8.00
    7 1/8" d.............................................10.00
    8" d.................................................10.00
    9 3/4" d.............................................15.00
Platter
    12" H-H.............................................25.00
    14" H-H.............................................35.00
Relish Tray, 8" l.........................................15.00
Serving Bowl, 10" d...................................15.00
Soup Plate, 8 3/4" d...................................8.00
Sugar Bowl, Cov........................................25.00
Vegetable Bowl, 10 1/2" l.........................10.00

## COVENTRY PATTERN
Berry Bowl, 5" d..........................................6.00
Cup and Saucer ..........................................6.00
Plate
    6 1/2" d...............................................5.00
    7 1/2" d.............................................10.00
    10" d.................................................10.00
    10 1/2" d.............................................15.00
Serving Bowl, 9" d.....................................35.00
Soup Bowl, 8 3/4" d.....................................3.00

## DIANE PATTERN
Plate, 8 1/2" d............................................10.00

Gravy Boat, 9" l, Underplate, 14" l, "Bombay" pattern, $30.

Platter, 12" H-H .........................................20.00
Soup Plate, 8 1/2" d ..................................15.00

## DOGWOOD PATTERN
Bowl, 6" d ...................................................8.00
Celery Dish, 10" l.......................................25.00
Cup and Saucer .........................................10.00
Fruit Bowl, 6 1/2" d....................................10.00
Plate
    9 3/4" d .............................................15.00
    10 1/2" d ...........................................15.00
Soup Plate, 9 1/4" d ..................................10.00

## ELBERTA PATTERN
Plate
    8" d ...................................................5.00
    9 3/4" d ...............................................7.00
Soup Bowl, 6 1/4" H-H, tab handles.............6.00

## EVENING STAR PATTERN
Cup and Saucer ..........................................8.00
Plate
    6 1/4" d ...............................................5.00
    8" d ...................................................5.00
Platter, 12 1/2" H-H ...................................25.00

## FINESSE PATTERN
Platter, 12" l...............................................25.00

## GOLDEN SEEDS PATTERN
Cup and Saucer ..........................................3.00
Plate
    6 3/4" d ...............................................2.00
    8 1/4" d ...............................................2.00

## GOVERNOR CLINTON PATTERN
Cup and Saucer .........................................12.00

Plate
    8" d ..............................................4.00
    10" d .............................................5.00

## GRANDMA MOSES DESIGNS
Plate, 12" d, "Taking in the Laundry" ...........60.00

## INDIAN TREE PATTERN
Berry Bowl, 5" d ...................................5.00
Plate
    6 1/2" d ..........................................10.00
    7 3/4" d ..........................................10.00
    10 1/2" d .........................................10.00
Salad Bowl, 6 3/4" d ..............................10.00

## LADY LOUISE PATTERN
Plate
    6 1/4" d ...........................................5.00
    10 1/4" d .........................................13.00
Platter, 12" l .......................................30.00

## LYRIC PATTERN
Cup and Saucer ....................................4.00
Plate
    6 1/4" d ...........................................4.00
    8" d ...............................................5.00
    10 1/4" d ..........................................6.00
Platter, 12" l .......................................20.00

## MARLENE PATTERN
Berry Bowl, 5" d ...................................5.00
Cup and Saucer ....................................4.00
Plate
    6 1/4" d ...........................................5.00
    7" d ...............................................6.00
    10" d ..............................................8.00
Soup Plate, 8 3/4" d ...............................8.00

## MAYFLOWER PATTERN
Plate, 8" d, red .....................................6.00

## MAYVIEW PATTERN
Berry Bowl, 5" d ...................................8.00
Plate, 6 1/2" d .....................................3.00
Vegetable Bowl, 9 3/8" d ..........................10.00

## MEADOW BREEZE PATTERN
Bread and Butter Plate .............................10.00
Cup and Saucer ...................................20.00
Dinner Plate .......................................25.00
Platter, 14 1/8" l ...................................64.00
Sugar Bowl, Cov ...................................45.00

## MINUET PATTERN
Creamer, 2" h ......................................10.00
Plate, 8" d .........................................20.00
Sugar Bowl, 2" h ..................................18.00

## OAKLEIGH PATTERN
Berry Bowl, 4 1/2" d ...............................10.00

Pitcher, 4" h .......................................15.00
Platter, 12 1/2" l, oval .............................20.00

## OLD ABBEY PATTERN
Dish, 9 1/2" l ......................................10.00

## PEACOCK PATTERN
Plate
    6 1/4" d ...........................................7.00
    8" d ..............................................15.00
    10" d .............................................15.00

## PENDLETON PATTERN
Bowl, 8" d ..........................................7.00
Cup and Saucer ....................................6.00
Plate
    6 1/2" d ...........................................5.00
    7" d ...............................................7.00
    8" d ...............................................7.00
    10" d ..............................................8.00

## RADCLIFFE PATTERN
Platter, 16" l, oval .................................45.00

## ROMANCE PATTERN
Platter, 12" l .......................................40.00

## ROSE MARIE PATTERN
Cup and Saucer ....................................5.00
Plate
    8" d ...............................................6.00
    9" d ...............................................6.00
    10" d ..............................................8.00

## ROSLYN PATTERN
Teapot, 4" h .......................................25.00

## SELMA PATTERN
Bouillon Cup and Saucer, 6 1/2" H-H ............10.00
Bowl, Cov, 7 3/4" d ...............................25.00
Creamer ............................................5.00
Cup and Saucer ....................................4.00
Fruit Bowl, 5" d ....................................3.00
Plate
    6 1/4" d ...........................................3.00
    9" d ...............................................5.00
    9 3/4" d ..........................................15.00
Platter, 14 1/8" l ...................................20.00
Soup Bowl, 7 1/2" d ...............................6.99
Sugar Bowl, Cov ...................................10.00
Vegetable Bowl, 10" l .............................10.00

## SHARON PATTERN
Cup and Saucer ....................................5.00
Fruit Bowl, 5" d ....................................5.00
Plate
    7 1/4" d ...........................................7.00
    9 3/4" d ..........................................10.00
    10 1/4" d .........................................10.00
Soup Bowl, 7 1/2" d ...............................8.00

## SHERWOOD PATTERN
Berry Bowl, 5" d......................................................3.00
Bread and Butter Plate..........................................5.00
Cream Soup, 5" d, w/underplate, 6 1/2" d..............28.00
Cup and Saucer....................................................10.00
Gravy Boat...........................................................10.00
Plate
    6 3/8" d............................................................3.00
    8" d...................................................................3.00
    9 3/4" d............................................................10.00
Platter
    12" H-H............................................................15.00
    14" H-H............................................................15.00
    16" H-H............................................................18.00
Salad Plate............................................................6.00
Serving Bowl, 10 1/2" l........................................10.00
Soup Plate, 8 3/4" d............................................15.00

## STANSBURY PATTERN
Creamer................................................................18.00
Cup and Saucer....................................................30.00
Fruit Bowl, 5" d.....................................................14.00
Gravy Boat and Stand..........................................60.00
Plate, 10" d...........................................................32.00
Platter
    12" l.................................................................40.00
    14" l.................................................................50.00
Soup Bowl, 8" d....................................................30.00
Sugar Bowl, Cov...................................................15.00
Vegetable Bowl, 10 5/8" l....................................45.00

## SUZANNE PATTERN-FEDERAL SHAPE
Cereal Bowl, 5 1/8" d.............................................8.00
Fruit Bowl, 5 1/8" d.................................................6.00
Gravy Boat and Stand..........................................70.00
Plate
    6 3/8" d............................................................6.00
    7 1/4" d............................................................4.00
    8" d...................................................................6.00
    10" d.................................................................7.00
    10 1/2" d...........................................................9.00
Soup Bowl, 8 1/8" d..............................................24.00
Vegetable Bowl, 10 3/4" l....................................42.00

## TEMPLE BELLS PATTERN
Plate, 8" d...............................................................8.00

## TREND PATTERN
Cereal Bowl, 5 3/4" d.............................................5.00
Cup and Saucer......................................................6.00
Plate
    6" sq.................................................................6.00
    8 1/2" sq...........................................................8.00
    10 1/4" sq.........................................................10.00

## VICTORIA PATTERN
Creamer................................................................25.00
Plate
    10" d.................................................................30.00

10 1/2" d...............................................................28.00
Platter, 14" l.........................................................75.00
Sugar Bowl, Cov...................................................35.00

## WAYSIDE PATTERN
Plate
    8" d...................................................................10.00
    10" d.................................................................10.00
Platter, 11" l.........................................................10.00

# Taylor, Smith, and Taylor
### Chester, West Virginia
### 1901-1981

**History:** John Taylor and Charles Smith organized a company to make plain and decorated semi-porcelain in 1899. Taylor's sons and Joseph Lee also joined the firm, and they built a pottery in Chester, West Virginia. Two years later, Lee dropped out, and the name was changed to Taylor, Smith, and Taylor.

For a brief time, the plant was closed and reorganized. In 1906, Smith and his son acquired the Taylor interests, but they kept the same factory name. The pottery was very successful after the Taylors left, and they enlarged their facilities many times. They made semi-vitreous dinner and toilet sets along with wares for hotels and restaurants.

A very long list of patterns, shapes, and designs was made. Two of the most popular lines were "Lu-Ray" and "Vistosa" from 1938. "Lu-Ray" came in soft solid colors of pastel blue, lilac, green, turquoise, and yellow. "Vistosa" came in green, blue, yellow, and red.

Cooking and oven wares were made in the 1960s. Many different marks were used. In 1972, the company was sold to the Anchor Hocking Corporation. The pottery was closed in 1981 due to a depressed market for dinnerwares.

**References:** William C. Gates, Jr. and Dana E. Ormerod, *The East Liverpool, Ohio, Pottery District: Identification of Manufacturers and Marks*, The Society for Historical Archaeology, 1982; Kathy & Bill Meehan, *Collector's Guide to Lu-Ray Pastels U.S.A.*,Collector Books, 1995.

## APPALACHIAN HEIRLOOM PATTERN-BONNIE SHAPE
Berry Bowl, 5 1/2" d...............................................3.00
Cup and Saucer......................................................4.00
Plate
    6 3/8" d............................................................3.00
    9" d...................................................................4.00

## AUTUMN HARVEST PATTERN-EVER YOURS SHAPE
Creamer................................................................12.00
Cup and Saucer......................................................5.00
Dessert Bowl, 5 1/4" d............................................3.00
Plate
    6 3/4" d............................................................5.00

10" d.............................................................12.00
Platter, 11" l..................................................12.00
Sugar Bowl, Cov............................................18.00
Teacup and Saucer ......................................12.00
Water Jug, 8" h.............................................30.00

## AZURA PATTERN
Creamer .........................................................4.00
Cup and Saucer .............................................3.00
Fruit Bowl, 5 3/4" d.........................................4.00
Plate
    7" d............................................................2.00
    8" d............................................................3.00
    10 1/4" d....................................................5.00
Serving Bowl, 8 1/2" d.....................................9.00
Soup Bowl, 7 1/4" d.........................................4.00
Sugar Bowl, Cov..............................................6.00

## BAMBOO PATTERN
Bowl, 7 1/4" d .................................................4.00
Cup and Saucer .............................................2.00
Plate
    6 3/4" d......................................................2.00
    10" d..........................................................3.00

## BLUEBIRD PATTERN
Plate, 9" d ....................................................10.00

## BLUE DELFT PATTERN
Creamer .........................................................4.00
Cup and Saucer .............................................2.00
Plate
    7 1/2" d......................................................3.00
    10 1/2" d....................................................4.00
Platter, 12 1/2" d............................................6.00
Soup Plate, 8" d..............................................4.00

## BOUTONNIERE-EVER YOURS PATTERN
Berry Bowl, 5 1/4" d.........................................5.00
Bowl
    8" d..........................................................12.00
    9" d..........................................................15.00
Carafe, 9" h .................................................28.00
Casserole, Cov, 10 1/2" d..............................30.00
Creamer, 4 1/4" h ...........................................7.00
Cup and Saucer .............................................8.00
Plate
    6 3/4" d......................................................5.00
    10 1/4" d....................................................8.00
Platter
    13" l.........................................................15.00
    14" l.........................................................16.00
Sugar Bowl, Cov, 5" H-H .................................9.00

## BREAK-O-DAY PATTERN
Cereal Bowl, 6 3/4" d.......................................4.00
Cup and Saucer .............................................3.00
Dessert Bowl, 5 1/2" d.....................................3.00
Gravy Boat ......................................................5.00

Plate
    6 3/4" d......................................................2.00
    10" d..........................................................5.00

## CATHY PATTERN
Bowl, 6" d .......................................................5.00
Creamer, 4" h .................................................6.00
Cup and Saucer .............................................6.00
Plate
    6 1/2" d......................................................3.00
    8" d............................................................4.00
    10 1/2" d....................................................8.00
Platter, 13 1/2" l............................................10.00
Soup Plate, 7 3/4" d.........................................4.00

## CONVERSATION SHAPE
Chantilly Pattern
    Coffeepot, 8" h...........................................10.00
    Fruit Bowl, 5 1/2" d.......................................2.00
    Plate, 6 3/8" sq...........................................3.00
    Platter, 13 3/8" l.........................................10.00
    Soup Plate, 8" d...........................................6.00
    Vegetable Bowl, 9" d.....................................5.00
Coffee Tree Pattern
    Plate
        6" sq......................................................8.00
        10 1/4" sq............................................18.00
    Platter, 13" l..............................................20.00
Day Lily Pattern
    Berry Bowl, 5 1/2" sq.....................................4.00
    Coffeepot....................................................25.00
    Plate
        6" sq......................................................5.00
        8 1/4" sq................................................6.00
        10 1/4" sq............................................12.00
    Platter
        11 1/8" l..............................................20.00

**Plate, 10 1/2" sq, "Daylily" pattern, green border, "Conversation" shape, $10.**

13 1/2" l ..................................................20.00
Vegetable Bowl, 10" l ..........................10.00
King O'Dell Pattern
Plate, 6 1/4" sq. ...................................5.00

## CURRIER AND IVES PATTERN
Chop Plate, 12 1/4" d ...............................35.00
Plate
6" d ......................................................6.00
10" d ....................................................8.00

## DWARF PINE PATTERN
Cereal Bowl, 6 3/4" d..................................5.00
Creamer, 6" w .............................................5.00
Cup and Saucer ..........................................3.00
Dessert Bowl, 5 1/4" d ................................3.00
Plate
6 1/4" d..................................................3.00
8 1/2" d..................................................4.00
10 3/8" d................................................5.00
Sugar Bowl, Cov.........................................6.00

## EMPIRE PATTERN
Creamer .....................................................7.00
Dessert Bowl, 5 3/8" d................................7.00
Plate
6 3/8" d................................................10.00
7 1/2" d................................................10.00
10" d ...................................................20.00
Platter, 13 1/2" l ......................................18.00
Sugar Bowl, Cov.........................................8.00

## ENGLISH ABBEY PATTERN
Berry Bowl, 5 1/4" d ...................................4.00
Plate, 9 3/4" d ..........................................10.00

## LU-RAY
Bowl
8 3/4" d, Sharon Pink .............................70.00
10" d yellow............................................25.00
Cereal Bowl, 7 3/4" d, Surf Green ..............10.00

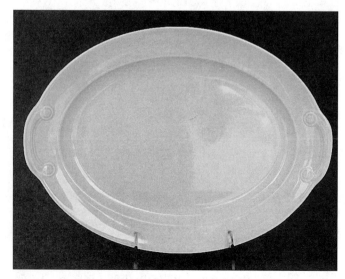

**Platter, 11 3/4" l, "LuRay," Sharon Pink, $16.**

Chop Plate, 12" d, Chatham Gray.............20.00
Coupe Soup, Surf Green...........................18.00
Creamer and Cov Sugar Bowl, Sharon Pink
................................................................34.00
Cup and Saucer, Sharon Pink....................15.00
Grill Plate, 10" d, Windsor Blue.................30.00
Lug Soup, Surf Green ................................20.00
Plate
6 1/4" d
Persian Cream ..................................6.00
Sharon Pink .....................................4.00
7 1/4" d, Sharon Pink ..........................10.00
8 1/4" d, yellow ...................................16.00
9" d, Surf Green ..................................10.00
10" d
Sharon Pink ...................................28.00
Surf Green ......................................28.00
Windsor Blue .................................28.00
Platter
11 1/2" l, Surf Green .............................15.00
12" l, Windsor Blue ..............................20.00
13" l, Windsor Blue ..............................25.00
Relish Dish, 9 1/2" d, 4 section, center handle, Surf Green
................................................................35.00
Shakers, Pr, Persian Cream......................20.00
Soup Plate, 7 3/4" d, Windsor Blue ...........12.00

## MISCELLANEOUS
Beverage Set, pitcher, 13 1/4" h, 4 mugs, 4 3/4" h, multicolored bust of sad-eyed dog, dk brown ground, c1906
..............................................................250.00
Mug, 5" h, Fraternal Order Of Eagles, multicolored eagle decal w/banner, shaded brown ground...................35.00
Plate
6 1/4" d, decal of elephant w/howdah on back, lt to dk brown shaded ground, "gold You Are Always Welcome" below, shaped rim .................................25.00
9" d, decal of kitten chasing butterfly, shaded brown ground, molded border........................50.00
9 1/4" d, medieval youth holding tankard and scroll in center, brown shaded ground...........................20.00

## PEBBLEFORD PATTERN
Cup and Saucer, Sunburst .........................4.00
Plate
6 3/4" d Sunburst .................................4.00
10" d, Sunburst......................................5.00
Vegetable Bowl, 8 1/2" l, Sunburst...............8.00

## PETAL LANE PATTERN
Berry Bowl, 5" d.........................................3.00
Cereal Bowl, 6" d........................................4.00
Cup and Saucer ..........................................2.00
Gravy Boat w/attached undertray.................8.00
Plate
7" d .......................................................2.00
10" d .....................................................4.00
Platter, 13 1/2" l.......................................10.00
Serving Bowl, 8 1/2" d.................................5.00

## PINE CONE PATTERN

Plate

6" d .............................................................. 5.00

8 1/4" d ........................................................ 7.00

9 1/4" d ...................................................... 12.00

## RANCHERO PATTERN

Plate, 6 1/2" d .................................................. 5.00

Soup Bowl, 7 1/4" d .......................................... 6.00

Vegetable Bowl, 10" d ...................................... 10.00

## REGAL PATTERN

Cup and Saucer ................................................ 7.00

Fruit Bowl, 6 1/4" d ............................................ 3.00

Plate

7" d .............................................................. 5.00

9" d .............................................................. 7.00

Platter, 10 3/4" l .............................................. 10.00

Soup Bowl, 7 1/2" d .......................................... 4.00

## REVEILLE PATTERN

Bowl, 9 1/2" l .................................................. 27.00

Cereal Bowl, 6 1/2" d ........................................ 4.00

Creamer ........................................................... 4.00

Cup and Saucer ................................................ 5.00

Mug, 3 1/2" h ................................................... 5.00

Plate

6 1/2" d ........................................................ 7.00

10" d ............................................................ 8.00

Platter

8 1/4" l ......................................................... 8.00

13" l ........................................................... 32.00

Serving Dish, 11 1/2" l, divided .......................... 8.00

Serving Plate, 12" d .......................................... 5.00

Sugar Bowl, Cov ............................................... 5.00

## ROOSTER PATTERN-EVER YOURS SHAPE

Creamer ......................................................... 12.00

Sugar Bowl, Cov ............................................. 16.00

## SHASTA DAISY PATTERN

Vegetable Bowl, 8 1/2" l .................................. 10.00

## SILHOUETTE PATTERN

Cereal Bowl, 6" d ............................................ 30.00

Cup and Saucer .............................................. 24.00

Fruit Bowl, 5" d ............................................... 12.00

Plate

6" d .............................................................. 8.00

7 1/4" d ...................................................... 12.00

8 1/4" d ...................................................... 18.00

9 1/4" d ...................................................... 24.00

Serving Bowl, 8" d .......................................... 18.00

Soup Plate, 7 3/4" d ........................................ 24.00

## VERONA PATTERN

Vegetable Bowl, Cov, 11 1/2" H-H ..................... 15.00

## VISTOSA

Berry Bowl, 5 3/4" d, yellow .............................. 7.00

Chop Plate, 12" d ............................................ 45.00

Cup and Saucer, green .................................... 25.00

Plate

6" d, orange .................................................. 8.00

7" d, Mango Red ........................................... 25.00

9" d, green ................................................... 20.00

10" d, Mango Red ......................................... 25.00

Platter, 13" l, yellow ......................................... 60.00

Water Pitcher, 7" h, yellow .............................. 130.00

## WEATHERVANE PATTERN

Plate, 10 1/4" d ................................................. 3.00

## WHEAT PATTERN-VERSATILE SHAPE

Creamer ......................................................... 12.00

Cup and Saucer .............................................. 10.00

Plate

8" d .............................................................. 7.00

10" d ............................................................ 8.00

Sugar Bowl, Cov ............................................. 16.00

## WILD QUINCE PATTERN

Cup and Saucer ................................................ 4.00

Plate

6 3/4" d ........................................................ 4.00

10" d ............................................................ 5.00

# Teco/American Terra Cotta and Ceramic Company

### Terra Cotta, Illinois
### 1886-1930

**History:** William Gates established the American Terra Cotta and Ceramic Company in Terra Cotta, Illinois in 1886 to make sewer pipe, drain tiles, and brick and terra cotta decorative architectural items. Many Chicago landmarks feature architectural terra cotta pieces made by Gates' company.

"Teco Art Pottery might very appropriately be called the art ideal of Mr. William D. Gates, its creator. Desiring to produce an art ware that would harmonize with all its surroundings, which, while adding to the beauty of the flower or leaf placed in the vase, at the same time enhanced the beauty of the vase itself, he has devoted a lifetime to experimenting with different combinations to produce his ideal art pottery." (From *Hints for Gifts and Home Decoration*) Copyright 1905 by The Gates Potteries.

Gates started experimenting with pottery along with Elmer Gordon and two of Gates' sons, William Paul and Ellis Day. Gates designed many of the forms that were eventually used on the Teco pottery examples. Many other artists and architects also designed for Gates. Though a few pieces were thrown, Teco pottery was sculpted in clay and then cast in molds. The glaze was applied with a sprayer. Designs were identified with pattern numbers. Some shapes were made in a variety of sizes. Nearly twelve hundred designs were made.

The first Teco wares were glazed in shades of red, then buffs and browns. Surfaces were also marbled or mottled. Teco is best known for its matte green glaze, "Teco green" that was used exclusively for nearly a decade. Often the green had a silver blush or gunmetal frosting to the finish. Teco green was the hallmark of the pottery.

At the 1904 St. Louis Exposition, Teco won two gold medals for its innovative crystalline artwares. In addition to matte green, new glaze colors introduced about 1910 included shades of brown, grays, blue, rose, purple, and yellow. Designs were influenced by the Prairie School, aquatic plants, leaves, and flowers.

Teco garden pottery examples included window boxes, large urns and vases, fireplace mantels, fountains, and such. Pottery shapes were vases, pitchers, bulb pots, low bowls, ashtrays, wall pockets, mugs, steins, and lamp bases, Surfaces were mostly smooth with graceful lines and soft curves.

Faience tiles were added in 1912. Teco also made ten terra cotta panels depicting the life of Abraham Lincoln. Architectural terra cotta continued while the pottery was being made.

Production of art pottery stopped during World War I, but was resumed shortly after that. The terra cotta business also expanded at that time. With the approaching Depression, Teco ceased to be made since the business declined. The pottery was sold to George A. Berry Jr. in 1930 who changed the name to The American Terra Cotta Corporation.

The mark used on Teco was the impressed long stemmed T. Model numbers also were used.

**References:** Sharon S. Darling, *Chicago Ceramics and Glass: An Illustrated History from 1871-1933*, Chicago Historical Society, 1979; _____ *Teco: Art Pottery of the Prairie School*, Erie Art Museum, 1989.

**Museums:** Chicago Historical Society, IL; National Museum of History and Technology, Smithsonian Institution, Washington, DC; New Orleans Museum of Art, LA; Western Reserve Historical Society, Cleveland, OH; Worcester Art Museum, MA.

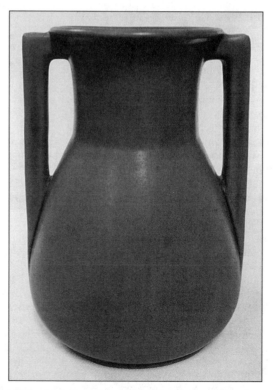

**Vase, 8" h, matte green glaze, imp mk, (A), $1,980.**

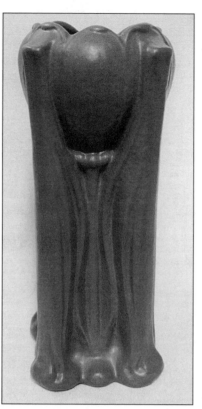

**Vase, 11 1/2" h, matte green glaze, imp mk, (A), $2,530.**

Bowl

    4 1/2" d, closed rim, ridged, matte dk red raspberry glaze, "Imp TECO" mk, (A) ......................................... 220.00

    7" d, rolled rim, matte green glaze, imp mk, chip on rim, (A) ................................................................. 230.00

    9 1/2" d, prairie form, 4 sided ft, matte green glaze, imp mk, (A)......................................................... 2,090.00

Bud Vase, 4 1/2" h, bulbous body, short, rolled rim, matte green glaze, (A) ..................................................... 412.00

Jardiniere, 16" h x 21" d, 4 flared feet, matte green glaze, #157, repairs...................................................... 1,650.00

Planter, 17" h x 27" d, tapered shape, applied rosettes, unglazed, #508, hairline and chips, pr, (A) ......... 1,100.00

Vase

    3 3/4" h, straight sides w/dimples, rolled rim, matte dk green glaze w/charcoaling, "incised Teco 519" mk, (A) ......................................................................... 605.00

    4" h, bag shape, bulbous base, matte green glaze, "stamped Teco" mk, (A).................................... 385.00

    4 1/2" h

        Ovoid, rolled rim, lt matte green glaze, (A)........ 440.00

        Shouldered form, matte brown glaze, (A) ......... 495.00

        Tapered body, squared shoulder, curdled matte green glaze, "imp Teco" mk, (A)............................. 550.00

    5" h

        Bulbous, short collar, matte green glaze, imp mk, (A) ................................................................. 467.00

        Cylinder shape, horiz ribbing, matte green glaze, #370 ................................................................. 850.00

        Squat base, flared neck, wavy rim, matte green glaze, (A)................................................................. 605.00

    5 1/4" h, bulbous, flared, scalloped rim, matte dove gray glaze, "imp Teco" mk, (A) ................................. 385.00

5 1/2" h

Cylinder shape w/2 buttressed handles, matte dk blue glaze, "imp TECO" mk, (A) .......................... 825.00

Slightly tapered shape w/2 sm open handles on shoulder to rim, matte beige to pink ground, chip repair, (A) ............................................................... 523.00

6" h, ball shape, 4 cutout open handles on shoulder, molded stylized floral design, shaded pink to beige matte glaze, (A) ........................................ 1,650.00

7" h, 2 handled form, matte brown glaze, imp mk, (A) ......................................................................... 990.00

8" h, 3 sided, matte green glaze, imp mk, (A) ..... 1,045.00

10 1/2" h, 4 vert buttresses, flared lip, matte dk green glaze w/charcoaling, imp mk, (A) ................... 2,420.00

11" h, cylinder shape w/4 cutout handles at top, matte pink to lavender glaze, imp mk, (A) ............... 6,050.00

11 1/2" h, tapered cylinder shape, flared rim, architectural handles, matte green glaze, c1905 ................ 2,800.00

11 3/4" h, molded narrow leaf handles, flared neck, matte green glaze, "stamped Teco" mk, (A) ........... 16,500.00

13" h, cylinder shape, everted rim, matte green glaze, "imp Teco" mk, (A) .......................................... 1,100.00

13 3/4" h, cylindrical neck, flared base, matte gray glaze, (A) ............................................................... 1,650.00

16 1/2" h, organic, squat base, tall, flared neck, matte green and charcoal glaze, "stamped Teco" mk, restored chips, (A) ............................................ 1,320.00

c.1910–1930s

1868
Thompson's
Old Liverpool
Ware

# C.C. Thompson Pottery Company

**East Liverpool, Ohio**
**1868-1938**

**History:** The company was started under the name Thompson and Herbert in 1868. The partners built a small pottery to make Rockingham and yellow Queensware. Two years later, Herbert was bought out. The firm became C.C. Thompson and Company and expanded.

It made a wide variety of pieces in cream-colored ware, and continued to make the same pieces in Rockingham and yellowware, except for the toilet sets. In 1899, it incorporated as C.C. Thompson Pottery Company. It added white ironstone toilet and dinnerware.

In 1917, it phased out yellowware, Rockingham, and cream-colored ware in favor of semi-porcelain dinnerware. Production stopped in 1938 due to poor business conditions.

A wide variety of marks was used on the company's wares.

**Museums:** Museum of Ceramics at East Liverpool, OH.

Berry Bowl

4 7/8" sq, "Seville" pattern ........................................ 3.00

Platter, 15 5/8" l, bluebird design, $20.

**Bowl, 9 1/4" d, yellow, pink, and red roses, orange luster border, black "REICHART FURN. CO., Salem, Ohio COMPLETE HOME FURNISHINGS" on reverse, $40.**

5" d, "Chatham" pattern, mauve exotic flowers, green leaves in center, green inner band, relief molded border, shaped rim .................................................... 3.00

5 1/2" d, "Mayfair" pattern .......................................... 3.00

Bowl, 9 1/4" d, multicolored scene of Venice in center, ribbed border, orange luster border, mkd ................ 40.00

Butter Dish, Cov

9" H-H, oct cov, orange poppies, sm blue flowers, orange striping .................................................................. 15.00

12" H-H, molded curlicues and beading, wavy body, flower knob, "Thompson's Old Liverpool 1868" mk ................................................................................ 32.00

Casserole, Cov

11" H-H, brown flowers on molded sections, gold trim, "1868 Thompson's Old Liverpool Ware" mk ................................................................................ 10.00

12" H-H, bluebird pattern ........................................ 12.00

Cream Pitcher, 6 1/4" h, raised diamond thumb rest, white glaze ........................................................................ 7.00

Cup and Saucer, "Mayfair" pattern ................................ 6.00

Grill Plate, 10" d, orange-red poppies and garden flowers pattern ........................................................................ 8.00

Plate

5 7/8" sq, "Seville" pattern ........................................ 4.00

6 1/2" d, "Mayfair" pattern ........................................ 4.00

9 1/4" d

    Decal of multicolored sailing galleon, pink and white shadow leaf border .........................................12.00

    Multicolored exotic bird in center, orange luster border w/white shadow birds, mkd............................10.00

9 1/2" d, "Mayfair" pattern .........................................8.00

Platter

    11" l, "Mayfair" pattern...............................................10.00

    11 1/2" l, rect, "Seville" pattern ................................6.00

    13 1/4" l, oval, bluebird design................................10.00

Serving Bowl, 9" d, "Mayfair" pattern...........................10.00

Serving Plate, 12" d, bouquet of poppies at side, relief molded dots, leaves, and curlicues, gold outlined shaped rim, "Thompson's Old Liverpool Ware" mk..............12.00

Vegetable Bowl, 8 1/2" lx 8 1/4" w, rect, "Seville" pattern .................................................................25.00

# Tiffany Studios

## Corona, New York
## 1898-c1920

c.1906

**History:** Tiffany started experimenting with pottery at his studio in Corona, New York in 1898. Tiffany Furnaces Favrile was first shown at the Louisiana Purchase Exposition in St. Louis in 1904. The next year, he offered pottery for sale to the general public.

    Previously, he purchased ceramic lamp bases from other art potteries, but now they made lamp bases, vases, and bowls that were individually designed and hand made. Art Nouveau influences were obvious in the designs along with all sorts of native flora. The original Favrile pottery was a light yellow green with shading to darker tones and was called "old ivory." By 1906, they used shades of green. Glazes employed were matte, crystalline, and iridescent. Some examples were biscuit finished without glaze. Painted decorations were not used on Tiffany pottery.

    In 1911, pieces were made with the interior glazed with a gloss finish and the exterior with a bronze plating called Bronze Pottery. Tiffany stopped producing pottery sometime before 1920.

    All Tiffany pottery was marked. Most often the L.C.T. cipher was incised. Some examples had "L.C. Tiffany," "Favrile Pottery," or "Bronze Pottery" etched into the base. Pieces were not artist signed since all wares were attributed to the studio.

**Museums:** Chrysler Museum, Norfolk, VA.

Bud Vase, 5 1/2" h, carved and incised leaf design, matte brown and cream glaze, "incised L.C.T., Favrile Pottery P930" mk, (A).....................................1,210.00

Cabinet Vase

    3 1/2" h, cylinder shape, spread ft, emb mushrooms design, mottled green glaze, restored base chip, "LCT/P1946/LCT Favrile Pottery" mk, (A) ......1,760.00

    4 3/4" h, gourd shape, amber, gunmetal, and ivory glaze, "incised LCT" mk, (A) .....................................2,090.00

Urn, 12 1/2" h, bulbous body, 3 handles, frothy, drip crystalline glaze, textured body, restored chip, "incised LCT/87A-Coll.L.C.TIFFANY/Favrile Pottery" mk, (A) ...........................................................................8,800.00

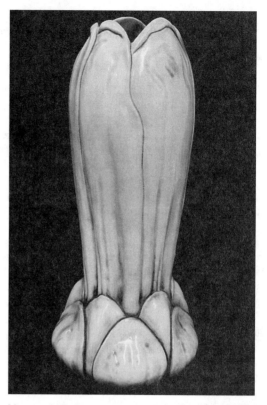

**Vase, 11" h, matte, yellow, green, and ivory glaze, "imp LCT" mk, repaired hairline, (A), $2,860.**

Vase

    3" h, celadon and beige microcrystalline glaze, "incised LCT" mk, (A).....................................................220.00

    5" h, shouldered w/short collar, cream drip panels over brown body, mkd ............................................1,600.00

    5 1/2" h, bronze clad w/relief of leaves on shoulder, dk patina, "incised LCT" mk, (A) ........................2,200.00

    6 1/2" h, corset shape, rolled base, emb wisteria pods, apple green and turquoise glaze, "incised LCT" mk, hairline and chips, (A) ......................................990.00

    8 3/4" h, relief molded and reticulated arrowroot plants, blue and green lustered glaze, "incised LCT, etched L.C.Tiffany-Favrile Pottery" mk, hairlines, (A) .. 15,400.

    9 1/2" h, Art Nouveau organic form w/4 lobes and undulating rim, gloss metallic black and green finish, "incised LCT" mk, (A) ....................................7,700.00

    9 3/4" h, modeled lg oak leaves, Old Ivory glaze, restored top, "incised LCT/909" mk, (A) ......................3,850.00

    12" h

        Cylinder shape, bisque finish w/low relief foliage design, green glazed int, "inscribed L.C.T." .............................................................................2,700.00

        Ftd cylinder shape, emb jonquils and leaves, shellac and moss satin matte finish, "incised LCT" mk, (A) .............................................................................5,500.00

    15" h, rolled rim, green and ivory flambe glaze, restored base chip, "L.C.Tiffany/Favrile Pottery" mk, (A) 880.00

Vessel

    5" h 7" d, relief of mushrooms, amber and cream flambe glaze, "incised LCT" mk, hairline, (A) ............2,970.00

    6 1/4" h x 10 3/4" d, squat shape, ribbed shoulder, thick, mottled cobalt and matte green glaze, "incised LTC" mk, chips, (A) .................................................1,120.00

## A.E.T.Co.

*J & JG LOW
PATENT
ART TILE WORKS
CHELSEA MASS USA
COPYRIGHT 1881 BY
J & JG LOW*

# Tiles

## Eastern Half of United States and California c1870s-Present

**History:** American tile making increased in importance after Philadelphia's Centennial Exposition of 1876, which displayed numerous European decorative ceramics. This provided the impetus for American tile makers to develop their own designs.

The majority of the tile factories were in the eastern half of the United States since there was ample clay available there. Several companies were located in California. There were at least one hundred firms making art pottery tiles. Some factories made tiles along with their art pottery lines, while others concentrated on tiles and made small amounts of art pottery.

Some early art tiles were machine manufactured by large potteries, but the Arts and Crafts movement at the turn of the century placed the emphasis on hand-crafted works. Tiles were then pressed and decorated by hand.

## J. & J.G. Low Art Tile Works, Chelsea, Massachusetts, 1877-1907

The first important American art tile factory was the Low Art Tile Works founded by John Gardner Low in Chelsea, Massachusetts in 1877. Following the Victorian themes, his favorite motifs were pastoral scenes, mythological subjects, or nymphs for tiles with colored, transparent glazes.

Three methods of tile production were used at Low Art. First they used a dust process where powdered clay was die-pressed onto a solid clay backing that resulted in sharp, heavily embossed designs. Then artists undercut the design with hand tools to give a crisp appearance to the design. A lot of attention was devoted to each individual tile. They also utilized a technique where leaves and flowers were pressed into the wet clay leaving a delicate life-like impression. Some tiles were made with hand-cut designs into the tiles themselves leaving the picture in very high relief.

Low Art won many awards for its tiles. The most common sizes were 6 x 6 and 4 x 4, but they were made in a variety of sizes.

Arthur Osborne who came from England worked at Low Art from 1879-93 and was known for his "plastic sketches" which were low relief pictures using clay instead of oil paint. They were up to 18" in length and featured farm scenes, animals, birds, monks, cupids, and women. They were signed "AO" on the face of the sketch. Osborne also made tiles in a variety of motifs.

Starting in c1882, Low Art made pottery and tile decorated objects such as clock cases, ewers, fireplace tiles, planters, inkwells, and flower holders. Brass objects with tiles included candlesticks, boxes, paperweights, lamps, and trivets. Tiles were made in a wide variety of colors, but most used the green and brown earth tones. Low Art even made soda fountains starting in 1899.

## Beaver Falls Tile Company, Beaver Falls, Pennsylvania, 1886-1927

Beaver Falls Tile Company was organized by Francis Walker in 1886 and also made tiles in the Victorian style. Many tiles depicted bust portraits of men, women, children, and classical scenes. Numerous tiles were used for stove decorations. Isaac Broome was a major sculptor-ceramist who worked for Beaver Falls in 1890 after working at Ott and Brewer. He also made large panels of The Muses, and a famous 12" tile of George Washington.

## American Encaustic Tile Company, Zanesville, Ohio, 1875-1935

American Encaustic Tile Company was in an ideal location in Zanesville, Ohio since there was plenty of clay deposits. By the early 1920s, they were the largest tile company in the world, and made a tremendous variety of tiles.

Victorian style motifs were used under clear, colored high glazes for some examples. They also made hand-cut, hand finished, unglazed terra cotta tiles. These were mostly made by Herman Mueller who later formed his own company in Trenton, New Jersey. American Encaustic also used the cloisonné technique where designs were usually die-stamped into a tile leaving thin walls between the sections. These depressions were filled in with colored glazes.

Floor tiles were their first product. Frederick Rhead was hired as a designer in 1917. In the 1920s, they made faience tiles. All sorts of decorative tiles were made here with a wide variety of techniques. Novelties and souvenir plaques and tiles as gifts for customers and commemorative pieces also were made.

American Encaustic closed in 1935, and several years later reopened as Shawnee Pottery.

## Mosaic Tile Company, Zanesville, Ohio, 1894-1967

Mosaic Tile was started in 1894 by Karl Langenbeck and Herman Mueller from American Encaustic. Their first product was floor tiles. "Florentine mosaic" was a dull finish floor tile inlaid with an assortment of colored clays. Langenbeck and Mueller left in 1903, and William Shinnick became manager in 1907. The company expanded with several branch offices and had numerous artists working there.

Faience tiles were made for walls in 1918 in pastel colors. They also made ceramic mosaic, white wall tiles, and fireplace tiles. Numerous commemorative tiles and plaques depicting famous people and events were made along with souvenir pieces. Some tiles had molded figures like Wedgwood Jasperware in a variety of shapes. Many different decorating techniques were used including embossing, impressing, and decals.

## United States Encaustic Tile Company, Indianapolis, Indiana, 1877-1939

United States Encaustic Tile Company made floor, wall, and fireplace tiles in matte finish, unglazed, or brightly colored glaze. Relief tiles were made in three or six section panels.

## Moravian Pottery and Tile Works, Doylestown, Pennsylvania, 1877-Present

Henry Chapman Mercer's earliest tiles were Moravian inspired examples for floors, fireplaces, walls, ceilings, and large decorative panels. Mercer created his designs using medieval motifs, Indians, plants, animals, tapestries, and architectural finds to inspire him. His brocade tiles were done in high relief with irregular shapes which were often set into concrete. Some examples were unglazed, some were glazed in matte or shiny finish. Mercer used a variety of decorating techniques. His tiles were often cut into the shape of the figure, and not into squares.

## Grueby Pottery, Boston, Massachusetts
### (see Grueby for history)

The Grueby Pottery was the best of the Arts and Crafts tile makers. They utilized the cloisonné technique to make tiles for fireplaces and bathrooms with a wide assortment of decorations such as tulips, castles, landscapes, and such. Most of the tiles were designed by Addison B. Le Boutillier. The design was die-stamped on the tile and then glazed by hand.

## Rookwood Pottery, Cincinnati, Ohio
### (see Rookwood for history)

Rookwood Pottery made faience tiles intended for exterior garden use or to be set into walls. Most of their tiles were large, heavily embossed mural type tiles.

**References:** Norman Karlson, *American Art Tile, 1876-1941,* Rizzoli International, 1998; Ralph and Terry Kovel, *American Art Pottery,* Crown, 1993; Cleota Reed, *Henry Chapman Mercer and The Moravian Pottery and Tile Works,* University of Pennsylvania Press, 1989.

**Collectors' Club:** Tile Heritage Foundation, Box 1850, Healdsburg, Ca 95448, quarterly bulletin, *Flash Point.*

**Museums:** Chrysler Museum, Norfolk, VA; Mercer Museum, Doylestown, PA; Museum of History and Technology, Smithsonian Institution, Washington, DC; Newark Museum, NJ.

3" d, incised brown and tan Paul Revere riding horse, green landscape, med blue sky, dk blue rolled rim and body, Paul Revere, rim chips, (A) ..................................275.00

3" w x 6" l, cuenca design of purple berries, green leaves, blue ground, Grueby, pr, (A)..................................495.00

3" sq, white kitten with pink ribbon, turquoise ground, Pewabic ..................................................................295.00

3 1/2" sq
Blue, green, and ivory stylized flowerheads and leaves, tan-orange ground, North Dakota School of Mines, (A) ......................................................................88.00

5 1/2" d, yellow peacock feathers, dk blue center and rim, Rhead, (A), $385.

Incised framed reindeer through blue ground glaze, North Dakota School of Mines, (A) ...........................130.00

Painted primitive black and blue sailing ship on green waves, blue frame w/black dots on border, tan ground, North Dakota School of Mines, (A)....................220.00

Relief molded fleur-de-lys, chartreuse glaze, unmkd, (A) ........................................................................110.00

3 3/4" sq, incised and painted red cross on cream shield, med blue ground, Newcomb College, c1925, (A)..660.00

4" sq
Arts and Crafts, yellow flower, brown leaves in black vase, green bkd, Rookwood, oak frame, (A).....468.00

Brown Cheshire cat in lt brown tree w/green foliage, Grueby/Pardee, chips, (A)...............................770.00

Incised and painted matte green, blue, white, and yellow landscape, Grueby, framed, (A) ....................1,045.00

Matte blue and white
Mayflower, Moravian, c1915 ...............................65.00
Woman dipping candles.....................................60.00

Relief molded jester in club shaped cartouche, gloss yellow and blue mottled glaze, Moravian.................75.00

4 1/2" sq
Brown leaf and berry design, American Encaustic Tile Co...................................................................25.00

Gray and brown elephant, tan bkd, blue-gray grass, American Encaustic .........................................245.00

Rampant lion on shield, geometrics in corners, unglazed buff clay, Weller.................................................350.00

4 3/4" sq
Blue raised floral w/raised circle surround, sm florals in corners, J. & J.G. Low..................................25.00

Brown herringbone design, J. & J.G. Low ..............25.00

Raised green coil design, J. & J.G. Low..................30.00

Raised green sunflower design, J. & J.G. Low........30.00

5" sq, faience, emb 4 yellow and brown abstract flowerheads on blue ground, Walrich ...........................285.00

5 1/2" sq
Arts and Crafts style yellow flowers, green leaves, brown textured ground, wood frame, (A) .....................220.00

Cuenca yellow haystack on green ground, blue sky w/white clouds, Grueby, set of 4, (A).............7,700.00

White 3 masted ship, dk turquoise crackle ground, Newcomb College, "incised HB/LN/NC" mk, (A) ......................................................................1,045.00

6" h x 3" w, cuenca, Arts and Crafts style pink and yellow tulips, "A.E.T. Co." mk...........................................135.00

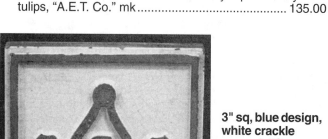

3" sq, blue design, white crackle ground, "Cambridge Tile Co." mk, c1929, $45.

6" sq

Arts and Crafts

Emb matte green circles w/matte black centers, matte mustard yellow ground, matte gold edges, "imp Grueby" mk,(A) ............................385.00

HP bust of Dutch girl wearing cap, windmills in bkd, brown shades, Columbia Encaustic Tile Co. ........................................135.00

Incised and painted yellow, lt and dk brown butterfly in center diamond, filled corners, oak frame, (A) ........................................286.00

Lt yellow tulip head, green ground, Owens, imp mk, (A) ........................................275.00

Raised purple grapes, green leaf, tendril, textured ground, Owens, pr ........................................413.00

Raised stylized black peacock, black framing w/filled corners, white ground, chips, (A) ...................50.00

White and yellow water lilies, green lily pads, blue ground, Grueby, oak frame, (A) ................1,320.00

Blue, brown, and dk blue geometric squares, oak frame, Saturday Evening Girls, (A) ........................825.00

Brown shell design, Providential Tile Works ...........45.00

Buff clay donkey on white ground, Moravian ...........75.00

Cuenca stylized white seagulls and waves, blue ground, framed, Grueby, (A) ........................1,540.00

Faience, relief molded blue and ivory sailing ship, red clay, Moravian, corner chip........................200.00

Imp white tulip, green leaves, matte mustard yellow ground, Grueby, (A) ........................1,870.00

Molded flower design, gloss mustard glaze, Hamilton Tile Works ........................................159.00

Photo picture of waterfall, gold-brown glaze, American Encaustic........................................295.00

Portrait of woman w/lacy collar and cap, mauve glaze, Isaac Broome ........................................350.00

Profile of classic woman, mauve glaze, American Encaustic Tile ........................................130.00

Red bisque "EROS" Cupid figure, mustard yellow ground, (A)........................................330.00

Red stylized mermaid or monk drinking, matte mustard yellow glaze, Grueby, pr, (A) ...................357.00

Relief molded

Bust of Robin Hood, teal green glaze, Hamilton ........................................75.00

Child w/balloons, brick red bkd, Grueby, (A) .....467.00

Flaming torch and branches, chocolate brown glaze, American Encaustic........................................35.00

Gargoyle and stylized leaves, green glaze, "J. & J.G. LOW" mk, c1881 ........................................115.00

Oriental style chrysanthemums, black glaze, Trent ........................................125.00

Peapod and swirls, dk green glaze, American Encaustic ........................................115.00

Portrait profile of gypsy, olive green glaze, American Encaustic ........................................175.00

Profile of man wearing ruffled collar, gloss blue glaze, Trent........................................225.00

Waffle pattern, brown shades, Beaver Falls ...........32.00

Yellow, blue, pink, and black mosaic design, American Encaustic Tile Co., (A) ........................33.00

6 1/8" l x 3" w, relief of intertwined geometric circles, pebble ground, blue glaze, Low........................30.00

6 1/2" sq

Emb white sailing ship and waves, dk blue ground, crackle ground, "imp ship" mk, Marblehead, (A) ........................................330.00

Incised and painted yellow tulip, matte green ground, set in Tiffany bronze frame, Grueby, (A) .............2,090.00

6 3/4" l x 5" w, white relief of 4 monks in swirled border, blue ground, American Encaustic Tile ...........................40.00

7 1/2" h

3 1/2" w, yellow, blue, green, and yellow raised landscape design, Claycraft, framed, (A) ........................1,540.00

8 1/2" l, emb yellow owl holding yellow and red coat of arms, blue-gray ground, "imp Rookwood Faience" mk, (A) ........................................330.00

8" sq

Cuenca ochre and ivory tall sailing ship, green sea, blue sky, leathery matte glazes, (A) ........................990.00

Faience, pink, ochre, and green geometric design, mtd in oak frame, Rookwood, (A) ........................358.00

Painted green, blue, and yellow Hispano-Moresque design on orange ground ........................115.00

Semi-matte turquoise, pink, yellow, black, brown, purple, and green bowl of flowers on pedestal, Claycraft ........................................350.00

9" sq, black stylized nude woman riding horse or black stylized man with spear riding horse, silver ground, American Encaustic Tile Co., pr........................................375.00

9 3/4" sq, emb medieval knight on rearing horse, semi-gloss dk orange ground, "imp ship" mk, Marblehead, (A)302.00

11 1/2" h x 3 1/2" w, incised and emb brown, yellow, blue, and green landscape of road through trees and mountain, Claycraft, framed, (A)........................1,760.00

11 3/4" sq

Cuenca mountain landscape design, matte ochre and green shades, "imp Owens" mk, (A) .............2,970.00

Relief molded bust of George Washington, burgundy glaze, "BEAVER FALLS ART TILE CO." mk .....950.00

12" h x 6" w, relief of 2 cherubs fishing, gloss green glaze, unmkd, (A) ........................................275.00

12" l x 6" h, relief of cherubs w/goat, gloss green glaze, Hamilton Tile Works, (A)........................................275.00

12 3/4" l x 8 1/2" w, emb yellow, black and white oriole, white and blue floral ground, scalloped border, Grueby, c1917, (A) ........................................770.00

15" l x 3 1/2" h, brown, tan, and green incised and emb landscape, mountains, trees, and rising sun, Claycraft, (A) ........................................2,640.00

18" h x 5 7/8" w, relief molded design of colonial lady w/fan, scrolling bkd, gloss brown glaze, "imp American Encaustic Tiling Co. Limited New York Works Zanesville, O." mk, (A)........................................330.00

**TILE PICTURES**

12" h x 18" l, 6 tiles, relief molded Cupid w/bow and arrow facing woman w/coal fire, pink glaze, Hamilton ........................................1,350.00

13" sq, 9 tiles, 3 flying bluebirds over hills, white sky, Mosaic Tile Company........................................225.00

15" w x 9 1/2" h, relief of cherubs in tree branches playing musical instruments, yellow glaze, Providential Tile Works, set of 2, (A) ........................................440.00

18" h x 6" w, 3 tiles, relief molded lady in Renaissance dress, green glaze, American Encaustic ...............395.00

18" l x 6" h, cuenca design of ivory and yellow water lilies, lt green leaves, dk green ground, "stamped GRUEBY BOSTON/63" marks, set of 3, (A) ...................... 4,675.00

21 1/2" h x 9 1/2" w, relief of hunter w/shotgun in forest, yellow glaze, Providential Tile Works, set of 3, (A) ............................................................................... 385.00

22" l x 13 1/2" h, 15 tiles, yellow and maroon tropical fish, brown and tan coral, lt and med blue water ........ 1,200.00

24" h x 6" w, 4 tiles, relief molded day lilies in urn, olive green glaze, American Encaustic ...................... 375.00

# Trenton Potteries Company

## Trenton, New Jersey
## 1892-1969

**History:** Trenton Potteries Company was formed in 1892 from combining five individual Trenton operations into one. Crescent, Delaware, Empire, Enterprise, and Equitable Pottery Companies combined their resources, but continued to operate separately after the merger.

For the most part, four of the companies made vitreous china sanitary wares, while Equitable made more tablewares and other items for hospitals. The companies experimented to make porcelain sanitary wares which had to be imported from England. A new plant called Ideal Pottery was constructed to make the porcelain bathtubs. With the addition of the tunnel kiln in 1922, operations to produce sanitary wares were improved greatly. Slip casting was also substituted for pressing clay into molds.

In 1924, Crane got a controlling interest in Trenton Potteries. They continued in operation until fires in 1967 and 1969 and then closed down.

The French artist Lucien Boullemier decorated excellent urns made by Empire Pottery that were exhibited at the Louisiana Purchase Exposition in St. Louis in 1904. His paintings on the porcelain were exquisite; four different craftsmen worked on the urns.

From the mid 1930s until sometime after World War II, some art pottery was produced by TEPECO which was fired in the same kilns as the sanitary wares. Most pieces were produced for florist shops. The same pastel colors used for the sanitary wares: pale green, yellow, blue, pink, off white, dark red brown, and charcoal shades were found on wares that were usually undecorated with thick walls. Shapes were both Art Deco types and classic in design. They made vases, planters, wall pockets, flower pots, centerpiece bowls, console sets, bud vases, rose bowls, candleholders, ashtrays, and umbrella stands. Many of the forms were made in varying sizes and shapes, and always were marked with a stamped mark. Some of the ashtrays were made for advertising and promotional purposes.

**References:** Dr. M.W. Lerner, "The Art Pottery of the Trenton Potteries Company," *The Antique Trader Weekly Annual of Articles*, Volume XV, 1983.

**Museums:** Brooklyn Museum, NY: City of Trenton Museum, NJ; New Jersey State Museum, Newark, NJ.

Bowl, 7"d, Art Deco style, blue glaze............................ 40.00
Cache Pot, 5" h, red and purple tulips and florals w/greens on side, gold banded ft and rim, 2 sm gold handles, pr ............................................................................... 95.00

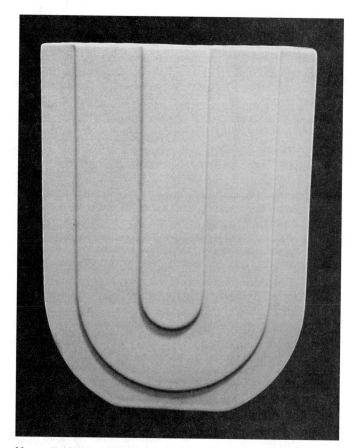

**Vase, 6" h x 6 1/2" w, turquoise glaze, $65.**

Candlestick
 3 1/4" h, egg shape, domed base, matte lt blue glaze ......................................................................... 25.00
 5" h, raised vert ribs, flared base, med blue glaze, pr ....................................................................... 145.00
Flower Dish, 9 3/4" w, shell shape w/frog at end, white glaze ........................................................................ 135.00
Pitcher, 12" h, disc design, cream ............................ 175.00

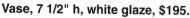

**Vase, 7 1/2" h, white glaze, $195.**

Planter, 4" h, flared shape, paneled, blue, green ......... 20.00
Urn, 6" h, 2 horiz handles, sq base, aqua blue glaze, pr
.......................................................................... 35.00
Vase
    4" h, cornucopia shape, oval base, white glaze, pr
    ................................................................ 70.00
    5 1/2" h, orbit or ball shape, gloss maroon glaze ..... 95.00
    5 3/4" d, ball shape, 3 horiz grooves at middle, gloss
        white glaze ................................................. 95.00
    6" Sq base, 4 lobes at top, aqua glaze ................. 185.00
Urn form, gloss turquoise glaze ............................... 60.00
    7" h, tapered shape, figure, I cross section, white ... 75.00
    7 1/2" h, trumpet shape stepped base, dk blue ground,
        gold lined rim and base, gold curved ball and stick
        handles, "THE TRENTON POTTERIES CO." mk 75.00
    Yellow glaze, mkd ............................................ 250.00
    7 3/4" h, lobed, fan shape top, scalloped base, green ext,
        pink int ......................................................... 32.00
    8 1/2" h, 3 graduated disks at sides, ivory ........... 125.00
    9" flat sides, wide middle, narrow base and rim, relief
        molded vert leaves on stems, aqua glaze ......... 220.00
    Six sides and base, scalloped rim, cobalt ............... 85.00

# Uhl Pottery

### Huntingburg, Indiana
### 1849-1944

**History:** August Uhl and Henry founded a pottery business in Evansville, Indiana in 1849 when they came to America from Germany. In 1854, the A & L Uhl Pottery Company was founded by August and Louis Uhl. They produced stoneware, as well as stone pumps, sewer pipe, stove flues, and flower pots. The company operated under a series of names until it was changed to the Uhl Pottery Company and moved to Huntingburg, Indiana in 1909.

It made an extensive line of utilitarian wares of all types. Crocks were made in a wide range of sizes. Churns and covers, milk pans, mixing bowls, drinking jars, covered casseroles, bean pots, canister sets, 6-cup drip coffee makers, bud vases, piggy banks, and such were just some of its production.

Wren houses were made in terra cotta or glazed dull colors. Frogs and turtles were glazed. The company also made bird baths, flower pots, and sundials for outdoor use.

Despite the fact it made a really extensive line, it was unable to compete with foreign markets. The business closed in 1949. Some pieces were marked "Uhl Pottery, Huntingburg, Ind." but most wares were unmarked.

**References:** Earl F. McCurdy and Jane A. McCurdy, *A Collectors' Guide and History to Uhl Pottery*, Ohio Valley Books, 1988.

**Collectors' Club:** Uhl Collectors Society, Lloyd Martin, 1582 Gregory Lane, Jasper, IN 47546, bimonthly newsletter, $10.

Basket, 7 1/2" d x 5 1/4" h, 3 loops for hanging, red
.......................................................................... 50.00
Bowl, 6" d, molded hanging drape, gloss yellow glaze
.......................................................................... 15.00
    8 1/2" d, Picket Fence, dk blue glaze ..................... 45.00
    8 3/4" d, emb tulips, tan ground ........................... 125.00
Casserole, Cov, 7 1/4" H-H, ear handles, med blue
.......................................................................... 42.00
Crock
    7 3/4" h, gray stoneware ....................................... 25.00
    13" h, "blue 5, UHL POTTERY COMPANY, acorn" mk
    .................................................................. 50.00
Ewer, 5 1/4" h, dk blue glaze, #34 ............................. 20.00
Figure, 4" h, cowboy boot, rose glaze ......................... 35.00
Flowerpot
    8" h, ribbed, blue .............................................. 140.00
    8 1/2" h, cream base w/multicolored transfer of American
        Indian, dk brown top, mkd, (A) ......................... 60.00
    19 1/2" h, tan ground, black oval "UHL POTTERY
        WORKS, 5" ..................................................... 175.00
Pitcher
    4 1/2" h, disc shape, dk brown ............................... 15.00
    5" h, barrel shape, green glaze ............................... 60.00
Sugar Bowl, 4" h, imp handles, med blue ..................... 20.00
Sugar Bowl, Cov, 4" h, red ......................................... 40.00
Vase
    5 1/2" h, handled, rose design ............................. 210.00
    8 1/4" h, trumpet shape, med blue glaze ................. 40.00

**Mug, 4 1/2" h, tan glaze, #6, $35.**

1879-1891

# Union Porcelain Works

## Greenpoint, Brooklyn, New York
## 1861-1904

**History:** Thomas Smith purchased the Boch Brothers Pottery in 1861 in the Greenpoint section of Brooklyn, New York and established the Union Porcelain Company. First he concentrated on porcelain house trimmings. Utilitarian wares such as pitchers, spittoons, bowls, shaving mugs, cups and saucers for coffee, tea, and chocolate, and heavy oval dishes all were made.

Smith had studied hard paste porcelain making in France and Union Porcelain Works was the first American pottery to produce a true hard paste porcelain. He utilized the underglaze method of decoration on his pitchers, tete-a-tete tea sets, vases, and such. In 1874, Karl Muller became artistic director at Union and created sculptures for the Philadelphia Centennial International Exhibition in 1876. His Century vase was considered the finest example of American ceramics at the Centennial. The design detailed the progress of America through its first century. Muller also made pedestals, statues, and vases with plant and animal motifs or classical designs.

The company used a variety of marks on its wares.

**Museums:** Brooklyn Museum, NY; Henry Ford Museum and Greenfield Village, Dearborn, MI; Metropolitan Museum of Art, New York, NY.

**Collectors' Club:** Oyster Plate & Collectibles Society, P.O. Box 632, Brigantine, NJ 08203-0632, $20. per year.

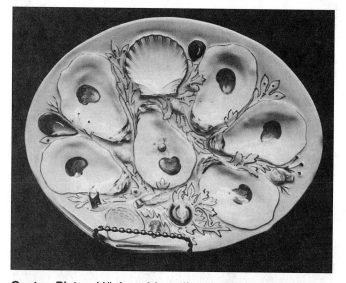

**Oyster Plate, 11" l, gold outlined white molded shell wells, red, purple, and black snails, shells, and seaweed, blue and brown accents, tan border, green "UPW" bird head w/banner, Patent Jan. 4, 1881" mk, $790.**

Oyster Plate
  8 1/2" l x 6 1/2" w, 5 shell molded wells, molded pink and black shells on border, olive green molded seaweed, off white ground ................................................. 495.00
  8 3/4" l x 6 3/4" w, clam shape, 4 wells, separate sauce well, lt green int, mkd ....................................... 595.00
  9 1/2" d, 6 wells, salmon pink ground, c1879, mkd
  ...................................................................... 995.00
  10 1/4" l x 5 5/8" w, clam shape, 6 wells, turquoise int, sauce well, c1881, mkd ................................... 895.00
Paperweight, 2 3/4" h, modeled bulldog head top inscribed "THE MURPHY VARNISHES PERFECTION OF QUALITY" on yellow band, gold bands, stamped "U.P.W.," (A) ...................................................... 168.00

# Universal Potteries, Inc.

## Cambridge, Ohio
## 1934-1976

**History:** Universal Potteries acquired the Atlas-Globe Company in 1934 and made semi-porcelain dinnerware, baking dishes, utilitarian kitchenwares including refrigerator wares in Cambridge, Ohio. Tiles were started in 1956. Dinnerware was made until 1960, and then stopped in favor of decorative tiles. The name of the company changed to the Oxford Tile Company in 1956 until 1976 when the factory closed.

Universal Promotions distributed Universal Potteries products from 1937-1956, when Universal Potteries switched to floor and wall tiles. Some other potteries made dinnerware and kitchenware for Universal Promotions after 1956. Homer Laughlin, Taylor, Smith, and Taylor, and Hull Pottery made pottery with the Universal Ballerina marks for Universal Promotions, Inc.

The Cat-Tail pattern from the 1930s-40s was a very popular decal pottery that was used on a variety of shapes. Calico Fruit from the 1940s was sold in department and catalog stores. Ballerina from the late 1940s-1950s originally came in four solid colors: Periwinkle Blue, Jade Green, Jonquil Yellow, and Dove Gray. Chartreuse and Forest Green were added in 1949. Designer Charles Cobelle added five new patterns for the Ballerina shape in 1950 including: Painted Desert, Mermaid, Passy, Gloucester Fisherman, and The Fountain. In 1955, pink and charcoal were added in solid colors, and Moss Ross was made for the Ballerina shape. Ballerina Mist was done in blue/green with decals.

Walter Kail Titze designed Upico in 1937, which was one of the most extensive of Universal's shapes in both dinnerware and kitchenware. Decorations included solid colors, decals, and combinations of both.

Many other patterns and shapes were made. Elaborate marks were used.

**Anemone Pattern**
Platter, 10" H-H ......................................................... 15.00

## Ballerina Shape

Berry Bowl, 5 1/2" d, Wheat pattern ............................. 4.00
Bowl, 9" d, Harvest pattern ........................................ 10.00
Cup and Saucer
    Green Day Lily pattern .................................... 5.00
    Mist pattern, floral design, blue-green ground ........ 10.00
Plate
    6" d, Mist pattern, floral design, blue-green ground
    ................................................................. 6.00
    6 1/4" d, Green Day Lily pattern ............................... 4.00
    10" d
        Green Day Lily pattern ...................................... 11.00
        Mist pattern, floral design, blue-green ground
        ......................................................... 12.00
        Multicolored florals, Universal, Ballerina Oven Proof E45 Union Made in USA ............................... 10.00
Platter, 10 1/2" H-H, Iris pattern .......................... 15.00
Vegetable Bowl, 7 3/4" d, Dove Gray ............................ 5.00

## BITTERSWEET PATTERN

Bowl, 6 1/2" H-H, tab handles ...................... 45.00

Bowl, 9" d, "Calico Fruit" pattern, $32.

Pitcher, Cov, 7 1/2" h, "Calico Fruit" pattern, $42.

Casserole, Cov, 8-1/2" d ...................................... 20.00
Mixing Bowl
    7" d ............................................................ 30.00
    10" d ........................................................... 10.00
Plate, 9" d ......................................................... 28.00
Refrigerator Jar, Cov .......................................... 30.00

## CALICO FRUIT PATTERN

Bowl, 9" d ......................................................... 33.00
Casserole, Cov, 10 1/4" d ....................................... 35.00
Grill Plate, 10" d ................................................ 10.00
Jug, Cov, 9" h ..................................................... 85.00
Pitcher, 7" h ...................................................... 35.00
Plate, 9 1/8" d .................................................... 55.00
Platter, 11 1/2" l ................................................ 20.00
Shakers, 3 3/4" h, pr ............................................ 45.00
Soup Bowl, 7 3/4" d ............................................... 20.00
Teapot
    5" h, 1 cup ..................................................... 85.00
    7" h ............................................................ 45.00

## CAT-TAIL PATTERN

Berry Bowl, 5 1/4" d ............................................... 5.00
Bowl
    6" d ............................................................ 12.00
    7 1/2" d ........................................................ 18.00
    8 1/2" H-H, tab handles ........................................ 15.00
Butter Dish, Cov, 6" l x 3 1/2" w ................................ 75.00
Cup and Saucer ..................................................... 18.00
Leftover, Cov, 4" h ............................................... 20.00
Mixing Bowl, 6" d ................................................. 15.00
Plate
    6" d ............................................................ 6.00
    7" d ............................................................ 7.00
    9 3/4" d, 3 section ............................................ 7.00
Platter
    12" l .......................................................... 18.00
    13 3/8" l ...................................................... 20.00

Mixing Bowl, 4 1/2" h x 6 1/4" d, "Cat-Tail" pattern, $15.

Leftover, Cov, 5" h, "Cat-Tail" pattern, $10.

Serving Bowl, 9" l ................................................20.00
Shakers, 4 1/4" h, pr.............................................16.00
Soup Bowl, 7" d .....................................................8.00
Water Jug, 6 1/4" h.............................................25.00

## CIRCUS PATTERN
Bowl, 9" d ...............................................................35.00
Butter Dish, Cov, 4 3/4" d...................................22.00
Casserole, Cov, 9 1/2" d.....................................40.00
Cup and Saucer ...................................................22.00
Pitcher
　　4 3/4" h.............................................................30.00
　　6" h, ice lip ......................................................60.00
Platter, 12" ............................................................25.00
Shakers, Pr............................................................24.00
Tray, 13" H-H..........................................................20.00

Dish, 9 1/2" l, "Harvest" pattern, $5.

## HOLLYHOCK PATTERN-OLD HOLLAND SHAPE
Cereal Bowl, 6" d.....................................................5.00
Cup and Saucer .......................................................6.00
Plate
　　6 1/4" d ...............................................................6.00
　　9" d ......................................................................8.00
Platter, 13 1/2" l......................................................15.00

## IRIS PATTERN-BALLERINA SHAPE
Cup and Saucer .......................................................5.00
Pitcher, 5 1/2" h.....................................................30.00
Plate
　　6 1/4" d ...............................................................4.00
　　7 1/2" sq.............................................................5.00
　　10" d ....................................................................8.00
Sugar Bowl, Cov, 4 1/2" h....................................10.00

## LAURELLA PATTERN-CAMBRIDGE SHAPE
Soup Plate, 7" d ......................................................6.00

## MISCELLANEOUS
Platter, 13 5/8" l, 3 red roses on lt border, silver rim, Ivory
............................................................................10.00
Punch Set, bowl, 10 1/4" d, 12 mugs, 3" h, orange border
　　band, gold Tom And Jerry.............................98.00
Refrigerator Jar, 7 1/2" h, decal of lg red, yellow, and blue
　　morning glories on side .................................28.00

## MOSS ROSE PATTERN
Berry Bowl, 51/4" d..................................................5.00
Casserole, Cov, 9 1/2" H-H ..................................10.00

## NETHERLAND PATTERN
Soup Plate................................................................5.00

## ORANGE POPPY PATTERN
Creamer ....................................................................5.00
Plate
　　6" sq....................................................................4.00
　　9" d ......................................................................5.00

## RAMBLER ROSE PATTERN
Bowl, 8 3/4" d ...........................................................6.00
Custard, 3 1/4" d......................................................8.00
Gravy Boat ...............................................................8.00
Plate, 9" d.................................................................5.00
Serving Plate, 9 1/2" H-H .......................................5.00

## RED POPPY PATTERN
Mixing Bowl, 7 1/2" d.............................................20.00
Plate, 9 1/8" d.........................................................10.00
Soup Plate, 7 3/4" d.................................................8.00
Vegetable Bowl, 9 1/4" l........................................24.00

## RODEO PATTERN
Platter, 13 1/4" H-H, yellow ..................................10.00

## WOODVINE PATTERN
Bowl, Cov, 4"d, 5" d, 6" d, set of 3............................35.00
Mixing Bowl
　　6 1/2" d ..............................................................20.00
　　7 5/8" d ..............................................................28.00

8 5/8" d...............................................................45.00
Pitcher, 7" h .......................................................45.00
Plate, 10" d.........................................................20.00
Platter, 13" H-H..................................................20.00
Tray, 13" H-H ......................................................35.00

1914

# University City Pottery

## University City, Missouri
## 1908-1915

**History:** Edward Gardner Lewis founded the American Woman's League in 1907 to provide more opportunities for women. Superior students were invited to study at University City and the Art Institute.

An excellent group of potters worked at University City, though it was only in existence for a short time. The school was headed by Taxile Doat who brought his extensive ceramic collection from France. Many of these shapes were used at University City. Frederick Rhead, Adelaide Robineau, and Julian Zolnay were just a few of the fine artists who worked with Doat on the low fired earthenware, porcelain, and art porcelain. This notable group of ceramic artists received many prizes for its works.

They used superior quality bodies and glazes in both matte and gloss finishes, both colored and colorless. Many matte greens had various textures such as Alligator Skin, Crystalline, Oriental Crackle; a matte white similar to Rookwood's Vellum finish also was used.

In 1911, both Rhead and Robineau left, and Doat continued to work with other potters. The pottery was reorganized in 1912 and continued until 1914, but University City stopped work in 1915. Not all pieces were marked, but most were in a variety of different marks. The earliest mark was an impressed U-P.

**Museums:** Atascadero Library, CA; University City Library, MO.

Bowl, 4 1/2" d, low shape, excised band of stylized green, brown, and teal squirrels, incised "UC" restored hairlines, (A) .................................................................3,080.00
Jardiniere, 8 1/4" h, incised stylized plants, matte periwinkle blue glaze, incised UC/5122 mk, restored rim chips, (A) ..........................................................................440.00
Paperweight, 2 1/2" d, carved cameo of 2 twinned carp and waves, blue and gray ground, incised TD mk, (A) ..........................................................................990.00
Vase
  7 1/2" h
    Bottle shape, mottled pea green microcrystalline glaze ..........................................................................2,000.00
    Pate-sur-pate and modeled blue maple leaves and white berries, cross-hatched white bisque ground, U.C. 1913/MCL (A) .....................................4,125.00

9" h, tall, slender shape, celadon and ochre crystalline glaze, Mabel Lewis, (A)................................. 1,760.00
9 1/4" h, bottle shape, ivory crystalline glaze, incised "UC/1913" 3353344 mk, (A)..........................4,400.00

# Van Briggle Pottery Company

## Colorado Springs, Colorado
## 1900-Present

**History:** Artus Van Briggle joined Rookwood in 1896 and was a senior designer by 1891. Rookwood sent him to Paris to study in 1893. When he returned to Rookwood three years later, he worked to perfect the matte glaze from the Ming dynasty on his pottery. He finally succeeded in 1898. Due to severe tuberculosis, Van Briggle was forced to leave Rookwood and relocate to Colorado Springs, Colorado where he established the Van Briggle Pottery Company in 1900.

Upon arrival in Colorado, he continued his glaze experiments at Colorado College. With Mrs. Storer's help from Rookwood, his pottery was immediately successful, and his first exhibition was sold out. Utilizing the Colorado clays, Van Briggle's low relief decorations attracted a lot of interest. With his marriage to Anne Gregory, an artist, the company expanded with Anne working alongside since Van Briggle was already quite ill. Numerous medals and awards came from the Paris Exposition of 1903-4 and other expositions. Van Briggle died in 1904, Anne became president, and reorganized the company as the Van Briggle Company. Construction was soon started on the Memorial Pottery in 1908 to honor her husband's memory.

A large number of items was being made. All sorts of tiles for utilitarian purposes plus decorated tiles for inserts both indoors and outside. Garden pottery, as well as nearly 300 designs in the art pottery line, were made. Novelty pieces included bookends, paperweights, flower frogs, letter holders, and the like.

The period from 1901-12 saw some of the finest designs and glazes utilized by the company. Glazes ranged from a semi-matte finish, to pebbled and curdled effects. Some pieces were slightly glossy. Glazes were applied with an atomizer run by compressed air. Sometimes a second glaze was used as an overspray to highlight certain parts of the design. Greens, blues, browns, and reds were the first colors used. Glaze colors reflected the Colorado landscape. Designs were influenced by the wildflowers and fauna of the region. At first, there were mostly small vases, but by 1908-09, large vases with Art Nouveau and dramatic shapes were made. One of the most famous designs by Artus Van Briggle was the Lorelei vase with a mermaid wrapped around the top rim of the vase.

Anne remarried in 1908. The pottery was reorganized as Van Briggle Pottery and Tile Company in 1910. By 1912, when it was leased to Edwin DeForest Curtis, Anne was no longer involved. Curtis had the company until 1915 and sold to Charles B. Lansing who continued to expand until the fire in 1919. He sold it in 1920 to I.F. and J.H. Lewis, who renamed the company in 1931 to Van Briggle Art Pottery Company. There was a major flood in 1935.

In 1953, the Midland Terminal Railroad roundhouse was purchased and used as an auxiliary plant until 1968, when Memorial Pottery was sold to Colorado College and all operations moved to Midland. Kenneth Stevenson became the owner in 1969 and continued to produce art pottery with new glazes and designs. When he died in 1990, Craig, his son, and Bertha, Kenneth's wife, continued the operation and still produce art pottery to this day.

From 1912 until the 1920s, Turquoise Blue or Ming Turquoise, Mulberry, and Mountain Craig Brown glazes were used. Persian Rose, a lighter maroon than Mulberry, was used from 1946-68. Other colors included Moonglo, Honey Gold, Jet Black, and Trout Lake Green, to name a few. From 1970 until the present time, Ming Turquoise continues to be used along with variations of Moonglo, Russet, Midnight and other colors.

The logo for Van Briggle pottery was the double "A" enclosed in a square for Artus and Anne. To date pieces, it is important to know the various bottom markings. Up until 1920, pieces usually had the date or a particular pattern.

**References:** Scott H. Nelson, Lois K. Crouch, Euphemia B. Demmin, and Robert Wyman Newton, *A Collector's Guide to Van Briggle Pottery*, Holldin Publishing Company, Inc, 1986; Richard Sasicki and Josie Fania, *Collectors' Encyclopedia of Van Briggle Art Pottery*, Collector Books, 1998.

**Museums:** Chrysler Museum, Norfolk, VA; Colorado State Historical Society Museum, Denver, CO; Everson Museum of Art, Syracuse, NY; National Museum of History and Technology, Smithsonian Institution, Washington, DC; New Orleans Museum of Art, LA; Newark Museum, NJ; Pioneer Museum, Colorado Springs, CO.

**Reproduction Alert:** False Van Briggle marks appear on reproductions of original Van Briggle shapes, on new fantasy shapes never made by Van Briggle, and on old pottery from other makers to which forgers have added the Van Briggle mark.

Bookend, 5" h, figural seated dog, matte green over brown ground, c1930, pr ................................................. 425.00

Bowl

6" d, rolled rim, emb poppy pods on stems, matte green glaze, incised AA/VAN BRIGGLE/162/190 hairlines, (A) .............................................................. 1,100.00

11" d, emb mistletoe, mottled mauve glaze, incised AA/VAN BRIGGLE/1905/387 mk, (A)............. 4,125.00

Bud Vase, 7" h, ovoid body, incised pedestal base, emb leaf design on base, mulberry glaze w/teal overspray on base, VAN Briggle/Colo. Sprgs mk, (A) .................. 77.00

Cabinet Vase, 4" h, narrow base, wide shoulder, rolled rim, dk blue and green glaze, incised VAN BRIGGLE/1902/101/OD/III, (A) ...................................... 990.00

Candlestick, 4 1/2" h, 3 figural cornucopia feet, matte turquoise, pr ............................................................ 150.00

Chamberstick, 7 1/4" h, blue to lt green shaded ground ................................................................................ 210.00

Conch Shell, 16" l, Persian Rose glaze..................... 135.00

Figure

7" h, seated nude holding open scallop shell, matte rose glaze, (A)............................................................ 330.00

10 1/2" h, seated nude on rock, rose glaze .......... 275.00

12 1/4" h, Indian brave or squaw, turquoise, pr ................................................................................ 400.00

15" h, seated cat, blue-purple matte glaze ........... 395.00

Mug, 5" h, emb flying eagle, textured matte green glaze, incised AA Van Briggle/1906/355 mk (A)............... 440.00

Paperweight, 4 1/2" d, amber figural horned frog on matte green disk base, (A) ............................................. 990.00

Plaque, 4 5/8" l x 2 3/8" w, Indian design, blue/green ................................................................................ 95.00

Plate

8 1/4" d, emb purple grape clusters, textured turquoise ground, AA/VAN BRIGGLE/COLO. SPGS/15 mk, (A) ................................................................................ 605.00

8 1/2" d, incised poppies, leaves, and stems, lt green glaze, AA/VAN BRIGGLE/1902/ mk, (A) ........ 1,540.00

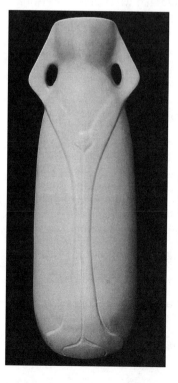

Vase, 15 1/2" h, matte yellow glaze w/green wash top, dtd 1903, (A), $1,540.

Plate, 8 1/2" d, molded grapes and leaves, matte green and maroon glaze, c1907-12, (A), $750.

Pot, 10" h, 2 small handles, emb desert flowers, matte green and burgundy glaze, incised AA/VAN BRIGGLE/1904/V. mk, (A) .................................................2,475.00

Vase

2 1/2" h, carved floral design, suspended multi-tone matte green glaze, c1907-12, (A) ......................825.00

4"

Ball shape, incised and molded floral design w/whip-lash stems and leaves, green, brown, and blue matte glaze, c1915, (A)................................495.00

Bulbous, emb circ stylized flowers, matte gray-green glaze, c1907, (A)...........................................498.00

5"

Bowl form, figural overlapping leaves, maroon glaze w/blue shades................................................125.00

Squat base, tapered neck, emb yucca leaves, curdled brown glaze, incised AA/VAN BRIGGLE/Colo. Spgs./162 mk, (A).........................................990.00

5 1/4" h, emb trefoils, green and purple matte glaze, incised AA BRIGGLE/COLO.SPGS. 1912/26 mk, (A) ....................................................................1,430.00

5-1/2" h

Bulbous, emb trefoils, curdled matte green glaze, red clay body, incised AA/VAN BRIGGLE/COLO. Springs mk, (A) ...............................................825.00

Tapered form, matte green glaze, brown clay body, c1905, (A) ...................................................770.00

6" h, cylinder shape, black glaze, blue-gray drip on rim, engraved PAT-N-TERRY on front, ANNA VAN BRIGGLE COLO. SPRINGS mk ...........................35.00

6-1/2" h, emb flower design, matte lt green glaze, incised AA/VAN BRIGGLE/1903/210 mk, (A).............1,100.00

6 3/4" h, swollen cylinder shape, emb daisies and stems, frothy mustard glaze, incised AA/VAN BRIGGLE/Colo. Spgs. mk, (A) ..............................................1,760.00

7" h

Bottle shape, emb papyrus blossoms on base, vert stems, semi-matte turquoise glaze, AA/Van Briggle/Colo.Spgs. mk, (A) ..........................1,045.00

Cylinder shape, emb stylized daisies, matte blue-green shaded glaze, c1920, (A)....................220.00

Emb jonquils on long stems, dk green dead matte glaze, incised AA VAN BRIGGLE/1902/III mk, (A) ....................................................................2,750.00

Molded dragonflies, matte rose-blue (A) ...........253.00

Ovoid shape, collared rim, curdled and heavily textured matte green glaze, incised AA/Van Briggle mk, (A) ......................................................2,640.00

7 1/4" h

Swollen cylinder shape, emb daisies, matte turquoise glaze, imp AA/USA mk, (A)...........................193.00

Wishbone handles, incised feather design on waist, mulberry glaze w/plum overspray, (A)...........247.00

7-1/2" h

Bulbous, base and shoulder, emb crocuses, matte green glaze, imp AA/VAN BRIGGLE/COLO SPG/692 mk, (A)..........................................770.00

Tapered cylinder shape, sm neck, raised and incised floral designs, multi-tone blue matte glaze, (A) ....................................................................468.00

7 3/4" h, emb stylized leaves, flowing matte green glaze, red clay, incised AA/VANBRIGGLE/1905 mk, (A) ....................................................................3,300.00

8" h, trumpet shape, incised and painted leaves, tobacco brown and green matte glaze, c1918, (A) .........495.00

8 1/2" h, emb green leaves, red berries, matte raspberry red glaze, AA VAN BRIGGLE, 1904/164 mk, (A) ....................................................................3,300.00

8 3/4" h, bottle shape, emb stylized papyrus, matte blue-green glaze, imp AA/VAN BRIGGLE COLO SPGS/639 mk, (A).......................................................1,320.00

9" h, emb poppy pods on long curved stems, matte burgundy glaze, incised AA/VANBRIGGLE/1902/II mk, (A) ..............................................................12,100.00

10" h

Bulbous shape, emb spade shaped leaves, frothy green glaze, beige clay, c1905, (A) ...........3,575.00

Emb stylized irises, semi matte turquoise glaze, AA Van Briggle/Colo. Spgs/40 mk, (A) ............1,100.00

Swollen cylinder shape, thick rim, carved stems w/Queen Anne's Lace, dk maroon matte glaze w/blue highlights, c1907-12, (A) ...............1,485.00

10 1/2" h, tapered cylinder shape

Long slender molded flowers, matte purple and maroon glaze, dtd 1915, (A) ......................1,210.00

Two sm handles, fissured and veined matte green and burgundy glazes, AA/VAN BRIGGLE/224/1904/V mks, (A) .............................................................2,420.00

11" h, Lady of the Lily, nude leaning against calla lily, matte lt green glaze, incised AA/VAN BRIGGLE/1902/III mk, (A) ....................................41,250.00

11 1/4" h, emb cornflowers, long stems, curdled raspberry red glaze, beige clay, incised AA/VAN BRIGGLE/COLO.SPGS/146 mk, (A) .....................2,640.00

11 3/4" h, cylinder shape, emb stylized peacock feather under yellow and turquoise butterfat glaze, burgundy ground, incised AA/VAN BRIGGLE/VX/1905 mk, (A) ....................................................................1,980.00

12 1/2" h, Despondency, carved figure of man on rim, matte green glaze, AA/Van Briggle/Colo. Springs/1909 mks, (A)............................................................21,280.00

13" h, emb irises, frothy blue-gray glaze, red clay, c1905, (A) ...................................................................3,850.00

Vessel, 4" h, spherical shape, emb mistletoe, frothy dk green glaze, brown clay, (A)...............................770.00

c.1913

# Vance/Avon Faience

### Tiltonville, Ohio
### Wheeling, West Virginia
### 1900-1908

**History:** The Vance Faience Company was incorporated in West Virginia in 1900 by Nelson Vance, J.D. Culbertson, and Charles W. Franzheim, who had founded Wheeling Pottery Company in 1879, but used the Tiltonville, Ohio plant. They experimented with both utilitarian and ornamental lines. They reissued the four quart Greatbach pitcher, and then expanded to issue in it three sizes in a 1904 reproduction, and in a variety of glazes including orange shading to brown, high gloss blue and white, and matte green. They were marked with Vance impressed in the base.

Artwares were designed and made by William P. Jervis who became manager in 1902. The company name was changed to Avon Faience Company. Jervis worked with Frederick Hurten Rhead who joined in 1903 to make artwares. Pieces were decorated underglaze with Art Nouveau motifs in a wide range of colors. Sometimes designs were outlined in squeezed white slip, which was the forerunner of the Weller Jap Birdimal line introduced by Rhead and also made at Roseville. In-mold decorations in high relief were used by Rhead and other artists who worked there.

In 1902, Wheeling Potteries Company absorbed Avon Faience, and it was operated as a department of Wheeling. Avon continued to make artware with a heavy body and experiment with decorative techniques. They leaned more toward utilitarian objects. Jervis and Rhead left in 1903. Vases, jardinieres, umbrella racks, steins, tobacco bowls, and teapots were made.

All art work was stopped at Tiltonville in 1905, and the Avon line was moved to Wheeling. The ceramic body changed from earthenware to semi-porcelain, thus ending the production of artwares. The Ohio plant was retained for the manufacture of sanitary ware.

In 1908, they stopped making general wares and only made sanitary wares. The firm entered into receivership. Art pottery examples first had the Vance Faience marks. Some pieces were incised "Avon" after 1902. Other marks had "W.Pts. Co." for Wheeling Potteries Company.

Bud Vase, 6" h, bulbous base, tapered neck, shaded gloss brown glaze, imp mk, (A) .......................................... 70.00
Jardiniere, 7" h x 9" d, emb stylized cats, shaded brown, green, and black glaze, hairline, imp mk, (A)........ 550.00
Mug, 4 3/8" h, multi-colored decal of man drinking from wine bottle, dk green border band w/gold accents ........... 10.00
Pitcher
   5" h, tankard shape, red strawberries, green leaves and stems, wide dk green border band w/gold stripe
   ........................................................................................ 15.00
   8" h, cylinder shape, lg red daffodils, green leaves and stems, blue ground, "Avon Faience" mk, repairs
   ...................................................................................... 100.00
   10" h
      Figural hound handle, relief molded vines and grapes on upper section, hunt scene on lower section, amber-tan glaze w/green accents on base, (A)
      ...................................................................................... 880.00
      Tankard style, raised yellow jonquils, green leaves, white ground, mkd ......................................... 50.00
Vase
   7" h, ovoid shape, curled rim, squeezebag design of brown, umber, and tan stylized heartshaped trees, (A)
   ...................................................................................... 880.00
   7 1/2" h, bottle shape, squeezebag design of roses on shaded brown and green ground, stamped Vance mk, pr, (A)..................................................................... 515.00
   11 1/4" h, tapered shape, stepped collar, incised green and brown stylized trees in landscape, amber ground, (A)................................................................... 1,650.00
   12" h, ball shape, wavy rim, relief molded mermaids, shellfish, and waves, brown-yellow swirled glaze, chips, (A) ............................................................... 1,43.00

SALAMINA
Designed by
Rockwell Kent
VERNON KILNS
MADE IN USA

Designed by
WALT DISNEY
Copyright 1940
VERNON KILNS
Made in U.S.A.

VERNON KILNS
MADE IN
U.S.A.
CALIFORNIA

# Vernon Kilns

## Vernon, California
## 1931-1958

**History:** Faye Bennison purchased the Poxon China Company in 1931 and changed its name to Vernon Kilns. During the early years of the company, he established an artware department and made vases, bowls, candlesticks, and figurines, along with dinnerwares. Due to economic problems, they stopped the artware line in 1937. The Coronado shape was used in 1938 for solid color premium ware.

Vernon Kilns employed many famous and gifted artists and became a leader in the dinnerware market. Gale Turnbull was hired as art director in 1936 and created the Ultra shape for solid-color dinnerware. Rockwell Kent used this shape for his Salamina, Our America (scenes and regions of America), and Moby Dick (ships and scenes from the novel) with transfer printed designs.

Vernon contracted with Walt Disney to make figures from "Fantasia," "Dumbo," and "The Reluctant Dragon." Figures from "Fantasia" were produced from actual models used in production of the film. "Fantasia" vases and bowls also were made along with an accompanying dinnerware pattern. All of these pieces were marked. Due to high production costs, Disney designs were sold for less than two years.

Don Blanding used the Ultra shape for his tropical floral and fish designs. His Lei Lani was one of the most popular Vernon patterns of all time.

Royal Hickman designed the Melinda shape in 1942 that was used for fourteen different patterns, including solid color Native California and English look-alike traditional patterns. The San Fernando shape was used for Early Days and P.F.D., both transfer printed patterns.

The hand painted Organdie and Brown Eyed Susan were very popular during the war years. Many variations of the brown and yellow plaid of Organdie were sold in later years.

In the mid 1940s, the San Marino shape was a complete change from the earlier shapes. Three solid color lines included Casual California, California Shadows, and California Originals with drip glazes.

Vernon Kilns was a pioneer in the transfer printing process. All sorts of commemoratives, French opera reproductions, and the Bit Series sold well. Collectors have identified more than one thousand different souvenir plates from Vernon Klins. Almost every possible subject found its way to souvenir plates. Cities, states, national parks, famous people, businesses, universities, World War II commemoratives, advertising, transportation, churches, organizations, and historical events were depicted. The same shapes used for dinnerware were also used for souvenir plates that were 10 1/2" in diameter.

Other shapes included Chatelaine in 1953 that was square with embossed leaf corners, leaf handles and finials and was made in four solid colors. Anytime shape in 1955 designed by Eliot House was used for nine different patterns. A large variety of shapes was used on the lightweight dinnerwares that were made until 1958 and sold in department, jewelry, and gift stores.

After World War II, the United States was flooded with imports from Japan, England, and Scandinavia. Edward Fischer took over when Faye Bennison retired in 1955. With ever increasing costs and the continuing foreign competition, the pottery was unable to survive and closed in 1958. Metlox Potteries bought the Vernon Kilns molds and modified some shapes. They continued to make some patterns for several years using both Vernon backstamps and "by Metlox."

Almost all of the Vernon Kilns pieces were marked, and some were artist signed.

**References:** Jack Chipman, *Collector's Encyclopedia of California Pottery, 2nd Edition*, Collector Books, 1998; Bess Gedney Christensen, *Souvenir Plates from Vernon Kilns*, *The Antique Trader Weekly*, June 3, 1992; Maxine Feek Nelson, *Collectible Vernon Kilns*, Collector Books, 1994; Mike Schneider, *California Potteries, the Complete Book*, Schiffer Publishing Ltd. 1995.

**Newsletter:** *Vernon Views*, P.O. Box 945, Scottsdale, AZ 85252, Pat Faux Editor, quarterly, $10 per year.

Teapot, 4 5/8" h, "Brown Eyed Susan" pattern, $15.

## ARCADIA PATTERN
Berry Bowl, 5 3/4" d ........................................... 2.00
Cereal Bowl, 6 1/4" H-H ..................................... 4.00
Chop Plate, 12" d .............................................. 25.00
Cup and Saucer ................................................. 3.00
Plate, 9 1/2" d .................................................... 4.00
Platter, 12 1/4" d ............................................... 10.00
Vegetable Bowl, 9" d ......................................... 15.00

## BEL AIR PATTERN
Butterpat, 2 1/2" d .............................................. 45.00

## BITS OF THE OLD SOUTH
Chop Plate, 14" d, Down on the Levee .................. 135.00
Plate, 8 1/2" d
    "Down on the Levee" ...................................... 50.00
    "Off to the Hunt" ............................................ 45.00
    "Southern Mansion" ....................................... 45.00

## BROWN EYED SUSAN PATTERN
Cereal Bowl, 7 1/2" H-H ..................................... 8.00
Chop Plate, 12" d .............................................. 25.00
Pitcher, 3" h ...................................................... 9.00
Plate
    7 1/2" d ......................................................... 7.00
    9 1/2" d ......................................................... 9.00
Sugar Bowl, 3" h ................................................ 6.00
Teapot, 4 3/4" h ................................................ 15.00

## CALIFORNIA ORIGINALS
Platter, 13" l, almond yellow ............................... 14.00

## CASA CALIFORNIA PATTERN
Chop Plate, 12" d, yellow and brown ................... 85.00
Gravy Boat, 10" l, yellow ................................... 10.00
Plate, 9 1/2" d .................................................. 30.00

## DESERT BLOOM PATTERN
Coffeepot, 8 cup ............................................... 75.00
Plate
    7" d .............................................................. 6.00
    9" d .............................................................. 10.00

## DOLORES PATTERN-MELINDA SHAPE
Chop Plate, 12" d, maroon, blue, and yellow .............. 32.00

## EARLY CALIFORNIA PATTERN
Bowl, 10" l, pink ............................................... 12.00
Chop Plate, 12" d, maroon ................................. 20.00
Plate
    6" d, orange .................................................. 6.00
    9 1/2" d
        Pink ........................................................ 10.00
        Turquoise ................................................ 9.00
Platter
    12 1/2" l, aqua ............................................. 5.00
    14" l, orange ................................................ 15.00
Serving Bowl, 8 3/4" d, yellow ........................... 10.00

## FRUITDALE PATTERN
Bowl, 9 1/2" l ................................................... 5.00
Cup and Saucer ............................................... 12.00
Plate
    6 1/2" d ........................................................ 3.00
    7 1/2" d ........................................................ 3.00
Platter, 12" d ................................................... 10.00
Soup Plate, 8 1/2" d .......................................... 14.00

## 1860'S PATTERN
Fruit Bowl, 5 1/2" d ........................................... 10.00
Creamer ........................................................... 15.00
Cup and Saucer, Demitasse ............................... 20.00
Plate, 10 1/2" d ................................................ 18.00
Sugar Bowl, Cov ............................................... 25.00

Vegetable Bowl, 10" l...................................................25.00

## FANTASIA
Bowl, 2 1/2" h, Winged Nymph, pink, #122 ...............350.00
Figure
    5" h, ballerina elephant, #25 .................................450.00
    5 1/2" h
        Ballerina elephant, #27........................................550.00
        Pegasus, #21 .........................................................450.00

## FROLIC PATTERN
Pitcher, 8 3/4" h.............................................................30.00

## GINGHAM PATTERN
Chop Plate, 12" d ........................................................24.00
Mixing Bowl, 8" d.........................................................40.00
Plate, 9 1/2" d..............................................................10.00
Salad Bowl, 5" d ..........................................................16.00
Shakers, Pr..................................................................15.00
Sugar Bowl, Cov...........................................................15.00

## HAWAIIAN FLOWERS DESIGN
Bowl, 5 1/4" d, burgundy ............................................45.00
Coffeepot, 8 1/2" h, blue.............................................275.00
Chop Plate
    12 1/2" d, orange .................................................39.00
    14" d, blue ...........................................................155.00
Coffeepot, 8" h, blue...................................................275.00
Creamer, orange ........................................................15.00
Cup and Saucer, burgundy..........................................45.00
Plate
    6 1/4" d
        Blue ..................................................................20.00
        Orange .............................................................15.00
    9" d, burgundy.....................................................65.00
Shakers, pr, pink.........................................................75.00
Vegetable Bowl, 9 1/4" d, orange ...............................35.00

## HOMESPUN PATTERN
Beverage Set, pitcher, 6 tumblers ............................180.00
Butterpat, 2 1/2" d.......................................................45.00
Cereal Bowl, 5" d.........................................................15.00
Chop Plate, 12" d ........................................................20.00
Creamer ......................................................................12.00
Cup and Saucer ...........................................................5.00
Plate
    6 1/2" d..................................................................5.00
    9 3/4" d................................................................18.00
Platter, 12" l ...............................................................20.00
Soup Plate, 8 1/2" d....................................................24.00
Sugar Bowl, Cov...........................................................15.00
Vegetable Bowl, 9" d ..................................................25.00

## LEI LANI PATTERN-ULTRA SHAPE
Maroon
    Berry Bowl, 5 3/4" d..............................................12.00
    Cup and Saucer, Demitasse ..................................65.00
    Gravy Boat.............................................................165.00
    Nappy, 9" d...........................................................165.00

Chop Plate, 14" d, "Moby Dick," maroon and white, Rockwell Kent, $250.

Plate
    9 3/8" d................................................................28.00
    10 1/2" d..............................................................50.00
Salad Dish, 5 1/2" d....................................................45.00

## MAYFLOWER PATTERN
Creamer ......................................................................10.00
Platter, 12 1/2" l..........................................................20.00
Serving Bowl, 9 1/8" d.................................................20.00
Sugar Bowl, Cov...........................................................12.00

## MEXICANA PATTERN
Cereal Bowl, 5 3/4" d....................................................3.00
Cup and Saucer .............................................................3.00
Plate
    6 1/8" d..................................................................2.00
    7 5/8" d..................................................................3.00
    10 1/8" d................................................................4.00

## MODERN CALIFORNIA PATTERN
Chop Plate, 12" d, straw..............................................20.00
Cup and Saucer, azure ...............................................10.00
Plate, 7" d, pistachio.....................................................8.00

## MONTEREY PATTERN
Coffeepot.....................................................................75.00
Creamer and Sugar Bowl.............................................22.00
Teapot .........................................................................65.00

## NATIVE CALIFORNIA PATTERN
Chowder Bowl, 6" d, blue ............................................10.00
Coffeepot, 8 cup, blue................................................120.00
Cup and Saucer, Demitasse, blue................................15.00
Fruit Bowl, 5 1/2" d, green ............................................5.00
Plate
    5 3/4" d, green ......................................................4.00

6 1/2" d, green .................................................PRICE
9 1/2" d, blue.................................................5.00
Soup Plate, 8" d, blue................................... 15.00
Teapot, 7" h, cream yellow .......................... 35.00

## ORGANDIE PATTERN
Butter Dish, Cov, 7 1/2" l ............................. 30.00
Cereal Bowl, 7 1/4" H-H ................................. 6.00
Chop Plate
    12" d ...................................................... 20.00
    14" d ...................................................... 25.00
Cup and Saucer .............................................5.00
Mixing Bowl
    5" d........................................................ 22.00
    6" d........................................................ 25.00
    7" d........................................................ 30.00
    8" d........................................................ 35.00
    9" d........................................................ 38.00
Pitcher
    3 1/2" h....................................................7.00
    11" h...................................................... 40.00
Plate
    6" d..........................................................2.00
    7" d..........................................................5.00
    9" d..........................................................6.00
Shakers, Pr ................................................. 10.00
Soup Plate, 8 1/2" d..................................... 12.00
Vegetable Bowl, 8 1/2" d .............................. 15.00
Vegetable Bowl, Divided, 12 1/2" H-H .......... 18.00

## ROCKWELL KENT DESIGNS
Creamer and Cov Sugar Bowl, Moby Dick, maroon
.................................................................. 195.00
Chop Plate, 17" d, Salamina design ........... 650.00
Plate
    6" d, Moby Dick, brown ........................... 38.00
    6 1/2" d, Salamina design ........................ 65.00
    7 1/2" d Salamina design ....................... 120.00
    8 1/2" d, Our America Series-Fishing Schooner, blue
.................................................................... 75.00

**Cup and Saucer, "Salamina," multicolored, Rockwell Kent, $75.**

9 1/2" d
    Moby Dick-blue ....................................... 75.00
    Our America Series-Chicago From the River,
      walnut brown ...................................... 40.00
    Salamina kneeling .................................. 230.00
10 1/2" d, Our America Series-New York City Harbor, wal-
    nut brown ................................................ 75.00
Vegetable Bowl, 9 1/2" d, Moby Dick, dk blue ............ 135.00

## SANTA ANITA-MELINDA SHAPE
Plate, 10" d
    Hibiscus ................................................. 35.00
    Red Ginger ............................................. 35.00

## SANTA BARBARA-ULTRA SHAPE
Chop Plate, 14" d ....................................... 125.00
Coffeepot .................................................... 235.00
Plate, 10" d .................................................. 65.00

## SOUVENIR ITEMS
City Plates
    10 1/2" d
      City of Miami Florida, dk blue transfer................. 10.00
      Los Angeles, California, burgundy transfer ......... 20.00
State Plates
    10 1/2" d
      Alaska, brown transfer of bear and state designs
      ............................................................. 22.00
      "Picture Map of Kentucky," maroon transfer........ 12.00
      State of Lousiana, dk blue transfer .................... 10.00
      State of Maine, multicolored transfer ................. 35.00
      State of Missouri, dk red transfer ....................... 15.00

## TAM-O-SHANTER PATTERN
Creamer ...................................................... 15.00
Cup and Saucer ............................................. 8.00
Mixing Bowl
    5" d........................................................ 25.00
    6" d........................................................ 30.00
    7" d........................................................ 35.00
    8" d........................................................ 40.00
Plate
    6" d..........................................................3.00
    9" d..........................................................8.00
Platter, 12 1/2" d......................................... 40.00
Soup Plate, 8 1/2" d..................................... 15.00
Sugar Bowl, Cov .......................................... 15.00
Vegetable Bowl, 8 1/2" d ............................. 20.00

## TASTE PATTERN
Chop Plate, 14" d, maroon with enamels ................. 140.00
Cup and Saucer ............................................. 6.00
Plate, 9 1/2" d, maroon with enamels ......................... 45.00

## TICKLED PINK PATTERN
Bowl
    7 3/4" d ....................................................7.00
    9" d..........................................................8.00
Cup and Saucer ............................................. 3.00
Fruit Bowl 5 1/2" d......................................... 5.00

Plate, 10" d .................................................. 15.00
Platter
  11" l ........................................................ 8.00
  13" d ...................................................... 10.00
Teapot, 6 1/2" h ........................................... 25.00
Tumbler, 5" h ............................................... 16.00
Vegetable Bowl, 9 3/4" l, divided .................. 10.00

**VERNON ROSE PATTERN**
Platter, 14" d .............................................. 45.00

**WINCHESTER 73 PATTERN**
Chop Plate, 12" d ....................................... 160.00
Plate, 6" d .................................................. 32.00
  Platter, 12 1/2" l ........................................ 130.00

1879-1888

# Volkmar Kilns

### Metuchen, New Jersey
### 1903-1914

**History:** Charles Volkmar and Leon, his son, established Volkmar Kilns in Metuchen, New Jersey in 1903 after Charles closed his pottery in Corona, New York. They used both the high gloss and semi-matte glazes that were previously developed at Volkmar Pottery.

Artwares, tiles, panels, and plaques were made with a variety of excellent glaze techniques used on the simple forms. Vases and bowls were made with a matte finish in dark gray, green, pink, blue, and dark red-brown. They won a bronze medal at the St. Louis Exposition in 1904.

After 1905, a porcelain body was used for their work. Charles and Leon worked together until 1911 when Leon left. Charles continued to work until his death in 1914.

The most often used mark was the incised stylized "V." An incised "Volkmar" mark also was used.

**Museums:** The Newark Museum, NJ.

Bowl, 9 1/4" d, organic, molded broad leaves, matte green glaze, mkd, (A) ...................................... 495.00
Candlestick, 13" h, twisted stem, grained gold glaze, (A)
.................................................................. 165.00
Centerpiece Bowl, 13 1/2" d x 6 1/2" h, flared shape, thick, crackled Persian blue ext, Persian turquoise int, incised Durant/1928 mk, (A) .............................. 770.00
Plaque
  11" d, Delft style, blue residence of George Washington, G.W.M.A. at top wavy blue border, stamped VOLK-MAR mk, (A) ............................................. 40.00
  15 1/2" l x 9" h, rect, barbotine type painted animals in creek w/forest bkd, framed, sgd Chas. Volkmar
.................................................................. 3,500.00
Vase
  5 1/2" h, spherical, short neck, mottled med blue vellum glaze, incised Volkmar ............................. 550.00

**Vase, 4" h, 8 sides, black gunmetal glaze, incised mk, (A), $330.**

6 1/2" h, bag shape, flared rim, mottled and frothy purple glaze, incised Volkmar mk, (A) .................... 440.00
7" h, bulbous
  Crackled Persian blue glaze, incised Durant 1913, (A)
.................................................................. 303.00
  Persian blue glaze, incised Volkmar/Durant, chips, (A)
.................................................................. 358.00
7 1/2" h, bulbous, cylinder collar, feathered matte blue glaze, incised V mk, (A) ............................. 550.00
8" h
  Classic shape, thick matte green glaze, incised V mk, (A) ......................................................... 440.00
  Tapered shape, flared rim, incised arched panels, rust and green glaze, mkd, chips, (A) ................. 198.00
9 1/2" h, incised vert leaves, matte green glaze, (A)
.................................................................. 1,760.00
10 1/2" h, tapered shape w/bulbous base and spherical neck, flared lip, curdled green glaze w/dk brown accents, white over brown int glaze, incised V mk, (A)
.................................................................. 495.00
12 1/4" h, pillow style, barbotine sepia scenes of horses pulling carts in forest, Chas. Volkmar, chips, pr, (A)
.................................................................. 5500.00
Vessel, 3" h x 4 1/4" d, squat faceted shape, short, flared rim, matte green glaze, (A) ......................... 247.00

# Wallace China Company

### Vernon, California
### 1931-1964

**History:** The Wallace China Company was founded in 1931 to make vitrified hotel china in Vernon, California. Both plain and transfer printed dinnerwares were produced for institutional use. During the '30s and '40s, much Willow design china was made in blue, green, brown, and red.

George Poxon brought his Poxon China designs to Wallace when he was hired by the company. The M.C. Wentz Company of Pasadena commissioned Wallace in 1943 to produce "Barbecue Ware" which became part of the Westward Ho housewares.

Till Goodan, the well-known Western artist, created three patterns: Rodeo, Boots and Saddle, and Pioneer Trails that he usually signed somewhere in the design. A three-piece Little Buckaroo Chuck set was produced for children. El Rancho and Longhorn were also designed by Goodan for restaurants.

Shadowleaf, originally designed for restaurants, was available as an open stock pattern as well. In 1959, Wallace became part of the Shenango China Company of East Liverpool, Ohio and was closed in 1964. A variety of backstamps was used on Wallace pieces.

**References:** Jack Chipman, *Collector's Encyclopedia of California Pottery*, Collector Books, 1992.

**Reproduction Alert:** Westward Ho Rodeo reproductions are being sold through catalogs and retail locations, mostly in the southwest. The mark on the new china does not include "California" and "Wallace China," but the patterns are identical. The china is made by True West pottery in Texas.

## BOOTS AND SADDLES

Ashtray, 5 3/8" d ....................................55.00
Chop Plate, 13" d ..................................295.00
Creamer, 4" h .......................................95.00
Cup and Saucer .....................................50.00
Plate
    7" d....................................................30.00
    10 1/2" d.............................................50.00
Serving Bowl, 12" l ................................250.00
Shaker, 5" h .........................................50.00

**Chop Plate, 13" d, "Westward Ho-Pioneer Trails," sgd "Till Goodin," brown, $225.**

Sugar Bowl.............................................45.00
Water Pitcher, 7 1/2" h ...........................425.00

## CHUCK WAGON PATTERN

Ashtray, 5 1/2" d ....................................75.00
Bowl, 5" d .............................................10.00
Butter Pat, 3" d ......................................45.00
Mug, 2 1/2" h .........................................20.00
Plate, 9 1/4" d ........................................50.00
Platter, 12" l ..........................................75.00

## EL RANCHO

Ashtray, 5 1/2" d ....................................30.00
Bowl, 4 3/4" d .........................................90.00
Cereal Bowl, 6 1/2" ................................25.00
Cup and Saucer .....................................40.00
Plate
    5 1/2" d ..............................................35.00
    6 1/4" d ..............................................20.00
    7" .......................................................50.00
    9 1/2" d ..............................................50.00
    10 1/2" d .............................................40.00
    12" d ...................................................70.00
Platter
    6" l .....................................................75.00
    9" l .....................................................75.00
    12 1/2" l ..............................................85.00
    14" l ..................................................125.00

## 49er PATTERN

Soup Plate, 9" d .....................................20.00

## PIONEER TRAILS

Cereal Bowl, 5 5/8" d...............................85.00
Creamer, 4 3/8" d ....................................50.00
Cup and Saucer, Demitasse ......................60.00
Creamer, 4 3/8" d ....................................50.00
Plate
    6 1/4" d ............................................135.00
    10 3/4" d ...........................................130.00
Platter, 13 7/8" l ...................................165.00
Shakers, Pr ...........................................50.00

## RODEO PATTERN

Cereal Bowl, 5 1/4" d ..............................25.00
Chop Plate, 13" d ..................................295.00
Creamer, 3 5/8" h ...................................70.00
Cup and Saucer, AD ...............................50.00
Dessert Bowl, 4" d ..................................20.00
Mixing Bowl, 7" d ..................................265.00
Mug, 3 1/2" h .........................................40.00
Plate
    7 1/4" d ..............................................40.00
    9" d ...................................................125.00
    10 1/2" d .............................................85.00
Platter
    11" l ....................................................75.00
    15" l ..................................................175.00
Salad Bowl, 13" d ..................................600.00
Shakers, Pr ..........................................140.00

Sugar Bowl, Cov........................................................50.00
Vegetable Bowl
    12" l......................................................80.00
    15" l......................................................90.00

## SHADOWLEAF PATTERN
Plate
    8" d, red ...................................................4.00
    9" d, red .................................................15.00
    10" d, gray...............................................16.00

# Walley Pottery

## West Sterling, Massachusetts
## 1898-1919

**History:** At first, Joseph William Walley made pottery in Portland, Maine from 1873-1885. In 1898, he bought Wachusett Pottery in West Sterling, Massachusetts and operated it until his death in 1919. He used the local red clay and did most of the work himself on the handmade art pottery.

Pieces made by Walley included vases, planters, candlesticks, lamp bases, tea tiles, bowls, mugs, hair receivers, and powder jars that were cast or hand thrown. He used mostly green glazes in both matte and gloss finishes. Other colors were variations of greens and brown. Pieces were marked with an impressed "W J W."

Bowl, 5 1/2"d, squat shape, closed rim, matte green glaze, imp WJW mk, (A) ...................................523.00
Creamer, 4" h, figural grotesque spout, blue cabochon on handle, brown and gunmetal glazes, unmkd, (A)...550.00
Urn, 9 1/2" h, ftd, 2 wing handles, frothy gloss green glaze, (A) ........................................1,210.00

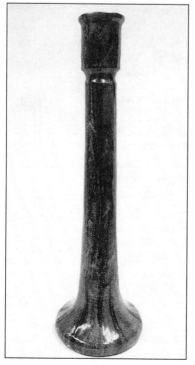

**Candlestick, 14" h, multi-toned blue drip glaze, imp mk, (A), $260.**

Vase
  3 3/4" h, bowl shape, dk green glaze over brown, brown bisque int,(A) ................................ 165.00
  4" h, spherical, periwinkle blue glaze w/ curdled accents, dk blue speckling, imp W.J.W. (A).................... 302.00
  5" h, ovoid, imp lg stylized leaves, semi-matte apple green glaze, imp WJW mk, (A) .................... 413.00
  6 1/2" h, sculpted and applied vert leaves, matte green and brown glaze, (A)................................. 3,190.00
  6 3/4" h, bulbous body, short collar, mahogany flambe glaze, imp WJW mk ................................ 1,200.00
  7" h
    Bulbous bottle shape, thick gloss green and brown streaky glaze, imp WJW mk, (A) .............. 2,420.00
    Corset shape, mottled brown and green glaze, imp WJW mk,(A) ................................................ 935.00
    Spherical shape, short collar, gloss mahogany glaze, imp WJW mk, (A)................................ 1,210.00
  7 3/4" h, ovoid, applied vert leaves, mottled gloss green and brown glaze, imp WJW mk, (A)
    .................................................... 1,045.00
  8" h
    Gourd shape, mottled matte yellow and green streaked glaze, imp WJW mk, (A) ............. 3,190.00
    Tapered shape, short collar, semi-matte gloss brown glaze w/ a green mottled green base, stamped WSH mk,(A)................................... 770.00
Vessel
  3 1/4" h x 4 1/4" d, squat shape, short collar, gloss teal and blue flambe glaze, imp WJW mk, (A) ......... 528.00
  4 1/2" h x 6 1/2"d, thick, leathery dk blue glaze, stamped WJW mk,(A) ..................................... 220.00

# Warwick China Company

## Wheeling, West Virginia
## 1887-1951

c.1905-1920

**History:** The Warwick China Manufacturing Company was incorporated in 1887 in Wheeling, West Virginia by C.E. Jackson and a group of four other men and continued operating until 1951. Vitreous china was its specialty, and it was one of the first American companies to produce these wares.

A wide assortment of pieces was made including jardinieres, clocks, umbrella stands, dresser sets, shaving mugs, bowls, dinnerware sets, platters, pitcher and bowl sets, garden ornaments, and other decorative and utilitarian items. Pieces were either hand painted or decorated with decals. Many lines included florals, fraternal order pieces, Indians, monks, and such.

At the height of its production, Warwick made over ten thousand sets of dinnerware per month. After 1912, hotel and restaurant china was made as well as china for several railroads. Some bone china was made after 1940.

Style names were impressed in the base of a piece. Hand painted letters, usually in red, indicated finish or coloring. A number, usually in red, indicated the type of decoration used. There were at least 47 different back marks used on Warwick examples. "IOGA" appeared on some early wares.

**References:** Donald C. Hoffmann, Jr. *Why Not Warwick,* published by author, 1975 and *Warwick A to W* Supplement; John R. Rader, Sr. *Warwick China*, Schiffer Publishing Ltd. 2000.

**Collectors' Club:** Warwick China Collectors' Club, Don Hoffmann, 1291 N. Elmwood Drive, Aurora, IL 60506.

Bowl
   10"d, country house, road and pole in center, blue trans-fer, molded border w/blue accents, lobed rim, "WAR-WICK CHINA" mk ............................................... 130.00
   10 1/2" H-H, Blue Onion pattern ............................. 20.00
Bulb Vase, 7 5/8" h, red flowerhead w/ green leaves, shaded brown ground, gold rim ........................................ 170.00
Dresser Tray
   8" l x 6 " w, flowing blue floral design .................... 115.00
   12 1/2" l, purple clover and green leaves, relief molded design on border w/ matte green glaze, "WARWICK CHINA" mk ............................................................ 12.00
Jar, Cov, 5 1/4" h, twisted shape, blue florals w/ green leaves, speckled gold trim, "WARWICK CHINA" mk
   ........................................................................ 50.00
Jardiniere, 4 3/8" h, pink and white shading, gold outlined petals on border, sponged gold in trim, WARWICK CHINA mk ............................................................... 30.00
Mug
   3 5/8" h, multi-colored monk reading newspaper, brown shaded ground, IOGA mk ................................... 18.00
   4 1/4" h, man playing guitar, brown shaded ground, IOGA mk ..................................................................... 95.00
Pitcher
   7 1/4" h, lobed body
      Bust of sailor smoking pipe, brown shaded ground, WARWICK CHINA mk ..................................... 67.00
      Multi-colored bust of monk w/red skullcap, brown shaded ground, IOGA mk ........................... 100.00
   10 1/4" h, multi-colored monk ............................... 235.00
   10 1/2" h, Egyptian scene around base, hanging fraternal order symbol under spout, matte multi-colors ... 150.00
Plate
   6" d, Dresden flowers, scalloped gold rim, set of 12 72.00

9 1/2" d
   Bust of Indian chief w/headdress on side, shaded brown ground ............................................... 45.00
   Monk drinking from bottle, brown to beige shades, IOGA mk ......................................................... 25.00
Platter
   8 1/2" d x 4 3/4" h, red flowers and berries, green leaves, brown shaded ground, 4 feet, IOGA mk ............. 60.00
   11 1/2" l, 4 groups of hanging red berries, green foliage, shaded brown border, shaped rim, WARWICK CHINA mk ..................................................................... 35.00
Soup Tureen, 9 1/2" d, June Bride pattern .................. 25.00
Spittoon, 8 1/2" d x 6 1/2" h, multicolored crab apples, shaded brown ground ........................................... 195.00
Vase
   4" h, bowl shape, lg red and white lily w/green foliage, tan to brown shading, IOGA mk .............................. 50.00
   8" h, pillow, multi-colored garden flowers, yellow to brown shaded ground, IOGA mk ................................ 175.00
   8 1/4" h, pillow, blue trimmed bust of woman, brown shaded ground, #A-17 ...................................... 195.00
   9" h
      Flattened lobe shape, flared rim, sm red flowers, yel-low to brown shaded ground, IOGA mk ........ 115.00
      Trumpet shape, multicolored carnations and leaves, shaded brown ground .................................. 255.00
   10 1/2" h
      Ruffled rim, twist handles, flared base, lg red flowers, red to dk brown shaded ground, IOGA mk
         ................................................................. 230.00
      Two sm handles, portrait bust of girl w/blue ribbon in hair, blue and tan trim, shaded brown ground, IOGA mk ................................................................. 285.00
   12" h
      Hour-glass shape, yellow and red scattered flowers, brown shaded ground, IOGA mk .................. 110.00
      Lobed, tapered shape, 2 sm handles, gray, pink, and green standing storks, cream ground, gold rim
         ................................................................. 295.00
         Yellow pinecones, green needles, yellow to dk brown shaded ground, IOGA mk ............. 185.00
         Tapered shape, twist handles, flared ft, bust of woman in thin blue ground holding red rose bou-quet, shaded brown ground, IOGA mk .... 265.00
Vegetable Bowl, 9 3/4"d, dk red and green flowers, folded border, gold washed rim, matte finish ..................... 20.00
Wash Set, pitcher, 12" h, bowl, 15 3/4" d, pitcher, 7 1/4" h, chamber pot, 11" d, toothbrush holder, 4 1/2" h, mug, 3 1/4" h, cov soap dish w/drain, white ground, gilt line trim, chips ................................... 250.00

# Watt Pottery Company

### Crooksville, Ohio
### 1922-1965

**History:** After working at Ransbottom Brothers Pottery until 1921, W.J. Watt purchased the Globe Stoneware Company in Crooksville, Ohio and renamed it the Watt Pottery Com-pany. The company was run by Watt, his sons, and additional family mem-

**Flower Pot, 6" h, multicolored portrait, shaded yellow to orange-brown ground, dk brown handles and edges, $245.**

bers. From 1922-35, they made stone containers in the form of jars, jugs, Dutch pots, milk pans, preserve jars and mixing bowls. At first, all pieces were done on the potter's wheel; later they used a "jar machine."

In 1925, they diversified their production and made jardinieres, chicken waterers, mixing bowls, and churns with dashers. When they added a tunnel kiln, their capacity increased to over 15,000 pieces daily.

By the mid-1930s, they discontinued stonewares and made plaster molds for new items. The Banded Watt Ware from the late 1930s was cream colored with various colored bands. There were kitchenwares of all types: mixing bowls, cookie jars, covered casseroles, pie plates, bean pots, pitchers, salt and pepper shakers, spaghetti bowls, creamer and sugar sets, mugs, grease jars, etc. In the 1940s, the banded mixing bowls were made in graduated sizes. One of the earliest combinations featured blue and white bands on cream pottery.

The Pansy Pattern in 1950 was the first attempt at hand painted pottery. The rose-colored clay had a small flower with a yellow center and green leaves. Many variations were made including Raised Pansy, Cut-leaf Pansy and Cross Hatch. No two pieces of Watt Pottery were exactly alike since they were all hand painted.

The Apple Series introduced in 1952 was made for ten years. This was the best-selling pattern and is the most sought after today. Deep red apples with green leaves were set against the cream ground. Variations included Reduced Decoration Apple, Open Apple, and Double Apple. Some of these pieces were ordered as grocery and hardware store premiums for sales promotions. The Starflower Series from the early 1950s was made in dinnerwares in several variations. The most popular was a deep red starflower with green leaves.

The mid-1950s saw two versions of the Tulip Series. The Standard Tulip had one large royal blue tulip and one deep red tulip with deep green leaves. Dutch Tulip had a cobalt blue tulip with green and red leaves in a "folk art" style.

Other series from that period included the Cherry Series and Tear Drop or American Red Bud Series. In 1955, the Rooster Series showed a crowing rooster outlined in black with green and red feathers standing in grass. American Foliage Series from 1959 featured brown leaves on brown stems.

During the late 1950s, the Morning Glory Series had an embossed lattice design with raised morning glory flowers and leaves in several color combinations. In addition to all the regular series, much Watt Pottery was made in a wide variety of color schemes and patterns.

Markings were varied during the years of Watt production. Due to a lack of uniformity it is difficult to date pieces by their bottom marks. Most pieces usually have the circular impression on the bottom. Some have a number corresponding to the mold number. Some pieces were not marked at all.

**References:** Sue & Dave Morris, *Watt Pottery*, Collector Books, 1998; Dennis Thompson and W. Bryce Watt, *Watt Pottery: A Collector's Reference with Price Guide*, Schiffer Publishing Ltd. 1994.

**Collectors' Club:** Watt Pottery Collectors USA, Dennis Thompson, Box 26067, Fairview, OH 44126, quarterly newsletter *Sproutings,* $12; Watt Collectors Association, *Watt's News*, Wendy Stinocher, P.O. Box 1995, Iowa City, IA 52244, quarterly, $10.

**Reproduction Alert:** The Watt Policeman Cookie Jar is being reproduced. A casting is made from the original jar, so the resulting reproduction is a little smaller. Four Rivers Stoneware in Hazel, Kentucky reproduces Watt Pottery that is marked. However, pieces have been found with the bottom marks ground off or obscured. The Apple pattern is the most common decoration, but Rooster, Tulip, and Dutch Tulip are also being made. The Four Rivers clay is quite close in color to the Watt originals.

Additional Watt reproductions are being made in molds taken from original pieces and include the impressed marks found on authentic Watt Pottery.

## APPLE PATTERN

Baker, Cov, dbl apple, #96 .............................. 275.00
Bowl
    4" d, ribbed, #04 ..................................... 65.00
    9 1/2" d, #73 .......................................... 75.00
    10 3/4" d, #106 ..................................... 395.00
Coffee Server, 9 3/4" h, ............................... 2500.00
Creamer, 4 1/2" h, #62 ................................. 110.00
Grease Jar, 5 1/2" h, #01 ............................. 375.00
Mixing Bowls, 9", 7", 5"d, set of 3 ................ 325.00
Pitcher
    6 1/2" h, #16 .......................................... 90.00
    8" h, ice lip, #17 .................................... 250.00

## AUTUMN FOLIAGE PATTERN

Baker, Cov, 8 1/2" d, #96 .............................. 78.00
Bean Cup, 6 1/2" h x 7 1/2" d, #75 ................ 70.00
Fondue, 9" l, #506 ....................................... 325.00
Pitcher
    5 1/2" h, #15 ......................................... 100.00
    6 1/2" h, #16 ......................................... 145.00

## CABINART

Pitcher, 5" h, cream and brown ..................... 29.00

## CHERRY PATTERN

Baker, Cov, 7 1/2" d ..................................... 98.00
Cereal Bowl, 6 1/2" d, #52 ............................ 30.00
Pitcher
    5 1/2" h, #15 ......................................... 125.00
    6 3/4" h, #16 ......................................... 315.00
    8" h, #17 .............................................. 350.00
Spaghetti Bowl, 13" d, #39 ........................... 85.00

## EAGLE PATTERN

Baker, Cov, 8 3/4" d, #601 ........................... 210.00

**Bowl, 8 1/4" d, "Autumn Leaf" pattern, $55.**

## GOODIES
Jar, 6 1/2" h, #76 .......................................270.00

## KATHY KALE
Bowl
    5 1/2" d.............................................25.00
    6 1/4" d.............................................25.00

## KITCH-N-QUEEN
Coffeepot, 10 1/2" h..................................145.00

## KLA HAM'RD
Casserole, 9" d, 2 handles ..........................48.00

## KOLOR KRAFT
Bowl, 8" d, gray, #8....................................20.00

## MEXICAN PATTERN
Bowl, 6" d, #603 .........................................30.00

## PANSY PATTERN
Casserole, Cov, 7 1/2" l x 3 3/4" h, raised pansy design
....................................................................100.00
Cup and Saucer .........................................135.00
Pie Plate, 9" d, cut-leaf................................165.00
Pitcher
    7" h, raised design ...............................195.00
    8 1/4" h..............................................295.00
Spaghetti Bowl, 13" d, cut-leaf variety..........90.00

## RIO ROSE
Cookie Jar, #21 ...........................................88.00
Pitcher, 6 3/4" h, cutleaf, #16.......................135.00
Plate, 7 3/8" d.............................................115.00
Spaghetti Bowl, 13" d, #39 ...........................80.00

## ROOSTER PATTERN
Bean Pot, Cov, 6 1/2" h, #76 ......................325.00
Bowl
    6 1/2" d, #63.....................................110.00
    8 1/4" d, #67.......................................80.00
Bowl, Cov, 7 1/2" d, #66 .............................200.00
Casserole, Cov, 8" l x 4" h ..........................130.00
Creamer, 4 1/2" h, #62 ...............................175.00

Ice Bucket, Cov, 7 1/4" h ............................325.00
Pitcher
    5 1/2" h, #15 .....................................128.00
    8" h, #69 ............................................450.00
Shakers, 4" h, barrel shape, pr....................500.00

## STAR FLOWER PATTERN
Casserole, 7 1/2" l, pink on black, #18 ...........49.00
Mug, 4 1/2" h, #501 ....................................100.00
Pitcher
    5 1/2" h, #15 .......................................85.00
    6 1/2" h, #16
        Five petal flower...............................110.00
        Four petal flower ..............................150.00
    8" h, icelip, #17 .................................135.00
Plate, 10"d..................................................75.00
Spaghetti Bowl, 13" d, white on green, #39 ..............120.00

## TEARDROP PATTERN
Pitcher
    4 1/4" h, #62 .....................................195.00
    5 1/2" h, #15 .......................................85.00
    6 3/4" h, #16 .....................................175.00

## TULIP PATTERN
Cheese Crock, Cov, 8" h x 8 1/2" d, #80 ...................700.00
Cookie Jar, 8 1/4"h......................................350.00
Creamer, 4 1/4" h, #62 ...............................158.00
French Casserole, 8" l..................................185.00
Mixing Bowl, 6" d .........................................60.00
Pitcher, 6 1/2" h, #16 ..................................225.00
Pitcher, ice lip, 8" h, #17..............................350.00

**Pitcher, 5 1/2" h, "Autumn Leaf" pattern, gold advertising, imp mk, $90.**

# Weller Pottery Company

### Zanesville, Ohio
### 1872-1948

**History:** Samuel Weller founded the Weller Pottery Company in 1872 in Fultonham, Ohio. Working by himself, he made flower pots, vases, cuspidors, crocks, and milk pans. Ten years later, he moved his operation to Zanesville, Ohio, and over the years he added additional plants. By 1890, he built a new plant and made jardinieres, pedestals, hanging baskets, vases, and umbrella stands, and he was experimenting with a variety of glazes.

At the Chicago World's Fair of 1893, he was very impressed with William Long's Lonhuda ware. The following year he bought Lonhuda Pottery and William Long came to Zanesville to supervise production. Weller's version of Lonhuda was called Louwelsa Weller, which had the standard brown glaze and was decorated with fruits, flowers, dogs, American Indians, Dutch cavaliers, portraits and such.

Weller hired fine artists to work on Louwelsa to compete with Rookwood's Standard Glaze. Vases, jars, umbrella stands, oil and electric lamps, tobacco jars, and ashtrays were made from 1896-1920. The line was expanded to include high glaze green, red and blue Louwelsa plus Matte Louwelsa with pastel grounds. Louwelsa Perfecto from 1905 had delicate shades of sea green with pink and salmon matte finishes. Blue Louwelsa was a high glaze line. More than five hundred shapes were made for one of Weller's best sellers. Some rare pieces had silver overlays.

Charles Upjohn was head of decorating from 1895-1904 and was responsible for the Dickensware lines in matte, semi-gloss, and high gloss glazes. Dickenware II was decorated by the sgraffito method with browns predominating. Subjects included Dickens characters, as well as portraits of Indians, tavern scenes, monks, and natural subjects.

In 1899, Weller purchased the old American Encaustic Tiling Company plant and made cooking utensils, flower pots, and toilet articles there.

Jacques Sicard came from training with Clement Massier in France in 1902 and made Sicardo pottery for Weller with a metallic luster glaze for about seven years. Vases, umbrella stands, jars, jewel boxes, candy dishes, plaques, candlesticks, figurines, and lamp bases were made in magenta, green, gold, silver, and purple with flowers, stars, seahorses, and dolphins.

Karl Kappes replaced Charles Upjohn in 1904 as head of decorating. By 1905, they were producing about fourteen artware lines. There was a lot of copying going on among Weller, Owens, Roseville, and Rookwood. Many artists worked at more than one of these potteries in Zanesville.

Plaster of Paris molds replaced the potter's wheel about this time. Other important lines were Aurelian from 1898, Eocean from the same year, and Turada from 1897 with applied ornaments of pierced work on a high gloss, dark ground.

New lines continued to be introduced until 1910. Jap Birdimal was created by Frederick Rhead in 1904 with a tube lining technique. Japanese decorations, animals, and birds appeared on blue, sea green or brown grounds. Rhead also introduced L'Art Nouveau which had a high gloss finish with flowing figures in pastels or dark brown.

By 1910, competition from the Japanese potters interfered with Weller's business since they were able to make near perfect copies at about half the cost. Weller was always a family business. He purchased Zanesville Art Pottery in 1920. In 1922, Weller incorporated as S.A. Weller, Inc. and had three plants operating. When Sam Weller died in 1925, Harry Weller, his nephew, became President.

A variety of Weller Hudson lines was made from 1917-34. Other new lines were added each year during the teen years. Fairfield was brought out in 1916-17 to compete with Roseville's Donatello.

John Lessell was head of Weller decorating from 1920-24 and created luster lines and others. LaSa and Lamar were two of his designs. When Lessell left and Weller died, art pottery was replaced by industrial artwares. Modeler Rudolph Lorber came to Weller after World War I and was responsible for many less expensive molded lines.

With a big reduction of profits during the Depression, the three plants were consolidated into one in 1931, and freehand decoration came to an end. Some new lines continued to be introduced, but only molded wares were made.

All during its history, Weller made brown and white cooking ware in a wide assortment of pieces such as mugs sets, teapots, tumblers, mixing bowls, beanpots, and such. During World War II, they continued to make inexpensive lines.

After the war, the foreign competition from Europe and Japan increased and interfered with Weller's business.

Essex Wire took over the pottery in 1947 and it closed in 1948. Weller used a large assortment of different marks for each of its lines and time periods.

**References:** Sharon and Bob Huxford, *The Collectors Encyclopedia of Weller Pottery*, Collector Books, 1998; Ann Gilbert McDonald, *All About Weller: A History and Collectors Guide to Weller Pottery*, Antique Publications, 1989.

**Museums:** Chrysler Museum, Norfolk, VA; Museum of History and Technology, Smithsonian Institution, Washington, DC; National Road, Norwich, OH; New Orleans Museum of Art, LA; Zanesville Art Center, OH.

**Reproduction Alert:** There is a faked Weller 7" vase done in the style of Bonito in a shiny high gloss glaze. Almost all original Bonito is matte glaze.

The Weller Coppertone vase with figural frogs and water lilies has recently been reproduced. The new example is smaller than the original and the glazes are different. Also the new pieces are quite heavy.

## APPLE BLOSSOM
Jardiniere, 9" d x 7 1/2" h ............................................ 195.00

## ARDSLEY
Bowl, 12" d, (A) .......................................................... 260.00
Jardiniere and Pedestal, 30" h, hairline, (A) ............ 1,650.00

## ART NOUVEAU
Vase, 10" h, panels w/flowers and female, (A) ........... 357.00

## AURELIAN
Pedestal, 27" h, twisted shape, painted roses, (A) ..... 308.00
Umbrella Stand, 24" h, twisted shape, grapes, leaves, and vines, chips, (A) ...................................................... 605.00
Vase
    6" h, spherical, rose decor ..................................... 550.00
    9 1/2" h, lt yellow irises, lt yellow border, dk brown ground, Aurelian/Weller/678, K9, (A) ................ 913.00
    14" h, bulbous shape, spread rim, painted palm leaves, sgd Albert Halbrich, (A) ................................. 2,970.00

## BALDIN
Vase
    7" h, apples, brown ground, WELLER ................... 395.00
    11 1/2" h, apples ................................................. 795.00
    13" h, apples, (A) ................................................ 230.00

## BARCELONA
Vase, 7" h, loop handles ............................................ 145.00

## BLUE WARE
Jardiniere and Pedestal, (A) ..................................... 770.00
Vase, 10" h, (A) ........................................................ 231.00
Wall Pocket, 10 1/2" h, (A) ........................................ 242.00

## BONITO
Bowl, 3 3/4" d x 5 1/2" h, (A) ................................... 220.00
Candlestick,1 1/2" h x 4" d, script, pr, (A) ................. 220.00
Vase, 7" h, hairlines, (A) ........................................... 44.00

## BRIGHTON
Figure
    6" h, woodpecker, (A) ........................................... 297.00
    6 1/2" h, kingfisher, (A) ......................................... 467.00

**Console Bowl, 12 1/2" l, "Bouquet" pattern, $65.**

8" h, parrot, (A) ..................................................... 660.00

## BURNTWOOD
Jardiniere, 11 1/2" l.................................................... 300.00
Plate, 7" d, (A) ........................................................... 55.00
Vase
   5 1/2" h.................................................................. 165.00
   12" h, birds design ............................................... 225.00

## CAMEO
Basket, Hanging, 6" d x 5" h, blue, (A) ...................... 44.00
Vase, 7" h, blue, (A)...................................................... 44.00

## CHENGTU
Vase
   6 1/2" h, Chinese red, (A) ....................................... 55.00
   8 3/4" h, Chinese red ............................................. 145.00

## CLAYWOOD
Bowl, 4 1/4"d, pinecone design, (A) .......................... 220.00
Jardiniere, 6 3/4" h, California mission scenes, chips and
   hairline, (A)............................................................ 175.00
Pot, 4" h, spiderweb design........................................ 170.00

## CLINTON IVORY
Cider Set, tankard, 10" h, 4 mugs, 5" h, grape and foliage
   design ................................................................... 395.00

## COPPERTONE
Console Bowl, 11" l, figural flower frog on lily leaf ...... 895.00
Figure, 5 1/2" l, turtle, (A) ......................................... 310.00
Vase
   6 1/2" h, ovoid shape, flat rim, (A)........................... 440.00
   6 3/4 " h, bulbous base, trumpet neck, 2 loop handles,
     incised mk, (A)................................................... 330.00
   7" h, trumpet shape................................................ 295.00
   8" h, ball shape, green and copper glaze, (A)........ 495.00
   9" h, single frog on side, (A)................................... 935.00
   12 1/4" h, trumpet shape, (A) ................................ 605.00

## CORNISH
Urn, 7" h, tan shades................................................. 225.00

## DAHL ROSE
Candlestick, 7 1/2" h, pr, (A)...................................... 440.00

## DICKENSWARE
Jardiniere, 8" h x 11 1/2"d, painted nasturtiums, (A)
   ................................................................................. 495.00

**Vase, 8 1/4" h, "Coppertone" pattern, $1,895.**

Tankard, 11 3/4" h, incised cavalier in colors, flowering vines
   on handle, (A) ...................................................... 495.00
Vase
   6 1/2" h, incised and painted bust of Tame Wolf, (A)
   ................................................................................. 660.00
   11" h, tapered shape, leaf and berry design, (A)
   ................................................................................. 605.00

## DICKENSWARE II
Humidor
   6" h, bisque monk design, #176, chips, (A)
   ................................................................................. 275.00
   7" h, figural bisque Turkhead, turquoise and brown w/red
     trim, rim chips, (A) ......................................... 1,045.00
Jug, 7 1/2" h, mallard flying over fish ........................ 550.00
Mug
   5 1/2" h, incised flying ducks design, figural fish
     handle, (A)........................................................ 132.00
   6" h, forest scene.................................................. 325.00
   6 1/2" h, monk design ............................................ 125.00
Pitcher
   11 1/4" h, bisque, incised deer and stylized tree motif,
     blended teal, cream, and cream ground, slip tan swirl
     design on body and handle, (A) ......................... 660.00
   12" h, tankard shape, portrait of Chief Black Bear, imp
     mk, (A)............................................................ 1,540.00
Stein, 6 1/2" h, incised deer head on shaded matte brown
   and green ground, imp Dickensware Weller mk, (A)
   ................................................................................. 180.00
Vase
   6 1/2" h, incised portrait
     Native American, sgd "Black Bird," (A).............. 660.00
     Profile of monk, (A) .......................................... 440.00
   8 3/4" h, bisque, brown monk holding wine glass, slip
     decorated stylized floral vines, blended ochre and teal
     green ground, (A) .............................................. 825.00
   9" h, incised design of 2 children playing football, (A)
   ................................................................................. 880.00
   16" h, corset shape, incised Revolutionary War
     soldiers, (A) ...................................................... 715.00

## DUPONT
Basket, Hanging, 8" d x 3 1/2" h, molded floral design, (A)
   ................................................................................. 110.00
Bowl, 6 1/2" d, molded floral design, (A) ...................... 33.00

Vase, 10 "h ....................................................... 150.00

## ELBERTA
Strawberry Jar, 3 1/2" h, (A) ...........................88.00

## EOCEAN
Jardiniere, 8 1/2" h ....................................... 523.00
Mug, 6" h, hanging plums and leaves ....................... 450.00
Vase
    12" h, painted lavender water lilies, green ground, (A)
    ....................................................3,190.00
    12 1/2" h, pink, yellow, and green wild roses, lt green ground, sgd Stemm, (A) ................................. 1,430.00
    16" h, pink and gray painted hanging flowers and berries, pink to gray shaded ground, sgd "Leffler," (A)
    ......................................................1,430.00
    17" h, painted columbine flowers and stems, shaded ground, sgd "Claude Leffler," (A) ................. 10,450.00

## ETNA
Tankard, 14" h, gray grapes ......................................295.00
Vase
    14 1/2" h, cylinder shape, roses and olive branch
    .......................................................1,225.00
    15" h, molded blue to purple grapes, green to gray ground, (A) ...................................... 1,430.00

## FLEMISH
Basket, hanging, 4 1/2" h, molded floral design, (A)
.....................................................................88.00
Jardiniere, 11" h, apples and grapes ......................... 750.00
Vase, 7" h, matte green with magnolia blooms ..........320.00

## FLORETTA
Ewer, 4 1/4" h, floral design, #38, (A) .......................... 55.00
Jug, 6" h, (A) ........................................................ 121.00
Vase, 6" h, yellow-gold emb pears, blended dk brown ground, (A) .......................................... 165.00

## FOREST
Jardiniere, 11" h x 12" d, (A) ................................... 1,045.00
Planter, 2" h, dish shape ...................................... 300.00
Umbrella Stand, 20" h, cracks ................................. 440.00
Vase, 10 1/2" h, hour-glass shape ........................... 350.00

## GLENDALE
Bud Vase, 7" h, dbl, molded yellow bird and nest, hairline, (A) ................................................143.00
Vase
    7 1/2" h, dbl tree trunk with bird nest and eggs...... 450.00
    13" h, molded bird and nest w/eggs design, (A) . 1,320.00

## GOLDEN GLOW
Bowl, 3 1/2" h, ftd, molded floral design, (A) ...............77.00

## GREORA
Strawberry Jar, 5" h, (A) ....................................... 165.00

## HOBART
Candy Dish, 9 1/2" h, boy w/grapes, (A) ................... 220.00
Flower Frog, 6" h, figure of boy and swan, (A) ...........110.00

## HUDSON
Floor Vase, 19" h, painted birds on limb w/fruit, leaves, and branches, repaired top, (A) ....................... 1,430.00

Vase
    7" h, cherry on leaves design, sgd "Pilsbury" ........ 700.00
    8" h, 2 sm handles, painted robin on flowering branch, peagreen shaded to pink ground, sgd "LBM," (A)
    ..................................................... 1,760.00
    8 3/4" h, corset shape, painted floral bouquet, blue shaded to yellow ground, sgd "Timberlake," (A)
    ..................................................... 605.00
    9" h, lily of the valley, sgd "McLaughlin" ................. 500.00
    9 1/2" h, bulbous base, cylinder neck, slip decorated pink and lavender flowers w/yellow steps, matte blue ground, (A) ........................... 412.00
    10" h, white, painted pr of yellow birds in tree, (A)
    ..................................................... 1,540.00
    11 1/2" h, swollen middle, spread ft and rim, painted winter landscape, of road and fence, sgd "McLaughlin," (A) ..................................... 3,575.00
    12" h, blue and pink painted flowers w/green leaves, shaded green to blue ground, (A) ................ 1,210.00
    15" h, multi-colored painted irises, sgd "Timberlake," chips, (A) ................................................. 4,400.00
    15 1/2" h, painted grapes, leaves, and vines, gray to pink shaded ground, (A) ............................. 990.00

## IVORY
Jardiniere, 9" h, (A) ............................................. 154.00
Umbrella Stand, 20" h, ....................................... 242.00
Window Box, 20 1/2" l, molded classical design, (A)
................................................................ 495.00

## JAP BIRDIMAL
Jardiniere, 9 1/2" h, blue landscape, (A) ................... 357.00
Mug, 5" h, cobalt squeezebag stylized trees, blue-gray ground, (A) ............................................. 440.00
Pitcher, 11" h, squeezebag design off lying crane, shaded gray ground, imp Weller mk, (A) .......................... 440.00
Vase, 8 3/4" h, carved and painted row of stylized blue roses over white geese, green ground, chips, (A) ........ 2,750.00

## KNIFEWOOD
Planter, 5 3/4" h, emb birds and leaves, (A) ...............395.00
Vase, 7" h, molded yellow butterflies ........................ 100.00

## LAMAR
Vase
    6" h, ovoid, metallic black tree landscape, boats and mountains in bkd, shaded burgundy-maroon ground, (A) ................................................. 220.00
    9 1/2" h, baluster shape, flared rim, metallic black palms w/mountains, burgundy-maroon ground, (A)..... 385.00

## LASA
Lamp Base, 7 1/2" h, metallic landscape scene, (A) .. 385.00
Vase
    5" h, tapered shape, short collar, metallic landscape design, (A) ............................................. 495.00
    8 1/2" h ........................................................... 395.00
    10 1/2" h, trumpet shape, metallic landscape design, (A)
    ..................................................... 412.00

## LEBANON
Vase, 6 1/2" h, (A) ................................................. 120.00

## LORBEEK

Vase

5" h, bowl shape, pink............................................175.00

8 1/2" h, Art Deco-style, mauve, (A) .....................193.00

## LOUWELSA

Ewer

7 3/4" h, brown flowerhead ....................................295.00

14" h, daffodil design, sgd "M. Mitchell," (A) .........286.00

Jardiniere and Pedestal, 32" h, fluted rim, roses and thorns, (A) ................................................................715.00

Jug

5 1/2" h, blue cherries, blue shaded ground, (A) ....................................................................1,320.00

6 1/4" h, brown shaded cascading grapes from branches, sage green and brown shaded ground, (A).......220.00

Tankard, 16 1/2" h, painted bird seated on fence, sgd "Abel," (A) .....................................................................825.00

Umbrella Stand, mums and leaves, sgd "Ferrell," (A) ....................................................................1,540.00

Vase

4 1/2" h, bulbous shape, blue pansies design, matte finish ....................................................................225.00

5 1/4" h, yellow, white, and green daffodil, dk brown and green body, (A) ..................................................77.00

7" h, clover and leaves design, dk brown ground ....................................................................320.00

7 1/2" h, blue cherries, dk blue ground, (A) ........1,100.00

9" h, leaves and berries in blue shades, dk blue ground, (A) ....................................................................1,760.00

10 1/2" h, pink and dk red roses, dk red ground, (A) ....................................................................3,575.00

10 3/4" h, painted wisteria, shaded brown ground, mkd, (A)....................................................................240.00

13 1/2" h, portrait of Jean Francois Millet, sgd "L.J. Burgess," (A) .............................................................1,760.00

15" h, ruffled rim, lg daisies, (A) ..........................1,320.00

19 1/2" h, 3 feet, painted wildroses, artist sgd, (A) ....................................................................770.00

## MAMMY LINE

Creamer, 3 1/2" h ....................................................565.00

Sugar Bowl, Cov, 3 1/2" h........................................875.00

Syrup Pot, 6" h .......................................................425.00

Teapot, 8" h ............................................................650.00

## MUSKOTA

Flower Frog

4 1/2" w, dragonfly, (A)...........................................297.00

6" d, starfish, tan, (A) .............................................231.00

6 1/2" h, pagoda, (A) ..............................................253.00

7 1/4" h, fishing boy ...............................................395.00

7 1/2" h, standing nude on rock .............................695.00

Inkwell, 5" d, turtle body, frog on lid, (A) ................1,100.00

## NOVELTY

Figure

12" h

Squirrel seated on haunches eating nut, brown shades, (A) .............................................2,750.00

Standing bulldog, gray and tan, (A)...............1,430.00

20" h, seated pelican, blue-green shaded body, yellow beak, orange-brown webbed feet, (A)............5,500.00

Planter

6" h, figural duck, matte green glaze, (A) ...............99.00

8" l, figural dog, med brown, script mark, (A)...........66.00

## OAK LEAF

Bowl, 12" d ..............................................................75.00

Vase, 9" h, cream and brown ..................................110.00

## PANSY

Basket, 7 3/4" h, single handle, lt green...................110.00

## PARIAN

Vase, 13" h, gray stone w/set in tile effect.................395.00

## PATRICIA

Bowl, 10 1/2" l, (A)..................................................187.00

Vase

8 1/2" h, white glaze, swan head and neck handles ....................................................................130.00

18" h, tan and green streaking, figural swanhead handles, (A)....................................................495.00

## PUMILA

Console Bowl, 11" d, w/flower frog, molded floral design, (A) ....................................................................200.00

## ROMA

Bud Vase, 8" h, dbl, (A) ...........................................65.00

Console Bowl, 13" d, w/liner, molded florals, (A)........220.00

Jardiniere and Pedestal

27" h ......................................................................475.00

35" h, (A)................................................................880.00

Vase, 8" h, pink and blue flowers, cream ground.......120.00

Wall Vase, 10"h, (A) ...............................................176.00

Window Box, 15" l, (A) ............................................495.00

## SABRINIAN

Vase, 6" w, molded seahorses, (A) .........................253.00

## SELMA

Lamp Base, 11" h, (A) ...........................................1,605.00

## SICARD

Dish, Cov, 8 1/2" d, twisted and ribbed form, metallic floral design, chip, (A) .........................................715.00

Lamp Base, 14" h, metallic floral design, (A) ............935.00

Tray, 5 1/4" d, emb bust of Abraham Lincoln, purple luster glaze, (A) ...........................................................605.00

Vase

4" h, 3 sided, metallic floral design, (A) .................357.00

5" h, twisted shape, metallic floral design, (A) ....1,045.00

5 1/2" h, metallic mistletoe design, (A) ...................363.00

7" h, metallic floral design, (A) ...............................715.00

8 1/2" h, twisted and ribbed form, metallic floral design, (A) ....................................................................715.00

11 1/2" h, 4 lobed design, poppies design, (A) ...2,945.00

15" h, bulbous shape, flared rim, raised metallic leaf design, (A)....................................................7,150.00

## SILVERTONE

Bowl, 12" d, w/flower frog, 4" d, (A) .........................330.00

### Vase

7 1/2" h, handled, Brown Eyed Susans ................. 325.00
10" h, dbl vert handles, (A) ............................... 264.00

### SYDONIA

Vase, 5" h, fan shape, (A) ......................................... 110.00

### TURADA

Jardiniere, 7 1/2" h, (A) ......................................... 209.00
Lamp Base, 8" h x 10" d, 4 sm feet, raised burnt orange, blue, and lt yellow floral and scrolling on shoulder, dk brown ground, (A) ................................. 440.00

### TUTONE

Vase, 4 1/2" h, chalice shape ................................... 175.00
Wall Pocket, 10 1/4" h, paper label, repair, (A) ............. 88.00

### UTILITY WARE

Teapot, 6" h x 9" w, figural pumpkin, pale orange ground, brown-green stalk handle and knob, c1930 ........... 750.00

### VOILE

Jardiniere, 8" d x 7 1/4" h, (A) ................................ 286.00

### WOODCRAFT

Bowl, 3 1/2" d, molded squirrel design, (A) ................. 160.00
Bud Vase, 10 1/4" h ............................................. 195.00
Flower Holder, 10 1/2" h, figural tree trunk, blended tan ground w/pastel berries, (A) ................................. 77.00
Jardiniere and Pedestal, 29" h, molded squirrel design, (A)
.................................................................. 4,675.00
Umbrella, 23" h, molded pheasants in forest, (A)
.................................................................. 4,125.00
Wall Pocket
9" h, squirrel .............................................. 350.00
12" h, owl ................................................. 390.00
13" w, 2 squirrels, (A) ................................. 3,300.00

### WOODROSE

Jardiniere, 3 1/2" h ............................................. 150.00

### ZONA

Coffee Cup and Saucer, set of 4, (A) ...................... 110.00
Jardiniere and Pedestal, 32" h, (A) ......................... 660.00

**Coffee Set, pot, 6 1/2" h, creamer, 3 1/2" h, cov sugar bowl, 5 1/4" h, "Zona" pattern, $410.**

### Plate

7 1/2" d, set of 4, (A) ......................................... 88.00
9" d, set of 5, (A) ............................................. 121.00
Platter, 12 1/2" d ............................................... 44.00
Tea Set, pot, 5" h, creamer, cov sugar bowl, (A) ........ 198.00

# Western Stoneware (Including Macomb and Weir)

## Monmouth, Illinois
## 1906-Present

**History:** Western Stoneware Company was formed in 1906 in Monmouth, Illinois by merging seven companies: Monmouth Pottery and Weir Pottery; Macomb Pottery and Macomb Stoneware; D. Cultertson Stoneware from White Hall, Illinois; Clinton Stoneware from Missouri; and Fort Dodge Stoneware from Iowa. They identified their acquired plants with numbers One to Seven. Examples were marked with the stenciled logo, the maple leaf with WESTERN STONEWARE COMPANY and the Plant #.

By 1924, Western was producing more than 225 different sizes and varieties of stoneware containers including milk pans, jugs, jars, churns, preserve jars, butter jars, flower pots and such. Necessary items for dairy production, food and liquid preparation and storage were all made. Some were made by hand and some in molds. Western stoneware was sold through jobbers and salesmen.

The use of glass fruit jars cut into stoneware use during the 1920s, since glass cost less to produce, was easier to transport, was lightweight, and was made by machine at a lower cost. Dairy needs for stoneware were also reduced. Tin containers also became readily available.

Western experienced difficulties with labor problems, financial problems, and divided management resulting from the merger. In 1926, they realigned their plants again and shifted their concentration. Plant One made the Maple Leaf brand of standard kitchen and pantry utilitarian items, and the Colonial Design items. Westko chicken waterers also were made.

Plant Two was used for the new artware line that was made for a twenty-year period starting in 1926 under the "Monmouth Pottery" label. Lines such as "Burnt Wood Effect" in brushware patterns in brown including Egyptian designs, and "Dull Finish" in blue and green found form in fern dishes, jardinieres, ashtrays, candleholders, bowls, and lamps. "Bright Finish" in black, green, blue, gray, lavender, yellow and blue mottled was used on lamp bases, bowls, pitchers, bookends, candleholders, vases, urns, wall pockets, and cigarette holders. Many of these examples had paper labels. Westko Garden Pottery was made at Plant Three in Macomb.

Western Stoneware was also the last maker of Old Sleepy Eye items, but referred to their examples as "Indian Head" without using the chief's name. They made pitchers in five sizes, steins in two sizes, a sugar bowl, hot plate or trivet, jar, bowl, three sizes of mugs and a vase. Production was stopped by 1937, but not all of these items were made every year. Though cobalt blue on white was the most common color, there was also brown on white, green on white, and brown on yellow. Solid colors also were made.

In 1952, the molds were redesigned, and steins were made in chestnut brown, but only for one year. Very limited numbers of board of director steins were made from 1968-1973. Mugs were also made for the Old Sleepy Collectors Club of America, Inc. from 1976-1981. (See Old Sleepy Eye).

During the 1940s and '50s, there were frequent changes of ownership at Western. The focus was shifted to premium items in 1956. The Marcrest premium line was made for the Marshall Burns Company of Chicago including ovenproof stoneware in a wide assortment of pieces. Eva Zeisel designed a collectible line of stonewares for Western.

Additional changes in ownership occurred in the '60s and '70s. In 1985, the company ceased operations. Local residents formed a group to take over and renamed the company De Novo Ceramics Ltd. They are still in business making stone and earthenwares.

## Macomb Pottery, Macomb, Illinois, 1880-1906

**History:** Macomb Pottery Company was incorporated in 1880. It was one of the potteries that merged to form Western Stoneware in 1906. Its products included mass-produced Bristol or Albany slip glazed wares that were typical of the area. Items made were butter crocks in many sizes, jars up to thirty-gallon size, jugs from pint to fifteen-gallon size, a patented stone mason jar, umbrella stands, match safes, animals, cuspidors, pudding pans, churns, bean pots, flower pots with saucers, and jardinieres. The mark used was MACOMB POTTERY CO. MACOMB, ILL. stenciled or embossed.

## Weir Pottery, Monmouth, Illinois, 1899-1905

**History:** Banker William Weir incorporated Weir Pottery in Monmouth, Illinois in 1899 and then died two years later. In 1902, they had a major fire, but rebuilt immediately.

In 1903, Weir received a contract to produce 500,000 pieces of cast stoneware mugs, vases, bowls, and butter crocks for premiums given away by the Sleepy Eye Milling Company of Sleepy Eye, Minnesota. These pieces were glazed in the Flemish blue and gray and had the bust of a Sioux Indian chief. They were marked "Old Sleepy Eye." They also made pitchers with the chief's profile. (See Old Sleepy Eye)

One million patented Weir Stone Fruit Jars with bail tops were produced for the H.J. Heinz Company that were called the Weir Seal Jars. Cruets for various companies, jugs, and butter crocks also were made.

The logo for the company was the WEIR POTTERY CO. stamped within a circle. Weir was sold in 1905 for consolidation into the Western Stoneware Company in 1906. The Weir factory became Plant Number Two for Western Stoneware.

**References:** Jim Martin and Bette Cooper, *Monmouth-Western Stoneware*, Wallace-Homestead, 1983.

**Collectors' Club:** Collectors of Illinois Pottery and Stoneware, David McGuire, 1527 East Converse Street, Springfield, IL 62703, $15 per year, newsletter.

## Western Stoneware

Bowl, 5 1/2" d, w/underplate, pea green glaze, raised leaf mk ............................................................................. 5.00

Bowl, Cov, 7 1/2" H-H, brown sponging ...................... 50.00

Jug, 10" h, tan base, dk brown top, blue leaf mk, $45.

Churn, 13 1/2" h, blue leaf, 2 WESTERN STONEWARE CO. MONMOUTH, on front ........................................... 375.00

Crock

11 1/2" h, blue leaf Western Stoneware Monmouth, and blue ...................................................................... 50.00

13" h, blue 5, blue Western and leaf design ........... 45.00

13 1/2" h, blue 6, Western Stoneware and leaf design ............................................................................ 68.00

Floor Vase, brown relief molded leaves on shoulder, semi-gloss blue glaze body, mkd .................................... 150.00

Jardiniere, 6 1/2" h, Egyptian pattern, dk brown brush ware, Albany slip int ......................................................... 55.00

Mixing Bowl, horiz ribbing, dk brown, cream drip on rim, mkd ............................................................................ 10.00

Pie Plate, 9 1/2" d, dk brown glaze ............................. 50.00

Pitcher, 10" h, sq handle, vert ribbed base, matte brown glaze, mkd ................................................................ 15.00

Plate, 10 1/2" d, brown sponging, Western Stoneware Monmouth, Illinois U.S.A. leaf mk ..................................... 5.00

Platter, 11 3/4" l, Desert Tan glaze, maple leaf, Monmouth, Ill. USA mk ................................................................. 5.00

Vase, "Brush Ware"

8" h, corset shape, brick red tulip heads and curlicues, matte blue ground .............................................. 75.00

10 1/8" h, cylinder shape, tan ground w/vert streaks, matte blue ext, gloss blue int ............................... 35.00

### MACOMB STONEWARE

Bowl, 10 7/8" d, slip glazed int and ext, unglazed rim ............................................................................ 21.00

Crock, 5" h, salt glaze, imp MACOMB POTTERY CO. mk ............................................................................ 22.00

Jug

7" h, wide mouth, brown glaze, imp MACOMB STONEWARE CO. MACOMB, c1890 ............................. 22.00

8" h, Albany slip glaze ............................................ 26.00

### MARCREST PATTERN

Baker, 10" d, divided .................................................. 20.00

Bean Pot, 3" h, raised daisy and dot design, set of 4 ............................................................................ 140.00

Bowl, 8 3/4" H-H ......................................................... 10.00

**Plate, 10" d, Eva Zeisel design, blue and tan, $8.**

Casserole and Warmer, 8 1/2" d, daisy and dot design ...................................................................... 15.00
Cereal Bowl, 6" d, daisy and dot design ......................... 6.00
Coffee Cup, daisy and dot design ................................... 3.00
Cream Pitcher, 4 1/8" h ................................................... 15.00
Mixing Bowl, 8" d ........................................................... 24.00
Mug, 5" h ........................................................................ 10.00
Pitcher, Daisy and Dot design
    6 1/4" h ..................................................................... 10.00
    8 1/2" h ..................................................................... 10.00
Plate, 9 1/2" d, daisy and dot design .......................... 10.00
Shakers, Pr. ................................................................... 28.00
Tankard, 5" h ................................................................. 10.00
Vegetable Bowl, 10" l, divided, daisy and dot design ... 10.00

**MOJAVE PATTERN**
Platter, 11 3/4" l .............................................................. 8.00

**WEIR**
Canning Jar
    7 1/2" h, brown and tan .............................................. 25.00
    8" h, stoneware, dk brown top and lid, tan base, metal
        closure ................................................................... 39.00
    9" h, Bristol glaze ..................................................... 25.00
    9 1/2" h, Bristol glaze, metal closure ......................... 56.00

# T.J. Wheatley and Company

## 1880-1882

# Wheatley Pottery Company

## 1903-1936
## Cincinnati, Ohio

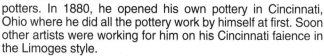

**History:** T.J. Wheatley was first associated with the Coultry Works and taught a decoration class there for other potters. In 1880, he opened his own pottery in Cincinnati, Ohio where he did all the pottery work by himself at first. Soon other artists were working for him on his Cincinnati faience in the Limoges style.

Wheatley patented a slip painted underglaze decoration method, but the patent did not hold up in court. The Cincinnati Art Pottery that was formed in 1879 provided some financial support for Wheatley. Even though he sold an extensive line to Tiffany and Company in New York, he left the pottery in 1882. Pieces from this period were marked with incised initials "T.J.W. & Co." or had the full incised signature "T.J. Wheatley & Co." Some pieces had dates too.

Wheatley built a pottery in Kentucky in 1882 that was destroyed by fire in 1884. In 1897, he was working for Weller Pottery in Zanesville, Ohio.

In 1903, T.J. Wheatley and Isaac Kahn established Wheatley Pottery Company back in Cincinnati, Ohio. They made art wares called Wheatley ware. Examples had colored matte glazes over the relief designs in dark shades. Garden ware and architectural items also were made. Some pieces only had paper labels.

Kahn took over after Wheatley died in 1917. Garden pottery was expanded to include pedestals, fountains, jardinieres, flower boxes, and lawn sets. Wheatley's Plymouth gray ware in ivory and buff tones was a specialty.

In 1927, they were purchased by the Cambridge Tile Manufacturing Company of Covington, Kentucky, renamed the Wheatley Tile and Pottery Company, and operated there until 1930. In 1930 they left Cincinnati for Hartwell, Ohio where all operations were stopped by 1936.

Many pieces from the Wheatley Pottery Company were unmarked. They usually had a paper label with "Wheatley/Cincinnati Ohio" with the firm's cipher.

**Museums:** Cincinnati Art Museum, OH.

Bowl
    6" d, corset shape, emb leaves on ext, thick matte green
        glaze, (A) .............................................................. 165.00
    9 1/2" d, low profile, emb leaves on ext, thick matte green
        glaze, stamped WP mk, (A) ................................. 220.00
Chamberstick, 4" h, emb leaves and scroll handle, leathery
    matte green glaze, chip on bobeche, unmkd, (A) .. 467.00
Figure, 12" h x 15" w, bust of Dante, matte green glaze,
    c1920 ................................................................... 2,400.00
Floor Vase, 26" h, architectural form, lt blue matte glaze drip
    over clay ground, imp mk, (A) ................................. 880.00
Garden Sculpture, 7 3/4" h, figural frog, rect base, matte
    green glaze, chips, (A) ............................................ 935.00
Jardiniere
    6" h, tapered rim, frothy matte green glaze, unmkd, (A)
        ............................................................................. 825.00
    7" h, dbl lobe shape, 4 buttressed handles, thick, matte
        green glaze, repaired base hole, (A)
        .......................................................................... 3,080.00
    8 1/2" h x 11 1/2" d, molded vert leaves, matte green
        glaze, hairlines, (A) ........................................... 1,760.00
Pitcher, 11 1/2" h, corset shape, emb grape clusters and
    vines, frothy matte green glaze, imp WP (A) ......... 770.00
Planter, 14" h x 24" d, oct, raised woven design, buff terra
    cotta finish, (A) ....................................................... 770.00
Stein, 7 1/4" h, emb coat of arms on front, pretzel handle,
    matte green glaze, incised "Compliments of the Fleischmann Co." (A) ........................................................ 165.00
Urn, 11" h, bulbous, collar rim, loop handles, frothy matte
    green glaze, hairline, (A) ........................................ 495.00

Vase
    5 1/2" h, bulbous shape, emb wide leaves w/alternating
        buds, thick and frothy matte green glaze, (A)
        .......................................................................... 1,320.00

5 3/4" h, squat base, flared neck and rim, loop handles from base to rim, frothy matte green glaze, unmkd, (A) ....................................................2,200.00

8 1/4" h, bulbous, tapered body, spread ft, frothy matte green glaze, imp WP, restored base, (A)...........495.00

9" w, bowl shape, short, straight neck, molded leaves and buds on stems, matte green glaze, (A) ...................................................................1,320.00

9 3/4" h, tapered ribbed rim, frothy matte green glaze, unmkd, (A).........................................................495.00

10" h, bulbous, frothy matte green glaze, unmkd, (A) ..............................................................................550.00

10 3/4" h, cylinder shape w/4 buttressed feet, curdled matte green glaze, unmkd, (A) ........................2,420.00

13" h, buttresses w/stems and buds on sides, matte green glaze, (A)...............................................3,575.00

14 1/2" h, bulbous base, cylinder neck, 4 buttressed handles, dripping matte green glaze, imp WP, 615 W restored hairlines, (A) ......................................3,080.00

# Wheeling Pottery Company

## Wheeling, West Virginia
## 1879-1909

LaBelle CHINA

**History:** The Wheeling Pottery Company was organized in 1879 in Wheeling, West Virginia, where it made plain and decorated white granite ware. In 1887, it formed a second company with the same management called La Belle Pottery Company and made plain and decorated Adamtine China and utilitarian wares. Two years later, the two companies joined together.

In 1903, Wheeling Potteries Company organized by combining Wheeling, La Belle, Riverside Pottery Company of Wheeling, and Avon Potteries of Tiltonsville, Ohio. Riverside made sanitary wares and Avon made artwares. The various factories continued making their semi-porcelain, sanitary ware, artware, and utilitarian pieces.

Products included Flow Blue wares, tankards, "Virginia Girl" plates, cracker jars, children's items, and a full line of dinnerware. In 1909, the name was changed to Wheeling Sanitary Manufacturing Company. The company went into receivership and was reorganized to make sanitary ware.

A variety of marks was used.

Celery Dish, 13 1/2" l, flowing blue design, "LaBelle" mk ..............................................................................275.00

Charger, 11 1/4" d, multicolored bust of woman wearing cap, dk blue flowing border w/gold overlay, "LaBelle" mk ..............................................................................375.00

Chocolate Cup and Saucer, HP dk red roses, green leaves, gold rims, fancy handle, LaBelle ..............................10.00

Cup and Saucer, flowing blue, "LaBelle" ......................25.00

Pitcher

6 1/2" h, bust of naval officer on side, battleship Maine on reverse, red, white, and blue panels, "LaBelle" mk ..............................................................................150.00

7" h, squat shape, HP purple violets, green leaves, molded rim w/gold dusting....................................35.00

Plate

6" d, 4 bunches of purple flowers, shaded purple ground, artist sgd..................................................................15.00

Plate, 10 1/4" d, multicolored scene of wild boars in center, flowing blue border w/raised design and gold accents, "LaBelle" mk, $375.

Wash Set, pitcher, 12" h, bowl, 15 1/2" d, sm pitcher, 7 1/4" h, mug, 3 5/8" h, cov soap dish, 6" d, toothbrush holder, 5 5/8" h, gold outlined raised blue periwinkles, raised gold swirls and molded swirls, $495.

8 1/4" d, Gen. Karney's Headquarters, Fort Scott, Kas. 1846, brown transfer, 4 bunches of lt pink and blue flowers on border, lobed gilt rim ...........................18.00

9" d, flowing blue border, scalloped rim, "LaBelle" mark ................................................................................30.00

Platter

Oval, 11" l, white granite ware ...................................5.00

15" l, gilt outlined scalloped border, "LaBelle China," mk ..................................................................................8.00

Serving Plate, 10" d, flowing blue, "LaBelle" mark .....150.00

Vase, 11 1/2" h, bulbous, slender neck, long tapered handles, clusters of flowers on sides, shaded brown bkd
.................................................................... 175.00

Water Pitcher, 7" h, HP lg pink tulips w/lg green leaves
.......................................................... 40.00

# White's Pottery

## Utica, New York
## 1834-1910

**History:** Noah White was the first in his family to make pottery in Utica, New York in 1834. At first he made stoneware at Addington Pottery. In 1839, he bought out Addington and another factory, and joined with Nicholas, his son, and two other potters. They made salt-glazed crocks and jugs with distinctive cobalt-blue designs. The early wares of the 1830s and 1840s were marked "N. WHITE, UTICA."

Another son, William, joined the pottery in 1843. In 1848, White made his two sons partners and changed the name to N. White and Sons. The pottery had a variety of names, as family members came and went during the firm's history. From 1850-1870, wares were marked "WHITE UTICA" or "WHITE'S UTICA."

An additional operation included a branch pottery in Binghamton, New York and used the marks "White's Binghamton" or "N. White and Co. Binghamton." A wide range of wares was being made by the 1860s at both locations. Noah died in 1865, and additional name changes followed. From 1876-1882, they used the mark "WHITES UTICA N.Y."

By 1907, they stopped making stoneware. The firm continued in business as C.N. White Clay Products Co. until 1910 and then closed completely.

**References:** Barbara Franco, "White's Pottery: Stoneware From Utica, New York," *New York-Pennsylvania Collector*, March 1996.

**Museums:** Munson-Williams-Proctor Museum, Utica, NY.

Bottle, 6" h, w/handle, blue accented relief of Dutch scene and "Federal Law forbids sale or reuse of this bottle" around scene, blue incised bands top and base, (A) .......................................................... 66.00

Butter Churn

15 1/2" h, blue accented incised geometric lines, imp "WHITES UTICA" on shoulder, c1865, (A) ........ 198.00

16 1/2" h, thick blue dbl flower design and imp "WHITES UTICA" on shoulder, c1865, (A) ........................ 908.00

Cake Crock, Cov, 7 1/2" d x 5" h, blue accented deer hunt scene, hairlines, (A) .............................................. 303.00

Canteen, 9 1/2" h, Bristol glaze w/blue accented drinking scene on front, imp blue accented "Take me back to Dep's Waxahachie Tex" on shoulder, chips, (A)..... 358.00

Cooler, 12" h, Bristol glaze, blue accented relief molded polar bear w/garden of flowers on reverse, (A)...... 330.00

Cream Pot, 7 1/2" h, blue parrot on stump design, imp "WHITES UTICA," c1865, restored hairline, (A) .... 247.00

Crock

10 1/2" h, blue running chicken w/long tail design, imp WHITES UTICA, NY, c1865, (A) ...................... 440.00

21" h, ovoid, thick blue orchid design on front, imp "N.A. WHITE & SON, UTICA, NY," 12 gallon, c1870, (A) .................................................................... 4,070.00

**Jug, 11" h, blue relief of Washington or Lincoln bust on sides, cobalt dog head on shoulder, cobalt "Prosit" on front, gray leaf and pebble designs, $625.**

Humidor, 6 1/2" h, bulbous shape, Bristol glaze, blue accented relief of hunting dog, (A) ........................ 248.00

Jar

7 3/4" h, blue flower and leaves, imp WHITE UTICA mark
.................................................................... 490.00

11" h, dk blue vine and floral design, imp N.A. WHITE & SON UTICA, NY on shoulder, c1870, (A) ......... 468.00

Jar, Cov

4" h, blue relief NOSEGAY TRADE MARK CLUB CHEESE on front, salt glaze, (A) ...................... 275.00

6" h, Bristol glaze, blue accented relief molded rose and leaf design, imp blue on reverse, (A) .................. 99.00

Jug

13" h, thick cobalt compote w/flowers design and "WHITES UTICA" on shoulder, c1865, staining, (A)
.................................................................... 633.00

13 1/2" h, blue lg breasted bird on flowering branch and blue imp "WHITES UTICA," on shoulder, c1865, (A)
.................................................................... 853.00

14" h

Cobalt quill floral design, "WHITE'S UTICA" on shoulder, (A)........................................................ 330.00

Dk blue paddletail bird, floral plume and 2, "N.A.WHITE & SON UTICA, NY" on shoulder, c1870, (A) ................................................................. 3,410.00

15 1/2" h, ovoid, cobalt brushed 3, incised "N. White, Utica," strap handle, hairlines, (A)..................... 358.00

17 1/2" h, cobalt quill design of flowering plant flanked by 2 exotic birds, imp "Whites Utica" dbl ear handles, (A)
.................................................................... 2,090.00

Mug

3" h, Bristol glaze w/blue accented MASONIC FAIR, blue geometric swirls on body, (A) ............................. 99.00

3 3/4" h, barrel shape, blue accented bands, imp DOL-GEVILLE TURNVEREN S 11, salt glaze, (A) ...... 55.00

4" h

Bristol glaze blue accented relief molded buffalo design, drinking couple on reverse, blue border bands, (A) .............................................. 55.00

Imp "PROSIT" and star designs, blue accents, imp sawtooth ext, (A) ............................................. 44.00

4 1/2" h, barrel shape, pedestal base, bands of blue accented tooling, blue wash, salt glaze, (A) ...... 165.00

4 3/4" h, blue incised "ROOT BEER" on side, 2 men drinking on reverse.................................. 70.00

5" h, raised cobalt grapes, leaves, and tendrils, gray pebble ground, blue stripes top and base, "PROSIT" on front, hairline.................................. 35.00

6" h, narrow blue band, gray ground, mkd.............. 50.00

7 1/2" h, relief of cobalt elves w/brown caps and dk brown beards, gray beards ......................................... 190.00

Mustard Jar, Cov, 3 3/4" h, blue accented sunflower design, salt glaze, (A) ...................................... 176.00

Pitcher

5" h, relief bark design w/blue accented relief of Diana the Huntress, roses on reverse, salt glaze, (A)
.................................................... 248.00

6 1/2" h, Bristol glaze w/blue accented relief of hunt or kitchen scene, rect handle.................................. 99.00

9 1/2" h, Bristol glaze, blue accented tavern scene, chips, (A)...................................................... 66.00

9 3/4" h, Bristol glaze, blue accented relief of 11 people dancing at farmstead, (A) .................................. 468.00

Stein

6 1/2" h

Bulbous, blue accented relief molded design of 4 people drinking and walking, framed German verse on reverse, pewter lid and thumblift, (A)
.................................................... 248.00

Relief molded hunter, fence and animals, reverse w/hearth, dog, and people, blue wash on gray body, blue rope handle ...................................... 75.00

10" h, Bristol glaze, blue accented relief molded card playing scene and framed German verse on reverse, pewter lid and thumblift, (A)................................ 413.00

12 1/2" h, blue accented incised court jester, incised pine branches on sides, pewter lid............................. 688.00

13" h, relief blue and brown woman playing tuba w/man, cobalt vines on reverse, gray ground, pewter lid
.................................................... 228.00

15" h, relief of bride and groom on front, ftd base, blue accents, pewter lid, "Whites Pottery Utica, NY" mk
.................................................... 468.00

Storage Crock, 10 1/2" h, overall stippled design w/star, blue accented rim band, imp 8 on front, salt glaze, (A)
.................................................... 165.00

Syrup Pitcher, Cov, 6" h, cobalt accented relief of children pulling log, salt glaze, chip, (A) ............................. 330.00

Vase

7" h, blue accented incised daffodils and butterflies, hairline, (A)........................................... 330.00

12" h, cylinder shape, relief of classical head w/cobalt wreath and florals, reverse w/classic woman in cobalt gown reaching to cobalt tree, gray pebble ground, blue stripes.................................... 700.00

OPAQUE PORCELAIN 1884-c.1890

BELLEEK WILLETS 1890s

# Willets Manufacturing Company

## Trenton, New Jersey
## 1879-1909

**History:** The three Willet brothers, Joseph, Daniel, and Edmund, purchased the Excelsior Pottery and changed the name to Willets Manufacturing Company in 1879 in Trenton, New Jersey. The plant was enlarged several times since they made a wide variety of wares including sanitary, earthenware, opaque china, white granite, white and decorated pottery, art porcelain, and decorated dinner and toilet sets.

Walter Scott Lenox, formerly at Ott and Brewer, became head of decorating at Willets in 1884. Willets began making hard porcelain in 1886, as suggested by Lenox. When William Bromley Sr. came to Willets from Ott and Brewer in 1887, he brought his formula for Belleek porcelains.

Willets Belleek, called Art Porcelaine, was first made in 1887 and very much resembled its Irish forerunner. The Belleek examples at Willets were exceptionally graceful and delicate. A group of outstanding decorators worked on these pieces. There were woven baskets, oval picture or mirror frames with tiny naturalistic flowers in high relief, and other fine examples. Each piece was a unique handmade work of art. Most Belleek was marked.

Belleek production was suspended for a short time in 1888, due to harsh economic times in the United States. Lenox resigned, and the factory was reorganized. In the early 1890s, Belleek was resumed, but there was increasing competition from other firms now making American Belleek examples. Willets also made porcelains with a variety of grounds, ormolu and gilding.

In 1909, the company went into receivership and was reorganized as the New Jersey Pottery Company. A wide variety of marks was used on Willets products. The mark on the Belleek porcelain was printed in the form of a twisted serpent with "WILLETS" printed below or above. Mark could be in red, brown, black, blue, or green.

**References:** Mark Frank Gaston, *American Belleek*, Collector Books, 1984.

**Museums:** Newark Museum, NJ: New Jersey State Museum, Trenton, NJ.

Bowl

6 3/4" H-H, pink roses, green leaves, brown stems, white ground, matte gold sculptured rim and handles 350.00

13" d, HP roses, gold dragon handles ................... 595.00

Chalice, 11 1/2" h, painted polychrome pinecones, berries, and leaves, shaded yellow, crimson red, and brown ground, gilded rim and int, (A) .............................. 282.00

Mug

5 5/8" h, painted grapes, yellow and green shaded ground, dtd 1908............................................. 280.00

6" h

Figural dragon handle, painted berries and leaves
.................................................... 275.00

**Bowl, 7 3/4" d, red-purple raspberries, brown and green leaves, shaded yellow ground, gold rim, lt green ext, $250.**

HP bust of black man w/red kerchief, blue to brown shaded ground, gold handle, artist sgd.........250.00

Pitcher, 4 1/2" h, figural woman's head, hat spout, matte and gloss cream glaze, gold accents...........................375.00

Platter, 15 1/4" l, "Princess" pattern, green transfer .....25.00

Tankard

5 1/2" h, Art Nouveau style green and yellow flowers and stems, cream to yellow ground.........................250.00

10 1/4" h, painted blackberries and blossoms, top and base gilt bands w/emb berries and blossoms, brown stamped "BELLEEK/WILLETS" mk, (A)
........................................................................450.00

11" h, hanging blackberries and leaves, shaded green to brown ground, molded face spout, brown dragon handle, snake mk ...................................................695.00

13 1/2" h, green, purple, and burgundy blended body, gold trim on rim and handle, sgd "Frances E. Schierholz," ........................................................................350.00

Teapot, 5 1/2" h, painted polychrome and gilt Arts and Crafts style scene of mountain and lake, dk green ground (A)
........................................................................275.00

Urn, 14 1/4" h, shield shape, curled handles on shoulder, lg pink and dk red flowerheads and buds, cream to green shaded and mottled ground, gold trim and rim, curled snake mk..........................................................500.00

Vase

8 1/2" h

Cylinder shape, painted pink and white orchids, green leaf bkd, sgd "L.E. Schick," c1880 ...............700.00

Tapered cylinder shape, HP yellow daffodils and green leaves, shaded cream ground, gold rim, sgd "B.M. Buchanan," (A)................................................265.00

11 1/2" h, bulbous elongated shape w/narrow top, yellow flowers, green leaves, brown branches, rust ground
........................................................................795.00

12 1/2" h, hourglass shape, purple berries, yellow-gold leaves, white ground ...................................285.00

15 1/2" h, HP lavender florals w/green and brown shades, gilt neck designs, c1885-1909 ..........1,100.00

# Winfield Pottery

### Pasadena, California
### 1929-1962

**WINFIELD 167 PASADENA**

**History:** Winfield Pottery was founded in 1929 by Lesley Winfield Sample in Pasadena, California. It began as a school and studio. Cast porcelain vases and bowls were made in both opaque and transparent glazes in a variety of colors.

Designer Margaret Gabriel made utilitarian dinnerware pieces. She designed the first square-shaped dinnerware in the United States in 1937. Her hand-painted patterns included Bamboo in 1937, Tulip, Avocado, and Geranium in 1938, and Citrus in 1939 in color combinations.

When Sample died in 1939, Margaret and Arthur Gabriel took over Winfield. They expanded production and built a new factory. Additional dinnerware patterns were Yellow Flower, Weed, Acorn, and Fallow. Tyrus Wong created dinnerware patterns in the '40s and '50s. He also used oriental motifs on large plates. Other artwares included glazed vases, low flower bowls, candleholders, and planters.

In 1946, American Ceramic Products of Santa Monica assisted with the tremendous backlog of dinnerware orders from W.W.II. "Winfield China" was used by Santa Monica on the expanded line, while Winfield Pottery used the trademark "Gabriel Porcelain."

Winfield incorporated in 1947 with a group of investors after the Gabriels retired. In the mid-'50s, Douglas Gabriel became the sole owner. With the influx of imported china, production slowed down until the plant closed in 1962.

Winfield examples are marked. Usually there is also a shape number incised on the pieces.

**References:** Jack Chipman, *Collector's Encyclopedia of California Pottery*, Collector Books, 1992.

## APPLE PATTERN

Bowl, 10 1/2" d ............................................................20.00
Vegetable Bowl, Divided, 8 1/2" sq ...........................20.00

## BAMBOO PATTERN

Berry Bowl, 5", green and white...................................3.00
Cup and Saucer, green and white................................9.00
Mug, green and white.................................................18.00
Pitcher, 6 1/4" h, green and white .............................15.00

Plate

6" d, green and white..............................................8.00
7" d, green and white..............................................4.00
10" d, green and white..........................................12.00

Soup Bowl, 6" d...........................................................6.00
Teapot, 7" h ..............................................................10.00

## BIRD OF PARADISE PATTERN

Ashtray, 4" l ................................................................3.00
Butter Dish, Cov, 7 1/2" l...........................................20.00
Casserole, Cov, 14" l.................................................43.00
Cereal Bowl, 6" d........................................................5.00
Creamer ....................................................................10.00
Cup and Saucer .......................................................10.00
Fruit Bowl, 4 3/4" d......................................................6.00

Plate

7 1/2" d ..................................................................8.00

10 1/2" d....................................................12.00
Platter
   12" l....................................................12.00
   14" l....................................................25.00
Serving Bowl, 9" d...........................................15.00
Vegetable Bowl, Divide, 13" l...........................20.00

## BLUE BAMBOO PATTERN

Ashtray ...............................................................4.00
Cup and Saucer ...............................................10.00
Plate
   6" d.......................................................10.00
   10 1/4" d...............................................12.00
Platter, 14 1/2" l...............................................22.00
Shakers, Pr.......................................................12.00
Vegetable Bowl, Divided, 13" l........................38.00

## BLUE SPRUCE PATTERN

Plate, 10" d.........................................................8.00

## DESERT DAWN PATTERN

Casserole, Cov, 9" d.........................................22.00
Cereal Bowl, 5 3/4" d..........................................4.00
Coffeepot, 7 1/2" h...........................................20.00
Cup and Saucer .................................................3.00
Fruit Bowl, 4 3/4" d.............................................3.00
Plate
   6" d.........................................................7.00
   10 1/4" d...............................................10.00
Platter
   11" l.....................................................12.00
   14" l.....................................................15.00
Serving Bowl, 9" d...........................................12.00
Serving Bowl, Divided, 13" l............................10.00

## DRAGON FLOWER PATTERN

Bowl, 9" d .........................................................40.00
Casserole, Cov
   6" H-H ..................................................65.00
   10" H-H ................................................65.00
   14" H-H ................................................75.00
Cereal Bowl, 5 3/4" d..........................................8.00
Cup and Saucer ...............................................10.00

Dessert Bowl, 5" d..............................................6.00
Plate
   5 3/4" d.................................................10.00
   7 1/2" d...................................................8.00
   10" d.....................................................12.00
Platter, 14 1/2" l...............................................20.00
Relish Dish, 8 3/4" l..........................................15.00
Sugar Bowl, Cov ................................................8.00
Teapot, 7" h......................................................55.00
Vegetable Bowl, 13" l, divided........................40.00

## GREEN BAMBOO PATTERN

Berry Bowl, 5" d..................................................3.00
Plate
   7" d.........................................................4.00
   10" d.......................................................6.00
Soup Bowl, 6" d..................................................6.00

## MISCELLANEOUS

Plate, 8 3/4" sq, yellow florals .........................12.00

## PASSION FLOWERS PATTERN

Cereal Bowl, 5 3/4" d........................................12.00
Cup and Saucer ...............................................12.00
Shakers, Pr.........................................................9.00
Vegetable Bowl, Divided, 13" l........................20.00

## TIGER IRIS PATTERN

Cup and Saucer .................................................6.00
Plate
   5 1/2" d...................................................4.00
   10" d.......................................................6.00
Sauce Bowl, 4 3/4" d..........................................4.00
Serving Bowl, 8 3/4" d......................................30.00

## TIGER LILY PATTERN

Platter, 11" l x 8" w...........................................15.00
Shakers, Pr.......................................................12.00

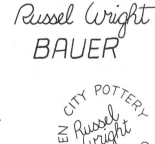

**Teapot, 7 1/2" h, "Passion Flower" pattern, $28.**

# Russel Wright

**New York, New York**
**1936-1967**

**History:** In 1936, Russel Wright and Mary, his wife, joined with Irving Richards to become the Raymor Company. For a five-year period, Wright did exclusive designs for Raymor. After five years, the Wrights sold the company to Richards and established their own design firm called Russel Wright Associates. Raymor continued to sell and distribute Wright designs plus many others.

American Modern dinnerware showed the new modern influences on American design. When it was designed by Wright in 1939, most of the Ohio River area potteries did not want to produce it. Steubenville Pottery in Ohio agreed to produce the designs if Mary and Russel Wright provided the financing. It was to be distributed exclusively by Raymor for a five year period. From 1939-1959 it became the largest selling dinnerware ever and forced Steubenville to expand several times to keep up with the demand. American Modern won the American Designers Institute Award for the best ceramic design of 1941.

This strictly functional, amorphous-shaped dinnerware was sold in starter sets, 53-piece sets, open stock, and in other groupings. It was highly advertised in the mass media of the period and mass produced for the middle class. Originally the colors were Seafoam Blue, Granite Gray, Chartreuse Curry, Coral, Bean Brown, and White. In 1950, Black Chutney and Cedar Green were added, followed by Cantaloupe and Glacier Blue in 1955. Bean Brown was discontinued during World War II. The shapes were non-traditional and very new for the times. The finish had a muted, soft glow with a textured feeling. A tremendous assortment of pieces was made with new shapes being added all during the time of production. Several different marks were used on Steubenville's American Modern designed by Wright.

Iroquois Casual China by Russel Wright was designed in 1946 and made by the Iroquois China Company. Garrison Products of New York City was the distributor. Featuring oven-to-table pieces, this, too, became a best-selling dinnerware. Original colors were Sugar White, Lemon Yellow, and Ice Blue, followed by Nutmeg, Avocado Yellow, and Parsley Green. Lemon and Parsley were short lived. The original shapes had a "pinch" style, and the glaze was mottled. Major design changes in 1951 gave Iroquois Casual a more polished look. By 1951, colors included Charcoal, Ripe Apricot, Pink Sherbet, Lettuce Green, Oyster, Cantaloupe, Aqua, Brick Red, and Forest Green. Not all items were made in all colors. Even with changes in color intensity and finish, buyers mixed pieces. Iroquois was restyled again in 1959 and sold in 45-piece sets.

Russel Wright designed solid color institutional dinnerware made by Sterling China Company starting in 1949 in Ivy Green, Straw Yellow, Suede Gray, Cedar Brown, White, and Shell Pink. Sterling put customers' logos and such on these designs.

For Paden City Pottery Company, Russel Wright designed Highlight in 1948 that was marketed by Justin Tharaud. Original colors were Blueberry, Nutmeg, Pepper, Citron, and later White and Dark Green. First it had a soft matte glaze, and later a high gloss finish. This design was more sophisticated than American Modern and Iroquois Casual, but due to struggles between Wright and the marketer, it was only produced until the mid 1950s.

The first patterned line by Wright was White Clover for the Harker Pottery Company. It had a silk screened engraved-like decoration and was made in Meadow Green, Golden Spice, Coral Sand, and Charcoal from 1951-1955.

In 1955, Wright designed an oriental-inspired line for Knowles in the Esquire shape that had naturalistic designs. The first colors were beige, white, pink, yellow, and blue in a matte finish with an underglaze rubber stamped pattern and an overglaze gold stamping. Patterns included Seeds, Grass, Queen Anne's Lace, Snow Flower, Botanica, and Solar with a gold back stamp mark which named the pattern.

This line was designed as a lower price line for stores such as Sears, Wards, and premium stamp companies, but was not successful. It came to an end in 1962.

Wright's first project after American Modern was an art pottery line for Bauer Pottery Company of Atlanta, Georgia that was marketed by Raymor. Though there were twenty shapes involved and sixteen different glaze colors, there was a tremendous amount of difficulty with the glazes, and the line was only produced for about six months.

Russel Wright used numerous marks on his wares since he designed dinnerware for Steubenville, Harker, Iroquois, Paden City, Sterling, and Knowles, and art pottery for Bauer. He closed his studio in 1967.

**References:** Ann Kerr, *Collectors' Encyclopedia of Russel Wright Designs*, Collector Books, 1990; *Second Edition*, 1998; _____, *Russel Wright Dinnerware*, Collector Books, 1985.

## BAUER

Ash Bowl, 4" sq, lt blue ext, gunmetal int, #10A......... 500.00
Ashtray, 6 3/4" l, lt blue and gray ext, dk blue int ....... 565.00

**Casserole, Cov, 12" l, "American Modern" pattern, granite gray, $65.**

**Water Pitcher, 11" h, "American Modern" pattern, coral, $75.**

Bowl, 10" l, celadon micro-crystalline ext, gunmetal int, unmkd, (A) ...............660.00
Bulb Bowl, 8 1/2" l, Georgia Brown ext, aqua int, #19A ...............550.00
Pillow Vase, 8 1/2" h x 9 3/4" w, lt blue ext, Georgia Brown int, #1A ...............1,250.00
Vase
  8 1/2" h, Atlanta Brick, #2A ...............600.00
  10 1/2" h, Georgia Brown, #6A ...............1,250.00

## HARKERWARE-WHITE CLOVER

Chop Plate, 11" d
  Charcoal ...............45.00
  Golden Spice ...............40.00
Clock, Golden Spice ...............80.00
Creamer, Meadow Green ...............35.00
Cup and Saucer
  Coral Sand ...............15.00
  Golden Spice ...............15.00
  Meadow Green ...............30.00

Plate
  6" d, no design
    Charcoal ...............15.00
    Golden Spice ...............5.00
  7 1/2" d, no design, charcoal ...............17.00
  9 1/4" d
    Golden Spice ...............13.00
    Golden Spice, no clover ...............12.00
    Meadow Green, no clover ...............12.00
  10" d
    Charcoal ...............30.00
    Golden Spice ...............17.00
    Golden Spice, no clover ...............16.00
Shakers, Golden Spice, pr ...............50.00
Vegetable Bowl, Open, 7 1/2" d, Coral Sand ...............25.00

## IROQUOIS CASUAL

Casserole, 8" d, divided, Ripe Apricot ...............35.00
Casserole, Cov, 4 qt, 8" d
  Nutmeg ...............250.00
  Oyster ...............425.00
  Pink ...............300.00
Coffee Cup and Saucer, Restyled
  Early Nutmeg ...............60.00
  Parsley Green ...............65.00
Coffeepot
  Oyster ...............375.00
  Parsley Green ...............350.00
  Ripe Apricot ...............265.00
Cream and Sugar, Stacked
  Oyster ...............75.00
  Parsley Green ...............65.00
  Ripe Apricot ...............45.00
Creamer, Restyled
  Aqua ...............350.00
  Charcoal ...............75.00
  Mustard Gold ...............75.00
  Ripe Apricot ...............35.00

Sugar White ...............65.00
Cup and Saucer
  A.D.
    Avocado ...............225.00
    Pink ...............250.00
Cereal Bowl, 5" d, Original
  Avocado ...............17.00
  Lettuce Green ...............25.00
  Oyster ...............30.00
  Restyled
    Aqua ...............100.00
    Lettuce Green ...............25.00
    Mustard Gold ...............40.00
    Pink ...............20.00
Chop Plate, 13 7/8" d
  Avocado ...............85.00
  Charcoal ...............125.00
  Nutmeg ...............85.00
Fruit Bowl, 5 1/2" d
  Parsley Green ...............30.00
  Pink ...............20.00
  Ripe Apricot ...............20.00
Fruit Bowl, Restyled, 5 3/4" d
  Aqua ...............100.00
  Brick Red ...............100.00
  Cantaloupe ...............75.00
  Lettuce Green ...............40.00
  Nutmeg ...............30.00
Plate
  6 1/2" d
    Ice Blue ...............15.00
    Lettuce Green ...............25.00
    Oyster ...............25.00
    White ...............20.00
  7 1/2" d
    Aqua ...............95.00
    Brick Red ...............95.00
    Lettuce Green ...............30.00
    Parsley Green ...............35.00
    Ripe Apricot ...............20.00
  9 1/2" d
    Ice Blue ...............25.00
    Oyster Gray ...............16.00
    Ripe Apricot ...............13.00
  10 1/2" d
    Aqua ...............165.00
    Avocado ...............20.00
    Cantaloupe ...............75.00
    Lemon Yellow ...............20.00
    Parsley Green ...............35.00
    Ripe Apricot ...............20.00
Platter
  12 3/4" l
    Avocado ...............45.00
    Lemon Yellow ...............19.00
    Pink Sherbet ...............19.00
    Sugar White ...............22.00

14 1/2" l
- Lemon Yellow .................................................55.00
- Mustard Gold ...............................................125.00
- Ripe Apricot ..................................................35.00
- Sugar Bowl, Restyled
- Pink ...............................................................55.00
- Nutmeg .........................................................65.00

Teacup and Saucer
- Ice Blue .........................................................25.00
- Parsley Green ...............................................35.00
- Restyled
  - Charcoal ....................................................35.00
  - Ice Blue .....................................................25.00
  - Nutmeg ......................................................25.00

Teapot, Restyled
- Ice Blue .......................................................300.00
- Lettuce Green .............................................375.00
- Nutmeg ........................................................265.00

Vegetable Bowl, 8" d
- Avocado ........................................................35.00
- Ice Blue .........................................................22.00
- Lemon Yellow ...............................................35.00
- Parsley Green ...............................................75.00
- Pink ...............................................................35.00
- Restyled
  - Brick Red ..................................................225.00
  - Lemon Yellow .............................................40.00
  - Pink ...........................................................40.00
- 10" d
  - Lettuce Green .............................................95.00
  - Oyster ........................................................95.00
  - Parsley Green .............................................85.00
  - Ripe Apricot ................................................50.00

Vegetable Bowl, Divided, 10" d
- Ice Blue .........................................................50.00
- Parsley Green ...............................................65.00

Vegetable Bowl, Divided, Cov, 10" d
- Charcoal ......................................................125.00
- Ice Blue .........................................................85.00
- Oyster ..........................................................125.00

**KNOWLES-ESQUIRE**
Cup and Saucer
- Grass .............................................................25.00
- Queen Ann Lace, ivory ..................................18.00
- Seeds .............................................................12.00

Fruit Bowl, 5 1/2" d
- Queen Ann Lace ............................................10.00
- Seeds .............................................................20.00

Plate
- 6" 1/4" d
  - Antique White ..............................................15.00
  - Grass ..........................................................15.00
  - Queen Ann Lace ............................................5.00
- 8 1/4" d
  - Grass ..........................................................20.00
  - Queen Ann Lace ..........................................10.00

10 1/4" d
- Antique White ................................................25.00
- Grass .............................................................25.00
- Queen Ann Lace ............................................14.00
- Seeds .............................................................25.00

Platter
- 13" l
  - Queen Ann Lace ..........................................38.00
  - Seeds ..........................................................40.00
  - Snowflower ..................................................60.00
- 14 1/4" l
  - Grass ..........................................................55.00
  - Seeds ..........................................................85.00
  - Snowflower ..................................................85.00

Serving Bowl, 12 1/4" l, Grass ...........................45.00
Soup Bowl, 6 1/4" d
- Grass .............................................................30.00
- Seeds .............................................................25.00

**STERLING**
Creamer
- Individual, Suede Gray ...................................35.00
- Table, Straw Yellow .......................................30.00

Cup and Saucer, Straw Yellow ...........................40.00

Plate
- 6" d
  - Shell Pink ....................................................15.00
- 7 1/2" d
  - Cedar Brown ..................................................9.00
  - Shell Pink ....................................................12.00
  - Straw Yellow ................................................10.00
- 9" d
  - Cedar Brown ................................................28.00
  - Straw Yellow ................................................10.00
  - Suede Gray ..................................................25.00
- 9 1/2" d
  - Black palm frond, white ground ....................15.00
- 10 1/4" d
  - Cedar Brown ................................................25.00
  - Straw Yellow ................................................28.00
  - Suede Gray ..................................................30.00
- 11 1/2" d
  - Straw Yellow ................................................35.00
  - Woodrose ....................................................35.00

Platter
- 7 1/2" l
  - Ivy Green .....................................................35.00
  - Straw Yellow ................................................38.00
- 10 1/2" l
  - Cedar Brown ................................................30.00
  - Straw Yellow ................................................18.00
- 11 3/4" l
  - Straw Yellow ................................................35.00
- 13 5/8" l
  - Shell Pink ....................................................35.00
  - Straw Yellow ................................................30.00

Salad Bowl, 7 1/2" d, Straw Yellow ....................45.00
Sugar Bowl, Cov, Straw Yellow ..........................95.00

Teapot, 10 oz, "Woodrose" ............................... 175.00

## STEUBENVILLE, AMERICAN MODERN

Celery Tray
    Cantaloupe ............................................. 125.00
    Granite Gray ............................................. 45.00
    Seafoam .................................................. 65.00
Coffeepot, 8" h
    Cedar Green ........................................... 395.00
    Coral ...................................................... 295.00
    White ...................................................... 595.00
Coffeepot, A.D., Glacier Blue .......................... 295.00
Cov Casserole, 12" H-H
    Coral ........................................................ 75.00
    Granite Gray ............................................. 65.00
Creamer
    Black Chutney .......................................... 20.00
    White ....................................................... 45.00
Cup and Saucer
    Bean Brown ............................................. 40.00
    Black Chutney .......................................... 25.00
    Granite Gray ............................................. 23.00
Cup and Saucer, A.D
    Chartreuse Curry ...................................... 33.00
    Granite Gray ............................................. 35.00
    White ....................................................... 50.00
Gravy, 10 1/2" l
    Chartreuse Curry ...................................... 30.00
    Coral ....................................................... 35.00
    Granite Gray ............................................. 25.00
    Seafoam .................................................. 40.00
Lug Fruit Bowl
    Coral ....................................................... 25.00
    White ....................................................... 40.00
Lug Soup
    Bean Brown ............................................. 40.00
    Granite Gray ............................................. 25.00
    Seafoam .................................................. 30.00
Pitcher, 10 1/2" h
    Chartreuse Curry ...................................... 75.00
Plate
  6" d
    Cedar Green ............................................ 15.00
    Chartreuse Curry ...................................... 12.00
    Seafoam .................................................. 15.00
    White ....................................................... 20.00
  8" d
    Glacier Blue ............................................. 40.00
    Granite Gray ............................................. 22.00
    Seafoam .................................................. 30.00
  10" d
    Cantaloupe .............................................. 40.00
    Chartreuse Curry ...................................... 15.00
    Coral ....................................................... 20.00
    Seafoam .................................................. 25.00
Platter, 13 1/4" l
    Bean Brown ............................................. 75.00
    Chartreuse Curry ...................................... 20.00

    Granite Gray ............................................. 45.00
    Seafoam .................................................. 42.00
Ramekin, Cov
    Chartreuse Curry .................................... 200.00
    Granite Gray ........................................... 225.00
Shakers, 5 Hole, Pr
    Coral ....................................................... 25.00
    Seafoam .................................................. 35.00
    Stack Set, Black Chutney ........................ 400.00
Sugar Bowl, Cov
    Bean Brown ............................................. 75.00
    Granite Gray ............................................. 30.00
    Seafoam .................................................. 40.00
Teapot, 6" h
    Granite Gray ........................................... 150.00
    Seafoam ................................................ 175.00
    Water Pitcher, Cedar Green ..................... 200.00

# Yellowware

## East and Midwest
## 1830-Present

**History:** Yellowware came to America from England in the 1820s. Pieces were made from heavy earthenware clays that fired to varying shades of yellow when coated with a clear alkaline glaze. Yellowware was quite durable and eventually replaced redware as a kitchen pottery since it was less fragile.

Peak years of production for yellowware occurred between the 1860s and '70s. More than eighty potteries were producing yellowware between 1830 and 1900. Several continue to make examples to the present day. Yellowwares were eventually replaced by whitewares and decorated porcelains.

Very little yellowware was marked. Some pieces did have impressed marks. At first it was made on the potter's wheel. By the late 1830s, molded pieces were made by slip casting, press molding, or drape molding techniques. Handles were applied by hand. Most of the clays were found in Ohio and New Jersey.

One of the first firms to make utilitarian yellowwares was David and James Henderson's Jersey City Pottery Company. Potters were brought from England from 1828-1833. Bennett Pottery from Baltimore was another important early yellowware maker.

The most common form of yellowware decoration was banding in either white, brown, or blue. Horizontal stripes were used in one or several colors. Other examples had sponge or mocha decorations. Some yellowware examples had the Rockingham glaze. The most desirable decorations was on teapots showing Rebekah at the well. These were made by many different potteries. Dog and lion figurals were also made in the Rockingham-glazed yellowwares.

There was a tremendous number of forms used for yellowwares. Most were utilitarian in nature. Mixing bowls were made in nests with sizes ranging from 3" to 17" in diameter. Pitchers came in an endless variety of sizes and shapes. Nappies came in sizes ranging from 3" to 13." Pie plates, custard cups, tobacco jars, soap holders, lidded storage jars, rolling pins, meat tenderizers, pepper pots, snuff boxes, and such all were found in yellowware. All types of food molds were made from the mini candy and chocolate types to cornbread, jelly, and Turk's Head molds. Batter bowls had a lipped edge and ranged in size from 7" to 15" in diameter. Much advertising and promotional ware also was made.

Additional potteries producing yellowwares were found in New Jersey, Vermont, Pennsylvania, Maryland, and Illinois. Ohio was the major source of yellowware production, and East Liverpool was the most important center. Many potters got their start there. Bennett, Harker, Goodwin, William Brunt, and such were all working there. By 1853, there were eleven different potteries in East Liverpool, all making utilitarian yellowwares. Chamberpots, milk pans, butter tubs, mugs, flower pots, pitchers, and bowls all were made in Ohio. Cincinnati also had a concentration of potters producing yellowwares.

During the 20th century, the Robinson-Ransbottom Pottery started yellowware production and continues to the present day. Both Hull and Red Wing made yellowwares as part of their production lines.

**References:** John Gallo, *Nineteenth and Twentieth Century Yellowware*, Heritage Press, 1985; William C. Ketchum Jr., *American Country Pottery: Yellowware and Spongeware*, Alfred A. Knopf, 1987; Joan Leibowitz, *Yellowware: The Transitional Ceramic*, Schiffer Publishing Ltd. 1985; Lisa S. McAllister and John L. Michel, *Collecting Yellowware*, Collector Books, 1992; Lisa S. McAllister, *Collector's Guide to Yellowware*, Collector Books, 1997.

**Museums:** Bennington Museum, VT; Henry Ford Museum and Greenfield Village, Dearborn, MI; Museum of Ceramics, East Liverpool, OH.

Bank, 6 1/4" l, figural pig, brown, green, and cream marbleized glazes, (A) ........................................83.00
Batter Pitcher, 5 1/4" h, relief molded vert florals and vines ............................................................495.00
Bean Pot, 6" h, center white stripe flanked by 2 brown stripes ...................................................200.00
Beverage Set, pitcher, 8" h, 6 mugs, 4 3/4" h, blue stripes, imp "100% Buckeye Pure," chips and hairlines, (A) ............................................................550.00
Bottle, 8 1/2" h, figural man w/fiddle, chips, (A) ..........715.00
Bowl
  5" d, blue and pink banding .................................. 115.00
  5 1/2" d, white band on border.............................25.00
  6 1/4" d, pink and blue banding ........................... 110.00
  8" d, dbl blue and white bands........................ 65.00
  9 1/4" d
    Brown banding ................................................. 125.00
    Incised geometric designs, 3 brown slip bands at center, (A) .............................................................55.00
  11" d, blue banding ............................................. 130.00
Bowl, Cov, 7" d, blue bands and stripes, crazing and stains, (A) ......................................................220.00
Bread Jar, 9" h x 9 1/4" w, straight sides, 3 white slip bands on upper section, brown "BREAD" on center band, chips on base, (A) ......................................252.00
Butter Jar, 5 1/4" h, 2 brown bands and black "Southern Dairies Pasteurized Milk Health Builders of the South" ............................................................295.00
Cake Mold, 8 1/2" d, ring shape ...............................295.00
Canister, 6" d, 6 3/4" d, 7" d, white bands and stripes, set of 3, (A) ...........................................................440.00
Canning Jar
  6"
    Paneled body, (A)............................................275.00
    Tin lid, (A) .................................................. 220.00
  6 1/4" h, barrel shape, (A)....................................185.00
  6 1/2" h................................................................150.00

Coffeepot and Percolator, 10 1/4" h, insert top w/filter and lid, (A) ..............................................................75.00
Colander, 6 1/4" d.....................................................550.00
Cup, Toy, 1 3/4" h, Morton Pottery ...........................185.00
Custard Cup
  2" h, wide green center band w/2 narrow green stripes ............................................................28.00
  2 1/2" h ............................................................75.00
Dish
  6" d, coggled rim, hairlines, (A)...........................135.00
  7 1/2" d, tub shape w/raised handles, white bands w/blue stripes, hairline, (A) ...................................440.00
Figure
  10" h, seated dog w/open front legs, mottled blue/black and clear glaze, Ohio, chips, (A) ............................................................ 4,400.00
  12" h, seated cat, sq base, dk amber brown glaze, (A) ............................................................ 1,265.00
Flask, molded morning glories and eagle, (A)......... 1,210.00
Food Mold
  4" d, interior spiral design, (A) ..........................50.00
  5 1/2" l, molded fruit, rect with cut corners............325.00
  6 3/4" l, molded ear of corn in center, (A) .............. 110.00
  7 3/4" l, fish, oval, rim chips ...................................295.00
  8 1/2" l, figural pineapple, (A) ...............................190.00
  9 1/4" l x 4 1/4" h, oval rabbit, hairline .................395.00
Foot Warmer, 13" l, cylindrical pillow shape, hairline, (A) ............................................................175.00
Jar
  3" h, rolled rim, (A).............................................35.00
  5 3/4" h, figural barrel .............................................185.00
Jar, Cov, 5 1/2" h, incised blue horiz lines.................575.00
Milk Bowl, 6 1/2" d, Rockingham glaze .....................149.00
Mixing Bowl
  4 1/2" d, flared rim, 3 white center bands, (A) .........60.00
  5" d, molded swirls on body....................................25.00
  8 1/4" d x 4 5/8" h, green and white stripes and molded rings, (A)............................................................55.00
  9 1/4" d, rust and white bands ...............................65.00
  9 1/2" d, 3 white stripes, (A)................................45.00

**Mixing Bowl, 9 1/2" d, blue stripes, $25.**

10 1/4" d, relief molded design of girl w/watering can, chips and hairlines, (A) .......................................85.00

11 1/2" d, molded ribs and brown stripes, "USA" mk .......................................................................65.00

12" d

    Brown stripes, molded half circles and fans .......................................................................150.00

    Wide red stripes, narrow white stripes .............150.00

14" d, relief molded swirl design .............................85.00

Mug

    2" h, white sanded center band, blue striped borders, (A) .......................................................................182.00

    3 1/2" h, hourglass shape, center brown and white bands .......................................................................250.00

    4" h, wide white center band w/brown stripes, (A) ...50.00

    4 7/8" h, tankard shape, blue stripes, (A)...............46.00

Mustard Pot, Cov, 2 1/2" h, applied handle, blue band and white stripes, (A) .............................................460.00

Pepper Shaker, 4 1/8" h, domed top, blue and white stripes, (A) .......................................................................640.00

Pie Plate

    9 1/4" d.................................................................130.00

    9 1/2" d, crimped rim, repaired................................65.00

    11 1/4" d, chips and hairline.....................................40.00

Pitcher

    4 1/2" h, molded swirl pattern ................................25.00

    5" h, strap handle, blue stripes, (A).......................578.00

5 1/2" h, strap handle, wide white bands w/brown stripes, (A) .......................................................................550.00

6 1/8" h, strap handle, white bands and black stripes, (A) .......................................................................688.00

6 1/4" h, imp vert streaks ......................................135.00

7 1/4" h

    Relief molded cow and tree, tan, green, and brown, stains and chips, (A) ....................................165.00

    Ribbed strap handle, white band w/blue seaweed and brown stripes, Ohio, repaired handle, (A).....770.00

7 3/4" h

    Flared base, dk blue and white stripes, (A).......743.00

    Green glaze w/dk flecks, (A) ...........................120.00

8 1/4" h, relief of peacock .....................................525.00

8 1/2" h, squat shape, wide white center band, ribbed handle, repaired spout, (A)...............................550.00

9 1/4" h, center cobalt band..................................135.00

Ramekin, 2 3/4" h, white band, brown stripes, set of 6, (A) .......................................................................248.00

Rolling Pin, 14 1/2" l, wood handles, (A) ...................360.00

Soap Dish, 5 5/8" d, (A)...............................................550.00

Sugar Bowl, Cov, 4 3/8" h, blue stripes, (A) .............475.00

Teapot, 8 5/8" h, relief molded basketweave base and spout, leaf border .......................................................525.00

Trivet, 5" d .................................................................495.00

Vase, 9" h, ovoid shape............................................185.00

Vegetable Bowl, 13 3/8" l, oval, imp "Fire Proof," (A) .......................................................................495.00

# Appendix

# CONTRIBUTING AUCTION HOUSES

The following auction houses cooperated with us by providing complimentary subscriptions to their catalogues for all ceramics auctions. Their cooperation is appreciated greatly. Without this help, it would have been impossible to produce this price guide.

Garth's Auction, Inc.
2690 Stratford Road
P.O. Box 369
Delaware, OH 43015

Sotheby's Chicago
215 W. Ohio Street
Chicago, IL 60610

Joy Luke Auction Gallery
300 E. Grove Street
Bloomington, IL 61701

David Rago Auctions, Inc.
333 North Main Street
Lambertville, NJ 08530

Horst Auctioneers
Catalogues by Clarence E. Spohn
50 Durlach Drive
Ephrata, PA 17522

Skinner, Inc.
357 Main Street
Bolton, MA 01740

Skinner, Inc.
Heritage on the Garden
663 Park Plaza
Boston, MA 02116

Smith and Jones, Inc.
12 Clark Lane
Sudbury, MA 01776

John Toomey Gallery
818 North Boulevard
Oak Park, IL 60301

Don Treadway Gallery
2029 Madison Road
Cincinnati, OH 45208

Cincinnati Art Galleries
225 East 6th Street
Cincinnati, OH 45202

Christie's at Rockefeller Center
20 Rockefeller Plaza
New York, NY 10020

Christie's East
219 East 67 Street
New York, NY 10021

Sotheby's
1334 York Avenue
New York, NY 10021

Strawser Auctions
200 North Main Street
Wolcottville, IN 46795

Vicki and Bruce Waasdorp
100931 Main Street
Clarence, NY 14031

Southern Folk Pottery Collectors Society
1828 N. Howard Mill Road
Robbins, NC 27325

# MUSEUMS

Museums listed have large general collections of American ceramics.

Art Museum, Princeton, NJ

Bennington Museum, VT

Brooklyn Museum, NY

Cincinnati Art Museum, OH

Cooper Hewitt Museum, New York, NY

DAR Museum, Washington, DC

Everson Museum of Art, Syracuse, NY

Henry Ford Museum and Greenfield Village, Dearborn, MI

Henry Francis duPont Winterthur Museum, DE

Jones Museum of Glass and Ceramics, Douglas Hill, ME

Los Angeles County Museum of Art, CA

Mint Museum of Art, Charlotte, NC

Museum of Ceramic Art at Alfred University, NY

Museum of Ceramics, East Liverpool, OH

Newark Museum, Newark, NJ

New Orleans Museum of Art, LA

Oakland Museum, CA

Philadelphia Museum of Art, PA

Yale University Art Gallery, New Haven, CT

Zanesville Art Center, OH

# PHOTO CREDITS

We wish to thank all those dealers and collectors who permitted us to photograph their American ceramics. Unfortunately we are unable to identify the sources for all of our pictures; nevertheless we appreciate all of those people who have contributed to this price guide.

Connecticut: Sara Sampson Antiques, Deep River. Florida: The Hallway, Port Charlotte; Tony McCormack, Sarasota. Georgia: Past-Tense Antiques, Swanee.

Illinois: Americana, Ltd. Chicago; Broadway Antique Market, Chicago; Canyon Company, Chicago; Chez Therese Antiques, Chicago; Chicago Antique Centre; Chicago Art Deco Society; Cothern House Antiques, Lanark; Gaslight Gallery, Chicago; Golden Oldies Antiques; Dennis Carl Hopp, Chicago; Lorraine K. Jaffe, Highland Park; KL Antiques, Ltd. Rock Island; Raymond Levin, Lake Forest; Lincoln Antique Mall, Chicago; Mello Antiques, Carterville; North Suburban Enterprises, Glenview; P.O.S.H., Chicago; Red Bandana, Chicago; Stephen F. Rhodes, Champaign; Somewhere in Time, Sycamore; V.J. Antiques, Downers Grove; Volo Antique Malls, I, II, III, Volo; D & F Collectibles.

Indiana: A Touch of Glass, Gary; Bill Spears, Butch Mikita, Indianapolis; The Antique Market of Michigan City. Iowa: William M. Bilsland III, Cedar Rapids. Kansas: American Spirit Antiques, Shawnee Mission; Rory Evans, McLouth. Kentucky: Vicki McLean, Louisville.

Michigan: Flo-Blue Shoppe, Birmingham; Gold Leaf Antiques, Grand Rapids; Grant's Antique Market, Galesburg; Norm Haas, Quincy; Things Remembered, Dexter; Vintage Style, West Bloomfield; Wendy Woodworth, Ann Arbor. New Hampshire: Etruria Antiques and Collectibles, Plainfield.

New Mexico: Adobe Gallery, Albuquerque. New Jersey: Andrea's Antiques, Brigantine; Falcon's Antiques, Warren; Flemington Antique Center; David Rago, Lambertville; Somerville Center Antiques, Valerie Owens-Echols.

Ohio: AAA I-70 Antique Mall, Springfield; AAA I-76 Antique Mall, Ravenna; Canale's Antiques, Delaware; Cincinnati Art Galleries; Medina Antique Mall; Gary and Judy Promey, Atwater; Seekers Antiques, Columbus; Springfield Antique Center; Third Edition Antiques & Collectibles, Mount Vernon.

Pennsylvania: Apple Hill Antiques, State College; Gillian Hine Antiques, Lancaster; Leonard's Antiques and Uniques Mega Mall, Chippewa. Virginia: Ken Forster, Falls Church. Wisconsin: The Carriage Barn, Pine River; Colonial House Antiques, Bug Bend; Victorian House Antiques, Bristol.

# AMERICAN CERAMICS PUBLICATIONS

The American Art Pottery Association
Patti Bourgeois, Secretary
P.O. Box 834
Westport, MA 02790-0697

American Pottery Journal
P.O. Box 14255
Parkville, MO 64152

Style 1900
The Quarterly Journal of the Arts and
Crafts Movement
17 South Main St.
Lambertville, NJ 08530

Ceramics Monthly
1609 Northwest Boulevard
Columbus, OH 43212

Pottery Lovers Newsletter
Pat and Ted Sallaz
4969 Hudson Drive
Stow, OH 44224

The Daze
P.O. Box 57
Otisville, MI 48463

The Pottery Collectors Express
Box 221
Mayview, MO 64071

Dorothy Kamm's Porcelain Collector's
Companion
P.O. Box 7460
Port St. Lucie, FL 34985-7460

# GLOSSARY

**Applied Design**-Ornamentation that is attached to the body or ground.

**Architectural Form**-The use of structural themes in the design of a piece of pottery. This type of design was used quite frequently during the Art Deco period and found form in art pottery.

**Baluster Shape**-Bulbous middle with a flared top and base.

**Belleek**-An eggshell thin decorative porcelain. It was manufactured at several locations in the U.S. such as Lenox, Willets, and Knowles, Taylor, Knowles. It was influenced by the porcelain from Ireland.

**Bisque**-The unglazed initially fired porcelain or pottery body.

**Cold Paint**-The use of non-fired color to accent or decorate. Cold paint is highly susceptible to wear and was used fairly extensively on cookie jars.

**Crazing**-Numerous surface cracks in the glaze resulting from different shrinking patterns of the glaze and body.

**Crystalline Glaze**-the recrystallization of particles during the cooling period resulting in a lustered sheen to the surface.

**Cuenca**-A technique of decoration for tiles and other wares that involved impressing the pattern on tiles to form ridges which prevented the colored glazes used from intermingling.

**Decalcomania**-The application of a lithographed print to a glazed or unglazed surface prior to glazing.

**Earthenware**-A lightly fired pottery which is often covered with a glaze to seal its porous surface.

**Engobe**-A French term for slip.

**Faience**-A French term for tin-glazed earthenware that is interchangeable with majolica. The term was used by several American manufacturers to describe their products.

**Flint Enamel Glaze**-A hard surfaced mottled glaze frequently found on Bennington pottery.

**Glaze**-A glass coating applied to seal a porous body rendering it non-porous.

**Glost Firing**-A second firing used to fuse the glaze over the biscuit body.

**Granite Ware**-A form of stoneware with a speckled appearance.

**Ground**-The basic body on which decorations are applied.

**Impasto**-A technique of applying pigment in such a way as to stand out from the glazed surface in slight but noticeable relief.

**Ironstone**-An opaque white vitrified china designed for utilitarian purposes. It often contains iron slag for strength.

**Jigger**-A device in which plastic clay is shaped in a turning mold, often mounted on a potter's wheel; the mold forms exterior of vessel, while a template cuts interior contour.

**Olla**-A wide mouthed bulbous pot.

**Overlay**-The application of a surface or overglaze decoration most often found on colored borders. The overlay is frequently a fine gold lattice treatment.

**Porcelain**-A highly vitrified ceramic ware with varying degrees of translucency depending on thickness.

**Pottery**-A generic term that includes earthenware, clay, and stoneware products, but generally excludes hard paste ceramics such as porcelain.

**Redware**-Low fired, porous pottery used for utilitarian purposes.

**Relief Design**-The raised design that projects from the ground or body.

**Rockingham Glaze**-Brown glaze with orange, blue, and yellow mottling. Associated with the Bennington potteries.

**Sagger**-A case composed of fire clay used to surround and protect objects during the firing process.

**Salt Glaze**-The application of salt during the firing of the glaze which produces an orange peel-type or finely textured finish.

**Sang-De-Boeuf Glaze**-A splotchy, ox blood red glaze. The color is obtained from reduced copper oxide and was used in American and European art pottery.

**Semi-Porcelain**-A type of porcelain that does not reach true vitrification associated with true high-fired porcelain. The body is somewhat duller in appearance than the smooth glossy body of true porcelain.

**Semi-Vitreous**-See semi-porcelain.

**Sgraffito**-The incision of a design through a layer of colored slip exposing the underlying red clay body.

**Shaped Rim**-A decorative technique whereby the rim features a regular or irregular pattern other than smooth.

**Slip Cup**-A small hollow cuplike device with tubes that are often made from turkey-feather quills or reeds; colored slip is trailed or dribbled through the tubes to create decorative patterns on a ceramic surface.

**Slip Decoration**-The use of liquid clay to produced a raised design on the body or ground. The slip is usually decorated with colored glazes.

**Sponging**-The application of color or glaze by dabbing with a sponge to produce a mottled effect.

**Squeezebag**-A decorative technique whereby liquid clay or slip is applied to a body through a means similar to cake decorating.

**Stoneware**-A refined, partially vitrified pottery that results in a strong, non-porous body.

**Terra Cotta**-An unglazed lightly fired reddish earthenware.

**Transfer Printing**-The application of a metallic oxide design by means of a tissue print on a ceramic body. Printing can be found under and over a glazed surface.

**Vitreous**-The fusion of ingredients at a high temperature resulting in a strong, glassy body or surface.

Additional glossary terms can be found in the following books:

Louise Ade Boger, *The Dictionary of World Pottery and Porcelain*, Scribners, 1971; George Savage and Harold Newman, *An Illustrated Dictionary of Ceramics*, Van Nostrand Reinhold Company, 1974.

# BIBLIOGRAPHIES

The following is a listing of general reference books on American pottery and porcelain that the reader may find useful. A list of marks books is also included.

## ART POTTERY REFERENCES

Paul Evans, *Art Pottery of the United States*, Feingold and Lewis Publishing Corp.1987; Lucile Henzke, *Art Pottery of America, Revised 3rd Edition* Schiffer Publishing Ltd.1997; Ralph and Terry Kovel, *American Art Pottery, The Collector's Guide to Makers, Marks, and Factory Histories*, Crown, 1993; David Rago, *American Art Pottery*, Knickerbocker, 1997; Dick Sigafoose, *American Art Pottery*, Collector Books, 1998.

## GENERAL CERAMICS REFERENCES

Edwin Atlee Barber, *The Pottery and Porcelain of The United States and Marks of American Potters*, Feingold and Lewis, 1976; Jo Cunningham, *Collector's Encyclopedia of American Dinnerware*, Collector Books, 1998; _____, *The Best of Collectible Dinnerware, Revised 2nd Edition*, Schiffer Publishing Ltd.1995; Ellen and Bert Denker, *The Warner Collector's Guide to North American Pottery and Porcelain*, Main Street Press, 1982; *Harvey Duke, The Official Identification and Price Guide to Pottery and Porcelain, Eighth Edition*, House of Collectibles, 1995; Alice Cooney Frelinghuysen, *American Porcelain 1770-1920*, Metropolitan Museum of Art, 1989; Harold F. Guilland, *Early American Folk Pottery*, Chilton Book Company, 1971; Joanne Jasper, *Turn of the Century American Dinnerware, 1880s to 1920s*, Collector Books, 1996; Dorothy Kamm, *American Painted Porcelain*, Collector Books, 1997; _____, *Comprehensive Guide to American Painted Porcelain*, Antique Trader Books, 1999; Lois Lehner, *Complete Books of American Kitchen and Dinner Wares*, Wallace-Homestead Book Company, 1980; Elaine Levin, *The History of American Ceramics 1607 to the Present*, Harry N. Abrams, 1988; Barbara Perry, editor, *American Ceramics*, Rizzoli International Publications, 1989; Harry L. Rinker, *Dinnerware of the 20th Century: The Top 500 Patterns*, Random House, 1997.

## MARKS REFERENCES

Gerald DeBolt, *Debolt's Dictionary of Whitewares and Porcelain: American Pottery Marks*, Collector Books, 1993; William C. Gates, and Dana E. Ormerod, *The East Liverpool, Ohio Pottery District: Identification of Manufacturers and Marks*, The Society for Historical Archaeology, 1982; Lois Lehner, *Encyclopedia of U.S. Marks on Pottery, Porcelain and Clay*, Collector Books, 1988.

## RESOURCE DIRECTORY

David J. Maloney, Jr., *Maloney's Antiques and Collectibles Resource Directory*, 5th Edition, Antique Trader Books, 1999.

# INDEX

# FROM THE LEADER IN HOBBY PUBLISHING

Provides the detailed, accurate and up-to-date information to make informed decisions in buying or selling pottery and porcelain. Covers the full range of ceramic products produced in the U.S., England and Europe from the 18th century through the mid-20th century. A convenient format, comprehensive listings and numerous photographs make it easy to locate and identify individual makers and their items. This volume also provides historical information and a variety of useful collecting tips that make it an indispensable reference.

Softcover • 6 x 9 • 416 pages
500 b&w photos • 50 color photos
**Item# PPOR3 • $18.95**

"The bible" for pottery and porcelain collectibles is not only all new from cover to cover, it is also in a larger format for easier reading. The only price guide of its kind, it features 300 new photos; more than 200 categories; and more than 10,000 new price listings of today's hottest collectibles in the antiques marketplace.

Softcover • 8-1/4 x 10-7/8 • 320 pages
300 b&w photos
**Item# ECPP3 • $27.95**

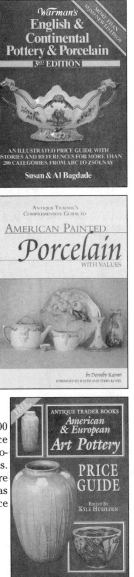

This all-new edition of the antiques and collectibles "bible," offers more than 500 categories, 50,000 updated price listings and hundreds of photos of the hottest items collected today. Major categories covered include advertising, Coca-Cola items, Depression glass, dolls, glassware, politics, sports and toys. This year's edition features a new category of American Paintings, more-detailed furniture and silver listings, and record-breaking prices set at various auctions across the country.

Softcover • 8-1/4 x 10-7/8 • 640 pages
600+ b&w photos
**Item# WAC34 • $17.95**

Complete, concise and well-organized, this beautifully illustrated reference and price guide tours a Victorian home and details which porcelain pieces would be found in each room. From how to identify and value painted porcelain, to each piece's function in the home.

Softcover • 8-1/2 x 11 • 192 pages
20 b&w photos • 400 color photos
**Item# AT1008 • $28.95**

Identify and value genuine Heisey glassware items produced from 1896-1924 using this book. As the earliest pieces produced by Heisey increasingly gain legitimate antique status, it is vital that collectors, dealers, and appraisers have access to accurate, comprehensive, detailed, and timely information relating to identification, pattern and color descriptions, production dates, variations, and values. This book provides the up-to-date prices and depth of identification information needed to confidently buy, sell, and trade in these colorful and treasured collectibles.

Softcover • 8-1/4 x 10-7/8 • 176 pages
50 b&w photos • 300 color photos
**Item# HEIS • $26.95**

This collector's reference contains over 2,000 listings that accurately describe and price items by major American and European producers from the 19th century to the 1930s. Features more than 40 artists, including more collectible lines by Rookwood and Weller as well as unique pieces by artists such as Clarice Cliff and Van Briggle.

Softcover • 6 x 9 • 224 pages
300 b&w photos
**Item# AT5412 • $14.95**

In the 1700s and 1800s, Limoges boxes were a traditional favorite of everyone. These beautiful boxes saw a renaissance in the last half of the 20th century, and they are continuing to be highly collectible and popular. This book has it all - collector tips, history, more than 400 beautiful and detailed photos and values for each box. It's the perfect guide for beginning or advanced collectors.

Softcover • 8-1/4 x 10-7/8 • 176 pages
400 color photos
**Item# LIMO • $29.95**

This reference and price guide is designed for collectors of teapots and lovers of tea. Nearly 2,000 price listings, along with historical backgrounds, nation-by-nation explanations of style, pattern, and composition, collector's guidelines, manufacturer's marks, advice on how to store and display a collection make this guide a must-have.

Softcover • 8-1/2 x 11 • 208 pages
400 color photos
**Item# AT0187 • $26.95**

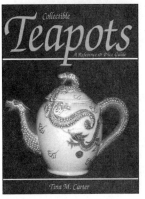

---

**Shipping and Handling:** $3.25 1st book; $2 ea. add'l. Foreign orders $20.95 1st item, $5.95 each add'l.
**Sales Tax:** CA, IA, IL, PA, TN, VA, WA, WI residents please add appropriate sales tax.

**SATISFACTION GUARANTEE**
If for any reason you are not completely satisfied with your purchase, simply return it within 14 days and receive a full refund, less shipping.

To place a credit card order or for a FREE all-product catalog call

# 800-258-0929
**Dept. ACBR**

M-F, 7 am - 8 pm • Sat, 8 am - 2 pm, CST
**Krause Publications, Dept. ACBR, P.O. Box 5009, Iola, WI 54990-5009**
Visit and order from our secure web site: www.krausebooks.com
*Retailers call toll-free 888-457-2873 ext 880, M-F, 8 am - 5 pm*

# DETAILED COVERAGE OF NUMEROUS COLLECTING FIELDS

The best source possible for in-depth and detailed coverage of hundreds of collecting fields. Covers the major categories of ceramics, furniture and glass, plus a diverse range of others. New areas of collecting are also presented so readers can keep abreast of current market trends. Some 600 photographs highlight over 20,000 entries.

Softcover • 6 x 9 • 912 pages
3,000 b&w photos
**Item# AT2001 • $16.95**

*NEW EDITION 9/00*

More than 10,000 listings, 16 pages of color and 650 b&w photos of hundreds of different advertisers including Betty Crocker, Campbell's, Coca-Cola, Domino's Pizza, General Motors, Harley-Davidson, Kellogg's, Levi's, McDonald's, Pepsi-Cola, and Zero. Also includes collecting hints, history, references, collections, collector's clubs, websites and reproduction alerts.

Softcover • 8-1/2 x 11 • 304 pages
650 b&w photos • 70 color photos
**Item# WADV • $24.95**

Indulge your appetite for beauty with this charming work on the Shelley Pottery - renowned for their fine English tableware and figurines in the 1920s and early 30s. This guide covers all the collectibles of the Shelley Pottery and gives you values in both pounds sterling and U.S. dollars and British pounds.

Softcover • 6-3/4 x 9-1/2 • 140 pages
200 color photos
**Item# SHPOT • $24.95**

Updated with 50 new chapters to reflect today's hottest trends, the book offers introductory histories of many collecting specialties, general collecting guidelines, 10,000 values for representative collectibles in over 90 categories, tips on buying and selling on the Internet, and club information for the specialty collector.

Softcover • 8-1/2 x 11 • 356 pages
1,300 b&w photos
**Item# CGA02 • $24.95**

*NEW 9/00*

This lavishly illustrated volume will quickly become the market leader for Carnival collectors worldwide. Includes chapters on identifying manufacturers and covers all forms of Carnival (U.K., European and Scandinavian). Prices listed in both U.S. dollars and British pounds.

Softcover • 8-1/4 x 10-7/8 • 164 pages
8-page color section
**Item# CARGL • $19.95**

This is the best encyclopedic, photo-intensive price guide and reference book for more than 16,000 vintage and obscure toys from the late 1880s to today. All of the 45,000 prices have been reviewed and updated from the eighth edition, with many increasing.

Softcover • 8-1/2 x 11 • 768 pages
3,500 b&w photos
16-page color section
**Item# CTY09 • $28.95**

Did you know that there are more than 100 different patterns of Depression glass in several different colors? And that the pattern and color greatly affect the value? Don't pay more than you should. Use this comprehensive guide to identify the pattern and find the appropriate value range for more than 10,000 pieces.

Softcover • 8-1/4 x 10-7/8 • 256 pages
155 patterns • 400 color photos
**Item# WDG02 • $25.95**

You're sure to enjoy this unique and informative guide to the fascinating world of desk accessories and other writing-related implements. With full chapters devoted to inkwells (including the history of ink and inkwells), pens, blotters and desk sets, advertising items, letter openers, and rulers, this colorful and carefully researched book will help round-out your collection. Includes historical information, photos of original catalog ads and rare items, and up-to-date market-place values–all the information a savvy collector needs to idenity and value these intriguing items.

Softcover • 8-1/2 x 11 • 208 pages
250+ b&w photos • 32-page color section
**Item# AT5862 • $26.95**

**To place a credit card order or for a FREE all-product catalog call**

**Shipping and Handling:** $3.25 1st book; $2 ea. add'l. Foreign orders $20.95 1st item, $5.95 each add'l..
**Sales Tax:** CA , IA , IL, PA, TN, VA, WA, WI residents please add appropriate sales tax.

**SATISFACTION GUARANTEE**
If for any reason you are not completely satisfied with your purchase, simply return it within 14 days and receive a full refund, less shipping.

# 800-258-0929
**Dept. ACBR**

M-F, 7 am - 8 pm • Sat, 8 am - 2 pm, CST
**Krause Publications, Dept. ACBR, P.O. Box 5009, Iola, WI 54990-5009**
Visit and order from our secure web site: www.krausebooks.com
*Retailers call toll-free 888-457-2873 ext 880, M-F, 8 am - 5 pm*